HOGARTH

Detail from 'The Country Dance', *The Analysis of Beauty Plate 2*, etching and engraving, 1753

HOGARTH

LIFE IN PROGRESS

JACQUELINE RIDING

P

PROFILE BOOKS

ALSO BY JACQUELINE RIDING

Peterloo: The Story of the Manchester Massacre (2018)

Jacobites: A New History of the '45 Rebellion (2016)

HOGARTH

First published in Great Britain in 2021 by
Profile Books Ltd
29 Cloth Fair
London
EC1A 7JQ
www.profilebooks.co.uk

1 3 5 7 9 10 8 6 4 2

Typeset in Garamond by MacGuru Ltd
Printed and bound in Great Britain by
Clays Ltd, Elcograf S.p.A.

ISBN 978 1 78816 347 7
eISBN 978 1 78283 611 7

For Jack & Pat

Contents

PROLOGUE

*'Wond'ring Muse'**

From deep within the infinite realm, tentative light beams pulse and flicker, hinting at unnumbered stars, of untold planets. Close by, the dense black yields to the sun's glorious warmth and burning colour, illumining our fragile globe and her pale moon. Then, from the region of this world, a pointed flame appears. It passes quickly over and on, weaving through the universe, dipping here and there, skimming across the surface of those distant spheres, observing all fresh wonders. In the heightened imaginings of the poet, stirred by discoveries too incredible to be the product of mere human thought, this comet is the soul of nature's philosopher, mankind's wondering muse, great Newton on his daily orbit of divine creation. Through him the innermost recesses of the conquered heavens are thrown open, the archives of hidden truth unlocked.

Now turning towards that shining orb, we pass down through the regions of the sky, the winds and cloud, and then, further still to mortality's low province, the mass of earth and water. Lordly Nineveh and Babylon are no more; noble Palmyra's exposed ruins the sentinels of empire long lost. Next, across the middle sea to Eternal Rome where we behold the extremes of fate. For among the emblems of her modern boasted state, Rome's temples are open to the sky, her columns dreadful in decay, her ancient greatness sunk. Onward, passing lofty mountains, valleys, forests and low plains, over the figs and vines of proud King Louis's fertile dominions towards the island cluster on Europe's western edge. As the sun sinks below the horizon, its last rays glister the curling form

---

*John Hughes, *The Ecstasy*, London, 1720

of a mighty river, on whose banks now sprawls, so the inhabitants claim, a new Rome: the metropolis of London.

This is our destination, or rather, to be exact, the upper floor of the Bedford Arms tavern in the district called Covent Garden. We are here because on Friday 26 May 1732, in the fifth year of King George II's reign, the tavern's club members have gathered to drink, to eat and to engage in conversation of a bluff and convivial nature. Only five of the original party are now present.

These are the dwindling hours of a glorious late spring day: a day that signals summer's imminent approach, with all the hope and promise this might bring. On such an occasion an Englishman, whether a Londoner by birth or circumstance, who rarely has time or need to leave his beloved city, and while gazing absently from an upper window into the familiar, hectic streets below, might feel the sudden impulse to go far away: to succumb, however briefly, to the lure of simple pastoral pleasures and yearn, then, to follow the ancestral siren-call of the ploughman, the cockle-seller, the peasant bard. To venture, like the pilgrim, beyond the confines of the city, through the verdant land, to the estuary of a great river and to glimpse the vast terrains and oceans beyond.

One of the company is indeed gazing from the tavern's open window at the last of the sunset already described. What happened next has never been explained fully. Perhaps a wayward spark from that disciple of Phoebus, Sir Isaac's happy lighted spirit, dropped to earth, setting aflame these desires in its unsuspecting host. Or, as likely, it was nothing more than an ardent wish that the night's revelries should not, must not end so soon: the remaining club stalwarts neither too sleepy nor boozed enough to need the immediate comfort of bed and bolster. Whatever its path hither, an inspiration came, took root, the resulting idea voiced to those gathered, the company responded in accord and so, after scrawled notes to nearby wives and family were exchanged for fresh shirts and coin, these five friends ventured into the night on their own journey of discovery, along that same river, the Thames and his sister the Medway, as far as the Kentish Isle of Sheppey off England's south-eastern coast, with no particular idea or expectation of what would happen next.

Now you may be thinking that countless such journeys have occurred over the centuries, some, frankly, far more noteworthy than this appears to be and, in fairness, you would be right. Excepting that such workaday travels are rarely recorded in any detail and are, therefore, an aspect of our forebears' lives that is all but lost to us. And, more important still, a member of this particular group of travellers will be described justifiably, indeed within his own lifetime, as one of the most significant individuals to have been born in these islands: supplying posterity with a ready shorthand, not just for a style of graphic satire or comic grotesque, but a type of character or behaviour and even, rightly or wrongly, an entire era of British history.

The fact that we know anything at all about this modest adventure rests on the survival of a manuscript, written just after the event and rejoicing in the ponderous title, 'An account of what Seem'd most Remarkable in the Five Days Peregrination of the Five Following persons Viz^t. Messieurs Tothall, Scott, Hogarth, Thornhill & Forrest' with the accompanying exhortation, 'Abi tu et fac Similiter' ('Go and do the same').[1] The text was later transformed into a doggerel poem by the Reverend William Gostling, a resident of Kent and friend to the participants.[2] The manuscript, in a neat hand using a quill pen and brown ink (typical of the period), plots the towns and villages they passed through and the inns they stayed at, the various repasts enjoyed with expenditure itemised, the modes of transport used, the characters they encountered and the incidents that occurred. This chronicle is further enlivened by the presence of several picaresque drawings and a map. In this way it is both the record of a journey and the means to relive it, whether alone or in company, as part of the deliberations at the Bedford Arms tavern club for example, in the imagination or in person. The claim that the account concerns a peregrination or pilgrimage, coupled with the promise to recount what was 'most remarkable' during the five days, encourages the expectation of philosophical depth or, at the very least, events of some importance. Yet, to be clear from the outset, *The Peregrination* (as it shall be known) is not, in any traditional sense, a pilgrimage. And it is debatable whether anything remarkable, as we might define it, happens at all.

Of the five individuals, our focus here is, of course, Mr William
Hogarth, now in his thirty-fourth year, a painter and engraver
known to his close friends as Billy.[3] His progress, from birth in
1697 to this moment, will be charted in due course but, for now,
it should be observed that the year 1732 signalled a transformation
in the fortunes of this gentleman: indeed his recent publishing of
a set of engravings following the decline and fall of a young naïve
woman turned prostitute may have been the stimulus for the
gathering – a celebration of sorts – and the impromptu five-day
journey a respite from a business that had increased dramatically,
almost overnight.

Hogarth's companions are Ebenezer Forrest, lawyer, playwright
and scribe of *The Peregrination*, William Tothall, former merchant
seaman now draper and appointed treasurer for the duration,
and fellow artists John Thornhill and Samuel Scott, who, with
Hogarth, supplied the drawings. These men are not well known;
they are not of the status of his other collaborators and friends,
such as the author, playwright and magistrate Henry Fielding or
the actor-manager David Garrick. Yet they represent Hogarth's
friendships from the years before he was firmly established as an
artist and when his fame, specifically as a commentator on modern
life, had not yet fully taken hold: a circumstance which, counter-
intuitively perhaps, became something of a burden to his artistic
ambition in later years.

Surprisingly, given his subsequent renown, very little information exists with which to construct entirely Billy Hogarth's life up
to 1732, the mid point of his allotted span, beyond those engravings and paintings that survive. Tantalising glimpses can be found
in the core sources for his life as a whole, some of which are in
Hogarth's own hand, notably his unpublished drafts for *The Analysis of Beauty* (1753) and the somewhat random, at times incoherent
notes for an uncompleted autobiography.

But we have a very good idea of his appearance in that crucial
year. Hogarth was not, as a rule, a vain man, and like most he was
neither handsome nor ugly but somewhere in between. The earliest surviving self-portrait, created around the time of the trip to
Sheppey and considered by Mrs Jane Hogarth and others to be

very like, is testament to his ambitions and his hard-won success to date (Col. Fig. 1). It is painted with vigour and an infectious sense of expectation: the thick curls of his shoulder-length wig and the linen neck stock are both brilliantly dashed off using touches of grey, highlighted with thick smudges of bright white. This frames a face alert with intelligence and intensity – an expression, to an extent, encouraged by the method of self-portraiture, that is glancing back and forth between canvas and looking glass and hence immortalising, along with everything else, an enquiring air. The head is tipped back just a little, adding to that mood of deep concentration, his blue eyes under lightly arched eyebrows are neither arrogant nor proud, just direct, his nose a little stubby, and with thin lips parted. The dense brown of the background and coat directs all attention towards the person and personality, a trick learned from the seventeenth-century Dutchman Rembrandt van Rijn and the Flemish masters Sir Peter Paul Rubens and Sir Anthony van Dyck, artist ancestors much favoured by British painters of Hogarth's generation. The portrait remained unfinished, in comparison, that is, to the more polished state of his other endeavours in that line. But the image, as it is, may have served its purpose – a record of the artist, addressed in the first instance to and for himself, at the moment of public recognition, at the very cusp of enduring fame.

Apart from its handling, the other hint that this is an unfinished portrait is the faint presence of a feature that Hogarth was particularly proud of: a distinctive, deep and long scar above his right eye, the result, as described by an early biographer, John Ireland, of a mysterious 'accident' in his youth. Decades on, 'the mark remained ; and he frequently wore his hat so as to display it'.[4] From this it seems that Hogarth placed his black tricorn hat, the correct headwear for gentlemen in public spaces, tipped back, to expose fully his forehead, or tilted at a jaunty angle to his left, drawing attention to this scar and lending him the air of a raffish veteran of the battlefield. As Henry Fielding observed of Captain John Blifil in the 1749 novel *The History of Tom Jones*, 'He had a Scar on his Forehead, which did not so much injure his Beauty, as it denoted his Valour.'[5] Whatever had caused the wound, an inch or two lower and a promising career in fine art would have been seriously imperilled.

The other key aspect of Hogarth's appearance, which the portrait cannot even suggest, concerns his physical stature. John Thomas Smith in *Nollekens and his Times* recalled, referring to David Garrick, 'Whenever Garrick's name was mentioned, it was generally accompanied with the appellation of *little* ; but I have often heard my father observe, that he never knew any one who spake of *little* Hogarth, though he was half a head shorter.'[6] Davy Garrick was known for his extreme affability, not something readily said of Hogarth, and so was far less inclined to take offence. Our artist was many things – loyal, kind, jovial company – but also chippy and, at times, easily affronted. Perhaps no one dared allude to Hogarth's build. Still, stature, whether physical, social or professional, was fundamental to his sense of worth, and although presence is so much more than mere height, nonetheless it is useful to imagine Hogarth, both figuratively and physically, expanded to his full elevation and breadth, chest out, chin lifted, legs slightly akimbo, hands clenched on hips, like a wee 'Bluff King Hal'. In a letter to 'T. H.', Hogarth stressed the need for proportion relative to height and used the slim, handsome Garrick, whether diminutive or no, as the exemplar of good proportion, and his fellow actor and friend, James Quin, thickset, large of limb and head, as the very opposite.[7] Proportion, Hogarth insists, is (almost) everything.

So, in sum, was the be-scarred, compact Billy Hogarth, a man of honour and action, or, perhaps, a common street bruiser, perpetually on his guard against insult? Or else, simply, a one-time accident-prone youngster. No doubt he enjoyed and encouraged such speculation, and shedding light on this maddening, delightful, contrary individual is the very purpose of our journey over the following pages.

Hogarth was, instinctively, a great storyteller. But as we shall see, he yearned to be recognised as much more than a satirist. The single-word motto for his one foray into art theory, 'Variety', was as much an appeal for a fair, unbiased judgement from his contemporaries and, he would hope, posterity, as it was a statement of fact in regard to his astonishing inventiveness and range. The

1. *The Proportions of Garrick and Quin, 21 Oct 1746*, detail from a
letter to 'T.H', pen with brown ink, over pencil on paper
The recipient has not been identified, but the ideas expressed,
with the date, connect the letter to *The Analysis of Beauty*,
Hogarth's main contribution to art theory.

caricature, or cliché, of William Hogarth as, on the one hand, an
unrefined urban chronicler and, on the other, a fiercely nation-
alistic John Bull figure, does not allow for the ambitious history
painter, the grand-manner portraitist, his extensive knowledge of
western European art and deep admiration for European as well as

British artists, ancient and modern, and his breadth of reading, all of which he funnelled into his work, whether painting or engraving or theory. Hogarth aimed to rival, through art, the great literature of his day – the learned elegance of an Alexander Pope, as well as the satirical heft and bite of a Jonathan Swift. A central aim of this biography is to seek out the less familiar – portraiture, history and religious painting, art theory – that our subject pursued with a relentless focus.

In quest of this more rounded Billy Hogarth, no little detail, no matter how apparently inconsequential, will be left unexplored. As Henry Fielding sagely points out: 'In reality, there are many little Circumstances too often omitted by injudicious Historians, from which Events of the utmost Importance arise. The World may indeed be considered as a vast Machine, in which the great Wheels are originally set in Motion by those which are very minute, and almost imperceptible to any but the strongest Eyes.'[8] *The Peregrination* is just such a sequence of little circumstances which, uniquely, provides a precious glimpse into Hogarth's activities as separate from, as well as inherent to that of a professional artist and, in his fellow travellers and their interactions during the five days, even into his character. For *The Peregrination*, in its undramatic, gentle way, sees this Londoner, born and bred, out of his sphere of comfort and influence, while serving as a tiny window on to an England far away (in distance and mentality) from the metropolis. And weaving through this landscape is the very reason London exists at all: the river Thames. This is a part of England, echoing Fielding's incisive comment, that speaks brilliantly of national and even global events, past, present and future, due to its geography, topography and history, with references to trade and the Royal Navy, Good Queen Bess and the Spanish Armada, the devastating mid seventeenth-century Dutch raid on the Medway, and the ongoing threat of invasion and war at home and abroad.

Meandering and random, yet with a clear purpose, *The Peregrination* acts as one model for our journey through Hogarth's life and world. As such it will interweave, as a sequence of interludes through the coming chapters, assisting us in pursuit of that life and world. First, and whimsically, as an intermittent parade of palate refreshers offered up, continuing the analogy, to offset the richer flavours served in the chapters, of succulent roast beef and claret, of hearty puddings and frothing beer, or, in contrast, the necessary often bitter correctives for overindulgence, venality, disease and corruption, all of which make up the expected Hogarthian fare. Second, as an invaluable and unusual opportunity to spend time with our subject over an entire five-day period as he goes about his life, while offering an opportunity to travel through eighteenth-century London and the surrounding area, seeing along the way the sights and sounds that made up Hogarth's world at a crucial point in his career, when all lay before him.

By way of example, two humorous ink and watercolour drawings, which, as it happens, open and close *The Peregrination*, go some way to encapsulating Hogarth's personal philosophy for life and thus his art. The first depicts 'Some body' who, as the name asserts, is a legless and headless figure armed with a walking staff and wearing a curious coat, half buff, half blue, one side back to front. The suggestion is that this somebody might have trouble finding his arse, even when both hands are freely deployed. He is accompanied by the ruins of a castle and a classical column, and so on one level must be a parody of those peculiar tribes, the antiquarians and connoisseurs: the former (some might say) revel in tedious detail that few others care much about and the latter, Hogarth would argue, see nothing yet profess to know everything and impose their opinions on everyone else.

The second drawing is of 'no body', a curious assemblage of maniacally smiling head – in appearance, strangely akin to Hogarth himself – with hat and wig, a pipe, knife, fork and spoon hanging from the latter, supported by a pair of splayed legs and two oars, from which dangle an onion-shaped wine bottle and a large rummer or drinking glass.

Somebody, by long-standing tradition, is a futile creature who pompously thinks himself worthy of notice, 'a somebody'. Often characterised as a villain or hypocrite, but in practice he or she could be anyone with pretensions and a false sense of their importance in the world. Hogarth might list a few aristocrats, merchants and even fellow artists who would fall into this category.

The nobody, as the name suggests, is an unassuming 'every-man' with simple appetites and expectations – symbolised here by laughter, pipe-smoking, food and wine – just trying to make his way in a difficult, often uncaring world and, through the lack of pretension, a common hero. Characters as variable as John Bun-yan's Christian from *The Pilgrim's Progress*, Swift's Lemuel Gulliver and Daniel Defoe's Robinson Crusoe and Moll Flanders take on this role. And, given the resemblance, so too could Billy Hogarth. This idea, rooted in European folklore and popular philosophy, is utilised, adapted and updated by Hogarth throughout his career, with the inspired influence of, in particular, Bunyan, Swift, Defoe and the like, in the common man and woman villains and heroes in his own work: sometimes adding greater realism to the archetypes, as these authors do in turn, by blurring the line between the two opposites.

Hogarth developed this idea in a 'no Dedication' to his proposed but abandoned history of the fine arts, in which he declared that no prince, no man of quality, no learned body, that is a somebody (as was the norm), not even a particular friend would be named in connection with the publication and therefore, by extension or default, his book was dedicated to 'nobody'. 'But,' he continues in a riddling manner, 'if for once we may suppose Nobody to be every body, as Every body is often said to be nobody, then is this work Dedicated to every body.'[9] Taken as a whole, Hogarth's art is evidence of a life dedicated to everybody and nobody. His subject may be the nobility as a whole, or a particular aristocrat; the crimi-nal underclass or a lone lawbreaker; the love of mankind or a single abandoned infant, but his overarching theme is human nature and experience. Like another hero and exemplar, his namesake William Shakespeare, whom, Hogarth declared, 'had the deepest penetra-tion into nature', Hogarth's art, as he himself defined it, 'was my Stage and men and women my actors.' Like Shakespeare, his art might be rooted in the everyday or the specific, while, at the same time, it is high-minded and universal. And, again like Shakespeare, humour and high art are not mutually exclusive, nor is comedy an end in itself.

Hogarth recalled the pleasure that came from watching a

country dance, with many and varied participants, during which he alighted on one elegant dancer in particular. He describes pursuing her eagerly with his eyes as she moved among, around and through her companions. He imagined a ray of light marking her graceful windings, which 'was bewitching to the sight, as the imaginary ray ... was dancing with her all the time'. The effect, in Hogarth's own beautiful phrase, was 'to lead the eye a wanton kind of chace'.

So, in line with Hogarth's own inclinations and in the spirit of these and other journeys, great and small, whether physical or imagined, of the body or the mind, contemporaneous or historical, and with *The Peregrination*, like the Thames, curling through the familiar and unfamiliar landscape, we will move through Hogarth's life: sometimes in a straight line, sometimes not, stopping off at unexpected or shocking locations en route, but always with a clear purpose, to illuminate the life and work of our subject while revealing the humanity and inhumanity of this so-called Age of Hogarth. Our guides and companions will come from high to low life (often interchangeable, as Hogarth's work reminds us) and everywhere in between – the somebodies and the nobodies. Alongside Messrs Bunyan, Fielding, Swift and Defoe, we will be accompanied by the exiled prince, the philanthropic shipwright and patriot, the condemned thief on his final journey from Newgate to Tyburn, the characters and settings of Hogarth's life and art. We will witness great collective triumphs and agonies, alongside individual examples of everyday kindness and cruelty.

Let Hogarth and his world, in these pages, lead you a wanton kind of chase – not so much the progress of a life step by step, structured and logical, cradle to grave, but life, as it invariably is, a rambling work in progress. To that end we will continue as we have begun, that is, in the middle of Hogarth's life, and follow the five friends on their very modern pilgrimage, commencing, as it should, in the heart of London.

INTERLUDE ONE

EARLY SATURDAY 27 MAY, AT AROUND HALF PAST MIDNIGHT. The five friends set off from the Bedford Arms tavern, with spare linen shirts stuffed into their coat pockets and carrying, between them, enough money to cover the necessary expenditure for a trip to and from the Isle of Sheppey. This may have been the first time that three of the party have ventured so far down river, to the estuary meeting place of the Thames and the Medway. John Thornhill had journeyed to Flanders via Gravesend six years before, while Will Tothall had only recently exchanged a career at sea for shop work, so of all the pilgrims, he was by far the most seasoned traveller and an experienced sailor into the bargain. If you are wondering at the logistics of their baggage arrangement, or lack thereof, the answer lies in the early Georgian gentleman's coat pocket, which was of a style and scale similar to a medium-sized saddle bag, so a folded spare shift could be carried very neatly in this manner.[1] Besides, the journey would be achieved in days, not weeks, and the services of a local laundress could be called upon if required.

As an introduction to Hogarth's metropolitan world, it is fortunate that *The Peregrination* began where it did, in London's cultural and artistic heart, Covent Garden, although it is no coincidence that Hogarth and his friends set off from this place and this tavern. In 1732, all five were resident within a few streets of each other and naturally they had chosen a watering hole at 1 Tavistock Row, a short walk from their respective homes. In this particular acreage of London it would be difficult not to bump into, accidentally or otherwise, fellow artists, authors and playwrights.

The Bedford Arms had been converted from a private dwelling into a public house by February 1731, only a year or so before this great adventure occurred. The change of purpose hints at the flourishing environment for new places and spaces for such like-minded gentlemen to gather.[2] The said 'Bedford' was the ground landlord (also commemorated in 'Russell' Street) of Covent Garden, which was itself named from the medieval convent vegetable garden of nearby Westminster Abbey, the land granted to Bedford's ancestor by King Edward VI. The third earl's building plans for this part of his extensive estate was an early sign of London's developing 'West End', which had been made more urgent by the devastation of the City to the east during the Great Fire of 1666. Both the fire and the plague that had preceded it were within living memory, and the new city was still rising from the ashes, with Sir Christopher Wren's masterpiece, St Paul's Cathedral as the most prominent and symbolic of the new buildings.

Covent Garden sits between St Martin's Lane and Leicester Fields to the west, the latter where Hogarth was to establish his practice; Long Acre and Great Queen Street to the north, Lincoln's Inn Fields, Temple and the Inns of Court to the east and, running along the southern edge, the Strand, the main thoroughfare between the City and the West End. At its most westerly point lies Charing Cross, the new church of St Martin-in-the-Fields, the Royal Mews (where the National Gallery now stands) and the entrance to Whitehall. To the south of the entire length of the Strand is the river Thames. This residential and commercial area of central London will be home to Hogarth for much of his adult life. And at its heart is the commodious public space, the Great Piazza, planned from the 1630s, which, among other things, hosted a fruit and vegetable market from the late 1650s.

In addition to the market, the Piazza is dominated on its western side by the Anglican parish church of St Paul, designed by Inigo Jones, the most prominent and influential English architect working in the early Stuart period.[3] Jones was also the designer of the Banqueting House on nearby Whitehall and the Queen's House in Greenwich, Kent (roughly six miles down river), both buildings that Hogarth knew well – the latter, the companions would pass on their way to Gravesend. According to legend, the Earl of Bedford had asked Jones to design an inexpensive chapel for the well-to-do he was actively encouraging to move to the area, declaring, in short, that the building should be no better than a barn. 'Well, then,' cried the nation's greatest living architect, 'you shall have the handsomest barn in England.'[4] Inigo's barn is an austere, imposing presence still, with its doughty Doric columns topped by a bold, simple pediment and, both externally and internally, unhindered by overt flamboyance and embellishment.

In the last years of the seventeenth century, the author Edward 'Ned' Ward (1667–1731) championed a style of publication, the satirical account of a journey, most famously through his metropolitan journal (published from November 1698 to May 1700). *The London Spy* is written in the moment, with Ned and an unnamed friend passing through the city like a modern-day Dante and Virgil, the latter acting as the explanatory guide to his cheerfully unworldly companion. Only what is described is not some imaginary Heaven and Hell, and this Divine Comedy is at times (as will become abundantly clear) resolutely earthbound, intentionally extreme and determinedly comic: Hogarth's urban visions in word form. It could be seen as the wayward parent of *The Peregrination*, alongside popular one-off tracts such as *The Merry Travellers: or, A Trip upon Ten-Toes from Moorfields to Bromley* of 1712.[5]

In the preface, Ward declares that he seeks to scourge the villanies, vanities and vices of London's citizenry '*without levelling Characters at any Person in particular*'. Giles Jacob, in his *The Poetical Register* of 1719, described Ned Ward as 'A very voluminous Poet ... Of late Years he has kept a publick House in the City (but in a genteel way) and with his Wit, Humour, and good Liquor has afforded his Guests a pleasurable Entertainment.'[6] This description should signal the style and content of Ward's famous creations, and Hogarth would repeat *The London Spy*'s stated philosophy in his wholly Ned-Wardian engraving, *A Midnight Modern Conversation* of March 1733 – '*Think not to find one* meant Resemblance *there, we lash the* Vices *but the* Persons *spare.*'

Ned Ward and his anonymous friend wander from Whitehall along the Strand, observing young men and women who seem, to the author, unusually keen to attend church service. As Ned recalls, 'we over-took [an] abundance of Religious Lady-birds, Arm'd

2. *A Midnight Modern Conversation*, etching and engraving, 1733
Individuals within this assembly of carousing men will inspire
future characters, notably (foreground) Tom Rakewell. The scene
also foreshadows the mayhem of *An Election Entertainment*.

against the Assaults of *Satan* with *Bible* or *Common Prayer-Book*,
marching with all Good speed to *Covent-Garden*-Church ... These,
says my Friend, are a Pious sort of Creatures that are much given to
go to Church, and may be seen there every Day at Prayers, as Constantly as the Bell rings.' The reason for such feminine enthusiasm
is equally clear to the keen observer, for 'if you were to walk the
other way, you might meet as many Young-Ge[n]tlemen from the
Temple and *Grays-Inn*', the Inns of Court to the east, 'going to Joyn
with them [in] their Devotions'.[7] The habit, of some locals, of using
the church and daily service as an opportunity to observe each
other at close quarters and even to flirt with members of the opposite sex – in other words, acting as any social gathering, such as a
ball or assembly – would be of interest to the recorder, visual and
literary, of the social foibles of their fellow Londoners. Hogarth
put such circumstances to good satirical use in his painting and

3. *The Four Times of the Day Plate 1: Morning*, etching and engraving, 1738
The Great Piazza, with St Paul's church top right and, beneath, 'Tom
King's' Coffee House. This 'Religious Lady-Bird' (centre) ignores her
young servant's discomfort as she ogles Widow King's clientele.

print 'Morning', from *The Four Times of the Day*, the print, *The
Sleeping Congregation* (Fig. 38 p. 259), and later, with no critical
purpose intended, as one venue in the virtuous courtship of the
Industrious Apprentice, Francis Goodchild, and his lady.

By 1732, besides the everyday Covent Garden folk at prayer, or flirtation, many illustrious people had been buried within St Paul's and adjoining churchyard, and their various occupations point to the distinctive, even eccentric character of the Piazza and its environs. People attending service or visiting the church would have been mindful of those who had gone before, as they glanced at the tombs and memorial plaques, all bearing witness to lives sometimes allowed their full three score years and ten, usually less. If Hogarth had ever attended a service here – and he would almost certainly have been at the baptism at the church of Sam and Ann Scott's infant, Ann Sophia, in 1724 – or sought a moment's quiet reflection, away from the hurly-burly, within the church's reassuring walls, he would have taken inspiration from some of the names and lives so honoured. Our travellers in 1732, as they weaved their way through Kent and its history, modern and ancient, made a particular point of inspecting the churches and graveyards they encountered, noting the more amusing or intriguing memorials and epitaphs as they went.

So, in the spirit of *The Peregrination*, perusing the memorials in St Paul's Covent Garden, the visitor would chance upon one dedicated to Sir Peter Lely (d.1680), the ebullient Dutch-born painter of King Charles II's court. Lely's entire career, give or take a few years, was founded and flourished in England, and he lived and worked in a house on the north side of the Great Piazza. Moving on through the church, the visitor would alight on the memorial to Grinling Gibbons (1648–1721), an Englishman born in Rotterdam, the chief sculptor and master wood-carver to all the monarchs of the British Isles from Charles II to his cousin, the first Hanoverian king, George I. As with Sir Peter, Grinling was an exemplar, and an Englishman at that, for any up-and-coming artist. A court sinecure or pension provided a regular income and therefore a cushion against the vagaries of fashion and the capricious contemporary art market, and was, for obvious reasons, highly prized. The associated glamour, influence and encouragement of royal patronage would continue regardless, or despite the personality and particular interests of the present incumbent. This too was motivation for the next generation to attempt to follow in Sir Peter and Grinling's footsteps, not least one William Hogarth.

4. *Hudibras Plate 2: Hudibras Sallying Forth*, engraving, 1726
Sir Hudibras and Squire Ralpho set off on their
adventures and immediately cause disruption.

Among the luminaries of literature celebrated in St Paul's
Covent Garden can be found Samuel Butler (1613–80), a staunch
royalist and author of the mock-heroic narrative poem, *Hudibras*, a
spoof on the radical Protestant factions, the roundheads and puritans of the Civil War of 1642–51. It tells of Sir Hudibras, so called
from a knight in Edmund Spenser's *The Faerie Queene* (1590–96)
'not so good of deeds as great of name', and his squire, Ralpho, in
imitation of Miguel de Cervantes's *Don Quixote* (first published in
1605 and 1615) venturing forth through England at a time

When *civil Dudgeon* first grew high,
And Men fell out they knew not why ;
When hard Words, *Jealousies* and *Fears*,
Set Folks together by the Ears,
And made them fight, like mad or drunk,
For Dame *Religion*, as for Punk [whore]:

Whose Honesty they all durst swear for,
Tho' not a Man of them knew wherefore.[8]

Lines for every epoch and every occasion. So well known was this poem, which remained extremely popular for over a century after Butler's death, that the term 'Hudibrastic', in the manner (metre, style and satirical purpose) of *Hudibras*, was a common description, much like the expression 'Hogarthian', and for good reason (as we shall see). John Nichols, publisher of an early biography of Hogarth (in collaboration with George Steevens and Isaac Reed), described *The Peregrination* in the hands of Reverend Gostling as being 'in *Hudibrastic* verse',[9] while Giles Jacob defined Ned Ward, in very similar terms, as 'an Imitator of the famous *Butler*'.[10]

Among those who had carried Samuel Butler to his final rest in St Paul's church was John Aubrey (d.1697), the eccentric antiquarian, writer of *Miscellanies* (published 1696) and what became known as *Brief Lives*: an intended biography of the post civil war age, left at Aubrey's death as random, fascinating scraps of incidentals and gossip. Here Aubrey observed of his friend Samuel that 'satirical wits disoblige whom they converse with, etc; and consequently make to themselves many enemies and few friends; and this was his manner and case'. A caution indeed to any would-be satirist. Given the synergy between Butler's *Hudibras* and Hogarth's developing brand of graphic satire, it should come as no surprise that one of the first major projects and corresponding successes of Hogarth's early career will be his engraved scenes from Butler's work.[11]

Theatre, too, lent a particular character to the area, with the Theatre Royal in Drury Lane to the east (the first built in 1663, the second in 1674) which, coupled with the Lincoln's Inn Fields Theatre (built in 1661) was founded in the wake of the restoration of the monarchy. As the pilgrims ventured forth from Tavistock Row, a new theatre was under construction adjoining the Great Piazza's north-east corner, between Bow Street and Great Hart Street, which would open in the December, with great fanfare, as the Theatre Royal, Covent Garden. In addition to actors and playwrights, theatre provided another opportunity for artists – whether interior decoration for the building itself, production design or scenery. John Thornhill, son of an artist and, as it happens, Hogarth's brother-in-law, was probably designing and painting scenery for the local theatres at this time. In 1732 and like Ebenezer Forrest, a young author and playwright called Henry Fielding was attempting to establish himself in this milieu. This was a vibrant cultural environment, building on the innovations of the post-Restoration generation represented, in art, by Lely and Gibbons, which offered plenty of opportunities and inspiration for young and ambitious artists. Hogarth, young and extremely ambitious, was emerging at a propitious time.

From the beginning, Ebenezer's account of *The Peregrination* has the air of an enchantment with all routines suspended, as if the only rule governing the entire expedition was to live in the moment. Leaving the Bedford Arms, they sauntered on in great spirits, singing the ditty 'Why shou'd wee Quarrell for Riches', or 'The Sailor's Rant', as it is titled in Allan Ramsay's popular *Tea-Table Miscellany: a Collection of Scots Sangs* (first published in three volumes, 1723–7). The song had been reused only recently in the pantomime entertainment *Perseus and Andromeda* at Lincoln's Inn Fields Theatre – Hogarth had produced two illustrations for the published libretto – which may have brought it readily to mind.[12] It was certainly well chosen, with apt references to journeying by water and the simple joy of travelling light, unburdened (as, eventually, Bunyan's pilgrim would be) and carefree:

> How pleasant a Sailor's Life passes,
> Who roams o'er the wat'ry Main!
> No Treasure he ever amasses,
> But chearfully spends all his Gain.
> We're Strangers to Party and Faction,
> To Honour and Honesty true,
> And would not commit a base Action,
> For Power, or Profit in View.

Chor.   *Then why should we quarrel for Riches,*
        Or any such glittering Toy?
        A light Heart, and a thin Pair of Breeches,
        Goes thorough the World, brave Boy.[13]

These words set the tone of their wanderings and, although not
quoted in full within the memorial manuscript, the song would
have been immediately recalled by the listeners, perhaps trigger-
ing a raucous rendition as part of the regular performances by the
assembled Bedford Arms club. By this date Hogarth was a subscriber to the Academy of Ancient Music, together with his friend
and librettist William Huggins, a group of professional musicians
and keen amateurs who championed 'old' music.[14] The regular
bouts of singing during *The Peregrination*, with engravings such as
A Chorus of Singers (Hogarth's 1732 homage to Huggins's oratorio
Judith) and *The Enraged Musician*, point to Hogarth's enthusiasm
for music and the camaraderie of a shared interest and activity.

They crossed the Strand, warbling as they went, towards the
nearest place on the Thames to hail a boat heading east. This was
likely to have been Somerset Watergate (as on their return), which
was the landing point for Somerset House. In 1732, with only one
bridge over the river within London, crossing the Thames by horse
and foot ferry, or travelling along it in a variety of craft, was as
common as taking a modern taxi.

From the watergate, Hogarth and his friends caught a wherry
boat, a shallow craft rowed by one or two oarsmen or 'watermen'.
Such craft had carried patrons up and down the Thames for centuries, including audiences to and from Shakespeare's Globe Theatre
in London's main borough of Southwark, lying to the south of the
Old Bridge. Apart from carrying Londoners and visitors over and
along the great river, the watermen were at the centre of one of
London's great annual river events, first run on 1 August 1715 at
the instigation of Thomas Doggett (1640–1721), an Irish comic
actor and the manager of the Theatre Royal, Drury Lane. Called
'the wager', it was a race for watermen who had just completed
their apprenticeship, and the course stretched from Swan Stairs
near the Old Bridge to the White Swan Tavern at Chelsea, a village

about four and half miles upstream.[15] There had been racing on the Thames before, but this was different. Doggett had established the contest to honour the first anniversary of the accession (in 1714) of King George I. There was a cash prize and a striking dark reddish-orange livery coat with a solid silver badge, weighing about twelve ounces, displaying the White Horse of Hanover and 'Liberty' as the motto. 'All which,' Doggett declared, 'I would have to be continued for ever yearly in Commemoration of His Majesty King George's happy Accession to the Brittish Throne.'[16] Among the early winners of the coveted red livery and solid silver badge was, in 1730, John 'Jack' Broughton of Hungerford Stairs, later to become one of England's most famous and successful prize-fighters.[17]

As this annual display of physical endurance made clear, watermen required particular strength in the upper body, spending their working hours, day in day out, in a sitting position. As he was ferried across or along the Thames, Hogarth had countless opportunities to observe the peculiar physical characteristics resulting from such employment: 'Watermen too, are of a distinct cast, or character, whose legs are no less remarkable for their smallness ... There is scarcely a waterman that rows upon the Thames, whose figure doth not confirm this observation.'[18] The everyday nature of ferrying Londoners across this wide and deep expanse of water must have attained a strange power at night, with the dense black of a barely lit river so close you could touch it, the splosh of the oars and the wherrymen calling to each other or chatting, as they were wont to do, to their passengers. Within the darkness, the only respite for the eye were the little flickering lights of the wherries and other small craft skimming over the water.

The dangers of travelling at night were heightened, in an emergency, by the fact that most people could not swim; most Londoners simply did not learn. In the case of the Thames, a passenger being carried over might have called to mind the Greek mythological character of Charon, the ferryman of Hades, transporting the souls of the recently deceased across the Styx and Aceron – the rivers dividing the worlds of the living and the dead. Ned Ward introduces 'Part VII' of *The London Spy* with a journey by river, where 'a Jolly Grizzle-Pated Charon handed us into his Wherry'.[19] Like

Ward but with less whimsy, Hogarth established this connection between modern London and ancient myth and how he might apply his observations from nature and real life in his art. Noting the broad shoulders and thin legs of the Thames watermen and echoing Ward's description, he mused, 'were I to paint the character of a Charon, I would thus distinguish his make from that of a common man's ; and, in spite of the word *low*, venture to give him a broad pair of shoulders, and spindle shanks'.[20] Charon, a figure from 'high' culture is brought 'low', in the guise of a London waterman. It is in this application of everyday observations to his art – whether high or low – that distinguished Hogarth from his contemporaries and brought him into conflict with received wisdom, as to what was or was not appropriate, particularly in regard to the highest form of art, 'history painting' – precisely the context in which the figure of Charon might appear.

The wherry passed Somerset House and its formal gardens lying next to the river and then, running parallel to Fleet Street, the Temple legal district, with the ancient Knights Templar church and, after more gardens, walks and a timber yard, those places of misery, Bridewell and the Fleet prison to the north, and the outlet of the Fleet Ditch. From here they could see more clearly the distinctive domed shape of St Paul's Cathedral as they passed Puddle Dock and the wharfs and alleys lining the riverbank up to Fishmongers' Hall and, directly ahead, the Old Bridge, visible in the moon's light.

This ancient bridge was built as a demonstration of penance by King Henry II, after the murder of his friend and the popular London-born Archbishop of Canterbury, Thomas Becket in 1170: it is to pay homage at Becket's tomb that Geoffrey Chaucer's medieval pilgrims travel from London to Canterbury. The use of the term 'peregrination' by Hogarth and his friends encourages the forming of connections, tenuous or otherwise. We might note, for example, that they are heading from London to Kent, as were Chaucer's pilgrims in *The Canterbury Tales* before them. Both journeys begin at a tavern, spring and its bounty are in the air and, in the case of the furthest destination, the Isle of Sheppey and Canterbury Cathedral respectively, tombs and wells (holy or otherwise) are prominent features. The unspoken hint to such illustrious literary ancestry allows the spirit of these medieval pilgrims to hover over the early Georgian narrative: what they hope to gain from such a journey, their own histories, their fallings out and makings up, and the (mainly) ribald yarns told to each other as they travelled, all of which form the greater part of Chaucer's work. In the association, further layers of potential meaning and not a little comedy arise in the 1732 account. And, as a reflection on Hogarth's art, the connection to Chaucer – described by Giles Jacob as the 'Father of the English Poets, and HOMER of our nation'[21] – the mixing of high and low, the moralistic and the realistic, places Hogarth in a long line of English artistic (in the general sense) endeavour.

At the north and south entrance on to the bridge there was a gate house, over which, on the southern or Southwark side, the heads of executed traitors were displayed. On either side of the central roadway, running the entire length, was a mass of rickety residences and businesses, many overhanging the river. The bridge was a survivor of the fire of 1666, which had broken out in Pudding Lane, just to the north-east. And in commemoration, here stands the column with a gilded ball of flame at its summit, called The Monument. The deep bas-relief carved into the facing side of the pedestal depicts Charles II and his brother, James Duke of York (later James II), leading the fire rescue.

By the early eighteenth century, negotiating the narrow gaps between the numerous starlings driven into the river bed, which supported the pillars and held the bridge aloft, must have been a little alarming for river passengers. The pillars required continual reinforcement, narrowing the gap between them and through which the little craft had to steer. The bridge makes an appearance, seen through the lead-and-glass window of the City merchant's house, in the last scene of Hogarth's *Marriage A-la-Mode*. This tiny detail anchors the narrative, where greed and monetary accumulation override compassion by a father towards his dying daughter, to a precise London location and a recognisable professional type. Incidentally, we can also see the plucky craft and crews who negotiated daily this dangerous but necessary river passage.[22]

The pilgrims' little boat may have attempted to pass under the

5. Gérard Jean Baptiste Scotin II after William Hogarth, *Marriage A-la-Mode Plate 6: The Lady's Death*, etching and engraving, 1745
The window view locates this old-fashioned merchant's house to near Billingsgate. The countess has taken poison after reading the notice (lying at her feet) of her lover's execution.

Old Bridge, but, given the well-known adage that the bridge was 'for wise men to pass over, and for fools to pass under', they may have thought it prudent to land just before at Swan Stairs, the starting point for Doggett's watermen race. This was the nearest passenger landing for Billingsgate, the site of the famous fish market a little to the east of the Old Bridge and from where the boats left for Gravesend. The arrival here signals that the pilgrims had left behind the City of Westminster and were now within the parameters of the City of London, Hogarth's place of birth.

As Hogarth and his friends headed east towards Kent, fishing boats around the coast near Sheppey and along the Thames and Medway estuaries were loading fish and shellfish for delivery to Billingsgate, the capital's central fish market. These marshy regions of Essex and Kent were deemed less visually attractive than the lush orchards and market gardens around Maidstone, where the cherries and apples heading for Covent Garden were grown. Yet, despite their ugliness and associated putrid, unhealthy air (as the early Georgian traveller might view them), one visitor, the novelist, pamphleteer, government spy and travel writer Daniel Defoe at least acknowledged that the region provided a common staple of the late Stuart, early Georgian diet, that is the 'best and largest Oysters, such as they call Stewing Oysters : which are generally call'd also *Milton* Oysters' from the town of Milton near Gravesend. He continues 'the whole of the City of *London* is chiefly supplied with Oysters from this Part of the *Thames*'.[23]

Jonathan Swift, author of *Gulliver's Travels*, with reference to the unlikely appearance of the mollusc, apparently declared 'He was a bold man that first ate an oyster.' Whether he said it or not, it is a fair comment, although this did not reduce the popularity of this cheap foodstuff.[24] In fact oysters were so abundant that Dr Samuel Johnson, the famed lexicographer, wit and man of letters, fed them to his cats. James Boswell provides a delightful picture of the doctor's love of the animals he had 'taken under his protection', a sentiment with which Hogarth would have wholeheartedly agreed, and one called Hodge in particular: 'I never shall forget the indulgence with which he treated Hodge, his cat ; for whom he himself used to go out and buy oysters, lest the servants having that trouble should take a dislike to the poor creature.'[25]

Rather than cats, Hogarth's favoured domestic pets were dogs, specifically pugs, the most famous, immortalised in paint and even ceramic, named Trump – possibly because he was plagued with gastric wind, or as a reference to the card game. Trump was living with Hogarth from about 1730 to about 1745, so had been Hogarth's companion for several years before *The Peregrination* occurred and seems to have been the replacement for another pug, imaginatively called Pugg, who disappeared in late 1730. Hogarth treasured the dog enough to put an advert in *The Craftsman* in the hope of his return.[26] His distaste for the abuse of animals will be expressed in his 1751 series, *The Four Stages of Cruelty*. Being an admirer rather than simply an owner of dogs, the artist clearly considered them personalities in their own right. Of course 'pugnacious' chimed perfectly with Hogarth's own appearance and character, and the pug will become, most overtly in his 1745 self-portrait, an expression of Hogarth's self-identity – an animal incarnation of the artist. Samuel Ireland declared that Hogarth 'had conceived a greater share of attachment than is usually bestowed on these domestic animals',[27] although, for any dog lover, that reveals more about Ireland than his subject.

The artist and author William Henry Pyne (aka 'Ephraim Hardcastle') published a series of anecdotal articles (gleaned from various sources but using 'Uncle Zachary' as his named authority) concerning Hogarth and his contemporaries, originally in the *Literary Gazette* then collated in 1823 under the title *Wine and Walnuts*.[28] One anecdote, revealing that Hogarth was not alone in making a close connection, metaphorically and otherwise, between man and dog, tells how Hogarth produced a caricature portrait of a young apprentice, who, we are told, '*unfortunately* looked more wicked than he was' – Hogarth noted his 'hanging look'[29] – on the back board of a cupboard in the weaving attic of the apprentice's place of work. In revenge, the said apprentice, Kit Sugars, daubed a portrait of Hogarth and his dog with the title 'The two Pugs' nearby.[30] Having demonstrated his wit in this original and provocative manner, Kit became concerned (justifiably) that Hogarth would not take kindly to the comparison. But Samuel Scott, who was present, declared, 'The devil a bit ; Hogarth is too fond of genuine humour to take offence at this.'[31] And so it proved, for when Hogarth saw Kit's handiwork 'he laughed loudest of the group ; when, flying back again he exclaimed, "Kit, you witty dog, I love you from my heart !" and going to the wall, he, in spite of all the struggles of his friends to spare it, obliterated his own caricature ; then turning to him whom it represented, he said, "Kit, if you rub out *me* and *my dog*, I'll break your bones."' And so there they stayed, artist and canine muse, on the back panel of this cupboard, 'until the old premises were clean swept away'.[32] Trump is not mentioned as joining the pilgrimage, so he must have remained at the house in Covent Garden, guarding his mistress while her husband was away.

Apart from the delivery of Kent and Essex oysters, Billingsgate dock and market was populated by the market sellers and workers from the various craft that landed the catch brought from the coast. Again, thanks to Ned Ward, we have an extremely evocative description.[33] He and his friend, like the five pilgrims, ventured to the area at night, a time of day that increased the sense of adventure and, it has to be said, menace. Ned's chronicle is far from sympathetic towards the people he encounters. Instead he summons up a hellish vision, populated by characters that are barely human – crowds of '*Thumb-Ring'd Flat-caps*' ranging from seven years old to seventy, 'who sat Snarling and Grunting at one another, over their *Sprats* and *Whitings*, like a pack of *Domestick Dogs* over the *Cook-maids* kindness, or a parcel of hungry *Sows* at a Trough of *Hogwash*' and all as wily 'as a strol[l]ing *Fortune-teller*; that I fear'd they would have pickt my Pocket with their Eyes'.[34]

Ebenezer Forrest, the official chronicler for *The Peregrination*, did not care to describe the area in any detail at all, nor the company that he and his friends now found themselves among. Rather, he simply notes they arrived at the 'Dark House',[35] likely so named because its exterior was painted a dark colour, although the name also hints at murky activities within. Some sense of what the ominously titled hostelry might have been like, located on the river at the south end of Dark House Lane, is provided by Ned Ward in his section, '*On* the Dark-House *at* Billingsgate', although a fair amount of artistic licence (one would hope) had been expended in the process: 'in a narrow Lane, as dark as a Burying Vault, which Stunk of stale Sprats, Piss, and Sirreverence' (human excrement), 'we groped about, like a couple of Thieves in a Cole-hole, to find the Entrance of that *Nocturnal Theater*, in whose delightful Scenes we propos'd to terminate the Nights felicity.' After further stumbling about, at last they happened upon the Dark House or 'Gloomy Cavern ; where, at a distance, we saw, Lights burning like Candles in a Haunted Cave, where Ghosts and Gobblins keep their Midnight Revels'.[36]

It was here, among the local ghouls and goblins, that Hogarth, always ready with his paper and pencil (then, either thin sticks of graphite or, like a modern pencil, encased in wood) sketched a portrait of the Gravesend-ferry porter and self-named 'Duke of Puddle Dock'.[37] The pilgrims had passed this wharf, to the west of

Billingsgate, now only remembered in a street name. With Ned Ward's additional information to guide us, we can imagine how the presence of His Grace of Puddle Dock may have inspired the artist, but wonder at Hogarth's daring in such an environment. The portrait of the porter, described pithily as 'grim' by the Reverend Gostling, was completed in quick time and Hogarth, whether on a whim or as an act of discretion being the better part of valour, surrendered it to his subject, who pasted it up, in pride of place, 'on the Cellar Door'.[38]

Meanwhile, within the Dark House the five friends were highly entertained by the tavern regulars and what Forrest calls the 'Humours of the Place', which is a play on the ancient 'Physical senses', that is, blood (hotness), phlegm (coldness), choler (dryness) and melancholy or 'Black Bile' (moistness), connected to health and temperament. The term 'humours' also conveys the character, style, spirit and behaviour or actions regarded as whimsical, odd, quaint or amusing. Hogarth uses the term in his satirical works, *The Humours of the Fair*, or *The Humours of an Election*. A flavour of what these humours might be can be found in Ned Ward's recollection of the women of Billingsgate, also regulars at the Dark House. (Forrest only mentions the common terms 'Gaffer' and 'Gammer', an old man and old woman, being lent a bawdy twist by a fellow drinker, considered by the pilgrims 'a Litle Obscene' in the presence of two members of the 'Fair Sex'.)[39] As Ned goes on, he and his friend encounter the women fish workers and, not wishing to engage with them, as the author continues, 'Come, come away, says my Friend, let's seek another Apartment : These saucy Tongu'd old Whores will tease us to Death.' Unfortunately, these 'unhappy words one of them over-heard ; and starting up like a Fury, thus gave her Lungs a Breathing'. And here, apparently, is the tirade verbatim that Ned's squeamish guide received from this particular representative of the gentle sex: '*You White-liver'd Son of a* Fleet-street Bumsitter, *begot upon a Chair at Noonday, between* Ludgate *and* Temple-Bar. *You Puppily off-spring of a* Mangy Night-walker, *who was forc'd to Play the Whore an Hour, before she cry'd out, to pay the* Bawd *her* Midwife, *for bringing you, you Bastard, into the World.*' Concluding, '*Who is it that you call Whore?*'[40]

Now, Ned Ward is deliberately caricaturising for comic effect and succeeds brilliantly. As noted his pen portraits of London were extremely popular and influential. But rather than simply mock, we might at least ponder on the desperate lives of the people who eked out a living in the environs of Billingsgate. In the main, Hogarth deals very sympathetically with London's workers and street criers, particularly girls and women: the Savoyard girl, belting out her songs while accompanying herself on a hurdy-gurdy; the pretty milkmaids in *The Enraged Musician* and *The March of the Guards to Finchley*, the former standing proudly and centrally, returning your gaze with a calm confidence (see endpapers). In the stunning unfinished oil on canvas called *The Shrimp Girl* (Col. Fig. 2), painted in the early 1740s, he captures, from the life, one of the women who collected the shellfish from Billingsgate, dressed in oilskins and a fisherman's sou'wester over her cap and tied-back hair, on top of which she balances a shallow basket with shrimps, cockles and mussels. From the market, she would wander the streets hawking her wares, one of the famous Cries of London, with the shellfish priced per half pint, the measuring jug also carried in the basket. The aroma will become more and more pungent as the freshness turns to putrefaction, the liquor dripping over her protective head ware and down her back. Yet, in Hogarth's hands, she is the very essence of good health and joy. (Equally, Hogarth can depict such figures with no empathy at all. The three fish wives to the left of the painting *Calais Gate* are closer to Macbeth's witches, unsexed as it were, than prime examples of the fair sex.)

But, continuing in the spirit of Ned Ward's description, we are left to imagine the nature of the obscenity to which Hogarth and his friends were witness. The popularity of *The London Spy* and their own experiences would mean that they and their fellow club members would require no additional information or prompting with regard to the regulars at the notorious Dark House. But in any case, Forrest's account concludes this section by stating that the pilgrims lingered happily enough in this mercurial ambience, spending eight and a half pence on refreshments, until the clock struck one.

CHAPTER ONE

GOOD CHILD

Very little is known about Hogarth's ancestry and, as previously noted, details of his early life and career prior to 1732, when he was already in his mid thirties, are curiously patchy. We know he was born on 10 November 1697 in Bartholomew Close, opposite Middlesex Court in Smithfield, properly called 'West' Smithfield, to the north-west of Billingsgate.[1] Hogarth was born in the house where his father, Richard, had been lodging from 1690 (initially as a single man) just a few years after his arrival in London from the county of Westmorland in England's north-west. The house, within a 'close' or network of lanes and small inner courtyards, lay to the east of Smithfield's central open ground and adjoining St Bartholomew's Hospital. The hospital's legendary founder, the twelfth-century English priest Rahere, had been miraculously cured of a terrible illness during a pilgrimage to Rome and, in gratitude, founded a priory and hospital for the poor on his return to London. Within its confines, just beyond the stone gate topped by the distinctive swaggering effigy of King Henry VIII, is the church of St Bartholomew the Less. The fellow Anglican church of St Bartholomew the Great (what remains of the priory), the place where the infant William Hogarth's arrival into this world and his baptism were recorded in the nonconformist register, is located between the hospital and the close named after it.[2]

This area of the City, lying between Clerkenwell and Charterhouse to the north, the Old Bailey and Newgate prison to the south, the Inns of Court to the west and St Paul's Cathedral to the south east, brought together institutions that balanced life with death – it still does. Apart from St Bartholomew's Hospital, the area's past and present spoke of different forms of 'butchery'.

Smithfield was used as a place of execution in the medieval period, and it was here that the Scottish hero, William Wallace, and Wat Tyler, the leader of the Peasants' Revolt, came to their grizzly ends in 1305 and 1381 respectively. The same area hosted London's main livestock market, within a stone's throw of Hogarth's first home, so anyone living locally would have been familiar with a very particular and unusual urban soundscape: the lowing and bleating of penned animals awaiting auction and, for some, slaughter nearby; the shouts and cries of farmers, herders, market traders, slaughtermen and butchers. As well as noise, the market would have presented a nasal assault, with the ground covered in straw, dirt and various shades of farmyard dung and effluvia.

Surely spending his childhood in close proximity to the livestock market made Hogarth more sensitive to the welfare of animals. Samuel Ireland, in reference to the artist's love of pugs, suggests he was unusually fond of such creatures – as, too, was Dr Johnson of his cats.

Thousands of animals, herded through the metropolis to Smithfield market, simply exacerbated the filth on London's streets. Tens of thousands of horses provided the main mode of transport (apart from walking) in Hogarth's time, and London houses (great and small) had private stables or access to stable yards nearby. Human waste was carried by night soil men through the streets, or dumped in open sewers (or conduits), including tributaries of the Thames, like the Fleet Ditch, which lay just to the south of Smithfield. Human urine was a valuable product in the leather-tanning process, and Hogarth introduces a soil man carrying fresh piss through the streets of Charing Cross in the night scene of *The Four Times of the Day* (Fig. 45 p. 311).

But the herding of animals through the streets of a densely populated city like London had its hazards, beyond the need to sidestep the steaming manure piles that inevitably covered the roads and walkways. A tiny detail in the background of Plate 2 of Hogarth's *The Four Stages of Cruelty*, set in the streets near Thavies Inn, Holborn, is of a rampaging ox tossing a man into the air as frantic herders attempt to stop it. This is not fantasy, as illustrated by a dramatic report from the *Grub Street Journal* of 1737.

6. *The Four Stages of Cruelty Plate 2: Second Stage
of Cruelty*, etching and engraving, 1751
Lawyers clamber out of the over-turned carriage, uncaring of
their part in the horse's abuse, while (right) a dozy wagoner,
through negligence, is about to run over a young boy.

The incident described in great detail also occurred in the
streets around Holborn, situated on the northern route west to
east (via Tyburn Road, Oxford Street and High Holborn) to and
from Smithfield market. As seen in Hogarth's engraving, an ox was
being herded too fast, and the irritated animal began charging pas-
sers-by, tossing aloft and injuring six, including a woman, before

careering into the ground floor of a house on Rathbone Place some distance away. Within was a Mr Pantillo, who was playing games with his child in the back parlour, while chatting over a cup of tea with a young man, probably his lodger, who used this room as a living and sleeping space. As the ox burst in, Mr Pantillo threw his infant under the bed while hurling himself on top. Luckily the ox followed Mr Pantillo, which allowed time for the quick-thinking parent to grab his child and flee the room. The lodger, not so lucky, was gored in the chest. The report goes on to describe how the ox was startled by its own reflection (or 'shadow') in the overmantel mirror – which hints at the scale of the beast – and proceeded to crash about the room, breaking the mirror and all the furniture. There were several attempts to shoot it, but, at the second, the now wounded and terrified animal forced its way out through the ground-floor window, carrying with it the wood frame and glass entire, and fell into the open basement area. Here it broke a rack of bottles, before smashing all the basement kitchen windows, finally arriving in the vault, where it was shot dead by the owner.[3]

Hogarth's engraving foregrounds the everyday cruelty meted out to animals on these urban streets and in plain sight to all those passing by – the whipping of horses, the clubbing of donkeys and sheep – animals, lest they forget, that Londoners depended on for transport, haulage and sustenance. The tiny detail of the ox, whose power and destructive behaviour should be viewed, in the spirit of Hogarth's print, as connected to the abuse displayed in the foreground is illustration of a moment when nature, bullied and beaten, finally and dramatically turns on its human abuser.

Hogarth, as any Londoner, indeed any human being, would have some compassion for the people injured and potentially killed by the ox in the *Grub Street* report – 'there but for the Grace of God &c.' – but, turning to those mishandling the animal, he would say, what do you expect? And to those silently witnessing and ignoring such behaviour, what are you going to do about it? Hogarth does not answer these questions: he is prodding his audience's conscience and leaving it to them to respond, whether to challenge abuse against animals, or not, as they see fit. But, he observes, through these four connected prints, inactivity by good citizens allows such aggression and disdain for life to breed. And who can say that abusers will limit themselves to animals? If animals are mistreated, humans will eventually suffer, as did Mr Pantillo with his wrecked house, terrorised family and gravely injured tenant. But here Hogarth makes a direct association between animal and human abuse: the child, in the First Stage, who tortures a dog – an abuse Hogarth would have seen himself – becomes the youth, in the Second Stage, who flogs a horse, already collapsed on the ground, and then, inured completely to the fear and agony of others, by the Third Stage has turned into a murderer in adulthood, cutting the throat of his pregnant partner. The fourth and final stage, the protagonist's comeuppance, is execution. The only hope for humanity within the entire series comes in the form of a boy in the first image, weeping as he attempts to defend the dog from the sneering child torturer.

Beyond the livestock market, and on a lighter note, the Smithfield area was also famed for the annual Bartholomew Fair, originally located in the street called Cloth Fair (as the name suggests, the carnival had formerly been associated with the sale of textiles). By the mid seventeenth century the fair had relocated to the south side of the livestock market. This ancient and popular local tradition, staged since the year 1133 – it was Rahere who secured the charter for the fair to provide financial support for the priory and hospital – and occurring over several days around 24 August (the saint's day), brought a further barrage of noise, smell and spectacle to Hogarth's childhood experience, and was another significant and enduring influence on him. Ned Ward devoted an edition of *The London Spy* to the fair – written and published when Hogarth was two or three years old – dubbing the scene that greeted him on entering the precincts as 'Belfegors Concert'. 'Belfegor', or 'Belphegor', known as the 'Lord of the Opening' and representing discoveries and ingenious inventions, is a demon or prince of hell alongside the better known Beelzebub ('Lord of the Flies') and Satan. This hellish concert, as Ned recalled, is formed from 'the rumblings of *Drums*, mix'd with the Intolerable Squeakings of *Cat-Calls*, and *Penny-Trumpets*, made still more Terrible with the shrill Belches of *Lottery Pick Pockets*'.[4] It is a common observation that Hogarth's scenes are full of sounds and noise, whether the cacophony that sends the musician into an impotent rage, or the collapsing stage in Southwark Fair, or the raucous hubbub at Tottenham Court Turnpike. The scene at night, as experienced by Ned Ward, would have been lit with torches and fires, contrasting with the surrounding darkness, and adding to the appearance of an urban Hades or Pagan Sabbat.

In an attempt to protect themselves from the full sensory onslaught, Ned and his companion sought refuge in a tavern overlooking the fair and observed the goings-on from this safer distance, while smoking pipes and drinking wine. They watched the mountebanks tout their dubious wares, the Merry-Andrews' buffoonery, and the street-booth entertainers performing their ribald plays, usually combining slapstick comedy with folksy home-spun morality, to the delight of the immense jostling crowds 'Sweating and Melting with the heat of their own Bodies'. This accompanied by the pungent odours, or 'unwholesome Fumes' arising from whole roasting pigs, sizzling and spitting among the roar and cackle. Densely populated gatherings inevitably attracted pickpockets, as Ned recalled, and other criminals who plied their trade with impunity.[5] Such scenes appear in Hogarth's paintings and engravings as varied in subject as *Southwark Fair*, a similar annual carnival based in London's southern borough, and the execution of Tom Idle at Tyburn in *Industry and Idleness* – both situations deemed entertainment, at least by those who thronged to them.

Beyond the melding of all human life, it is in the plays, performed on temporary stages or booths, that a direct connection can more broadly be made with the character and substance of Hogarth's work and in his sets or narrative series in particular. One such entertainment, again described by Ned Ward, presents and challenges certain social conventions and mores by revealing the various circumstances where human beings make arrant fools of themselves, all wrapped up to a common purpose, the learning of a moral lesson:

The *Show* being thus ended, my Friend asked me how I lik'd it? Truly, said I, 'tis a very Moral Play, if the Spectators have

7. *Southwark Fair*, etching and engraving, 1733
Southwark's dilapidated parish church, St George the Martyr,
like the staging to the left, was in danger of collapse. With the
banner, a White [Trojan] Horse, Hogarth hints that King
George's grip on national matters may be a little shaky too.

sense enough to make use of it. At which saying, my Friend
burst into a Laughter. Prithee, says he, wherein lies the Morality of it? Why, said I, it will serve to let us know how familiar
a Priest, notwithstanding his Holy Orders, may be with the
Devil. How easily Clergy may impose upon the Vulgar a belief
of those things which never were, or can be. What a Blockhead
may be a *Justice of Peace*. How a Rich Cunning Knave may have
a Fool to his Son: How Old Men love Young Bed-fellows : How
a Woman will cheat her Father to oblige her Gallant : What
Stratagems Lovers will project to Accomplish their Ends ; and
what *Jack*-Puddings Men will make of themselves to get a little
Money. On my Word, says he, you have made a rare use of it
indeed : But I very much Question whether any Body else will
be half so much the better for it ; for it may be observed that

Bartholomew-Fair Drolls are like *State-Fire-Works*; they never
do any Body good, but those who are concern'd in the Show.[6]

Hogarth, as a child as well as an adult, would have been very familiar with this '*Hell* in an Uproar'.[7] He recalled, 'I had naturally a
good eye' and that 'shews [shows] of all sort gave me uncommon
pleasure when an Infant'.[8] It is a beguiling thought, that the child
William, holding his father's hand while giggling at the antics of
the Merry Andrews and the street players, is learning the indis-
pensable basic tools for storytelling and entertainment.

Hogarth would have known well the West End actors who performed at the fair, including John Mills, William Bullock, Henry
Norris and William Penketham and the famous stages on which they
performed, Heatley's Booth, Thomas Doggett's Booth, the instiga-
tor of the annual Thames watermen race, and Mrs Mynn's Booth,
where *The Siege of Troy* was performed, the entertainment later
depicted by Hogarth in his *Southwark Fair*.[9] In the recollections of
his childhood, Hogarth states that 'mimickry common to all children was remarkable in me',[10] which could refer both to his ability
to reproduce a character or scene with his trusted pencil, but also in
an 'impersonation' in the modern sense. No wonder Hogarth was
considered such good company. But beware a man who can imitate
the idiosyncrasies of his fellows in person as well as in paint. The
simple folk morality played out here at the Bartholomew Fair booths
should chime with anyone familiar with Hogarth's work: untrust-
worthy officials, men and women behaving badly, parents ruining
the lives of their children and so on. In a challenge to *The London's
Spy*'s assumption that the moral lessons will have little or no impact
on their audience, Hogarth, for one, was paying attention.

In *The Analysis of Beauty*, published towards the end of his life,
Hogarth recalled, from his experience of theatre in general and
Bartholomew Fair in particular, certain comic turns as examples
of how inappropriate visual combinations create humour through
absurdity: 'When improper, or *incompatible* excesses meet, they
always excite laughter ; more especially when the forms of those
excesses are inelegant, that is, when they are composed of unvaried
lines.' He goes on to use examples he himself had witnessed:

For example ... a fat grown face of a man, with an infant's cap on, and the rest of the child's dress stuff'd, and so well placed under his chin, as to seem to belong to that face. This is a contrivance I have seen at Bartholomew-fair, and always occasion'd a roar of laughter. The next, is of the same kind, a child with a man's wig and cap on. In these you see the ideas of youth and age jumbled together, in forms without beauty.[11]

Such observations translate into Hogarth's designs: the pug, for example, sitting upright on its haunches, wearing a man's wig, holding a scroll, and looking out at us with a wry expression. In another note, Hogarth describes a scene from Christopher Marlowe's *Dr Faustus*, a popular play which, in adapted form, would have been produced at Bartholomew Fair. He selects the moment where a canvas sack leaps up, by itself, and then jumps across the stage, which 'makes a whole audience burst into laughter'.[12] And then there is Falstaff, that larger than life Shakespearian character of *Henry IV Part 1–2* and *Henry V*, a source for humour as well as pathos: 'Falstaff's Humour<ous saying> as *stand before me boy I would not be seen* to his little page when the lord Chancelor [*sic*] was passing by' a classic device, where the character professes to hide in plain sight.[13] In any case such comic juxtapositions would be translated into pairings within Hogarth's compositions, notably the full-figured wife and puny husband in 'Evening' from *The Four Times of the Day* (Fig. 18 p. 124).

Hogarth was naturally attracted to fictitious tragicomic characters like Don Quixote, Hudibras and Falstaff, all of whom he would illustrate. And Hogarth's affection for such lovable rogues or hapless dreamers may have encouraged the selection of a scene from Thomas Betterton's adaptation of *Henry IV, Part 2* (Act IV, Scene 3), *Falstaff Examining his Recruits* (1730), as an early foray in narrative painting.[14] Another juxtaposition, at the time considered more ridiculous and unnatural than strictly humorous, is the young man and the much older woman, as seen in Tom Rakewell's desperate marriage to the one-eyed, toothless but wealthy widow (Fig. 22 p. 138). The lines beneath declare, '*Now to ye School of hard Mishap, Driven from ye Ease of Fortune's Lap, What Shames will*

Nature not embrace, T'avoid less Shame of lean Distress? Gold can the Charms of Youth bestow, And mask Deformity with Shew; Gold can avert ye Sting of Shame, In Winter's Arms create a Flame, Can couple Youth with hoary Age, And make Antipathies engage.' John Nichols observes that this widow, the epitome, in his opinion, of mutton dressed as lamb, made more incongruous still by continental modishness, 'has received so high a polish, that she might be mistaken for a queen mother of *France*'.[15]

When Richard Hogarth arrived in London in 1690, the main occupants of the house in Bartholomew Close were John and Ann Gibbons and their children, from whom Richard rented a room, probably (for economy and as a single man) on an upper floor. Residing within a family or individual's home, as Mr Pantillo's unfortunate lodger had done, was a standard and relatively cheap way for a single person or couple, even those with children, to find accommodation. Aside from providing an income, the arrangement could be very beneficial to the landlord or lady – offering companionship as well as security, in a city where housebreaking as well as personal robbery and mugging was rife. Indeed, opening your home to a stranger – whether a lodger or a servant – could, in isolated cases, also come with significant risk (as we shall see).

Among John and Ann's children still resident with them at this time was their daughter Anne, unmarried at the mature age (for the period) of twenty-nine. A handwritten reference in the family bible, the King James version with a Book of Common Prayer, confirms that Richard and Anne married on 4 November 1690, just after Richard had moved in.[16]

John Gibbons died soon after and the newly-weds took over a floor of the house, living alongside the mother, now 'Widow' Gibbons, who continued to own and manage the property. Between 1691 and 1694, three children were born to the Hogarths – John, Elizabeth and Anne (or Ann). All three died within weeks of their baptisms.[17] In early eighteenth-century London, infant mortality was between 350 and 400 per 1,000.[18] But however common, losing three newborns was a high mortality rate. This sequence of tragic deaths was followed by the birth of Richard in 1695, two years later by William and then Mary and a second Ann.

These last three were the only Hogarth children to survive into adulthood, Richard dying in late 1705, aged just ten.[19]

If little is known about William Hogarth's early life, even less is known about his father. 'Hogarth' may have been a later modification of the Westmorland surname of Hogart or Hogherd.[20] The adaptation of the surname – from the honest if admittedly inelegant association to pig keeping – hints at the desire to move the family on and up the social ladder. Sometimes surnames associated with geographical places become adapted through time. John Thornhill's grandfather had been a 'Thornhull' despite hailing from Thornhill in Dorset.[21]

John Nichols provides two stories concerning the change in spelling, the first associated with Mrs Hogarth: '*Hogart* was the family name, probably a corruption of *Hogherd*, for the latter is more like the local pronunciation than the first. This name disgusted Mrs. *Hogart*; and before the birth of her son, she prevailed upon her husband to liquify it into *Hogarth*. This circumstance was told to me by Mr. *Walker*, who is a native of *Westmoreland*.' Nichols then offers another explanation, this time from Dr Thomas Morell, Hogarth's collaborator on *The Analysis of Beauty*, who stated that it was William himself who made the transformation: 'I was informed that his real name was *Hoggard*, or *Hogard*, which [he] himself altered, by changing the *d* into {þ}, the Saxon *th*.'[22]

Either way, Richard Hogarth is thought to have hailed from the vale of Bampton, the village of that name located fifteen miles north of the market town of Kendal. He is recorded as being the third son of a 'plain yeoman', who worked a small tenement farm.[23] Bampton is in the Eden district of the old county of Westmorland, named after the river that flows north to Carlisle in what is now Cumbria, at the edge of the Lake District. The creativity of J. M. W. Turner, William Wordsworth and Samuel Taylor Coleridge would later establish the sublime and romantic allure of the region in the mind of the British public, but that is over a century and many lifetimes away. In the late seventeenth century, such wild landscapes were places that the ambitious would, if possible, leave in all haste and travellers would pass through, occasionally looking out of the carriage window, rather than linger a moment longer than necessary.

The information on Hogarth's ancestry, provided by John Nichols, came from local historian Adam Walker, who also identifies Richard's elder brother as the picaresque character, the 'ploughman' playwright and poet Thomas or 'Ald Hogart'. Thomas (d.1709) provides his own play on his surname: 'A Hogg, a Heard, A Haire, a Hart's delight/ Smile on his name that did these fancies write. THOS. HOGGART'.[24] Crucially he is described as notable for his 'jollity and whimsicality, as much as for his habit of spinning rhymes, constructing plays, and getting up dramatic entertainments'.[25] Regarding our William Hogarth, Walker's declared purpose is 'to shew you, that his family possessed similar talents', and thus knowledge of Thomas brings greater understanding and appreciation of his famous nephew. The 'songs and quibbles' of 'Ald Hogart', the 'simple strains of this mountain *Theocritus*', the Sicilian-born inventor of the pastoral form of ancient Greek poetry, 'were fabricated while he held the plough, or was leading his fewel [fuel] from the Hills'.[26]

The similarities as emphasised by Walker between the two Hogarths, uncle and nephew, does not rest with a native knowledge, wit and creativity. For Thomas 'was as critical an observer of nature as his nephew' albeit from 'the narrow field he had to view her in'. Hence, in the context of Bampton and its vicinity,

> not an incident or an absurdity in the neighbourhood escaped him. If any one was hardy enough to break through any decorum of old and established repute ; if any one attempted to over-reach his neighbour, or cast a leering eye at his wife ; he was sure to hear himself sung over the whole parish, nay, to the very boundaries of the *Westmoreland* dialect ! so that his songs were said to have greater effect on the manners of his neighbourhood, than even the sermons of the parson himself.[27]

This attempt to present William Hogarth, years after his death, as springing from a family of eccentric, north-country rustics is appealing. Ald Hogart's songs, through which he exposed the hypocrisy and immorality of his neighbours to the scrutiny of each other, chime brilliantly with William Hogarth's use of his art to that very same purpose.

Thomas Hoggart's work seems to have existed in manuscript form, but was mainly recalled, according to Adam Walker, through an oral and aural tradition within Westmorland. In 1853 his work became more widely available via a pamphlet entitled *Remnants of Rhyme by Thomas Hoggart of Troutbeck (uncle to the great painter)*, derived, according to the cover's puff, from those autograph manuscripts still in the possession of the poet's descendants. Here Thomas is described as 'a rustic untutored rhymester'. The book includes poems and epitaphs for the recently departed. The one to 'William Idle' (note his surname) observes: 'Here lies a man who, in his life,/ Was blest in all things but a wife.' Having then late in life acquired said wife and now on his last legs,

> Death hovering by him did the sick man spy;
> On wife and death at once he fixed an eye,
> Revolving then what way might be the best,
> With wife to tarry, or with death to rest.
> 'Come, throw thy dart, he said, and take my life,
> With thee I'll go, but, pray thee, leave my wife.'[28]

Unfortunately, there is no evidence that the ploughman bard is a direct relative of the artist and, given this, it speaks more of a desire to project Thomas on to William as a less refined version of the latter than anything else. Perhaps William's father had heard of his namesake and through the local oral tradition imbibed and passed on his particular brand of moralising? The connections between them do highlight general aspects of Hogarth's source material and style. We could almost say it indicates a certain type of national character, crossing county and national borders, rural–urban experience and even cultural and political divides. It offers a fundamental reason for the broad recognition Hogarth's characters and narratives enjoyed across the British Isles (indeed, beyond) and thus their universal appeal. Although it is important to note that the expendable income required to own a majority of Hogarth's prints (other than those produced cheaply, precisely to attract a broader audience), let alone his paintings, was limited to a very small percentage of the population.

Richard Hogarth, it is thought, attended Archbishop Grindall's Free School at St Bees, a coastal village in the old county of Cumberland. Certainly Hogarth senior had acquired traditional classical learning, as his means of achieving gainful employment on arrival in London confirm. In any case, Richard would leave Westmorland and venture to the capital at a momentous time. In the late 1680s the British Isles were once more in turmoil. Charles II had died in 1685, with his brother, the Catholic convert James II, ascending to the throne. Charles had attempted to confirm a Protestant succession through his nieces, Mary and Anne, children of James's first marriage. But in June 1688 the new king's second and Catholic wife gave birth to their first child, a son, o'er leaping the claims of James's daughters, as heir apparent and Prince of Wales. The prospect of a Catholic monarch ruling the predominantly Protestant England after James II's death was now a reality. The child's arrival after so many years of marriage raised an eyebrow, fuelling the ludicrous rumour (which few intelligent people actually believed) that the prince was a bastard of lord-knows-who, perhaps a bricklayer, smuggled into the queen's bedroom via a warming pan. In any event James fled abroad after the invasion in November 1688, supported by prominent parliamentarians of his Dutch (and Protestant) nephew and son-in-law William of Orange, setting in train the so-called Glorious Revolution, a tentative form of constitutional monarchy enshrined in the Bill of Rights (1689), and the reign as joint monarchs of King William III and Queen Mary II.

Like many others before and since, Hogarth would, in the future, use the legend of the warming-pan baby to refer to James's only legitimate son, James Francis Edward, also known as the Old Pretender. But as a demonstration of just how ludicrous this idea was, we need only refer to the testimony of the royal portrait painter, Sir Godfrey Kneller, recorded soon after the death of James II in 1701 at his place of exile, Saint Germain-en-Laye near Paris.

Louis XIV of France, James's cousin, had declared James Francis Edward King James III of England, despite the fact that an Act of Settlement had been passed in the English parliament, confirming that the succession to the English and Irish thrones (Scotland remained separate) was now 'settled' on Protestants only, bypassing James's Catholic offspring. Kneller, who had painted every monarch, their consort and children since Charles II, had travelled to Corpus Christi College, Oxford to paint the portrait of a Dr Wallis at the behest of Samuel Pepys (diarist and Royal Navy official). As a supporter of James's claim, he was one of those known as Jacobites.[29] The topic of the warming pan and the bricklayer came up and Sir Godfrey, with his heavy German accent, cried, 'Vat de devil! De prince of Wales de son of de brickbat ouman? It is a lie. I am not of his party, nor shall not be for him. I am satisfied with what de parliament has done, but I must tell you what I am sure of, and in what I cannot be mistaken.' He continued, 'His fader and moder have sat to me about thirty-six times a-piece, and I know every line and bit in their faces. I could paint king James just now by memory. I say the child is so like both, that there is not a feature in his face but what belongs either to fader or Moder ; this I am sure of … I cannot be out in my lines.'[30] Sir Godfrey's testimony was so devastating that all who had witnessed it signed a transcription. The very fact that detractors felt the need to invent such a story in order to undermine the prince's parentage simply confirmed that such legitimacy was important if not, in itself, crucial.

Perhaps, as an ardent Protestant, Richard's arrival in London at this moment was a conscious move. Whether coincidence or not, the last three children born to Richard and Anne Hogarth had the names of the last Protestant Stuart monarchs of England: a sign of the political times and a hint as to where Richard and Anne's loyalties lay.

Soon after, Richard was running a school in Ship Court off the Old Bailey, so finding accommodation in the nearby Smithfield area made great sense. Alongside teaching, Richard was also keen to publish and, as we might expect of the son's father, those traceable examples are full of strong opinions and moral observations. His *Thesaurarium Trilingue Publicum: Being an Introduction to*

English, Latin and Greek (published 1689) includes, in section two, a sequence of lessons for children, split between morning and afternoon of each day of the week from Monday to Saturday, 'Being Wholesome *Precepts* containing several *Vertues* necessary to be instill'd into young *People*'.[31] The lesson for Wednesday mornings is set out as follows:

> Custom makes every thing easy : Accustom but your selves to laugh and you will not, without Difficulty leave the foolish Habit. Use not your self to Women or Wine; nay even almost to Sleep, and you may easily abstain from them. If you use your self always to ride a Coach, you will lose the Benefit of walking by disusing it. Plunge not your selves in Pleasures, lest afterwards you should not be able to live without them, and so make your selves miserable, by making that become necessary which before was Superfluous : So prevalent is Custom, That if you set your self resolutely to that which is *good*, or that which is *evil*, you shall not easily relinquish the one or the other.[32]

This has a direct echo in Hogarth's own creations, whether for the benefit of children, youths or adults. Tom Rakewell's plunge into pleasures, on inheriting great wealth, his addictive usage of 'Women' and 'Wine' certainly makes for a miserable life as revealed in *A Rake's Progress*. There are many examples in Hogarth's work where a clear moral and instructive purpose, offering black-and-white choices made by individuals which lead to divergent life journeys, is offered with all humour and entertainment stripped away. *Industry and Idleness* (1747) balances, within the same series, two diametrically opposed journeys taken from the same starting point, of Francis Goodchild, a diligent and virtuous apprentice and Tom Idle, a bad or immoral apprentice. More extreme still are *The Four Stages of Cruelty* (1751) and the paired prints *Gin Lane* and *Beer Street* of the same year.

Similarly, Richard Hogarth's Thursday afternoon lesson, on '*Every Man the Causer of his own Happiness or Unhappiness*'[33] leads on to the Friday morning subject, more optimistic in its mood, for, the reader is pleased to learn, '*'Tis never too late to be Good*':

As no Man ought to presume to instruct others, having not
first given good Counsel to himself ; so I think it absolutely
necessary for every one to endeavour to be good at one time
or other, and the sooner the better, though 'tis never too late
to repent ; or as the Divine *Seneca* has it, *'Tis never too late to
learn, what it is always necessary to know ; nor Shame, so long
as we are ignorant, and that is, all our Lives.* When any thing
ails us in our Bodies or Estates, we have presently recourse to
the Physician or Lawyer ; and why not to God, the Soveraign
Good, in the Disorders of our immortal Souls, that best and
most valuable Part of us? 'Tis worth your Notice and Observation to keep good and wise Men Company, for 'tis a fair
Step to Happiness and Vertue so to employ our time.[34]

The Saturday morning lesson, '*A wise Man is provided against all
the Accidents of Fortune*', could be a proverb or axiom associated
with any one of William Hogarth's more stridently moralistic
works:

To persist in an Opinion, I mean, not to be given to Change,
is the certain Mark of a wise Man, for Fools are various ; one
while Thrifty and Grave, another while Profuse and vainly
Conceited : But happy is that Man that sets himself right at
first, and continues so to the end. A prudent Man carries his
Treasure within him; what Fortune gives she can take, therefore he so providently orders the Matter as to leave nothing
to her Mercy : He stands firm, and keeps his Ground against
all Misfortunes, without so much as changing Countenance :
He will not murmur at any thing that comes to pass by Gods
Appointment : He is not only Resolute but Generous and
good Natured, and for the publick Safety is ready to Sacrifice
his own.[35]

Reading these examples, it becomes obvious that Richard had a far
greater influence on his son than has been previously allowed. The
adult Hogarth will not abandon his prosperity to fortune alone, he
will stand firm against adversity with unswerving resolution and

will be public spirited and generous. Further, it is not too fanciful to suggest that one impetus for Hogarth's translation into graphic form of such tenets as set out in Richard Hogarth's publications was a homage of sorts to his father and his own upbringing, as well as the firm belief, even certainty, of their accuracy and efficacy.

By the time the second Ann was born in 1701, the Hogarths and their young family had moved to a house at the lower end of St John's Street, just to the north of Bartholomew Close, and a few years later they had moved again, to nearby St John's Gate. The gate was part of what remained of the old priory church of St John of Jerusalem, the crusade-period Knights Hospitaller. While here, Richard, an enterprising man attempting to play to his education, experience and strengths, opened a coffee house that encouraged conversation in Latin, as his advertisement in the *Post Man* trumpets with pride and optimism:

> At *Hogarth's* Coffee house in St Johns Gate, the mid-way between Smithfield Bars and Clerkenwel, there will meet daily some Learned Gentlemen, who speak Latin readily, where any Gentleman that is either skilled in that Language, or desirous to perfect himself in speaking thereof, will be welcome. The Master of the House, in the absence of others, being always ready to entertain Gentlemen in the Latin Tongue.[36]

The use of the spelling 'Hogarth' in this advertisement suggests, of the two stories, that the one connected to Mrs Anne Hogarth is the more likely. But returning to Richard's new enterprise, in view of the status and use of Latin in professions like the Law and, generally, its importance in signalling a gentleman's education, a coffee house where said gentlemen could practise Latin is not as madcap a proposition as some later commentators have suggested. Further, apart from access to classical languages, it means that when William was a child, the coffee house and club setting, where men with social, professional and intellectual affinities gathered together over coffee or something stronger, was a familiar environment. This followed him throughout his life, from the Bedford

Arms tavern club, to the artists' gathering place, Slaughter's Coffee House on St Martin's Lane and, as a founder member, the Beef-steak Club.

The district encompassing Clerkenwell, St John's Gate, West Smithfield, Little Britain and as far south-east as the churchyard of St Paul's Cathedral was renowned for publishing, printing and bookshops, so Richard's relocation from Westmorland to this particular corner of London was a canny move for an aspiring author. A few decades later the young Benjamin Franklin would travel from Philadelphia to Smithfield in order to train as a printer at Palmer's, 'a famous Printing-House in Bartholomew Close'[37] and soon after, Samuel Johnson, after walking to London from his native Lichfield, would be submitting his weekly sketches as a parliamentary reporter, describing the activities in 'the Senate of Lilliput', also known as the House of Commons, on behalf of the *Gentleman's Magazine* printed at their offices in St John's Gate.

Some elements of the father's learning and scholarship would have been transferred to his only surviving son. In *The Analysis of Beauty*, Hogarth quotes or paraphrases the writing of, among others, Socrates, Pythagoras, Pliny and Aristotle. In 1712 Richard published a book to help children learn to speak and write Latin, so it is difficult to imagine that William did not benefit from his father's expertise when he was young, and particularly when he reached school age.[38]

William's mature handwriting is well formed, even if, when in the mode of free-flowing thought, his sentences have little struc-ture or punctuation and his spelling is, at best, haphazard. This is not unusual for the period, prior to any concerted attempts at standardisation – Dr Johnson's dictionary of the mid 1750s, for example – where randomly phonetic spellings are often used and punctuation is considered desirable but not necessary. The notebooks of George Vertue, habitual chronicler of London's art world and a wonderful source of information on Hogarth and his career (as an alternative voice and perspective) are, to be fair, barely more decipherable. It is clear from William's writings and in the way he could make jokes and puns, that he understood some basic Latin and Greek, although not in any learned way. A supper invitation Hogarth sent to his friend, Dr Arnold King, illustrates this.[39] At the centre is a sketch of a platter, on which is a pie or tart, with a two-pronged fork (the usual fork type at this time) and knife on either side. The text around the pie reads, 'Mr Hogarth's Comp[limen]ts to Mr King and desires the Honor of his Company at dinner on Thursday next to Eta Beta PY.' This little joke, inviting his friend to join him at his house 'to eat a bit of pie' is an indication of Hogarth's wit, and nods to a basic knowledge of ancient Greek alphabet, but is whimsical, clever and charming. It also, like *The Peregrination*, gently pokes fun at classical learning. After all, as John Nichols declares, 'A quibble by *Hogarth* is surely as respectable as a conundrum by *Swift*.'[40]

That said, a turn in the fortunes of Richard Hogarth, and therefore of the whole family, soon occurred which would limit his son's access to formal learning, in the process reducing dramatically his immediate prospects and setting him back some years from pursuing a career in fine art. No matter how well read Hogarth was, there is an element of the autodidact's sense of inferiority, particularly when in the presence of easy familiarity with the Classics and the like. He certainly carried through his life a heightened awareness of his deficiencies, which made him sensitive to condescension and slights – real and imagined.

Between 1707 and 1708, when William was ten or eleven years old, Richard was imprisoned for debt in the Fleet prison, which lay to the south-west of Smithfield and near to those other sites of misery, Newgate prison and Bridewell house of correction. He was still there on 23 September 1710, when he was begging for respite from his confinement in a letter to Robert Harley, Queen Anne's chief minister. The choice for Richard was either to have his debts declared void by his creditors, or for someone to pay them off. There was little opportunity to earn money while within the prison and, as a resident, you were expected to pay your way, which simply compounded the financial crisis, the sense of powerlessness and despair. Hogarth would bring conditions in the Fleet to painful life in the seventh scene of *A Rake's Progress*, just before Tom Rakewell's journey terminates at the infamous asylum, 'Bedlam' (from 'St Mary Bethlehem' or Bethlem Royal

8. *A Rake's Progress Plate 7: The Prison*, etching and engraving, 1735
Harangued by his wife, whose wealth he has squandered (along with
his own), his new play rejected and the gaoler (or jailer) demanding
'garnish' money, Tom's state of mind is visibly disintegrating.

Hospital). Given his direct personal experience of the prison, it
can be presumed that the depiction here is accurate in atmosphere
if not detail: from the overall gloom, the exposed stone walls, the
small, high and barred window, the dirty floor, the corner stove at
which meagre food is cooked, the remnants or wreckage of a life
represented by the clothes the inmates stand in and little else. The
text beneath, written by Hogarth's close friend, the Reverend John
Hoadly, resounds with hope lost and desolation: '*Talents idle &
unus'd, And every Gift of Heaven abus'd. The Sea of Sad Reflection
lost, From Horrors still to Horrors tost.*'

The day-to-day existence within the Fleet, much like Charles
Dickens's later narratives concerning the Marshalsea in Southwark, could surely send many inmates from penury to madness

– 'Reason *the Vessel leaves to Steer, And Gives the Helm to mad*
Despair' – although there is no indication that Richard's mental
health suffered to that extreme extent, no one emerges from such a
circumstance unscathed. It is probable, however, that his physical
health did deteriorate, indicated by his death less than a decade
later. While Richard languished within the Fleet itself, Anne
Hogarth was attempting to feed and clothe her little family, while
having to live within the liberty or rule of the prison, a defined
area beyond its walls, by advertising the sale of home remedies,
including a medicine for infants 'call'd The GRIPE OINTMENT'
– revealing a resourcefulness in the face of extreme adversity.[41] In
tandem, as a debtor, Richard's possessions, at least anything with
any value, would have been sold to offset debt. But Richard's circumstances were far from unusual – in fact he was in good company.
Daniel Defoe declared himself bankrupt twice and then spent
time in the Fleet and King's Bench prison in 1692 and 1702.[42] The
daily and weekly newspapers regularly advertised extensive lists of
bankrupts. The imperative to declare your resources, as part of the
bankruptcy process, could literally be a matter of life and death,
with the death penalty one outcome if the bankrupt neglected to
provide a full disclosure of assets or attempted to hide them.[43]

Richard and his family survived the period of his incarceration,
but soon after his release a further setback seems to have ruined,
once again, Hogarth senior's hopes and ambitions and, in the
process, finally broke his spirit: in a proverb familiar to the early
Georgians, it would be the last feather that broke the horse's back.

Before any accusations are made against Richard's choice
of employment as the source of the family's distress, it must be
stated that William's father was (as far as the evidence can suggest)
innovative, persistent and hardworking. His attempts at gaining
employment were usually on a speculative basis, as was often the
case with publishing, and, unlike a commissioned or sponsored
publication, his efforts were more vulnerable to failure. Crucially,
with no upfront fee that a publisher's commission or a patron's
largesse would provide, there was no financial safety net against
any unforeseen difficulties, or simply on which to live before
copies could be sold. And with Richard's fading hopes, the family's

immediate circumstances collapsed, along with the dreams of his son.[44]

By 1712 John Nichols states that Richard was teaching at a school in the parish of St Martin's Ludgate and, around this time, he was advertising in the *British Mercury* 'to all Gentlemen and others, that have any Thing to translate, transcribe, Indexes to gather, or any Business of that kind, that they may have it readily and carefully done, by Richard Hogarth, at his House in Angel-Court on Snow-Hill, over against St. Sepulchers [*sic*] Church'.[45] But it became increasingly difficult for Richard to afford to have a son in school, rather than training for a profession. While a schoolboy, possibly at the institution where his father was employed, Hogarth had already developed an interest in drawing, a skill he later described as coming naturally to him. In his autobiographical notes Hogarth hints that a local artist stimulated this early interest in art: 'an early access to a neighbouring Painter drew my attention from play' and after this contact, 'evry oppertunity was employd in attempt at drawing'.[46] It is not clear who this local artist may have been, although a John Dalton had been established in Bartholomew Close from the late seventeenth century.[47] He also recalls that 'when at school my exercises were more remarkable for the ornaments which adorn'd them than the Exercise itself'. He notes that 'Blockheads with better memories' beat him at the exercise, but for the adornments 'I was particularly distinguish[e]d'.[48] Perhaps it was in frustration with the 'blockheads' and lashing out that Hogarth received that wound above his eye? Hogarth would later observe that the experience and example of his father's ongoing difficulties as a writer turned his natural ability in drawing and 'mimickry' into an ardent desire to be an artist, rather than a writer or a learned man of letters: 'Beside the natural turn I had' – that is, for drawing – 'I had before my Eyes ... the precarious State of authors and men of learning I saw not only the difficulties my father went through whos dependence was cheifly on his Pen' but 'the cruel treatment he met with from Bookseller[s] and Printers.'[49] And here we might consider Hogarth's painting and engraving of *The Distress'd Poet* in his garret, his young wife mending clothes by an unlit fire, with a grumpy infant in the only bed. The accompanying lines by Alexander Pope read 'Studious he sate, with all his books around,/ Sinking from thought to thought, a vast profound!/ Plung'd for his sense, but found no bottom there;/ Then writ, and flounder'd on, in mere despair.'[50]

William then recalls, with further bitterness and indignation on behalf of his poor beloved father, that it was a protracted situation around a Latin dictionary that finally did for Richard and, indeed, for his son's hopes of an education. Despite receiving letters of support for the project from 'the great schools in England Scotland and Ireland', among which were no doubt Eton, Winchester and Harrow, which should have guaranteed the production of the dictionary (the major schools and libraries being chief beneficiaries and promoters) and, again, despite the many years his father had spent compiling the volume and with the manuscript then being deposited with 'a certain printer', the culprit remaining nameless, the project failed.[51]

Hogarth later declared, using the third person, that 'His Fathers Pen like that of many other authors was incapable of more than putting him in a way to shift for himself.'[52] William was therefore removed from school and set on a new path. One route to professional training and therefore the prospect of regular employment was through apprenticeship, which tied the youngster to a master for seven years. Hogarth was in the event apprenticed, against his inclinations, to a silver engraver. Although not unconnected to the fine art field he so desperately wanted to be part of, engraving items such as plates and cups was still a very long way down the artistic hierarchy. That said, a trade's a trade, and Hogarth would benefit immensely from the skills he developed in this line of work, as he later grudgingly admitted. John Nichols states that an unnamed assay master at Goldsmiths' Hall confirmed that Hogarth had been consigned to the sole monotonous activity of engraving arms and cyphers 'on every species of metal'. This gentleman, sadly not identified, knew this because he had been apprenticed to a silversmith in the same street as Hogarth, and was 'intimate with him during the greatest part of his life'.[53]

Hogarth's master was Ellis Gamble, himself the son of the silver engraver William Gamble, who had entered his mark at

Goldsmiths' Hall in 1697 and was based in Foster Lane, the location of the silver engravers' guild, the Goldsmiths' Company, between around 1692 and 1703.[54] There is a silver tankard dated 1697 engraved by William Gamble, 'The gift of the Directors of the Bank of England to Sir John Houblon', which is indicative of the type of work Hogarth was now training to do. William Gamble was succeeded by his son, Ellis, Hogarth's master, who then, from 1713, soon after joined by his new apprentice, Master Hogarth, established himself to the west, beyond the City, in Blue Cross Street, just south of Leicester Fields (now Square) in the parish of St Martin-in-the-Fields.[55]

The street was described by John Strypes in 1720 as 'Blue Cross-street, new built with Houses fit for good inhabitants: It cometh out of Hedge-lane, crosseth St. Martin's-street, and falleth into Orange-street.'[56] Leicester Fields itself is pronounced 'a very handsome open Square, railed about, and gravelled within. The Buildings are very good, and well inhabited, and frequented by the Gentry ... especially the North, where is Leicester House, the Seat of the Earl of Leicester: Being a Large Building, with a fair Court before it, for the reception of Coaches; and a fine Garden behind it ... Next to this House is another large one, inhabited late by the Earl of Aylsbury, now by His Royal Highness George Prince of Wales', that is the heir apparent to King George, the future George II.

Leicester Fields and its environs were, indeed, a very suitable place for a young, intelligent chap with ambitions to find himself. Hogarth's apprenticeship ran from February 1714 to, probably, early 1720, so he was training and boarding with Ellis in Blue Cross Street during the working week. In so doing, the expense of his upkeep was no longer a burden to his parents: one reason why apprenticeships were popular for families like the Hogarths. As Hogarth's traineeship started only a year after Ellis had established himself, it is likely that the master was not much older than his apprentice. At sixteen years of age, Hogarth was some years older than was usual at the start of an apprentice's journey. The delay is clearly connected to the original plan that Hogarth would have been in school, acquiring that longed-for gentleman's education, rather than training in an artisan skill. Hogarth was not the only would-be painter to have his ambitions thwarted by family concerns or difficulties. Joseph Highmore, his contemporary (b.1692), also a Londoner and, later, established in Lincoln's Inn Fields as a portrait painter, had hoped to be apprenticed to his uncle, Thomas, sergeant painter to William III, but mysteriously he was instead articled – very much against his inclinations – to a City attorney. He was not released from his articles until he was twenty-two years old but, determined, like Hogarth, to keep his hopes alive for his chosen career, he schooled himself in the theory of art (perspective, geometry), attended anatomy lectures and signed up to a new drawing academy, established in 1711 under the governorship of Sir Godfrey Kneller, at Great Queen Street.[57] The notion that a career in fine art was not a stable profession prevailed and therefore, through family pressure, other routes to earning a regular wage were required. Hogarth considered this period as his wilderness years: 'the chief part of my time was lost <till I was three and Twenty> in a business that was rather detrimentall to the arts of Painting and Engraving I have since pursued'.[58]

Perhaps this is why, being dismissive and a little embarrassed (as Hogarth was) of this period of his life, we have so little information about it, just a few precious indications of his time with Ellis Gamble through the anecdotes gathered and published many years later. Writing in the early nineteenth century, John Thomas Smith, recalling the Flemish-born painter Joseph Francis Nollekens, called 'Old' Nollekens, wrote 'I have several times heard Mr. Nollekens observe, that he frequently had seen Hogarth, when a young man, saunter round Leicester-fields, with his master's sickly child hanging its head over his shoulder.'[59] Samuel Ireland described a portrait by Hogarth, now lost, allegedly painted during his apprenticeship and therefore the first known oil by him, which was said to be of Ellis Gamble's young son, possibly the same child seen by Old Nollekens hanging its head over Hogarth's shoulder.[60] The anecdote presents a striking image: a confident, perhaps on the face of it cocky young man, sauntering around his patch, while carrying a frail child on his back. Whether true or not, although there is no reason to think it invented, the story points to Hogarth's youthful energy, his ease with children, the defenceless and vulnerable, and a forthright, unshowy compassion and protectiveness. The use of the word 'saunter' to describe the young Hogarth, suggesting a gentle swagger, is wholly appropriate: indeed it is a word he used to describe himself.[61] Old Nollekens may have recalled these small incidents in later life because, at the time of publishing, they would have had greater resonance with Hogarth's known character and career, given his close and active association with, for example, the Foundling Hospital (founded in 1739).

Even now, Hogarth was supporting his parents and indeed Ellis Gamble, as John Nichols states, 'the skill and assiduity of *Hogarth* were, even in his servitude, a singular assistance to his own family, and to that of his master'.[62]

John Nichols provides another anecdote which reflects on Hogarth's determination to move on from silver engraving as swiftly as possible. He records a Sunday jaunt to Highgate, then a village to the north of London, which Hogarth made with his fellow apprentices. The company walked the four or so miles from Leicester Fields to Highgate, much of it uphill. The most direct route, in the early stages of the trip, would have taken them along Tottenham Court Road (then a track through open fields) to the turnpike, on to the fork in the road, left to Hampstead, or right to Highgate via Kentish Town where more or less the last buildings stood between London and their destination. Hogarth and his contemporaries would have thought very little of an eight-mile round hike. Even within London, walking was usual, the city being a fraction of its modern size. As the apprentices made their way north on their one free day, a warm sabbath during the summer season, the bells of the parish churches would have been sounding and beyond, on the horizon, Highgate and her sister village Hampstead would have been visible on the hills before them. It is the same route that, in 1745, the King's Guards will take on their march to Finchley.

Nichols describes the event in the following manner:

he set out one *Sunday*, with two or three companions, on an excursion to *Highgate*. The weather being hot, they went into a public-house, where they had not been long, before a

quarrel arose between some persons in the same room. One
of the disputants struck the other on the head with a quart
pot, and cut him very much. The blood running down the
man's face, together with the agony of the wound, which had
distorted his features into a most hideous grin, presented
Hogarth, who shewed himself thus early 'apprised of the
mode Nature had intended he should pursue,' with too laughable a subject to be overlooked. He drew out his pencil, and
produced on the spot one of the most ludicrous figures that
ever was seen. What rendered this piece the more valuable
was, that it exhibited an exact likeness of the man, with the
portrait of his antagonist, and the figures in caricature of the
principal persons gathered round him.

Nichols supports the truth of this anecdote with the comment that
it 'was furnished by one of his fellow apprentices then present, a
person of indisputable character, and who continued his intimacy
with *Hogarth* long after they both grew up into manhood'.[63]

Unfortunately it is not known who this fellow apprentice was,
and frustratingly Nichols again does not disclose his source, but
the story is a superb illustration of a habit that Hogarth developed
early in life, as stated in his autobiographical notes, of sketching
wherever and whenever the inspiration struck. Hogarth clearly
considered a pencil and sketchbook, or, at the very least, a bit of
paper or cloth, as vital kit while he moved through and around the
city – as essential, indeed, as a hat and shoes. John Nichols recalls: 'A
gentleman still living informs me, that being once with our painter
in the *Bedford Coffee-house*, he observed him to draw something
with a pencil on his nail. Enquiring what had been his employment,
he was shewn the countenance (a whimsical one) of a person who
was then at a small distance.'[64] Further details of this extraordinary
event are provided by William Pyne, apparently quoting Hogarth
himself, where he describes sketching the firebrand theatre critic,
John 'Griffin' Dennis (1658–1734) 'on my thumb-nail – I did not
dare have a scrap of paper before me in his presence, or he would
perchance have broken my bones. His malicious eye was every now
and then glancing towards me, but he did not find me out. I went

thence, holding my glove loosely to guard the pencil sketch on my nail, directly to the Rainbow, and showing it to Colley Cibber [the actor] bid him guess. "By all that's sacred," said he, "if that's not Griffin Dennis ! – For God's sake do not rub it off."[65]

As he developed this technique, it seems he also settled on a method through which an intricate form can be reduced to a few simple lines – a very personal and idiosyncratic type of hieroglyph. This process will find full expression in his *The Analysis of Beauty*, but another example, perhaps tested out during an idle hour in a tavern, involved a famous conundrum with which Hogarth delighted in teasing new companions. Hogarth would announce to onlookers that he could draw a serjeant carrying a pike, going into an alehouse with his dog following, in just three strokes of the pencil. The audience would wonder at how such a complex composition could be achieved so simply. Hogarth would then draw the following, with 'A. The perspective line of the door. B. The end of the Serjeant's pike, who, is gone in. C. The end of the Dog's tail, who is following him.'[66]

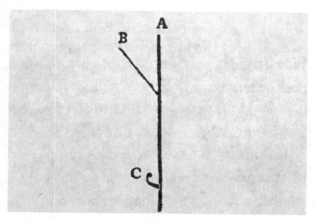

9. Illustration from John Nichols, *Biographical Anecdotes of William Hogarth*, 3rd edition, London, 1785, p. 63

The younger Hogarth alighted on the process of sketching from life at every opportunity, alongside this reduction of forms to hieroglyph, both an *aide-memoire* (mnemonic) as well as a puzzle, in order, by his own admission, to bypass the need for the more laborious aspects of the traditional artists' training. This included the continual copying (relentless and tedious copying, as Hogarth would view it) of casts, or copies, of famous sculpture – typically ancient Roman/Greek examples, such as the renowned *Apollo Belvedere* and the *Laocoön*, the originals of which were in the papal collections at Rome. And, in addition, copying drawings by other artists considered, again, exemplars – depending on availability (a connoisseur's collection for example) by experts of the drawing technique such as Rembrandt, Van Dyck and Rubens. Kneller and the portrait painter turned art theorist Jonathan Richardson both collected drawings, which were made available for students and young professionals to study.[67] Such training in Great Britain, previously offered within the studio master–pupil system, was now more broadly available for a fee through the informal London art academies, including Kneller's at Great Queen Street, to which we will return.

The description, early in *The Peregrination* account of Hogarth sketching the porter at the Dark House, is the first but far from the last mention of this habit in the narrative. The anecdote reflects exactly his constant awareness of and interest in the people around him – in appearance, personality and behaviour – and his deft ability to capture, quickly, a likeness to great comic effect. Another example is mentioned by John Nichols, in his *Biographical Anecdotes*. No date offered but still in his youth, according to Nichols, Hogarth's then landlady demanded payment of twenty shillings (a not insignificant sum) which Hogarth, being poor, did not have. (Another source, an obituary, states that, at this juncture, he was arrested and bailed.)[68] And so in revenge he drew her in as ugly a manner as possible: 'in that single portrait', Nichols continues, 'gave marks of the dawn of superior genius'. However, Nichols introduces some doubt as to the truthfulness of this story. He notes that a not dissimilar tale was told of Antonio Verrio (1636–1707), an Italian painter of vast painted interior schemes, who, while painting the ceiling in St George's Hall, Windsor Castle for Charles II, borrowed the face of the irritable housekeeper, Mrs Marriot, for the screaming visage of one of the mythical furies.[69]

Perhaps this was simply one of many artist-related tropes, much like marine painters strapping themselves to ship masts to experience a storm, used to enliven the artist biography and to introduce a rite-of-passage element to what can be a very mundane, uneventful narrative. The moral being, beware the ire of one who can capture your likeness. Indeed, as John Nichols continues, regarding Hogarth's landlady: 'This story I had once supposed to be founded on certainty ; but since, on other authority, have been assured, that had such an accident ever happened to him, he would not have failed to talk of it afterwards, as he was always fond of contrasting the necessities of his youth with the affluence of his maturer age.'[70] So, when in his pomp, at the height of his powers, these wilderness years served one crucial purpose – to show just how far William Hogarth had come.

In addition, using every opportunity to improve his sketching skills was a way of keeping his artistic ambitions alive. Hogarth felt that his enforced apprenticeship, which, as noted, started later than was usual and in silver engraving, had set him back years in comparison to his artist peers, and he was impatient to pursue his dream of becoming an artist, with all its associated dignity and renown. Yet even during his apprenticeship, painting was not necessarily his ambition in the short term, for, as he later recalled, again in the third person, 'Engraving on copper was at twenty ... his utmost ambition'[71] – that is, around halfway through his apprenticeship period. This was a perfectly sensible ambition, because silver engraving was piece work, whereas copper-plate engraving was the means of generating multiple print copies and was considered the most refined and skilful of all the printmaking techniques: reproduction in this way was highly prized, particularly if the print run was limited.

The standard artist training, aside from copying, also included life drawing; drawing from the live, usually nude human figure. As an adjunct to studying the naked form, students were also encouraged to attend anatomy classes, delivered by surgeons or physicians. Hogarth considered this aspect of traditional training crucial, because it involved looking at nature in the flesh – whether alive or dead – rather than once removed, as with a classical sculpture, for example. The object of that observation, translated into chalk or graphite or ink strokes on paper, was the very basis for all great art, whether portraiture or, greater still, history or narrative painting. Both genres, to varying degrees, dealt with the nature of human life and experience, but history painting was considered the noblest, because it required artistic ability fused with an extensive knowledge of history and literature and the ability to select and depict a telling moment, or combination of moments, that turns a story of the particular into the universal.

This focus on observing nature refers not only to the comic or extraordinary but also to the subtle, the attractive and the everyday. Hogarth's observations on women's costume and hair suggest an interest in impression and effect – necessary in a portrait painter, whose very work requires close looking, and for the creation of distinctive characters in a narrative painting. Another wonderfully evocative example of everyday observation, which would be used in his art at the appropriate time, concerns watching servants, surely his own employees, washing clothes. Of particular interest are 'the hand and arms ... plunging suddenly from warm into cold water' which 'become as red as beef'.[72]

Such an observation could be the work of a moment: after glancing up from a book and noticing a companion or stranger's hair artfully styled, or while walking around London's streets and squares. Although, having described the appeal in such details, Hogarth also notes that there is a moment when a pleasing but innocent curl, for example, stimulates more than just attraction: 'A lock of hair falling thus cross the temples, and by that means breaking the regularity of the oval, has an effect too alluring to be strictly decent, as is very well known to the loose and lowest class of women: but being pair'd in so stiff a manner, as they formerly were, they lost the desired effect, and ill deserv'd the name of favourites.'[73] Such a wanton curl can be seen and to great effect (considering its subtlety) gracing the forehead of Lady Squanderfield in *Marriage A-la-Mode* (Fig. 12 p. 76), as she stretches, cat-like, after an illicit night with her lover. Similarly Hogarth observes, 'This principle also recommends modesty in dress, to keep up our expectations, and not suffer them to be too soon gratified'[74] – a rule Moll Hackabout has abandoned by scene three of *A Harlot's Progress* (Fig. 26 p. 158).

Such observations are not the exclusive property of the elite; anyone – man, woman or child – can see such little, everyday delights, if only they took the time to look for, acknowledge and appreciate them. Returning to ancient sculptures of Apollo or Venus, which had come to define what is beautiful for art connoisseurs, a breed Hogarth loathed as tyrants of taste, he argues they are mentioned within *The Analysis of Beauty* only because they are 'generally known : nor would we have it thought, that either of them have ever yet come up to the utmost beauty of nature. Who but a bigot, even to the antiques, will say that he has not seen faces and necks, hands and arms in living women, that even the Grecian Venus doth but coarsely imitate ?'[75] Here the opportunity to mention *The Shrimp Girl* once more cannot pass – a true London Venus, flesh and blood. However, these are Hogarth's mature contemplations, and we are in danger of getting ahead of ourselves. So with the observation that the seeds for *The Analysis of Beauty* are sown very early in Hogarth's life, we shall leave the artist and return to the apprentice.

Such sketches, on the spot, in the moment, sparkling with immediacy and candour, will act (as already stated) as aides-memoire, Hogarth called them 'memorandum' for future compositions. By way of example, imagine Hogarth's sketch at the Highgate tavern, the victim's hideous grin, the blood dripping down his face, being filed away and then appearing, adapted, decades later, as the battered figure in the foreground of a chaotic election banquet and, earlier still, in his caustic (and all too realistic) homage to a drunken night out going horribly awry, *A Midnight Modern Conversation*. In a similar vein, Hogarth recalled, 'I remember to have seen a beggar whose head was clouted up artfully enough to excite pity but his features were so unfortunately formd, tho they were thin and pale enough for his purpose that what he intended for a grin of pain and misery ... was rather a joyous laugh.'[76]

We should not assume that it was all work and no play for young Billy. Hogarth was more than aware that apprentices and young male workers were almost a social archetype, representing that period between childhood and manhood where good and bad habits were formed, perhaps to dominate the adult life for good and ill – as his father's lessons for children declared. In detailing the paths of two apprentices in *Industry and Idleness*, where character and choices are crucial to the onward journey, the boisterous and convivial Hogarth may have used his own wrestle between dedication to a craft and a love of the pleasures of life. In fact, Hogarth demonstrated that both could be achieved, with a little guile and ingenuity. In the autobiographical notes he recalls: 'He never accustomd himself to coppy but took the short way of getting objects by heart so that w[h]ereever he was [he] cau[gh]t some thing and thus united his studies with pleasure' meaning he could be sitting in a tavern, in Highgate for example, and be observing and noting faces, postures, 'humours'. And thus 'by this means he was apt [to] catch momentary actions and expressions'.[77] Besides which, Hogarth felt he had no time to lose, so a shortcut, while allowing some relaxation and pleasure, was a necessity.

With so little to construct Hogarth's years as an apprentice, the experience of his contemporary, young Benjamin Franklin, as he negotiated the highs and lows of life in London is of interest and value. As stated earlier, Franklin, future founding father of the independent America, spent two years learning his trade as a printer in London, at exactly the time that Hogarth was finding his way in the engraving and, eventually, printmaking business across town. During the year he was with his first employer, Palmer's in Bartholomew Close (who had two apprentices), Ben lodged with the charming ne'er-do-well James Ralph at nearby Little Britain, paying three shillings and sixpence a week, which was, as he recalled, 'as much as we could then afford'.[78] Franklin and Hogarth's experiences in youth chime exactly – both were inclined to hard work and understood the need for thrift, but both were more than capable of being distracted. For Ben, temptation came in the form of James Ralph, who had left behind a wife and child in America, never to return.[79] And while Hogarth may not have met the young Franklin during his first stay in London (although Franklin would write to him in later life), he would soon come to know James Ralph, a vocal supporter as well as a friend and collaborator.

Ben recalled, 'I was pretty diligent; but spent with Ralph a good deal of my Earnings in going to Plays and other Places of Amusement. We had together consum'd all my Pistoles, and now just rubb'd on from hand to mouth. He seem'd quite to forget his Wife and Child.' Ben was far from innocent himself in affairs of the heart, for by degrees he in turn forgot his 'Engagements with Miss Read, to whom I never wrote more than one Letter, and that was to let her know I was not likely soon to return. This was another of the great Errata of my Life, which I should wish to correct if I were to live it over again.' In fact, such were their expenses, that Ben was constantly unable to raise the money for his passage home.[80] The mature Franklin was aghast at the behaviour of his young self – the carelessness with the feelings of others and recklessness with his modest wages. He was not the first nor the last young man to turn a little wild away from home.

Meanwhile, Ben had moved to another, even bigger printing workshop, Watt's near Lincoln's Inn Fields, just to the west of Smithfield, with fifteen apprentices and fifty workmen. In a detail with which Hogarth would have been all too familiar, Franklin describes himself agog at the behaviour of his fellow apprentices and workers: 'I drank only Water; the other Workmen, near 50 in Number, were great Guzzlers of Beer.'[81] He continues, still incredulous, fifty years on: 'My Companion at the Press drank every day a Pint before Breakfast, a Pint at breakfast with his Bread and Cheese; a Pint between Breakfast and Dinner; a Pint in the Afternoon about Six o'clock, and another when he had done his Day's Work. I thought it a detestable Custom. But it was necessary, he suppos'd, to drink *strong* Beer that he might be *strong* to labour.'[82] Ben tried to persuade his fellow worker that beer was not the source of strength, quite the opposite, but he 'drank on however, and had 4 or 5 Shillings to pay out of his Wages every Saturday Night for that muddling Liquor; an Expense I was free from. And thus these poor Devils keep themselves always under.'[83] In contrast, Ben's hearty working breakfast encompassed, 'a large Porringer of hot Water-gruel, sprinkled with Pepper, crumb'd with Bread, and a Bit of Butter in it, for the Price of a Pint of Beer, viz, three halfpence'[84] – a repast Hogarth, as apprentice, would in all probability have enjoyed too. Ben Franklin and his fellow, the inebriated worker, could have stepped straight out of the first plate of *Industry and Idleness* (overleaf).

10. *Industry and Idleness Plate 1: The Fellow 'Prentices
at their Looms,* etching and engraving, 1747
Tom Idle sleeps off his liquid lunch, while a cat (slang for prostitute)
toys with his dangling shuttle. Frank Goodchild, meanwhile,
pursues his trade with diligence and will soon be rewarded.

Two years before William Hogarth was released from his
apprenticeship, his father died (11 May 1718), as recalled by his
son, 'of Illness occationd by partly the useage he met with from
this set of people' – that is, publishers – and partly by 'disapoint-
ments from great mens Promises'. Richard Hogarth was buried at
St Bartholomew the Great. William blames directly the behaviour
of publishers and the contrariness of patrons, who blew hot and
cold on projects of great significance to the author concerned,
little caring the impact on that individual and their dependents.
But young Hogarth felt the impact keenly, and a distrust of the
word or promises of so-called 'great' men, aristocrats who had no
comprehension of living hand to mouth from one's own labours,
would be carried throughout his life. That is not to say that he
did not court the patronage of the elite, but he would strive not
to depend on them – indeed the interaction, wherever possible,

would be on his terms. Even so, a degree of bitterness remained with him, to surface more aggressively in later years.

When finally released from his apprenticeship, William Hogarth signalled his freedom and independence by designing and printing his own shop card, dated 23 April 1720 – Shakespeare's birthday and St George's Day – and embarked on a career as an engraver, not turning away work on silver if it was offered, but, hopefully, encouraging commissions for prints.[85] The card design includes elegant figures representing poetry and history, cherubs and intricate festoons, all competently wrought, with what would become the Hogarth signature idiosyncrasies and light humour already in evidence. The cheeky cherubs hold a silver cup and a print, a declaration of the engraver's versatility, and the central 'W. Hogarth' is lightly rendered, with swirls and twiddly flourishes demonstrating a steady, precise hand.

And it worked. Over the following years Hogarth took on a variety of commissions, including shop cards, funeral tickets and book illustrations, as well as the occasional piece work on silver. The paucity of surviving examples of the latter hints that he had achieved his immediate ambition, to move from silver to copper engraving, very successfully. Regarding a tankard, as recalled by William Pyne, he engraved for 'Spiller's Club', 'Several years after the death of Hogarth, an impression from a large silver tankard which he had engraved for the use of this club – a sort of *loving cup*, sold for ten pounds. Such was the rage for any relic of this ingenious graver.'[86]

Where Hogarth was living and working in 1720 is not clear, and most surviving versions of his shop card do not include the usual detail of a business address – no doubt he put off adding this information until he was settled. Ronald Paulson states that Hogarth had briefly returned to West Smithfield.[87] It is also possible that this was the period when he boarded with Will Tothall, as the latter's friend, Captain Bulstrode, later recalled. Or the anecdote about his landlady's portrait may date from this period.

In any case, Hogarth's transfer from apprentice to independent craftsman was not without its pain – and he no longer had the encouragement and support of his father. His mother and sisters

were maintaining themselves through a sequence of haberdashery and garment businesses in the vicinity of Bartholomew Close,
Little Britain and later Leicester Fields. Billy Hogarth's sauntering,
as described by Old Nollekens, is an indication of pride and a cock-
of-the-walk brio, but it could so easily be replaced with mild, even
heavy despair if money was running low. John Nichols records: 'It
happened, however, that when he was first out of his time [appren-
ticeship], he certainly was poor. The ambition of indigence is ever
productive of distress. So it fared with *Hogarth*, who, while he was
furnishing himself with materials for subsequent perfection, felt
all the contempt which penury could produce.'[88]

Opportunity existed, but this was still a tough, unforgiving
environment, with little to assist individuals trying to find day-
to-day employment, let alone a flourishing career, other than
luck, the faith that hard work will deliver and the kindness and
support of others. Hogarth would have been acutely aware of the
example of his father. And young William could not allow this to
happen again. John Nichols hints that signs of poverty – perhaps
a frayed, over-repaired coat, holes in the shoes, a gaunt, hollow
face – would be greeted with disdain rather than compassion from
onlookers. Hogarth himself may have felt deep contempt for his
lowly circumstances. He recounted this period in his life, quoted
by companions, 'I remember the time when I have gone moping
into the city with scarce a shilling in my pocket ; but as soon as I
had received ten guineas there for a plate, I have returned home,
put on my sword, and sallied out again, with all the confidence of
a man who had ten thousand pounds in his pocket.'[89] So although
Hogarth would empathise with anyone down on his or her luck,
or struggling to get established, having suffered and endured it
himself he would have no sympathy for anyone taking an easy
option – crime for example – or those unwilling to put their all
into making a success of themselves, and, understandably, would
have little patience for someone who was elevated beyond their
talent. For all his faults, Hogarth could justifiably take full credit
for his career – for he, as described by Nichols, 'by indefatigable
industry and uncommon strength of genius has been the artificer
of his own fame and fortune'.[90]

John Nichols describes one early 'patron' or employer, the print publisher and seller John Bowles at the Black Horse, Cornhill in the City, who (Nichols was told) 'bought many a plate from *Hogarth* by the weight of the copper', in other words, paying little for Hogarth's engraving work. Nichols believed this had in fact happened only once, and not by John, but his father Thomas Bowles operating from St Paul's churchyard, who had 'offered, over a bottle, half a crown a pound for a plate just then completed'. Hogarth's 'friend in that line was Mr. *Philip Overton*, who paid him a somewhat better price for his labour and ingenuity'.[91] It was, perhaps, these payments from the Bowles elder and junior and Phillip Overton that transformed Hogarth's mood, as he recalled, from moping to strutting. The bargain these publishers had struck with the young artist can be described as either supporting a new talent or, as Nichols infers regarding Bowles senior, short-changing a desperate man not in a position to argue. The London printselling and publishing environment was a limited one, dominated by a small group of individuals such as Bowles and Overton, the latter part of a powerful dynasty, who invariably paid 'in-house' engravers (who sold their services outright), owned the plates, controlled print production and took the associated profit.[92] And there was profit to be had, for the metropolitan market alone was extensive among those with disposable income, who would purchase prints for framing and display, or would keep them in a portfolio for private inspection. Besides which the printed image, as with text, could be viewed in the print-shop window, or shared at a coffee house or club. The young Hogarth was happy to take the ready cash (or 'rhino', as was the slang) for his plates, but this would have impressed upon him the need to be in a more commanding position, as soon as possible, as an independent engraver, with greater control over his work, distribution and prices. Another thought would have been the need to diversify – spread the risk – as a way of building up reserves and reducing the unstable hand-to-mouth existence.

Someone who would have empathised with Hogarth at this time was Ben Franklin. Now independent of his wayward friend, but still living on very frugal means, needing as he did to save for his passage home to Philadelphia, Franklin, like Hogarth, was buckling down to working hard. After moving to Watt's, Ben also changed his lodgings and remained at Duke Street until he returned to America. These lodgings were kept by an elderly widow with a daughter and a colourful array of residents. After receiving character references, then as now, Ben's landlady offered him rent on a reduced rate, as she considered the presence of a young well-behaved lad in her home would be beneficial to her safety and protection. Suffering from gout, she rarely left her chamber, but Ben joined her for supper, sharing 'half an Anchovy each, on a very little Strip of Bread and Butter, and half a Pint of Ale between us'. In their mutual poverty they found companionship, the old lady regaling her lodger with thousands of anecdotes concerning people of distinction, stretching back to the reign of Charles II.[93]

Like Franklin, Hogarth, no doubt, had started to think about his next move, towards a career as a painter. But for now engraving was his focus, in the hope of bringing in regular money. As he later wrote, 'Engraving in the first part of life till near thirty did little more than maintain myself in the usual gai[e]ties of life' yet this was 'in all a punctual paymaster'.[94] Although Hogarth was determined eventually to move away from engraving, he nonetheless was to find it financially expedient, while establishing himself, to engrave his own plates until such time as he could afford, if needs be, to commission others. In fact Hogarth would continue to engrave plates for the whole of his career. Of course this meant greater control over quality, and even when contracting the services of other engravers, for the series *Marriage A-la-Mode* for example, he still preferred to complete the faces himself, maintaining the touch of the master that no other engraver, no matter how good, could imitate.

Hogarth used copper-plate engraving with etching for his more refined prints. The plate was cut with a burin (a sharp gauging tool), the ink rolled over it (the ink contained in the cuts) and then the paper pressed on to it, leaving the ink on the paper. Usually, the engraved image is the reverse of the painted image, as the engraver copies the painted image directly on to the plate.[95] And it was engraving, whatever his thoughts later in life, that would soon provide him with his first great success, setting him on the path to fame and indeed fortune.

INTERLUDE TWO

SATURDAY 27 MAY, SOME HOURS BEFORE DAWN. Hogarth and his companions, having hired for themselves a boat to carry them to Gravesend, were awaiting the ringing of the bell which would signal their imminent departure, in the lively surroundings of the Dark House inn, Billingsgate. At one o'clock in the morning, the tide being with them and a strong south-east-by-east wind blowing, they answered the chime and, guided by the porter's lamp, walked the short distance to the landing place at Billingsgate Stairs through the pitch darkness and a rainstorm that had burst forth in the intervening hours. They clambered aboard and set off on the next stage of their adventure.

The boats, or 'tilts', that shuttled the winding route between London and Gravesend (twenty-two miles as the crow flies) were so-called, as Nathan Bailey notes in his *Dictionarium Britannicum*, because they were 'covered with a Tilt, to keep off rain, &c'.[1] These nippy craft, seventeenth century in origin, had a single main mast, a sprit topmast and, their defining feature, a canvas awning over the deck, under which passengers could sit or lie on straw — although in this instance not much sleep was had by any of the company, with the wind swirling about the little boat and unseasonal rain lashing down.

According to Samuel Denne and William Shrubsole, in their *History and Antiquities of Rochester and Its Environs*, the Gravesend crews had been plying their trade since the reign of King Richard II in the late fourteenth century: 'They go to London with every flood tide, and return from Billingsgate with the ebb. Their departure from each place is regulated by ringing a small bell [every] quarter of an hour. Great numbers of people use this passage, the boats being very safe and commodious.'[2] The rates for travel on the river were advertised in the most recent edition of *The Constitutions of the Company of Waterman and Lightermen*. In 1730 the cost 'For the whole Tilt-Boat, when one or more Persons have occasion to hire it to themselves' was '£1 2s 6d',[3] although Will Tothall's final account of expenditure notes the fare for the five pilgrims to Gravesend to have been just five shillings.[4]

The tilt-boat passed the Customs House and the Tower of London on the north bank – then the location of the Royal Armouries and headquarters of the Board of Ordnance – and, a little further on, St Saviour's Dock and Timber Wharf to the south. This is the section of the river, to the east of the Old Bridge, where such wharfs and docks for the loading and unloading of trade goods were packed more closely together on both north and south banks. Such ships moved goods manufactured in Great Britain, mainly wool-based textiles, around the world. They returned with a multitude of commodities, responding to increasing customer demand. These goods would then be sold by businesses such as Mrs Holt's Italian Warehouse on the Strand, at the sign of the Two Olive Posts. A shop card produced for Mrs Holt by Hogarth in the 1720s emphasises the warm climes from which her goods had come – Rome, Naples, Venice, Florence, 'Leghorn' (Livorno) and Genoa – and shows the stern of a British ship with men loading cases and large terracotta jars. These cases and jars would have been packed with rich textiles – silk lustrings, satins, paduasoy (from *soie*, French for silk, heavy corded or embossed), velvets, damasks – fans, wide-brimmed straw 'Leghorn' hats, lute and violin strings; medicinal items such as books of essences, 'Venice Treacle', a potion touted as a 'cure-all', balsams, wines, Florence cordials, oil, olives, anchovies, capers, vermicelli, Bologna sausages, parmesan, cheeses and 'Naples Soap' for shaving.

Trade in Asia under the East India Company included bullion, textiles and tea, while goods from the colonies in North America and the West Indies included tobacco and sugar, with Jamaica in addition exporting coffee, cotton and indigo. It is an inescapable fact that England and then Great Britain's transatlantic trade, from the seventeenth century onwards relied increasingly on the labour of enslaved Africans. It was under Charles II that the Royal African Company was established (in 1672), led by his brother James, then Duke of York, to trade in slaves along the west coast of Africa, with the specific purpose of challenging the dominance of the Dutch, at the time England's greatest maritime competitor in this region. From here men, women and children continued to be shipped to the colonies in North America and the West Indies to work in brutal conditions on sugar and tobacco plantations. Every time Hogarth, his companions and countless others across the country sweetened their tea, drank chocolate with sugar or puffed on a pipe of tobacco, they were encouraging the maintenance, and indeed, as the eighteenth century advanced, the expansion of the transatlantic slave trade. Further, certainly some and probably many of Hogarth's patrons and subscribers would have had direct connections to this appalling trade, for example as directors and shareholders in organisations such as the South Sea Company like the Strodes, or sugar planters like the Mackinens: Hogarth's portrait of young William and Elizabeth Mackinen hung in their house in Antigua.[5]

Of the five pilgrims, only Will Tothall would have understood what, exactly, that would have meant. British colonial activities offered a myriad of opportunities to young men like Tothall, with nothing to recommend them but their intelligence and drive. Will was the son of an apothecary in Fleet Street and his lady, a midwife. Trained as a fishmonger, his uncle's profession, Tothall was by inclination an adventurer and jack of all trades, with a keen eye for a business opportunity. Abandoning fishmongering, he ran away to sea, serving on merchant ships heading to far-flung places including Newfoundland and the West Indies. So, unlike a majority of his fellow Britons, he would have witnessed first hand what life was like in these islands, or, at the very least, would have been told tales by his fellow mariners too terrible for any humane person to contemplate, of torture and punishment meted out to the enslaved, from severe beatings that left them bloodied and raw, to the use of pottocks – iron rings fixed around the neck with a spur for the mouth – to amputation and castration.

Yet away from such atrocities, when on his travels Will acquired an interest in natural history and the collecting of curiosities – a passion and an interest in scientific enquiry that he shared with Sir Hans Sloane, who had also journeyed to the West Indies and who, in his published journals, recalled the living conditions and treatment of the enslaved Africans alongside close study of the local flora and fauna.[6] Sloane later married Elizabeth Rose, the wealthy daughter and widow of Jamaica sugar planters, and his tens of thousands of objects (animal, mineral, etc.) would form the core of the new British Museum (established in 1753) and later the Natural History Museum. No doubt Tothall's father's profession, similar to that of a modern pharmacist, was good grounding for an interest in such things. Tothall is described by his neighbour in later life, Captain Bulstrode, as 'indefatigable in the collecting of shells' and, during his period of travel, 'brought home several utterly unknown in *England*'.[7]

Tothall was still in the sea service in his late twenties, and on one voyage had the misfortune to be captured by the Spanish, probably during the Anglo-Spanish War of 1727–9, when Great Britain blockaded Puerto Bello (present-day Panama) and Spain attempted to retake Gibraltar. Dressed in a woollen cap, a waist-coat and precious little else, being shoe- and stocking-less, and with only a large walking staff for his comfort and protection, Tothall was marched across country under guard and remained a prisoner until, eventually, he was exchanged. It reveals something of a stoical or eccentric character, or both, that in honour of what must have been a harrowing experience, he had his portrait taken (now lost) in this wretched, semi-naked state.

By 1732 William Tothall had swapped a life of misadventure abroad for something altogether less risky back in England. This hardworking, resourceful lad had been hired as a shopman by a London woollen draper and, with the encouragement and financial backing of his master, expanded into trimmings and shalloon (a thin worsted fabric). At the same time, via a contact in the West Indies, he also began selling a puncheon (large barrel) of rum in small measures from his master's cellar. Eventually his master retired, leaving this trainee shopman the remaining stock, and the younger man continued to trade as a woollen draper as well as a

11. *A Rake's Progress Plate 1: The Heir*, etching and engraving, 1735
Tom starts as he means to go on by splashing out on new clothes. Will
Tothall's bale of black cloth and note can be seen bottom right.

brandy and West Indies rum merchant.[8] Hogarth would give his
friend a welcome puff just a few years later, in the first image of *A
Rake's Progress*: a bale of black cloth, for the mourning suit young
Tom Rakewell is being measured for, in honour of his departed
miserly father, has the attached note 'London Bought of Wm.
Tothall Woollen Draper in Covent Garden'.[9] Perhaps the tailor
measuring Tom is a portrait of Mr Tothall himself? At some point
Hogarth had lived with Tothall, as noted by Captain Bulstrode,
'on the footing of a most intimate friend' and this friendship was
lifelong, despite Tothall's eventual move away from London to
the Kent coast near the port of Dover. Here Tothall continued his
interest in natural history, adding fossils to his burgeoning collection, considered important enough to be sold by the prominent
London auctioneer, Abraham Langford.[10]

12. Bernard Baron after William Hogarth, *Marriage A-la-Mode*
Plate 2: The Tête à Tête, etching and engraving, 1745
The dishevelled young lord slumps in his chair, a dog sniffs at the girl's
cap in his pocket, while the black patch on his neck hints at syphilis.
The steward, despairing, exits stage right with unpaid bills.

Natural history and the collecting of intriguing items from
across the globe was not a personal obsession for Hogarth, although
he included such details in his paintings and engravings. If in a portrait, then this feature would add a biographical dimension. But in
one of his satirical works they were invariably intended to show
that his protagonists, in assembling such curiosities and in contrast
to Tothall and Sloane, had no interest or understanding of them
beyond a mindless desire to follow fashion. In scene two of *Marriage A-la-Mode*, for example, the newly-wed Squanderfields are
seen the morning after their respective night's debauch in a grand
sequence of rooms hung with silk damask and, knowing Hogarth,
what are probably dubious Old Master paintings. Equally dodgy
are the oddities on and around the mantelpiece, which Hogarth's

German admirer, Georg Christoph Lichtenberg, writing in the late eighteenth century, described as 'the most outrageous artistic motifs', including 'Puffy and pregnant Chinese idols ... Vases ... little bottles ... artificial *naturalia*', an 'antique bust ... its head is modern and the nose even newer than the head' and a mechanical cat clock, with elaborate carved decoration of 'fish in the trees and its cat amongst the fish' which, he suspects 'meows the hours as cuckoo clocks cuckoo them'. For such clocks, he observes, Englishmen are willing to pay substantial sums.[11] That was true for mechanical objects of varying levels of sophistication. When Hogarth recalled the destruction of the original paintings of *A Harlot's Progress* and *A Rake's Progress* in 1755 (in fact the latter series survived the devastating fire at Fonthill House, the seat of William Beckford, a major Jamaican sugar plantation and slave owner), what he considered most 'remarkable in the disaster ... as reported is that a most magnificent clockwork organ in the house being set ago[i]ng by some accident [and] was heard in the midst of the flames to play of a great variety [of] pleasing airs'.[12] There are several interesting aspects to this recollection, not least that Hogarth's wry almost gallows-style humour never left him.

The manner of collecting, or, a better description, random assembling, typified by the aristocratic Squanderfields, lay at the heart of an establishment which was one of the sights of Georgian London, made famous by Richard Steele's short-lived but influential publication, *The Tatler*. Aimed at a male and female readership, *The Tatler*'s jaunty, whimsical style chimes exactly with *The Peregrination*, on one level parodying travel journals to places much further afield, while, at the same time, imitating and popularising the more serious idea, that a journey up or down the river Thames (for example) can be approached in the same manner as those to distant lands and exotic climes. Applying the same cool eye to the character and behaviour of our near neighbours and the goings-on in our immediate vicinity, highlighting the charms and absurdities as well as the daily lives of our fellow inhabitants of England, has as much educational worth and amusement as any voyage narrative, real or imagined. The same is true of Hogarth's graphic adventures around London's streets.

In late June 1709, Steele ventured to a Chelsea 'Coffee-house where the *Literati* sit in Council'. This establishment was then under the management of James Salter. A former servant of fellow Irishman, Sir Hans Sloane, Salter had travelled extensively, and was used to living in somewhat eccentric surroundings, mingling with learned folk of science and the arts.[13] Ben Franklin recalled venturing to Salter's coffee house, and Hogarth certainly visited, probably in the company of Will Tothall, whose own collection of shells and other curiosities, given they shared lodgings at some point, would have been familiar to Hogarth.[14] Colonial expansion and global trade increased from the late-seventeenth century, as then did, in turn, a peculiar fascination for collecting everything and anything, and no one was more peculiar in the collecting line than James Salter. The 'museum' he established in Chelsea was open to generous donations, and there seems to have been a fair amount of competition to provide the most curious items, or, indeed, the most hilarious and imaginative descriptions for workaday tat, whether human, animal, plant or mineral.[15] Among Salter's benefactors, listed in the catalogues of the collection pro-duced for the visitors' edification, can be found presidents of the eminent Royal Society, notably local resident and Hogarth's friend Martin Folkes – another reason Hogarth would have visited – and, of course, Sloane. Other supporters included the physician Dr Richard Mead, whom Hogarth knew through his art collection and, later, the Foundling Hospital.

As recalled by Steele, on entering the coffee house 'I had not Time to salute the Company, before my Eye was diverted by Ten thousand Gimcracks round the Room and on the Sieling.' Steele dismisses Salter's self-description as a descendant of the famed botanist during Charles II's reign, John Tradescant, considering him, rather, as the fictional character Sancho Panza, companion of Don Quixote. Steele notes one exhibit that the host had drawn his attention to, a straw hat which, Steele observes, 'I know to be made by *Madge Peskad*, within three Miles of Bedford' yet Mr Salter will tell you 'it is Pontius Pilate's Wife's Chamber-Maid's Sister's Hat'. This is demonstrably fake, but, at the very least, in satirising Salt-er's pretensions, Steele points to the imaginative as well as eclectic

nature of the proprietor's collecting habits. It is not for Salter –
renamed in the article, 'Don Saltero', a nickname that stuck – to
prove or not the declared provenance of these items. But the discussions that sprang from such far-fetched labels and notions can
be enlightening in their own right. Steele himself, in response to
the nonsensical idea that a straw hat, which he deduces was made
near the Midlands town of Bedford a few weeks before his visit,
could have any association with the biblical governor of Judea,
hypothesises 'that the Covering of Straw was never us'd among the
Jews, since it was demanded of 'em to make Bricks without it'.[16]

Salter died around 1728, after which his daughter, May (b. 1682),
ran the business, now located in Cheyne Walk.[17] A glance through
the catalogue certainly backs up Steele's dismissal of the collection as essentially a promotional gimmick for the main business.
Among the 'rarities' listed are '3 Boxes of Relicks from Jerusalem', '24 A Handkerchief, made of the Abestus Rock, which Fire
cannot consume', '36 A Fairy, or Elfe's Arrow' and '67 The Pizzle
of a Raccoon' (a pizzle being an animal's penis – this, no doubt,
to be compared to that of the whale in an adjoining cabinet). This
bizarre assembly is followed, naturally enough, by '70 A Giant's
Tooth', '105 The Effigies of an Egyptian Mummy', '135 A Turkish
Ladies Dress', '136 A Pair of Nun's Stockings' to match '137 A Nun's
Whip', which may be an instrument of religious chastisement but,
given 'nun' and 'convent' were period slang for prostitute and
bawdy house, could as easily be a dominatrix's implement. This
leads on to '168 A Chinese Idol', like those on the Squanderfields'
mantlepiece, '173 The Pope's Infallible Candle', '191 An Embrio of
a Child', '235 A China Ladies Shoe', '269 A Canibal's Habit and
Shirt' and '328 A young Crocodile'. Some of the last items listed
are '380 Queen Elizabeth's Prayer Book' and '381 Mary Queen of
Scott's Pincushion'.[18]

The shoe of a Chinese woman would be intriguing to a European due to the ancient custom of foot binding. Hogarth for one
expresses an interest in such customs, when he wrote, in a rejected
passage for *The Analysis of Beauty* concerning John Bulwer's 1650
classic, *Anthropometamorphosis: Man Transform'd, or the Artificial
Changeling*, which 'hath set the amazing force and folly of custom

and Fashions of Dress in the most rediculous and almost shocking light imaginable by not only shewing the most extravagant wild and uncouth man[n]ers of coverring the body in different ages and countrys but their disgustefull and sometimes cruel methods of moulding and forcing the human form out of its natural figure and collour.' Indeed, Hogarth continues, 'many of his Instan[c]es remain to this day, one in China of bandaging the feet of the females to prevent their growing, which shocking disproportion in Women is become a Beauty to them by force of custom'. Hogarth enlists this example to further his argument that nature is best when he concludes that whereas creativity and expression are important in dress fashions, 'nothing should be restr[a]in'd but the folly I had almost said wickedness of Changing natures form or Colour'.[19]

One of Hogarth's earliest commissions in book illustration were the fifteen engravings for Aubry de la Motraye's *Travels through Europe, Asia, and into Part of Africa* (1723/4). The prints cover a gamut of subjects, from 'An Emerald Vessel' at Genoa Cathedral, thought to be a gift from the Queen of Sheba to Solomon and/or, used by Christ at the Last Supper; 'The Inside of a Mosque'; 'The Seraglio'; 'A Silver Mine at Sala' in Sweden; and 'A Lapland Hut'.[20] Likewise, at Don Saltero's establishment, the visitor, while contemplating the tiny shoe of an adult woman from China, might then glance up at the Turkish lady's dress, next to the nun's stockings, via the Egyptian mummy, a Native American peace pipe and '*Muscovite*' or Russian 'habit' and wonder at the diversity of human life occupying this astonishing, complex planet. At the same time the wealth of natural history, whether accurately described or not, would surely encourage feelings of wonder, together with those of queasiness, at God's Creation. Just a few years after La Motraye's *Travels*, Hogarth depicted a scene from *Hudibras* (Plate 8) where the knight accosts the astrologer Sidrophel and his servant Whacum. Dangling from the ceiling and walls are a crocodile, bats, frogs, snakes and other curiosities; a skeleton, with an owl on one bony shoulder, is suspended in a cupboard; and on the floor is a small child in a jar of alcohol (note '328 A young Crocodile' and '191 An Embrio of a Child'.) And if

13. *Hudibras Plate 8: Hudibras beats Sidrophel and his*
man Whacum, etching and engraving, 1726
The horoscope the astrologer has cast for the knight, full of ill omens, lies on
the table. In response Hudibras draws his sword, crying 'You are no Conj'rer'!

we separate out the fantastical and downright ridiculous, some of
Salter's items are of genuine scientific interest, if a little concerning from a health and safety perspective, notably the proliferation
of asbestos.[21] The inclusion of objects related to monarchs of the
British Isles, as well as a plethora of items representing a variety
of religions, adds to the encyclopaedic quality, on a national and
global scale, of Don Saltero's very curious Cabinet of Curiosities.

As the pilgrims continued on, passing the great trade ships anchored
in the Pool of London and approaching the shipwrights' wharfs of
Shadwell to the north and Rotherhithe to the south, the company
may have discussed Tothall's experiences of the colonies, his love
of shells, the wealth and variety of the cargo being unloaded at the
docks and the distant lands from which they have come. Alternatively, being the early hours, they may simply have closed their eyes,
in the hope of a much-needed kip.

CHAPTER TWO

MOCK KING

Recalling the period of his apprenticeship, Hogarth singles out 'the painting of St Pauls and gree[n]wich hospital which were during this time run[n]ing in my head'.[1] These paintings were the work of John Thornhill's father, Sir James Thornhill, the most famous and successful English artist in living memory. As soon as his apprenticeship ended, aged around twenty-three and while establishing himself as an engraver, Hogarth enrolled in a new drawing academy under the direction of the veteran French-born history painter, Louis Chéron and the young Englishman, John Vanderbank. That Vanderbank, like Hogarth a Londoner (baptised at St Giles-in-the-Fields) and just a few years older, was in such an elevated, influential position must have been galling. And yet, at the same time, this may have provided further impetus to raise his own status with all speed. Hogarth felt keenly the burden of disadvantage, but he was also extremely competitive. According to Hogarth, the building where the academy was held had been converted from 'an old <presbyterian> meeting house' in Peter's Court, off St Martin's Lane.[2] The surgeon and lecturer in anatomy, William Cheselden, had also subscribed, as had John Ellys, a pupil of Thornhill's, who quickly became Billy's firm friend, as well as one William Kent, fresh from his Grand Tour and extended sojourn in Italy. The annual subscription was two guineas, or £2 2 shillings – a not insignificant sum, given the income of most families – and women were among the life models. Hogarth later stated that this was in order 'to make it more inviting to subscribers'.[3] It also attracted eminent local visitors, such as George, Prince of Wales, in 1722.[4] It should be noted that female nudes would not be employed in the academies of France or Italy for another century.[5]

14. *Study of a Female Nude,* graphite, black and
white chalk on brown paper, early 1720s
This drawing is dated to Hogarth's membership of the first St
Martin's Lane Academy. Louis Chéron, a French protestant
(Huguenot), had trained at the Académie royale in Paris.

At the time, John Vanderbank was considered the most prominent painter of Hogarth's generation and a potential leading light
of London's art world. By the early 1720s there was a sense that the
decline of the previous generation, notably Sir Godfrey Kneller
(who died, after prolonged illness, in October 1723) and his dominance of royal and court portrait production through a factory-style
studio practice, would create opportunities in the very near future:
not least a significant and highly prized vacancy at court. George
Vertue certainly considered John Vanderbank as someone who
could fill that vacancy and in the process, carry all before him.
Vanderbank had great natural artistic skill and financial backing
from his family, his father being 'chief arras' or fine tapestry maker
to the crown, and owner of the Soho Tapestry Manufactory: a
solid foundation for success. In 1725 the playwright Benjamin
Victor published an anonymous poem which judged the current
competition to replace Kneller, Jonathan Richardson and Joseph
Highmore among them, with Vanderbank emerging the clear

winner, but with provisos.[6] In the event, Vanderbank failed to rise to his potential, or the faith his supporters, like Victor, had placed in him, due, almost solely, to a fundamental lack of professional focus and an inherently weak character. Vertue, tutting under his breath, noted down stories doing the rounds, from sources close to Vanderbank, which stressed his carelessness and ingratitude. Worse still were the 'Blemishes of his Vanitys', frittering his money on '*high-liveing*'[7] and the aping of upper-class behaviour, from expensive clothes to keeping a mistress, to the extravagance of maintaining several coaches and teams of horses for use in the country as well as around town. Having pissed and fornicated his inheritance away, as Hogarth might phrase it, Vanderbank then stole the academy's subscription money, as recalled by Hogarth. Inevitably, 'the lamp stove etc were seized for rent and the whole affair put a stop to'.[8] All of which caught up with Vanderbank in May 1724, when he was forced to flee to France to avoid being imprisoned for debt.[9] By the time Chéron, Vanderbank's long-suffering business partner, died in May 1725 and was laid to rest in St Paul's church, Covent Garden, the academy had collapsed completely. Over the next four years, having learned nothing from his difficulties, John Vanderbank, on returning to London, would be in and out of the Fleet prison with his debts mounting: a situation that may have stirred Hogarth to pity but, given that he was largely responsible (unlike Richard Hogarth) for his dire situation, never to empathy.[10] However, Vanderbank's behaviour and corresponding woes have a familiar twang: for Hogarth, it was another real-life model, to be filed away in his memory under 'Rake', cross-referenced to 'Wastrel'.

In 1725 Hogarth was in his late twenties and, while making a name for himself as an engraver, was nowhere to be seen as a future leading light among British and London-based painters (from Benjamin Victor's point of view at least). This makes his shift from engraving to painting over the next five years, and the enormous success he achieved in the process, even more astonishing. There are many reasons for this achievement, but the key is Hogarth's relationship with Sir James Thornhill. Initially, from a distance, Thornhill provided the template for success, which later, as their connection became personal and then familial, developed into vital support and contacts. Thornhill was a man of wit, intelligence and drive, very much in the mould of his contemporaries born and raised in the restoration period, such as Richard Steele, Joseph Addison and the playwright and architect, Sir John Vanbrugh. He was the professional mentor Hogarth needed, as well as the father figure he longed for after the death of his own. And, in John Thornhill, Hogarth would find a much-cherished brother. In short, Hogarth was dazzled.

There would be no particular impetus for a man engraving business cards to attend evening life-drawing sessions and to mingle with established and up-and-coming professional artists, other than the ambition to join them. So even as he was developing his technique in print engraving, copper plate in particular, Hogarth was also honing his skills in figure drawing, with a view to improving his abilities in design and composition. Given his comments on Thornhill's painted schemes, it can be safely assumed that moving beyond engraving to painting was already on Hogarth's mind. During his regular journeys from Leicester Fields back to his mother and sisters still living in West Smithfield, the looming dome of St Paul's Cathedral, located on a rise beyond Fleet Street and above Ludgate, would have been a constant presence: a guiding light, as he walked through Covent Garden, Lincoln's Inn Fields and along High Holborn. And the very fact that Thornhill's paintings in the Great Hall at the Royal Hospital for Seamen are twinned with those within St Paul's in Hogarth's recollection, tells us that he, perhaps with his fellow apprentices and friends, made trips down the Thames to the maritime town of Greenwich, to see the painted decoration of the Great Hall while in progress and on completion.

Little wonder that Sir James Thornhill and his paintings filled young Billy's waking and dreaming hours. They were major contemporary art commissions, located, not in a private house, hidden from all but a select few, but in civic spaces – national, royal, spiritual and charitable – and by their very nature accessible to the public. As such they would be of great interest to anyone with the ambition to be an artist – specifically a great artist. That they were the creation of an Englishman gave them an immense totemic status to those who cared about such things. And Hogarth was one such person. This was the type of artistic greatness that leaves a prominent mark on the city, its citizens and on posterity.

Born in 1675 or 1676, only twenty or so years before Hogarth, in Melcombe Regis, Weymouth, James Thornhill was from a family who had sided with parliament against the Stuart king Charles I during the civil wars, continuing their support after the king's execution in 1649 and, as a result, had lost everything at the Restoration. One key impetus for the young James was the regaining of his family's dignity and status along with their ancestral home in Dorset. In 1689 Thornhill began training with the royal painter, Thomas Highmore, uncle of Hogarth's fellow painter and future collaborator Joseph. In the mid to late seventeenth century the guild and studio systems were still prevalent, and restricted access to the nuts and bolts of artistic training. That said, Sir Peter Lely had set up an informal drawing school in his home in Covent Garden, which became the model for such academies, including at St Martin's Lane, into the next century – led by prominent seasoned practitioners and self-funded by an annual membership fee.

In this period, artists were more flexible in the commissions they accepted and the genres and media in which they worked. Hierarchies existed: flower painting, still life and scenes of everyday life ('genre') were considered the lowest in status, followed by landscape, then portraiture, and finally history or narrative painting at the apex. Similarly engraving was lesser to painting; watercolour and pastel lesser to oil and so on. Artists specialised accordingly but, nonetheless, practically and commercially there was no rigid separation between designing for the theatre, decorative arts and fine art, for this would be unnecessarily self-defeating in a risky contemporary market. As an example, in 1705 Thornhill designed scenery for Thomas Clayton's opera *Arsinoe, Queen of Cyprus* at the Theatre Royal, Drury Lane, while at around the same time he was painting the Sabine Room at Chatsworth, Derbyshire. Both schemes, which existed within different contexts but were equally ambitious in scale and conception, were examples of Grand Theatre – the lives of royalty and aristocracy, ancient and modern, played out within Thornhill's scenery. Immediately after Chatsworth he won his greatest secular commission at the Royal Hospital, Greenwich, and was employed there from 1708 to 1726.

In 1711 James Thornhill had been elected one of the twelve directors of a new art academy, under the governorship of Sir Godfrey Kneller (the academy that Joseph Highmore had attended), and in the same year he was inspired, during a journey to the Low Countries, to design a set of delftware dinner plates, each representing one of the twelve signs of the Zodiac.[11] And even as he achieved fame through his painting, including portraiture and design, Thornhill harboured the ambition to add 'architect' to his list of accomplishments – an ambition he eventually achieved. Ambition coupled with variety was Thornhill's driving force. This multifaceted career path, varying genre and context, is something Hogarth will himself develop, along with a deep respect for history painting and the type of grand interior schemes for which Thornhill was famed.

In June 1715, when Hogarth was entering his second year as an apprentice, and while still working on the scheme at Greenwich, Thornhill was awarded the commission to paint the cupola at St Paul's Cathedral. The competition had included the highly experienced Italian, Antonio Pellegrini, and the equally qualified Frenchmen, Louis Chéron and Louis Laguerre. George Vertue noted that, on the announcement that the only Briton in the competition had won, the artist Marco Ricci, sensing a change in mood, left London for Italy, never to return.[12] As legend has it, the clinching argument was delivered by the Archbishop of Canterbury, Thomas Tenison, who is quoted as saying: 'I am no judge of painting, but on two articles I think I may insist: first that the painter employed be a Protestant; and secondly that he be an Englishman' – which would have narrowed the field immeasurably.

The year 1715 was an interesting moment to assert the principle that such commissions should go to a native of the British Isles and a Protestant. Queen Anne, James II's second daughter, had died in 1714, leaving the Kingdom of Great Britain (after the Union of Scotland and England in 1707) to George I. (George's mother, Sophia, niece of Charles I, had been heir presumptive, but died a few months before Anne.) A year after his accession, the first

Jacobite challenge to the House of Hanover occurred, with the support of Catholic France and the pope. Putting their Protestantism to one side, this new dynasty, who remained (while monarchs of Great Britain and Ireland) the Electors of the German state of Hanover, was generally perceived to be more overtly foreign than the exiled family. The Stuarts had over time intermarried with most of the leading royal European houses, but had ruled England for just over a century (both Charles II and James II were born in London) and Scotland since Robert II (1316–90). The idea that the German Hanoverians had usurped the hereditary (or even divine) right of the Stuarts carried weight through all levels of society: it seemed possible that the element of doubt, as well as enduring support, could carry the day for the Jacobites. The situation had been somewhat muddied while the daughters of James II, Mary, then Anne, had occupied the throne. The survival into adulthood of Queen Anne's son, the Duke of Gloucester, would have answered the dynastic question perfectly well, being a male Stuart, but his death in 1700, a few days after his eleventh birthday, ruined any prospect of a peaceful transfer on his mother's own death. A distant cousin from Germany and speaking little English, even if a great-grandson of James I and VI, the first Stuart king of both England and Scotland, George was a different prospect altogether. Certainly, in such a fraught broader context, the idea that a Catholic Frenchman or Italian could be employed to paint the interior of London's newly completed Protestant cathedral was thought bizarre. After all, it was a building made necessary after a fire that had been blamed – bogusly – on London's Catholic population, a lie written on the base of The Monument.

Unfortunately for James Thornhill, who was more than capable of winning the competition in his own right, this introduced a nagging doubt that he was only succeeding against foreign competition because he was English, not because he was the best artist for the job. The situation proved that art too was highly political.

The painted scheme, within the interior of the cupola, the inner skin of the great dome, entailed a sequence of compartments with surrounding decoration, all in the *grisaille* style, that is, using a very limited, almost single-colour palette – in this case shades of brown imitating stone. Each compartment illustrated an episode in the life of St Paul, heavily influenced by the Raphael Cartoons depicting the Acts of the Apostles, one of the royal treasures at Hampton Court Palace. The area concerned rises above the Whispering Gallery to a vertiginous height of two hundred and twenty-five feet from floor level. Compare this to the Sistine Chapel, at sixty-eight feet from ground to ceiling, where Michelangelo spent four uncomfortable years on a scaffold. The logistics of building a similar platform, supported by scaffolding, gradually rising to the necessary levels as the artist and his assistants worked around the cupola's circular wall, was an engineering feat in itself. The danger inherent with such working environments is illustrated by some of the stories in circulation while Thornhill was at his labours. The following was recalled by Joseph Highmore: 'a Gentleman of his acquaintance was one day with him on the scaffolding, which, though wide, was not railed : he had just finished the head of one of the Apostles, and running back, as is usual with painters, to observe the effect, had almost reached the extremity : the Gentleman, seeing his danger, and not having time for words, snatched up a large brush, and smeared the face,' at which Thornhill ran hastily forward, crying out 'Bless my soul, what have you done?' 'I have saved your life!' replied the friend.[13] For the young art student, these stories stressed the thrillingly heroic nature of such artistic endeavours.

Even as this monumental scheme progressed, Thornhill was taking on other commissions. In June 1716 he was at work at Blenheim near Woodstock, Sir John Vanbrugh's great baroque palace, completing the hall with scenes celebrating the recent military exploits of the Duke of Marlborough. In a signal of what was to come, however, this commission ended in great acrimony between Thornhill and the formidable Duchess of Marlborough and former favourite of Queen Anne, Sarah Churchill. In October 1716, Thornhill replaced Kneller as governor of the Great Queen Street Academy, and on 2 May 1720 he was knighted – the first English-born artist to be so honoured, and following in the illustrious footsteps of Rubens, Van Dyck, Lely and Kneller. In 1721 he was elected a member of parliament for Weymouth and Melcombe Regis in Dorset, the place of his birth. It was not completely unheard of for artists to take on civic duties – Sir Godfrey was a justice of the peace for Whitton, his country residence to the west of London.

In the same year that he entered parliament, Sir James Thornhill was commissioned to paint the interior walls of the chapel of Wimpole Hall, Cambridgeshire for Edward Harley, 2nd Earl of Oxford, and in March, the royal gardener Charles Bridgeman, James Gibbs (chapel architect), John Wootton (painter) and Thornhill journeyed together in a coach to Wimpole. This seemingly everyday event was hindered by a sequence of minor catastrophes, which Thornhill commemorated in the humorous ballad, 'A Hue and Cry'.[14] In this comical account the germ of another jaunt ten years later can be found. Thornhill describes himself whimsically as 'MONTESPINOSA', the Italian for Thornhill, declaring himself as having 'A Brownish Complection, a lover of drink,/ A drawer of Devils they say was his trade' although, in the present circumstances, 'My Landlord drew worse in his House, I'm afraid'.[15] Having set off from London, the four colleagues endured an uncomfortable journey, packed together in the coach, as 'things like men, that look'd something Wild'. Having reached Royston, about eight miles south of Wimpole Hall, the coachman abandoned them at an inn 'To shift for themselves'. In the morning they arose, 'They Yawn'd & they Gap'd, & look'd cursed simple/ Lord! how shall wee four get ever to WIMPLE?' Eventually they are rescued by the Earl of Oxford himself, who 'smelt them all out', sending four horses, a groom and a boy. Two of the company, described as 'Dons', perhaps as a humorous nod to the fictional rake, Don Juan or, more likely, Don Quixote, 'on palfreys did ride/ a Spurr on one Heel, But a sword by the side'. And thus 'Nobly equip'd they gallop'd away'.

But in March 1722, Sir James Thornhill's onward march, which must have seemed (from the outside at least) unstoppable, hit a significant obstacle from which, in the event, he did not recover personally or professionally, despite the great acclaim he received for his work at St Paul's and Greenwich. In his role of Sergeant Painter to the King, which he assumed after the death of his master Thomas Highmore, the decoration of the royal palaces was firmly within his remit and demonstrable talents. This position in the royal household had been augmented by another title, History Painter in Ordinary to the King (1718), which, you would think, was an emphatic statement of affairs at court. But in an extraordinary move, Thornhill lost a commission to decorate the king's apartments at Kensington Palace, which George Vertue describes as a 'mighty mortification' for Sir James personally. It signalled that court machinations were at play, and that Thornhill and his supporters no longer had the upper hand. The commission was given to William Kent, Hogarth's fellow student at the St Martin's Lane Academy and the favourite of Richard Boyle, 3rd Earl of Burlington (b.1694). Burlington was nicknamed 'Apollo of the Arts' because his interests covered most cultural bases, from music to painting and architecture. Burlington, accompanied by Kent, had returned from Italy in December 1719, and was mooting some sort of academy on the Italian lines.[16] The sheer scale of the commission at Kensington kept Kent employed for several years: the new 'Cupola Room', the king's drawing room, privy chamber, bedchamber, presence chamber, council chamber, the king's gallery, great and little closets, and the grand staircase.[17]

Possibly in response to Sir James's mortification at court, or perhaps just very well timed, Hogarth began to issue a sequence of prints which attacked Kent directly and, by extension, Lord Burlington. The general point was an aversion to the artistic and cultural taste being promoted by the likes of Burlington – importing rigid Italian-style art academies alongside Italian opera and entertainments, like masquerades, in the process diverting energy and, crucially, funding away from native art forms and artistes – and a gut disapproval at the rise, as he saw it, of talentless individuals, simply because they were the willing creatures of some overbearing and overly influential patron. Personalities and cliques based on partialities, then as now, could make or break a career. In Kent's case, with Burlington's heft behind him, fairness (the sharing out of what little royal and civic commissioning there was) and relevant talent were of little or no consequence whatsoever. Hogarth had already come into personal contact with Thornhill through the latter's short-lived drawing academy, based from 1724 at his Great Piazza home in Covent Garden, which Hogarth and

John Ellys effectively managed on Sir James's behalf.[18] (At the same time Hogarth would have encountered Thornhill's collection of paintings and drawings, among them works by Rubens and Poussin, which Sir James would have made accessible to academy members.)[19] But it was the prints, *Masquerades and Operas*, and the parody on Kent's dismal altarpiece for St Clement Danes church in the Strand that signalled his very public criticism of the Burlington clique and, therefore, his support for Thornhill in the latter's public struggle to defend his reputation, status and income. Of course Thornhill was far from an innocent when it came to pulling rank or leaning on his own patrons and contacts for competitive advantage. But Hogarth's loyalty lay with him and with what, in Hogarth's mind, Thornhill represented.

In justice to Kent, his talent did not lie in painting; he was certainly a far better architect and garden designer, and he was of the same social class as Hogarth, so in as much need of paid employment as anybody else. He had an easy, cheerful way about him, and a useful talent for ingratiating himself into the lives and homes of his patrons – traits guaranteed to raise Hogarth's hackles.

The machinations of Burlington led to the rise and eventual dominance of Kent, as George Vertue noted in his journal: 'M[r]. Kent has been greatly favour[e]d by this Noble Lord. who has patronized and encouraged him above any other Artist living [-] constantly keeping him in his house' and has vigorously recommended him at Court for 'several imployments'.[20] In other words, Kent was exactly the type of talentless aristocrat's poppet that Hogarth detested. The fact that he was not simply lording it over his hero but ruining Thornhill's reputation and dignity as a pre-eminent artist made Hogarth see red. And this will not be the last public spat that Hogarth will gleefully enter into. Loyalty is one of Hogarth's defining traits, coupled with the laudable need to act. The public snubbing of Thornhill in favour of Kent happened at the same moment that Hogarth was establishing himself as a print rather than silver engraver and aiming to raise his public profile. So moral outrage and self-interest, in this instance, aligned perfectly – another leitmotif of Hogarth's life and career.

The fact that Kent was himself an Englishman, born in Yorkshire, might have tempered Hogarth's ire, but his travels in Italy – making him part of the connoisseur gang that privileged all things Italian, symbolised by his faintly nauseating nickname 'Kentino' – would have trumped any camaraderie for a fellow Briton. Kent, with the encouragement of his patron, developed a new wave of interest in the Italian Palladian style (introduced almost a century before by Inigo Jones) over the English Baroque, of which Wren, Vanbrugh and Nicholas Hawksmoor were the main exponents. As this style crept in and eventually dominated British architecture, the eminent architects of the late-Stuart vintage were gradually pushed out, and with them, the great painted schemes in which Sir James Thornhill specialised. It could be argued that this is simply what happens; tastes change. But the dominance of the Palladian architectural style was swift and complete and very much to Kent's advantage. It should be noted that James Gibbs, Thornhill's colleague at Wimpole Hall, maintained a canny flexibility in his use of architectural style – not confining himself to one or other side in this particular culture war. Through these means, despite his Catholicism, which, in any case, he succeeded in keeping private, Gibbs rode the stylistic storm, keeping himself very busy indeed in the process.[21] Through their mutual connection to Thornhill, Gibbs would prove a very useful contact for Hogarth in the near future.

Masquerades and Operas was, as Hogarth announced in the *Daily Courant* on 24 February 1724, a satire on the 'bad taste of the town'. This was the first engraving that Hogarth published or issued himself, independent from printsellers like Bowles and Overton. Among the many places where the print could be bought, the advertisement notes 'at Wm. Hogarth's, the Engraver thereof, at the Golden Ball in Little Newport-street'. Four years since leaving his apprenticeship, Hogarth was now firmly established as an independent craftsman within the vicinity of Leicester Fields. Little Newport Street lay just to the east of Leicester House and near Ellis Gamble's new premises (since 1723) at the Sign of the Golden Angel, Cranbourn Street, which runs eastwards from the north-eastern corner of Leicester Fields.[22] This street (usually called Cranbourne Alley), a passage with pavement populated by shops and shoemakers' studios, leads into Little Newport Street. One of Hogarth's

15. *Masquerades and Operas*, etching and engraving, 1724
At the window, top left, is the King's Theatre manager, the Swiss-born
masquerade and Italian opera impresario John James Heidegger.

earliest commissions, confirming his maintainance of good relations with his former master, is a trade card for Ellis's new enterprise,
with the said angel, Ellis's shop sign, dominating the design and the
text (in English and French) declaring that he made and dealt in 'all
sorts of Plate, Rings, & Jewells &c'.[23] Ellis, like Hogarth's father and
countless others, would be declared bankrupt only ten years later.

   Masquerades and Operas is signed 'Wᵐ Hogarth Invᵗ et sculpᵗ'
– that is, invented and engraved by William Hogarth. Following on from the burlesquing of the South Sea Bubble in 1721, this
new print, with its proud statement of authorship, was part of
Hogarth's move into graphic satire, a high-risk but potentially high-
return venture. The price of the print, one shilling, would certainly
encourage its purchase and circulation, although the market for
such items, for those with an expendable income, was, as observed,
a limited one. It has been calculated (as far as it can be) that in the
eighteenth century only six per cent of families in England had an

annual income as high as £100 and three per cent of £200, so a shilling (one twentieth of a pound) was a significant outlay for a vast majority of Hogarth's fellow citizens.[24] Another opportunity for promotion was the print- and bookshop window, where new and topical engravings were displayed for all to see and at no cost. In this engraving, both new and topical, Hogarth's attack on the rage for imported forms of entertainment and art would have been well known, beyond those buyers and collectors of prints. It is notable and no coincidence that on the same page of advertisements in the *Daily Courant*, the King's Theatre in the Haymarket was promoting a new opera in Italian, *Julius Caesar* by George Frideric Handel, in which the male lead, the warrior Caesar, is trilled by the castrato Senesino, with fellow-Italian Francesca Cuzzoni as Cleopatra. The casting of Senesino was considered, beyond rarefied aristocratic circles, as ludicrous. The production was supported by the new Royal Academy of Music, created to encourage Italian opera in London and with Lord Burlington among the subscribers. Tickets sold at half a guinea for the stalls and five shillings for the gallery.

The same theatre is represented daringly on the left of Hogarth's print, with a devil and a fool leading a parade of people in masquerade costumes through the entrance. A banner hanging above represents overpaid and exotic Italian singers, including Cuzzoni and Senesino, who are being offered a princely £8,000 by fawning admirers and theatre managers. Opposite the King's Theatre, another crowd are flocking into the pantomime *Dr Faustus*, while between these two modish competing entertainments, a wheelbarrow is pushed through the street containing waste paper, in fact the unnamed works of the classic English playwrights, William Congreve (*The Double Dealer*, 1694, and *The Way of the World*, 1700), John Dryden (*The Indian Emperor*, 1665, *Marriage-a-la-Mode, a Comedy*, 1673), Thomas Otway (*Venice Preserv'd*, 1682), Joseph Addison and no less a personage than William Shakespeare.

And as Lord Burlington was an enthusiastic supporter of all things Italian, in the background of the print is seen the monumental gate of an imagined 'Accademy of Arts', which is recognisably Burlington's town house on Piccadilly (now integrated into the Victorian Royal Academy of Arts). The gate is crowned with a slightly camp effigy, Kentino himself, to whom, below and on either side, the crouching, adoring figures of the High Renaissance artists Raphael and Michelangelo pay due homage. In the street below, three posturing gentlemen, art connoisseurs, gesture towards Kent as if indicating where great art is represented and, with Burlington's protégé placed above the Renaissance masters, where the correct balance is struck (or not).

No sooner had Hogarth issued this print (and not for the last time) he discovered that cheaper pirated versions were being sold in the print shops. Thus undercut by unscrupulous printsellers, with many unsold copies of his own engraving returned to him, Hogarth was eventually forced to sell the plate.[25] Hogarth recalled, with reference to the publishers, 'I found this Tribe as my father left them when he died.'[26] Hogarth lost money, but these poor, crude versions were also an attack on his reputation as an engraver. At this point in his career Hogarth had neither the wherewithal, nor high-powered supporters, to do anything about it. It was simply a misfortune of life, that creativity and popularity would be preyed upon by such vultures. How long the resourceful Hogarth, a man of action as well as opinion, would be willing to allow this to continue is another question.

Masquerades and Operas was followed by an anonymous print, alleging to be a precise copy of William Kent's altarpiece at St Clement Danes. The church had been designed by Sir Christopher Wren, with its spire completed by James Gibbs, and Kent's altarpiece was part of the completion of the church's interior. Alas, Kent was no better a painter of oil on canvas than he was of vast interior schemes, not that this prevented him scooping up every available commission, or so it seemed. Hogarth's clear intention was to highlight every inch of its incompetent draughtsmanship, clunky anatomy and limitless individual inadequacies, the subscript, to leave no room for doubt, confirming that 'This Print is exactly Engriv'd after ye Celebrated Altar-Peice'.

Others found the altarpiece's alleged Roman Catholic and even treasonous overtones, rather than its sheer artistic incompetence, beyond the pale. One of the angels, it was said, was a portrait of the Princess Maria Clementina Sobieska, wife of James II's son, the

'Old Pretender' James Francis Edward Stuart. They had married in 1719 after another failed Jacobite rising, this time supported by Spain, producing the longed-for Jacobite heir apparent, Prince Charles Edward Stuart, a year later. In 1725 a spare, Prince Henry Benedict, had also arrived at the Palazzo del Re in Rome, the new Jacobite headquarters. Given Kent's association with Burlington, often suspected but never quite outed as a Jacobite, this so-called likeness could be added to the growing evidence against him. The controversy was such that the altarpiece was removed on the orders of the Bishop of London. The satirical description beneath Hogarth's engraving expressed the hope, having argued against the covert presence of Maria Clementina, that the altarpiece could be returned to the church as soon as possible, 'by which means ye Parishes 60 pounds which thay wisely gave for it, may not be Entirely lost'. The key fact was that '1st Tis not the Pretenders Wife and Children as our weak brethren imagin'. Having drawn attention to the presence or not of the Catholic pretender's wife and offspring (thus planting in the viewer's mind the idea that they may indeed be represented) and confirming the high price paid (read wasted) by the parish – a majority of English families were living off less than £60 over an entire year – Hogarth then proceeds to dismantle the validity of it as a work of art, while appearing to be simply and innocently describing it. For example, figure E is 'an Angel tuning an Harp', while F is 'the inside of his Leg but whether right or Left as yet undiscover'd'. Moving on, G is 'a hand Playing on a Lute', while H 'is the other leg judiciously Omitted to make room for the harp', and so it goes on. Kent's altarpiece has disappeared, but if Hogarth's print is anywhere near a fair reflection of it, the mocking criticism was wholly justified. The serious point here is why, with so few opportunities to paint such prestigious commissions, was this opportunity squandered on an incompetent who may be a Jacobite to boot?[27]

Meanwhile, Hogarth's own compositions were improving and developing in ambition, thanks in no small part to his attendance at the various drawing academies. After the pirating of his independent print, *Masquerades and Operas*, he had been forced to return to engraving plates on behalf of publishers and printsellers. Two small designs for John Milton's *Paradise Lost*, 'The Council

in Hell' and 'The Council in Heaven', intended as book illustrations, reveal great imagination, spatial depth and myriad detail.
Greater still, and anticipating his first print series, is *The Mystery
of Masonry brought to Light by the Gormogons* (December 1724)
for Robert Sayer on Fleet Street. This is essentially a satire, with
complex and exotic imagery worthy of Aubry de la Motraye, on
the factions within freemasonry, particularly the 'Gormagons'.[28]
Hogarth was a mason himself, although somewhat ambivalent
and, as the years went on, increasingly half-hearted. Many artists
of his generation were freemasons. Joseph Highmore, Samuel
Scott, William Kent, George Lambert, John Pine and, from a previous generation, Sir James Thornhill, all joined for a variety of
reasons personal to themselves. But universally, the camaraderie
this extended brotherhood offered, the regular opportunities for
entertainment – lodges usually gathered in the upper rooms of
taverns – and the openness across the classes, religions and, technically, political divides meant that the contacts made through the
masonic fraternity as a whole, and the individual lodges in particular, could prove extremely useful. From the early 1720s the Grand
Master of the Grand Lodge was a leading aristocrat, and royalty
too were increasingly involved in the movement.[29]

What inspired Hogarth to even greater intellectual heights,
scale and compositional complexity than *The Mystery of Masonry*
was Samuel Butler's *Hudibras*. *Hudibras* was published after the
civil war, the Interregnum (England's only republic) and restoration of the monarchy (1660). Crucially, as one model for Hogarth's
own satires – Hogarth described him as 'the inimitable Butler'[30] –
the poem expands beyond the fable and allegory of its inspiration,
Cervantes' *Don Quixote*, by blending the imaginary with specific
individuals and real-life events. Although puritans were the main
focus, zealotry, in whatever guise, was also targeted.

The idea of a sequence of images, as well as Butler's narrative
style, will combine to influence Hogarth's innovative series schemes
in the near future. Again, this was not an independent enterprise,
but was under the banner of the printseller Philip Overton, to
whom Hogarth sold the plates.[31] Within the twelve large-scale
prints there are several details which will make a reappearance,

adapted appropriately, within his works over the next decade or so – whether a tumbling table, symbols of cuckoldry, a night-time masquerade scene or a quack doctor's den. Overton's advertisement, setting out the ambition of the series, stated:

> Proposals are publish'd for Engraving and Printing by Subscription twelve Historical and most diverting PRINTS of Hudibras and his Man Ralpho, describing, in a pleasant Manner the Humour and Hypocrisy of those Times, finely engraved on 12 Copper Plates of about 14 inches in Length, excepting the Skimmington and Burning the Rumps at Temple Bar, which are 12 inches long. The Price to subscribers, who are sure to have the best Impressions, is Fifteen Shillings the Set. Seven Plates are already finish'd, and Specimens of them to be seen at Phil. Overton's, Printseller near St. Dunstan's Church, Fleet-street, and John Coopers in James-street, Covent Garden, where subscriptions are taken in.[32]

Hogarth's name does not appear, Overton sensing that the subject rather than designer/engraver was of greater importance. Four months later, there was no need for such reticence. This earlier omission was rectified when it was announced on 3 February that subscriptions for the twelve prints 'Designed and Engraved by Mr. *Hogarth*' would remain open until the 12th of that month and then, on the 25th, that these prints 'Invented and Engrav'd by William Hogarth, and printed on a fine super Royal Paper' were now available for delivery to subscribers.[33]

This confidence was based on the large number of subscribers who had been attracted to support the project, including the Edinburgh-based poet and bookseller, Allan Ramsay (1686–1758) of *Tea-Table Miscellany* fame. The frontispiece to the set included a pictorial allegory, with Samuel Butler's genius represented as a 'satyr', a play on 'satire', also a symbol of earthiness and nature. The foolish puritan Hudibras and his sidekick, Ralpho, represent 'Rebellion, Hypocrisy, *and* Ignorance, *the Reigning Vices of his time*'. Published only ten years after the 1715 Jacobite rising, themes of rebellion and civil war were startlingly contemporary. Both sides of the divide could accuse the other of hypocrisy and ignorance, so Hogarth's subject appeals to pro-Stuart or pro-Hanoverian, Jacobites and Loyalists alike.

One (at this time at least) with overt Jacobite sympathies and, among his circle and clientele many like-minded folk, was Allan Ramsay.[34] His stance was more anti-Union than pro-Stuart, but while the 'King over the Water' advocated a dismantling of Great Britain, a return of this dynasty was wholeheartedly supported. Ramsay's fame as a man of wit and earthy humour had already been established by the popularity of his poetry, plays and miscellaneous publications, so it should come as no surprise that he was an enthusiastic supporter of this project, subscribing to no less than thirty sets, when a vast majority of the subscribers required only one. Subscription meant a payment up front (usually, as in Overton's original advertisement, offered at a special reduced price) in anticipation that the subscribers, after viewing a sample of the engravings, here available at Overton's and John Cooper's, would make the judgement to give their support. This upfront payment, if enough people subscribed, would allow the scheme to become a reality.

Ramsay would, of course, sell on most of these sets, or would have been acting as the agent for a third party.[35] Even so, this was a resounding endorsement of the creative brains behind the project, as well as the quality of the engraving, and was suitably and gratefully acknowledged by the humble dedication to 'Mr. *ALLAN RAMSAY*, of *Edinburgh*', which appeared alongside the published frontispiece.[36] John Nichols states that, because in need of cash Hogarth had sold the plates to Philip Overton, 'he often lamented to his friends the having parted with his property in the prints of the large *Hudibras*, without ever having had an opportunity to improve them'.[37] Still, the popularity of *Hudibras* would have signalled to Hogarth what a suitable subject might require – contemporary resonance combined with humour – for such an ambitious and expensive enterprise. Occasionally his choice of subject and the manner of its execution misfired – notably, as we will see, in his late work *Sigismunda* – encouraging a barrage of disdain and ridicule from his critics. A lifetime of holding up a mirror to the vanities and failings of his fellows would inevitably result in gleeful reciprocation in kind – as John Aubrey had predicted – but the manner of the attacks included snobbery and the judgement that Hogarth was straying into areas to which his intellect and artistic skill were unfitted: a circumstance Hogarth recognised and railed against.

As Hogarth was gaining in confidence and renown he continued to align himself with Sir James Thornhill, even as his idol's sparkle was beginning to dull. Yet Thornhill was a man of many parts, and even as the situation around his lessening power and reduced number of commissions at court continued, perhaps stirred by it, he became more entrepreneurial than usual. In 1724/5, despite the machinations at court, Thornhill became a Fellow of the Royal Society which, at the time he joined, included Sir Christopher Wren, Sir Hans Sloane and its president, Sir Isaac Newton. In that same year Sir James paid the gaolers (jailers) at Newgate prison to allow him access to a noted thief then awaiting execution, with the aim of taking his likeness. John 'Jack' Sheppard was briefly the most famous criminal in London and, beyond creating a portrait, Thornhill would have been intrigued to meet him in person.

Modern crime and punishment is an unusual theme for Thornhill, but it will be a consistent and important strand for Hogarth throughout his career as an artist – forming the basis of some of his best-known and most successful works. It was also, as we shall see, something that inspired writers and dramatists. This was simply because, then as now, it was part of everyday life – most people would be affected by crime or know someone who had been. Unlike now, much of the punishment – custodial sentencing being very limited – whether the pillory or execution, occurred in public. Of course Sir James could have joined the crowds lining the streets on execution day, a charged atmosphere like no other, with the hordes surging around the lone cart as it journeyed the two and a half miles from Newgate via High Holborn, Oxford Street and Tyburn Road, to the 'Hanging Tree' at London's most north-westerly edge (now Marble Arch). Instead, Thornhill had arranged to meet Sheppard alone, in the bleak, intimate space of the condemned man's cell in the notorious Newgate prison.

Bernard Mandeville (1670–1733), a Dutch-born philosopher,

political economist and satirist, described Newgate and its occupants in a pamphlet of 1725 entitled *An Enquiry into the causes of
the frequent executions at Tyburn*. (Mandeville held a club at the
'Horns' pale ale house in Cheapside, visited by young Ben Franklin, who described Mandeville as 'a most facetious entertaining
Companion'.)[38] Received wisdom declared that execution was
an effective deterrent, and its associated parade from Newgate
to Tyburn, of roughly a two-hour duration (depending on the
crowds) was a crucial part of it. Mandeville, with the eye of an
informed outsider, begged to differ, by noting that, if it worked as
a deterrent, why were so many put through it month after month,
year after year? He challenged the use of receivers of stolen goods
and thief-takers as part of the justice system – something that had
become a racket in its own right, led by the likes of the aptly named
Jonathan Wild – alongside the advertised rewards for lost goods
in newspapers, again encouraging the crime in the first place. He
also challenged those who did not correct bad behaviour early, at
the first crime, rather erring on the side of mercy and therefore
demonstrating that petty crime has no adverse ramifications – the
unintended consequence being further encouragement and even
greater crimes in the future: 'The oftener a young Rogue steals
with Impunity, the sooner he'll be a thorough-paced Villain, that
will venture on more hazardous Undertakings.'[39]

This idea, common at the time, acted as one driver within the
later narratives of both *Industry and Idleness* (1747) and *The Four
Stages of Cruelty* (1751) – bad behaviour, poor company and petty
crime leading to greater crimes and, eventually, the gallows. But,
crucially, society's culpability in this seemingly relentless cycle
is also laid bare, which suggests that Hogarth had empathy with
much of what Mandeville's tract described and argued. Mandeville
did not veer away from the responsibility of individuals to look
after their property as best they could, to be on their guard when
out in the streets, particularly at night (which should be avoided,
if at all possible), not to get drunk, not to consort with prostitutes,
and to maintain security at home.

Conversely he highlighted those 'who are unthinking, and
never mind what Companies they thrust themselves into; or such

as will be drunk, go home late in the dark unattended, and scruple not to talk and converse with lewd Women, as they meet them',[40] which brings to mind Tom Rakewell in the Rose Tavern scene of *A Rake's Progress*, giddy-drunk with alcohol and the quarry of a seasoned troop of prostitutes, one fondling him as she picks his pocket.

Most evocative of all, and to which Mandeville devoted a greater portion of the pamphlet, bringing all these arguments together, is his description of execution day itself, commencing with the journey of the condemned. In reality this intended warning to would-be criminals only served to expose the worst of human instincts and behaviour. He described how those with only a few hours left to live might, you would think, display some sorrow, or signs of contrition, and that throughout the prison, in honour of those about to die, a contemplative silence, or, at the very least a sober sadness might pervade. And further, those preparing the condemned, the gaolers and their men, might aim, for common decency's sake, to bring some solemnity to this terrible occasion. You might think, even hope this. But the reality was very far from it: strong liquor, to dull the senses, was handed out liberally by individuals with black hands 'and Nastiness all over', with the cries of 'More!' ringing throughout the prison; the 'howling in one Place, scolding and quarrelling in another, and loud Laughter in a third'; the dinginess, with little light penetrating, the squalor, the constant rattle and clank of the chains and fetters, with different weights emitting varying depths of sound, all contribute to the melancholy scene. The Ordinary, or priest, bustles about dispensing godly thoughts to people who are not listening, while the executioner, the hangman, grumbles and swears at any delay. Mandeville had little patience with anyone involved – everyone is culpable.

You could pay a fee, as Thornhill did, to enter Newgate prison, and other institutions had similar access. Hogarth shows two women, gawping and sniggering behind their fans, while visiting the asylum of 'Bedlam' in the last scene of *A Rake's Progress* (Fig. 30 p. 198). But in reality most people would have, at best, only an inkling of Newgate's horrors, as powerfully described by Mandeville. His pamphlet is a useful literary accompaniment to those prints by Hogarth that focused on criminals and their journey, via Newgate, to Tyburn: whether obliquely, as seen with the murderers Silvertongue and Tom Nero, or, overtly, Tom Idle.

At last, the gate of the prison opens and the cart carrying the condemned moves off, accompanied by a human torrent, pushing, shoving and shouting. The vast majority of the crowds gathered in the street to watch or follow the cavalcade, according to Mandeville, are of the lower level of society, including 'working People, the idlest, and such as are most fond of making Holidays, with Prentices and Journeymen to the meanest Trades, are the most honourable Part of these floating Multitudes. All the rest are worse.' Mandeville observes that as executions are advertised well in advance, the day becomes a draw to thieves and pickpockets in their hundreds, even thousands, and the sheer scale of the crowds, as at Bartholomew Fair, act as cover to their activities; in fact, he draws a comparison with an extreme type of Bartholomew Fair, with whores, rogues and 'rakehells' partnering up in plain sight, befuddled gin sellers dressed in rags and with putrefied wigs touting their brain-curdling wares. As little can be done, given the level of criminality and the lack of a police force in the modern sense, the day is in effect a thieves' jubilee, an outlaws' amnesty, who, usually more reticent, eagerly crawl out of their holes (as he describes it) to ply their trades unhindered.[41]

These 'undisciplined Armies', as he calls them, who have no particular enemies other than 'Cleanliness and good Manners', are royally entertained by what havoc can be made with a dead cat or dog, preferably one covered in dirt and of some vintage. These 'ill-boding Meteors' are flung as high in the air as possible, dirt and entrails spilling in all directions, only to land where the throng is at its most dense, causing maximum discomfort to those beneath. The joy and satisfaction of the onlookers becomes even greater 'to see a good Suit of Cloaths spoiled by this Piece of Gallantry'. Mandeville observes that 'no People in their Senses would venture among them on Foot, in any tolerable Dress, yet there are young Rakes of Fortune, who care not what they lavish, or destroy: Of these the maddest sort will often, after a Night's Debauch, mix with Crowds, and thrust themselves in the midst of the most abominable Rabble, where they seldom fail of meeting with such Adventures.'[42]

The condemned were drunk prior to setting off. But this, of course, would wear off over the two to three hours it took to reach Tyburn. Therefore the cart stopped en route at several places along the grim progress, including the George Inn at St Giles, the area depicted in *Gin Lane*, lengthening (again) the journey time. Meanwhile the crowds got bigger the more often the cart stopped, particularly if there were notorious criminals among the mob. Jonathan Swift burlesqued this procession in his poem, '*Clever* Tom Clinch *going to be hanged*' of 1726–7:

> As clever *Tom Clinch*, while the Rabble was bawling,
> Rode stately through *Holbourn*, to die in his Calling,
> He stopt at the *George* for a Bottle of Sack,
> And promis'd to pay for it when he'd come back.
> His Waistcoat and Stockings, and Breeches were white,
> His Cap had a new Cherry Ribbon to ty't.
> The Maids to the Doors and the Balconies ran,
> And said, lack-a-day! he's a proper young Man.
> But, as from the Windows the Ladies he spy'd,
> Like a Beau in the Box, he bow'd low on each Side;
> And when his last speech the loud Hawkers did cry,
> He swore from his Cart, it was all a damn'd Lye.
> The Hangman for Pardon fell down on his Knee;
> *Tom* gave him a Kick in the Guts for his Fee.
> Then said, I must speak to the People a little,
> But I'll see you all damn'd before I will * *whittle*.
> My honest Friend Wild, may he long hold his Place,
> He lengthen'd my Life with a whole Year of Grace.
> Take Courage, dear Comrades, and be not afraid,
> Nor slip this Occasion to follow your Trade.
> My Conscience is clear, and my Spirits are calm,
> And thus I go off without Pray'r-Book or Psalm.
> Then follow the Practice of clever *Tom Clinch*,
> Who hung like a Hero, and never would flinch.

[* *A Cant Word for confessing at the Gallows.*][43]

So rather than a grim example, the condemned are heroes, with young men fighting their way to the cart to shake their hands and gaining reflected glory in the process. At the gallows the jostling between the mob and the gaolers becomes more violent, with clubs and sticks randomly used, men falling to the ground and trampled on. While the noise and cries and laughter becomes louder and more dissonant, 'together with the Sound of more distant Noises, make such a Discord not to be parallel'd'. A different kind of Belphegor's Concert.

The nooses are put around their necks. Even now some are still hoping for a reprieve, but as this tends to arrive too late and, besides, everyone concerned on the official side is keen to get on with it, the cart moves off and each falls – there is no 'drop' – and is hanged, or strangled, one by one. The death could take minutes, or much longer. This again, the death-throes jig, the pissing and soiling, are very much part of the entertainment. At last, the 'Ordinary and Executioners, having performed their different Duties with small Ceremony, and equal Concern, seem to be tired, and glad it is over'.

But the entertainment is far from over, for now there is the tussle over the bodies, between the surgeons who need cadavers for dissection, and the mob. The latter, paraphrased by Mandeville, cry 'They have suffer'd the Law ... and shall have no Barbarities put upon them: We know what you are, and will not leave them before we see them buried.' Mandeville then makes the following observation, based on the proviso that 'I have no Design that savours of Cruelty, or even Indecency, towards a human Body' but, as he continues, 'the superstitious Reverence of the Vulgar' (the lower class) 'for a Corpse, even of a Malefactor, and the strong Aversion they have against dissecting them, are prejudicial to the Publick'.[44] Surgeons need to learn from bodies; medicine or 'physick' can only be improved through such exploration. And, given the abhorrence revealed by the mob at the executions, who show little compassion at any other moment, dissection as an automatic rule might actually have acted as a much-needed deterrent. This would become the core tenet of the Murder Act of 1751, whereby the body would be either hung in chains or given to the surgeons for dissection – the latter the final stage of cruelty in Hogarth's 1751 series.

Such descriptions, alongside personal experience, fed directly and largely unedited into Hogarth's art throughout his career. Hogarth, for the first years of his life, lived just north of Newgate, so the dismal tolling of the nearby St Sepulchre bell every month, signalling the commencement and estimated duration of the journey (so at least two hours) would have been very familiar. It is difficult to imagine not experiencing a sinking sensation at the sound: a reminder, too, of your own mortality. After all, as another Londoner and Dean of St Paul's Cathedral, John Donne, observed, 'No Man is an *Iland*, intire of itself; every man is a peece of the *Continent* ... Any Mans *death* diminishes *me*, because I am involved in *Mankinde* ; And therefore never send to know for whom the *bell* tolls; It tolls for *thee*.'[45] Mandeville makes a direct comparison between Smithfield's livestock market and Tyburn: 'and should we compare the Droves that are carried to *Tyburn* for Slaughter, with those others that are sent to *Smithfield* for the same Purpose, we would find the modern Thief-Catcher subservient to the Executioner in the same Manner, as the wealthy Grazier is to the needy Butcher; and that of the Cattle in either Sense, few are kill'd by the one that were never cherish'd by the other'.[46]

Tyburn's 'hanging tree', originally set up in the Elizabethan period and a permanent fixture, was a distinctive 'three-legged stool' form, and appears on the notice of execution in the last image of *Marriage A-la-Mode*, (Fig. 5 p. 25, painting *c.*1743, engraving 1745) as the countess's lover, Silvertongue, having killed her husband in a duel, is hanged (off stage) for the murder. A more direct graphic description occurs in the penultimate plate of *Industry and Idleness* (overleaf), where Tom Idle's catalogue of poor decisions stimulated by laziness, the desire for easy money and instant gratification, brings him to Tyburn. A ballad seller, standing centrally, is hawking the dying speech or confession (as Swift describes it, the '*whittle*') of the condemned, the gin sellers are making good sales, the unaware, ogling the 'dead man' passing, are being divested of their valuables, and people are fighting, shouting and laughing. Simply for research, or just curiosity, Hogarth may well have attended a hanging at Tyburn, but, even so, Mandeville's evocative blow-by-blow description would have served as

16. *Industry and Idleness Plate 11: The Idle 'Prentice*
Executed at Tyburn, etching and engraving, 1747
The three-legged gallows is centre right, with spectator seating
behind. Elements of this print (e.g. the central hawker) will reappear
adapted in *The March to Finchley* and *The Four Stages of Cruelty*.

good source material – certainly, Hogarth here visualises Mandeville's 'undisciplined Armies'. Tom Idle himself appears more
contrite than Mandeville or Swift's protagonists, visibly reading
from a religious book, possibly the Bible, his gaunt, hollowed-out
eyes gazing heavenward. Perhaps Hogarth hopes for Tom to show
some contrition, right at the end. But no one else seems to care.
His demise is mere entertainment. And thus the cycle continues.
For among the crowd, as Mandeville warns, more Tom Idles are
already being moulded. The proverb attached to the image gives
little consolation: 'When fear cometh as desolation, and their
destruction cometh as a Whirlwind: when distress cometh upon
them. Then they shall call upon God, but he will not answer'
(Proverbs 1:27–8). Two skeletons flank the composition, like sinis-
ter heraldic supporters, hinting that the dissection table and, once
finished with, the boiling down of the body to the bare bones for
permanent display, is Tom's perpetual destiny. This final stage in
the process is shown in full in the fourth plate of *The Four Stages
of Cruelty*. In depicting the complete cycle, including the ultimate

17. *The Four Stages of Cruelty Plate 4: The Reward
of Cruelty*, etching and engraving, 1751
The skeletons (echoing those adorning the print of Tyburn) are what remain
of the real-life 'Gentleman Highwayman' James MacLaine and boxer-turned-
thief James Field (executed October 1750 and February 1751 respectively).

deterrent, Hogarth's prints are intended as moral instruction. The
production of this image as a cheap woodcut, as well as an engraving, stresses his aim that these images should be as accessible as
possible, to be seen by the intended beneficiaries of this instruction, for example, apprentices like Jack Sheppard. Yet here, too, it

is the state's culpability in the perpetuation of this cycle that is the focus. Still, God remains silent while the surgeons are all attention.

The best advice Hogarth and Mandeville can offer is to avoid this scenario with every fibre of your being. For once on this road, everything and everyone conspires against you and any hope of reformation diminishes with relentless predictability. A weak, persuadable character will always be easy prey to the unscrupulous, the self-serving and the callous, who, in London's burgeoning population, are legion.

The criminal Jack Sheppard, sitting manacled in his cell and with all this bleak pageantry before him, would have been delighted, no doubt, that such an esteemed artist, the king's painter, would take the time to sketch his likeness for posterity. And, of course, for the artist, the resulting image had great commercial potential, given the celebrity of his subject. Jack allegedly wrote a short autobiography, generally believed to have been ghostwritten by the prolific Daniel Defoe, delivered from within the 'Middle-Stone-Room in Newgate', in which he recounts his feats of daring and general criminality.[47] Jack signs off 'A clear and ample Account have I now given of the most material Transactions of my Life, and do hope the same will prove a Warning to all young Men.'[48] Not least 'I hope none will be so cruel as to reflect on my poor distressed Mother, the unhappy Parent of two miserable Wretches, my self and Brother; the last gone to America for his Crimes, and my self going to the Grave for mine; the Weight of which Misfortune is sufficient surely to satisfy the Malice of her Enemies.' Concluding *'I beseech the infinite Divine Being of Beings to pardon my numberless and enormous Crimes, and to have Mercy on my poor departing Soul.'*[49]

Sir James Thornhill's portrait, from which an engraving was made, helped to establish Jack Sheppard as the tragic example of how a life that starts with some hope can spiral out of control through a lack of guidance and a flawed character. For despite the abject poverty of his birth in Spitalfields, East London, Jack's life of crime commenced while he was a shop boy to a kindly draper on the Strand called William Kneebone, who taught him some reading and writing and encouraged him to become an apprentice carpenter. The seven-year indenture was signed in 1717 with Owen Wood of Covent Garden. Regular visits to the Black Lion public house off Drury Lane brought him into contact with the young prostitute Elizabeth Lyon, known as Edgworth Bess, as well as the criminals Joseph 'Blueskin' Blake and the notorious receiver of stolen goods and thief-taker, Jonathan Wild – Tom Clinch's 'honest friend'. By 1723 Jack had abandoned his apprenticeship and was living with Bess, who seems to have had expensive tastes. Penalties for theft were severe, the level of severity depending on the value of the property taken. For Jack, minor theft turned to house-breaking (burglary) for which the penalty was death. The protection of property was one core focus of the justice system. It was, after all, levels of property that allowed you to vote and stand for parliament, so not for the vast majority of the population.

As his 'autobiography' establishes, Jack was accompanied on his criminal spree with his brother Tom, who had been caught the previous year and branded on the hand. In fact it was Tom who betrayed his brother. Perhaps it is no surprise that Hogarth's reprobates and criminals tend to be called Tom – Tom Rakewell, Tom Nero (*The Four Stages of Cruelty*), Tom Idle – and in the latter series, Hogarth modelled the idle apprentice's career on Jack's life, but, in a poetic flourish, in Hogarth's version it is 'Tom' who is hanged. The presence of Tom Idle's long-suffering mother within the series accords with Jack's reference to the 'distress'd' parent in his *Life*, and Hogarth includes an Edgworth Bess figure in scenes seven and nine. The infamous thief-taker Jonathan Wild – who was in possession of a sizeable criminal organisation himself – was keen to get his hands on the £40 bounty and, as was his 'legitimate' role in the criminal justice system, turned Jack in to the authorities. Wild's technique was to hold off until the criminal was no longer of use or profit to him – indeed at the moment when they became more valuable dead. As Tom Clinch declares 'He lengthen'd my life with a whole year of grace.'

But Jack was transformed from a common everyday thief, a nobody of no particular interest to anyone, into a celebrity because of his talent for gaol breaking. In one escape, he managed to smash a hole in the ceiling of his cell and pull himself up and through it, manacles and all, eventually appearing on the prison roof. He then dropped down on to the street and joined the crowd, who, on hearing of his escape, were gathering outside. Jack casually pointed towards the roof, announcing that he had seen someone up there, and, having distracted the crowd, calmly walked, or more likely hobbled away in the opposite direction. It was this level of confidence, or brass neck, that captured the public imagination. And, although a notorious and prolific thief, he was not a murderer, so could be converted more easily into a folk hero.

Jonathan Wild, no folk hero, unless one at which the audience might hiss, eventually paid the price for his own criminality and was, like Sheppard, executed at Tyburn only a year after (24 May 1725). His immortality came in a very different guise: dissection at Surgeon's Hall and, following, no Christian burial but as an exhibit, like the skeletons pointing and laughing, a deathly, silent laugh, in the last plate of *The Four Stages of Cruelty*. ('Tom Nero's corpse is in preparation to join them.) Wild remains on display in the Hunterian Museum, London.

Jack Sheppard was only five years younger than Hogarth, and both would have been working their apprenticeships in the same district at the same time, as too, a little later, would Will Tothall – the idle and industrious apprentices in action. Jack was only twenty-two when he died, and although young, he would have been considered personally responsible for his choices, limited as they might have been, his associated deeds and far from satisfactory life path. But Thornhill's portrait belies expectation, by presenting Jack as a slight, callow youth, with doe-eyes, dark lashes and enigmatic expression – not despairing, perhaps contrite, certainly not the face of evil – his cropped hair, neckerchief and coat, one hand lying on the wooden table, the other, to which it is manacled, pointing towards an unseen door. His glance back allows the sunshine from the high and barred window to cast a raking light over his face – perhaps God's light shines on him yet. Sheppard, sitting in the Middle-Stone-Room of Newgate, from which he will not, this time, escape, appears to be recounting one of his adventures.

The resulting engraving by George White is in mezzotint, a medium which is quicker to complete than copper engraving, so used for a fast turnaround of topical subjects, while also producing a soft, painterly effect, allowing for dramatic contrasts in light and shade. As a development from Thornhill's drawing, at the artist's direction the engraver has introduced a shadow against the wall, created by the bright light covering Sheppard's body and particularly his face and hands. The manacled wrists, with the face of youthful innocence, are highlighted, with the pointing finger now indicating towards his own dark shadow – the criminal's dark soul within, or a portent of his imminent death? The viewer can provide their own interpretation. But Jack now turns away from the darkness, towards the light and redemption, while justice too is seen to be done. A poem published in the *The British Journal* and addressed to Thornhill declared simply that:

> Thornhill, 'tis thine to gild with Fame/ Th'obscure, and raise the humble Name,
> Thy Pencil brings a kind Reprieve,/And bids the dying Robber live.[50]

Here the poet uses 'pencil', from the Latin *pencillus* 'little tail' referring to a thin brush or graphite stick, or the French 'pincel', 'little brush', to mean all pictorial representation, whether brush or pencil. Once again Hogarth was learning from Thornhill's example – observing the popular interest in depictions of crime and criminals and therefore the career-enhancing potential in such subject matter. And very soon he will be putting Thornhill's example into action, in a way that will transform his career. For within a few years of his execution, Jack Sheppard, along with the spirits of hundreds of young men just like him, would strut life's stage once more and in an equally spectacular style. It was the opportunity that Hogarth had been waiting for.

In early 1728 Hogarth was in the audience for a new theatrical entertainment, *The Beggar's Opera*, first performed, as was his friend Ebenezer Forrest's *Momus*, at Lincoln's Inn Fields Theatre, but, in striking contrast to Forrest's offering, a sensation. Hogarth immediately began a painting inspired by what he had witnessed, and as one of the earliest datable oil on canvases by him, it signals Hogarth's shift from engraver to painter.

The abundance of examples in this particular medium by Hogarth and his contemporaries cloaks the fact that painting in oils is a highly complex technique, requiring great skill and knowledge of fundamental rules, not least that oil layers can take days or weeks to dry and a completed canvas up to six months. How Hogarth achieved the requirements in practice is uncertain, but can be guessed at. He had attended the St Martin's Lane Academy from 1720, led by two experienced painters, John Vanderbank and Louis Chéron, so some guidance beyond the main activity of life drawing may have been forthcoming. There were prominent painters who were extremely happy to demonstrate their skill to an admiring audience of anyone and everyone. One such was Sir Godfrey Kneller, whom George Vertue noted 'let any body see & be by him,'[51] a reason why Kneller's technique was followed by the next generation of portrait painters. Crucially, for any would-be portraitist, Sir Godfrey painted with an assured manner and at speed. Stories about his bravura performances as a young man at the court of Charles II were still circulating decades later – part of the London artworld's folklore. One such story concerned Kneller and Sir Peter Lely painting the king's portrait at the same sitting. As their time in His Majesty's presence came to a close, the king no doubt bored to tears (one key skill of a portrait painter was keeping their sitters entertained), to everyone's amazement the young Kneller had almost finished, while Sir Peter was barely completing a preliminary third layer of 'dead' or grey colour. 'After this,' Vertue recalled in 1713, 'his reputation daily increase[e]d', so much so 'that most noblemen & Ladies would have their pictures done by him.'[52] The lesson was lost on no one with any commercial nous – a good likeness done at speed increased, dramatically, the viability of a portrait practice.

But given Hogarth's evident admiration, the key influence for his move into oil painting must have been Sir James Thornhill. Aside from Hogarth's involvement with Sir James's own drawing academy, in 1727 Thornhill, alongside John Vanderbank, had been witnesses for Hogarth against one Joshua Morris, concerning a tapestry design with which Hogarth had furnished him, only for Morris to declare it was not fit for that purpose and refuse to pay. Thornhill and Vanderbank, the latter particularly well placed, given his father's profession, gave testimony in Hogarth's favour.[53] Perhaps flattered by Hogarth's attention and support, while sensing something of himself in this young man's character and professional drive, Sir James began to tutor William in the oil on canvas technique. Given that Hogarth married Jane Thornhill, Sir James's only daughter, in 1729, a close acquaintance had clearly been developing over the years leading up to this event. Thornhill would also have shown Hogarth how elevating through art the criminal and celebrity Jack Sheppard, produced, in turn, associated fame and financial benefit for the artist. No doubt the creator and producer of *The Beggar's Opera*, John Gay and John Rich respectively, had also taken note. Jack Sheppard, the charming scallywag who comes good in the end, in so far that his 'confession' recording his life and death acts as a warning to other would-be criminals, was one model for an anti-hero, with Jonathan Wild a recognisable archetype as villain.

The structure of this theatrical entertainment was new. Plays often had a song or two for variation. Grand Operas, like *Julius Caesar*, were sung completely. But a play with songs, not only sprinkled throughout the piece, but crucial to the narrative drive and character development, was fresh and exciting. Alone this would have guaranteed *The Beggar's Opera*'s place in theatrical history. But the originality did not end there. A quick glance at the plot, characters and cultural sources provide countless reasons for its popularity and why it appealed to Hogarth as a suitable subject to assist his professional transformation.

As the title declares, the narrator is a man of the street – a nobody – and, usually, marginalised. But this nobody is master of ceremonies. Continuing with this carnivalesque world turned upside down, more extraordinary still, London's under- and criminal class are here centre stage, not the usual classical gods and Roman generals or pastoral lovers. The British folk airs and ditties, both jaunty and plaintive – many assembled by Thomas d'Urfey in his ever popular *Wit and Mirth, or, Pills to Purge*

Melancholy (published in six volumes between 1698 and 1720)
– were lightly reworked by the Prussian-born composer Johann
Christoph Pepusch, director of the Academy of Vocal Music (soon
after renamed the Academy of Ancient Music, with Hogarth as a
subscriber) and then cleverly blended with high culture, notably
some popular tunes from the Opera Seria of the newly minted
Briton (after his naturalisation in 1727 on the accession of George
II) George Handel. This repurposing of such grand, aristocratic
and regal music – in the process plunging it from high heaven to
street level – added to the joyousness and glee of the production. It
was a new, essentially British form of entertainment, the descendant of the wheelbarrow's discarded contents as seen in Hogarth's
Masquerades and Operas.

Within this mix of high and low culture there are further
layers. The dramatis personae, dialogue and action mimic real
people, circumstances and events in such a contemporary, up-
to-the-minute way, that audience members were left tittering in
amazement at the sheer audacity of it. And nothing represents
this more than the central love triangle between Macheath, the
charismatic captain of a brotherhood of thieves and rascals, loosely
based on Jack Sheppard, and his 'wives', Lucy Lockit, the Newgate
gaoler's daughter, and Polly Peachum, the child of a criminal-gang
leader and thief-taker, a surrogate for Jonathan Wild. That said, any
number of contemporary figures could be slotted into the place of
these three characters. For example, the prime minister Sir Robert
Walpole, his wife, Catherine, and his mistress, Maria Skerrett, with
whom he had been living openly at his house in Richmond Park
and Houghton Hall, Norfolk; the old king, George I, his imprisoned wife, Sophia Dorothea (who had died in 1726), and mistress,
Melusine von der Schulenburg; the tired, overblown tropes of
Opera Seria alongside Handel, its main London champion, and
the public spats with his warring Italian divas, Faustina Bordoni
and Francesca Cuzzoni; and so the list goes on.

In terms of contemporary satire, *The Beggar's Opera* eclipsed
everything else, even Jonathan Swift's hit, *Travels into Several
Remote Nations of the World*, better known as *Gulliver's Travels*,
published just over a year before (Fig. 33 p. 221). Swift declared

ruefully, 'The Beggar's Opera hath knocked down Gulliver', although he had hopes that Alexander Pope's new mock-heroic poem *The Dunciad*, a votive offering to the goddess Dullness and dedicated to Swift, will 'knock down the Beggar's Opera, but not till it hath fully done its job'.[54] Dullness and her acolytes, listed over several parts commencing in 1728, represent, in Pope's mind, the progress of 'decay, imbecility and tastelessness' in the Kingdom of Great Britain. *The Beggar's Opera* too had a message, but was great fun, a lot less effort and, thus, targeted at the many rather than a learned few. Swift's defence of *The Beggar's Opera* is of interest, not least if, as we read it, we replace the named theatrical satire with (say) *A Harlot's Progress*. Pondering humour over wit, that is, for example, *The Beggar's Opera* over *The Dunciad*, he notes the former is more universal, across class and education. It is 'in some Manner fixed to the very Nature of Man' ... 'I know very well, that this happy *Talent* is contemptibly treated by *Criticks*, under the name of *low Humour*, or *low Comedy*; but I know likewise that the *Spaniards* and *Italians*, who are allowed to have the most Wit of any *Nation* in *Europe*, do most excel in it, and do most esteem it.' He continues, 'It is certainly the best Ingredient toward that Kind of Satyr, which is most useful, and gives the least Offence; which, instead of lashing, laughs Men out of their Follies and Vices.'[55] *The Beggar's Opera*, 'by a Turn of *Humour*, entirely New, placed Vices of all Kinds in the strongest and most odious Light; and thereby done eminent Service, both to *Religion* and *Morality*.'[56] He has little truck with the court chaplain, Dr Thomas Herring, who preached against *The Beggar's Opera* at Lincoln's Inn, adjoining the theatre, rather Gay's entertainment 'will probably do more Good than a thousand Sermons of so stupid, so injudicious, and so prostitute a Divine'. Moving on, in terms that Hogarth would have cheerfully applauded, Swift declares, 'This *Comedy* likewise exposeth, with great Justice that unnatural Taste for *Italian* Musick among us, which is wholly unsuitable to our Northern *Climate*, and the *Genius* of the People, whereby we are overrun with *Italian Effeminacy*, and *Italian Nonsense*.' And after an invasion of Italian opera, singers and the like, what next? Why, 'we should want nothing but stabbing, or poysoning, to make us perfect *Italians*'.[57]

The climactic scene of the opera, Act III, Scene 2, brings all five major players on to the stage for the first time, with the said love triangle at the heart, and, in a further *coup de théâtre*, is set in the grim confines of Newgate prison itself. Unsurprisingly, this is the scene that captured Hogarth's imagination, and a drawing, using black and white chalk on blue paper, with splats of white and red oil paint (Col. Fig. 3), so full of life and immediacy, may have been drawn by Hogarth while sitting in the audience. Certainly, given his established modus operandi, he would have been watching the performance, sketchbook and pencil at the ready. As *The Beggar's Opera* ran for sixty-two nights (unlike poor Ebenezer's play), there was ample opportunity to pin down the presence and likeness of the performers, notably Thomas Walker as Macheath and Lavinia Fenton as Polly, and the general spirit of the production and performance. This drawing will form the basis of the variations in paint, as the splats suggest, that he produced over a three-year period (Col. Fig. 4).

But still more hardhitting, as Swift touches on, was the exposure of an iniquitous criminal justice system in general and, specifically, as Bernard Mandeville had described only three years earlier, such practices as the advertising of rewards for stolen goods, simply encouraging more theft as a route to easy money, and the systemic use of corrupt thief-takers, such as Jonathan Wild. So in its irreverent and whimsical way, *The Beggar's Opera* had a very serious core message, highlighting the disparity between rich and poor, the powerful and the downtrodden, the privileged and the disadvantaged. Criminals are criminals, wherever they come from, whoever they are. The legal system will endeavour to punish the lower class, on whom its pitiless gaze is largely fixed, but who monitors the behaviour of the elite, those very men who *are* the system? No doubt the reader can offer some modern examples that would fit this scenario perfectly. And, like the parading and execution of criminals, this was all played out, ironically in the context of *The Beggar's Opera*, for the purposes of instruction and entertainment.

The comic possibilities of the love triangle will make a reappearance, in various guises, in Hogarth's later compositions. One example, on a different scale but continuing the connection to theatre, was a frontispiece for a publication, *The Tragedy of Tragedies* by Henry Fielding – possibly the commission that first brought them together, as friends and mutual supporters. Tall and, by his own admission, not handsome, with a long nose and protruding chin, Fielding might have excited some sympathy in Hogarth for his misaligned proportions but for his aristocratic relations and Eton education – a significant head start, along with that easiness in any company and context which Hogarth would have envied. By 1725 Henry had achieved some notoriety for pursuing, perhaps with a little too much vigour, his young cousin, Sarah.[58] That matrimonial attempt failing, Fielding had ventured to London and, needing to write for a living, despite his background and connections, commenced publishing plays and poetry. After a few false starts, the satire *The Grub-Street Opera*, evidently inspired by Gay and Pepusch's extravaganza, achieved some success, playing at the Theatre Royal, Haymarket, until, that is, it was withdrawn in June 1731 due to its lampooning of the Hanoverian dynasty and its Walpole-led government. But Fielding's *Tom Thumb: A Tragedy* of 1730, later improved as *The Tragedy of Tragedies, or, The Life and Death of Tom Thumb the Great* established him and, with other such plays published under the name 'Sciblerus Secundus', he claimed his place alongside Jonathan Swift, Alexander Pope and John Gay. That is exactly the company with which William Hogarth also wished to be associated, intellectually and otherwise, so it would come as no surprise that he provided a frontispiece for *The Tragedy of Tragedies*. By the time of *The Peregrination*, Fielding was ensconced as house playwright at the Theatre Royal, Drury Lane, then managed by Colley Cibber, and that year he published *The Modern Husband* dedicated to Walpole, in an attempt at a rapprochement.

The dramatis personae of *The Tragedy of Tragedies* include Tom Thumb himself, described by Fielding as 'A little Hero with a great Soul, something violent in his Temper', which could almost describe William Hogarth, Lord *Grizzle* 'Extremely zealous for the Liberty of the Subject', the 'Courtiers in Place' that is, placemen (read sycophants) 'and consequently of that party that is uppermost', namely *Noodle* and *Doodle*, alongside *Foodle*, 'A

Courtier that is out of Place, and consequently of that Party that is undermost' and so on. Hogarth's frontispiece, taken from Act II, Scene 7, perhaps based on a performance, shows Princess Huncamunca inspecting the features of her rival, the amazon Glumdalca, by candlelight, with the tiny form of Tom Thumb – like a mini Roman general, a Caesar indeed, his helmet plume as wide as he is tall, arms folded – at her feet. Fielding seems to have taken the Polly/Lucy/Macheath template from another street opera, with all its contemporary resonances, including Grand Opera (which their costumes ape most distinctly) and given it a further comic twist. The distorted heights and breadths thus displayed is another example of comedy deriving, as Hogarth will term it, from visual inappropriateness.[59]

Yet, despite the popularity of *The Beggar's Opera*, both drama and painting – Hogarth produced at least six painted versions for various clients, including John Gay himself – no engraving was made from any of these canvases during his life. Hogarth had not, as yet, arrived at the method of using a painting (which can only be the property of one owner at a time) as the basis and marketing tool for engravings – purchased by hundreds or even thousands of individuals, and through which the fame and popularity of the artist spreads far beyond single commissioners, while, crucially, generating a rolling income. This commercial model would be exploited by Hogarth only a few years later, just before the pilgrims embarked on their journey to Kent, and with outstanding results.

In fact it would be another London artist called William, Mr William Blake, who would supply the demand much later in the century for an engraving of *The Beggar's Opera*, revealing Hogarth's high status and market worth over two decades after his death.

INTERLUDE THREE

EARLY MORNING ON SATURDAY 27 MAY. The first location beyond Billingsgate mentioned in *The Peregrination* is Cuckold's Point, and some years later, Samuel Scott, who specialised in Thamesside and maritime subjects, would return to paint this intriguing section of the Thames near Rotherhithe.[1] A few years younger than Hogarth and John Thornhill, Sam was the son of a barber surgeon. In 1723, he had married Ann Bolton at St Mary's church, Newington Butts, then a village located a mile south of London's Old Bridge and, in tandem with Hogarth, had over the subsequent decade achieved success in his chosen field, culminating (around 1730–31) in a commission from the all-powerful trading leviathan, the British East India Company. This commission, six canvases for the company's Leadenhall Street headquarters, each depicting a view of the settlements of the company (Bombay; Tellicherry Kerala; the Island of St Helena; Fort St George, Madras; Cape of Good Hope; Fort William, Calcutta) was in collaboration with George Lambert, a mutual friend of Scott, Thornhill, Hogarth and Tothall.[2] A year or so later Scott had begun painting scenes of the Thames, at first around Wapping and Limehouse to the east of the City, which might explain his enthusiasm for the impromptu trip along the river, for there was much to inspire Samuel during their five days away. Not least there were the ships of the Royal Navy at the Royal Dockyards, Chatham and the Fort at Sheerness, with the seas around Sheppey and the Nore, a sandbank located in the estuary (the key rendezvous point for Great Britain's formidable fleet, ever watchful of England's old enemy, France, a mere twenty miles away).

To mark his growing reputation, Samuel had recently sat for the newly popular portraitist, Thomas Hudson, from which a print, by the mezzotint-engraver John Faber, has been made and circulated.[3] Vanity aside, this was considered a standard and necessary tool for self-promotion, for both marine and portrait painter alike. Samuel was of a prickly temperament as will become clear, hinted at by his unsmiling expression in the portrait and his guarded blue eyes under slightly frowning black brows. But he was another loyal friend to Hogarth, clearly attuned to his fellow artist's foibles and temper, as the Kit Sugars 'two pugs' anecdote noted earlier suggests, and an active supporter in his various campaigns and schemes. Hogarth, being who he was, would have need of such allies throughout his life.

But for now the five friends, weary and a little rain-sodden, revived their spirits with a raucous rendition of the song 'Sir John', probably referring to 'Sir John got him an ambling nag', sung to the tune of 'John Dory'. Believed to have been composed by Sir John Mennis, the ditty concerns the threatened invasion of England by the Scottish Covenanters in 1639. Sir John Suckling had raised a troop of horse to fight for King Charles I and kitted them out in flamboyant style – to which the king is quoted as saying, with suitable irony, 'Scots would fight stoutly, if it were but for the Englishmen's fine cloaths'. As predicted, the rugged Scots proved more than a match for their showy Southern cousins.[4]

> Sir *John* got him an ambling Nag,
> To *Scotland* for to ride *a*;
> With a hundred Horse more then his own,
> To guard him on each side *a*.
> No arrant Knight e'er went to fight,
> With half so gay a *Serado*;
> Had you seen but his look, you'd a sworn on a book,
> He'd conquer'd a whole *Armado*.[5]

The landing place at Cuckold's Point lay between two river-facing timber yards, which backed on to Lavender Street. Up to the seventeenth century, on the shore alongside the lone tavern in the vicinity, stood a tall post upon which was displayed a large pair of animal horns. This was the sign of the cuckold, a man whose wife was unfaithful and who, as a result, was invariably characterised in novels, plays and folktales, as also in paintings, prints and book illustrations, as a ridiculous booby. Certainly cuckolds received no sympathy from their neighbours, if the popular literature and folk ceremonies are anything to go by. The word 'cuckold', according to John Brand in his *Popular Antiquities*, 'is plainly from the Latin *Cuculus*, the *Cuckow* [or cuckoo], a Bird, that as Aristotle says, builds no Nest herself, but deposits her Eggs in that of some other Bird, who hatches and adopts *her* Offspring as the *Mari Cocu*† [† French for Cuckold] does the Children who are none of his.' Brand, unusually, has some sympathy for the victim of a faithless wife if, that is, 'the Husband was not to blame', considering 'it is highly ungenerous, and an Instance of that common Meanness in Life of confounding a Person's Misfortunes with his Faults'. Indeed, the 'Cruelty of such wanton Reflections will appear, if we consider that a Man, plagued with a vicious Wife, needs no Aggravation of his Misery'.[6]

Such protestations for understanding and even kindness were largely ignored by the authors of the many bawdy ballads on the subject. Notable among them is the mid seventeenth-century folk song *Cuckolds Haven: OR, The marry'd mans miserie, who must abide/ The penaltie of being Hornify'd*. One verse, hardly flattering towards the wife or the husband in the scenario, declares, 'A woman that will be drunk,/ will eas'ly play the Punck [whore];/ For when her wits are sunk,/ all keyes will fit her Trunk.' The verse concludes with the rousing reprise, 'Then by experience oft is tride,/ poore men that way are hornify'd'.[7]

Hogarth introduced a cuckolded man in the print 'Evening', part of his 1738 series (paintings 1736), *The Four Times of the Day* (overleaf), in which the visibly feeble husband carries a child, likely not his, beside his taller, broader and decidedly lustier wife. The disparity in height and girth, as already observed in the context of the absurd, is intended to underscore the evidence of her full figure and flushed face, suggestive of a plethora of appetites that require constant satiation: something the husband, we are expected to sense, is constitutionally incapable of providing. To signal this in no uncertain terms, the husband is seen as he passes in front of a cow, whose horns, at that very moment, sit either side of his head. Everyone can see the reality, symbolised by the horns sprouting

18. Bernard Baron after William Hogarth, *The Four Times of the Day Plate 3: Evening*, engraving, 1738
The scene is Islington Spa next to Sadler's Wells Theatre (left), by the 1730s no longer a fashionable resort for the elite, but where tradesmen took their wives.

from his foolish noggin, except, of course, the cuckold himself. The spouse here is the very essence of Chaucer's lusty Wife of Bath, for 'Bold was her Face, and ruddy was its Hue'.[8] Shakespeare, one of Hogarth's heroes, is littered with jokes about cuckoos and cuckolds, the following from *Love's Labours Lost*:

The cuckow then on every Tree
Mocks married men ; for thus sings he,
Cuckow !

> *Cuckow ! cuckow ! O word of fear,*
> *Unpleasing to a married ear !*[9]

And not forgetting the Miller's yarn from *The Canterbury Tales* – a story of mishaps that spring from a cuckolding so obvious, you wonder at mankind's propensity for self-delusion. Of course a cuckold's fate can be avoided, Chaucer tells us, or certainly the possibility lessened, by the aged would-be husband marrying his match in years and sexual energy – a point repeated in the booth shows at Bartholomew Fair. Chaucer's Middle English verse tales had been modernised in the late seventeenth and early eighteenth century by some leading literary figures, including John Dryden. This allowed the style, narratives and characters to be better understood in an age where this medieval form of English was not widely read. In the updated versions, the bawdy humour, the social and professional stereotypes – from John the 'Dotard' husband, the 'buxom', sexually ripe Alison, his young wife and her priapic lover Nicholas – become so fresh and contemporary, it is as if the intervening centuries have simply evaporated.[10] As already observed, in this fundamental sense William Hogarth is a direct descendent of Chaucer as well as Shakespeare.

Hogarth's most famous telling of a wife's unfaithfulness is within *Marriage A-la-Mode*, where the countess's extramarital liaison with the lawyer Silvertongue turns from high-jinks to tragedy in just six canvases. After arranging a rendezvous at a masked ball in scene four – a scene in which we see the pageboy pointing and laughing at a roughly hewn model of Actaeon, the mortal transformed by the goddess Diana into a deer and then ravaged by his own dogs, but here mid transformation and therefore a horned man – the couple's night of passion is interrupted by the earl in scene five (overleaf), a duel is fought and, as the cuckolded husband faints back, Silvertongue is spotted clambering out of the window in his shift, his chubby arse in the air. So far, so Chaucerian. But, as noted before, the earl dies of his wound, and the lawyer's execution at Tyburn

19. Simon François Ravenet after William Hogarth, *Marriage
A-la-Mode Plate 5: The Bagnio*, engraving, 1745
The countess and Silvertongue have rented a room in a 'bagnio' (a term for
both 'Turkish' Baths and brothels) for their post-masquerade tryst. The
night watch burst in as the earl expires and his wife begs forgiveness.

is announced in scene six, where the countess is seen dying from
self-inflicted poisoning. All three in this particular love triangle die
unnatural, hideous deaths: a significant escalation from the traditional fate of the cuckold, that of social humiliation.

The legend associated with Cuckold's Point offered a twist on
the old chestnut of cuckoldry, as it concerned a miller who encouraged and then benefited from the adultery of his wife. The story
was clearly an oft-heard yarn for those journeying up and down
the river via the local watermen. The legend had given birth to
a carnival, the Horn Fair, much like that of Bartholomew, which
was celebrated annually on 18 October. Ned Ward, in *A Frolick to
Horn-Fair* (1700), recalls being told the foundation story by 'the
Dame of the tenement', the landlady of the public house at Cuckold's Point, which begins as follows:

That in the time of King *John*, when Religion could no more keep a Prince's Codpiece Button'd, then it can now infuse Charity in a Priest, *In the room of this House* says she, *here then stood a Water-Mill, and Providence having blest the* Knave *the* Miller, *with a very handsome Wife, King* John *coming often this Way to Hunt upon* Greenwich-Heath, *& thereabouts, happen'd to see her, and became so Enamour'd with her Lovely Looks, that he could by no means restrain his Inclinations, but must needs Cuckold the* Miller; *to which, when an Opportunity stood fair, the Dame Consented.*[11]

In one version of the story, the said miller, described as hailing from nearby Charlton, barters with the king, who consents to give him, as a willingly cuckolded husband, all the land he can see from the door of his mill. In return, the king insists that every year the miller must parade to what became known as Cuckold's Point wearing a pair of bucked horns on his head. The king's subject, canny and opportunistic as he may be, is suitably put in his place and presented to his neighbours, like poor John in another 'Miller's Tale', for what he is. Among other things, the story addresses the quandary – how willingly would we accept public humiliation and reputational destruction in exchange for material wealth?

The centrepiece of the Horn Fair was a type of charivari parade and re-enactment of the miller's penance. This folk ceremony was not unlike the 'skimmington', a form of people's justice for the moral crime of adultery, where the offenders themselves, or a surrogate (either a different person or an effigy) were paraded through the community, sitting backwards on an ass, accompanied by loud banging of pots and shouting, or 'rough music'. This parade featured in Samuel Butler's *Hudibras* (overleaf), and was included among the drawings and engravings by Hogarth. In Hogarth's imagining, a man standing centrally in a strutting posture blows on a hunting horn, another carries a pole displaying a shift and a pair of horns, the cringing man riding backwards on the nag holds a phallic symbol, and hovering above is the tailor's sign of The Shears (the ceremony is 'castrating' him), the said tailor laughs heartily at the victim, while the woman standing behind him holds her hand

20. *Hudibras Plate 7: Hudibras Encounters the Skimmington*, engraving, 1726
Hudibras, a foolish puritan killjoy, describes the folk ceremony, with a plethora of
horns and phallic symbols, as a 'Devil's Procession' and an 'Anti-Christian Opera'.

above his head – two middle fingers held against the palm with
the thumb, the two remaining fingers erect – in the sign of the
cuckold. The noise and clamour of banging pans, shouts, laughter and cries of anger and groans of despair is palpable. Hogarth's
work throngs with sound as well as visual detail.

The knowledge of Cuckold's Point and its legend would surely
have inspired Hogarth's rendition of a skimmington (for both
the *Hudibras* book illustration and print set), as the yearly Horn
Fair continued to draw revellers like Ned Ward to the area in their
droves. The significance of the date of the annual fair and re-enactment, 18 October, St Luke's Day, lies in the saint's symbol, a horned
creature, the winged Ox. And in its particular connection to sex
and overindulgence, the Horn Fair loosely echoes the 'Vanity Fair'
of Bunyan's *The Pilgrim's Progress*.

Cuckold's Point and the pilgrims' next stopping-off place,
Blackwall Reach or Point (the northernmost part of the Greenwich peninsula), were both the site of gibbets, specifically where
the tarred bodies of the most notorious criminals executed under
the jurisdiction of the Admiralty, who were responsible for crimes
at sea including mutiny, piracy and smuggling, were displayed in
cages or 'hung in chains'.[12] This aspect of the area's appearance is

not mentioned in the account of *The Peregrination* because, as with other familiar places and features they encountered or passed by, it was too well known to Hogarth and his companions to warrant specific reference. En route to Cuckold's Point, the pilgrims had passed Wapping and the eerie gallows at Execution Dock, where such capital punishment took place, which may have been visible through the night gloom and rain. Piracy was associated with the seas around the West Indies, again a situation of which Will Tothall would have had some experience. Trials and executions were usually carried out locally, but the Admiralty would, on occasion, go to the effort and expense of bringing some miscreants back to London. In 1721 the *Weekly Journal* reported that 'About 40 Pirates have been brought Home by the Mary Man of War from Jamaica, to be try'd here by the Court of Admiralty, because several Masters Ships are now in London, who have been robb'd by them, and who are the proper Evidence for convicting them.'[13] It has been calculated that between 1716 and 1726 four to five hundred pirates were executed in London.[14]

The gallows was located on the foreshore, with the execution itself occurring at low tide. What made the process different, in addition to the riverside location, from those hangings occurring at Tyburn or in other sites around the capital (Kennington Common, for example) was the stipulation that while suspended the condemned's feet must dangle below the high-water mark, signalling that they were executed within the Admiralty's purview. These executions, like those at Tyburn, were public spectacles, and crowds would gather in boats on the river and around the shore to watch the invariably slow death by strangulation. Part of the entertainment was watching the jerking dance as they were throttled. The most famous pirate executed at Wapping was the Scotsman, Captain William Kidd, in 1701.

The hanging corpse was then taken down, chained to a post on the Wapping shore and left there for three tides, the rising water immersing and symbolically baptising the body, and then, as the tide went out, exposing it again to the gaze of onlookers, sharp talons and pecking beaks. After this, what was left was taken down and buried, sent to the surgeons for dissection or, if a notorious

21. *Industry and Idleness Plate 5: The Idle 'Prentice turn'd
away, and sent to Sea,* etching and engraving, 1747
In one unused design (British Museum) Hogarth depicts
Tom stealing from his mother's place of work. The paper
he has thrown away (bottom left) is his indenture.

pirate, covered in tar and then suspended once again at the gibbets
located to the east, including at Cuckold's Point. However, people
living locally had successfully petitioned to have the gibbet moved
further away – which suggests, rather than being inured to such
hideous sights, which ringed the main land and water access ways
into London, many people did not want to live within the orbit of
a tarred and gradually disintegrating corpse for years on end.

Hogarth was aware of the gibbet, now lying some distance away
from Cuckold's Point itself, as it appears in the fifth plate of *Industry and Idleness*, the scene where Tom Idle, accompanied by two
sailors and his weeping, long-suffering mother, is being rowed in a
wherry towards a ship and a second chance at a better life (than the
one he has been living thus far at any rate) on the high seas.[15] One
of the sailors points towards the ships in the mid distance but is, at

the same time, indicating towards the gibbet, surrounded by windmills, from which a pirate's body is suspended. Tom forms his hand, positioned against his forehead, into the shape of the cuckold's horns, as seen earlier in Hogarth's 'The Skimmington', while the sailor behind him smirks and dangles a short piece of rope. Tom, with no self-awareness, adds weight to the prophecy that his life will end swinging from one of London's many gallows – whether for piracy, theft or another capital crime is yet to be determined. And who is rowing Tom towards this destiny? A Thames Charon in neckerchief, hat and billowing shift, pulling on his oars, while grimacing with the effort as he puffs on his pipe. The drawing from which the print was taken, whether by design or accident, gives the waterman the appearance of a grinning skeleton.

Before arriving at Blackwall Reach, as they passed Deptford, they sang 'Pishoken', a ditty no one has been able to trace. It is possibly a drunken mangling of a song long forgotten, or simply a red herring. In any case, they landed at Blackwall and the pilgrims feasted on hung beef and biscuit, washed down with 'Right Hollands',[16] that is 'geneva' or gin at a total cost of one shilling, probably at the most famed hostelry in the area, the suitably Bunyanian Folly-house.

One eighteenth-century recipe for hung beef, not for the faint hearted, instructed the cook to 'Make a strong brine with bay-salt, salt-petre, and pump-water, and put into it a rib of beef for nine days. Then hang it up in a chimney where wood or saw-dust is burnt. When it is a little dry, wash the outside with blood two or three times to make it look black; and, when it is dried enough, boil it for use.'[17] The biscuits were probably made with a recipe familiar to modern Britons, that is a batter of eggs, sugar and flour, often, if *The Cook's and Confectioner's Dictionary* (1723) is any indicator, with coriander seeds and then oven baked on trays greased with butter.[18]

When thinking of gin and Hogarth, the image of *Gin Lane* (Fig. 35 p. 235), surely his most recognisable print, springs immediately to mind. References to gin, created by the re-distillation of malt spirit or wine with juniper berries and botanicals, can be found in the medieval period as an aid to digestion or to ease ailments relating to kidneys, stomach or gout. By the late seventeenth century in Holland, 'jenever' (from the Latin for juniper, altered to 'genever' in Britain and then shortened to 'gin') was drunk between jugs of ale. It was this form of the drink that made its way to England with the Dutch-born king, William III, achieving popularity partly because of the accompanying restrictions on the import of French brandy. What may have been a perfectly pleasant tincture in the early seventeenth century was, by the mid eighteenth century (at least if produced in the slums of St Giles, where Hogarth's scene takes place), very far from refined, and definitely not a route to healthy living. In fact, the production of gin had been debased to such a degree that any ingredients, using the distillation process, was sold under its banner. The epidemic or 'gin craze' was made possible due to the removal of licensing and the wholesale production of cheap drink using low-grade barley, considered unfit for the brewing of beer. This mass-produced gin was addictive, brain-addling and seen as encouraging crime and general self-destruction among the lower orders of society (as Bernard Mandeville indicates).

Although not a stopping-off point, therefore not mentioned in the account, the most significant site between Cuckold's Point and Blackwall Reach on the Kent side of the river was the town, former royal hunting park and residence of Greenwich, described by Defoe, with unusual enthusiasm, as 'the most delightful Spot of Ground in *Great-Britain* ; Pleasant by Situation, those Pleasures encreas'd by Art, and all made compleatly agreeable by *the accident of* fine Buildings, the continual passing of Fleets of Ships up and down the most beautiful River in *Europe* ; the best Air, best Prospect ... in *England*.'[19]

The old royal residence had been established by Henry VIII and extended and improved by the Stuarts, with the aforementioned Queen's House, designed by Inigo Jones for James I and said to be the first classical building in the British Isles since the Roman legions withdrew. It was certainly a dramatic contrast to the red-brick Tudor palace it originally adjoined on this dramatic Thames-side location – as if a villa from the warm climes of the Italian Veneto had unexpectedly landed at the royal gateway to London, all futuristic clean lines and dazzlingly white.

James's grandson, Charles II, continued to expand and develop the royal park at Greenwich, first within the Tudor complex, then as a new hospital (or refuge) for navy veterans, the companion to that housing army veterans at Chelsea, both designed by Sir Christopher Wren. Charles also commissioned the building of the Royal Observatory, primarily to find accurate calculation for longitude (a ship's location relative to the 'lines' north to south pole, the lines of latitude being those parallel to the Equator) before the wily French king Louis XIV did. He also commenced the building of a great baroque palace, one wing (the only one completed) of which was integrated into the Royal Hospital for Seamen after the king's death. Defoe continues his description of the hospital: 'the Front to the Water-side is extreamly Magnificent and Graceful; embellish'd with rich carv'd Work and fine Devices, such as will hardly be outdone in this, or any Age for Beauty or Art'.[20]

The significance of Greenwich for John Thornhill and William Hogarth, as they bobbed past in their tilt-boat, would have been the paintings in the Great Hall of the hospital, completed by Sir James Thornhill only six years before their trip to Sheppey. Sir James had produced a description of the interior paintings, which was printed and sold for six pence to the many visitors who thronged to see this new spectacle. The entrance fee to the hall made 'an excellent Fund for the yearly Maintenance of not less than Twenty poor Boys who are the Sons of Mariners that have been either slain or disabled in the SERVICE of their COUNTRY'.[21] These lads were not only fed and clothed but schooled locally, at Mr Weston's Academy, in mathematics and were therefore prepared for a career in 'the SEA *Service*, and consequently helps to make a perpetual Supply of skilful Seaman, who are the Safeguard of our COUNTRY'. Here is an early example of art attracting visitors to a charitable institution, through which the hospital can raise money as well as its profile, in this instance to support the care and education of children. Hogarth took note of this elegant symbiosis, and would soon apply it in practice.

The Great Hall, dimensions one hundred and six feet long, fifty-six feet wide and fifty feet in height, was originally intended as a dining room for the navy pensioners, but given its magnificent scale and spectacular decoration it fast became a venue for ceremonial occasions and a resort for visitors and fundraising events.

The overarching narrative, covering the entire ceiling and walls, is the national story, history as very much written by the victors. It covers the formation of Great Britain, the Protestant succession established by William and Mary in 1688 and then embodied in the House of Hanover after 1714, and the central role played by the navy – both the armed forces and the merchant fleet – in the past, present and future greatness of the nation. The scheme was commissioned during the early years of the reign of Queen Anne, in the seminal year 1707, when the Acts of Union between England and Scotland were signed. The last paintings to be completed, in 1726, were those in the upper hall: the north wall facing the visitor as they entered and the short return walls either side. The *Weekly Journal or British Gazetteer* on Saturday 27 August 1726 declared them 'so beautiful and ornamental as to strike with Admiration the Eyes of all Spectators, which begin already to be very numerous'. The side walls had a scene each, completed in *grisaille* or '*Basso-Relievo*' heightened with gold leaf, one depicting the landing of the future William III at Torbay, Devon on 5 November 1688 and the other, the landing at Greenwich of George I, fresh from Hanover, in 1714. Both stressed the arrival in England of the two kings, both foreign born. Indeed they depict, in a highly allegorical manner, the very moment the two men set foot on English soil. In Thornhill's own description, the former subject 'is the REVOLUTION', that is, what will be termed the Glorious Revolution of 1688–90, 'or the *Landing* of the *Prince of Orange*, who is welcomed on Shoar by *Britannia*, attended by *Reason* of *State*, and *Love* of her *Country*'.[22] The symbolic significance of the date of his landing was not lost on William: 5 November being bonfire night, which celebrates the failure of a Catholic plot to blow up the Protestant King James I, his court and parliament, and 1688 being the centenary of the defeat of the Spanish and Catholic Armada by the Protestant English under their sovereign, Queen Elizabeth.

The second scene 'is the ACCESSION or *Landing* of *King* GEORGE at *Greenwich*', Greenwich being a convenient place to break up a journey from the European continent to London, and resonant as a royal site. On George's right hand is the figure of 'PEACE' and on his left 'HAPPINESS': 'He is led on by TRUTH and JUSTICE, RELIGION and LIBERTY; before him falls REBELLION.'[23] The last is a clear reference to the failed 1715–16 and 1719 Jacobite rebellions, whose very purpose was the removal of 'the usurper' George, his progeny and government. Presumably this entire interior would be whitewashed, or repainted, perhaps with another glorious apotheosis, should the exiled Stuarts ever succeed in restoring their dynasty to the throne.

And with that thought, we will leave our travellers as they pass Greenwich and Blackwall Point and sail on towards Gravesend.

CHAPTER THREE

MORAL SUBJECT

Billy Hogarth and Jane Thornhill, or rather, as he called her, Jenny, were married by licence, which was registered on 23 March 1729 at St James's church, Paddington, then a village to the north-west of Tyburn.[1] To become a family member of such a significant well-connected figure as Jenny's father, and one that it would not be too much to say Hogarth revered, must have seemed wonderful. But it was not all plain sailing: Sir James initially refused to bless the marriage, as John Nichols declares, 'This union, indeed, was a stolen one, and consequently without the approbation of Sir *James*, who, considering the youth of his daughter, then barely eighteen, and the slender finances of her husband, as yet an obscure artist, was not easily reconciled to the match.' At thirty-one years old, Hogarth was over a decade senior to Jane, which may have added to parental anxiety, as Nichols states. In fact the new Mrs Hogarth was baptised on 25 March 1710, so at the time of the wedding, older than 'barely' eighteen but not twenty-one. Hogarth probably attained the licence by swearing that there was no 'just cause or impediment' and leaving a bond, should that ever prove not to be the case. It was common to marry young, for men to be single in their early thirties and, indeed, for them to be life-long bachelors. Society was less accommodating of unmarried women, particularly after youth's bloom had faded, as the custom of loaning the courtesy title 'Mrs' signals. Like the old wealthy widow, the figure of the ageing maid, which Hogarth introduces in his image of Covent Garden at early morning, one of *The Four Times of the Day* (Fig. 3 p. 16), is a comic archetype, usually viewed with disdain and not a little fear. The said spinster, as seen with Tom's elderly wife in *A Rake's Progress* (Fig. 22 p. 138), inappropriately (that is youthfully) dressed, pauses before St Paul's church (her destination, apparently) and stares intently, with a mixture of attraction and repulsion, at all-night revellers, male and female, cuddling and kissing in front of Mrs King's, a public house of ill repute. Years later, Henry Fielding will defer to this print when describing another woman unlucky in love and now 'somewhat past the age of thirty', Miss Bridget Allworthy: 'I would attempt to draw her Picture; but that it is done already by a more able Master, Mr. *Hogarth* himself, to whom she sat many Years ago, and hath been lately exhibited by that Gentleman in his Print of a Winter's Morning.'[2]

Incidentally, this figure is thought to have cost Hogarth a significant legacy, for all the reasons we can imagine. According to John Nichols, the 'Old Maid' 'was taken either from an acquaintance or relation of his'. At first, somewhat surprisingly, 'she was well enough satisfied with her resemblance ; but some designing people teaching her to be angry, she struck the painter out of her will, which had been made considerably in his favour'. This smacks of an apocryphal tale – the satirist, unable to restrain himself, even to his advantage, being hoisted by his own petard. Yet Nichols insists: 'This story we have heard often related by those whom, on other occasions, we could readily believe.'[3]

It seems unlikely, therefore, that the age difference was the main reason for parental disapproval. On balance, as Nichols also says, whatever career potential Hogarth had shown in the period leading to the marriage, it was not yet deemed sufficient. William's lowly position, as others perceived it, just a few years before *The Peregrination* occurred, was certainly too lowly for a knight's daughter, yet the couple were determined to marry despite parental opposition. In an age where much rested on the ability of a young man to support a wife and, hopefully, family, we should not judge a concerned and loving parent too harshly. Certainly the circumstances around Richard Hogarth's bankruptcy and the major setback his son had suffered as a result had also impacted on any cherished dreams for William's personal life. Perhaps an additional hope in tackling *The Beggar's Opera* was that it might produce some sort of thawing towards the couple on Sir James's part. After all, its subject was one he would have found appealing, and indicated a necessary

22. *A Rake's Progress Plate 5: The Marriage*, etching and engraving, 1735
As the widow and Tom tie the knot, imitated by two dogs to
the left, the groom's abandoned lover, their baby and her furious
mother are causing a disturbance in the background.

commercial spirit not unlike his own. The resonance, closer to
home, of the scene Hogarth depicted, where Polly Peacham, kneeling before her father, pleads for the man she loves, no matter what
he is or has done, might yet soften another parent's heart.

Soon after, an announcement appeared in the *London Evening
Post*: 'Mr. Hogarth, an ingenious Designer and Engraver, was lately
married to the Daughter of Sir James Thornhill, Knt. Serjeant-
Painter, and History Painter to his Majesty.'[4] Quite what Sir James
and Lady Judith Thornhill made of this shameless puff remains
unknown. The fact that the ceremony occurred at a church
outside London, rather than the bride's parish church of St Paul's,
Covent Garden, confirms the 'stolen' nature of the arrangement.
When Tom Rakewell marries the ancient widow in scene five of
A Rake's Progress, it is at the church in Marylebone to the east of

Paddington, at the time sufficiently distant from London, as John Nichols observes, 'as to become the usual resort of those who, like our hero, wished to be privately married'.[5]

From the earliest surviving portrait by Hogarth of his young wife (Col. Fig. 5), possibly dated from around the time of their wedding, it seems that Jane was a handsome woman, the image of her father, with warm-brown hair, a longish nose, strong, thin, dark eyebrows arching over light-brown eyes. The portrait, apparently cropped from a larger canvas, has Jane posing as St Agnes, gently holding the saint's symbol, a lamb. This type of portrait, using classical and allegorical symbols and allusions, is unusual in Hogarth's oeuvre, but typical of an earlier style, notably used by the Restoration court painter, Sir Peter Lely. (Hogarth depicts Miranda, daughter of the magician Prospero, feeding a lamb as a sign of her innocence in his *A Scene from The Tempest, c.*1732–5, Nostell Priory, National Trust.)[6] Presenting Jane as St Agnes might hint to the circumstances of her marriage, for Agnes kept to her path and choice of 'bridegroom' (in Agnes's case, Jesus Christ), in the face of parental and societal pressure.[7] Whatever their meaning to the sitter, such allusions also elevated a straightforward image of a particular person into something more universal and profound.

It is thought that the Hogarths were living in South Lambeth as newlyweds, on the Surrey or south side of the Thames, where Hogarth made the useful acquaintance of the new proprietor of the nearby Vauxhall Pleasure Gardens, Jonathan Tyers.[8] This is according to a note attached to a watercolour in the Royal Collection (possibly written by John Thomas Smith, author of *Nollekens and his Times*): 'This original Picture in some degree explains the obscurity all the Biographers complain of in the Early part of the Life of Hogarth, as it [con]firms [?] the Spot where he lived or at least exercised his pencil.'[9] The Sun public house, again according to the note, 'stood at the farthest Corner of Grays Buildings South Lambeth'. It also declares that this is the 'View from Mr Hogarth's lodging ... from an original Painted by Mr Hogarth about the year 1730 – not engraved.' Hogarth maintained his friendship with Tyers over the coming years by designing 'supper-box paintings', such as *The Four Times of the Day*, for the garden rooms where visitors could dine in some privacy, and membership tokens for the revamped gardens, launched in time for the summer season and just after *The Peregrination* on 7 June 1732.[10] In recompense for lending his name and artistry to the enterprise, the year after the grand opening Hogarth was given life membership, his badge made of gold, with 'Hogarth' engraved on the reverse, the figures of Virtus (Roman manly virtue) and Voluptas, the offspring of Cupid and Psyche (meaning pleasure or delight) on the face. The loop at the top of the badge allowed it to be worn around the neck attached to a ribbon, or hung from a watch chain.[11]

Something must have happened prior to the wedding, in addition to his canvases for *The Beggar's Opera*, that encouraged Hogarth to think that in this instance, Sir James Thornhill's judgement was flawed regarding his marriage and his prospects. George Vertue's first comments on Hogarth in his notebooks occur from late 1728 and early 1729 (written as 1728/9 in the old 'Julian' calendar, which Great Britain followed, the new year beginning – in England – in March not January) suggesting that something extraordinary had happened to bring this individual to Vertue's attention. After describing Hogarth's satirical engravings (including *Masquerades and Operas*) from a few years earlier, Vertue moves on to what has struck him as worthy of observation: 'but finding it more agreable to his mind, took up the pincill & applyd his studyes to painting in small conversations. or fancyes'. Vertue then notes that these 'conversations' are 'wherein he now has much reputation. & lately married to ye daughter of S^r. James Thornhill. without,' he concludes, 'his consent.'[12] So Vertue, at least, made a specific connection between Hogarth's success at 'conversations', small-scale group portraits and 'fancyes', paintings in a genre style with an element of storytelling, and his marriage.

Vertue's journal moves on to other important events occurring in the art world in general, until he returns again, in January 1730, to the intriguing subject of this Mr Hogarth: 'The daily success of Mr Hogarth in painting small family peices & Conversations with so much Air,' meaning with lightness or breeziness, '& agreeableness Causes him to be much follow[e]d, & esteemd. whereby he has much imployment & like to be a master of great reputation in that way'.[13] Vertue recalls Hogarth's early career as an engraver on silver, 'afterwards got some little insight & instructions in Oyl Colours. without Coppying other Paintings or Masters', which appears to challenge any idea that he received standard 'instructions' in the oil technique from the likes of Chéron and Thornhill, rather that he learned by trial and error, which is surely unlikely. Finally he achieved success 'immediatly by the force of Judgment a quick & ready Conception. & in exact immitation of Natural likeness'. So here, as observed by Vertue, Hogarth is applying his strategy, developed while an apprentice, for improving his drawing – constant observation and practice – to oil painting, with, as ever, nature and what is natural or true-to-life the guiding principle. And this diligence and determination, stirred by the ongoing need to make up for lost time, had certainly paid off. As Vertue concludes, through this, Hogarth 'became surprizingly forward to be the Master he now is'.[14] Vertue's observations were not published during his lifetime, but his summary of Hogarth's career and motivations to date chime exactly with the artist's own autobiographical notes written late in life.

The style of portrait, the conversation piece or 'conversation' that Hogarth was finding so beneficial to his career and reputation, and one he did so much to popularise, was a recent innovation in British portraiture. Conversation, as a Georgian would understand it, has a slightly different meaning from our modern usage. Both eras would have agreed on a conversation as verbal interaction, but beyond this, in the eighteenth century the term embraced, more broadly, the manner in which a person behaved in the world and dealt with others and, like the word 'intercourse', had a suggested intimacy which in certain contexts was sexual. The legal term 'criminal conversation', for example, referred to adultery. Another type of conversation was a salon, a regular social gathering for the purpose of discussion and entertainment. A portrait described as a conversation was, by definition, a group portrait, and had as its principal characteristics a sense of ease and informality alongside intimacy. It is usually of family or friendship groups, sometimes with a professional or intellectual connection, but always depicting affable interaction, whether in a parlour gathered around a tea table, in a garden, or a club over a bowl of punch (hence Hogarth's ironic usage in his engraving *A Midnight Modern Conversation*).

Another defining characteristic of a conversation was size. Unlike standard group portraits, they were full-length 'in little'. The small-scale format fitted very comfortably into the interiors of the 'middling-sort' and aristocrat alike and, therefore, the potential market was vast in comparison to the traditional, large, formal group portraits of previous generations – a singularly aristocratic and royal portrait-type, or, for those with masses of expendable income, the social ambition and wall space to match. For many portrait painters, particularly those like Hogarth who usually worked alone, without an assistant or drapery painter (artists who finished off the costume and surrounding detail), this smaller scale was a welcome addition to their repertoire: it required ingenuity, particularly in the placing of many figures together within a small space and in creating interest through incident, gesture, humour, complexity and variety. As important, it could be produced relatively quickly and therefore helped to make a painter's practice commercially sustainable.

And through such portraits Hogarth found his recent foray into oil painting very sustainable indeed, so much so that Vertue returned to the subject again and again, and in glowing terms: 'Mr Hogarths paintings gain every day so many admirers that happy are they that can get a picture of his painting.' In fact Hogarth's paintings were enjoying popularity beyond the artist–client relationship that is, in the auction room. Vertue notes 'a small peice of several figures representing a Christ[e]ning' which Hogarth had completed in around 1728 (now in a private collection) 'being lately sold at a publick sale for a good price. got him much reputation'.[15] Hogarth would not have resisted attending the auction at Christopher Cock's auction rooms in Soho in May 1729 (Cock moved to the Great Piazza in 1731), nor sketching the moment when his little picture (about to go under the hammer) is held up by the assistant. The auctioneer, Mr Cock, located in his pulpit, gavel raised and 'trumpeting forth', as Henry Fielding described him, in extravagant praise for this 'superb' item, then enquires who would care to start the bidding, soon after declaring, with astonishment, that '*Nobody bids more!*' Within the crowded room, standing room only at the back, some will bid, but many more are simply there to see and be seen, as Fielding goes on to satirise in his play *The Historical Register* (in which Mr Cock is rendered as 'Mr. *Hen*'):

Dang.	Fy upon it, Ladies, What are you going here? Why are not you at the Auction? Mr. *Hen* has been in the Pulpit this half Hour
1 *Lady.*	Oh, dear Mr. *Hen*, I ask his Pardon, I never miss him.
2 *Lady.*	What's to be sold to-day?
1 *Lady.*	Oh, I never mind that; there will be all the World there.
Dang.	You'll find it almost impossible to get in.
All Ladies.	Oh! I shall be quite miserable if I don't get in.
Dang.	Then you must not lose a Moment.
All Ladies.	O! not a Moment for all the World.
[*Exeunt Ladies*][16]	

An unfinished oil on canvas sketch by Hogarth of an auction in progress, dated from this time, is perhaps such a memento, or a commission from Kit Cock himself; a shop sign for his new establishment, from 1731, as Hogarth's neighbour in Covent Garden.

Vertue concludes his entry on Hogarth with the comment, 'many other family peices, & conversations' all done 'with great spirit a lively invention & an universal agreeableness'.[17] So his prosperity was, for now, assured. Hogarth himself wrote, 'Then mar[r]ied and turnd Painter of Portraits in small conversation Peices and great success.'[18] How long such painting will satisfy a restlessly ambitious spirit like Hogarth is another matter.

In retrospect it is surprising that Hogarth established his business through portraiture. This was certainly the opinion of Horace Walpole, the youngest son of prime minister Sir Robert, an art connoisseur and an early biographer of the artist, who was painted as a youth by Hogarth during this early period. In his influential, partial and highly flawed assessment of early Georgian art and artists, *Anecdotes of Painting in England*, Walpole declared that portraiture was 'the most ill-suited employment imaginable to a man whose turn certainly was not flattery, nor his talent adapted to look on vanity without a sneer'. Now this is fair enough, but portraiture, good portraiture, is much more than mere flattery. Walpole continues, 'Yet his facility in catching a likeness, and the method he chose of painting families and conversations in small, then a novelty, drew him prodigious business for some time. It did not last, either from his applying to the real bent of his disposition, or from his customers apprehending that a satirist was too formidable a confessor for the devotees of self-love.'[19] Walpole, for all his talents, was one of the vainest, most self-satisfied and sneering individuals of the entire eighteenth century – quite a distinction, given the competition. And Hogarth's known portraits of this period completely belie this assessment: *The Beckingham Wedding*, (c.1729–30, Col. Fig. 6), *The Jeffreys Family* (1730, Yale), *The Cholmondeley Family* (1732, Private Collection), *Miss Wood, with a Dog in a Landscape* (c.1735, Col. Fig. 7) and Walpole's own image, aged ten (1728–9) are exquisite.[20] One explanation is that Walpole was simply unaware of the scale of Hogarth's output in this genre and the quality of individual examples, or, as likely, ignored it to fit his idea of what were Hogarth's strengths. Unfortunately Walpole's assessment set the course of Hogarth's posthumous reputation for centuries and, with irony, given the artist's personal and heartfelt appeal that people should look and think for themselves, blinded commentators to the value and quality of this work.

Even so, by 1729 William Hogarth must have felt that he had proved himself to his father-in-law as well as to the world at large. And, ever inventive, at the same time as painting conversation pieces, Hogarth was developing a strand of portrait that crossed over into narrative painting, what George Vertue had described as 'fancyes'. One example, recorded by Vertue, suggests Hogarth was flying a little too close to the wind in pursuit of fame. It concerned 'a prodigious penurious' magistrate of the City of London called, aptly, Sir Isaac Shard. An advertisement appeared in the papers, according to Vertue, around the beginning of 1731, declaring 'that a Curious and ingenius Painter. of reputation was painting a picture which when done woud be hung up in justice Hall in the Old Baily'. As a result, people flocked to see it and were mightily delighted with what they saw, especially, so Vertue continues, the Lord Mayor of London himself, who had commissioned the image in order to ridicule Shard. Vertue goes on to describe the painting: 'this picture was the person in his habit and manner, being remarkably singular seated in a great chair in judgment as it were upon a Malefactor'. Only the culprit was not a human, but 'a great Hungry dog' indeed, who had stolen 'from his Honours kitching a pitieous lean scraggy shoulder of Mouton which his cook had surpriz[e]d and taken from the dog'. The poor ravenous mutt was duly brought before Sir Isaac Shard, who, as was his wont, 'pronounced the Sentence of death on him'. The furious cook was the dog's accuser, and an old cobbler lined up to act as executioner, all of which Hogarth had introduced into his painting, which he titled, according to John Nichols, *The Miser's Feast*.[21] Vertue declares that 'many other incidents remarkable for the Subject made this picture an entertainment for all that saw it. and a high Caricature of the chief person represented'.[22]

Hogarth must have been delighted at such a spectacular response from the curious and the corresponding fame or notoriety this generated. However, he would soon have reason for some regret. For although the gentleman thus satirised, according to Vertue, 'was too grave or too old to resent the affront', his son on the other hand, Isaac Pacatus Shard, was not.[23] On viewing the painting and having the meaning explained to him, as it had been to every gleeful visitor, 'It raisd his spirit of resentment', so much so that he drew his sword and 'swore he would Sacrifice the Author or Painter of it'. As far as is known, Hogarth received no injury, the son instead venting his ire on the offending painting itself, by cutting out his father's face with a knife.[24] Now although he had been commissioned to paint the 'portrait', Hogarth did not have to advertise the fact. So if he was indeed the source of the advertisement, this dramatic and angry response was largely brought upon himself. Hogarth had a habit of acting on impulse before thinking through fully the risks, and although sometimes he regretted his actions, more often than not he would double down, as we would now say, by refusing to apologise or make recompense. These attempts to ride out, or, more accurately, brazen out the ensuing storm would in some instances make the situation infinitely worse.

A handwritten list of fourteen paintings in Hogarth's studio which were unfinished as of 1 January 1731, almost two years after his marriage, is completely dominated by these small portraits and conversations. Some involve many figures and were for high-ranking clients. For example, *The Assembly at Wanstead House* (Philadelphia Museum of Art) here listed as 'A Assembly of 25 figures' was commissioned on 29 August 1729 by Richard Child, Lord Castlemaine (in June 1731 elevated to the title of Earl Tylney), with half of the fee paid in advance. One portrait was commissioned as far back as November 1728, and another, a single figure of Sir Robert Pye, was dated from 10 November 1730.[25] This list alone indicates how quickly Hogarth had established a reputation as a painter within aristocratic circles. His talent may well have been driving custom to his door, but one suspects the fact of his marriage, rather than being a hindrance, had turned to his advantage.

Hogarth's developing reputation at this time is beautifully evoked in a letter written by the widowed Mary Pendarves to her sister Ann Granville in July 1731. Mary had become acquainted with the artist while he was painting the group portrait of her close friends the Wesley family and Miss Donnellan.[26] In the letter she declares she does not like the painting she saw at Hogarth's studio of Sir Andrew Fountaine's family, a six-figure conversation with a delightful pug pup in the mid foreground, nibbling on a basket, ordered by Christopher Cock and also on Hogarth's 1731 list. But, she goes on to write, 'I am grown passionately fond of Hogarth's painting, there is *more sense* in it than any I have seen.' Regarding the Wesley family portrait, 'I have had the pleasure of seeing him paint the greatest part of it ; he has altered his manner of painting since you saw his pictures ; he finishes more a good deal', which might refer to a more polished, rather than loose or unfinished effect. This conjures up an image of Mary joining the family at their sittings, where the greater focus would have been on capturing facial likeness, or even visiting Hogarth on her own while he completed the painting. Mary was highly intelligent and extremely good company, so her visits would have been much enjoyed. She then admits, 'I have released Lady Sunderland from her promise of giving me her picture by Zinck [the Dresden-born miniaturist Christian Freidrich Zincke], to have it done by Hogarth. I think he takes a much greater likeness, and that is what I shall value my friend's picture for, more than for the excellence of the painting.' Mary's keen eye acknowledges that at this time the artist still requires some refinement in his technique, but likeness and a sense of personality are already achieved. Indeed, 'Hogarth has promised to give me some instructions about drawing that will be of great use, – some rules of his own that he says will improve me more in a day than a year's learning in the common way. When he has performed his promise I will communicate to my dearest sister.'[27]

What Hogarth is referring to here is his method of observing, sketching and memorising from nature, rather than relentless copying from casts and drawings from other masters ('the common way'). Mary, already interested in developing skills in pastel and pencil, would, in later life, invent, in her own words, 'a new way of imitating flowers'[28] cut from paper. She had noticed that a geranium in her room was the same bright scarlet colour as some Chinese paper lying on a nearby table, 'and taking her scissors she amused herself with cutting out each flower, by her eye, in the paper which resembled its hue'.[29] The manner of discovery, observation, and Mary's description of them as 'Plants Copied after Nature in paper Mosaick' would have delighted Hogarth greatly.[30]

Marrying against the wishes of a parent had been a risk, not least because of the possibility of a lasting rift. In fact, contrary to reports in the early biographies, it is possible that the Thornhills and Hogarths had been reconciled very soon after the marriage – so Hogarth's advertisement may not have been a shameless plug, but placed, with the agreement of Sir James, to announce that all was now well in the Thornhill–Hogarth household. If so, this did not stop rumours spreading, as noted by George Vertue. Yet in late 1729 Hogarth had been requested to paint a group portrait in commemoration of the parliamentary investigation into the management, or rather mismanagement, of the Fleet prison. The canvas was still in his studio in early 1731, commissioned by the committee's chairman, Sir Archibald Grant.[31] It was a subject very close to Hogarth's heart and evident in his empathetic preliminary sketch (Fitzwilliam Museum) of an inmate, dressed in rags yet dignified, addressing the committee, while demonstrating the shackles that had been placed upon him by the deputy keeper of the prison, Thomas Bainbridge, who stands, scowling, to the left.[32] This commission may have come with the encouragement of Sir James Thornhill as a member of parliament himself. Certainly, by 1730 Hogarth and Thornhill were collaborating on an innovative portrait of the prime minister, Sir Robert Walpole, standing next to Speaker Arthur Onslow, seated on Speaker's Chair within the House of Commons debating chamber. At least two of the figures on the front bench, including the very lively portrait of Thornhill himself, are attributed to Hogarth.[33] Beyond parliament and government, Sir James's son-in-law was also seeking and gaining contacts at court, which must have been instigated or encouraged by Thornhill. The month before the journey through Kent there had been a performance of John Dryden's *The Indian Emperor, or The Conquest of Mexico*, in which, unusually, the cast were children, before an audience of royalty and aristocrats. Hogarth was commissioned to paint the youthful thespians and their illustrious spectators. The result (Private Collection) is one of, if not the most spectacular of his group portraits in little.

Between 1725 and 1728 Thornhill had been employed as architect and decorative painter for Moor Park in Hertfordshire, his client the City of London financier Benjamin Styles. Thornhill's bill was challenged by Styles in two court cases (1728 and 1730), both finding in Thornhill's favour. Vertue considered the situation had been encouraged by 'Mr Kents friends & interest', who 'no doubt endeavourd to foment this difference & slurr the reputation of Sr James'.[34] But Styles, losing a battle, would win the war. Between 1730 and 1732, under the cloak of changing tastes and fashion, he hired the Venetian Giacomo (aka Jacopo) Amigoni (1689–1750), recently arrived on these shores, to create canvases that replaced those of Thornhill, to the latter's evident dismay.

Around the same time, Hogarth achieved a royal commission. As Vertue noted, 'he had some time ago begun a picture of all the

Royal family in one peice by order', presumably commissioned or by royal order 'the Sketch being made. & the P. William the Duke had sat to him for one'. In fact Hogarth produced two sketches, one exterior (Col. Fig. 8), one interior, of the entire family of the new monarch, George II, alongside a small full-length portrait of the king's second surviving and favourite son, William Augustus, Duke of Cumberland.[35] The portrait of the Duke of Cumberland is finished, although for whom is unknown. However, for reasons that are not totally clear, Vertue recounts, the royal family portrait 'has been stopt. so he can't proceed'.[36] The sudden withdrawal of royal largesse suggested some insider politicking had occurred, which was soon confirmed, for Hogarth had been granted permission to be present at the wedding of the Princess Royal in order to make an engraving. Planned for the October of 1733, the event finally took place in March 1734. This time his entrée had been through 'some Lady about the Queen'. So certain was Hogarth that everything was proceeding to plan that on 17 November 1733 it was announced in the *London Journal* that 'Mr. Hogarth is permitted to be at the Royal Wedding, to take a View of the Procession, Gallery, and Chappel; and is afterwards to oblige the Publick with a fine Print thereof.'[37] Hogarth duly turned up to the chapel to sketch the assembly, but was very quickly and unceremoniously removed from the premises. Apparently William Kent, now safely ensconced as a royal painter, complained that Hogarth was encroaching on his territory (something Kentino did not find an issue, when the boot was on the other foot). We can surmise that Hogarth's intimate association with Thornhill and his spirited defence of his now father-in-law – stretching back to 1724 – had stymied, for now, the commissions he was attempting to gain at court. However, the alternative court established by Hogarth's regal neighbour, the king's heir apparent Frederick Louis, Prince of Wales, now resident at Leicester House, Leicester Fields, provided some work – namely the heads for a large hunting scene by John Wootton (Royal Collection). It is conceivable the commission was intended to rile the cliques around his father and mother, neither of whom much liked him, nor he them.

However, such frustrations, maddening as they might be at

the time, would never intimidate a character like Hogarth – any wounds to his dignity, coupled with a desire to be avenged and an innate competitiveness, would spur him on. The seeking of a royal commission was now on hold, but other irons were in the fire.

Perhaps as a development from *The Beggar's Opera*, springing from the bawdier aspects of the work, Hogarth had painted two paired images showing sexual encounters between young men and women, entitled, with deceptive brevity, *Before* and *After*. The version showing a couple in a glade has more humour and is a gentle (while also graphic) skit on the popular *fête galante* (courtship party) genre. This was a staple of French contemporary art – notably by Jean-Antoine Watteau (1684–1721) and his followers – and tended to feature lovers floating through arcadian landscapes or flirting, in a chivalrous or, occasionally, unchivalrous manner, in gardens and interiors. Watteau had visited London in 1720 in search of treatment for tuberculosis from Dr Richard Mead, and his canvases – Mead owned *The Italian Comedians* (c.1720) – and those of his followers Nicolas Lancret and Jean-Baptiste Pater, were known in Britain, although their compositions would achieve far greater impact through engraving.[38] Hogarth himself owned 'A port-folio' of prints 'with a parcel various, by Watteau'.[39]

In this version of *Before*, a young gallant with amorous intentions is attempting to charm a maid, even if his leg is firmly thrust between her legs and her hand may be grasped just a little too tightly. She flutters, feigning (or not) alarm at his forwardness. All this is in keeping with Watteau's ambiguities of courtship and so-called 'seduction', but Hogarth presses on still further with *After*, which sees the two now on the ground in ungainly, flushed post-coital collapse, with the dishevelled and disorientated male unaware that everything, quite literally, is hanging out. Gallantry be damned! cries Hogarth, this is the reality of sweaty sexual congress, red in cheek and groin.

The second pairing is altogether different. Here there is overt aggression, violence, the very real possibility of rape. The man pulls, or drags the woman towards the bed, she grabs at the dressing table in a bid to save herself, which topples over, everything crashing to the floor along with her chastity and reputation. After the fact,

23. *Before*, etching and engraving, 1736
Cupid (left of the bed) lights a rocket labelled 'Before'. The
girl has been reading the poetry of the Earl of Rochester, the
infamous Restoration rake (be careful what you wish for).

24. *After*, etching and engraving, 1736
Perhaps contrary to Nichols's assertion of Hogarth's regret, these prints
continued to be sold by him and then Jane for as long as there was demand.

the male, with a dazed expression, simply pulls up his breeches, while his 'love' kneels, weeps and begs him not to abandon her. Sexual politics is a minefield, then as now. But rape, regardless of whether it was dressed up and passed off as mere seduction, was a capital offence, and contemporaries would have recognised the distinction. The fact that the same artist had produced both versions suggests that it was the taste of his patron that had influenced the specific scenario. Even so, Hogarth had agreed to take that individual's *penchant* and visualise it. John Nichols observes that they 'display almost the only instance in which Hogarth condescended to execute a subject proposed to him ; for I am assured by one who knew him well, that his obstinacy on these occasions has often proved invincible. Like Shakespeare's Tully, " – he would never follow any thing/ That other men began."'

Before and *After*, what George Vertue described as 'fore & after enjoyment'[40] represents the taste among some patrons for highly sexualised images, in some instances violent sexual assault. John Nichols, in offering an example of Hogarth's obstinacy, declares, regarding the second *Before* and *After* set, that they 'were painted at the request of a particularly vicious nobleman ... Hogarth repented of having engraved them'. One of these sets, probably the interior version, was owned by John Montagu, 2nd Duke of Montagu. If we see them as part of a chain of commissions from the Fleet prison to the various versions of *The Beggar's Opera*, it helps to explain, or at least contextualise, Hogarth's next significant venture.

Recalling this moment many years later, Hogarth observed that, having married, his success in painting conversations and small portraits 'was not sufficiently paid to do every thing my family requir'd', since his responsibilities now expanded to include his wife, as well as his mother and sisters, Ann and Mary. However, all of these women were very far from helpless. In 1730, Ann and Mary had moved their business from 'the old Frock-shop' facing the cloisters of St Bartholomew the Great to the King's Arms in Little Britain, where, according to the trade card their brother had designed for them, they sold 'ye best & most Fashionable Ready Made Frocks, sutes of Fustian, Ticken & Holland, stript Dimmity & Flanel, Wastcoats, blue & canvas Frocks & bluecoat Boys

Dra[we]rs' this last possibly a reference to the Bluecoat charity school children's uniforms; 'Likewise Fustians, Tickens, Hollands, white stript Dimitys, white & stript Flanels in ye piece; by Wholesale or Retale at Reasonable Rates.'[41]

Nonetheless, it was William's traditional role, as head of the family and the only man, to earn the main income, so he was constantly looking for new ways to make money. Apart from financial pressure, the tedium of being limited almost exclusively to portraiture of one type or another must have played a part. He therefore refused any further commissions, and if approached, recommended other painters, who must have been extremely grateful, 'and turn[ed] my thoughts to still a more new way of proceeding, viz painting and Engraving moder[n] ... moral Subject[s]'. A 'Field unbroke up', that is he was breaking new ground, 'in any Country or any age'.[42] If his print satires, the *Hudibras* illustrations as well as the small portraits and conversations, were notable, at least for George Vertue, it was the creation of *A Harlot's Progress*, the first of his series, painted and engraved, described here by Hogarth as 'modern moral subjects', that indicated a path on which his fame could be firmly established. In fact he took everything he had learned so far, including his multi-print sequence based on Butler's *Hudibras*, and harnessed it to the creation of something essentially new – not unlike John Gay's theatrical hit. It was the first time where paintings were the basis and led immediately to engravings – a process that did not occur with his paintings of *The Beggar's Opera*, arguably a prime example of a modern moral subject – as well as the promotional tool to drive up demand for print subscriptions.[43] The series was also created independently, with Hogarth controlling all aspects of production, promotion, subscription and vending. According to Vertue, a fellow engraver so very interested in such things, the 'remarkable' story of a common harlot 'captivated the Minds of most People persons of all ranks & conditions from the greatest Quality to the meanest'.[44]

That Hogarth was addressing raw human nature, up close and laid bare, was signalled by the subscription ticket for this series: *Boys Peeping at Nature* – cherub-like figures, one drawing a figure of the multi-breasted goddess Diana or Artemis of Ephesus (Hogarth's adopted totem for 'Nature'), whose lower body has been covered with a drape, which two of his naughty companions have lifted, to peep at what lies beneath. The version at the British Museum is written out to Hogarth's friend, George Lambert, an indication that his friendship network was enlisted to get the project off the ground.

One question that immediately arises: why would the progress of a prostitute, from initiation, success, demise and death, stir such widespread interest? Titillation played a part, as seen with *Before* and *After*, along with an interest, vicarious or otherwise, in everyday immorality. And given Hogarth's own definition of this series as 'modern' and 'moral' in subject, the scruples of the viewer, as well as the viewed, are called into question or at the very least tested. Purchasers may delight in laughing along with Hogarth, without realising that the joke might well be on them.

Hogarth's use of the term 'moral' establishes a solid ethical core – a sense of right and wrong – but also a personal and critical distance from his subject. It is certainly too great an assumption to think that because of this series Hogarth had any direct experience of prostitution, such as using sex workers himself. Hogarth is very far from a prude, but his attitude towards the characters he has invented, based on archetypes who regularly use prostitutes, like Tom Rakewell, or, as we shall see, those from real life, is derisive rather than empathetic. The sex trade was an obvious presence on the city's streets: Bernard Mandeville describes prostitutes conspicuously plying their trade at executions, for example, so this, coupled with a lively imagination, hearsay – from friends who were lawyers or justices of the peace – and reports published in newspapers would be more than sufficient material to go on.

Hogarth eventually chose to call his series *A Harlot's Progress*, which would naturally call to mind John Bunyan's nonconformist Christian allegory, *The Pilgrim's Progress* subtitled, *from This World, to That Which Is to Come*, of 1678. The story concerns Christian travelling from his home, the 'City of Destruction', to the 'Celestial City', encountering difficulties on the way while carrying a weighty 'burden' (knowledge of his sins). The entirety of

Bunyan's narrative is styled 'in the similitude of a dream', while contributing new metaphors and phrases to the English language – 'The Slough of Despond', the 'Hill Difficulty', 'Valley of the Shadow of Death', with 'Vanity Fair' the most enduring – as well as characters aptly named, revealing their primary trait or purpose within the story, including 'Goodwill' and 'Faithfull'.

Ben Franklin considered John Bunyan 'my old favorite Author'. Honest John, as he fondly called him, 'was the first that I know of who mix'd Narration and Dialogue, a Method of Writing very engaging to the Reader, who in the most interesting Parts finds himself as it were brought into the Company and present at the Discourse'.[45] The same could have been said of William Hogarth. Bunyan died only nine years before Hogarth's birth so, rather than being obscure, ancient text, to Hogarth's generation *The Pilgrim's Progress* was modern literature. Certainly Hogarth's delight in symbol and layering, alongside the innovative notion of 'progressing' through a sequence of images, establishes him as Bunyan's literary, spiritual and moral descendant.

Vertue provides the background to the way in which Hogarth arrived at the final six-image scheme, suggesting the painting that is to become scene three was the starting point. He describes how, among other designs Hogarth was painting, which would include the *Before* and *After* sets, he began a small picture of a 'common harlot', presumed to live in the Drury Lane area of Covent Garden, shown as she is rising from her bed at noon for breakfast, a bunter, or brothel servant, waiting on her. This whore's state of undress, her carefree air, her pretty countenance, all within Hogarth's initial thoughts for a composition, apparently 'pleasd many'. Clearly the drawing (of which there is an example in the British Museum) or oil on canvas was available to view in Hogarth's painting room. This single scene was thought sufficiently pleasing, as an image and subject by those who saw it to warrant another to extend the story – for how did she get to this situation and where might it lead her?[46]

Hogarth's friends and visitors were intrigued enough to ponder on such things and then make their own suggestions. As Vertue goes on, 'some advisd him to make another ... as a pair ... which he did', which suggests a type of before and after pairing – perhaps the Duke of Montagu was one of the admirers of Hogarth's harlot. To chart such a progress requires some thought as to cause and effect. But an additional picture attempting, within a single image, to show how innocence might be corrupted – that is, what would become scene one of the completed series – would mean too swift a leap from this to the garret in Drury Lane. So in attempting to explain the harlot's journey, more questions arise and so more ideas and images are required, and thus 'other thoughts encreas'd, & multiplyd by his fruitfull invention'. Until, as Vertue says, 'he made six. different subjects which he painted so naturally. the thoughts, & strikeing the expressions that it drew every body to see them'.[47]

These six images as a sequence would fit the individual stories of thousands, tens of thousands of women, spanning time and place. That Hogarth is presenting a nobody, rather than a some-body, is signalled by the precise selection of 'a' rather than 'the' harlot's progress. No one should be under any illusion that this story is unique.

However, it still does not explain where the idea came from in the first place. John Nichols observes that Hogarth, in eventually naming his heroine 'M' or 'Moll Hackabout', 'has appropriated a name ... which belonged to a well known wanton then upon the town'. He also refers to a notice in the *Grub Street Journal* dated 6 August 1730 regarding a *'Kate Hackabout* (whose brother was lately hanged at *Tyburn*), a woman noted in and about the hun-dreds of *Drury, &c'*.[48] The brother hanged at Tyburn must refer to one Francis Hackabout, who was executed on 17 April 1730 for highway robbery. He appeared at the same Old Bailey court session as the degenerate aristocrat, Colonel Francis Charteris, who was convicted for the rape of his servant, Anne Bond.[49] While Charteris, known as the 'rape-master general', was safely behind bars in Newgate prison, *Fog's Weekly Journal* reported archly, 'We hear of no Rapes to have been committed for three weeks past.'[50] Anne was one of many victims of this unrestrained, utterly corrupt and desperately unpleasant individual. But it was not only thieves and rapists who found themselves on the wrong side of the law:

on 3 August 1730 the *Daily Journal* reported that 'On Saturday Last Sir John Gonson and Several other Justices of the Peace ... met at the Vestry-Room of St. Paul's Covent Garden, and committed the Keepers of several disorderly Houses (who were taken into Custody the Night before) to Tothill-Fields Bridewell to hard Labour, in particular Katherine Hackabout, alias Wooton, and Anne Lewis, alias Low, alias Brown.'

However, unlike Francis Hackabout, who was just another expendable member of the lower orders, Charteris, with his contacts in high places, was eventually pardoned by his peers and his estates restored to him: a situation that confirmed what most already knew, that there was one rule for the aristocracy, the elite, and another for everybody else. As a result of the ensuing furore, Gonson extended his raids to include the more notorious brothels, among them Elizabeth 'Mother' Needham's in St James's (a known procuress of women and girls for, among many others, Colonel Charteris). Needham was herself arrested and successfully prosecuted. Her sentence was to appear in the pillory in Park Place, near where her brothel was located, on 30 April 1731. Her treatment by the crowds that swarmed to see and pelt her, as the punishment required, was severe – some, it was reported, throwing dead cats, felines being one symbol for prostitutes, alongside the usual rotten food and muck. The barrage was so extreme that it almost killed her there and then. She actually died three days later, it is said, in terror at the prospect of returning to the pillory for the second obligatory appearance before the baying, jeering mob.

The progress of Hogarth's harlot begins with her arrival from York as a fresh-faced girl, unprepared for the ways of the metropolis. She is approached by a brothel bawd, Mother Needham, who will arrange the girl's 'initiation' by none other than the recognisable villain, preparing himself for the task in the background, Colonel Francis Charteris. John Nichols identifies the character standing near the convicted rapist as John Gourlay, 'a Pimp, whom he always kept about his person'.[51] The transformation scene, from girl to harlot, is not depicted by Hogarth, although the interior version of *Before* and *After* could easily stand as proxy. Thus inducted into brothel life, Moll then finds herself in the relatively elevated status

25. *A Harlot's Progress Plate 1*, etching and engraving, 1732
Mary or 'Moll' Hackabout's luggage (right) in the Bell (or 'belle') Inn's yard
includes a dead goose in a straw basket, mimicking Moll in her 'Leghorn' hat.

26. *A Harlot's Progress Plate 3*, etching and engraving, 1732
Sir John pauses on the threshold of Moll's miserable Drury Lane
abode. Now a common prostitute, her need to promote and
expose herself is symbolised by the cat, its rear in the air.

of the kept woman of a Jewish merchant, surrounded by luxuries. But she overplays her hand by cuckolding her keeper and ends up as a common prostitute in her dilapidated Drury Lane garret, about to be arrested by a justice of the peace, the real-life terror of prostitution, Sir John Gonson. That one of her clients, perhaps even a lover, is the famous real-life highwayman James Dalton (executed 11 May 1730) is signalled by his wig box sitting on the bed's tester and a print of Captain Macheath on the wall next to her pillow. This is a creative extrapolation from the circumstances of the real-life Hackabouts, brother and sister. Moll's arrest leads (we can suppose) from Gonson's court, held at the vestry of St Paul's church, to the humiliation of hard labour at Bridewell, the fate of the real Kate Hackabout, and then a swift decline, ravaged by venereal disease, to an untimely death. Even as she lies in her coffin Moll's fellow prostitutes are picking up punters – notably a pleasantly surprised vicar – and so the whole hideous cycle rolls on, and on: whether Moll or Kate, Hogarth's harlot is one of many.

So here Hogarth has adapted the idea of the celebrity criminal's portrait – Charteris, Needham, even the Hackabouts – in order to add topicality, veracity and interest to his invented tale. The three apparently separate news stories concerning the highwayman Frank Hackabout, the bawd Needham, the rapist Charteris and the whore Kate Hackabout, reported months and even years apart, are key elements of the narrative that became *A Harlot's Progress* – expanded by the imagination and experience of the artist. It is surely no coincidence that while *A Harlot's Progress* was in train, both Needham and Charteris were dead and unable to protest.

By the time the six scenes had been painted, to the approbation of his advisors, Hogarth had already begun work on the engravings, which, given the popularity of the theme, was an extremely canny decision. Painted copies might reduce the value of the original, unless, as with *The Beggar's Opera*, significant enough changes or variations are made to the composition – each being, as it were, an original. But much more crucial was the time required to make painted versions. Far better to tap into the interest in poor Moll Hackabout and her misfortunes with engravings after the paintings. Vertue noted that the pre-publication price for the six prints

was 'one guinea each sett' and, once announced, the subscriptions
flooded in, providing 'fifty or a hundred pounds in a Week – there
being no day but persons of fashion and Artists came to see these
pictures'. Vertue, as an art-world observer as well as a professional
engraver, is noticeably astonished by the success, which he simply
cannot stop writing about in his notebooks. He scribbles that
Hogarth has achieved around twelve hundred subscribers, but also
that Hogarth had initially proposed to hire the best engravers in
London to do the work, 'but none that he employed pleasing him.
he has set about them himself', concluding, 'I believe he has not
met with so much encouragement as heretofore.'[52]

The striking likeness of the magistrate, Sir John Gonson, alone
was a draw. It made the series particularly entertaining to the lords
of the Treasury, according to Hogarth's friend William Huggins, as
reported to John Nichols.[53] At a meeting held just a few days after
A Harlot's Progress was published, one of the lords brought along a
copy for the entertainment of the gathered gentlemen, and it gave
such 'universal satisfaction ; from the Treasury each lord repaired
to the print-shop for a copy of it, and *Hogarth* rose completely
into fame'. It is a lovely image, the treasury lords all filing out of the
chamber on Whitehall and, presumably, into Westminster Hall in
the Palace of Westminster, where Hogarth's engravings were sold
by the warring printsellers, John Stagg and the vociferously Jacobite Widow Chilcott.[54]

That Hogarth originally intended to hire engravers, or may
have done so and then, finding them not up to his standard, took
on the work himself, is an example of where Hogarth's unusual
experience – as an accomplished engraver as well as painter – was
of great benefit to him, not least from the view of quality control.
However, it is also true that he had to commit much more of his
own time to the project than he had intended originally, which
might well have necessitated turning away portrait commissions,
although having saved the cost of hiring engravers, the profit, if
successful, would have been even greater. Vertue, still demonstrably amazed, noted again the extraordinary success of *A Harlot's
Progress*: 'before a twelve month came about whilst these plates
were engraving he had in his Subscription. between *14 or fifteen*

hundred'. He was also told by Hogarth's printer that over twelve hundred sets had already been produced. And all this 'without Courting or soliciting subscriptions' but through word of mouth, everyone 'comeing to his dwelling'.[55]

Although based on realities and the experience of countless sex workers, the very fact that Hogarth had essentially invented a story, painted the sequence and then engraved it, was quite an achievement, as acknowledged by James Ralph, Benjamin Franklin's erstwhile friend, in the 3 June 1732 *Weekly Register*: it was through his journalism and political writing that Ralph achieved some semblance of stability after his theatrical and poetical disappointments. In his article Ralph opines:

> Now nothing is a greater Objection to the genius of the Painters than their Want of Invention; few of them have Spirit enough even to touch upon a new Story, or venture on a Subject that has not been very often handled before ... But fewer still have commenc'd Authors themselves, that is to say, invented both the story and the Executions; tho' certainly 'tis as much in their Power as the Poet's, and would redound as much to their Reputation, as the late *Progress of a Harlot* by the ingenious Mr. *Hogarth* will sufficiently testify.[56]

If Hogarth did not know James Ralph before this juncture, then surely this high and timely praise was the means of introduction.

John Nichols observes that both the familiarity of the subject and the 'propriety', the aptness 'of it's [*sic*] execution, made the "Harlot's Progress" tasted by all ranks of people'.[57] Unlikely as this might sound, Moll Hackabout's legend was engraved on to fan leaves, for young ladies to flutter. Examples printed in red on chicken skin exist, and we know from advertisements in the *Country Journal or The Craftsman* (1 July 1732) and elsewhere that they sold for two shillings and sixpence.[58] The etching was by Giles King, at the 'Golden Head' in Brownlow Street, Drury Lane, in collaboration with Martha Gamble, who traded from the 'Golden Fleece' (also in other advertisements called the 'Golden Fan'), St Martin's Court: 'on a Fan, three on each Side, curiously engraved.

Wherein the Characters are justly preserv'd, and the whole not varied from the Originals. Printed in divers beautiful Colours, Price 2s. 6d.'[59] And again in 1733, Martha, who is likely to have been a relation of Ellis, advertised, 'For those that are curious a small Number are work'd off on fine Paper, fit to frame. Likewise a new Edition of the Harlot's Progress in Fans, or singly to frame.'[60] John Nichols notes, 'It was customary in *Hogarth*'s family to give these fans to the maids'[61] as a friendly warning, in case they were ever tempted towards a wrong path.

Nichols states that *A Harlot's Progress* was the means of reconciliation between father and son-in-law. He quotes Sir James Thornhill declaring that the man who painted this series can keep a wife without a dowry.[62] According to Nichols, Thornhill made the remark concerning Hogarth's ability to keep his wife so that he would not have to part with any money himself – a tight-fisted miser in other words. This simply does not accord with Thornhill's character, but given that Hogarth 'ran away' with his daughter, against his will, he could simply be calling the young man's bluff. Yes, we are reconciled, but you must live by your decision and the confidence you have in your own talent. However, as even Nichols admits, Sir James 'soon after, became both reconciled and generous to the young couple'.[63]

This idea appears to be a retrospective fancy. George Vertue notes that people had come to see the paintings of *A Harlot's Progress* in their droves at the Hogarth abode, 'in common [Covent] Garden' that is 'where he livd with his father in Law Sr. James Thornhill'.[64] Other sources suggest that William and Jane were living in a separate house nearby, on the Little Piazza.[65] Either way, the people keen to see the portrait of Justice Shard had also come to the Covent Garden house, and the portraits listed from 1731 would have been worked on at the same location. It also means that Hogarth may have set off from Sir James's house (William and Jane's home too, for now) to the Bedford Arms directly opposite, on that late May day in 1732.

But with such great fame came risk, particularly from the shameless pirates of original designs and prints. Hogarth had fallen foul of them before, notably with his *Masquerades and*

Operas engraving. But what happened around *A Harlot's Progress* was unprecedented. Vertue observes that the sales would have been even greater, but 'no Soonner were these publisht but several Copies were made by other. hands & dispersd all over the Countries'. One advertisement declares that both Thomas and John Bowles were still making money at Hogarth's expense: '*This Day is Published, By* Tho. Bowles, *Printseller, in St. Paul's Church-yard, and* John Bowles *at Mercers-Hall in Cheapside*, THE HARLOT'S PROGRESS, in Six Prints, the same Size as Mr. Hogarth's ... These Plates are all of them curiously engraved by Mr. Foudrinier and other the best Masters in Town.'[66] Aside from pirated images, there were poems alleging to be the key to Hogarth's creation: 'This Day is publish'd, THE HARLOT'S PROGRESS: Or, The Humours of Drury-lane. In Six Canto's. Being the Tale of the noted Moll Hackabout, in Hudibrastick Verse, containing her whole Life ; which is a Key to the Six Prints already publish'd by Mr. Hogarth.'[67] Everyone, it seemed, was jumping on the bandwagon – even Thomas Bowles, the printseller who had paid the younger Hogarth so little for his plates – to Hogarth's financial distress.

Unfortunately there was very little that Hogarth or any other designer and engraver could do about this as the law stood. But the experience would be the last straw, and very soon, if not already, Hogarth was consulting his legal friends concerning an act of parliament for copyright. For he was developing a new series – almost certainly conceived in tandem with *A Harlot's Progress* – focusing on a male protagonist and likely to be as popular as the female counterpart, which Hogarth could not, would not allow to be hijacked in the same way. Beyond the loss of income, it was an issue of artistic reputation. Why should the artist not have full rights and associated benefits of their own creativity for as long as they lived?

While all this was fomenting, and still basking in the glorious success of his *A Harlot's Progress* (the irritant of piracy aside) another opportunity, not unconnected, presented itself. The events around the trial and execution of Sarah Malcolm were sensational. Not because the criminal was a woman per se but because she was found guilty of murder. Women gave birth and nurtured, they created and sustained life. It was this that had made the rabbit-woman fraud of 1726 so ridiculously deplorable. Hogarth's engraving of that year, 'The Cunicularii or the Wise Men of Godliman in Consultation', made merry with this sensational story of a hoaxer, Mary Toft of Godalming, who had allegedly given birth to rabbits. Perhaps more astonishing, was that some well-known men of sense and science (the 'Wise Men', worshipping at Mary, or the Virgin Mary's lying in), including the royal surgeon Nathaniel St André, had actually believed her. Toft was probably the victim of peer and family pressure. Certainly the desperation suggested by inserting skinned rabbits into her vagina, then 'giving birth' to them presumably in the hope of some financial return, should have encouraged pity as well incredulity.[68] Still, while Toft's fraud was bad enough, a murderess was the very antithesis of womanhood.

Sarah Malcolm, then a charwoman for the lawyer John Carrol (also called 'Kerrel'), was condemned for the murders of Ann Price, a maidservant of seventeen years; Lydia Duncomb, a bedridden widow about eighty years old, with 'her Memory much decay'd'; and Elizabeth Harrison, another servant aged about sixty, regarded as frail, on 4 February (at the turn of 1732 to 1733) in Mrs Duncomb's upper-floor apartment in Middle Temple. Carrol was her neighbour: his chambers and Mrs Duncomb's apartment shared a main staircase. The murder scene was described in the trial. The door was locked, so the neighbour Ann Oliphant climbed through the window and let in Mrs Duncomb's friends, Mrs Rhymer and Mrs Love:

> They enter'd: But the Surprize, the Horrour they were in, is not to be express'd, when the first Object they fix'd their Eyes on was the poor unhappy young Maid murder'd! inhumanly murder'd! and lying weltring in her own Blood, her Hands clench'd, her Hair loose, and her Throat cut from Ear to Ear! A terrible Spectacle. But this was not all, the tragical Scene did not close here; the honest old Servant lay strangled on her Bed, and a little farther, her good Old Lady robb'd of her Life in the same manner.[69]

The surgeon, Thomas Bigg, who inspected the bodies, made the observation that Ann 'seem'd to have struggled hard for her Life'.[70] Sarah Malcolm was discovered nearby, but accused others, including her master, even, it was said, planting some items taken from Mrs Duncomb's home to implicate them – Carrol discovered blooded linen under his bed and a silver tankard in his close-stool, or toilet.[71] It was reported that Mrs Duncomb had £54 in a money box, a sizeable lump sum in itself, but on which she was required to eke out her existence. The sum of £53, 11 shillings and 6 pence was found on Sarah Malcolm, hidden under her cap. The inference being that she had begun spending the money immediately after the crime.

In the *London Evening Post* of 3–6 March, and repeated in *The Craftsman or Country Journal* on 10 March, the following announcement appeared: 'Monday [5th] Sarah Malcolm sate for her Picture in Newgate, which was taken by the ingenious Mr. Hogarth ; Sir James Thornhill was likewise present.' It is totally in keeping with his interests and character that Sir James accompanied Hogarth to Newgate prison. And Hogarth, in turn, was following his father-in-law's lead in gaining access to a notorious criminal a few days in advance of execution, in order to sketch her image for swift translation into print form.

Two days later Sarah was taken to the temporary gallows on Fleet Street, close to the scene of the murders. The crowds were so dense that a Mrs Strangeways, attempting to cross Fleet Street from her home near Serjeants' Inn to her friend Mrs Coulthurst's abode on the other side, was carried over the heads and shoulders of the mob. At this point the condemned woman, 'dress'd in a black Gown, white Apron, Sarsenet Hood and black Gloves', was 'very penitent and devout ... She was very desirous to see her Master Mr. Carrol, and looked about for him, whom she acquitted of all Manner of Aspersions or Imputations laid on him at her Trial, but confess'd nothing concerning the Murder'.[72] The *Universal Spectator* takes up the story, declaring she 'appeared very serious and devout, crying and wringing her Hands in an extraordinary manner ... During the Time she was in the Cart, what with praying, Agony and Passion, she fell down ; but immediately was rais'd, and laid

27. *Sarah Malcolm*, etching and engraving, 1733
Pirated versions appeared on broadsheets, often with a vignette of
the execution. Unlike the painting a rosary is not shown here.

her Head against [the executioner] Jack Ketch ... At length she was
turn'd off, and hung about half an Hour, and then cut down.' Her
body was taken in a coach to the pump house at Newgate, though
another report states it was an undertaker's on Snow Hill, *'where
Multitudes of People resorted, and gave Money to see it'*, among them
a mysterious gentleman *'in deep new Mourning, who kiss'd her ; and
gave the People Half a Crown'.*[73] Finally 'last Night she was bury'd'.[74]
She was about twenty-two years old.

In the painted version of his portrait, Hogarth has depicted Sarah as a working woman with a white apron over her grey dress. She is staring into her cell, having turned away from the window and with her back to the door, but her face and upper body are lit by an ethereal light, which also picks out the beads of her rosary – defining her as a Roman Catholic. Her arms are folded, and she leans forward on to them. Her face has the ruddiness of a servant, and the red of her cheeks provides the only warmth of tone in an otherwise sombre medley of black, brown, grey and white. Her face is expressionless, her gaze vacant.

The painting (National Gallery of Scotland), full-length, is very small in scale, and may have been worked up from the *ad vivum* sketch that Hogarth used to produce the engraving. This version, published as a memento and priced six pence, is only a half-length, and concentrated on Sarah's upper body. In the *Genuine Works*, John Nichols and George Steevens quote the artist: "'This woman,' said Hogarth, after he had drawn Sarah Malcolm, "by her features, is capable of any wickedness."[75] Yet, like Thornhill before him, there is no suggestion here that Hogarth intends to present the face of evil; rather it is poignant how ordinary Sarah is, how unexceptional and, therefore, the inference being, that a character – a propensity to wickedness – may not always be read in the face. What is there, as depicted in the first scene of *A Rake's Progress* (Fig. 11 p. 75), in the wide-eyed pleading of the young Tom Rakewell, that might point to his recent past and present as the debaucher and abandoner of Sarah Young, seen weeping as she is paid off in the first image, leading to his relentless progress to full-blown depravity, disease and then madness? As Hogarth later declared, in a comment which throws serious doubt on John Nichols's quotation:

How often is it said, on the slightest view, that such a one looks like a good-natur'd man, that he hath an honest open countenance, or looks like a cunning rogue ; a man of sense, or a fool, &c. And how are our eyes riveted to the aspects of kings and heroes, murderers and saints ; and as we con-template their deeds, seldom fail making application to their looks. It is reasonable to believe that aspect to be a true and legible representation of the mind, which gives every one the same idea at first sight ; and is afterwards confirm'd in fact : for instance, all concur in the same opinion, at first sight, of a down-right idiot.[76]

Yet, he continues, 'Very handsom[e] faces of almost any age, will hide a foolish or a wicked mind till they betray themselves by their actions or their words.' Indeed, 'the bad man, if he be an hypocrite, may so manage his muscles, by teaching them to contradict his heart, that little of his mind can be gather'd from his countenance, so that the character of an hypocrite is entirely out of the power of the pencil, without some adjoining circumstance to discover him, as smiling and stabbing at the same time, or the like'.[77] What a powerfully simple image: straight, as it were, to the point – 'smiling and stabbing' – reminiscent of the sneering child torturer of *The Four Stages of Cruelty*.

By October 1733 Hogarth was ready to announce the imminent arrival of a new modern moral series. He and Jane had also left the Great Piazza and set up in what will be their London home and business address for the rest of their lives: a modest, three-bay building on the south-eastern corner of Leicester Fields. Above the door Hogarth placed the equivalent of the shop sign or business marker, like Ellis Gamble's Golden Angel and his, Hogarth's earlier sign, the 'Golden Ball'. This new talisman was a bust or head representing Sir Anthony van Dyck, with short hair, a cavalier's trimmed moustache and slim, pointy beard, which Hogarth had fashioned himself from layers of cork and then gilded.[78] 'The Sign of the Golden Head' will be used in advertisements; it is where all his paintings would be viewed, subscriptions received and from where engravings could be collected and purchased. Van Dyck, the knighted principal painter of Charles I, signalled where Hogarth's ambitions lay. It may be in honour of his new home and business address that, soon after moving in, he painted his self-portrait and that of Jane, for display in this their first permanent home and joint venture.

Such was the runaway success of *A Harlot's Progress* that, regardless of any other ambitions Hogarth may have had, or continued to have, cashing in on the success of his new form was too tempting. As Hogarth was to later confirm, with this format at least he had complete control over production, and by combining the paintings (advertising the project and maintaining his reputation as a painter) and the prints (the income generator and reputation disseminator), he had hit on a highly commercial format. The new series, following on from his *Harlot*, was extremely ambitious: eight rather than six individual canvases and prints, each painted and engraved by Hogarth.

In this new story, the behaviour of men and women, their motivation and choices, are still at the heart, but with the focus shifted to a male archetype, the libertine or rake. Among the many aspects that unite the two series is the absence of parental guidance or, indeed, any sound adult counsel. Thus, like Moll, abandoned to the foibles of his own character and with only the miserly attitude of his father to kick against, the young Tom Rakewell becomes a willing magnet to all the chancers, wastrels and artificers in town.

In the third edition (1785) of his *Biographical Anecdotes*, John Nichols notes that some of the characters in *A Rake's Progress* are based on real people, going on to say, 'I am also assured, that while *Hogarth* was painting the *Rake's Progress*, he had a summer residence at *Isleworth* ; and never failed to question the company who came to see these pictures, if they knew for whom one or another figure was designed. When they guessed wrong, he set them right.'[79] Further, in the first edition of his biography, dated 1781 (not repeated in the third), Nichols asserts that a surgeon called John Ranby 'sat for the hero'.[80] He goes on to describe a portrait of John Ranby (b.1703) by Hogarth, being in the collection of Samuel Ireland in the 1780s, but this painting has not been identified.[81]

At the time Hogarth was developing his new series, Ranby, the son of an innkeeper in St Giles, the area notorious for gin distilling and a stopping-off place for Tyburn, had been in practice as a surgeon for ten years. In 1724 he had been elected into the Royal Society, supported by William Cheselden and Sir Hans Sloane – Cheselden and Hogarth had both attended the Vanderbank-Chéron drawing academy in Peter's Court, St Martin's Lane, so Hogarth may have met Ranby through this connection. In 1729

Ranby had married a wealthy widow, Jane (b.1684), the daughter of the Hon. Dacre Barrett-Lennard, many years his senior. The union was one of convenience, and if there was any affection between them at the start, it soon disappeared. By 1737 Ranby had been appointed surgeon-in-ordinary to the king's household, and in that year, while attending to Queen Caroline, sadly for the condition that was to kill her, the queen joked that Ranby would rather be treating 'his own cross wife that he hated so much'.[82] Apart from potentially offering the physical model for Tom Rakewell, John Ranby's marital circumstances might have inspired image five of *A Rake's Progress*, where Tom, having squandered his inheritance, marries the old widow for her money. There was also the example of John Vanderbank, still resident in London, old before his time and living, pitiably, off the largesse of friends and supporters.

At the same time as Hogarth was doing battle with the plagiarists over his *Harlot* prints, *A Rake's Progress* had been advertised as in train, with the paintings available to be viewed: 'MR. HOGARTH being now engraving nine Copper-plates from Pictures of his own Painting, one of which represents the Humours of a Fair, the other eight, The Progress of a Rake ... Subscriptions will be taken in at Mr. Hogarth's, the Golden Head in Leicester-Fields, where the Pictures are to be seen.'[83]

Hogarth had already anticipated that some attempt would be made to pirate his new series – through necessity he had had to advertise its imminent arrival, exposing him to skulduggery – but he hoped that with the new copyright act, 'An Act for the encouragement of the Arts of designing engraving and etching Historical and other prints by vesting the properties thereof in the Inventors and Engravers during the time therein mentioned', he could finally stop these scoundrels in their tracks. Among the signatories was George Vertue. In his advertisement, stating that the prints for both *Southwark Fair* and *A Rake's Progress* were completed, he concluded:

> N.B. Mr. Hogarth was, and is obliged to defer the Publication and Delivery of the abovesaid Prints till the 25th of June next, in order to secure his Property, pursuant to an Act lately pass'd both Houses of Parliament, now waiting for the Royal

Assent, to secure all new invented Prints that shall be published after 24th of June next, from being copied without
Consent of the Proprietor, and thereby preventing a scandalous and unjust Custom (hitherto practised with Impunity)
of making and vending base Copies of original P[r]ints, to
the manifest Injury of the Author, and the great Discourage-
ment of the Arts of Painting and Engraving.[84]

But as Hogarth was about to release his prints for *A Rake's Progress*, the plagiarists had already attempted to circumvent the new
copyright law by covertly viewing the paintings in advance and
producing their own versions before the deadline. Hogarth's anger
is plain to all from a sequence of advertisements. First, at the sheer
breathtaking audacity of stealing another's designs from under his
very nose, second, degrading the artist by producing third-rate versions, which would reflect badly on Hogarth himself, and third, at
making money out of the theft. This time Hogarth was ready for
them, and in addition to calling out the perpetrators, he aimed
to ruin their money-making venture by undercutting their cheap
prints himself:

Certain Printsellers in London, intending not only to injure
Mr. Hogarth in his Property, but also to impose their base
Imitations (of his Eight Prints of the Rake's Progress) on the
Publick, which they, being oblig'd to do only by what they
could carry away by Memory from the Sight of his Paintings,
have executed most wretchedly both in design and Drawing,
as will be very obvious when they are expos'd; he, in order to
prevent such scandalous Practices, and that the Publick may
be furnished with his real Designs, has permitted his Original Prints to be closely copied, and the said Copies will be
published in a few Days, and sold at 2s. 6d. each Sett, by T.
Bakewell, Print and Mapseller, next Johnson's Court in Fleet-
street, London.[85]

The advertisement concludes, 'NB original engravings sold at two
guineas each set, the above are cheaper copies executed with the

consent of Hogarth.' John Nichols believed that Hogarth bought up 'great quantities' of the pirated copies, which remained with Jane long after her husband's death.[86]

Whether the original engravings by Hogarth or the various products of plagiarism, *A Rake's Progress* proved another hit. So much so that it drew the unlikely attention of Jean-Bernard, abbé le Blanc, an art critic from the Parisian literati and later patronised by Louis XV's most famous mistress, Jeanne Poisson, Madame de Pompadour. In his observations addressed to a 'connoisseur', later published as *Letters on the English and French Nations*, the abbé dismisses Sir James Thornhill outright, declaring if viewing the paintings at Greenwich or St Paul's, 'you would be puzzled to decide, not in what part the painter excelled, but that in which he is less faulty'. Indeed, he is the only English painter who aspires to this great form of art 'which requires a genius that nature had refused him'.[87] While staying in London the abbé could not fail to notice the way Hogarth's *Rake* had exploded on to the scene, but was extremely sniffy about the talent the English had, as he sees it, in the production of the grotesque:

> To succeed in the grotesque, as well as to hit the agreeable, invention alone is not sufficient: the great secret is to know where to stop, and our neighbours, who over-do every thing, know no bounds in a sort that permits them to give full scope to their imagination. But yet it is certain that the English would have less regard for this somewhat ignoble way of painting, if they were as much hurt as we by low disgusting objects, which are the foundation of it. In that which requires a nobleness and elevation, they have shewn an insufficiency, or rather a total inability.[88]

Le Blanc explains this deficiency by the fact that the English live in and breathe a thicker sort of air, and do not have the refined sensations of the southern European countries: 'To conclude, those of them who have the talent to paint nature in burlesque, ennoble it by the use they make of it : they employ it to give disrelish to vice.' He then moves on to *A Rake's Progress*, without naming the artist responsible, observing that two famous, highly regarded and monumental schemes, the Marie de' Medici cycle by Rubens, then at the Palais du Luxembourg, and Charles Le Brun's Alexander the Great, 'never had a greater run in our country, than a set of prints actually have in England, engraved lately from pictures of a man of genius in this way, but who is as bad a painter, as he is a good subject'. The unnamed engraver has made a fortune from these prints, indeed, 'the whole nation has been infected by them, as one of the most happy productions of the age. I have not seen a house of note without these moral prints, which represent in a grotesque manner the Rake's Progress in all the scenes of ridicule and disgrace, which vice draws after it; sometimes even in those circumstances, the reality of which, if tolerably expressed, raises horror: and the English genius spares nothing that can inspire it.' He admits that even 'the ancients were of opinion, that nothing could give such an aversion for intemperance, as the very sight of a person labouring under the effects of it. I verily believe that such pictures make a deeper impression on a people like this, who delight in strong representations, than the most sensible reflections, or the most pathetic discourses. What do I say? The human kind are the same every where : whatever end is proposed, it is surer and easier to make an impression on the senses, than to convince the understanding.'[89] In short, and on this point Hogarth might agree, pictures speak louder and more directly than words.

A Rake's Progress, fast on the heels of *A Harlot's Progress* and the groundbreaking Copyright Act, meant that Hogarth had very much arrived professionally. And the following accolade would have been the pinnacle of what was, professionally, a brilliant period:

> How I want thee, humourous *Hogarth!*
> Thou, I hear a pleasant rogue art;
> Were but you and I acquainted,
> Ev'ry monster should be painted:
> You should try your graving tools
> On this odious group of fools;
> Draw the beasts as I describe them;

Form their features, while I gibe them;
Draw them like, for I assure ye,
You will need no *car'catura*;
Draw them so, that we may trace
All the soul in ev'ry face.

Note the rhyming of 'Hogarth' and 'rogue art', perhaps a wink to the name's rustic origins. The tribute was from no less a personage than Jonathan Swift, Dean of St Patrick's, Dublin. Hogarth's fame now reached across the British Isles.[90] A personal connection with the artist may have been established by Patrick Delany, a close friend and future husband of Hogarth's admirer Mary Pendarves, who was in regular correspondence with the prominent printseller, publisher and Swift's friend, George Faulkner. A few years later, Faulkner wrote to Hogarth concerning three prints of which Delany had made him aware together with a gift, perhaps an engraving, which the artist had sent to Dr Swift:

Sir

I was favoured with a letter from Mr Delany, who tells me, that you are going to publish three Prints. Your Reputation here is sufficiently known to recommend any thing of yours and I shall be glad to serve you. The Duty on Prints is ten per cent in Ireland. You may send me 5 setts, provided, you will take back what I cannot sell. I desire no other profit than what you allow in London to those who sell them again. I have often the favour of drinking your Health with Dr. Swift, who is a great admirer of yours, and hath made mention of you in his Poems with great Honour, and desired me to thank you for your kind present, and to accept of his service,

I am, Sir
Your most Obedient, and Most humble servt.

George Faulkner[91]

But in the meantime Hogarth had suffered two significant personal family losses: 'Thursday Night was buried Mrs. Hogarth, Mother to the celebrated Mr. Hogarth, who died on Tuesday Morning at her House in Cranbourn-alley, of a Fright, occasion'd by the Fire in St. Martin's-court. She was in perfect Health when the unhappy Accident broke out, and died before it could be extinguish'd.'[92] John Nichols recalls that thirteen houses had been burnt, observing, 'The fire began at the house of Mrs. *Calloway*, who kept a brandy-shop. This woman was committed to *Newgate*, it appearing among other circumstances, that she had threatened "to be even with the landlord for having given her warning, and that she would have a bonfire on the 20th *June*, that should warm all her rascally neighbours".'[93] Anne Hogarth senior, in the wake of her husband's prolonged difficulties, had been, through her determination and resourcefulness, a steadying influence on the Hogarth family. Her death in her mid seventies was quite usual for the time, although, as she was reported to have been in 'perfect Health' before the fire, does suggest she could have hoped for a longer life.

And the year before, when Sir James Thornhill had died (just short of his fifty-eighth birthday, on 4 May 1734), an announcement appeared in the newspapers as follows: 'DEATHS. The following Character being drawn in Honour of a famous English Painter, we shall give it at Length. On Saturday, the 4th Instant, died at Thornhill, in the County of Dorset, Sir James Thornhill, Kt. the greatest History Painter this Kingdom has in any Age Produced.' After surveying his most acclaimed creations, including 'his elaborate Works in that noble Structure of Greenwich Hospital ; the Cupola of St. Paul's Cathedral', the entry continues by mentioning Sir James's daughter Jane, 'now the Wife of Mr. W. Hogarth, admired for his curious Miniature Conversation Paintings, as well serious as humourous, in which he excels all of his Time.' For Hogarth, even an obituary is an opportunity for publicity – note, also, it is the 'celebrated Mr. Hogarth' burying his mother. The short memoir concludes, 'Sir James has left a most valuable Collection of Pictures, and other Curiosities, and died in the 57th Year of his Age.'[94] George Vertue describes Thornhill's final illness, having spent a year 'much out of Order' and for some years 'afflicted with the gout' but, in a new development 'one of his leggs swelling as if dropsy the last years of his life, but always a man of high Spirit. but not long before he died he had a more violent Illness in London that had taken away his Voice'.[95]

Other than his constant lifelong admiration for Sir James and his protectiveness towards his father-in-law's legacy, at the time of his death, Hogarth was emulating his hero and second father in both a practical and artistic manner, through paintings combining the promotion of history painting, religion and charity. In fact, after this period of great success, with significant improvement in his professional and financial circumstances, even if tempered by family tragedy, Hogarth had already embarked on his first great history painting scheme.

INTERLUDE FOUR

SATURDAY 27 MAY, STILL EARLY MORNING. After passing the magnificence of Royal Greenwich and enjoying a swift repast at Blackwall Point, the five pilgrims resume their journey towards Gravesend. This section of the Thames continues to loop and meander, passing Woolwich on the south bank, roughly nine miles (as the crow flies) from their starting point. Sitting under the flapping canvas tilt, a little soggy and weary, in the pre-dawn darkness they could just see the collection of buildings and slipways of the Royal Dockyard, originally founded in 1514 by Henry VIII and where the ship *Henry Grace à Dieu* ('Great Harry') was built. It remained as the principal royal shipbuilding wharf on the Thames. It was here that the *Sovereign of the Seas*, the most powerful ship at the time, was built in 1637 by Phineas Pett, Charles I's shipbuilder, to the designs of his father Peter, the commissioner at Chatham Dockyard. She became the model for all one hundred gun ships – men of war – of the Royal Navy.

Passing Erith on the south side of the Thames, they were now thirteen miles from Covent Garden. The next landing place was on the north bank, the Essex side of the Thames at Purfleet. Here the five friends admired the Royal Navy ships at anchor, towering above the little craft. One of these was HMS *Gibraltar*, a twenty-gun sixth rate, built in 1711 and the first command of John Byng, the unfortunate admiral who was later court-martialled and executed on the deck of his ship *'pour encourager les autres'*,[1] as Voltaire ruefully observed in his satirical novella, *Candide, ou l'Optimisme* (1759). The rating system used in 1732 was an updated version of that devised by Samuel Pepys in his capacity as Secretary to the Admiralty in 1677, by which time the rating (sixth to first) was based on the number of guns rather than the number of men. That something or someone was 'first-rate', meaning the best, soon entered common parlance. The next named vessel is HMS *Dursley Galley*, another sixth-rate ship. The last ship noted at anchor near Purfleet is the curiously named *Tartar Pink*: the nautical term 'pink' being a type of ship with a narrow, overhanging stern. This was built in 1702, a thirty-two-gun fifth rate. One of the more unusual military personnel to board HMS *Tartar* would be Hannah Snell, a woman who served in disguise as a marine during the War of the Austrian Succession; but in 1732 this war was still a few years into the future. In any case, such fifth- and sixth-rate ships were not ships of the line – that is, ships that were deployed in battle – but tended to be escort, convoy and post ships. Their presence signals that the travellers had now entered the section of the river, continuing to the estuary itself, that was very much a working zone of the Royal Navy.[2]

The *Tartar*'s pilot, a sailor who guides ships through dangerous or busy waters, requested that he join Hogarth and his companions as far as Gravesend.[3] This might explain why the pilgrims' fare was reduced from that advertised (if they had had the boat to themselves for the entire trip from Billingsgate to Gravesend). Their new companion, a 'grateful'[4] gentleman, earned his passage by entertaining them with tales of a nautical nature – how, for example, the Spanish had treated English officers in recent encounters, certainly meaning the Anglo-Spanish War of 1727–9, a subject that would have had particular interest for Will Tothall – 'and other Affairs of Consequence'. This, Ebenezer Forrest observes, rather than keeping them wide awake, 'Naturally Made us Drowsy', suggesting that the pilot droned on with little regard for his audience's waning attention. Hogarth, having succumbed completely to Morpheus' charms, while the pilot chatted, soon after awakened with a jolt, as Forrest recalls, and attempted to recount a dream to his companions – perhaps a salty vision flavoured by the seafarer's tales. But, before recalling any of it, he dropped straight back to sleep again and then, on waking for a second time, had by then forgotten that he had dreamt anything at all. The setting down of this utterly nonsensical sequence of events in an attempt to elevate it, could be a whimsical nod to the dream narrative of *The Pilgrim's Progress* and Bunyan's anxieties due to fraught dreams foretelling expulsion from God's Grace and relentless punishment. Hogarth's confusion over whether he did or did not dream, one minute thinking it worthy of repetition, the next recalling nothing whatsoever, may have been a result of too much gin and too little sleep.

Hogarth was known for forgetfulness and, in the words of the artist and scientist, Benjamin Wilson, telling 'the *wrong story*'. On one occasion, in the company of David Garrick, Wilson and others, Hogarth 'said he had an excellent story to tell which would make them all laugh. Everybody being prepared he told his story, but instead of laughing all looked grave, and Hogarth himself seemed a little uncomfortable. After a short time, however, he struck his hand very suddenly upon the table and said that he had told the wrong story. This caused no small amusement, and when he told the right one at last it was so good in its way that all the company laughed exceedingly.'[5]

Thus, in this eventfully uneventful manner, the five friends and their new companion travelled the remaining miles to Gravesend. Daniel Defoe, with reference to the Kent side of the Thames between Woolwich and Gravesend, observed, 'there is little remarkable upon the River [...] the whole Shore being low, and spread with Marshes and unhealthy Grounds'.[6]

Arriving, then, at the shores of the town of Gravesend, twenty-one miles east-south-east, as the crow flies, from Covent Garden, they attempted to land, but with some difficulty, as they encountered an obstruction in the form of a churlish lad or, as Forrest describes him, an 'Unlucky Boy', a term used to denote a bringer of bad luck, ill-omened, troublesome or mischievous, who, in a gesture far from hospitable, refuses to move his boat.[7] Now this is hardly a monumental obstacle, yet it is, in the context of this adventure, worthy of note. The use of the term Unlucky Boy, with all its associations, hints again at a mystical element to the journey. In stepping out of their usual surroundings, the travellers are now exposed to the attitudes and rhythms of the people and communities they encounter. But eventually and inevitably, given, as pilgrims, they are a force for good, 'Virtue', Forrest declares, overcame 'all Obstacle's'[8] and, on landing safely, they made their way to the hostelry of Mrs Bramble, just as the clock struck six in the morning.

At this time in late May the sun would be rising, or would have already risen. At some point, then, in the previous hour or so, the friends would have experienced the kind of glorious sunrise (if a clear sky) which, one hundred years later, would inspire another great English painter, J. M. W. Turner.

Hogarth, although essentially an urban artist, occasionally offers a hint of his abilities in depicting vistas beyond the cityscape. Often he enlisted the expertise of his friend, the landscape painter George Lambert. But even in paintings in his hand entirely, those we might consider urban, like *The March of the Guards to Finchley*, are in fact at the very edge of the city, where the buildings grouped around a turnpike (itself surrounded by fields) signal the last wisps of urban sprawl: beyond are fields, pastures, heaths, until the next settlement, a village or farm, crosses the wanderer's path. Unhindered by buildings, the immense skies above and the landscape beyond the dense human activity at Tottenham Court Turnpike are brilliantly observed – vivid blues, dashes of thick white and cream, with Highgate itself exquisitely rendered. We can see this again in his quartet of canvases recounting the *Humours of an Election* in Oxfordshire (1753), a rare country setting away from the metropolis. The third painting shows the corrupt vote in progress, which might distract us from the beautiful (probably imagined) Oxfordshire landscape beyond, the little church on the rise, the hills in the distance and that vivid blue, once again, touched with pink and creamy clouds. A reminder that with Hogarth, we should always look beyond the main narrative, search for the seemingly incidental details at the furthest distance compositionally, as well as those in the foreground that demand our immediate attention.

Gravesend lies across the Thames from the fort of Tilbury in Essex, a military gathering place for centuries. John Thornhill's map offers a little image of the fort, and it was here that the pirate Captain Kidd's tarred corpse was displayed, as a greeting to travellers. Henry VIII, once again, had built the first fort here, which was extended during the Spanish Armada crisis in the 1580s. Nearby is where Queen Elizabeth delivered her famous speech, 'I know I have the body of a weak and feeble woman, but I have the heart and stomach of a king, and a king of England too.'[9] Gravesend also had a blockhouse, located just to the east of the town, and established during the reign of Henry VIII, in concert with the fort at Tilbury – the two guarding the vital ferry crossing. The presence of such defensive structures stirred Daniel Defoe to observe that this part of the river 'may justly be looked upon, as the Key of [the] River of *Thames*, and consequently the Key of the City of *London*'.[10]

After the first full stage of the journey, completed in five to six hours but with barely any sleep, the travellers urgently needed a refreshing wash of face and hands, and their wigs tidied up and re-powdered, at a cost for the barber of ten pence. Thus respectable, they partook of a light repast, their 'third breakfast' in fact, according to the Reverend Gostling, of coffee, toast and butter, morning fare familiar to any modern Briton.[11] The company paid Mrs Bramble two shillings and tuppence for their refreshments, and by eight o'clock they were on their way.[12] They would return to Gravesend en route home, but this was a short wander through the town before venturing on to the small cathedral city of Rochester.[13]

The travellers were now walking away from the Thames, south towards the river Medway, but after staying overnight in Rochester, they would eventually change direction, traversing the Hoo Peninsula in an easterly direction and then on to the Isle of Grain, before crossing the estuary of the Medway to the nearby Isle of Sheppey and its fort at Sheerness. Edward Hasted describes the Thames and Medway 'being thus united at the Nore, they flow together into the German ocean',[14] now called the North Sea.

The travellers noted Gravesend's 'new church' of St George, which was rising from the ashes of the old – the latter completely destroyed by fire only five years before. The founding of the new church was achieved with great speed via the Commission for Building Fifty New Churches, which was set up through a 1711 Act of Parliament passed in the wake of the Great Fire of London.[15] The first stone was laid on 3 June 1731, and the church was eventually completed by Michaelmas (29 September) 1732, meaning that it was unfinished at the point the travellers were passing by. The most famous burial here was that of Rebecca Rolfe, the married name of Pocahontas, daughter of Chief Powhatan of the Algonquian nation, who died in 1617 travelling home to Virginia with her husband, John Rolfe, and son Thomas. The previous year she had been resident in London, at the Bell Savage Inn on Ludgate Hill, received by King James I, and then moved to Brentford, a village to the west of London.[16] She was buried beneath the chancel of Gravesend's destroyed church, and her remains are now lost. The enigmatic reference by Ebenezer Forrest to 'The unknown person's Tomb and Epitaph'[17] also noted by the Reverend Gostling, may be an allusion to Pocahontas, or simply another reference to an 'unknown person', neither male nor female, a nobody.

Following a brief wander around Gravesend, including across the market place, the travellers strolled to the sister town of Milton, as marked on Thornhill's map but not mentioned in the text, famed for its oysters. Forrest's journal, meanwhile, simply notes how pleasant the countryside was as they wandered through. The Reverend Gostling elaborated with the lines, 'The beauteous prospects found us talk, And shorten'd much our two hours walk',[18] suggesting that their conversation was mainly concerned with the broad views, while pointing out various topographical details around them.

Eventually the company called in at another hostelry, the Sign of the Dover Castle, where they had three pots of beer each at a cost of nine pence.[19] While three pots of beer might seem excessive, for a mid morning refreshment at least, the beer is likely 'small beer', that is, watered down. The term was already in use to mean something of little consequence or worth. In *Beer Street*, a celebration, in Hogarth's words, of 'the invigorating liquor' as the healthy alternative to cheap gin 'in order to drive the other out of vogue', Hogarth presents an urban pastoral, gently playing out under 'The Barley Mow' tavern sign, with its joyful rustics dancing hand in hand around a bale. The streets of London are populated by contented jovial folk, rotund of girth, relaxing among 'thrivieing Industry' with a frothing pot and a clay pipe, and the only building in ruins is the pawnbroker.[20] The accompanying text declares, in terms with which many a modern Briton would concur:

1. *Self-Portrait with Palette*, unfinished oil on canvas, c.1732–5

2. *The Shrimp Girl*, unfinished oil on canvas, *c.*1740–50

This painting remained in Hogarth's house in Leicester Fields and was only sold after Jane's death in 1789. Its unfinished state reveals the artist's characteristic grey 'ground' and his vigorous method of building up layers, colour and detail.

3. *A Scene from The Beggar's Opera*, black and white chalk on blue paper, *c.*1728–9

4. *A Scene from The Beggar's Opera*, oil on canvas, 1729
By the time Hogarth painted this version, the production had achieved further celebrity
(or notoriety) through the affair between Lavinia Fenton (as Polly, dressed in white)
and the married Duke of Bolton (seated furthest right), who gazes intently at her.

5. *Jane Thornhill, Mrs William Hogarth, as St Agnes*, oil on canvas, *c*.1735–46
This canvas appears to have been cut down from what could have been a double
portrait of the newly married couple. The manner in which Hogarth has painted
his young wife's hair falling over her right shoulder is an example (here intimate and
sensual) of, in his own words, 'the flowing curl' and how 'the naturally intermingling
locks ravish the eye with the pleasure of the pursuit'. (*The Analysis of Beauty*)

6. *The Beckenham Wedding,*
oil on canvas, *c.*1729–30

7. *Miss Wood, with a Dog in a*
Landscape, oil on canvas, *c.*1735

8. *George II and Family, in a Park*, oil on canvas sketch, *c.*1732–3
The sitters in this proposed royal conversation piece are (left to right) Prince
William Augustus, Duke of Cumberland, George II and Queen Caroline
(seated), princesses Louisa (with spaniel pup) and Mary, and their elder siblings
(standing) Amelia, Anne (the Princess Royal, the oranges on the table symbolic
of her impending marriage), Caroline and Frederick Louis, Prince of Wales.

9. *The Good Samaritan*, oil on canvas, 1736–7
The composition brings together several moments in the parable: the priest
and Levite have already passed their injured compatriot without helping him.
This is left to the Samaritan, who disregards the traditional enmity between his
countrymen and the Jewish people to show kindness and practical assistance.

10. *The Pool of Bethesda*, oil on canvas, 1736

To the immediate right of Christ's extended hand, a mother with her sick
baby (suffering from rickets) is being blocked by a guard. This detail may be an
indication of where Hogarth's charitable instincts would soon be focused.

11. *Captain Thomas Coram*, oil on canvas, 1740

28. *Beer Street*, etching and engraving, February 1751
Two female fish sellers are among those gathered. The spire
of the royal church, St Martin-in-the-Fields, displays a flag,
indicating it is 30 October, George II's birthday.

Beer, happy Produce of our Isle
Can sinewy Strength impart,
And wearied with Fatigue and Toil
Can chear each manly Heart

Labour and Art upheld by Thee

Successfully advance,
We quaff Thy balmy Juice with Glee
And Water leave to France.

Genius of Health, thy grateful Taste
Rivals the Cup of Jove,
And warms each English generous Breast
With Liberty and Love.

Beer was also drunk undiluted: Ben Franklin, as already noted, was flabbergasted by the amount of strong beer consumed by his fellow printers only a few years before *The Peregrination*.

Ebenezer Forrest observes that they were later informed that 'The Dover Castle' tavern was 'an Evil House' – no explanation is offered as to why. Perhaps the effects of consuming three beer pots each was devilry enough and the idea of 'Evil', or temptation, is another quirky nod to *The Pilgrim's Progress*. Having succumbed, and thus full of vim and vigour, they set off again. As they traipsed through the landscape, via Chalk, Shorne and 'Gadshill', where Falstaff commits robbery at the start of *Henry IV, Part 1*, Samuel Scott became irritable after getting bogged down in wet clay, the result of the recent downpour. During the journey others would suffer some mild misfortune, but Scott does seem to have been the most accident prone. If a possession was lost, an incident occurred or some other calamity befell them, it was usually Sam who was at the sharp end of it. But despite this, the countryside was sufficiently pleasant for his good humour to return swiftly and a contented equilibrium within the group to be restored. Besides, in the near distance, bathed splendidly in the morning light, the pilgrims could see, with some relief, their destination.

Crossing the bridge over the Medway, with a view of the imposing castle and just behind it the cathedral's distinctive tower and short steeple, they arrived at the famous city of Rochester, on the river's south bank, just as the clocks struck ten and took up temporary residence at the Crown Tavern located near the bridge.

Rochester sits at a strategic point on the river Medway. The cathedral later was made famous by Charles Dickens's *Mystery of*

Edwin Drood, but in 1732 the city was better known for its former bishop, Francis Atterbury, a staunch Tory and Jacobite. In November 1721, stirred by the social and financial chaos in the wake of the South Sea Bubble, a Jacobite plot was hatched which Atterbury cheerfully joined, along with other Tories who were fearful of the increasing dominance of the Whigs under Sir Robert Walpole.[21] The Tories had much to be fearful about, as they would be effectively in the political wilderness for decades. George I and II both feared Tory support for the exiled Stuarts, their anxiety stoked by Walpole. Although true to an extent, it was also a self-fulfilling prophecy. For this situation, with no hope of ending the dominance of Walpole and his cronies (as Atterbury and his colleagues would see it), simply increased Tory desperation and was therefore a breeding ground for Jacobitism. The plot, named after Atterbury, collapsed (as many had before and since), and arrests were made. Despite a spirited defence in parliament, the bishop was found guilty in the House of Lords, not of treason (which would have required the death penalty) but a fate some would consider worse – convicted under a bill of pains and penalties. He was stripped of all preferments and then sent into perpetual exile. Atterbury found himself at the Jacobite court in Rome, but, uneasy with its Catholicism, he left for Paris, where he died a broken man on 22 February 1732.

Hogarth himself inclined towards the Whigs, who were supported in parliament by his father-in-law. Equally, he was certainly no admirer of rigid hierarchies or a 'natural order', so would have made an unlikely Tory or Jacobite sympathiser. Hogarth rarely engaged directly with party politics – there are no heroes in *The Humours of an Election*, while his one foray in the early 1760s ended in personal disaster. That said, idiots, charlatans and self-serving blaggards, of whatever political or religious stripe, were not to be countenanced, and Hogarth would dole out chastisement to either side if he thought it was merited.

Rochester's castle keep is of Norman vintage, originally built in 1127, and even in its ruined state stands one hundred and thirteen feet in height. The pilgrims considered it 'well worth Observing' and 'a Very High Building ... strong Built But almost Demolish'd'.

They decided to scale the keep and 'With some Difficulty wee Ascended to the Top of the Battlements and took a Veiw of a Beautifull Country a Fine River and Some of the Noblest Shipps in the World.'[22] 'Difficulty', usually stressed with a capital 'D', is a description used more than once on the pilgrimage, offering a connection to 'Hill – Difficulty' in *The Pilgrim's Progress*. Ebenezer Forrest's last observation must refer to the nearby Royal Dockyard at Chatham, to which the group would venture later on that same day. Daniel Defoe was less impressed by Rochester, observing that 'There's little remarkable in *Rochester*, except the Ruins of a very old Castle, and an antient, but not extraordinary Cathedral', yet, like the pilgrims, he is impressed by 'the River, and its Appendices', which 'are the most considerable of the kind in the World'.[23] Such comments are both a personal opinion and a reflection of what was deemed of value more broadly in the early eighteenth century. It is fair to say that medieval ruins were of little interest to the vast majority of Britons, although fascinating to antiquaries: it is Rochester's castle that appears alongside 'Some Body' in Hogarth's drawing.[24] After their precarious clamber to the top of the castle battlements and admiring the spectacular views across the surrounding countryside, they watched a young boy scamper down 'a Very Curious Well' carved out of an inner wall, from top to foundations as they supposed, using small holes cut into the side, and then return just as swiftly via the same route to where they were all waiting. He was clutching a 'Young Daw' or jackdaw (in Old English 'dawe'), which he had stolen from a nest located in the bowels of the castle.[25] To the naturally pessimistic at the time this might have appeared a portent of death.

After admiring the lad's bravery (or foolhardiness) and nimble climbing skills, the travellers picked their way back down to ground level, via a more regular route, and then wandered along the city's high street, noting the Town House and, in particular, Watt's Hospital.[26] The latter was a charity, the building still extant, established with a legacy left by Richard Watts (*c.*1529–79), a naval administrator, formerly of West Peckham, Kent, and owner of nearby Satis House on Bolly Hill. During the early reign of Queen Elizabeth, Watts was an accounting officer for the new works at Upnor Castle nearby (a stopping-off point for our pilgrims) and the creation of a blockhouse 'for the savegarde of our Navy'.[27] Watts also sat in parliament as the member for Rochester, and was host to the queen during her progress of Surrey and Kent in 1573. Legend has it that in response to her host's apology for the modest nature of Her Majesty's billet, Elizabeth simply declared 'Satis!', 'Enough!', and the house was thus renamed.[28] In his will, through the sale of Satis House, its contents and the adjoining orchards and gardens, Watts made provision for a new charity, a hospital or refuge, in Ebenezer Forrest's words, 'for Releif of Six Travelling Persons by Entertaining them with one Nights Lodging and giving to each four pence in the Morning, Provided' that is 'they are Not Persons Contagiously Diseased, Rogues or', worst of all, 'proctors'.[29] The offending proctors, a term with a variety of meanings, is here likely to refer to men who collected alms (donations) on behalf of those barred from begging themselves, such as lepers.[30] In addition to the six travellers, who only rested there one night, the charity was the residence of six poor locals, whose role was to maintain the rooms, each with a bed and mattress and other unspecified but termed good-quality furniture, and who welcomed the travellers, allowing them some warmth from a fire if requested.[31]

On the other side of the bridge, at 'Stroud' or Strood, where the company would venture the following morning, was a work-house for the poor founded in 1671, very much inspired by Watt's Hospital and the recipient of a portion of that worthy gentle-man's largesse as decreed by the administrators of Watt's request. The purpose of the charity was written on an inscription above the door, which read 'in which the Sick and Aged are taken care of; ye Ignorant instructed, Such as are Able to Work Imployed, & a Comfortable. Maintenance Provided for All', finishing with the motto 'Go and do Thou Likewise', Christ's exhortation at the end of the parable of the Good Samaritan and quoted (in Latin) at the beginning of Ebenezer's manuscript. The parable's message, in short, was 'Love thy Neighbour' for, as the proverb tells us, 'He that despiseth his neighbour, sinneth: but he that hath mercy on the poor, happy *is* he.'[32]

CHAPTER FOUR

HISTORY MAKER

Later in life, Hogarth recalled that 'the puffing in books about the grand stile of history painting put him upon trying how that might take'.[1] This statement may seem straightforward enough, but in attempting to encourage the commissioning of history painting in Britain, Hogarth was challenging, head on, several fundamental issues. The hierarchy of genres, with its explicit relative values, had existed little changed in principle for centuries, and was essentially codified by the Académie royale de peintre et de sculpture in Paris under its director, the history painter Charles Le Brun (director 1663–90). As the academician André Félibien observed, although requiring skill, 'one who can only draw Portraits, has not as yet attained to this high Perfection of Art, and cannot pretend to the same Honour with abler Painters'. To achieve this the artist must move from painting one figure to several, but more important still 'he must paint History and Fable; he must represent great Actions like an Historian, or agreeable ones as the Poets. And soaring yet higher, he must by allegorical Compositions, know how to hide under the Vail of Fable the Virtues of great Men, and the most sublime Mysteries. He is esteemed a great Painter who acquits himself well in Enterprizes of this Kind. 'Tis in this that the Force, the Sublime and Grandeur of the Art consists.'[2]

The high status or 'puffing' enjoyed by history painting, here writ large, unquestioned – almost – within artist and connoisseur circles, placed British artists at a distinct disadvantage. Put simply, as Hogarth himself admits, religion had been traditionally 'the great promoter of this stile in other countries', yet England had 'rejected it'.[3] In reality, 'religion' meant the Roman Catholic Church. Here, a desire to express the glory of God and, it should be said, Roman Catholicism itself – made more urgent after the Protestant Reformation – was through grand building, decorative schemes, free-standing sculpture and painting, which kept architects, artists and artisans very gainfully employed. England and Scotland in the sixteenth century had embraced Protestant Christianity as the state religion, but its patronage of the arts was on nowhere near the scale of the Catholic Church – such expenditure, alongside the creation of 'graven' images having been one impetus for reformation. Artists had therefore to turn to the aristocracy and monarchy to provide a demand.

In Britain this source of patronage was patchy to say the least, unlike France, where the arts not only had the support of the Catholic Church, but had been formally mobilised through royal academies and manufactures (run centrally by the Bâtiments du Roi). These were tasked with expressing the power and magnificence of the French state, effectively the monarchy, with the palace of Versailles, where king, court and government resided, the greatest example. No doubt British artists turned envious eyes towards the high status and regular employment enjoyed by their cousins across the Channel. There was some consolation, however, in the thought that Frenchmen, whether artists or not, had traded their liberty, rights and independence in an unequal exchange with the state – a popular notion that will become an increasingly prominent feature of Hogarth's art. And the prospect, looking back over the Channel towards London, was not an unpleasant one either. The freedoms that artists enjoyed, in a lively contemporary art market unshackled from the state, coupled with enthusiasm for all things new and/or foreign were very attractive indeed. In short, there were opportunities for foreign-born artists to make money and, as a result, London was a magnet for them.

The Académie royale in Paris and the equivalent systems in Italy, as elsewhere, provided training as well as opportunity, and this was another key difference with Great Britain. There was no formal state training for British artists, and even the guild/apprenticeship system, under the aegis of the Worshipful Company of Painter-Stainers, which had, to a degree, nurtured Sir James Thornhill's career, was, even by the early eighteenth century, fast losing significance. Even so, the Church of England, the monarchy and aristocracy, with their vast buildings and wealth (relative to a majority of the population), provided vital, if limited, platforms for creating and sustaining certain types of art, notably grand history painting schemes, such as those at St Paul's Cathedral, Greenwich and Chatsworth. But Sir James Thornhill and even William Kent aside, this meant, inevitably, that those artists who had the training and experience – particularly French and Italian artists – were best placed to scoop up the few commissions that came along. The particular situation at St Paul's had worked in Thornhill's favour, but in practice, little had changed by the time Hogarth was contemplating his move into history painting. To succeed with so much stacked against him took resilience, boldness and luck. Thornhill had led the way, his abiding legacy to the next generation.

The commissioning of artwork to embellish the offices of organisations like the British East India Company was one potential outlet for British artists. Another was the boom in redeveloping and establishing civic and charitable buildings including hospitals. The significant improvement scheme at St Bartholomew's Hospital, under the supervision of James Gibbs, and specifically the completion of the new administration block in 1732, opened up another precious opportunity for artists. The block contained a sequence of interiors – ante-rooms, a grand stair leading to a Great Hall – intended as semi-public spaces where the charity presented itself to visitors, as well as existing and potential donors in stone, brick and mortar. Built into the design, therefore, was some form of decorative scheme that would promote the work and beneficiaries of the hospital in scale, quality and, just as important, with an appropriate theme. Rumours began circulating that the Venetian and rival to Thornhill, Giacomo Amigoni, had been offered the commission. Arriving in around 1729–30, this was precisely the type of work that Giacomo had ventured to London to secure. Once again, it seemed the self-fulfilling prophecy would whirr into action.

Hogarth veered between on the one hand simply wanting a level playing field, to, on the other, expecting preferential treatment. After all, he would argue, not only were these commissions as rare as hen's teeth, but no one was vying with Italian artists in their native Italy. So why should British artists suffer unfair treatment on their home turf? And then there was the personal element: Thornhill's 'mortification' at Moor Park only a few years before, when Amigoni had replaced Sir James as part of Styles's humiliation of the English painter. The Venetian had literally, figuratively and symbolically expunged Thornhill from the house he had himself designed. That this was the artist being mooted for St Bartholomew's was unthinkable. And Amigoni had already been commissioned to paint a scene for John Rich's new Covent Garden theatre – Shakespeare being presented to Apollo – a commission Hogarth would surely have coveted for himself.[4]

Again Hogarth's attitude, so often characterised as a straightforward example of xenophobia, is revealed to be highly complex. An anti-foreigner stance is certainly there, and he would not have been unusual in this at the time. But so too is loyalty to his father-in-law's memory, which in turn has a self-reflective quality, coupled with a sizeable dollop of self-interest. To point to any one reason in particular is fundamentally to miss the point. What happened next must have occurred with the assistance of the hospital's resident architect, James Gibbs. Gibbs had collaborated with artists who would figure in Hogarth's plans in the near future, notably the sculptor John Michael Rysbrack, and with Sir James Thornhill at Canons, near Edgware (1716–20) for James Brydges, first duke of Chandos and, of course, Wimpole Hall. As noted Thornhill's *A Hue and Cry* celebrated this project, where Gibbs is described as 'Gibbesius ... a man of great Fame'.[5]

Gibbs's first public building, St Mary-le-Strand, was consecrated at the turn of 1723 and 1724, he designed the Radcliffe Camera in Oxford and then won the commission to rebuild the royal parish church of St Martin-in-the-Fields, still one of the most distinctive features on what is now Trafalgar Square and a building Hogarth knew intimately. Of this beautiful church, consecrated in 1726, the antiquary and fellow Scot Alexander Gordon declared if 'such Buildings as the great Artist Mr. Gibbs has adorn'd London with, continues to be carried on, very few Cities in Europe ... will contend with it for Magnificence'.[6]

Gibbs had become a governor of St Bartholomew's Hospital in April 1723, after which he proposed four buildings for the redevelopment of the hospital site, providing his designs and time free of charge. The North Wing, the administration block containing the court or 'board' room, Great Hall and staircase was completed nine years later. It was certainly with the encouragement of James Gibbs that the following announcement could be made in the *General Evening Post*, in July 1735: 'Mr. Hogarth is going to make a Present of the Painting of a Stair-Case at St. Bartholomew's Hospital, of which, he was lately chosen a Governor.'[7]

This announcement occurred just a few months after the death of Hogarth's mother. No doubt a grand, ambitious scheme was exactly what Hogarth needed, with his mother's untimely death and in such horrific circumstances, and the ongoing battle with plagiarists. Hogarth threw himself into this project with gusto – despite his instinctively suspicious nature, he does seem to have been a genuine optimist, or, at least certain that his drive and ambition could win over his detractors and that he could establish himself as a versatile genius, an artist of variety, like his great mentor, Sir James Thornhill. Remember, Hogarth recalled Greenwich and St Paul's Cathedral together as his guide, his talisman, whilst labouring over engraving on silver. It was these great schemes that propelled him forward. How much more so, was in forming a close bond with the architect who had worked with Sir James, as if the son-in-law was now emulating the father, taking on his mantle. The courage shown in his paintings at St Bartholomew's Hospital would, as ever, bring him applause and vitriol in equal measure. But the guiding spirit behind them was Thornhill.

The apparent appointment of Amigoni was a significant obstacle, but in the governors' defence, the greatest British practitioner capable of such a scheme, Thornhill, had just died, and Hogarth had displayed no interest whatsoever in doing anything in the grand interior style. Rather, he was the famous creator of modern scenes such as *A Harlot's Progress*, with a line in small group portraits and satirical prints. Where Hogarth differed from most of his compatriots – and where he lives up to Thornhill's example – is that he did not simply complain from the sidelines, but rolled up his sleeves and, in dramatic style, did something about it. In this instance he placed the hospital governors in a difficult position, considering their overtures to Amigoni, by offering to do the commission gratis, as James Gibbs had done as resident architect. No charity can be seen to be wilfully diverting funds away from its core purpose. And in the event Hogarth delivered on his promise and the faith that the governors – grudgingly or not – had put in him.

Yet this was a risk on both sides. Hogarth had no experience of history painting, beyond small single canvases such as *Falstaff and his Recruits* or *The Scene from the Tempest* or *Satan, Sin and Death* (Private Collection; National Trust; Tate). The progresses were narrative paintings, but of contemporary subjects and of a different order to that required in traditional history painting. He had, however, viewed and analysed examples by others, including Thornhill, of painting on this scale and in this genre. Even so, as Hogarth recalls gleefully, he received the commission 'without haveing a stroke of this grand business before'. His notes continue with the boast, a fair one given the amazing aspiration and confidence it demonstrates, 'imediatly from family picture[s] in smal he painted a great stair case at Bartholomews Hospital'.[8] The first scene was *The Pool of Bethesda*, an example of Christ's miracles, specifically where he bids a paralysed man to have faith, rise up and walk. The second was the parable *The Good Samaritan*, a story told by Jesus with a moral purpose, wholly suitable as a demonstration of fellow-feeling and practical help (Col. Figs 9 & 10). It is worth dwelling on the style of the parables. Here, in 'The Good Samaritan', Jesus tells the story in response to a question, Who is my neighbour?, and rather than answering the question directly, having told the story, he offers the question back to the original questioner. The latter, having followed Jesus's philosophical journey, responds by saying, 'He who showed mercy on him', that is, the Samaritan who showed kindness towards a man, a stranger, lying robbed, beaten and left for dead on the road. Jesus responds, 'Go and do thou likewise.'[9] The celebrated fables of Aesop follow a similar process, as indeed do Hogarth's modern moral subjects. In their own particular way Hogarth's creations have a parabolic quality, teaching through storytelling. We are presented with a

Sketch for the Harlots Progress
but never engraved

29. *Operation Scene in a Hospital*, graphite and red chalk on cream paper, undated
This scene with physicians treating a patient, who may have an ulcerated
leg, is thought to be an unused design for *A Harlot's Progress*.

scenario or story, and it is for us to ponder the moral whys and
wherefores and arrive, ourselves, at an answer. Understandably,
given the limited evidence to the contrary from Hogarth's own
writings, his motivation can appear to be restricted, almost exclusively, to a burning desire for artistic, commercial and reputational
success, rather than springing from any sense of humanity, or spiritual, even religious conviction. Yet, in addition to absorbing his
father's strong moral code, and following Hogarth's own urging to
use our eyes, there is the evidence of the images themselves.

Hogarth continues his recollection, with evident amazement
at his own success, that the figures in these paintings were '7 foot
high', that is larger than life and, because of 'the pother [*sic*] made
about the grand stile', he 'thought might serve as a specimen to shew

that were there any inclination in England for Historical painting such a first essay whould Proove it more easily attainable than is imagined'.[10] And this ease, with his own idiosyncratic approach to process at its core, meant a laborious, continental-style training was not necessary, thus levelling the playing field for all British artists with a fancy to have a try. The commission was completed over several years, with *The Pool of Bethesda* the first to be unveiled. As so often with Hogarth's surprising changes of direction, as he himself argued, he rose to the challenge both for personal ambition and, as crucially, for the betterment of his fellow artists, in this instance British artists, and for the dignity and appreciation of art in general within Great Britain.

In addition to all the reasons listed above, there was another very personal impetus for the commission to come to him, at whatever cost – whether time, money or, potentially, reputation. St Bartholomew's Hospital was, after all, the very institution in whose shade he had first drawn breath. And any joyful childhood memories of the area would be tempered by the sadness and anger, possibly a lingering sense of humiliation, at his father's treatment at the hands of local publishers, alongside Richard's imprisonment nearby, the family's ensuing hardships and William's lost decade: personal ghosts that required exorcising. Hogarth's offer, a donation in kind, was accepted and, in honour of his generosity, this local-boy-made-good was duly elected a governor, one of the hospital's volunteer managers (much like a trustee) on 25 July 1734. Another possibility is that he wrangled the governorship in order to guarantee his offer would be accepted.[11] In fact an announcement, written once more by James Ralph (who seems to have been something of a cheerleader), had already appeared in the *Weekly Register* on 23 February 1734, no doubt with Hogarth's encouragement, to avoid any last-minute wobbles from the governors regarding their decision: 'We hear that the ingenious Mr. *Hogarth*, is to paint the Great Stair-Case in St. *Bartholomew's-Hospital*.'[12]

This circumstance may have been an additional motivation for Hogarth's re-establishment in 1735 as co-manager, with his friend John Ellys (now a successful portrait painter) of the St Martin's Lane Academy at Peter's Court, using the equipment left to him by his father-in-law.[13] Certainly there are academy-style life drawings by Hogarth that relate directly to 'Bethesda', notably a female nude (Royal Collection), echoed in the figure of the wealthy woman being carried to the pool by her servants to the right of the central Christ grouping. In the finished painting her knee is inflamed and she has visible patches of ulceration, suggesting a sufferer from syphilitic arthritis due, we can presume, to promiscuity.[14] This seems to have led to the following anecdotal information connected to this figure and recalled by John Nichols: 'I am assured by an old acquaintance of Mr. *Hogarth*, is a faithful portrait of *Nell Robinson*, a celebrated courtezan, with whom, in early life, they had both been intimately acquainted.'[15] One recent biographer of Hogarth, Ronald Paulson, identifies the 'old acquaintance' as Ebenezer Forrest.[16] The intimacy, or friendship, may have sprung from Nell being one of the regular life-class models at the first St Martin's Lane Academy under Louis Chéron and John Vanderbank, which (unusually) hired both women and men for the purpose. This would indeed support the assertion that Hogarth, and therefore Forrest, knew Nell 'in early life'. Alternatively, the courtesan, whether Nell or another, may have been a model at Hogarth's establishment, which also promoted itself as a place where both male and female models were hired, although in 1735 Hogarth, aged thirty-seven, could hardly be described as a young man.[17]

No matter how extraordinary the opportunity, and the determination with which he pursued it, there must have been moments when Hogarth paused and wondered whether it would be worthwhile. He had produced oil sketches, to show the governors the scenes he intended to depict and how.[18] But despite preparation, the task ahead was enormous. The area within the administration block that he was to decorate was the grand staircase, the first and last key space into and out from the Great Hall. It was high profile enough for his success or failure to be weighed in the balance in as public a manner as was possible. Given the challenge and the recent loss of his natural mentor for such a project, the help and encouragement of another, preferably with experience of painting on such a scale, would be crucial. The medium was oil on canvas, but the magnitude was far beyond anything he, or many others for that matter, had attempted – 'Bethesda' is thirteen feet six inches by twenty feet, and *The Good Samaritan* sixteen feet six inches by thirteen feet six inches. It is generally assumed, a reasonable assumption in the circumstances, that Hogarth painted the majority of the composition off site, to then finish in situ, on a scaffold, once the canvas was stretched and fixed over a wooden frame. The most obvious place for offsite painting of this type was a scene-painting room at a theatre. The skills and experience of the landscape artist, scene painter and Hogarth's close friend, George Lambert, would have been extremely useful and, luckily for Hogarth, Lambert had recently taken up residence in such a studio space, the loft of the Covent Garden theatre, built on the proceeds of *The Beggar's Opera* which had opened on 16 December 1732.

In fact, both canvases have the appearance of elaborate staging, particularly 'Bethesda', with the events around the pool itself enveloped by the ornate sweep of the arched colonnade to the rear and the scroll work forming wings and a proscenium. Unsurprisingly, there are references to Lambert not just providing work space, but assisting Hogarth in *The Good Samaritan*, where, according to John Nichols, '*Hogarth* paid his friend *Lambert* for painting the landscape in this picture'.[19] Hogarth was clearly a great admirer of Lambert's skill, and was ever keen to promote his friends. When referring to the beauty of graduating colour in *The Analysis of Beauty*, using the example in nature of the rising or setting of the sun, Hogarth observed that the translation into paint was the revered French seventeenth-century artist, Claude Lorrain's, 'peculiar excellence' and, among modern masters, 'is now Mr. Lambert's'.[20]

Lambert, a few years younger than Hogarth, lived in a house on the Great Piazza, Covent Garden, a minute's stroll from Rich's new theatre.[21] He was named as an executor in John Thornhill's will, was a signatory of Hogarth's copyright bill of 1735, had taught Theodosius Forrest, Ebenezer's only child, to paint and, like Hogarth and Scott, was a freemason.[22] Lambert shifted between scene painting and landscape, in the latter viewed as in the style of John Wootton,

30. *A Rake's Progress Plate 8: The Madhouse*, etching and engraving, 1735
Among Tom's fellow inmates are (left to right) a man who
acts like an ecstatic saint, another trying to calculate longitude
on the wall and, in the middle cell, a mock king.

an older artist who also collaborated with Hogarth on outdoor
portraits. By December 1726 he was on the payroll of the Lincoln's
Inn Theatre – it is therefore possible that Lambert had worked on
the set of *The Beggar's Opera* – and then moved to the new Theatre
Royal, Covent Garden, with John Rich. From 1740 he was paid a
tidy £100 per year for his services. Lambert was also involved with
Hogarth's new venture, the St Martin's Lane Academy.

Adjoining the academy was Slaughter's Coffee House, a place
of resort for artists and their friends. Several anecdotes point to
Hogarth being a regular prior to 1735, at just the moment he was
contemplating the St Bartholomew's project and working on *A
Rake's Progress*. One such story concerns the circumstances around
a satirical image of Jonathan Richardson and his son, also Jonathan.

Joseph Highmore was a regular at Slaughter's too, and recounted the story to his grandson. Artists and their associates met at the coffee house twice a week to partake of a rummer or two and share any work in progress. The Richardsons, father and son, were composing what was to become *Explanatory Notes on Paradise Lost* (published in 1734), and Jonathan senior would bring segments of the draft to read out to the assembled group. Old Richardson, like Hogarth, had been apprenticed against his will to a scrivener (or notary) and recalled, echoing Hogarth, that he was 'put into a wrong Path at ye first setting out'. Again, in a statement curiously close to Hogarth's own autobiographical notes, Richardson would observe that 'Those first Years of my Life were in a manner lost to me, & I began to learn [painting] when it was almost time to live by a Profession.'[23] When at last free, he trained with John Riley, a London-born painter and then established himself as a portraitist. There was much in the older man's life with which Hogarth could empathise and sympathise.[24] However, Richardson was the greatest admirer of his son's abilities, who was brought up as a gentleman, with learning in modern and ancient languages and a sizeable inheritance. It was young Richardson rather than his father who swanned around Europe in 1716 and then 1720 (while Hogarth was labouring through and just emerging from his apprenticeship), collecting information and forming opinions on the art he saw there. This was the research required for the production of some of the most important books on art published in English in the eighteenth century, including *An Account of Some of the Statues, Bas-Reliefs, drawings, and Pictures in Italy* (1722), and, although attempting to elevate art and art appreciation, something Hogarth would have applauded, the father and son assisted in promoting Italian art, and particularly the work of Raphael, almost to the exclusion of any other country.

For these reasons alone Hogarth would have found Old Richardson's company, at times, irritating. But Richardson was also an avid collector, a connoisseur, of 'Old Master' drawings, including those by Salvator Rosa, Rubens, Rembrandt, Van Dyck, Claude Lorrain and Ludovico Carracci, many now in the British Museum, to which he generously allowed fellow artists, including Hogarth, access. But he was forever talking about them. William Pyne recounted: 'The good old man, I've heard my uncle Zachary say, fancied every one equally far gone in the collecting mania; hence he sometimes interrupted better conversation, which made Hogarth impatient, and utter a thousand pishes and pshaws ; for "though he loved the man," as he used to say, "he hated the connoisseur".'[25] According to Pyne, Richardson would amble from tavern to tavern in order to read out his notes on Milton to any unsuspecting victim who had been hoping, in vain, for a quiet drink – from Slaughter's, to Button's and Will's, both in Russell Street, Covent Garden, to the Rainbow and Dick's near Temple to the east, and back again. One venue, however, was safe from his custom, for 'He would not put his foot on the threshold of the Devil', a tavern near Temple Bar and opposite St Dunstan-in-the-West on Fleet Street. Above the door hung a sign depicting the well-known legend connected to that saint, a keen blacksmith, who tricked the devil into having his hooves shod, so that everyone could hear the approach of the prince of darkness. This image Old Richardson considered profane and would not pass under it. On the subject of the artist, according to Pyne, Henry Fielding 'would run a furlong to escape him', no doubt to the sanctuary of the Devil, and nicknamed him 'Doctor Fidget'.[26]

So, at Slaughter's, as the story goes, with the artists gathered, Old Richardson produced a specimen of his imminent tome on Milton, declaring 'I know well enough my eye is no eye at all ; I must apply to my telescope ; my son is my telescope ; 'tis by his help I read the learned languages.' Hogarth simply could not let such a statement pass without a response, so reaching for an envelope in his pocket, as Highmore recalled, Hogarth sketched, on the reverse, the image of a seated Old Richardson, peering through a telescope protruding from young Richardson's arse – like the 'enema' the Lilliputians inflict on poor Lemuel Gulliver, as illustrated with relish by Hogarth in 1726 – while the younger man reads from Virgil's *Aeneid*.[27] The likeness was sufficiently good for it to cause much spluttering and guffawing among the company, as it was passed from man to man. Richardson, however, was visibly upset by it. He no doubt felt slights and ridicule as keenly as Hogarth, but, being a gentle man, did not lash out or rejoinder with a verbal or pictorial insult. To Hogarth's credit, according to Highmore, realising the subject's discomfort, he threw the offending image into the fire.[28] Yet the damage had been done – an example of an action of the moment, without due care or pausing for thought. Perhaps in recompense, Hogarth made sure he mentioned the older artist in *The Analysis of Beauty* as 'the ingenious Mr. Richardson', quoting his invention of the term '*the art of seeing*' from 'his treatise on painting'.[29]

Even as the gatherings at Slaughter's continued, Lambert and Hogarth established another more exclusive club. The Beefsteak Club, or to give its full title, 'The Sublime Society of Beef Steaks', was formally constituted at the turn of 1735 and 1736, under the patronage of John Rich, with the founding members Lambert, Hogarth, Ebenezer Forrest, Gabriel Hunt, John Thornhill, Will Tothall and Richard Mitchell all associated with the Bedford Arms tavern, the last its proprietor. Also a member was William Huggins and later the polemicist and politician John Wilkes (from 1754). The club met at two o'clock in the afternoon on Saturdays, from November to June, in the area of Covent Garden Theatre (so close to the Bedford Arms) known as the 'Thunder and Lightning'. The presidency rotated and the incumbent paid for the beef, which was grilled in a no-frills fashion on a stove. It is said that the idea came from Lambert cooking himself this simple meal while he was working late, and then sharing the steak with visitors. He considered himself such a dab hand that he even challenged the fiery tempered cook at Slaughter's to a duel by steak and gridiron, witnessed by Hogarth, Henry Fielding and others, which the cook, known as 'Grecian' (no one knows why) narrowly won.[30] Various rituals were associated with the Beefsteak Club meetings, many nonsensical and some suggesting a parodying of other fraternities, notably the freemasons. There was, for example, a regular prize for the best 'catch' – an unaccompanied song for several voices, sung as a round and with the words, when sung in this way, forming a comical pun.[31] 'Beef and Liberty' was the motto, with the gridiron on which the steak was cooked standing as the emblem and mascot. On a more serious note, the club members were instrumental in supporting Hogarth's copyright bill.[32]

In 1736, a year after the original announcement regarding Hogarth's commission at St Bartholomew's Hospital, the *London Evening Post* reported that 'The ingenious Mr. Hogarth, one of the Governors of St. Bartholomew's, has presented to the said Hospital a very fine Piece of Painting, representing the Miracle wrought by our Saviour at the Pool of Bethesda, which was hung up in their great Stair-case last Wednesday [7 April]. The same Gentleman is preparing another Piece, representing the Story of the Good Samaritan, which he intends to present to the said Hospital.' Hogarth may have been receiving accolades in public from apparently independent authors such as James Ralph, but in private there were grumbles among his fellow artists, as revealed by George Vertue's personal journal. Vertue noted that, in his opinion, the report was produced by Hogarth, and the use of 'Ingenious', a 'new public Title', was applied to the painter by himself. He declared Hogarth's genius thus far was for conversations and 'caricatures', yet now he promotes himself as a history painter, a presumption Vertue describes as 'a noble artifice'. In fact Vertue sees Hogarth's great strength as being 'a happy – natural talent a la mode', but he is also 'a Scheemist' coupled with 'a good Front', in sum, as it were, an 'all mouth and breeches' intriguer and self-promoter without the substance to deliver. There is an element of incredulity and 'How dare he!' in Vertue's tone. He concluded by damning with faint praise, 'but as to this great work of painting it is by every one judged to be more than coud be expected of him'.[33] This condescending attitude has persisted to the present, but Hogarth's spectacular paintings require no special pleading.

Any negative criticism can be explained by Hogarth's treatment of the subject: a disconcerting mix of the traditional and his own idiosyncratic style. 'The Pool of Bethesda' narrative comes from the Gospel of St John (5:2–8), and offers an example of generosity and compassion to be copied by the visitors to the hospital. The figure of Jesus is elegantly poised, with the graceful downward gesture of his outstretched left hand – indicating towards the main central figure, the paralysed man, now rising – isolated at the very centre of the entire composition. This, therefore, is the focus, fellow feeling, the hand of love, friendship and succour. Jesus's posture, the right fist on his hip, almost impersonates the regal pose of Charles I in a full-length portrait by Sir Anthony van Dyck, which was the king's official state portrait and well known through engraving.[34] In fact, curiously, Christ does have a look of the saintly martyr monarch – the long curling natural hair, the trim pointed beard, the decidedly aristocratic, delicate pale face. This establishes a suitable contrast between the King of Kings and his people about him, every one of them suffering from a debilitating disease or condition – from jaundice and blindness, to gout, venereal disease and anaemia. It is this raw depiction of actual people with visible medical complaints, bringing the elevated genre down into the realm of the all-too-human, which jarred with many traditionalists.

This natural depiction – truth to nature – within the elevated genre of history painting continues in *The Good Samaritan*. The Samaritan shows concern, a furrowed brow, as he pours balm into the wounds of the victim of robbery. The latter is deathly pale, staring blankly, one hand clenched. (The hound to the left is licking the bleeding wound on its own leg.) Yet both figures are beautifully rendered, with dignity. The figure in the mid distance, a Levite who has ignored the victim, is also blithely disregarding the man kneeling and prostrate at his feet. The landscape is rugged and barren, a blasted tree offers some hope, with a tiny new shoot springing from it. Above are clouds and a piercing blue sky – the colour Hogarth would use in *The March to Finchley* and *The Humours of an Election*.

Hogarth's 'first essay' attracted attention among his fellow artists, and there was clearly, as Hogarth had hoped, an 'inclination in England for Historical painting'. Joseph Highmore ventured to St Bartholomew's – or may have seen the canvas at Covent Garden – but in any case sketched the central group of Samaritan, wounded man, horse and dog as a preparation for his own version of the New Testament story.[35]

These two paintings can still make for difficult viewing. The grotesque can so easily become comic, and rather than encouraging charitable thoughts, simply makes the viewer recoil or even laugh. Horace Walpole, writing after Hogarth's death, declared 'the burlesque turn of our Artist's mind mixed itself with his most serious compositions ; and that, in The Pool of Bethesda, a servant of a rich ulcerated lady, beats back a poor man who sought the same celestial remedy'. This is written as an implied criticism. John Nichols and George Steevens go further: 'the figure of the Priest, in The Good Samaritan, is supremely comic, and rather resembles some purse-proud Burgomaster, than the character it was designed to represent'.[36] But, as often was the case, such commentators simply highlight their own very conventional taste. The combining of the elegant with the grotesque is precisely why Hogarth's work challenges, jars even – if your idea of perfection is Laguerre, Chéron and even Thornhill – and why he is so innovative and unusual. It is this combination that sets him and his paintings apart: a refusal to see humour or the repugnant as separate from the great highs as well as the lows of human experience.

Crucially, the very people who rely on the charity of the donors are here brought into their presence, or perhaps, more accurately, the other way around – challenging complacency and snobbery, even as they appeal for money. But then, that is the reality: those suffering, those in pain, are rarely, in truth, aesthetically appealing, but they lie at the very heart of what the hospital exists to do. As these good people, donors and potential donors, enter the building via the elegant piazza, their first glimpse of Hogarth's work is of the gigantic figures of the Good Samaritan and wounded man looming above. They then process up the first flight of stairs to the half landing, passing below the Good Samaritan to the left, while facing Christ before them; then, from the half landing they turn to the right and walk under the Pool, past Christ's sandaled feet, only to turn to their right again, and up the last flight of stairs in parallel with the Good Samaritan. Here they might pause to look, leaning a hand against the balustrade's rail, and then continue on, arriving at the top and turning right one last time, where the full image of Christ and those who have come to be healed are finally laid out before them.[37] And here we might recall Hogarth's descriptions of the beggar in *The Analysis of Beauty*, who had been beaten to make him more appealing, or the man at the Highgate tavern, as witnessed by Hogarth and his fellow apprentices, who had been hit over the head with a bottle – his face contorted into a grimace. Hogarth observed all this and brought them into his art – whether sprawled on the rancid cobbles of *Gin Lane* or gathered around Bethesda's pool. Hogarth was turning 'art' on its head. He was using his observations of real life, real disease, real suffering – in all its dirty, nasty, tragic reality. But did anyone want to see this? Would it encourage donations and support for the hospital? Here Christ's example is the key. He does not flinch, he does not avoid suffering. Rather, he extends his hand in encouragement, even while exhorting those looking on, as they pass on the stairs, to go and do the same.

In 1737, three years after Sir James' death, Hogarth felt compelled to defend Thornhill in print after reading a derogatory comment, attached to the notice of the tragic suicide of the French history painter François Lemoyne, which appeared in *The Daily Post*. Lemoyne had occupied a similar position to Thornhill within Louis XV's court, *Premier peintre du Roi*, and for several years had been working on a magnificent ceiling at the palace of Versailles on the subject of the 'Apotheosis of Hercules'. Joseph Highmore, during a trip to Paris in 1734, had chatted amiably to Lemoyne while the latter was standing on the scaffold working on the ceiling, and in his journal noted, 'I think him the ablest painter I have seen in all respects.'[38]

The reason for Lemoyne's dramatic suicide, by stabbing with a sword in his chest and throat, has never been explained satisfactorily. The death of his wife and professional pressures surely combined to place him under acute stress, although *The Daily Post* repeats the announcement from French sources, who are clear as to the cause: 'his Head was out of Order ever since the four Faults that were found by some rigid Criticks in that vast Work, which he had been four Years about'. So Lemoyne, justifiably sensitive to criticism and in an already vulnerable state personally, killed himself in his despair. Any artist, indeed human being, would be saddened by this report. But it was the snide editorial comment appended to it, totally unprovoked and unwarranted, that stirred Hogarth's righteous anger, as *The Daily Post* concludes, 'The Painter of the great Hall of Greenwich Hospital had much more Resolution ;

notwithstanding there are as many Faults as Figures in that Work he died a natural Death, tho' an Englishman.'[39]

Hogarth's response under the pseudonym 'Britophil', first published in the *St. James's Evening Post* and then repeated in *The London Magazine*, includes one of the most famous statements in British art history, and his ire has been used by art historians over the ages, as another example of inherent xenophobia coupled with an aggressive 'John Bull' nationalist and popularist agenda.[40] Yet his argument, at least at the commencement, is measured and difficult to challenge: 'Every good-natur'd Man, and Well-wisher to Arts in *England*, must feel a Kind of Resentment, at a very indecent Paragraph in the *Daily Post* of *Thursday* last, relating to the Death of Mons. *le Moine* [sic], first Painter to the *French* King ; in which, very unjust, as well as cruel Reflections are cast on the noblest Performance (in its Way) that *England* has to boast of ; I mean the Work of the late Sir *James Thornhill* in *Greenwich-Hall*.' In fact it is apparent that Hogarth is speaking specifically about England, which he sees as particular. The once independent nations of England and Scotland continued to maintain very distinct identities (now as then), and in 1737 the concept of 'Great Britain' was, still in its infancy, a fragile entity. Even so, the sense of being a Briton and Britishness is gradually gaining form – note Hogarth's use of 'Britophil' rather than 'Anglophil' – initially around issues of religion, trade, the armed forces and a common foreign enemy.

Hogarth opens by drawing attention, quite rightly, to the inappropriateness or indecency of using Lemoyne's suicide as an opportunity to attack Thornhill, himself unable to offer a defence. The editorial's inference, unjust and cruel, is that Thornhill had more reason to respond as his French counterpart had done, given the scale of his perceived errors. But, having less scruple or artistic pride, the editorial suggests, Sir James Thornhill died a natural death (although in reality an agonising one) rather than having the decency, or sense of honour, to end it by his own hand. The final insult, 'tho' an Englishman' returns to a familiar trope, that Thornhill only got the commission at Greenwich, or indeed St Paul's, because he was English, being less able than foreign painters, and that, in turn, his 'substandard' performance should be expected, *because* he is English.

This short paragraph succinctly presents much of what Hogarth considered desperately wrong with the domestic art market, where the odds were stacked against English contemporary art, not least by the continuing and extreme prejudice of certain art buyers and commentators. Having warmed to his familiar theme of attacking gullible, ignorant *milordi* as uncritical Grand Tourists, hoovering up second- and third-rate art simply because it is foreign, he trains his guns on self-serving, fraudulent art dealers: 'There is another Set of Gentry more noxious to the Art than these, and those are your *Picture-Jobbers from abroad*, who are always ready to raise a great Cry in the Prints, whenever they think their Craft is in Danger.' Indeed, he continues, 'it is their Interest to depreciate every *English* Work, as hurtful to their Trade, of continually importing Ship Loads of dead *Christs, Holy Families, Madon[n] a's*, and other dismal dark Subjects, neither entertaining nor ornamental', that is, particularly to a Protestant, neither use nor ornament, 'on which they scrawl the terrible cramp Names of some *Italian* Masters, and fix on us poor *Englishmen*, the Character of *Universal Dupes*'. Hogarth returned to this fixation on all things foreign, regardless of quality or, worse, exposing the unknowing and credulous to copies and fakes, in his *The Analysis of Beauty*, where he observes, referring to Samuel Butler, 'For ought I know, the emolument [compensation] may be equal between the *bubler* and the *bubled* : at least this seems to have been Butler's opinion : Doubtless the pleasure is as great/ In being cheated, as to cheat.'[41]

In a truism, familiar through the centuries, including to E. M. Forster's readership and beyond, admiration for all things foreign, in this instance Italian, did not necessarily extend to the people of that country. In his popular travel guide, *The Grand Tour* (published in 1749) the Irishman Thomas Nugent, regarding the character of the Italians, dares to summarise the traits of an entire peninsula, not yet a unified nation but a patchwork of duchies, kingdoms and republics, as a warning to the young gentleman tourist. Italians are, apparently, driven by jealousy without reason and revenge, suspicious, apt to rage, easily offended, masters of dissimulation,

in 'outward appearance they shew a great deal of civility and kindness, but their complaisance is frequently a mixture of flattery and
design. They are too much addicted to pleasure and idleness, and
extravagantly violent in their amours.' He concludes this warning
to vulnerable Britons with the observation that 'They have a great
contempt and aversion for foreigners whom they slightingly call
Oltramontani' – they who live beyond the mountains, presumably
the Alps – 'though we must except the English to whom they shew
much greater marks of respect than to other nations.'[42]

The reference to the greater marks of respect towards Englishmen may be a nod to a famous proverb, *'inglese italianato è un
diavolo incarnato'* ('an Italianate Englishman is a devil incarnate').
This Roger Ascham, author and tutor to the young Elizabeth
Tudor, declared, in criticism of his compatriots, 'the Italian saith
of the English Man ... that is to say, *"You remain Men in Shape
and Fashion, but become Devils in Life and Condition"*'.[43] Some
believe the proverb can be traced back to the violent antics of the
English mercenary or 'condottiero' Sir John Hawkwood, who was
born *c.*1320 in Essex, died 1394 in Florence and was honoured
in that city's duomo. Alternatively, the Italian hosts treated the
English with greater courtesy because their guests were wont to
spend lavishly, without discernment or restraint, and thus easily
diddled into buying indifferent examples of those 'Ship Loads of
dead *Christs*, *Holy Families*, *Madon[n]a's*, and other dismal dark
Subjects'. Worse still were the off-the-peg or, more accurately,
off-the-conveyor-belt modern Venetian scenes and Roman vistas
– from the brush of Giovanni Antonio Canal 'Canaletto', Giovanni Paolo Pannini or, more likely, their many imitators – that
Hogarth found so completely absurd and, from the perspective
of the livelihood of the embryonic native school, utterly infuriat-
ing. Any reasonable Briton, mercifully unblinded by the raptures
of connoisseurs and after touring a number of English country
houses, might agree with Hogarth: all festooned with the spoils
of the respective milord's Grand Tour, all, as a result, curiously and
relentlessly similar in content and appearance.

Hogarth was not unique in highlighting the slavish devo-
tion, as he would see it, of a tired artistic model that naturally

prejudiced the foreign over the native. James Ralph had written in *The Weekly Register* (24 November 1733), concerning the statue yards rammed with copies after the antique, 'sorry I am that they afford a judicious Foreigner such flagrant Opportunities to arraign and condemn our taste. Among a hundred Statues, you shall not see one even tolerable, either in Design or Execution: nay, even the Copies of the Antique are so monstrously wretched, that one can hardly guess at their Originals.' He does not blame the craftsmen for the shoddy workmanship and 'this Prostitution of so fine an Art', but rather the 'Ignorance and Folly' of the purchasers. Concluding, 'Hence Excellency is never thought of, and the Master, like the Highwayman in the *Beggar's Opera*, is happy when he has turn'd his *Lead* that is, his pistol's shot, 'into *Gold*.'[44]

Hogarth's attack is not on foreign artists directly, and his published and unpublished writings are littered with references to European artists he admires, whether old, modern or contemporary masters. He is, after all, a European – that is, from the European continent, with its common philosophical and cultural heritage – as well as a Briton, an Englishman and a Londoner. His references within his own compositions to non-British art, particularly Italian, French, Flemish and Dutch, can be found in the style or nature of a figure, the colouring and handling of brushwork, or even in knowing details such as paintings within the painting. A good example is the appearance of the Italian renaissance artist Antonio da Correggio's *Jupiter and Io* (painted 1532–3), a sensuous love scene by an artist Hogarth very much admired, on the wall of the adulterous Countess Squanderfield's bedroom (in scene four of *Marriage A-la-Mode*, Col. Fig. 17).[45] This is not an attack on Correggio, but a detail that brings additional information to the story: a time-honoured device in western European art.

No, his greatest ire is not directed at his fellow artists, but ignorant patrons and self-serving dealers. And those other 'connoisseurs', art critics, like the patronising Frenchman the abbé le Blanc, who denigrated Thornhill's work at Greenwich, while, in the same breath, being equally haughty of *A Rake's Progress*. Hogarth would challenge Le Blanc in *The Analysis of Beauty*: 'let any one take a view of the cieling [*sic*] at Greenwich-hospital, painted by Sir

James Thornhill, forty years ago, which still remains fresh, strong and clear as it had been finished but yesterday : and altho' several french writers have so learnedly, and philosophically proved, that the air of this island is too thick, or – too something, for the genius of a painter, yet France in all her palaces can hardly boast of a nobler, more judicious, or richer performance of its kind.' He then moves on to correct a falsehood, still circulating, regarding the group portrait of George I and his family (which, incidentally, includes an image of Sir James himself) on the north wall of the upper hall at Greenwich. Generally accepted at the time and since as flawed in execution, certainly less accomplished than the remainder of the decoration, Hogarth states: 'Note, the upper end of the hall where the royal family is painted, was left chiefly to the pencil of Mr. Andrea a foreigner, after the payment originally agreed upon for the work was so much reduced, as made it not worth Sir James's while to finish the whole with his own more masterly hand.'[46]

Given the full circumstances, do we blame Hogarth's actions in 1737, his anger, restrained at first, but gradually, line by line, unleashed, as he sets out clearly the unfairness of the situation? Where is the level playing field on which art – good or bad – is being judged? Why are patrons unable to use their own eyes and judgement on such matters? Perhaps this is why a part of him wanted artists to present a united front against the tyranny of connoisseurs and dealers at home and abroad – a position he was inherently unable to maintain, due to his competitiveness – and thus his despair and irritation when this unity was not forthcoming. It is a fine line: maintaining the sense of brotherhood, 'we're all in this together', while the reality is a daily, dog-eat-dog battle for survival.

Just as Hogarth was completing his paintings at St Bartholomew's Hospital, and after the spirited defence of his father-in-law, another Briton, like William Kent before him, was enjoying an extended stay in Italy. This gentleman was the son of Hogarth's early supporter, Allan Ramsay. Young Allan's continental adventure, in the company of his friend and fellow Scot, Alexander Cunyngham, began in 1736 (as Hogarth, full of pride and hope for the future, was unveiling *The Pool of Bethesda*) and would entail the very type of experience that Hogarth considered detrimental, or just plain unnecessary, to the development of young artists.[47] But despite Hogarth's protestations, it would soon be the standard for any artist of ambition, establishing connections to and shared experiences with fellow travellers, including influential art patrons, while lending the young artist polish, both cultural and artistic. This would continue to be the case into the next century.

One key reason why some did not undertake such a journey was lack of money or time, or both. Such travel, through relatively recent tradition, meant months and, in many cases, years abroad, and, whether a short or longer time, required extensive outlay for travel, accommodation and general expenditure. Young professionals would have to take time out from their art practice, while spending money hand over fist – so either a patron paid for all expenses, as seen with William Kent, or artists would need to find work for the duration of their travel to cover themselves financially. It was important for them to hook on to networks and potential clients while abroad, for their peers back home would be busy establishing themselves in their absence. Either way, those who did not have the independent means of an aristocrat or who were not the child of a wealthy merchant, keen for his family to rise socially through the gentlemanly education of his heir, or, like Ramsay, supported by a patron, would find such an enterprise beyond reach. It is on this fundamentally practical as well as philosophical level that Hogarth argued against such an investment. His use of examples of art and architecture more easily accessible to British artists, particularly London-based artists, served to establish a sort of 'them and us' between those who did travel and those who did not. Of course, it was also useful to Hogarth to make a virtue of not journeying great distances in order to achieve the depth and breadth of experience necessary to be a great artist. This division between the moneyed travellers, whether self-financed or sponsored, and the stay-at-home strivers, as Hogarth might characterise them, ran in parallel to the production of a different sort of art, based on personal, first-hand experience, focusing on the study of nature in all its variety, rather than being taught to see. Perfecting nature by way of improving upon it, as espoused by Jonathan Richardson senior and later Joshua Reynolds, first president of the

Royal Academy of Arts (founded 1768), was not an ethos with which Hogarth agreed.

The primary aim for such a journey and its itinerary was art and architecture related. In addition to the treasures of Rome, Ramsay studied with Francisco Imperiale, the most celebrated history painter in Italy at that time, although, it must be allowed, little known today. Yet, alongside, there was a highly political element, which for Allan Ramsay and William Hogarth, indeed all Britons, would have a very powerful impact on their careers and lives. Rome was where the Jacobite court and Britain's alternative monarch resided, and both Ramsay and Cunyngham were pulled into its orbit from the moment they arrived in the city, as were many Scottish, and indeed British, travellers: there meeting Charles Edward Stuart and his brother, Henry, becoming initiates of the Jacobite masonic lodge, carousing with exiled Jacobites in their regular haunts, and even attending Charles's extravagant birthday celebrations at the Palazzo Pamphilj in late December 1736.[48] Although enduring loyalty to the Stuarts existed throughout Great Britain and Ireland, Scotland and particularly the western Highlands were seen as the likely well spring for armed rebellion in support of a Stuart restoration.

On his return to Britain in early 1737, Alexander Cunyngham may have dismissed his recent experiences as a case of what happens in Rome, stays in Rome. Allan Ramsay (likely feeling the same way) finally arrived back in London via Naples, then Venice, Milan and Turin in June 1738, a year after Hogarth had proudly unveiled *The Good Samaritan*, having been away for two years. By the August Ramsay was living in the Great Piazza, Covent Garden, and declared, by family friend Alexander Gordon, as 'one of the first rate portrait painters in London, nay I may say Europe.'[49] Ramsay joined Hogarth and Ellys's St Martin's Lane Academy and, partly through novelty – his modish use of red ground rather than the standard grey that Hogarth preferred – partly through his Italian training and experience, but also his camaraderie with fellow Scotsmen, he became something of a celebrity. Within a year of his return, Ramsay had bagged the highest ranking Scots, the Dukes of Argyll and Buccleuch, and the English Lord Chancellor, Philip

Yorke, Earl of Hardwicke, as clients. Some choice Italian words and references utilised by Ramsay – presenting the persona of the well-travelled, Italian-trained artist – would not have been out of place and, in certain circles, positively encouraged, setting those who had travelled to Italy apart from the herd. We can imagine young Allan Ramsay, clubbable and, his father's son, equipped with a good turn of phrase and a talent for storytelling, regaling a gathering of artists at Slaughter's with his adventures – the story of a near-death experience during a storm at sea, for example – to much gasping and laughter in response.[50] Hogarth, if in a good mood, might have gasped and laughed along, all the while painfully aware of his shortcomings and inexperience in comparison, the result of a deficit of opportunity and the poor hand he had been dealt in his youth. Something with which Dr Johnson, speaking in 1776, would empathise: 'A man who has not been in Italy, is always conscious of an inferiority, – from his not having seen what it is expected a man should see.'[51]

At the time of Ramsay's return Hogarth was focused on history painting. With the arrival of the young, talented, charming, well-travelled and connected Allan Ramsay, his competitive spirit would be ignited once more, and portrait painting, a genre Hogarth had apparently abandoned, except for the occasional commission to keep this strand of his practice going, would be his new battleground.

If either man needed a reminder of the vagaries of fate, or how early promise can so easily be dissipated or, indeed, how difficult maintaining a career in art might be, in 1738 a four-volume edition of *Don Quixote* was published by Jacob Tonson. It was illustrated lavishly with engravings after the designs of John Vanderbank, designs first submitted way back in 1723, at the early stage of the process, which had been favoured by the publishers over those proposed by Hogarth. Fifteen years on, with much water (troubled or otherwise) having passed under the bridge, there was no doubting who, now, was a leader of London's art world. Vanderbank, still living off the generosity of his friends according to George Vertue, 'galantly or freely according to the custom of the Age',[52] died the following year, aged just forty-five.

INTERLUDE FIVE

SATURDAY 27 MAY, MIDDAY. After the exertions of the morning, including visiting Mr Watts' Hospital, the group returned to their lodgings, the Crown Inn, at twelve o'clock, and between that time and lunch, an hour's duration, they snatched a quick restorative nap, lying across chairs in the dining room, the occasional snore rising from among them and, as the Reverend Gostling states, 'with clos'd eyes again survey/ In dreams, what we have seen to-day'.[1] The Crown Inn was said to have been visited by Queen Elizabeth in the year 1573, during her progress of the region, when she inspired the renaming of Richard Watts' dwelling and echoed in another 'Satis' house, that of Miss Havisham.[2] Messers Denne and Shrubsole declared the Crown to be one of the most 'capital and spacious inns in this city, which will vie with most in England, as well for their good accommodations, as for their antiquity'.[3]

The early afternoon rest was followed by a leisurely two-hour meal, which contained several courses and dishes: a hearty mix of seafood and nose-to-tail fare, accompanied by some vegetables and alcoholic beverages, all described with more attention to detail than was given the castle, or indeed the cathedral, which barely registered in their account. But this is hardly surprising, if we consider that an army marches on its stomach. Ebenezer Forrest recalls the dishes, in order of arrival and consumption, as 'a Dish of Soles & Flounders with Crab sauce, a Calves heart Stuff'd And Roasted ye Liver Fry'd', alongside other 'appurtenances Minc'd', moving on to 'a Leg of Mutton Roasted, and Some Green pease, all Very Good and well Dress'd, with Good Small beer and excellent Port'.[4] This midday repast, you will be relieved to hear, is most certainly the main meal of the day. Flounders are small flat fish with large mouths and thus used as a common insult – 'You great Flounder-mouth'd Sea-calf',[5] for example – while soles are another flat fish, for which the port of Dover became celebrated.

For roasting mutton, Hannah Glasse, in her bestselling cookery guide of the time, recommended a 'quick clear Fire' and to 'baste it when you lay it down and just before you take it up, and drudge it with a little Flour; but be sure not to use too much, for that takes away all the fine Taste of the Meat'.[6] Another recipe from 1723 recommended sticking the mutton leg with cloves.[7] Mrs Glasse also has some observations, particularly regarding cost and unnecessary waste of ingredients, on the fashion for importing French cooks and fancy overpriced French cooking, rather than delighting in the simplicity and good value of English fare: '*if Gentlemen will have* French *Cooks, they must pay for* French *Tricks. A* Frenchman, *in his own Country, would dress a fine Dinner of twenty Dishes, and all genteel and pretty, for the Expence he would put an* English *Lord to for dressing one Dish. But then there is the little petty Profit.*' This has all the appearance of the gullible art connoisseur and Grand Tourist, as noted by Hogarth. Mrs Glasse goes on, simmering her theme, '*I have heard of a Cook that used six Pounds of Butter to fry twelves Eggs; when every Body knows, that understands Cooking, that half a Pound is full enough, or more than need be used: But then*,' she supposes, '*it would not be* French' and with an audible sigh, followed by irritation and then a shrug at the stupidity of wealthy men: '*So much is the blind Folly of this Age, that they would rather be imposed on by a* French *Booby, than give Encouragement to a good* English *Cook! I doubt I shall not gain the Esteem of those Gentlemen: However, let that be as it will, it little concerns me.*' For, she concludes, '*should I be so happy as to gain the good Opinion of my own Sex I desire no more, that will be a full Recompence for all my Trouble.*'[8]

That cookery and even particular dishes acted as a metaphor for national character – not unlike art – lies at the heart of Henry Fielding's comic song, 'The Roast Beef of Old England', for his *Grub-Street Opera* of 1731, later set to a new tune by the famous English bass singer, Richard Leveridge. Born in 1670, Leveridge was a member of the company for which Henry Purcell had composed music and, in 1731, sang Polyphemus in the first public performance of Handel's English pastoral, *Acis and Galatea*. Hogarth had provided a frontispiece to Leveridge's 1727 forty-three song collection in two pocket-size volumes – a female figure presenting Leveridge's songs to Venus (Love) and Bacchus (Wine). The sentiment of Fielding's words, set to Leveridge's tune, Hogarth would visualise years later in one of his most famous paintings, *Calais Gate*:

> When mighty roast beef was the Englishman's food,
> It ennobled our hearts, and enriched our blood,
> Our soldiers were brave and our courtiers were good.
> Oh the roast beef of old England,
> And old England's roast beef!
>
> But since we have learnt from all-conquering France,
> To eat their ragouts as well as to dance,
> Oh what a fine figure we make in romance!
> Oh the roast beef of old England,
> And old England's roast beef![9]

All in all, the Crown Inn had provided an abundant and tasty collation and, rightly, the Kentish cook 'was much commended for't'.[10]

While they ate, the inn's resident lad had cleaned their shoes, much needed after crossing boggy clay earlier in the day, after which the company, sufficiently cheered and rested, set out once more 'to Seek adventures'.[11] This included Hogarth and Scott playing 'Hop Scotch' at the Town Hall, on the High Street next door to Watts's Hospital. This very fine structure was built in 1687 in brick, supported by coupled stone columns of the Doric order. The area under was paved with Purbeck stone at the expense of Sir Stafford Fairborne, the MP for Rochester during the reign of Queen Anne. The large hall within had a ceiling 'curiously enriched with trophies of war, fruits and flowers, with the arms of this city, and of Sir CLOUDSLEY SHOVEL, at whose expence it was done, in 1695. The whole is executed in a masterly manner.'[12] The scheme was completed with two full-length portraits of William III and Queen Anne at the upper end of the hall, likely two examples of the many studio copies after Sir Godfrey Kneller.

Samuel Scott and William Hogarth would have known of Sir Cloudesley Shovell's mysterious death during the infamous Scilly Isles naval disaster of 1707, where four Royal Navy men o' war had been wrecked for want of accurate navigation (a reminder of why finding a means of calculating longitude on board ship was so crucial) with thousands of lives lost. However, as they did not enter the building, they may not have been aware of the Town Hall's connection to the ill-fated admiral. (It is thought Shovell, a man of humble origins who had worked his way up through the Navy Service, had survived the carnage, washing up on the beach, only to be murdered by a local woman for his emerald ring.)[13] Instead, Samuel and William were determined to have fun, and the paving stones within the colonnade were just too tempting to pass by untested.[14] Hop Scotch (or scoring) is an ancient and still familiar game, which involves dropping a pebble on to a defined pattern of squares set out on the floor – Hogarth and Scott improvised with the paving stones – and hopping along the pattern while avoiding said pebble and square. This activity, no doubt hilarious at the time and perhaps aimed at shaking off some of the heft of their recent feast, simply delayed their departure from Rochester for their intended visit to Chatham: as the Reverend Gostling elaborates, 'Come let's away to *Chatham-Dock*;/ We shan't get there till almost four;/ To see't will take at least an hour;/ Yet *Scott* and *Hogarth* needs must stop/ At the Court-Hall to play *Scotch* hop.'[15]

Chatham lies to the east on the Rochester side of the Medway, and the journey to the dockyard is roughly two miles; on foot between forty minutes to an hour. The company would buy some shrimps to eat as they walked, probably fresh and raw, costing nine pence.[16] While munching on their shrimp snack, in the distance the pilgrims would have seen the extensive mass of buildings that made up the King's Storehouses and Dock Yard, 'which,' Daniel Defoe declares, 'are Very Noble'. 'This,' he continues, 'being the Chief arsenal of the Royal Navy of *Great Britain*. The Buildings here are indeed like the Ships themselves, surprisingly large, and in their several kinds Beautiful', effectively being a street plan lined with a combination of warehouses and storehouses 'for laying up the Naval Treasure' and, Defoe declares patriotically, 'the largest in Dimension, and the most

31. Samuel Scott, *Two Boats with Crews, Study for The Royal William
at Sea*, brushed black ink, grey wash and graphite, undated
The *Prince* (flagship of James II when Duke of York) was
renamed in honour of William III. The sailor's nickname 'tar'
probably comes from the waterproof canvas 'tarpaulin'.

in Number that are any where to be seen in the World'.[17] The 'treasure' was the precious men o' war of the Royal Navy, the means by
which Britain was vying, successfully as the century advanced, for
command of the oceans – whether home or international waters.
Such domination was deemed fundamental to the nation's security
(foreign invasion) and prosperity (colonial expansion and trade).
However, during the reigns of George I and II, 'internal disunity',
notably Jacobitism, as the naval historian N. A. M. Rodger observes,
coupled with powerful enemies abroad (such as France and Spain)
made Britain vulnerable and 'fear ... the main determinant of foreign
policy ... dictated a large fleet in home waters'.[18]

Our pilgrims' visit to Chatham, indeed any of the navy-related
sites, was, therefore, so much more than a tourist excursion. The
sea (and sea service) was central, practically and ideologically, to
British society, as expressed in the Great Hall at Greenwich. As
an example, seven years after *The Peregrination*, Admiral Edward
Vernon, in an audacious move against Spanish colonial possessions in the Americas, was to seize the major trading port of Puerto
Bello (blockaded ten years earlier) with just six Royal Navy ships
and three hundred men. This event was then commemorated, with

32. Charles Grignion after William Hogarth, *The Humours of an Election Plate 2: Canvassing for Votes*, etching and engraving, 1757 The maimed veterans of recent naval campaigns (left) are drinking outside the 'Portobello' tavern, while an unscrupulous voter (centre) is the focus of less heroic or patriotic contest.

the motto 'six ships only', on coins, medals and everyday domestic items such as tankards and teapots. Seizing on the celebratory mood, the capture of Puerto Bello would be the subject of a large oil on canvas by Samuel Scott, and Hogarth would make reference to Vernon's victory in scene two of *The Humours of an Election*.[19]

The five friends boarded the *Marlborough*, which was originally *St Michael*, a second-rate ship of the line built at Portsmouth in 1669, mounting ninety to ninety-eight guns, rebuilt at Blackwall Yard in 1706 and renamed in honour of John Churchill, 1st Duke of Marlborough, and hero of the War of the Spanish Succession. The ship was to see action in the Seven Years' War (at Martinique and Havanna), fought in the final years of Hogarth life (1756–63). From the deck of the *Marlborough* the friends would have had a better sense of this self-contained town, dedicated to the building and ongoing maintenance of these most intricate, extraordinary and beautiful vessels, the men o' war.[20]

After the *Marlborough*, they then boarded the *Royal Sovereign*, which, Ebenezer Forrest notes, is 'reckoned One of the Finest Shipps in the Navy'.[21] *Royal Sovereign* was a one-hundred-gun first-rate ship of the line, built and launched at Woolwich Dockyard (passed by our travellers) in July 1701. Its portrait was painted by Willem van der Velde, the Dutch-born father of British marine painting, Scott's artist ancestor and, later, Turner's too.[22] It was not the first ship of this name. That was built by the master shipbuilder Peter Pett and launched in 1637 on the orders of Charles I and originally called *Sovereign of the Seas*, which then changed to *Sovereign* and later *Royal Sovereign*. This ship was partially destroyed by fire in 1697 and then broken up, with elements integrated into its namesake. The second ship was then 'repaired', but in effect rebuilt at Chatham and relaunched in September 1728 (it was finally broken up in 1768).

Daniel Defoe visited the dockyard while the second *Royal Sovereign* was still under construction. The term 'man-of-war' or 'man o' war' (plural 'men of' or 'o' war') refers to a heavily armed combat ship. At that time the *Royal Sovereign* 'was riding her Moorings, entirely unrigg'd, and nothing but her Three Masts standing, as is usual when a Ship is lay'd up'. But in just three days 'she was completely rigg'd ; all her Masts up, her Yards put too, her Sails bent, Anchors and Cables on Board' and thus seaworthy.[23] Defoe, commenting on the skill and organisation of hundreds of men in this monumental task, declares 'the Dexterity of the *English* Sailors in those things is not to be match'd by the World'.[24] The *Royal Sovereign*'s great cabin, used by the captain and at his invitation where his officers joined him to discuss strategy or dine, had a painted ceiling depicting an assembly of the gods – Mars, God of War being crowned by Neptune, God of the Oceans, surrounded by Hope, Peace, Justice and Plenty – possibly designed, although not executed, by Sir James Thornhill.[25] For both John Thornhill and his brother-in-law William, this would have made viewing this particular ship of very great interest. But as the finest ship in the navy she was, in any event, well worth a visit, and the

33. *The Punishment Inflicted on Lemuel Gulliver*, etching and engraving, 1726
Gulliver is punished for peeing on a fire at the Lilliputian royal palace
(representing the Hanoverian monarchy) and thus (ironically) saving
it. The 'enema' echoes Hogarth's spoofing of the Richardsons.

Royal Sovereign's scale was famous enough for her to be mentioned
in another great satire on travellers' tales, as well as human nature,
Gulliver's Travels. Lemuel Gulliver, a surgeon and then the captain
of several ships (so the title page tells us), accidentally arrives in
the land of giants (Brobdingnag, Part II of 4). Here, while dining
with the king, he notes the presence of the first minister standing
behind the monarch, holding a white staff (not unlike the Lord
Great Chamberlain) 'near as tall as the Main-mast of the *Royal
Soveraign*'. The king, addressing his thoughts to Gulliver, writing
in the first person, observes 'how contemptible a thing was human
Grandeur, which could be mimicked by such diminutive Insects as
I [Gulliver] : And yet, said he, I dare engage, these Creatures have
their Titles and Distinctions of Honour ...' The king also describes
the English as 'the most pernicious Race of little odious Vermin
that Nature ever suffered to crawl upon the Surface of the Earth',
which Gulliver considers a bit rum.[26]

Other ships then present at the dockyard and mentioned by
Ebenezer Forrest included the *London*, a ninety-six-gun first-rate

ship of the line, built by Christopher Pett at Deptford Dockyard, launched 1670, rebuilt at Chatham in 1706 as a one-hundred-gun ship. Her more famous namesake had been one of the vessels that escorted Charles II back from Scheveningen, Holland, to Dover after the restoration of the monarchy in 1660. This HMS *London* was accidentally blown up on 7 March 1665 and remains, vulnerable but surprisingly intact, on the bed of the Thames estuary between Canvey Island and the Isle of Grain. Another ship named by Forrest is the 'Royall Anne'.[27] The mention of the *Royal Anne* is curious, as this ship, a survivor from Sir Cloudesley Shovell's ill-fated fleet, had been decommissioned and then broken up in 1727. Perhaps the hulk remained at the dockyard, to be used for the refitting of other men o' war, and was still referred to by the ship's name. Finally, Forrest notes the presence of the 'Royall George', a first-rate man o' war, originally the *Royal Charles*, then the *Queen* (after Mary II, who died in 1693) and finally rebuilt and renamed in honour of the new Hanoverian monarch, George I, in 1715. As the transfer from Charles to George via Queen Mary suggests, the naming of a Royal Navy ship was a political statement, indicating the shift in fortune of dynasties and monarchs. This is particularly the case for ships called *Royal Charles*, which seem to embody the great national and international struggles of the seventeenth century and their seismic impact on the century that followed. All of our five pilgrims had been born under a Stuart and would die under a Hanoverian, and the struggle for survival between these dynasties and their support-ers would mark the whole of Hogarth's life. Indeed, as we continue to map that life, and the struggle turns once again into armed rebel-lion – the greatest domestic crisis of the early-Georgian age – it will, inevitably, achieve greater prominence and significance in his art.

After several hours perusing the dockyard at Chatham, perhaps listening to such tales of the vagaries of fate, the pilgrims returned to Rochester and were ensconced at the Crown Inn by six o'clock. Here they 'pass'd the time agreably till Nine', staving off hunger with a snack and pint pot, and then 'Quite Fatigu'd with Pleasure, Went to Bed',[28] perhaps dreaming of the Royal Navy, the skill of shipwrights, and hopscotch.

CHAPTER FIVE

FEELING FELLOW

On a cold night in March 1741 a large crowd had gathered in the street in front of a plain terraced house in Hatton Garden, London. Some had come out of curiosity, others necessity. At around eight o'clock the front door opened, the streetlight was put out and a bell was rung. On this signal, the crowd fell silent. A woman stepped forward holding a newborn infant. She followed the porter to the ground-floor parlour, where a physician, Dr Robert Nesbitt, and other officials were waiting. The child, perhaps asleep, perhaps mewling, was gently handed over and inspected, the secretary methodically noting down the sex, approximate age, clothing, and any item or 'token', something like a piece of fabric or ribbon left as identification, and then, without a question being asked, no mention of the infant's name or family, the woman left, quietly disappearing into the dark, anonymous back streets of the metropolis.[1]

One by one more women followed until, at midnight, the house had received thirty children and was declared full. The porter announced this to the crowd still gathered outside, adding that an advertisement would be placed in a local newspaper should any vacancies occur – meaning, should any of the babies admitted that night subsequently die. Then he closed the door.

Immediately, as recalled in the daily committee minutes of the institution, the air was filled with moans and cries, for 'the Expressions of Grief of the Women whose Children could not be admitted were Scarcely more observable than those of some of the Women who parted with their Children so that a more moving Scene can't well be imagined'.[2] Yet, after a twenty-year fight against prejudice and indifference, Britain's first refuge for the most vulnerable children in society had finally opened.

In this instance, the person who answered the parable of the Good Samaritan's call 'Go and do the same' was Captain Thomas Coram. As an indication of how important and personal this project was to Hogarth and, indeed, how closely he would have associated himself with Coram as a man and visionary, within the papers for the abandoned autobiography he wrote the words 'Story of Coram'.[3] They sit as a solitary statement in the midst of the ramblings, perhaps, being so clear and fresh in his mind, simply as a reminder that he must return to the subject and tell this story at some future time.

Hogarth's starting point would have been Coram's place of birth, Lyme Regis in Dorset. This merchant and fishing town was famed for its 'cobb', the wide sea wall that against all the odds created a safe harbour from the ravages of the sea and winds. Despite its small size, West Indies sugar and Virginian tobacco were imported here, and locally produced goods, mainly textile and leather based, exported back to the colonies direct.[4] Behind the town are hills; as recalled by Daniel Defoe, it 'was in sight of these hills that Queen Elizabeth's fleet, under the command of the Lord Howard of Effingham, then Admiral, began first to engage in a close and resolv'd fight with the invincible Spanish Armada'.[5] It was also at Lyme that James Scott, Duke of Monmouth, the favourite illegitimate son of Charles II and, more important still, a Protestant, landed in 1685 to claim the crown from his uncle, James II. Those of Coram's boyhood neighbours who rose up to support the duke would be executed in their droves on the orders of the infamous Judge George Jeffreys, during the trials that came to be known as the 'Bloody Assizes'. Monmouth himself could expect little mercy from his uncle, and was beheaded, in a desperately botched execution, at Tower Hill.[6] Of this, Defoe wrote, 'I need say nothing, the history of it being so recent in the memory of so many living.' Defoe was writing in the 1720s, when the events of the 1680s would still have felt like recent history, whether for or against the Protestant succession, which remained fundamental to current politics and the future of the nation for decades to come. Certainly Coram's words and deeds throughout his life, in his professional dealings and with foundlings alike, firmly establish his allegiance to the Protestant settlement and succession, embodied by William and Mary, then Anne and, since 1714, the Hanoverians and their Whig supporters in parliament.

Almost all we know of Coram's early life – and as with Hogarth the details are hazy – is contained in his letters to various business contacts and friends. He admits to little if any formal education, although the very fact that he can read and write, in an age when such skills were far from usual among the lower levels of society, indicates some solid, if basic learning. In one key letter, concerning a recent publication (in Latin) of Erasmus, Coram declares, 'for my part I am no Judge in Learning I understand no Lattin, nor English nither, well, for though Through Mercy I discended from, vertuous good Parentage on both sides as any Body, they were Famelies of Strict hon'r and honesty and always of Good Reputation amongst the better sort of people, Yet I had no Learning.'[7] It should be said, from this evidence, Coram's phrasing and spelling here is no better or worse than Hogarth's, the son of a well-educated professional man. Coram then expands with a short autobiography. He describes how his unnamed mother – now believed to be a woman called Spes, Latin for 'Hope', wife of John Coram, whose profession, it is also believed, was in merchant shipping – had died when he was young, and that his father had married again about four years later. Coram senior, by this point, was living in Hackney, then a village near London. From Lyme (suggesting that Thomas was not living with his father) the son went to sea aged only eleven and a half. Coram's first biographer, Dr Richard Brocklesby, simply states that Coram was 'bred in the Sea Service'.[8]

When Thomas was sixteen, his father sent for him and he duly ventured to London, where he was apprenticed to a shipwright (a shipbuilder and fitter) on the Thames. It was during his apprenticeship that the Monmouth Rebellion occurred, followed by the events leading to the Glorious Revolution. His talents were quickly recognised by some London merchants, and he was enlisted to establish a new shipyard in Boston, Massachusetts, then the largest town in the American colonies, and New England's most substantial port. A period of time in the colonies was, like the sea service in general, a tremendous opportunity for a young man from Coram's background – as he says, honest and of good repute, but with few contacts and little money behind him – and in 1694, three years before Hogarth was born, he set sail for America. In December 1707, the year Great Britain was created, Daniel Defoe considered such a move as being, to all intents and purposes, much like migration around the British Isles, that is 'Sending our People to the Colonies is no more, nor ought to be esteemed otherwise, than sending people out of Middlesex into Yorkshire ... [the colonists are] every way a Part of ourselves.'[9] As also seen with Will Tothall's experience of the sea service – whether on merchant ships in the West Indies or as an importer himself in London – Coram's life as a shipbuilder and fitter in London and Massachusetts demonstrates how intimately connected were Britain and her colonies.

Coram was demonstrably an enterprising self-sufficient character. He was also a staunch Anglican, now journeying to settle (for the time being) in Massachusetts, an equally staunch religious community, but dominated by non-conformist puritan Protestantism rather than the Church of England. Coram was also vehemently anti-Catholic, or 'popery' as he and indeed many Protestant Englishmen described it, and very vocal about French and Jesuit activity among Native American peoples, to the detriment of English, then British, interests in North America.[10] In 1700 Thomas married, at the Puritan First Church in Boston, a local woman, Eunice Waite, from a well-regarded congregationalist (a form of puritan) family, which must have helped the Englishman integrate into local networks.[11] The colony was dependent on, and in turn crucial to, the transatlantic slave trade, with enslaved Africans being bought and sold in Boston. The Waite family were not unusual in owning at least one slave, Sebastian, who worked in the family's house. However, despite his marrying into a local family, Coram was also famed for falling out with the puritan community and was, eventually, driven out of Massachusetts.

The decades he spent based in Boston and then Taunton, thirty-three miles due south, developed his focus and his methods. As Dr Brocklesby observed, 'His Experience was his principal Guide.' That experience would have included freedoms to act where, in Great Britain, greater restrictions, through both political and social habits of long standing, prevented innovation and the address-ing, head on, of well-known ills. Old-world bias, class distinctions and disdain for the lower orders played their part. Perhaps, too, Coram's clarity of vision was sharpened by the ongoing need to maintain these colonial settlements – some of very recent founda-tion – which meant that the continuance of life (at whatever social class) and the need for man and woman power was, on a funda-mental level, at a premium. So, before embarking on the project for which he is justly famed, Thomas Coram had already lived a full life of adventure, but also professional and personal struggle in Great Britain's American colonies.

Thomas's marriage to Eunice Wait was a very happy one, but no children are mentioned in any of the accounts concerning them. In an age when a family was one of if not *the* expected outcome of marriage, this circumstance may have been a trigger, alongside his sense of civic Christian duty and basic fellow feeling, for the entire Foundling Hospital project. Coram retired in about 1719 and returned to London, at some point living among the shipwright yards in Rotherhithe, near Cuckold's Point.[12] At this time he rec-ognised the need for a refuge for abandoned children, and began forming a plan and agitating for a Foundling Hospital. In tandem, Coram remained actively involved in the British North Ameri-can colonies, becoming a trustee of the new colony of Georgia (founded 1732). Horatio Walpole, writing to his brother Robert, the prime minister, stated that Coram was the 'honestest, the most disinterested, and the most knowing person about the plantations, I ever talked with'.[13] In 1738, determined that the British govern-ment and monarchy should play fair by their Native American allies, and equally aware 'of the Great Importance of having all the Nations of Indians in the English Intrest to prevent the Vast Designs of France upon our American Plantations',[14] he facilitated the delegation to London from the 'Mohegan' leaders, carrying a petition to King George concerning the defrauding of their land. They were accompanied by a Samuel Mason, who was financially supported throughout the trip, at Coram's instigation, but left without bothering to thank anyone concerned. This Coram found very shaming – 'who can ever shew favour to such Creatures of no

More thankfulness in them than in the baser sort of horses when that have eaten up their Provender turn their Railes and Shi-te in the Manger'.[15] As his phrasing here makes clear, Coram's manner could undoubtedly be rough and pithy. Men like Horatio Walpole, coming from the Norfolk squirearchy, who could be pretty rough and pithy themselves when the occasion demanded, had no issue with it. On his success at currying favour with Queen Caroline, who held great sway over her husband, George II, Robert Walpole simply observed that he 'took the right sow by the ear'. Hogarth admired Coram greatly and, being a straight-talking chap himself, no doubt enjoyed such unvarnished candour, and particularly the indignant reactions it produced.

But in circumstances that required the complete reversal of ingrained opinion – negotiating with ecclesiastics and aristocrats used to deference from the lower orders – where some delicacy and diplomacy would help, such plain speaking hindered more than it persuaded. Dr Brocklesby described Coram as 'Free from all Hypocrisy, he spoke what he thought with Vehemence', 'His Arguments were nervous', meaning vigorous, manly, 'tho' not nice, founded commonly upon Facts', 'When once he made an Impression, he took care it should not wear out; for he enforced it continually by the most pathetic Remonstrances. In short, his Logic was plain Sense, his Eloquence the natural Language of the Heart.'[16] The fact that Brocklesby felt the need to repeatedly defend his subject on this point suggests that Coram's manner was an issue, and the subject of much discussion.

Coram may have been abrasive, but his letters are full of schemes and suggestions, great and small, designed to alleviate the suffering of those in need and, he believed, to the betterment of the British nation. This seems to have been a natural way of being for Coram, always thinking, always prepared to take action, traits he shared with Hogarth and a basis for their camaraderie. Coram was a different sort of ally, perhaps, given his relative age and strength of character, even another sort of father figure for Hogarth. But where Hogarth tended to combine philanthropy, genuine and heartfelt, with commercial interests – he was not unusual in this – Coram, in the context of the Foundling Hospital project at least, had nothing, personally, to gain. He was also a zealous patriot, whereas Hogarth's patriotism, as we shall see, could have a more tempered, more questioning aspect.

That said, Hogarth would have heartily agreed with one fundamental purpose of Coram's project. A hospital for 'unwanted' infants would also offer, Coram believed, an alternative to an even greater crime against humanity than abandonment, that of newborn murder, the scale of which, within the city's rapidly expanding population, could only be hinted at in contemporary newspapers. Even so, the evidence within the local and national press was shocking. It is clear that some of these infants had been left to die from exposure and hunger: 'The Body of a new-born Infant was found in Lamb's-Conduit-Fields, supposed to have perished with Cold',[17] in stark contrast to those babies left with notes, or in some way protected, in the hope of rescue. (It is worth noting that foundlings were not necessarily illegitimate or parentless orphans; some came from families that simply could not afford to keep them.) Other dead infants, however, were discovered lying in side streets or in churchyards, displaying signs of violence such as bruising or worse. This pointed to premeditated murder.

Probably weary of such reporting, over decades, by September 1738 the *London Evening Post* appeared to be leading a modest campaign on the issue, given a recent spate of incidents: 'Yesterday Morning a female Infant was found in a Ditch half full of Water by Wimple-street, Cavendish-Square, in a Bandbox; it is suppos'd to be about a Week old, and is the third Infant that has been found dead near that Place lately.'[19] This followed other examples noted by the newspaper: 'On Wednesday last a new born Infant was found dead, bound up in a Handkerchief, in a Passage leading into the House of an eminent Merchant in Nicholas Land, Lombard-street; and on Thursday Night the Coroner's Inquest sat on the Body. A Midwife, who was summon'd, declar'd the Child was kill'd in its Birth, for want of proper Assistance (the Mother being willing, as is suppos'd, to conceal her Shame.)' There is a presumption that an unmarried woman would conceal pregnancy because of the shame, that such a condition confirmed sexual activity – whether consensual or otherwise is not discussed – outside of marriage. In any case, 'The Inquest were all bound over to prosecute the Mother, when found.' The report concludes, 'The frequent Barbarities of this Nature, shew the Usefulness of an Hospital for Foundlings, for probably this and many other Murders wou'd be prevented, if Women knew where to carry their Children when deliver'd of them.'[20]

A vulnerable newborn could die as easily from accident and neglect, 'want of proper assistance', as by nefarious means. So how might a court decide – if bruising and broken bones, rather than, say, stab wounds were present – whether murder had occurred? Among the Old Bailey trials there were forty-seven cases of killing by infanticide, all listed as unmarried women, in the two decades during which Coram was petitioning for the hospital. But this is likely to be the tip of the iceberg, given the difficulties of bringing such cases to court.

Anne Jones of St Giles-in-the-Fields was accused of murdering her 'Male Bastard Child' by throwing it into a 'House of Office', an outhouse for domestic use, here likely to have been a latrine, on 9 June 1720. Anne protested that she had made preparations for the child by buying bed linens, which was the standard defence against premeditated murder. She also declared that she had not realised how close she was to giving birth, and that the child had fallen from her and died as a result. She was found not guilty.[21] In fact, in a vast majority of cases, the woman accused of murder was acquitted. The stories relayed in the court followed a similar course. The (usually unmarried) woman had hidden her pregnancy or, in a few instances, had not known she was pregnant. She had complained about feeling ill – whether with stomach pains, a loosening of the bowels, colic, etc. – and in many instances had gone to the 'vault', a 'necessary' area in the basement of the building, to relieve herself and had there given birth. The child, suddenly, had fallen from her and died from the trauma of hitting a stone or wooden floor, or the woman had been sitting over the privy and the child dropped into the slurry beneath, drowning. Some of the children, so the women argued, were stillborn. Surgeons brought in by the coroner to inspect the body to judge whether violence had occurred could conduct a post-mortem, including immersing the lungs in water to decide whether drowning had been the cause of death. A non-medical test involved 'provision', as it was termed. This was evidence, as seen in Anne Jones's case, that the woman had prepared for the arrival of the child, specifically baby clothes and linens. Most of the acquitted women were able to produce such items, or could draw on witnesses willing to swear to their existence. In fact the acquittal or not could depend in large degree on whether the accused had support from her employer, neighbours and family. Character witnesses were crucial.

The brief details offered by the court transcripts hint at lives traumatised and in some cases ruined by the pregnancy, the fear of being discovered unmarried and pregnant overriding all other concerns, including a fear for their own health and that of the child. Very few had admitted to being pregnant, even in the face of all the evidence to the contrary, let alone sought assistance in the lead-up to the birth. This tragic circumstance is a stain on society, not that this society saw it as such. The burden was placed on the women – the father of the child is rarely mentioned. Within the transcripts you get a sense of why these women went to such lengths to avoid scrutiny from their fellow workers, employers and neighbours. In some, the lack of empathy or sympathy – in the main, from other women – is breathtaking.

A Foundling Hospital would, as argued by the *London Evening Post*, prevent or at least reduce the need for such clandestine behaviour. But Coram's motivation was pragmatic and patriotic, as well as humane. Abandoned children, if they survived, were prey to London's brutal criminal gangs, with many pressed into lives of mugging, house breaking and prostitution that ended, more often than not, in a terrible early death through venereal disease or the noose. Meanwhile Great Britain was either at war with France, or on high alert for fear of invasion, and her global empire was expanding: opportunities for success and advancement existed at every turn, as Coram himself had experienced, and manpower was in great need. Coram argued that saving, nurturing, educating and training thousands of abandoned Britons was not just a Christian or human duty; it was a national necessity. Through his projected hospital, at least some of the nation's vulnerable youth would join the ranks of the honest, industrious, god-fearing citizenry, rather than the godless criminal underclass, or die prematurely. Certainly, the hospital was a concrete, practical, unsentimental antidote to the type of damaged lives Hogarth depicted so vividly in *Industry and Idleness*, *The Four Stages of Cruelty* and *Gin Lane*. The boys, Coram declared, would be educated for the sea service, while the girls would be schooled in husbandry and domestic service. Coram had firm ideas about the education of girls, and believed it 'an Evil' that in England it was considered of far less importance than for boys. In fact, Coram goes so far as to argue that it is more important, 'for Girls when they come to be Mothers will have the forming of their Childrens lives and if their Mothers be good or Bad the Children Generally take after them so that Giving Girls vertous Education is a vast Advantge to their Posterity as well as to the Publick ... I know and have seen the Experience of it and I believe every bodys owne Experience must tel them the Great benefit of it.'[22]

In 1737, Thomas Coram wrote a letter outlining his progress to date, with references to the project's impact on his health. He had finally recovered 'from a Dangerous and I thought Long Sickness', but, he continues, 'God be praised, in as good health as ever, I eat and Drink and Sleep Comfortably and tho heavy can Walk 10 or a dozen Miles in a day and hope to live to see the accomplishment of the Designe of Re[s]cuing poor Miserable Exposed Newborn Infants or Foundlings from the Cruelties of their own Parents or Barberous Nurses.' He summarises the frustrating lack of interest from those who, you would think, might support such a project, for 'I could no more prevaile on any Arch Bishop or Bishop or Noble-man Britain or Foreigner or any other Great Man, I tryed them all, to speake to the Late King [George I] or his present Majesty on this affair than I could have prevailed with any of them, if I had tryed it, to have putt doun their Breeches and present their Back-sides to the King and Queen in a full Drawing room such was the unchristian Shyness of all about the Court.'[23] Yet he is upbeat and hopeful of success, although he refers to the difficulties and the 'round about Wayes I was forced to take, first to get the first Rank of Ladys, then the first of the Noblemen and other Gentlemen, then a Recomendation Suscribed by ma[n]y Justices and others'.[24]

As this letter confirms, eventually, weary of petitioning male aristocrats, clerics and parliamentarians to no effect, Coram appealed to the maternal instincts of their wives – taking, as it were, the right sows by the ear – some of whom, such as the duchesses of Somerset and Richmond, agreed to lead the campaign. By the 1730s a tangible change in attitude towards children, particularly within the middling-sort, coupled with the high value now given to displays of 'sensibility' or deep feeling, and responsiveness to the plight of others, greatly assisted in this collective change of heart. Yet although women, whether mothers or staff, such as nurses, and children were at the centre of this charity, and aristocratic women had led the charge that secured its success, the hospital was established, governed and managed by men.

Despite the success of finally getting his petition to the King-in-Council, the death of Queen Caroline in November 1737 (of whom Coram was quite critical, especially regarding her 'much talked of extencive Goodness and Charity'), with royal physician, John Ranby in attendance, suspended, for now, any firm decisions at court.[25] It is around this time, as Coram's petition (he might have feared) was mouldering with the king and his council over 1737 and 1738, that Hogarth probably became involved, artistically at first, in the project. The timing was just as Hogarth was coming out of the intense period of activity at St Bartholomew's Hospital. Hogarth was, no doubt, amenable to taking on another charitable cause, although he would have been less willing to immerse so fully so soon, unpaid, having himself and a family to keep. The specific artwork required at this moment, a headpiece for subscriptions or donations to the hospital, not unlike the printed subscription tickets to support the imminent publication of his engravings, was on a miniature scale and, in contrast to the years involved at St Bartholomew's, could be quickly dashed off.

This image, with Coram – a thumbnail portrait, so Hogarth must have seen or met him by this time – as a central figure, set the tone for how the organisation would aim to appeal to donors, and it is striking in how it addresses both abandonment and newborn child murder. It addresses the latter issue with decorum, relying on the imagination of the potential donor to complete the story.

34. *Study for the Foundlings*, pen and ink with grey wash on paper, *c.*1738–9
The distant parish church, on whose charity the poor are expected to rely, is
balanced by the hospital in the foreground, its window bars forming a cross.

A dagger lies on the ground before a kneeling woman who, foiled
in her attempt, turns away in shame and fear. Her rescued infant
is held by the imposing figure of the hospital's beadle, the officer
in charge of security. Sadly little imagination was required as to
what Coram's intervention (as the personification or embodiment
of the hospital) has prevented, given the regular reports in newspapers of infanticide and the trials of mothers accused of the crime.
The design presents two realities – despair on one side, hope on the
other, connected (from left to right in the drawing, reversed in the
engraving) by the kneeling mother, Coram, the rescued infant and
the beadle. Scenes of danger and abandonment, with babies lying
alone on the ground, or being placed there, are contrasted with
the saved children, in their neat uniforms and holding items such
as spindles, navigation equipment, representing their training and
future professions as useful British citizens.[26] Given such details
within the sketch, it is likely that the tradition is true, that Hogarth
himself designed the brown-and-red uniforms for the foundlings
to wear. He may have had the advice of his family, as owners of
haberdashery and drapers' shops providing, as the business card
stated, 'blue & canvas Frocks & bluecoat Boys Dra[we]rs'. In this

35. *Gin Lane*, etching and engraving, February 1751
In glaring contrast to *Beer Street*, the only winner here is the pawnbroker,
surrounded by chaos, suffering and death. Atop the distant steeple of
Hawksmoor's St George's, Bloomsbury, is the effigy of George I.

way Hogarth's foundling design contains everything the potential
donor needs to know, about who they would be supporting – the
vulnerable child and, to a lesser extent, the abandoning mother
and would-be murderer – and to what purpose: the raising of good
citizens and loyal Britons. That Hogarth, of all people, restrained

himself in the depiction of the dangers facing such infants suggests he had limits. Even the likely death through neglect, rather than cold-blooded murder, of the infant in *Gin Lane*, as it tumbles off its inebriated mother or wet-nurse's lap, is not shown. In fact it was the portrait painter Joseph Highmore, stirred by the known contexts that had made the Foundling Hospital a necessity, who attempted to depict a woman strangling her baby, a painting that, still, has the power to disturb.[27]

By the time the design was ready to be engraved, the king had, finally, granted the Foundling Hospital its Royal Charter, or rather, to give its official title, the 'Hospital for the Maintenance and Education of Exposed and Deserted Young Children'. After decades of inactivity, now everyone, from His Majesty himself down, began to support the charity. Hogarth, as a founding governor – he was both a financial donor as well as a donor 'in kind', through art and as a volunteer administrator – attending the meeting on 17 October 1739 when the hospital was incorporated, as announced in the newspapers: 'His Majesty has been most graciously pleased, upon the humble Petition of Thomas Coram, Esq; in Behalf of great Numbers of helpless Infants, daily expos'd to destruction, to incorporate John Duke of Bedford, Charles Duke of Richmond, and several other great Officers and Minsters of State, and their Successors, into one Body Politick and Corporate ... And on Thursday his Majesty's Royal Charter pass'd the Great Seal.'[28]

The Common Seal of the Corporation, as described by Coram, depicts a subject of his choice, that is 'the affair Mentioned in the 2d of Exodus of Pharoah's [*sic*] Daughter and her Maids finding Moses in the ark of Bulrushes which I thought would be very appropo for an hospital for Foundlings Moses being the first Foundling we read of'.[29] Hogarth was also present to hear Thomas Coram's address to the president, the Duke of Bedford and the committee at Somerset House on 20 November 1739. Coram, with his usual bluntness, was not allowing anyone who had dragged their heels to get away with it: 'I can, my Lord, sincerely Aver, that nothing would have induced me to imbark in a Design so full of Difficulties and Discouragements, but a Zeal for the Service of his Majesty, in preserving the Lives of great Numbers of his innocent Subjects.'[30]

On 14 May 1740, it was noted in the General Council minutes that Mr Hogarth had painted a 'whole length' portrait of Coram, which he was now presenting as a gift to the hospital 'to keep in Memory' Coram's success and soon after, on 25 June 1740, it was recorded that Hogarth had subscribed £21 to the hospital. George Vertue wrote in his journal that Hogarth's portrait of Coram 'is thought to be very well', concluding, 'this is another of his efforts to raise his reputation in the portrait way from the life'.[31]

Hogarth had a love–hate relationship with portraiture: one minute declaring, in a huff, his abandonment of it, next minute announcing triumphantly his return to the genre, to the evident irritation of George Vertue, among others. Portraiture, although not the highest genre, was considered to be a higher category than landscape or flower painting because the focus was on the human form. On a basic level, portraits depicted a particular individual or individuals – rather than universal concepts or human experience, as history painting demanded – the skill lay in achieving a recognisable likeness, no more no less. However, in Hogarth's opinion, simply 'copying' a face was not enough, in fact he compares this to still life, the lowest of all genres – in this he echoes the opinion of the French academician, André Félibien. A person trained to copy would do so, Hogarth believed and perfectly well, whether it was a bowl of fruit or a person. There is little judgement, invention or intellect required, he declares: 'correctness therefore in still life from an apple or a Rose to the face nay even an Whole figure if you take em merely as the object ... requires only an exact Eye and great practice'.[32] He cites a crucifix carver who did nothing well but crucifixes, because he was trained from youth to carve such things. Then there was the example of a well-known copier of Rubens, he observes, 'who is almost an Ideot'. Replication, copying, is part of the tools of painting, but it is not art – certainly not great art. For the 'Subject of most consequence are those that most entertain and Improve the mind and are of public utility'.[33] Hogarth is making a distinction between just replicating the features of an individual and producing something far greater – what was termed the grand-manner portrait.

Hogarth's decision to turn his hand to an elevated style of

portraiture, which coincides with the return of Allan Ramsay from Italy and the Foundling Hospital project, was stimulated by yet another circumstance: the arrival in London of a French portrait painter, Jean-Baptiste Van Loo, who, through novelty and a highly polished style, immediately gained attention and commissions from those more interested in fashion than encouraging native talent, including the Frenchman's great patron, Robert Walpole. Hogarth later recalled that Van Loo 'mono[po]lised all the people of fashion in the kingdom', driving well-established portrait painters 'into the utmost distress and poverty'. Initially, however, Hogarth did not wish to challenge Van Loo himself, 'my studies being in another way'. Instead 'I exorted the painters to bear up against this torrents and to oppose him with spirit.'[34] In other words, Van Loo was not challenging his livelihood, therefore it was for others to act.

But eventually, 'provoked at this', he decided to take on Van Loo on his own turf, and so, with the Foundling Hospital project as the context and Coram the subject, 'I set about this mighty portrait, and found it no more difficult than I thought it.' Hogarth may have allowed his enthusiasm and impatience with his fellow artists to tip into arrogance. A further paragraph in his autobiographical notes refers to a gathering at the St Martin's Lane Academy around the time of the Coram portrait, where Allan Ramsay was present, when Hogarth asked a question of those assembled: if anyone 'at this time was to paint a portrait as wel as Vandike would it be seen and the person enjoy the benefit'?[35] Van Dyck, as Hogarth's 'Golden Head', proudly displayed over his front door since 1733, declared, was the exemplar *par excellence* for great grand-manner portraiture. In response to Hogarth's question, Allan Ramsay stated 'No', a response to which everyone there agreed. Ramsay continued, that they, the portrait painters, would need to be consulted on the matter, 'and we will never allow it', meaning that Van Dyck was too great a genius, so no one could, conceivably, match him. So there was the challenge Hogarth needed, and 'Upon which I Reso[l]ved if I did do the thing, I would Affirm I [had] done it.'[36]

The influences or models from which Hogarth was consciously drawing were recent French portraits of royals and courtiers by

Hyacinthe Rigaud and Nicolas de Largillière. The latter had studied with Lely in London, both were major and veteran figures of the Académie royale, and were far greater portraitists than Van Loo – clearly a poke at the latest arrival in London, despite his academy training. And, closer to home, were examples by Van Dyck. Hogarth's self-identification with Sir Anthony, that he was best placed to take on the Flemish master's mantle, is clear from his own writing, and in the following anecdote. John Nichols describes the narrative as 'authenticated', and included it in his biography of Hogarth in order to 'serve to shew how much more easy it is to detect ill-placed or hyperbolical adulation respecting others, than when applied to ourselves'. The story proceeds thus: '*Hogarth* being at dinner with the great *Cheselden*, and some other company, was told that Mr. *John Freke*, surgeon of *St. Bartholomew's Hospital*, a few evenings before at *Dick's Coffee-house*, had asserted, that *Greene* was as eminent in composition as *Handel*. "That fellow *Freke*," replied *Hogarth*, "is always shooting his bolt absurdly one way or another! *Handel* is a giant in music ; *Greene* only a light *Florimel* kind of a composer."' Hogarth, in this anecdote, is probably referring to *Florimel, or Love's Revenge*, first performed in 1734, an English pastoral (in the tradition of Handel's *Acis and Galatea* of 1718) with libretto by John Hoadly.[37] It seems odd that Hogarth should effectively attack a composer associated with his intimate friend. Excellent as Maurice Greene undoubtedly was, a fellow member, with Hogarth, of the Academy of Ancient Music, most modern observers would agree wholeheartedly with Hogarth's opinion as quoted here. The narrative continues, "'Ay," says our artist's informant, "but at the same time Mr. *Freke* declared you were as good a portrait-painter as *Vandyck*." To which Hogarth immediately responded "*There* he was in the right ... and so by G[od] I am, give me my time, and let me choose my subject!"'[38]

In Thomas Coram, Hogarth had his subject, and with Van Loo as the competition, plus the gauntlet thrown down by Allan Ramsay et al, the time was right. In Britain, Van Dyck's sitters were almost exclusively Charles I's courtiers, the English aristocracy and gentry. So imitating his grand manner with a decidedly un-aristocratic subject was challenging in itself. But if we consider

Thomas Coram's humble roots, another group of portraits that Hogarth was consciously alluding to might include individuals who were not born to such elevated treatment. Such an example, dated 1686, would be the wonderful portrait by John Riley, master of, among others, Jonathan Richardson senior, of Bridget Holmes (Royal Collection). Holmes, the necessary woman of every monarch from Charles II to William and Mary, was a dignified, modest, loyal servant and subject. In Riley's portrait, Bridget has her sleeves rolled up and is holding her broom as if she is shooing away the cheeky page peeking out from behind the drape. But also included is a pedestal, flowers and other props typical of a 'beauty' portrait, associated with the women of the court who were considered the most beautiful of their generation – both Lely and Kneller produced a group of portraits called 'Beauties', well known through engravings and imitated.[39] There is humour in the treatment of this elderly necessary woman, but the joke is not on Bridget. On her death in 1691, aged one hundred, after decades of royal service, she was buried in Westminster Abbey. Such an elevated image, therefore, is appropriate for a loyal and highly valued servant of the House of Stuart.

In Hogarth's portrait (Col. Fig. 11), Coram wears his own hair – shoulder length, grey-white, almost fluffy – not so surprising for a man born just after the restoration of the monarchy, but certainly unusual for an older man in 1740. Hogarth clearly shaved his head at this time, while younger men were starting to wear their natural hair long, curled or buckled at the side and tied back with a ribbon, wearing a wig on top for formal occasions. Either way, Coram is distinctively unprimped. At first glance Coram's face is ruddy and genial, but there is a steeliness in his gaze. The captain wears plain black from his waistcoat to his stockings and shoes, excepting a flash of white stock and shift. His red great coat adds a mass of warm colour to the painting and completes his habitual workaday clothing and lack of grooming. Coram holds his gloves in his left hand, which is a detail sometimes seen in royal portraits, but balances the gesture of his right hand, which crucially holds the seal attached to the Foundling Hospital's Royal Charter. The hand clutching the gloves brings the eye down towards the globe, turned to the Atlantic and the British colonies, and in the distance, behind Coram, is the sea.

Coram is not a servant, in the standard use of the term like Bridget Holmes. But he would consider himself a true servant of his country, a loyal subject of his king and relentless protector of his fellow man. It was Thomas Coram who had the moral focus, the dignity, the tenacity, the courage and the leadership to address the foundling issue, not the men whom society considers his 'betters'. Coram does not mimic the aristocracy; he surpasses it, and, in so doing, shames it. The portrait is therefore more radical than perhaps most governors and visitors cared to realise. The production of a portrait on this scale (the completed work measures just less than nine feet by five feet), without the assistance of drapery painters is a considerable undertaking by one artist, and it cannot be stressed enough how unusual life-sized full-lengths were within Hogarth's oeuvre. The creation and gift of Coram's portrait to the new Foundling Hospital acted as a statement of intent, that he was as good, if not better, than those whose whole reputation and career had rested on 'face' painting. In his autobiographical notes, Hogarth declared 'The portr[ait] of Cap Coram in the foundlings was given as a specimen', much like the paintings at St Bartholomew's were specimens of history painting and, he continues, despite the 'effort that has been made since by every pa[i]nter that has since emulated it', his portrait 'still stand[s] in competition', and 'it has been left to the Judgement of the Public these twenty years whether [any] of the efforts are equall or not.' Yet he cannot resist noting that his portrait of Coram, 'which lowers the difficulty of this branch', in other words shows that such a painting can be executed by a modern painter, not just Van Dyck, 'was done without the practis of having done [a] thounsand [*sic*] which ever[y] other face painter has before he a[r]rives at doing as well'. This may be true, but it is unlikely that Hogarth kept such boasting to himself, a factor that must have made his company at times unbearable, particularly for an artist who focused predominantly or exclusively on portrait painting.[40]

The hospital opened in its temporary accommodation in Hatton Garden, to the west of Smithfield as described in the hospital's daily committee minutes (quoted at the start of this chapter) on 25 March 1741, perhaps with Hogarth's portrait prominently displayed in the entrance hall. A permanent home was being designed and eventually built on open land, Lamb's Conduit Fields, to the north of the city.[41] Soon Great Britain will be, once again, at war – the 'War of the Austrian Succession' – so a better and more timely demonstration as to why raising 'useful' citizens was a good idea, loyal to King George, the Hanoverian dynasty, the Protestant settlement and the British constitution would be hard to find.

Among those governors and officers present that first evening and therefore witnesses to the terrible scenes recorded in the minutes, were Captain Thomas Coram, William Hogarth, Martin Folkes, Theodore Jacobsen (architect of the new building) and Charles Lennox, His Grace the Duke of Richmond.[42] Hogarth, also in his capacity as a governor, was present a few days later when one of the children from the first night died, possibly from an inflammation of the bowel, while others developed illnesses – several, it was observed, were 'Stupifyed with some Opiate' (whether before or after arrival is not clear) – and the local specialist on infant care, Dr Richard Mead, living in Great Ormond Street, was called in to inspect them.[43]

Jane would join William at some of the baptisms in those early years, where the babies were given names (whether they already had them or not) in honour of the governors. There were several Thomas and Eunice Corams, William and Jane Hogarths, even 'Richmonds' and 'Lennoxes', until, as rumour had it, the fear that the grown foundlings might attempt to claim kin with their aristocratic namesakes put a stop to it. The source for names changed to, for example, characters from literature. 'Tom Jones', also a foundling, was one.

The significant success of establishing the institution was followed by a dispute between the governors, allegedly over 'irregularities', and then unfounded rumours against two governors in particular, but no details are forthcoming. Whatever the truth of it, the situation abruptly finished Thomas Coram's official connection with the hospital by 1743, even as the permanent building was rising from its foundation stone. He had given his all to the project and had, in the meantime, lost his wife, Eunice: she had died in mid July 1740 before the opening in Hatton Garden. By this time Coram was lodging near Hogarth's home on Leicester Fields. Coram's finances, too, were in disarray, confirming that, however off-putting his manner, this was a project for which he received no benefit, other than honouring God, King and Country. Dr Brocklesby had broached the idea of raising a subscription to support him in his final years, at which Coram declared, 'I have not wasted the little wealth of which I was formerly possessed in self-indulgence and vain expenses, and am not ashamed to confess that, in my old age, I am poor.'[44] Meanwhile, because of rising death rates among the infants at Hatton Garden, it was decided that the children should be sent out to wet nurses in the country, vital women who breast-fed and nurtured the infants, raising them until the age of four, at which time they were able to return to the hospital.

Hogarth provided the armorial shield which was displayed over the front door of the temporary building, and in 1747 he also designed the institution's 'coat of arms' – the multi-breasted Venus (symbol for 'nature') alongside Britannia, with cap of liberty and shield, acting as supporters to another shield, on which was a naked infant, the motto simply and powerfully 'HELP'. In the meantime, Hogarth was working on a scheme which would be of mutual benefit to both institution and artist, in the spirit of his donation of Coram's portrait.

As already seen at St Bartholomew's Hospital, art was to have a prominent role within the new hospital building – encouraging visitors (and therefore potential donors), while promoting the skill and largesse of artists. For as a result of Hogarth's gift, a sequence of full-length portraits were donated to the Foundling Hospital, including Allan Ramsay's majestic portrait of Dr Richard Mead and Thomas Hudson's *Theodore Jacobsen* providing a roll call of the key (admittedly only male) figures involved in the institution. In tandem, the Governors' Court Room was to have a complete scheme of sculpture, history painting and landscape/topography, again donated by the artists concerned. In the round, the art showcased not just the hospital, its supporters and its beneficiaries, but

contemporary fine art in all its vibrant variety, in the hope that visitors might be inspired to commission an artist who caught their
eye. Crucially, other than in semi-public buildings, or at the artist's
own house, there were no exhibiting spaces or an exhibition-going
culture in the modern sense. Not until 1760, with the advent of
the Society of Artists and their annual exhibition – part springing from the Foundling Hospital art programme and regular artist
gatherings – which, in turn, prefigured the Royal Academy annual
shows from 1769, would artists collectively exhibit their artwork
to a paying public. Until that time, the Foundling Hospital would
be a key location for the donation and display of contemporary British art, from established artists like Hogarth, Lambert,
Ramsay, Highmore, Hudson and Francis Hayman, to young men
just setting out, like Hayman's pupil Thomas Gainsborough and
later Hudson's former student, Joshua Reynolds. For this reason
the hospital is viewed as the first public art gallery in England. And
central to this forum to encourage interest in contemporary art
was history painting – Hogarth had not given up yet, nor indeed
had his fellow painters.

The first artwork to be located in the Governors' Court Room,
anchoring the scheme, was a marble bas-relief overmantel representing Charity, a bare-breasted woman, nurturing three infants
– the traditional symbol for this virtue – by Michael Rysbrack:
the sculptor who had worked with both James Gibbs and Sir James
Thornhill. Surrounding these figures, taking Hogarth's subscription roll design one stage further, were representations of trade and
husbandry: the stern of a ship, cattle, sheaves of wheat. As with the
parable of the Good Samaritan, this was a call for all citizens to
help their neighbour, defined as anyone in need and distress.

The Court Room offered wall space appropriate for four large
independent paintings in 'landscape' format either side of this
overmantel. The arrangement would eventually include eight
roundels, one either side of each history painting, depicting the
Foundling Hospital (Richard Wilson) among her sister institutions, for example *Charterhouse* by Gainsborough, *Greenwich* by
Samuel Wale and *Bethlem* by Edward Haytley.[45]

The process of selecting suitable artists for the history paintings must have been led by Hogarth, Rysbrack and Jacobsen, and of the following names arrived at, Hogarth would obviously be one, in the wake of St Bartholomew's if nothing else, followed by Frank Hayman, his close friend, who had focused on narrative painting rather than portraiture. Hayman's popular large-scale supper-box paintings at Vauxhall Gardens would help to draw folk to this new institution to the north of the city. Next was James Wills, again a friend of Hogarth's and mainly a portrait painter, and then finally Joseph Highmore, who had painted his own *Good Samaritan* in 1744, inspired, in part, by Hogarth's version, proving that he had the ambition and wherewithal to advance in this genre. The Foundling Hospital was a civic institution, founded for the betterment of society as a whole and the British state, but it was also a Christian foundation – indeed, to be absolutely correct, a Protestant foundation. These men were well read. Joseph Highmore, with his early schooling at Merchant Taylors', a City-based free grammar school and then legal training, was proficient in Latin, ancient Greek and possibly Hebrew, and was something of an amateur theologian. James Wills, fearing art might not provide him with a regular income, would be ordained as an Anglican clergyman. So we can imagine the four artists seated around a table, with their combined experience, working out what the scheme should say, what was the theme or message, and how this might be delivered in painted form. At some point in their deliberations they alighted on a clever combination: how to tell the story of the modern foundling using narratives connected to children from the Old and New Testament.[46] Scenes from the early life of Moses, as the most famous foundling in the Jewish and Christian traditions, was an obvious starting point. On Coram's suggestion, the scene where Moses is found in the bulrushes, 'very appropo for an hospital for Foundlings', graced the institution's charter seal. So too was the story, from the Book of Genesis, of Hagar and Ishmael, a mother and her illegitimate child abandoned by the father. And from the New Testament, the famous story of Christ telling his disciples to 'Suffer the little children, and forbid them not to come unto me: for of such is the kingdom of heaven' introduces, for Christians, their greatest role model into the scheme. But placed in

a particular order, further meaning becomes apparent: the image
of Hagar turning away from the dying Ishmael, just as an angel
appears to rescue them, is followed by the children welcomed by
Christ, then to the finding of Moses in the bulrushes by Pharaoh's
daughter, who hands him to the care of a wet nurse, and finally
(the subject assigned to Hogarth) to the older child Moses returning to the protection of his adoptive mother, Pharaoh's daughter.
This, neatly and in parallel, charts the modern foundling's journey:
separation from its birth mother, to reception at the hospital, to
being sent to the country for fostering by a wet nurse and, finally,
the now grown child's return to the hospital.

Having agreed the plan and the format of each painting –
the finished canvases are almost identical in size and were fitted
in identical frames – the four men would have ventured home to
their respective studios and commenced researching, imagining
and then, as and when their day-to-day activities permitted, to
start sketching and, eventually, putting brush to canvas. Further
discussions and presentation of work in progress could have taken
place at their homes or, as was their habit, over a bowl at Slaughter's Coffee House. The hospital's first stone had been laid on 23
September 1742, but as the building was rising from its rural surroundings, Hogarth and his colleagues may have been aware that,
in all likelihood, the wing, containing the sequence of administration rooms including the Court Room, would not be ready to
receive artwork much before late 1745.

In the meantime, Hogarth found time to design the headpiece
of the subscription roll for another new hospital, the London
Infirmary. In a rare depiction (for Hogarth) of Jesus himself, here
he focused on Christ's words, as the seated figure gestures towards
a hospital building, from the Gospel of St Matthew 25:40: 'In as
much as ye have done it unto one of the least of these my Brethren,
ye have done it unto me'; in caring for the poor and less fortunate,
the hospital is doing the Lord's work.

INTERLUDE SIX

SUNDAY 28 MAY, MORNING, THE CROWN INN, ROCHESTER.
The pilgrims awoke at seven and, while still abed, both Hogarth
and Thornhill spoke of the dreams they had had during the night.
If related to the previous day's adventures, their visions may have
had a nautical, martial or charitable theme. This stimulated some
discussion within the group, an attempt to analyse the meaning
of them, although, after some time churning the subject over, the
company 'left off, no Wiser than wee begun'.

The friends clambered out of bed and only then realised
that Samuel Scott was missing, he having risen earlier, as he later
informed them, to sit on the bridge spanning the Medway and
sketch the view in the early morning light: gently rising hills, the
spire of a church in the distance, the river at low tide exposing the
sloping shore and slipway around a building raised on a platform,
itself surrounded by beached vessels, and rowing boats with two or
three occupants skimming over the flat water, drawing the eye to a
prominent single-mast craft to the right ('Drawing ye 2d'). As he
sketched, Scott became aware that the locals passing by were more
than usually interested in his drawing, in fact, rather uncomfort-
ably, they were staring at him. But recalling that it was a Sunday,
the sabbath and in a cathedral city too, solved this mystery. In
fact the ringing bells from the nearby cathedral alone, calling the
community to gather in prayer, should have alerted Sam, but such
was his concentration on sketching, no doubt he had blocked out
all such distractions. On returning to the Crown Inn, his friends
demanded to see the said sketch, but Scott was unable to produce
it, at which 'Wee were all Desirous to have him reconcile this Con-
tradiction.' But as no explanation was offered by the early riser,

and with 'other affairs Intervening', namely breakfast, in sum this 'prevented our further Enquiry'.[1]

The company breakfasted at nine o'clock, paid their reckoning of one pound, seven shillings and threepence for a night's bed and board, which included that princely spread at lunch the day before, and soon after set off on the next stage of their journey. They re-crossed the bridge to Strood and then made their way through the Hoo Peninsula and on to the Isle of Grain. As they walked through the fields, clouds were gathering until the heavens suddenly opened. To avoid getting soaked completely, Sam Scott disappeared under a hedge where, after he emerged, it became apparent from his soiled coat that he had been lying on something nasty, or, as Ebenezer elegantly frames it 'Ordural Moisture of a Verdant Hue'.[2] The Rev-erend Gostling adds that Scott's companions, while suppressing giggles, 'work, all hands, to make him clean, And fitter to be smelt and seen'.[3] In the ensuing confusion Scott became frantic, fearing he had mislaid a dainty white handkerchief lent to him by his wife, Ann. It was soon after found, but his joy turned to consternation, because the delicate item, made more valuable by its sentimental association, had been torn. But persuaded that he was more 'afraid then [than] Hurt' they proceeded 'merrily' to Frindsbury.

At Frindsbury, 'fam'd for prospects fair',[4] they visited the Church of All Saints, considered 'pleasantly Scituated'.[5] The church is on a rise and its spire is a prominent feature from around about: probably the church seen in Scott's sketch from Roches-ter's bridge. Forrest declares that there were 'Some Bad Epitaphs' on the graves outside the church, so bad in fact that they were only deserving of a brief mention. And within the church, they agreed that the list of donations or 'benefactions', where only the vicar was named, 'seem'd a litle odd', but after sniggering over the anomaly and imagining that some inexplicable mystery lay behind it, they moved on. The Reverend Gostling attempts an explana-tion, namely 'the Churchwardens could not write',[6] a reminder that, at this time, reading and writing were not prevalent among working and labouring folk. Foundlings, faring slightly better than the average, were taught to read but not write.

Only an hour had passed since they had left Rochester. A short progress meeting was called, during which the members of the company were given the opportunity to leave if they so desired. And as none did, they continued on together in good heart to Upnor.

Upnor, dominated by its castle, is located at a strategically defensive position on the opposite bank of the Medway to the Royal Navy's dockyards at Chatham. Here the group lingered to inspect the fortifications and Hogarth (as attributed in an engraving published by Jane Hogarth), likely with Scott's input, spent some time drawing the castle and foreshore. Recording buildings within their surroundings, beyond his usual haunts in London and its immediate environs, for example the village and spa of Islington, was very unusual for Hogarth – his focus and expertise if you like, was the depiction of metropolitan life, rather than the English or British experience more broadly. Another much more famous example beyond the capital, which reveals a genuine interest in ancient fortifications, as well as his habit of sketching wherever he was, happened at Calais, where, as here in Upnor, he included a self-portrait. But even in this foreign setting, as he observes in his autobiographical notes, this was an English-built gate, once marking the entry into the English-ruled (since 1347) Pale of Calais.[7]

Ruins are not often seen in Hogarth's work, which is unsurprising, given that he dealt, in the main, with the metropolitan streetscape. There are two unusual drawings on blue paper both of a ruined castle in a landscape, a lake in front, trees framing the scene, one inscribed by Samuel Ireland as a sketch dated 1762 and sent to Joshua Kirby for use in his publication on perspective.[8] And, of course, there is the castle seen behind 'Some Body'.

In Ebenezer Forrest's account, Upnor Castle is described as 'Not very Large But Strong, Garrison'd with Twenty four Men and the Like Number of Gun's Tho[h] no More than Eight are Mounted'.[9] The castle, an Elizabethan artillery fort, was established in 1559, a year after the loss of Calais and the second in the young queen's reign. As noted, the philanthropist Richard Watts was for many years the accounting officer for the works here, which occurred between 1559 and 1567 to protect Royal Navy ships moored or refitting at Chatham. In more recent history, the castle garrison had tried but failed to protect the English navy in 1667, when the Dutch, a mercantile and maritime competitor at this time, sailed up the Medway and set fire to the entire fleet: a humiliation for the recently restored English monarchy under Charles II, and a major blow to the ambitions of England as a naval power. Defoe recalled these painful events, observing that

> this Allarm gave *England* such a Sense of the Consequence of the River *Medway*, and of the Docks and Yards at *Chatham*, and of the Danger the Royal Navy lay exposed to there, that all these Doors which were open then, are lock'd up and sufficiently barr'd since that time ; and 'tis not now in the Power of any Nation under Heaven, no, tho' they should be Masters at Sea, unless they were Masters at Land too at the same time, to give us such another Affront.

The building work could be seen the length of the river and beyond, as our travellers were discovering and as Defoe continues, 'for besides all the Castles, Lines of Guns, and Platforms on each side the River Medway, as we go up, as above [i.e. Upnor, etc.]; there is now a Royal Fort built at the Point of the Isle of Shepey, call'd Sheerness, which guards that Entrance into the River'.[10] The strategic importance of these defences, still necessary while the threat of invasion persisted, continue to echo in the account, as the travellers made their way through this landscape to Sheerness and the English Channel.

Hogarth and Scott's completed drawing (referred to in the manuscript as 'Drawing ye 3d') is a view towards the castle's south side, a view that a visitor even now would instantly recognise. The tide is still low, exposing the riverbed of earth, pebbles and the wooden palisade or stake wall, another distinctive defensive structure. The castle's main façade, punctuated by square and round towers, faces the river (dramatically foreshortened because of the side-on view), with the gatehouse and flagpole at the reverse or road side visible to the left. In the distance the low-rising land is more sparsely wooded in the drawing than now – an indication, perhaps, of the dramatic deforestation in England in the service of the navy and its need of 'Wooden Walls'. In the mid foreground, Hogarth has placed himself and Thornhill standing together chatting and pointing towards the river, like any interested traveller or enthusiast of antiquities. Both are wearing tricorn hats, wigs and full-skirted coats buttoned up to their neck stocks, and they are stockinged and shoed rather than booted, standard attire for this period. John is a good head and shoulders taller than his brother-in-law, as expected, while Forrest and Tothall (in a great coat), too, are taller than Hogarth: which supports the recollection that Billy was comparatively short. To his credit, his vanity has not interfered in his dedication to truth and nature, as reflected in the drawing. All four have walking sticks. Sitting away from the others, perched on some rocks and looking out towards the river and shipping is Samuel Scott, sketching. The ship to the farthest right, with its distinctive prow, is a man o' war; the three-master in the mid distance may be another, with its masts dropped; while other smaller craft bob gently nearby, or are being rowed to and from the shore.

Ebenezer Forrest recalls buying cockles from an old blind man and a half-blind woman – another male–female couple, as with the 'gaffer' and 'gammer' at the Billingsgate Dark House – who were on the river in a 'Cock Boat', a small rowing boat used to ferry goods from ship to shore and back again, as seen in the commemorative sketch.[11] No doubt this was absolutely true, and points to the couple's relentless need to scrape together a living in advanced age. The Reverend Gostling considered the purchase of the cockles as an act of charity, in view of their frailty, but, in any case, the molluscs, pulled from the estuary riverbed, were freshly caught and the friends, being a little peckish, made good use of these tasty articles.[12] And, as with London's Charons, the watermen, there is an almost mystical quality to the scene. Sightlessness holds a particular significance in ancient myth, as does rowing back and forth across a river. Or perhaps their appearance – and Forrest's inclusion of the event – nods to the maxim, 'In the land of the blind, the one-eyed man is king', the blind man relying on his half-blind companion. And of course, the cockle shell, like the scallop, with its distinctive fan shape, acts as a symbol of the pilgrim.

The gang, peckish rather than philosophical, 'made a Hurry scurry Dinner' as they walked a few hundred yards beyond Upnor Castle, towards The Smack, another tavern, 'at ye Ten Gun Battery', established as a support to Upnor Castle after the Dutch raid on the Medway. Here the friends, feeling a little frolicsome or 'like boys',[13] made a commotion inspired by the military nature of the topography, 'and had a Batle Royall with Sticks pebbles and Hog's Dung'. During this playfight, Will Tothall, rather than Sam Scott, the usual butt of jokes and misfortune, 'was the Greatest Sufferer and his Cloaths carried the Marks of his Disgrace some time this occasion'd Much Laughter'.[14] The regularity with which Hogarth and his companions wilfully cover themselves in dirt – invariably one or other type of animal dung – seems a bit rash, given they had limited changes of clothing and still several days to go before a complete overhaul of their attire could be achieved, for this was a trip undertaken on a whim and a tight budget.

Passing over the hills, away from the Birdsnest Battery, another example of the Medway's strengthened defences and 'keeping the River and Shipping Still in View'[15] they arrived at Hoo (meaning spur of land). The ancient church with its prominent spire, like All Souls, was dedicated to the Mercian saint Warburgh or Werburgh (b.650–40 BC).[16] As previously noted, there was a genuine interest in visiting churches and inspecting the graves and tombs within and without – the references litter the record of the journey, for this was one of the central activities during *The Peregrination*, other than walking, eating, drinking and horseplay.[17]

In *The Analysis of Beauty*, Hogarth noted the delight of a puzzle and attempting to solve it: 'It is a pleasing labour of the mind to solve the most difficult problems ; allegories and riddles, trifling as they are, afford the mind amusement.'[18] Aside from the frivolous or simple brain-teaser nature of grave epitaphs, more profoundly it seems that with death much more present (comparatively, that is, to the majority of their modern descendants and successors) within the day-to-day lives of early Georgian Britons – from distressing levels of infant mortality, as experienced by Hogarth's own parents, and death in childbirth, to public execution and the sight of gibbets, let alone perpetual warfare, untold incurable diseases and debilitating medical conditions – there was an accompanying fascination in the details presented by such memorials. And not simply the manner by which those who have gone before have met their end, or at what age, but how the dead speak to those who come after: whether through the bombast of an alabaster tomb and effigy, or the idiosyncratic text scored into wood, or the same carved into marble and stone. No matter how it is done, a desire to be remembered, the very human need to linger in the present here on earth is remarkable. Given that Hogarth and his companions defined their travels as a pilgrimage, even in jest, such observances are wholly appropriate.

In an age that fervently believed in (or hoped for) the existence of an afterlife, the thought that the dead could be present among the living in a more active way was accepted. In his autobiography, Benjamin Franklin recalled that he had made a promise with a friend, Charles Osborne, who died relatively young in the West Indies, 'that the one who happen'd first to die, should if possible make a friendly Visit to the other, and acquaint him how he found things in that separate State. But,' Ben concludes, ruefully, 'he never fulfill'd his Promise.'[19] They may have been encouraged by such books as Elizabeth Rowe's popular *Friendship in Death: In Twenty Letters from the Dead to the Living* (first published 1728), the first letter from 'Mr.-------' to the 'Earl of R------,' 'who had promised to appear to him after his Death'.[20]

At St Werburgh's the pilgrims were drawn to an epitaph carved on a wooden rail over one grave, 'which', Ebenezer recalled, 'being something Extraordinary I shall here Transcribe Verbatim'. The Reverend Gostling adds the detail that they all laughed at this epitaph, 'A servant maid, turn'd poetaster, Wrote it in honour of her master.'[21] This is a rather dismissive observation, a poetaster being an inferior poet, a mere versifier:[22]

And. wHen. he. Died. you. plainLy. see.
Hee. freely. gave. al. to. Sara. passaWee.
And. in. Doing. so. if. DoTh. prevail.
that. I on. him. can. Well. besTow. this. Rayel.
On. year. I. Sarved. him. it. is. well. None.
BuT. ThanKs. beto. God. it. is. all. my. One.[23]

Such rustic memorials, 'Their name, their years, spelt by th'unletter'd muse', were given greater dignity by Thomas Gray in *An Elegy Written in a Country Church Yard* (1751): 'Some frail memorial still erected nigh,/ With uncouth rhimes and shapeless sculpture deck'd,/ Implores the passing tribute of a sigh.'[24] The full meaning of this particular epitaph is not immediately apparent, but what can be gleaned (with the assistance of the Reverend Gostling) is that the maid, Sara, had paid for a very modest wooden marker for her master, keeping the rest of her inheritance to herself. It is possible that the master had used Sara ill, and that some delicious revenge, a form of natural or folk justice, had taken place, in the guise of his monument's almost derisory lack of pomp.

After pondering collectively this conundrum, delivered from the grave to perplex visitors still, Ebenezer Forrest recalls the following incident, which, over subsequent centuries, is invariably quoted to expose Hogarth's iconoclastic disregard for organised religion. As Forrest tells it, 'Hogarth having a Motion; untruss'd upon a Grave Rail in an unseemly Manner which Tothall Perceiving administred penance to ye part offending with a Bunch of Netles, this occasion'd an Engagement which Ended happily without Bloodshed and Hogarth Finish'd his Business against the Church Door.'[25] The Reverend Gostling adds a few more details:

> Our *Hogarth*'s guts began to grumble,
> Which he to ease, turn'd up his tail
> Over a monumental rail;
> *Tothall*, for this indecent action,
> Bestowing on him just correction
> With nettles, as there was no birch,
> He fled for refuge to the church,
> And shamefully the door besh-t;
> O filthy dauber! filthy wit![26]

Gostling gives the impression that Hogarth had been afflicted, suddenly, with something like diarrhoea rather than the average bowel movement, from which his only relief was to pull down his breeches and, dangling his backside over a grave rail, proceed to unburden himself in plain sight of all present, including, should they be looking down upon the scene, St Werburgh of Blessed Memory, Our Lord and the Deity. The punishment for this (in itself) indecent act, let alone the disregard for the bones of the dead lying underneath and in the shade of God's House, was a beating on his bare arse with stinging nettles, administered by the former merchant sailor Will Tothall, which sent the delinquent hobbling towards the church for safety, coat hitched up, breeches round his ankles, where he finished the job by beshitting the church door, no doubt to the sound of rough reproach mixed with uncontrollable laughter. Before giving way to modern squeamishness, in this period men pissed in pots located around tavern rooms and there was little qualm, when a rumble signalled a turd's imminent arrival, to find the nearest and most convenient place to deposit it. In several images Hogarth depicts a figure relieving himself – notably in *The Enraged Musician*, *The March of the Guards to Finchley* and *Chairing the Members*. And in Hogarth's defence, the church at Hoo sat exposed on a small hill and so there was little else he could have done – although crapping up the church door does seem an extreme as well as unnecessary flourish.

The Reverend Gostling's response, although an Anglican clergyman, is lightly chastising rather than condemnatory, describing Hogarth as a 'filthy dauber!' but also a 'filthy wit!', which could as easily describe some of his bawdier graphic satires. There may be a symbolic frisson to this essential and dirty act, although the friends have shown little regard to throwing around animal dung, a common enough sight and smell in the paths and streets here in Kent, as well as at home in London. (That the great satirist and Hogarth's hero, Jonathan Swift, was probably born in the parish of St Werburgh, Dublin, is pure coincidence.)[27]

A possible connection, or explanation, to this anecdote is the Greek philosopher, Diogenes the Cynic (*c*.400–325 BC), a famed contrarian and ironic wit, who spent much of his time sitting in a 'tub', eschewing comfort and convention.[28] One story concerns him wandering through Athens, during the day, holding a lighted lamp, declaring he was looking for an honest man. For this reason he is depicted within political satires – the last place you might

36. *Industry and Idleness Plate 3: The Idle 'Prentice at Play in the Church Yard, during Divine Service,* etching and engraving, 1747
The skulls and bones, like the pirate gibbet at Cuckold's Point, are an omen. Tom's new friend, sporting an eye patch, will turn informer.

find one – but also appears in Raphael's *School of Athens*, and was a popular subject among seventeenth-century artists, including Rubens, Jusepe de Ribera (a portrait holding a lamp), Salvator Rosa and Jacob Jordaens (all engraved).[29] As an advocate of natural uninhibited behaviour, Diogenes was also known for urinating and defecating in public, even during public lectures – a 'filthy wit' indeed. Unsurprisingly, and alongside his admiration for the virtues of dogs, this philosopher was known for dog-like conduct: the term 'cynic' derives from the Greek *kynikos* 'dog-like'. Hogarth's actions here were certainly antisocial. He might be described as a cynic and, with his admiration for dogs, he could well be called a modern Diogenes – a further layer, perhaps, to Hogarth's use of the pug dog as his alter ego.

Hogarth used the desecration of the sanctity of a graveyard and those buried within it in the third scene of *Industry and Idleness*. Tom Idle is gambling on a tomb, skulls and bones littering

37. *Industry and Idleness Plate 2: The Industrious 'Prentice Performing the Duty of a Christian,* etching and engraving, 1747
While Tom gambles with his life and soul, Frank continues his
steady progress towards the Lord Mayoralty of London.

the foreground, but neither he nor his companions are sensitive to
this, or care. Nor are they aware that they are about to be chastised,
by a parish beadle armed with a whipping cane. 'The Idle 'Prentice
at play in the Church Yard during Divine Service' is accompanied with Proverbs 19:29, 'Judgements are prepar'd for Scorners
& stripes for the back of Fools'. The companion image is 'The
INDUSTRIOUS 'PRENTICE performing the Duty of a Christian' accompanied by Psalm 119:97, 'O How I love thy Law it is my
meditation all the day'. But, for all that Hogarth might be thought
cynical in some respects, there is no reason to see any irony in the
meaning of these prints. Hogarth is very open about the intended
clarity and simplicity of his message. And Goodchild's face is the
picture of earnest concentration while he sings, in full voice, an
Anglican hymn. To his right is his master's lovely daughter, his
future wife. And again, Tom Nero, in the third stage of cruelty,
is discovered in a churchyard, having murdered his girlfriend and

their unborn child. Churches are seen, in the distance of *Gin Lane* and *Beer Street*, and as a backdrop in 'Noon' and so on, planting the action in a specific London area or even street, but also, in the first two, indicating perhaps a moral distance from human degradation.

Hogarth may not have been a regular attender of church services, but there is clear moral and even a spiritual quality to his words, images and deeds, certainly established in childhood under his father's guidance. The issue for Hogarth is how the actual teachings of Jesus, as described in the New Testament, have been interpreted, muffled, even deadened, through the mechanisms of organised religion. For example the tedium of a bad sermon, as seen in *The Sleeping Congregation*, engraved in 1736 from a painting some years earlier. In both, Christ's beautiful words of hope and respite for the body and soul are visible on the preacher's open book, 'Come unto me all ye who labour and are Heavy laden & I will give you Rest'. A grumpy curate glances sideways at a pretty woman who is slumbering, likewise the entire congregation – yet the preacher preaches on, oblivious, unconcerned, or simply just going through the motions.

And as we have seen and will see, religious paintings, although a limited part of his entire output (which would be true of any British artist of his generation), would, however, become a prominent feature in Hogarth's later life. But authority figures, whether priests, bishops or the pope, were not immune from justifiable criticism, and any whiff of Christian hypocrisy or extremism – consider his late work, using the original plate for *The Sleeping Congregation*, now focused on 'Credulity, Superstition, and Fanaticism' (*Enthusiasm Delineated*, created 1760–62) – was quite correctly ripe for the taking. Hogarth was not a zealot, but there is an element of subversive disruption against the established order throughout his work, whether friends were members of it or not, with the accompanying rumble of quiet thunder, or, perhaps closer to his character, a long and low growl.

In any case, after such an ignoble display, and with time marching on, it being four o'clock in the afternoon, the five friends prepared to leave Hoo, but not until they had partaken of another soul-reviving beverage. The landlady of the unnamed hostelry,

38. *The Sleeping Congregation*, etching and engraving, 1736
Priced one shilling, the print depicts an ancient country
(rather than urban) church. The young woman, her prayer
book open to 'Of Matrimony', dreams of love.

according to Ebenezer Forrest an 'agreable',[30] comely widow, in
the Reverend Gostling's words 'complaisant and kind', is notable,
aside from her tangible personal allure, for having buried four
husbands or, as Gostling elaborates, 'Had (as the phrase is) been

shod round.' This is likely to be a reference to the shoeing of the four hooves of a horse, the horseshoe then as now being associated with weddings as tokens of good fortune. Gostling adds that, four husbands on, yet she 'had no want of charms for more'.[31] As a seasoned campaigner in the matrimonial stakes, we might be reminded, once more, of Chaucer's Wife of Bath, of whom 'Not one of her five Husbands could be found,/ She lay'd 'em safe long since in holy Ground.'[32] Perhaps the alluring widow regaled her guests, three of whom were married (Hogarth, Scott and Forrest), with some feminine wisdom.[33] Or perhaps, like any good host and a prime example of the fair sex, she listened quietly, nodding and smiling benignly to the talk and chatter of her beguiled guests, while topping up their pots with refreshing local beer. Thus revitalised, the five men grudgingly bid adieu to the Kentish Circe in the midst of her charmed or, as Ebenezer Forrest describes it, 'Charming Country', and continued on very contentedly, bathed in the mid afternoon sunshine which, accompanied by a heady lightness of spirit, was 'exceeding pleasant'.[34]

As they progressed, Samuel Scott, 'according to Custom',[35] introduced a philosophical conundrum – whether 'a Man might go over but not through the World', attempting to prove the former correct by pointing to the ground and asking whether anyone present could physically move through this dense element. The proposition may have provoked some consideration, even discussion, but was soon given short shrift by the others for 'Our fix'd opinion was that his argument had less Weight than his Coat Pocketts.'[36] At this prompting, Scott discovered that his pockets had been filled gradually, as they walked, with pebbles, an increasing burden he had been carrying, unbeknown, for some time. Scott had acquired the role of the group's straw man, as well as a mock Bunyan's Christian: 'But at last Discovering y'ᵉ. Trick and being thereby in a Condicōn to knock Down all opposition to his Argument, Wee Acqiesc'd.'[37] Continuing, at five o'clock they arrived at Stoke (or Upper Stoke) Church, dedicated to St Peter, and, as was their habit, they wandered through the churchyard, 'but saw Nothing Worth Observaciōn' that was worth their notice, or observance as in religious ceremony or custom. This, despite the obvious historical interest in this beautiful little church. Collective disappointment was soon forgotten, however, when the company came upon another conundrum in the shape of an elm tree next to a nearby farmhouse, perhaps recalled still in the 'Elm Tree Cottages' next to St Peter's church, which made them pause for some time. For on top of the elm was fixed a high pole, at the end of which was a board with a painted cock or cockerel, above which was a weathercock or weathervane, a not dissimilar contraption to the first and therefore somewhat superfluous, and above this still, a shuttlecock: all fashioned by a local carpenter or the resident farmer, whether last week or last century, who knows. Unsurprisingly, 'This Variety of Cocks afforded much Speculation',[38] as indeed it should.

Moving on, the pilgrims came to another settlement that Ebenezer Forrest calls 'North Street'.[39] This was likely to have been a few buildings on the main track to Lower Stoke, where they decided to quarrel, again, 'and being near a Well of Water full to the Brim, Wee Dealt about that Ammunition for some time till the Cloaths and Courage of the Combatants were Sufficently Cool'd'.[40] A water fight on a warm late spring day is a very natural instinct, and no doubt Will Tothall was delighted to remove substances of an ordural nature that still clung to his coat from a previous encounter. After which, somewhat 'pleas'd' with themselves, they travelled on to 'Stock', or Lower Stoke, located near the Saltings.

On some late eighteenth-century maps of the Hoo Peninsula, including in Edward Hasted's *History of Kent*, Lower Stoke is called Osterland, believed to derive from the abundance of oysters.[41] It lies on the main and ancient route used to pass from Hoo to the Isle of Grain. As a result, here is where inns, offering rooms and repast, could be had for the weary traveller, including our pilgrims' billet for the night, the Nag's Head.[42] The close proximity to the Medway allowed for easy transport of goods, including salt, to Rochester and London, and it is thought that the Saltings around Stoke have existed here since the time of the Romans. While waiting for their supper (timed for around six o'clock), they ventured out to 'take a Veiw of the Low Countries thereabouts',[43] which would have included these Saltings and associated buildings.

After admiring the long vistas and immense skies – there is little here to interrupt a full panorama – they entertained themselves, yet again, by a 'Sharp engagement', during which the clothes of both Sam Scott and Will Tothall were daubed in soft cow dung. No sooner had they washed off whatever grime clung to them at the North Street well, after several hours walking through marshland in the bright sunshine, they were filthy again. All this ribaldry occurred over an hour and now, as supper was awaiting them, they returned to the tavern, cleaned themselves up, ate their food – no details here, but their total bill for one night's bed and board was eleven shillings and sixpence – and then sat by the tavern door, with the main track before them, sipping punch as the evening drew on and the locals wandered by. Here Hogarth sketched the company, standing and sitting, at their contented leisure. The text says 'see Drawing yᵉ. 3ᵈ', which is that of Upnor Castle from earlier in the day, so clearly the figures were added while at Stoke.

Night coming on, the clocks striking ten, and as there were three beds available to them, the group drew straws or 'Cutts' to see who would be lucky enough to sleep alone. Ebenezer Forrest notes there were no nightcaps either, so they would have to sleep with bald, uncovered heads. The straws were drawn and Will Tothall, lucky fellow, the winner. And so to bed.

But not before some further bawdy banter, as Forrest, sharing with Sam, recalled we 'had Much Laughter at Scott and I forced to Lye together. They Threw the Stocking Fought perukes and did a Great many pretty things in a Horn, and then left us.'[44] Writing as 'Uxorius' (having a great or excessive fondness for one's wife), the anonymous author of *Hymen: An accurate Description of the Ceremonies used in Marriage* of 1760 tells us that 'to throw the stocking' is part of the newly-weds' ceremony in England, where the bride and groom have been led to the bedroom by (respectively) their female or male friends and relations: 'The men take the bride's stockings, and the women those of the bridegroom; they then seat themselves at the bed's-feet, and throw the stockings over their heads, and whenever any one hits the owner of them, it is looked upon as an omen that that person will be married in a short time.' Although, by the mid eighteenth century, this folk

ceremony was 'looked upon as meer play and foolery', nonetheless 'new marriages are often occasioned by such accidents'.[45] This
element of their horseplay and the wig fight seem clear enough, but
what a 'Great many pretty things in a Horn' might mean, an echo
of Cuckold's Point, St Werburgh's church and the Three Cocks, is
thankfully less obvious and, as Forrest himself has done, can be left
to our imagination.

An hour after this conjugal sport, Scott and Forrest dressed
in the dark, their sheets being damp, and then returned to sleep.
But at three o'clock, they were up again, cursing the day, 'Our Eyes
Lipps and Hands being Tormented and Swell'd by the Biting of
Gnat's' – a hazard of marshland. Thus tormented, like the long-
suffering Job, by a small plague of flies, but very weary, they soon
turned once more towards slumber: 'Notwithstanding this the
God of Sleep being powerfull wee soon forgott our Miseries and
Submitted to be bound fast again in his Leaden Chains in which
Condicōn wee remain'd till Six.'[46]

CHAPTER SIX

NATURE'S DRAMATIST

All available evidence confirms that the Hogarths had a happy marriage. Unequal, as husband and wife, though they were in the eyes of society and, fundamentally, in law, nonetheless, like many others in similar circumstances, the union developed into a strong partnership, both emotionally and professionally. Although described as an elopement, the marriage ceremony in 1729 was performed in an Anglican church rather than clandestinely, albeit not St Paul's, Covent Garden, the bride's parish. Still, as declared by George Vertue in private and by Hogarth's biographers in public, and, it should be noted, during Jane's lifetime, the couple's initial attraction, which ripened into a strong affection, struggled and eventually rebelled against the strictures imposed by Sir James's pragmatism and fatherly concerns.

Thornhill may have hoped that his only daughter would marry into money and a title, shoring up his hard-earned success over several decades by raising his family's fortunes and status, rather than tie herself to a man of modest origins and uncertain income. But there is no sign that he was attempting to force the issue by demanding that his daughter marry another of his choosing. And as seen, any rancour had soon passed, suggesting that Sir James's fondness for the couple, even his arrogant pup of a son-in-law, overcame all else. The close friendship between Hogarth and the affable John Thornhill, fulfilling the role of brother that Hogarth had grieved for since young Richard Hogarth's death in infancy, is likely to have assisted in a swift reconciliation.

In the event, both Billy and Jenny, as they playfully called each other, had chosen for themselves wisely and well.[1] Jane, as the daughter of a high-profile, very prolific and successful artist, knew exactly

39. *Drawing for an unused subject, probably 'The industrious
'prentice married and furnishing his house'*, pen and brown
ink and grey wash over graphite on paper, 1746–7
A young married couple hold hands as tradesmen decorate their parlour. A
pet cat snoozes (bottom right), adding to the air of domestic contentment.

how a busy combined household, practice and showroom was
managed. And she would have been familiar (if not always at ease)
with the very particular atmosphere and pressures of living over the
shop – it is likely that the domestic spaces were firmly within Mrs
Hogarth's bailiwick. But after her husband's death, Jane continued
to run and expand the print business, which largely maintained her,
her dependants and sizeable estate (by then including two houses)
until her death twenty-six years later. In a letter dated 1781 she confirmed 'my whole dependence is upon the sale of Mr Hogarth's
Works'.[2] This included a bound collection of her husband's most
famous prints, with commentary by the Reverend John Trusler,
priced £1 18 shillings under the title *Hogarth Moralized* (1768).[3]
In parallel (as we shall see) during these decades the indomitable
Jane will defend her husband's reputation both artistic and personal
– *Hogarth Moralized* is one example – against the presumptuous

comments and limited understanding of the likes of John Nichols and Horace Walpole, who were keen to tap into the broad appeal and high esteem, which rarely if ever waned for William Hogarth.

The house on Leicester Fields, their home and business address since moving from the Great or Little Piazza in 1733 was where sitters, visitors, clients and browsers were received, subscriptions taken in, engraving plates made and prints collected or sold. It was a standard terrace property of the late seventeenth/early eighteenth century. It consisted of a three-bay (window) front, with kitchens in the basement, two parlours on the ground floor, the front door, with a casement above and the distinctive 'Golden Head' set to the right, leading to the staircase. There were grander rooms on the first or principal floor, bedchambers above and the servants' quarters in the garrets. It is likely that the cook lived out, but any manservant or maid would be resident. All in, this is a sizeable group of people, living and working together in a relatively small space. So *esprit de corps*, a sense of common endeavour – the smooth running and success of the business that everyone depended on – would have been vital. Hogarth could expect and indeed received loyalty from this little community. According to John Nichols, 'Some of his domestics had lived many years in his service.'[4] When they first moved in, Hogarth's mother, Anne, lived close by in Cranbourne Alley – possibly where Hogarth had lived prior to his marriage and one reason why the couple had since moved back to the area – and therefore conveniently placed for her son and daughter-in-law to keep a filial eye on his ageing, but healthy and resolutely independent parent. After her untimely death two years later, following Sir James by just a few months, walking by or through this alley en route to St Martin's Lane or Covent Garden must have brought a pang of melancholy to family members.

The Hogarths entertained at home like any couple of their social status. There are references to suppers with Davy Garrick, among others, and of course the joking invitation to Dr Arnold King, playing on ancient Greek letters, to join the artist at his house to 'eat a bit of pie'. Hogarth, it is said, did not play at cards, but this was an entertainment that Jane enjoyed. Popular games included piquet and quadrille. So while she and friends were thus in affable contest, Hogarth, loitering around and ever in need of an activity or useful distraction, would take a few of the fish-shaped quadrille tokens and etch further detail on them – scales, fins, faces – so that each became an individual character, but all, given they were fish, with that slightly wide-eyed, watchful expression. So whimsical were these little gems that John Ireland, in the spirit of his subject, reproduced them as 'A TAIL-PIECE' in his *Hogarth Illustrated*.[5] Other sources suggest a much earlier date for the card tokens, before their marriage, but the anecdote, even if invented as a hint of their domestic arrangements, is too lovely to ignore. The lack of interest in cards does hint at a character that was not interested in frivolities. Hogarth was conditioned to be constantly on the go, always thinking and doing, so enforced repose, or just sitting down for hours on end, ran counter to his temperament. He may have considered such activity dissipated, a habit of the bored aristocrat – the late work known as *The Lady's Last Stake*, originally entitled *Piquet: or Virtue in Danger* (c.1759), might suggest Hogarth's attitude – but this was something about which Jane, the daughter of a knight, was unconcerned.

Hogarth's sisters, Ann and Mary, had been running their drapery business in Little Britain from 1730, but by 1736 they were operating from Cranbourne Alley, possibly the very house that their mother had occupied. Around this time William painted their portraits in profile for display, facing each other, a sign of their affectation and professional as well as sisterly bond (Col. Figs 12 & 13). The family resemblance between the three siblings is remarkable. The sisters' portraits probably hung at the house in Cranbourne Alley, but when Mary died in 1741, Ann joined her brother and sister Jane in Leicester Fields, where these portraits would remain until 1790. The Hogarth family firm was fully supported and staffed, with Ann now joining the management of all activity including printselling. Her presence would continue to be a great assistance to the business, but, again, Hogarth proved himself a fond and supportive brother, as Nichols observes: 'Want of tenderness and liberality to his relations was not among the failings of *Hogarth*.' He would leave his sister an annuity of £80, a sizeable sum for a single woman living with her relations, as Ann continued to do.[6]

In addition to inherited items such as Sir James Thornhill's ornamental 'Zodiac' delftware dinner plates, the family portraits of Ann, Mary, Jane (with lamb) and Hogarth's self-portrait in oil painted around the time of his move to Leicester Fields, there was a life-size terracotta bust (head and shoulders) of Hogarth that may have been on display in the public rooms for visitors and clients to admire.[7] The sculptor, the Frenchman Louis-François Roubiliac, had caused a stir with the unveiling in 1738 of his life-sized marble figure of George Handel at Vauxhall Gardens. It was Handel's informal appearance in modern dress that initially attracted attention: a house coat and soft hat, one slipper dangling effortlessly from a raised foot, the other just stockinged, strumming a lyre like a lithe young swain rather than the fifty-something, somewhat gruff and rotund musical leviathan that he then was. It was also extraordinary that a sculpture for a public space was for anyone other than a monarch, an aristocrat or a member of the armed forces: another example of proprietor Jonathan Tyers's canny use of art to raise Vauxhall's profile and draw the crowds. Through this sculpture, the modern Apollo holds sway over the gardens, the genius of endless pleasure.

Roubiliac had arrived in London from Paris as early as 1730, but this commission established his reputation and business. He joined Hogarth and John Ellys at their St Martin's Lane Academy as a teacher. So little wonder that he was sought out to immortalise other men of status in the arts. Vertue mentions Hogarth's bust, within the entries book-ended by June and October 1741, as being part of a sequence of portraits from life by Roubiliac, and that the example of 'Mr. Hogarth' is 'very like'.[8] Although in terracotta or clay, which might usually be the preparatory stage towards the marble busts Roubiliac was famed for, the warmth of terracotta, more suggestive of the sitter's flesh tones in this instance, brings the portrait more readily to life. In other words, anyone standing before the bust, as with a life mask – which Roubiliac is known to have used to achieve his strong likenesses – is as close as is possible to actually meeting William Hogarth, to being in his physical presence.

The inner sanctum at the sign of the Golden Head was the

space where Hogarth painted and engraved. Ideally, an artist's painting room was north-facing, so that natural light remained as even as possible as the sun rose, passed over and then set.[9] The canvas would sit on an easel facing the window and at such an angle (perhaps turned as the day progresses) so that the artist's shadow would not fall across it. The house was on the south-east corner of Leicester Fields, with the larger windows at the front, facing west on to the open public space. For this reason Hogarth may have located his painting room on that side, rather than the rear of the house, with the potential for longer periods of natural light, but with constant noise from the street and square – a comforting background hum, with the occasional intriguing distraction, or an irritation, enraging an artist as much as it would a musician. As a naturally inquisitive and observant chap, yet more than capable of prolonged periods of concentration (as the sheer scale of his output tells us) Hogarth was more likely to be in the former camp. Besides which, an open square was a far more pleasant and relatively quiet environment than a narrow street at least, and Leicester Fields had been improved soon after the Hogarths moved there, as announced in the *Country Journal* in 1737, 'in a very elegant manner: a new wall and rails to be erected all round, and a basin in the middle, after the manner of Lincoln's Inn Fields'.[10] A telescope listed among the artist's paraphernalia suggests a curiosity for whatever was going on outside – in heaven or on earth.[11]

The sale of Jane's property, held at the house in 1790, suggests that the ground floor (as would be expected) was where their business was conducted. This floor could be maintained more easily as a discrete area of the house, allowing the upper floors to be domestic and family spaces. The sale included a 'large press', described as with 'glazed doors and sliding shelves, painted mahogany' and a cabinet for 'colours', both in the front parlour – surely where such heavy items would have been throughout.[12] From the description, the press (rather than a printing press) was like a linen press or cupboard, easily adapted to store paper, sketchbooks and engravings. The cabinet for colours (the precise nature of these 'colours' is not mentioned) is described as small, with twenty-four drawers. It would have contained a myriad of either ready-mixed oil paint purchased from a local colourman in pig bladders, like a small bulging balloon tied at the top and pierced with a pin to control the release of paint, a precursor to the tube developed in the 1830s, or pigments in bottles, probably ground already for preparation on site. (Or a combination of the two.) To that end the room would have had bottles of oils, known as binding media, usually linseed, walnut and poppy, into which the pigment was mixed; Hogarth used linseed for most colours (it was a fast drier) except for whites and blues, as linseed tended to yellow over time.[13] Hogarth's supports were invariably canvas (flax-based fabric), stretched over a wooden frame, the stretcher, either by the artist or, more likely, purchased ready-made in standard sizes (height then width: 'three-quarter' 30 × 25 inches; 'Kit Kat' 36 × 28 inches; 'half-length' 50 × 40 inches; 'whole length' 94 × 58 inches) again from a local artist supplier or colourman. Canvases were usually coated with a coloured priming or ground, which stopped the paint sinking into the fabric, and in Hogarth's case was a grey – standard for the period, and as had been practised by Sir Godfrey Kneller. (Hogarth had nothing but disdain for artists returning from their foreign travels and attempting to draw the gullible public to their studios by 'some new stratagem of painting the face all red or all blue or all purple at the first sitting'.[14] Allan Ramsay famously had returned from Italy having acquired the habit of using red.) Other materials would have included rags (painting is, inevitably, a messy business), easels, brushes, knives and palettes – of this last, one in particular would act as a favourite instrument, akin to a virtuoso's violin. J. M. W. Turner owned a palette associated with Hogarth shaped like a large rectangular games bat.[15] All three of Hogarth's painted self-portraits (excluding *Calais Gate*) include a palette, but of a more familiar, 'kidney' shape. The example in the earliest version, hanging proudly within the house, seems to be a slightly ungainly later addition, while that included in the 1745 portrait (which we will return to) is a standard shape, a stretched oval with a thumb hole to one side – a portrait of his own palette.

The last self-portrait (Col. Fig. 27) shows Hogarth in the act of painting, his canvas resting against the easel and on two pegs, at a height suitable for an artist seated rather than standing, deftly holding his palette, with pure paints, from white and red to yellow and blue, neatly arranged across the upper edge, and, in the same hand, five brushes of various thicknesses, all for use during the course of painting. Finally, in his right hand, is a palette knife. The canvas, as expected, is turned towards the even light filtering through the window behind him, the room decorated plainly in an olive or drab colour. Not seen in any of the self-portraits is a mahl or maul stick, a steadying tool held in the (usually at this time) left hand with the padded tip resting on the canvas and with the right or painting hand leaning against it, allowing the application of a detail without smudging any wet paint. Sir David Wilkie (1785–1841) owned such a mahl stick again associated with Hogarth.[16] The fact that artists like Turner and Wilkie owned the tools of their predecessors suggests that these very personal items had a totemic quality imbued, through their sweat and paint, with artistic pedigree and kinship. This was certainly true for Wilkie, who described the six *Marriage A-la-Mode* scenes as 'miracles of art'.[17]

Although preparatory sketches exist, there is evidence of extensive reworking on many of Hogarth's canvases, which Elizabeth Einberg has described beautifully as 'his restless, individual handling of paint – often more resembling a struggle with it, especially when it comes to compositions ... Almost every canvas bears witness to this struggle with multiple alterations, over-paintings and additions, and sometimes, as in the case of his famous Self-Portrait, these were of a very radical nature.'[18] In some cases Hogarth reused canvases: one was employed four separate times, with the artist turning it ninety degrees at each reuse.[19]

Given the intensity in which he worked it is not surprising to learn, from the recollections of a household servant, Mrs Chapel, that everyone, including Jenny, had to tread very carefully when Hogarth was labouring in his painting room, for 'when he was engaged with his pencil any interruption gave him great annoyance'. Mrs Chapel recounts a charming incident, when, overwhelmed by curiosity on account of a tradesman's bill which she thought extravagant, Jane, daringly, approached the painting room door and called out, '"Billy, Billy." "What is the matter, Jenny?" he inquired.' Surprised at his inviting tone, '"I may come in, then, may I?" she answered.' And so she did.[20]

Whether the painting room would be the same space in which a client came for sittings is not clear. Mary Pendarves, now in the early 1740s, very happily married to the Reverend Patrick Delany, recalled, in her letter of 1731, being with (rather than sitting for) Hogarth while he painted, although (given the date) not at Leicester Fields. Hogarth's friend and neighbour, the Swiss enamellist André Rouquet, wrote that 'Every portrait painter in England has a room to shew his pictures, separate from that in which he works' and that 'portraits, finished and unfinished, decorate the picture room'.[21]

The Reverend William Cole sat for Hogarth around the year 1736. At the time Cole was a student at Clare College, Cambridge, and his fellow student and friend, Thomas Western, had also sat for the painter.[22] In his recollection, the Reverend Cole says that tipping servants was still usual at the time, so, leaving Hogarth 'at the door, and his servant's opening it ... I offered him a small gratuity ; but the man very politely refused it, telling me it would be as much as the loss of his place, if his master knew it. This was so uncommon, and so liberal in a man of Mr. *Hogarth*'s profession at that time of day, that it much struck me, as nothing of the sort had happened to me before.'[23] Presumably Hogarth did not want his servants to make money from his clients and visitors. He could also argue that he was more than capable of paying and caring for his own household – anything other would be irresponsible, an abrogation of duty, about which aristocrats had no scruple.

Later in life Hogarth was disparaging about portraiture – 'face painting' or 'phiz-mongering', as he described it. He believed he had been forced in the early 1740s to withdraw from this genre because of internal fighting within the art community, an ungrateful community that he felt he had been trying to defend against an influx of voguish portrait painters from abroad, notably Van Loo. This may be a retrospective shift of reality, as well as a misconception of what was happening at the time. Portrait painting was the most sought after genre, and therefore the most likely to attract new blood. Inevitably, artists who had chosen to focus on portraiture – rather than use it as a stepping stone to greater things, as Hogarth's actions and words would have constantly reminded them – were sensitive to all competition, wherever it came from. Hogarth had launched his painting career in portraiture, after having been known for print production for almost a decade, and his own success may have been viewed by professional portrait painters of some standing as mimicking the opportunistic behaviour of fashionable foreign artists. Allan Ramsay, a young pretender, had arrived back in Britain to great fanfare in 1738, as Hogarth acknowledged. It was one reason why, in the late 1730s, the theatre of war, as it were, had seemingly shifted away from history painting – which, in any case, would be only an element rather than the main focus of any artist in the current climate – towards portraiture.

However, a glance through Hogarth's works dated to around the period of Thomas Coram's magnificent portrait, the painting he states was the crucible of his battle with 'phiz-mongers' and withdrawal, once again, from the genre, offers a different story. Clearly portrait painting continued to be a significant element of his practice, despite his later protestations. Among the sitters were a fair sprinkling of aristocrats, albeit not old families but of more recent creation, such as Gustavus Hamilton, 2nd Viscount Boyne, George Parker, 2nd Earl of Macclesfield, Captain the Hon. John Hamilton, RN, and no less a personage than William Cavendish, Marquess of Hartington, eldest son of the Duke of Devonshire (Col. Fig. 14): all resolutely of the Whig persuasion. The last mentioned had, in 1741, just returned from his Grand Tour, and was embarking on a political career as a member of parliament for Derbyshire. Already engaged to Lord Burlington's only child, a union against the wishes of his mother (probably due to Burlington's mounting debts as much as his politics), Hartington is portrayed here as a dashing, handsome young man sporting light-brown/auburn curls, probably his own hair, a heavily embroidered gold and floral pattern waistcoat and a moss-green coat, again heavily embellished with gold thread. His lordship, it can be said with certainty, and despite sitting to many artists, would never be portrayed in such a vivacious manner again.

Most distinctive are the three commissions connected to Lord
Boyne, dated around the late 1730s, *Sir Francis Dashwood at his
Devotions*, *A Night Encounter* and *Charity in the Cellar*, three
of the least well known and yet extraordinary compositions by
Hogarth.[24] Like the second version of *Before* and *After*, by their
nature they may have tested Hogarth's personal attitude towards
the aristocracy and certainly set new limits as to what he was
willing to do to court their patronage.

Dashwood's image, which is likely to have been a commission
from Lord Boyne, who certainly owned a version, plays on his
nickname 'St Francis', and is based on any number of paintings
of the mendicant saint reading the bible while contemplating the
image of the crucified Christ. Rather than this, Dashwood, dressed
in a Franciscan's brown robe, kneels within a cave or grotto, regarding a miniature naked woman – the object of his devotions – who
would not look out of place on his lordship's bed, legs slightly
apart, her breasts pert, head turning away so her master might
indulge himself without interruption or challenge. Such an image
would certainly be too blasphemous for a Roman Catholic, indeed
for most God-fearing Protestants, and reveals a casual disdain for
everything but Dashwood's self-indulgence and myriad urges.
Hogarth may have enjoyed creating this unusually, for him, outré
image, or simply shrugged off any qualms. What a man hangs on
his wall in the privacy of his own home is his business. And a commission is a commission. Hogarth certainly did not make a habit
of creating such images – they are a very small part of his total
output.

More typical, although still a minor strand, is the crossover
genre, the portrait as 'fancy' picture, seen with Justice Shard and
later (*c*.1755–60) with Francis Matthew Schutz, propped up in bed
while vomiting into a chamber pot after a particularly bibulous
night (apparently commissioned by his wife to shame him into
better ways).[25] In *A Night Encounter*, Boyne is himself represented,
along with his friend Sir Edward Walpole, the younger son of Sir
Robert.[26] The exact details of the event depicted are not known. A
scene at night on a London street, Boyne is fending off an assailant
with his walking stick, while Sir Edward lies on the ground, at risk

of being trampled under the hooves and wheels of a passing carriage. Certainly, the friendship of Boyne and Walpole was central to the commission and the event. The unusual depiction of the city at night is reminiscent of the last canvas and print from *Four Times of the Day* (Fig. 45 p. 311), the engravings issued in 1738, around the time this scene was painted and one possible reason why Boyne approached Hogarth to immortalise the incident.

Charity in the Cellar is another friendship painting, but of a different order altogether. Set in the dank darkness of a cellar rather than the street, family legend has it that it commemorates a bizarre pact, whereby no one present could leave until a hogshead of claret has been consumed – in pre-imperial measurements, a hogshead was fixed at a bladder-busting sixty-three gallons – a subject wholly appropriate for the creator of *A Midnight Modern Conversation* and the Rose Tavern scene from *A Rake's Progress*, which pre-date it by just a few years. Thought to represent men who were both members of parliament and founders of the Dilettanti Society, the scene explicitly blends two standard subjects from history painting: the personification of Charity, usually a nurturing or suckling woman with three infants, as seen in Rysbrack's Foundling Hospital overmantel; and Roman Charity, where Pero breastfeeds her imprisoned father, Cimon, who has been condemned to a prolonged execution by starvation.[27] In Hogarth's ribald rendering, the central figure, broad of girth, sits astride a large barrel with its tap open and dribbling wine, so that he appears to be pissing into a punch bowl on the floor in front – the direction of this tap is guided by a companion. Two large 'onion' bottles are held against him like fake female breasts, from which two companions are suckling. In the gloom, an unconscious figure is just visible, lying flat out on a bench to the left, and empty bottles are strewn about.

It is difficult to gauge Hogarth's own feelings for such commissions. The behaviours and attitudes depicted belong to that easy entitlement, which society will not or cannot condemn, that only comes from wealth and privilege. As an artist keen to be in control, as far as humanly possible, Hogarth's attitude would depend on the prescriptiveness of the client in defining not just what is being depicted, but precisely how. The latter would push

Hogarth perhaps too far towards the role of the hired craftsman, indulging the vanity and twisted humour of the elite and therefore too far away from the independent artist, the man in command of what he does and how he does it.

Even so, the three commissions, with the portrait of Boyne himself (of which there are several versions by copyists) confirms the Irish peer as a significant patron of Hogarth around this time, generating much-needed income and, potentially, further commissions from his lordship's friends and family. Word of mouth recommendation was a standard and vital marketing tactic for any portrait painter. Hogarth clearly benefited from friendship networks; the three paintings associated with Cole and Western fall into this category. Commissions from friends in the immediate post-Coram years included the Hoadly family.[28] Hogarth painted Benjamin Hoadly, Bishop of Winchester, at least twice between 1741 and 1742, the first of the two a magnificent painting of the bishop in his deep-blue velvet robes as prelate of the Order of the Garter, later more widely known through an engraving by the Frenchman, Bernard Baron, in 1743. Bishop Hoadly, according to his son, had suffered from smallpox as a child, and the botched intervention of a surgeon left him requiring, ever after, the use of crutches and the need to preach while kneeling.[29] Hogarth also painted the bishop's second wife Mary in around 1745, his eldest son, also Benjamin, in c.1738, a small full-length with Benjamin seated under a bust of Sir Isaac Newton again in 1740 and yet another c.1740–45, both more conventional formats, alongside Benjamin junior's wife, Elizabeth née Betts in 1741.[30] In the same year as he painted Elizabeth, Hogarth painted the ebullient John Hoadly (1741), younger son of the bishop and one of the artist's closest and most loyal friends. As John Nichols recalls: 'With Dr. *Hoadly*, the late Chancellor of *Winchester*, Mr. *Hogarth* was always on terms of the strictest friendship, and frequently visited him at *Winchester*, *St. Cross*, and *Alresford*. It is well known, that Dr. *Hoadly*'s fondness for theatrical exhibitions was so great, that few visitors were ever long in his house before they were solicited to accept a part in some interlude or other.'[31]

Another significant patron from the early 1740s was Mary

Edwards (b.1705), whom Hogarth painted in 1742 dressed in a magnificent red silk robe (Frick Collection, New York). It so happened that Mary was writing her will at the same time, so the portrait acts as a statement of Mary's circumstances in general, and her particular feelings and attitude at this crucial moment. This was not the first time that she had commissioned a portrait from Hogarth. In 1733 Mary's beloved only child, Gerard Anne Edwards, was painted by Hogarth in his cradle (Upton House, National Trust). Rather than a docile infant, Gerard is sitting up in his wicker cot, wearing a white 'dress', cap and apron (as all infants at this time were clothed) with a slightly testy expression, holding a wooden toy. However, his attention is directed towards the dog lying on the floor nearby, perhaps the reason for his scowl, who in turn is eyeing the child, but with trepidation at the imminent launch of the toy. Gerard had been born in March at the turn of 1732 and 1733 and his baptism registration hints at a great scandal. He is named as 'Gerard Ann[e] Son of Mrs Mary Edwards of this Parish' a 'Singlewom[a]n'.[32]

Gerard's status as illegitimate is somewhat surprising, given that he was the offspring of Mary and Lord Anne Hamilton (as the infant's name suggests), and that the marriage between them had been announced in the *Gentleman's Magazine* in July 1731.[33] Yet by November, in the same magazine and under 'Marriages and Births', appeared the following announcement: 'The Ld *Anne Hamilton*, to Miss *Edwards*, an Heiress with 100,000 l. This article was inserted also on p. 311. from the Public Papers, but we are informed it is false.'[34] The one aspect of the report which is beyond doubt is that Mary was extremely wealthy in her own right, and her husband, generally seen to be a profligate, had already made significant inroads into that wealth. So Mary, showing extraordinary strength of character and single-mindedness, first, in all likelihood, expunged all trace of the marriage, then registered her son as illegitimate and, finally, manoeuvred Lord Anne (named after his godmother, Queen Anne) to give up all claim to her fortune – but not before commissioning a family group portrait, her young son now grown by a year or so, with mother and errant father.

It is no wonder, then, that several years on Mary chose to be

presented in such a sumptuous bright-red silk brocade dress, with
fine lace at her décolletage, wrists and as a cap over her hair. She
is also spectacularly bejewelled – studded with lustrous diamonds
and pearls – and has an ornamental cluster of household items
hanging from her waist, including a cased pocket watch, believed
to represent the keys of a medieval chatelaine, a female form of the
Old French for governor or keeper of a castle. At her right elbow
a document reads:

> Remember Englishmen the Laws the Rights
> The generous plan of Power delliver'd down
> From age to age by your renown'd Forefathers
> So dearly bought the Price of so much Contest
> Transmit it careful to Posterity
> Do thou great Liberty inspire their Souls
> And make their Lives in [thy] possession happy
> Or their Deaths glorious in thy Just defence.

The text has been identified as an adaption of lines from Joseph
Addison's *Cato* (1713), where the eponymous ancient Roman
senator declares the rights and liberties of the citizen.[35] Appearing
as busts on the far wall are supporting symbols of English liberty
including Queen Elizabeth, the 'Virgin' Queen, and King Alfred:
Mary is a single woman, like Elizabeth, who rules alone and is most
certainly in control of her own destiny. Her left hand, with two
glittering rings, is resting on the head of a dog, signifying loyalty
but, rather than a 'lap dog', this is a hunting breed, usually associated with male sitters. Again she asserts her right, as any man
would, to independence.

In his autobiographical notes, Hogarth recalled the sequence of
events in his career through the 1730s to the early 1740s as follows:
that his marriage, he implies, had necessitated the painting of conversations, which brought success but not quite enough money 'to
do every thing my family requird'.[36] As a result he redirected all
enquiries for such portraits to other artists and turned his focus to
the painting and engraving of a new style or genre that is 'moder[n]

... moral Subject[s]'. 'But not,' he declares 'before I had entertain'd some notions of succeeding in what is call[ed] the grand stile of History', that is, his paintings at St Bartholomew's Hospital.[37] He then goes on to say that the failure, or, more correctly, lack of enthusiasm for such work – 'from which I found no Effects and the reason upon consideration was so plaine', there was simply no demand – meant 'that I dropt all the old Ideas' (his long-cherished desire to emulate Sir James Thornhill in grand history painting) 'and pursued the former', that is he returned to the modern moral subjects which had brought him such success in the early to mid 1730s. He concludes by saying that dealing directly with the public, in general, he found was the most likely to do well, 'provided', that is, 'I could strike the passions and by small sums from many by means of prints which I could Engrav[e] from my Picture myself I could secure my Property to my self.'[38]

Looking back over this journey, and with the benefit of hind-sight, Hogarth now, in retrospect, perceived *A Harlot's Progress* and *A Rake's Progress* – at the time opportunistic and seem-ingly not part of a grander, long-term scheme or strategy – as a testing ground for a style or genre that was yet to be fully real-ised or exploited. It was an acknowledgment that his hopes for grand manner history painting had stalled, forcing a reassessment of what he had been, until then, so dismissive – that which had brought him easy success – while in dogged pursuit of high art. This and the everyday circumstances of life, not least the need to maintain his family and household, while 'still unwilling to fall into the manufacture' (by which he may mean relentless, production-line painting for money) and desirous 'of being singular' he 'next conceived morality'.[39] So his early successes, in what he came to call modern moral subjects, would now be built on with gusto, using all his significant drive and ingenuity. Perhaps the production of portraiture per se and particularly the requirement to bend to the demands of others – losing complete control over his art and its production – also helped to galvanise another change in direction.

The encouragement of Mary Edwards may have been one catalyst for this return to modern moral subjects, for Mary also owned Hogarth's painting of *Southwark Fair* (1733, Cincinnati

Art Museum) and, at the same time as her own portrait, commissioned *Taste in High Life* – also known as 'Taste a-la-Mode'[40] in Mary Edward's delayed collection sale – a satire on the excesses of the day. Unlike *Masquerades and Operas* (also called *The Bad Taste of the Town*), an image targeting specifically Italian opera and masquerade-type entertainments, this painting was responding to all manner of bad taste displayed by women and effeminate – or 'frenchified' – men. It should be noted that the French fashions pilloried here were equally attacked on the other side of the channel in society and in print. Here the choice of clothing style, as well as the fabrics, the items furnishing the home, as well as choice of music and entertainment are collectively and, apparently, randomly or carelessly assembled: even the boy of African descent, finely dressed in a silk plumed and tasselled turban, a green silk suit and, most disturbingly, a collar, is, like the contents of the room, a fashionable possession to the other people in the image. A similar figure appears in the second scene of *A Harlot's Progress*, where Moll is the kept woman of a wealthy merchant. Collectively the result is an unedifying hotch-potch, signalling people with too much money and no propriety, sense or interest in, let alone love of, mankind – notably the slave trade, of which this child is evidence and in turn symbolises. The monkey front and centre, 'aping' human dress and behaviour, is a standard symbol for human folly, also a gesture to the fashion, again popularised in France, for such images, called *singerie*, or 'monkey trick' (see Antoine Watteau, *The Monkey Sculptor*, c.1710, engraved by Louis Desplaces, c.1726–31). Hogarth included a pet monkey in the second scene of *A Harlot's Progress* – here the folly this creature helps to expose is Moll's delusion that she is in control of her circumstances and will continue to be maintained in some luxury by the merchant, while she dallies with her lover, seen sneaking out of the parlour, stockings sliding down his legs.

In *Taste in High Life* (Private Collection), the monkey holds a list of French fare 'Pour Dinner', namely 'cocks combs' 'Ducks Tongues' 'Rabbits Ears' 'Fricasey of Snails' / 'Grande d'oeufs' 'Beurre' – reminiscent of Hannah Glasse's complaints against overwrought cuisine much favoured by gullible English aristocrats, but also, collectively, redolent of the figures standing before him, quacking in delight, as one chucks her child servant under the chin, the others gawp and tremble with pleasure over a tiny, insignificant ceramic cup. The 'beau' is intended to represent the affectations of every young aristocrat who, giddy with the French court, appears in extravagant French fashion on his return. The main visual giveaway of one suffering from such pretension is the enormous black bow attached to his highly primped wig, with its stiff platted 'tail' giving the appearance of some oversized insect, and the *talons rouges*, or red heels, instigated by Louis XIV and worn by nobility at Versailles.[41]

John Nichols declared that Mary Edwards had commissioned *Taste in High Life* for a 'rather whimsical' reason: 'By her own singularities having incurred some ridicule, she was desirous, by the assistance of *Hogarth*, to recriminate on the publick. As he designed after her ideas, he had little kindness for his performance, and never would permit a print to be taken from it.'[42] This is an intriguing comment, suggesting that Hogarth found Mary's specific directions inhibiting – naturally and understandably he preferred free rein. This resistance to an interfering client could apply to those images commissioned by Lord Boyne, suggesting they are, in everything but the basic story, of Hogarth's devising.

In 1742, the same year as he painted Mary Edwards and *Taste in High Life*, Hogarth produced one of his most superb portraits of children: the two girls and two boys of the royal apothecary Daniel Graham by his second marriage to Mary Crisp or Cripps (they married on 30 October 1732). Once again Hogarth's protestations, in later life, that he had abandoned portraiture at this time is not borne out by the facts. Graham's business, inherited from his father in 1733, was run under the sign of the mortar, 11 Pall Mall, close to St James's Palace, and Daniel had continued the family connection to royalty (Daniel's uncle had been apothecary to Queen Anne and George I). Daniel had amassed sufficient wealth for him to redevelop this extensive property, and the portrait of his four bonnie children (Col. Fig. 15) was no doubt part of this refurbishment, and intended to hang pride of place. The children are, left to right, infant Thomas, Henrietta Catherine, Anna

40. *Head of a Sleeping Child*, black and red chalk on grey paper, *c.*1740–42
The infant wears a linen cap (worn by boys as well as girls, see *The
Graham Children* Col. Fig. 15) and appears to be lying in a cot.

Maria and Richard Robert, the last mentioned turning the handle
of a bird organ, known as a *serinette*. What may have begun as a
standard depiction of four healthy children, is, in its completed
form, steeped with references to the passing of time, death as an
indiscriminate reaper of lives, vulnerability, and so on. This could
have been Hogarth's intention from the start, as such symbols
appear elsewhere in his work, but as the commission progressed it
became even more apposite when little Thomas died. The symbols,
although located around the painting, are positioned in such a way
as to lead back to Thomas. The carved bird decoration on Thomas's
elaborate carriage is echoed in the flapping bird in the cage – not
animated by the sound of the bird-organ, as the laughing Richard
Robert believes, but distressed by the ominous presence of the
cat, of which Thomas's brother is totally unaware. Thomas himself

lifts his hand, as if unconsciously aware of the drama occurring aloft and to his left. The clock with the cherub holding a scythe is above Thomas's head, meanwhile lying next to him is a silver basket, resplendent with fruit – cherries, grapes, apples – which although vibrant now, would inevitably and quickly perish. Henrietta Catherine, holding bright red-cherries and looking us in the eye, understands this, as she transitions from childhood to adulthood. The memento mori continues with the pink carnations lying at Thomas's feet – 'carnations' is a term used by artists for the colouring of pink bare skin and flesh, the blush on a cheek for example, but also here referring to 'incarnation' (made flesh). An exquisite sketch by Hogarth in the British Museum, currently catalogued as 'Head of a Child Sleeping' could as easily and tragically be a portrait of Thomas just after death.

Over a period of just a few years, therefore, Hogarth's work had touched on a wealth of subject matter, from marriage, families, inheritance, the fragility of childhood, men behaving badly and modish 'taste'. This experience would be channelled towards a new, ambitious project, and one that would prove to be his most enduringly famous creation, *Marriage A-la-Mode*.

On 2 April 1743 an advertisement appeared in newspapers including the *Daily Advertiser*, announcing Mr Hogarth's intention to publish six prints by subscription 'from Copper-Plates engrav'd by the best Masters in Paris, after his own Paintings'. The sequence represented 'a Variety of Modern Occurrences in High Life', and was called 'MARRIAGE A-LA-MODE'. This would have brought to mind the popular John Dryden comedy of that title, first performed at the Queen's Theatre (as it was during Queen Anne's reign) in the Haymarket in 1707, but the narrative was very much Hogarth's own. The advertisement goes on to state 'Particular Care will be taken that there may not be the least Objection to the Decency and Elegancy of the whole Work, and that none of the Characters represented shall be personal.'[43] A prudent anticipation of any attempts to name and shame, should any of the characters or scenarios chime with real-life examples, and one which draws a line between the recognisable individuals seen in the 'Harlot' and 'Rake' progresses.[44]

With this signal that *Marriage A-la-Mode* would be an advance on his previous series, over the period May to June Hogarth ventured to Paris, as far as we know his first trip abroad, to secure the said French engravers as promised in his announcement, having already begun working on the paintings themselves in London. Unfortunately, very little is known about this trip, other than what is mentioned in a later advertisement, placed by Hogarth in the *Daily Advertiser* on 8 November 1744, which was required to explain the delay in completing the engravings. Here Hogarth admits that his intention in going to Paris was to secure six engravers to take an image each: 'In the Month of June 1743, the following French Masters, Mess. Baron, Ravenet, Scotin, Le Bas, Dupré, and Suberan, had entered in an Agreement with the Author (who took a Journey to Paris for that sole Purpose) to engrave the above Work in their best Manner, each of them being to take one Plate for the Sake of Expedition.'[45]

However, while in Paris, Hogarth could not have avoided viewing examples of recent and contemporary French art associated with the game of love, masquerades, scenes of everyday life by Jean-François de Troy (*The Declaration of Love*, 1724; *The Reading from Molière*, c.1730; *Before the Ball*, 1735 and *After the Ball*, 1737), Jean-Baptiste-Siméon Chardin (*The Young Draftsman*, 1737 in London before 1740, *The Governess*, 1739), Nicolas Lancret (*The Four Times of the Day*, c.1737) and François Boucher (*A Lady fastening her Garter*, 'La Toilette', 1742) – all of which, in style and content, he would plunder for this new series. Even so, you sense that Hogarth is enjoying himself, that there is admiration, or affection, for these fellow artists, and that Hogarth is honouring the work of his French peers, even as he is using them for satirical effect – imitation, in itself, being a sincere form of flattery. Perhaps, too, the imitation is another repost to the patronising comments, discussed earlier, of the abbé le Blanc.

It seems likely, even if he were in Paris for only a short time, that Hogarth undertook some of the itinerary of the grand tourist, if only to see Versailles: the temptation would have been overwhelming, to satisfy himself that Louis's great palace really did not deserve its reputation, and to inspect Lemoyne's 'flawed' ceiling. Another venue, the mansion of the financier Pierre Crozat, was a must for any visitor, and Hogarth could have gained access through one of his contacts in Paris, as much for Crozat's Old Master paintings and drawings as the modern and contemporary French art, including a significant selection by Antoine Watteau.

The announcement concerning *Marriage A-la-Mode* was attached to an advertisement that declared, due to popular demand and if original subscribers were in agreement, a second impression of *A Harlot's Progress* would be available. The juxtaposition is interesting. Hogarth may have needed a quick injection of cash due to the prolonged gestation of his new series. He may also have felt that a reminder of the perils of Moll Hackabout was useful, in the context of this project. In any case, in his update Hogarth confirms that his intention had been for the new engravings of *Marriage A-la-Mode* to be executed in Paris, and that the six paintings were to have travelled to the French capital for that purpose. The engaging of six engravers, a print each, meant that the paintings would have been in Paris for the shortest period of time possible. It is inconceivable that Hogarth would have missed the opportunity for the paintings to be available for local artists and collectors to view during this time, as a means of promoting himself to this discerning audience for art. Hogarth's engravings were known in Paris, due to a thriving international print market and a corresponding community of collectors, but his paintings less so. Even the abbé le Blanc's highly critical observations on the phenomenon that was *A Rake's Progress* would have piqued the curiosity of his fellow countrymen in regard to the Englishman. Hogarth's friend and neighbour in London, André Rouquet, would soon publish a series of 'letters' explaining Hogarth's prints to date, including *Marriage A-la-Mode*, precisely to explain the baffling barrage of detail to an interested and intrigued French clientele. And Hogarth was extremely pleased that Rouquet should do so and trusted his friend to place him and his art in a good light, preferably without causing too much offence – a reliance on, or faith in the sophistication of French collectors to value fine art more highly than sensitivities around patriotism and nationhood. Indeed a refined viewer would see that it is the English, in imitating their French counterparts without understanding, that are the main target.

41. Bernard Baron after William Hogarth, *Marriage A-la-Mode Plate 3: The Inspection*, etching and engraving, 1745
The doctor is often misidentified as the tall, thin Jean Misaubin, who attends the dying Moll Hackabout and was known as 'M. de la Pillule' because of his pill 'remedy' for venereal disease.

That said, Rouquet makes an important observation querying Hogarth's accuracy when it came to French characters: 'I will not pretend to decide whether the Author is as happy when he chuses the object of his satire from amongst us', Rouquet was French-Swiss, 'as when he takes them from his own Nation, but it appears to me that he knows his own Countrys Foibles best.' He cites the example of the Quack Doctor in scene three, 'The Inspection', of *Marriage A-la-Mode*, who is presented as a Frenchman. Medicine is held in greater esteem in France than in England, observes Rouquet, and this character, evidently practising everything from surgery to chemistry to alchemy, and surrounded by his 'Don Saltero' curiosities, simply does not resonate with the profession in France. The French, Rouquet declares, can therefore dismiss such misreading and, he concludes, thank God Hogarth is not more attuned to their particular foibles, for 'what wou'd become of us, if he knew us well enough to paint us in our proper Colors?'[46]

The proposed process was complex in practice but simple in concept: paintings by an English artist, partly modelled on and adapted from French contemporary art, engraved in Paris, by Frenchmen. It combined showmanship and marketing nous, with a desire to go to any length to achieve the desired effect and quality: French engravers were considered the most refined in the world.

In the event only three engravers undertook the work. In the same advertisement of 1744, explaining the delay in printing, Hogarth announces the following piece of bad luck (although predictable, given the international political climate) which occurred after the six engravers had been engaged around June 1743: 'the War with France breaking out soon after, it was judged neither safe nor proper on any Account, to trust the original Paintings out of England, much less engrav'd at Paris'. Averting jeopardy makes for a good news story, while, in this particular instance, simultaneously denoting patriotic sentiment (which the original scheme may have ignored). The text continues, concerning Jacques-Philippe Le Bas, a highly experienced engraver, 'Dupré' and 'Suberan' (neither identified), that 'not being able, on Account of their Families, to come over hither, the Author was necessitated to agree' with the remaining three, already in England, 'to finish the Work here, each undertaking two Plates'.[47] Hogarth puts a good complexion on this, by saying that no one will surely complain about the engravings being executed on home soil, with the added benefit that Hogarth could now closely supervise their execution. Finally, Hogarth reassures his subscribers that the printing and publishing of a second set of *A Harlot's Progress* will not get in the way of the new project, the original copper plates not requiring much attention from wearing, and the French engravers having agreed to take on no additional work until the two plates for which they were responsible were completed.

The first of the three engaged by Hogarth was Gérard Jean Baptiste Scotin II (1698–after 1755), who was to execute Plates 1 and 6, and was also named as the engraver on the first state of Plate 2

A Rake's Progress (1735). He had engraved several works by Antoine
Watteau (*L'Indifferent* 1729, *Le Lorgneur*, *c.*1727, *La Cascade*, 1729,
Les Plaisirs du bal 1730 and *Les Jaloux* 1726–9 for *Recueil Julienne*), and also works after Nicolas Lancret. According to Vertue,
Scotin had been travelling back and forth across the Channel since
at least 1733. The second, Bernard Baron (1696–1762), would
undertake Plates 2 and 3, and had already engraved 'Evening' and
Hogarth's portrait of Bishop Hoadly. Baron was a good choice, as
he had been engaged, along with many other engravers, by Pierre
Crozat to work on prints after his extensive collection.[48] Lastly, of
the three, only Simon François Ravenet (1706–74), who studied
under Le Bas, was actually brought to England by Hogarth. He
would engrave Plates 4 and 5.[49]

The renewal of formal hostilities between France and Great
Britain, after an abortive invasion attempt early in 1744 (in support
of the Stuarts and nominally led by Prince Charles Edward)
covered, conveniently, the failure of the original scheme, which
may have been over-puffed in the first place.[50] If Hogarth was
irritated by foreign artists being used where British artists should
suffice, then in this instance he was in danger of gross hypocrisy.
However, given the subject matter, Hogarth's argument would be
that he needed that certain *je ne sais quoi* to make his point, the
'Frenchness' of the subject and treatment, even more forcefully.
Still, there is a tension between his behaviour here and his past
protestations on foreign art and artists. In another advertisement,
Hogarth added the following comment: 'the Heads, for the better
Preservation of the Characters and Expressions, to be done by the
Author'.[51] Whatever the style and desirability of a French touch to
the main body of the engravings, Hogarth always intended to complete the image himself, and in particular the faces of his characters,
so that the artist's hand, his signature – more acute in faces than
anywhere else – was present. After all, collectors wanted to possess
works by Hogarth, rather than Ravenet or Baron. Yet Hogarth no
doubt enjoyed the frisson this situation inspired and the delicious
irony that while poking fun at the fashions for all things foreign,
namely French and Italian, the purchasers were themselves buying
engravings by Frenchmen, to designs by an Englishman. Vertue

would later observe that Hogarth's future series, engraved by himself in a less sophisticated manner, were 'without being at that great expence he was, of good workmen when he publishd – his Marriage A la Mode – the costs of which works of engraving. he paid dear for'.[52]

One motivation for creating such a series, describing the progress of a couple, is as a development from his previous modern moral subjects focused on a female and then a male lead character. Both notable successes, the former in particular, meant that tapping back into this market made sense, because relationships between men and women and the marriage state was in the air after the publication of Samuel Richardson's bestseller, *Pamela or, Virtue Rewarded* in 1740 and its continuation, *Pamela in Her Exulted Condition* of 1742. The novel, in letter form, followed the trials and tribulations of Pamela Andrews, a highly moral fifteen-year-old servant, and the failed attempts of her young, parentless (and therefore unfettered) 'guardian', the squire Mr B, to ape the behaviour of libertine aristocrats, by debauching and then keeping her as his mistress – she, despite her many virtues and refinements, being too lowly for a wife. Through Pamela's example, in defence of her virtue, against what is relentless mental and physical abuse, Mr B undergoes what is almost a religious conversion, and he and Pamela, who has loved him all along, are married. Now in an exulted state, the last half of the extended novel deals with the prejudice Pamela encounters and her triumph as wife, mother and mistress of her husband's household and estates.

It is known that Richardson had approached Hogarth to create two frontispieces for the original two-volume novel. There has been much discussion over the motivation of both the author and the artist in initiating and agreeing to this project. It seems clear that Richardson's novel was itself inspired, in part, by Hogarth's modern moral subjects – the two men also coincide in their stated aim of using their respective arts to instruct as well as entertain – and his 'Harlot' and 'Rake' in particular. To have the famous Mr Hogarth embellish a deluxe edition seems on the face of it commercially astute. From Hogarth's point of view, Richardson's approach was a signal of the writer's faith in his intellectual and artistic variety and his empathy with Pamela Andrews and her sisters in circumstance, living at the mercy of their masters up and down the country, and whose stories of desperation had resulted in the Foundling Hospital project.

The subjects for the frontispieces were the least lascivious that could have been selected – not, for example, the preamble or effect, the before and after, of the various sexual assaults, which would more closely align in substance and character to the progresses. The subjects were: Pamela while fishing – making a connection between her current circumstances and the fish she has caught or trapped with 'false bait' (she returns it unharmed to the pond); and Pamela rejecting material wealth, as symbolised by the bundle of fine clothes Mr B has offered her as a bribe in exchange for her chastity, and embracing instead honourable poverty. Both subjects require subtlety and invention, a challenge Hogarth was very happy to accept, given his ongoing desire to expand into 'high art' (an ambition he had not, in reality, abandoned) and, no mean feat, to visualise the complex Pamela in such a way as to avoid disappointing her fans, who were legion. What hovered over the entire enterprise were Henry Fielding's spoofs, *Shamela* (*An Apology for the Life of Mrs Shamela Andrews*, first published in April 1741) – the heroine is now a scheming trollop and her victim, the gormless Mr Booby – and *The History of the Adventures of Joseph Andrews … Written in imitation of the manner of Cervantes* (1742). The latter is connected to Richardson's novel by being the equally virtuous brother of Pamela (rather than Shamela) who, in this second satirical configuration, is tempted and morally tortured by a 'Lady Booby', the widow of Sir Thomas Booby, a modern Potiphar's wife. In fact, Richardson's deluxe edition, indeed his continuation of the novel to include Pamela's marriage and motherhood, was part of a concerted effort to counter the anti-Pamela lobby, whose cheerfully iconoclastic leader Fielding was always ready to raise a laugh along with his profile. It seems that Hogarth produced at least one of the Pamela designs before 1742, by which time Richardson had cancelled the commission (the reason unclear and debated to this day) and brought in Hogarth's friend, the painter Francis Hayman and the Paris-born draughtsman and engraver Hubert-François Bourguignon, nicknamed 'Gravelot' from the French to engrave, *graver*, who, over the entire four volumes, created twenty-eight designs – including the two scenes attempted by Hogarth.

And there was other competition. An announcement in 1743 by Joseph Highmore, that he intended to paint twelve scenes from *Pamela* and have them engraved by 'the best French engravers' suggests that he considered Hogarth's modus operandi worth a try himself. Highmore also used models from contemporary French art, notably the servant figures and scenes of everyday life by Chardin.[53] Highmore's project runs exactly in parallel with *Marriage A-la-Mode*, and as both painting sets would have been available to view, one artist to the other, there should be every expectation of crossover. Highmore, like Richardson, referred directly and indirectly to Hogarth's *Harlot* and *Rake* – for example in scene seven, the preamble to an attempted rape, where Pamela is undressing in her bedroom, echoing Moll Hackabout in her attic chamber, and the prostitute in the Rose Tavern 'orgy' scene.

Hogarth may also have been encouraged to return to modern moral subjects in the wake of Henry Fielding's published support, which had, no doubt, been shared in private. In his introduction to *Joseph Andrews*, Fielding first coins the term '*Comic History-Painter*', applying it directly to Hogarth, whom he names, and then comparing Hogarth's work with what the Italians call *caricatura*.[54] Fielding contrasts what is within the bounds of the natural, '*where we shall find the true Excellence of the former to consist in the exactest Copy of Nature ; insomuch, that a judicious Eye instantly rejects any thing* outré ; *any Liberty which the Painter hath taken with the Features of that Alma Mater*', to what is distorted or amplified, or 'Caricatura' where '*we allow all Licence. Its Aim is to exhibit Monsters, not Men ; and all Distortions and Exaggerations whatever are within its proper Province*'. He then states that *caricatura* in painting is termed 'burlesque' in writing, '*and in the same manner the Comic Writer and Painter correlate to each other*'. He then observes that those '*who should call the Ingenious Hogarth a Burlesque Painter, would, in my Opinion, do him very little Honour: for sure it is much easier, much less the Subject of Admiration, to paint a Man with a Nose, or any other Feature of a preposterous Size, or to expose him in some absurd or monstrous attitude, than to express the Affections*

of Men on Canvas. It hath been thought a vast Commendation of a
Painter, to say his Figures seem to breathe *; but surely, it is a much*
greater and nobler Applause, that they appear to think.'[55]

Fielding is responding to the dedication in William Somervile's *Hobbinol, or the Rural Games. A Burlesque Poem* (London,
1740) to 'Mr. *HOGARTH*': 'Permit me, Sir, to make choice of you
for my Patron, being the greatest Master in the Burlesque Way. In
this indeed you have some Advantage of your poetical Brethren,
that you paint to the Eye; yet remember, Sir, that we give Speech,
and Motion, and a greater variety to our Figures. Your Province is
the Town, leave me a small Out-ride in the Country, and I shall
be content. In this at least let us both agree, to make Vice and
Folly the Object of our Ridicule; and we cannot fail to be of some
service to Mankind.' Somervile signs off *'Your admirer, and Most*
humble Servant'.[56]

Fielding had mentioned Hogarth before – in the preface to the
Familiar Letters, 'In the works of Cervantes or Hogarth, he ...', referring to anyone, 'is, I believe, a wretched judge, who discovers no new
beauties on a second, or even a third perusal' – and will continue to
do so, to their mutual benefit. But his observations in the preface
of *Joseph Andrews* were an important and very public intervention.
Hogarth may have found Somervile's dedication, no doubt considered by the author a compliment, as the exact opposite. Somervile
simply did not understand what Hogarth was trying to do. But
Fielding did, and managed to articulate it in such a way that Hogarth
could feel rightly vindicated and elevated. From here on, Hogarth
would define those aspects of his work that deal with 'the customs
manners fasheons Characters and humours of the present age in this
country' as moral comedy: 'I beg leave here to mention what first
put me upon this way of designing induced me first to enter into this
Comic and Moral rather than any other manner of Designing.'[57]
Now, re-energised, he could allow himself to describe his work as
he saw it, not how others did. It was theatre, the theatre of life. The
world was his subject, his style Hudibrastic *and* Shakespearian:
'Subjects I consider'd as writers do [,] my Picture was my Stage and
men and women my actors who were by Mean[s] of certain Actions
and express[ions] to Exhibit a dumb' – that is, silent – 'shew.'[58] He

continues: 'Whether they were comical or tragical what subjects have been done [,] for I mean to speak of only such Subjects as the human species are actors in And these were <Scenes> what I found had not been often done', nor, if done, in 'the manner I imagin'd them capable off [*sic*]'.[59] He, like Fielding, was forging a middle way: 'In the historical way of any intermediate species of subjects for painting between the sublime and the grotesque.'[60] Ultimately, and to repeat, the 'subject of most consequence are those that most entertain and improve the mind and are of public utility'.

When Joseph Andrews, in the presence of Lady Booby, is verbally defending his virtue, Lady Booby responds in utter surprise at the very mention of the word. Indeed, 'not from the imitable Pencil of my Friend *Hogarth*, could you receive such an idea of Surprize, as would have entered in at your Eyes, had they beheld the Lady *Booby*, when those last Words issued out from the Lips of *Joseph*. – "Your Virtue!" (said the Lady recovering after a Silence of two Minutes) "I shall never survive it. Your Virtue! Intolerable Confidence! Have you the Assurance to pretend, that when a Lady demeans herself to throw aside the Rules of Decency, in order to honour you with the highest Favour in her power, your Virtue should resist her Inclination? That when she had conquer'd her own Virtue, she should find an Obstruction in yours?"'[61] Later, Fielding mentions Hogarth again, in a sly reference to the St Bartholomew's Hospital controversy – for supporters of Amigoni at least. During a nonsensical exposition by his hero, on the concept of 'whose picture', Joseph declares 'for when it has been asked whose Picture that was, it was never once answered, the Master's of the House, but *Ammyconni, Paul Varnish, Hannibal Scratchi*, or *Hogarthi*, which I suppose were the Names of the Painters'. The mangled names are Amigoni, Paolo or Paul Veronese, Annibale Carracci – scratchy Carracci – and yet another Italian, Signor '*Hogarthi*'.[62] Surely Fielding's witty string of artists is intended to declare that Hogarth sits very happily among them, that he is as good as they are to the extent of being mistaken for one of them, while, at the same time, highlighting the connoisseurial bias – parroted out of the mouth of a young ignoramus – where every artist worthy of note must be Italian. We might also compare 'Hogarthi' with that *inglese italianato* 'Kentino', but rather than a fearsome fourteenth-century English mercenary, now misapplied to tubby Yorkshiremen who do poor battle with a brush.

In Joseph Andrews, Fielding articulates with simple precision Hogarth's intention, his innovation and the value of his 'middle way'. He has also legitimised the idea that comedy can be high minded, or be galvanised to a higher purpose. Hogarth is depicting neither Gods nor grotesques or caricatures, but characters taken from nature itself, not overblown and exaggerated for mere comic effect. It should also be said that caricatures or *caricatura* had been of interest to artists such as the named Annibale Carracci, a sixteenth-century Bolognese painter much venerated by art theorists and connoisseurs. What is good for the Italian goose is, surely, equally good for the British gander, if the latter so chooses. To say otherwise was simply prejudice, whether wilful or driven by ignorance.

To make this aim emphatic, and armed with Mr Fielding's explanation, the subscriber's ticket for *Marriage A-la-Mode* was entitled *Characters and Caricaturas*, and based on a crowd of heads produced by Carracci. There are some specific explanatory examples along the base: the heads to the left taken from the exemplars par excellence of elevated history painting, the Raphael Cartoons, to demonstrate the 'characters', and to the right, examples by Pier Leone Ghezzi (1674–1755, Hogarth owned copies), Carracci and even 'the great Leonardo da Vinci'[63] to illustrate the 'Caricaturas'.[64] The text reads '*For a farther Explanation of the Difference Betwixt* Character & Caricatura *See ye Preface to* Jo^h Andrews'. Hogarth and Fielding – dangerous enough in isolation: together, formidable.

In addition to the impact of *Pamela*, text and pictures, elements originally introduced into *Taste in High Life* reappear, with little modification, in *Marriage A-la-Mode*. Hogarth may have chafed at the restricting hand of his patron (as argued by John Nichols) but the association and the resulting painting certainly gave him fresh thoughts, and would have made up for any irritation.[65] Sadly, Mary Edwards had died in 1743, the year after writing her will and sitting for Hogarth's portrait, so may not have known the extent to which she had influenced her favoured artist.

42. *Characters and Caricaturas: Subscription Ticket
for Marriage A-la-Mode*, etching, 1743
Hogarth's general point is that artists are concerned with
the human condition, in all its guises, while the critic and
connoisseur are more narrow in their interests.

In the first scene (Col. Fig. 16), the Viscount Squanderfield
is the image of the beau, with his mannered posture, clothes, the
immense bow and those red heels. The figure of the alderman's

daughter, soon to be Lady, later Countess, Squanderfield, may
be a reference to Mary Edwards – a wealthy merchant's daughter married unhappily into the aristocracy, and with a profligate
husband. Assisting in the brokering of the marriage is Silvertongue
the Lawyer. Through the window, a Palladian-style monstrosity
is in the process of being built, but for which fresh 'trade' cash is
required to complete. A Medusa's head screams and writhes above
the ill-matched and ill-fated couple. The second scene, with the
arch Lady Squanderfield and her husband both recovering from
the activities of the night before, shows them sitting, as noted,
among tasteless gimcracks and oddities. Scene three sees the earl
at the quack doctor's, a composition developed from Hogarth's
earlier *Hudibras beats Sidrophel and his man Whacum* (Fig. 13
p. 81), but again, as noted, reminiscent of descriptions of 'Don
Saltero's' museum. The earl is requesting more pills to purge the
syphilis he has passed on to his extremely young and sickly mistress:
in reality there is no cure. The fourth scene (Col. Fig. 17), the countess's toilette or levee, shows her surrounded, like Tom Rakewell
before her, with all the accoutrement of fashionable modern living,
including a castrato and servants of African descent. The younger
of the two, a small boy with a turban and collar, as noted, is pointing towards a horned man, the cuckold, and laughing, echoing the
figure in *A Harlot's Progress* and *Taste in High Life*. A baby's teeth-
ing coral hangs from the back of the countess's chair – given the
cuckolding, this baby's paternity is in question. The fifth scene is
where the countess's lover kills her cuckolded husband in a duel:
the masks indicate that the lovers had met after one of these foreign
masquerade entertainments, which, because of the encouragement
for play acting and disguise, are mere hotbeds for such behaviour.
In a previous engraving, the *Masquerade Ticket* of 1727, the scene at
a masquerade includes a shrine to Priapus (a minor god of fertility
usually seen with a giant phallus, although not here) decorated by
cuckold's horns; another to Venus, with cupid's bow and bow arm
forming a phallus substitute; and 'a pair of Lecherometers shewing
ye Companys Inclinations as they approach em', from 'Hope' to
'Hot Desire' to 'Extreme Hot Moist' to 'Sudden Cold'. Hogarth
is nothing if not consistent on this subject. Finally, in scene six, as

the countess expires from the poison she has taken and her father removes a ring from her finger – waste not want not – a starving dog pulls at a pig's ear (which everyone concerned has made of their lives) while the disabled offspring of this disastrous marriage, marked by inherited syphilis, attempts to kiss its mother before she expires.

Even if the creation of *Marriage A-la-Mode* was ultimately inspired by the disappointments Hogarth had experienced regarding history and portrait painting, there is nothing cynical or world weary about the paintings – they are beautifully executed, some of his finest works, with deliciously vibrant colouring and a sense of joy, combined with his habitual struggle in the work.

However, this was not enough to keep body and soul together, so Hogarth decided to raise money – taking control over the process while generating a shiver of excitement in London's art world in an extremely novel manner. Even before the engraved sets for *Marriage A-la-Mode* were available for distribution to the subscribers, Hogarth made an extraordinary announcement, that he would sell the paintings of *A Harlot's Progress*, *A Rake's Progress* and the *Four Times of the Day* at a single auction, to be held at his own residence rather than Cock's auction house. The format of the auction was equally extraordinary and, again, we have Vertue's description of the event, hinting at how this 'new manner of sale' was received by contemporaries. Invitation was by printed tickets delivered only 'to Gentlemen Nobelmen & Lovers of Arts ... no painters nor Artists to be admitted to his sale', no critics, no auctioneer costs. On a fixed day the bidders arrived at Hogarth's house and bid for the paintings with 'Gold only by a Clock. set purposely by the minute hand – 5 minutes each lott. so that by this means he coud raise them to the most value'. By 'this sub[t]le means. he sold about 20 pictures ... for near 450 pounds in an hour', a handsome sum, although Hogarth would have been a little disappointed, given what he was selling.[66] *A Harlot's Progress* and *A Rake's Progress* were bought by William Beckford for £88 4 shillings and £184 16 shillings respectively.[67] But if we think of Hogarth's reaction to the reported destruction by fire of both progresses, the mechanical organ bursting into life being the most

'remarkable' element of the story, it might also suggest how little
he valued or how unsentimental he was about these paintings once
they had served their purpose, relative to the plates, as the means
of ongoing income.

The acknowledged success of his sale may have simply increased
Hogarth's confidence and renewed a sense of invincibility. Vertue
rounds up this most recent journal entry on the rise (and rise) of
the ingenious Mr Hogarth by observing that 'the Temper of the
people loves humourous spritely diverting subjects in painting',
so the sale of these particular works was bound to go well. Even
so, Hogarth's audacity in managing the entire process himself and
excluding certain interested parties rankled, 'as Hudibrass expres-
seth "yet He! that hath but Impudence,/ to all things, has a Fair
pretence"'.[68]

By the time the *Marriage A-la-Mode* project was nearing its
completion, Jane and William had been married for sixteen years.
Although they could still start a family themselves (he would be
forty-eight in the November, she around thirty-six or seven), there
is no evidence of a pregnancy at any time in these sixteen years,
nor would there be. It is often said, and a fair enough comment
given the pressures of the era, that their childlessness found an
outlet in the Foundling Hospital project, and it is worth remind-
ing ourselves of Old Nollekens's anecdote concerning the young
Hogarth carrying the sickly child of Ellis Gamble. In this the
couple were not alone – Thomas and Eunice Coram had been in
the same position, so too would be the very happily married David
and Eva-Maria Garrick – but the situation must have put stress on
their relationship. The advertisements in newspapers promoting
cures for barrenness and impotency can only suggest the anguish
of early Georgian couples, unable to fulfil a basic requirement of
marriage in this period, quite apart from their own personal yearn-
ings. However, Mrs Chapel recalled many years later that Billy and
Jenny 'lived in great harmony [...] They had no children, but that
does not appear to have disturbed them. Sometimes they felici-
tated themselves on being spared the cares inseparable from the
bringing up of a family.'[69]

It is likely that, at the same time as devising the disastrous

Squanderfield marriage, Hogarth was considering a contrasting series as a refreshingly uplifting antidote, later called *The Happy Marriage*. He had been painting cheerfully contented couples and their offspring for years, and he had his own marriage and those of his friends from which to draw inspiration. However, there are only remnants of the project, as it was eventually abandoned for reasons that are not clear and, as a result, much speculation, some overblown, has surrounded it.

To separate the two series geographically and culturally, *The Happy Marriage* was to be located within a rural rather than a metropolitan setting. This community is led by a family from England's squirearchy, a rank Hogarth here judges to have a greater connection with, and interest in, the land and its people than the self-serving aristocracy and City merchant class pilloried in *Marriage A-la-Mode*. On the evidence of surviving oil sketches, *The Happy Marriage* would have been a far less complicated depiction of contemporary life than that displayed in the *Harlot*, *Rake* and *Marriage A-la-Mode*, but then a life based on honesty and virtue is, comparatively, a far less complicated existence.

The three main canvases that can be confidently assigned to the series are *The Wedding Feast*, *The Staymaker* and *The Country Dance*. John Nichols, writing in the 1780s, was only aware of the first and on such scant evidence presumes to judge the entire project. It should be observed that he had not actually seen *The Wedding Feast* (Royal Cornwall Museum) himself, but was relying instead on 'a gentleman who, long ago enjoyed only a few minutes' sight of so imperfect a curiosity'.[70] Having described the surrounding detail, a hall in an old house with preparations for the banquet in train, Nichols turns to the face of the bride, seated next to her new husband, which, as the biographer states, is the only part that has been finished, the rest loosely blocked in: '*Hogarth* had been often reproached for his inability to impart grace and dignity to his heroines'; this figure, therefore, was 'meant to vindicate his pencil from so degrading an imputation'. However, although the bride is pretty, Hogarth is unsuccessful, Nichols believes: she 'might have attracted notice as a chambermaid, but would have failed to extort applause as a woman of fashion'. He continues: 'The painter sat down with a resolution to delineate beauty improved by art ; but seems, as usual, to have deviated into meanness ; or could not help neglecting his original purpose, to luxuriate in such ideas as his situation in early life had fitted him to express. He found, himself, in short, out of his element in the parlour, and therefore hastened, in quest of ease and amusement, to the kitchen fire.'[71]

Nichols feels confident enough in this opinion to state it in a biography of the artist published less than two decades after Hogarth's death, in the expectation that few, if any, would challenge it. If only Nichols had had some knowledge or understanding of French art from the 1730s and 1740s, the work of Chardin in particular being certainly one model for both *Marriage A-la-Mode* and *The Happy Marriage*, he might have had the wherewithal to make a better, more informed judgement. *The Happy Marriage* is focused not on the modish aristocracy, but the country gentry or squirearchy – a group Henry Fielding describes with relish in *Tom Jones*. In fact the novel offers a better understanding of Hogarth's inspiration for *The Happy Marriage*, for example, in regard to *The Wedding Feast*, in the ultimately tender relationship between the rough-talking Squire Western and his lovely daughter Sophia, Tom's true love.

In the canvas known as *The Staymaker* (Col. Fig. 18), the setting moves to a private room, balancing the bedchamber of *Marriage A-la-Mode* scene four. Rather than a large gathering of strangers and hangers-on, where the wife plots an assignation with her lover, here the virtuous wife is being fitted for a new dress, in front of her husband, children and nursemaid. The male dressmaker grapples with her bodice – an activity Nichols may prefer not to see, but a common enough experience for any Georgian woman – which cleverly introduces a little light comedy, as does the child pouring milk into the dressmaker's hat to feed the pet cats dozing, out of harm's way, under the table. The nurse and husband are paying close attention to the most recent addition to the family. The former is kissing the newborn's rosy bottom, while the father leans towards the infant's chubby face, to kiss these bonnie cheeks. (Compare this lovely affectionate incident, lightly sketched yet clear enough, with the grouping of dying mother, her grasping father, sickly child and servant in scene six of *Marriage A-la-Mode*.) This modest room is a suitable backdrop to the gentle scenes of everyday life, indicating, as with Samuel Richardson's *Pamela*, the rewards of virtuous living.

The oil sketch known as 'The Country Dance' (Tate), considered the finale of *The Happy Marriage*, would have brought this series to a boisterous close. The scene is at night, the moon appears at the window, with the room lit by a chandelier and wall sconces. Again, like *The Wedding Feast* and *The Staymaker*, it is only loosely painted – blocks and dashes of red, blue, pink, green, ochre, the white heat of the candles – but with this economy of brushstrokes Hogarth presents a community, in all its variety, celebrating their collective prosperity by dancing together in a 'country' or line dance: the participants are elegant, clumsy, slim, rotund, well matched and ill matched – in physique only, as far as we know – but all enjoying this moment. The edge of the canvas is cast into shadow, which gives the impression in this final scene of a theatrical stage: perhaps the dance of life, revels now ended to the sound of buckled shoes on board, the wheeze and scrape of a band of village fiddles and viols players. For exuberance and joy only *The Shrimp Girl* dated from the same period can match it, which makes the following comment utterly bewildering. John Nichols, with reference to *The Happy Marriage*, observes: 'Why he did not persevere in his plan ... we can only guess. It is probable that his undertaking required a longer succession of images relative to domestic happiness, than had fallen within his notice, or courted his participation. *Hogarth* had no children; and though the nuptial union may be happy without them, yet such happiness will have nothing picturesque in it ; and we may observe of this truly natural and faithful painter, that he rarely ventured to exhibit scenes with which he was not perfectly well acquainted.'[72]

On the contrary, Hogarth had experience of such scenes, and he has expressed it beautifully. But this does seem to be a common perception – or rather misconception. In fact this comment, repeated in John Nichols and George Steevens's *Genuine Works*, is accompanied by a restrained but angry response from Hogarth's friend Thomas Morell. After stating he began to know the Hogarths while at Chiswick, and that 'from that time was intimate with him to his death, and very happy in his acquaintance', he goes on, 'His excellencies, as well as his foibles, are so universally known, that I cannot add to the former, nor shall I attempt to palliate the latter. To assert, however, that he had little or no acquaintance with domestic happiness, is unjust. I cannot indeed say, I have seen much fondling between Jenny and Billy (the common appellation of each other); but I have been almost a daily witness of sufficient endearments to conclude them a happy couple.'[73] Unsurprisingly, Nichols's presumptuous, unfounded and hurtful reflections (among other things) angered Jane Hogarth herself, who declared, after reading a proof of Nichols's first edition in 1781, that 'through the <u>whole</u> work misrepresentation and error, abounds. It would require a book, to refute, all the mistakes' and therefore, unable to prevent it, the work would be published '<u>entirely against my Consent</u>.'[74] Nichols's biography, specifically the third edition (enlarged and corrected) remains informative, but has been used here with great care.

Regarding a conversation piece of her own family, Harriet Hesketh née Cowper wrote, 'Hogarth who excell'd so much and whose fame will never dye, made all his children Frightful!! He had none of his own, and my dear Father, who knew him well, often said that he believ'd his Friend Hogarth had an aversion to the whole Infantine Race, as he always contrived to make them hideous.'[75] Harriet has not the luxury of flicking through a catalogue raisonné of Hogarth's paintings, for if she did, she would immediately see how ridiculous is her assertion. The Graham, Mackinen and later John Ranby's children, hideous? Little Gerard Anne Edwards, with his crumpled scowl, is hardly the picture of sweetness, but it is an accurate image of a tetchy baby. It is possible that Ashley Cowper, whose family portrait was one of those incomplete in 1731, is jesting. Or perhaps his child, Harriet's sister, was a disagreeable infant – after all, not all children are as beautiful as their loving parents believe.

The first half of the 1740s was a period of intense activity and variety: if Hogarth had only produced *Thomas Coram* and *Marriage A-La-Mode* these years would be considered a success. But with *The Shrimp Girl, The Graham Children, The Happy Marriage* and the many portraits, this was an extraordinary five years in Hogarth's career. What he achieved over the next five years would confirm this decade as being nothing short of miraculous.

INTERLUDE SEVEN

MONDAY 29 MAY, MORNING. The Nag's Head, Lower Stoke. At six o'clock the five pilgrims arose, 'had our Shoes Clean'd were Shav'd and had our Wiggs Flower'd by a Fisherman in his Boots and Shock Hair without Coat or Waistcoat', all recorded in the drawing Hogarth made of the scene ('Drawing yᵉ 4th').[1] It is an everyday levee or 'toilet', where the travellers prepare themselves for the day while in company. Such a scene, with an entirely different cast and narrative purpose, serves as a subject in both *A Rake's Progress* and *Marriage A-la-Mode*, and the contrast between the necessary ablutions at the Nag's Head and the pretensions of Tom Rakewell and Countess Squanderfield is notable.

This is a splendidly factual sketch and rare, as one of Hogarth's habitual drawings while out and about, in the moment, that can be dated and located precisely. Hogarth is sitting (to the far left) hunched over while 'drawing this drawing' as Ebenezer Forrest's annotation informs us. Hogarth is holding a pencil and a sketch-book, head down in concentration. Standing nearest to him is Will Tothall, possibly (it is not clear) just wearing his shift, breeches, stockings and shoes, a small cloth around his head and, as ever self-sufficient, shaving himself with a razor, a sharp blade with a handle, which can fold to protect the blade (in later years this would be described as a 'cut throat'), looking into a small mirror hung from a peg in the wall. As someone used to shaving on board ship, Will would have a very steady razor hand. Between Tothall and the fisherman (who is shaving John Thornhill) is a leaded window, lending the scene an antiquated, even timeless charm. The fisherman, as Forrest notes, is less formally attired than most of the company. He has his own short-cut 'shock' (rather than close-cropped) dark

43. *Drawing ye 4th: The Nag's Head*, pen and brown ink, with
grey wash and watercolour over graphite on paper, 1732
Hogarth composes the scene first using pencil and then ink lines and colouring.
His own figure, defined more boldly than the rest, will have been worked up later.

curly hair and he is in his shirt sleeves, breeches, saggy stockings
and shoes. He pushes up and holds Thornhill's nose as he shaves
his client's upper lip, an activity and gesture Hogarth introduces
into 'Night' from *The Four Times of the Day* (Fig. 45 p. 311). Thornhill's head is tipped back, a cloth tied around his head, arms folded,
trying desperately hard to keep still during this tricky manoeuvre.
Forrest sits on the other side of the table enjoying, as described, a
breakfast of milk and toast, so likely, as was usual at the time, he has
soaked the lightly grilled bread in a bowl of fresh creamy milk and
is now eating this melange with a spoon. Like Tothall and Thornhill he has a cloth around his head, tied under the chin in the style
of a headscarf awaiting his newly dressed wig. And then, finally,
there is Sam Scott to the right, already shaved and ready to go,
sitting with his freshly 'flower'd' wig (meaning powered, spruced)
under his hat, one foot propped up on a stool while 'finishing a

drawing'.[2] No one is speaking, except, perhaps, the fisherman. All is quiet concentration, to the gentle sounds of the scrape of blade on stubble, the slop and slurp of milky breakfast and the scratch of pencil on paper.

They paid their reckoning of eleven shillings and sixpence and set off for Sheerness at eight o'clock. Walking through the Stoke Marshes, they were advised by a local to keep to the main road. But instead they got lost, having spied a quicker 'tempting'[3] way, and climbed over a stile to cross a field in pursuit of it. Eventually, finding the path less and less enticing as they ambled along it, they were forced to turn back to 'the Right Road', losing an hour in the process and with tempers fraying.[4] They had ignored good advice, taken the wrong path, suffered for it and were now back on the straight and narrow – a metaphor for life. A little behind schedule, they approached the Isle of Grain, 'so Called from it's Fruitful-ness as I Conjecture',[5] although, in reality, no longer an island as such, due to silting of waterways over time, more a village at the easternmost point of the Hoo Peninsula. And 'Grain', rather than abundance, derives from the Old English 'Greon', meaning gravel. They crossed over the small stream or creek called The Dray (to the south) and the North Yenlet (to the north), and then walked past Grain's only church, St James's, with no comment at all. Before them and of far greater interest than the church and graveyard was the Chequer Alehouse. The landlady here was one 'Gooddy Hubbard', Goody being a reduced form of 'Goodwife', a title given to a woman, usually married, of low social status, sometimes asso-ciated with folk medicine, a 'wise woman', or witchcraft.[6]

As it was now lunchtime they were treated to another hearty meal, this time of salt pork, black bread, buns and butter, washed down with good malt liquor, another term for a fermented alco-holic beverage using malt, such as ale, beer or stout.[7] As a core produce of this area was sea salt, it is unsurprising that the pork served by Goody Hubbard, from pigs locally reared, would be pre-served in brine.[8] The 'black bread' is a traditional coarse dark rye loaf, while the 'buns' with butter, may be similar to brioche.

Paying the three shillings for their meal, they now searched for someone to take them across the water to Sheerness. But they had difficulty finding a volunteer, for 'the Ferryman Did not Care to go', and another man who had seemed amenable later refused because the wind was blowing too hard. The usual means of crossing to Sheppey from the mainland, whether by carriage, on horseback, driving cattle or as a foot passenger, was with the ferry, called the Kings Ferry, which was certainly already in existence in the reign of Queen Elizabeth, when an act was passed for its maintenance. Edward Hasted tells us the ferry was moved by hand via a long cable stretching across the water about 'one hundred and forty fathoms, or more'.[9] The ferry's upkeep was managed through contributions from the locals of Sheppey and in addition, each year a ferry warden, two ferrymen and a constable were chosen from among the local folk to manage the operation, and appoint a ferry keeper. The traffic using the service increased dramatically after the building of the fort at Sheerness and the expansion of associated activities such as provisioning.[10]

But, for our pilgrims, all seemed lost, with their destination tantalisingly in sight but out of reach (even the ferrymen dared not venture on such a day) until, that is, Goody Hubbard, a wise woman indeed, came to their rescue with the suggestion that they walk down through the marshes to the 'Salt houses' lying to the south and 'hail the Shipps in ordinary and by that means gett one of their Boats'[11] – the term 'in ordinary' means a navy ship that was not in active service.[12] While walking around the shell-covered shore they spied a little boat braving the inclement weather and through Thornhill's ingenuity and charm it was secured for the passage to Sheerness: although boarding the craft was fraught with extreme 'Difficulty', once more like the hill in *The Pilgrim's Progress*, with the wind whirling and the prospect rough. This particular event, 'the Manner of our Embarking', is immortalised in Hogarth's vignette, with the surrounding terrain and distant Sheerness drawn by Sam Scott ('drawing ye 5th'). The situation, although comical in retrospect, appeared hazardous at the time, as the boat attempted to keep close to a raised landing point while moving up and down on the swell and with waves crashing around it. Will Tothall is already on board and, as an experienced sailor, has taken a commanding position at the helm, while Thornhill, also on the

A. The Boat
B. Mr Tothall at the Helm
C. Mr Thornhill lending a Hand to
D. Mr Hogarth

E. Mr Forrest Pushing forward
F. Mr Scott,
G. Sheerness.

44. William Hogarth and Samuel Scott, *Drawing ye 5th :
The Manner of our Embarking*, pen and brown ink, with grey
wash and watercolour over graphite on paper, 1732
The smaller craft around the men o' war would be similar to
those seen in Scott's sketch of the *Prince William* crew (Fig. 31,
p. 218) and the 'yawl' they encounter later in the day.

boat, reaches across to assist Hogarth, lying on his front, balanced
precariously between two thin planks, arms and legs wrapped
around, as he shifts his way gingerly over the choppy water. Forrest
and Scott, still on terra firma, await the issue of Hogarth's success or
failure, Forrest 'pushing forward' Scott to be the next to negotiate
the planks.

   In the mid distance are ships of war and associated craft, and
centrally can be seen the fortress of Sheerness. Three birds reel
just above the waves in the foreground, hoping for a catch themselves, and in the far distance more full-masted ships. Within this
nautical scene, a very human incident which could end in disaster
is playing out, not centrally, but to the left foreground, with the
remainder focusing on the intended destination, the breadth of

sea and sky, and the mass of shipping that characterises this stretch of the Kent coast. The section of water between Sheerness and the Isle of Grain, which the company would soon sail across, is called West Swale, and at its most northern point the Medway joins the Thames.

All now aboard and with a palpable sense of relief, perhaps some nervous laughter, the travellers set out for Sheerness: 'The Sea run High The Wind Blowing Hard at SW & by S. In our passage wee had the Pleasure of Seeing and hearing the Guns fir'd from the Fort and the Men of Warr.'[13] The sketch also shows the smoke blasting forth from the man o' war to the right and the distant fort. The reason for the gun salutes is explained by the date: 29 May. This was 'Restoration', 'Oak Apple' or 'Royal Oak' Day, the date that Charles II entered London after his restoration to the throne of England and, as it happens, the king's birthday. By act of parliament, this was a public holiday of thanks for the return of the monarchy. The 29th of May was one of the Royal Navy saluting days, alongside the accession, coronation and birth days of the current monarch and, in addition, on the anniversary of the foiled Gunpowder Plot, 5 November. Sir James Thornhill, on his travels to Flanders, noted the guns firing at Landguards Fort in Suffolk on this day in 1711.[14] At that time, with Queen Anne, the last Stuart monarch of Great Britain on the throne, the natural connection between the restoration of the monarchy per se and the Stuart dynasty in particular was not an issue. However, with the arrival of the Hanoverians and an alternative king and dynasty ever ready to unthrone them, such a commemoration became at best ambiguous, at worst, a cover for discontent and rebellion.

In 1700 Ned Ward, a staunch supporter of the Stuarts, describes a particular walk through the side streets and back allies of Charing Cross. As he and his companion emerged on to Whitehall, 'the first Object with which our Eyes were affected, was the Brazen Statue of that Pious Prince King *Charles* the First on Horse-back, whose Righteous Life, Unhappy Reign, unjust Sufferings, unparallell'd Martyrdom, shall bury Monuments, out-live Time, and stand up with Eternity'.[15] And those changing fortunes continued, as symbolised by the dilapidated condition of the sculpture by the

Frenchman, Hubert Le Sueur. By 1721, the male descendants of
Charles I's second son, James II, were in exile. Meanwhile, in that
year the Office of Works reported to the treasury 'the ruinous Condition of that fine Equestrian Statue at Charing cross, which is very
much out of repair', the bridle reins being broken and degraded, the
dirty pedestal decidedly unstable with stones loosened or missing,
and much of the iron fencing protecting the sculpture having been
stolen or was wasting away – a warning of the waxing and waning
of royal dignity to the current Hanoverian monarchy, perhaps, for
this Charles Stuart was a prominent, if a little careworn feature of
London's streetscape.[16] It is for this reason that Hogarth would
choose Charing Cross, with a view towards the bronze sculpture in
the mid distance, for his final painting and print of *The Four Times
of the Day* – the king's effigy roots the area of London in which the
action takes place, but also, as the spirit or genius of this area, cues
the viewer into the veiled meaning of the details and narrative that
Hogarth has introduced.

In truth this scene offers a confusion of meanings, perhaps on
purpose, with the descending night and a pale light from the moon
allowing London's citizens to flaunt their loyalties, whomever
they may favour, under cover. The significance of the oak and 'Oak
Apple Day' is to the tree – the Boscobel Oak – in which Charles II
hid after his defeat by Oliver Cromwell at the Battle of Worcester in
1651, leading to his weeks as a fugitive, his escape and exile. (Popular
accounts published on the Restoration included Thomas Blount's
Boscobel and John Danver's *The Royal Oake*.)[17] The oak leaf sprigs
decorating the barber's symbol of the striped pole might indicate a
loyalty to the Stuarts, as might the oak leaf favour worn by the freemason and the short, fiery gentleman in the foreground. The erect
pole, springing forth from the fuzz of oak leaves, might even be a different kind of reference to the notoriously randy 'Merry Monarch',
then again it might not. Perhaps Hogarth recalled the sound, sight
and smell of the guns at Sheerness as he painted this canvas just four
years later (the engravings published in 1738). Charles II will make
a cameo appearance in other Hogarth images, and in a similarly
ambiguous manner.

In themselves the presence of oak leaves, you would think, in

45. *The Four Times of the Day Plate 4: Night*, etching and engraving, 1738
Among the bagnios, the 'Rummer' Inn and the profile on the
barber's sign (suspiciously like James II or his son the 'Old
Pretender') may hint to Jacobite toasts. A piss-pot is emptied on
to the drunk freemason (in full regalia) as he totters home.

this 'Night' scene means it is set on 29 May, Oak Apple Day, but it
is more likely, or as likely, a representation of 5 November, Bonfire
Night, originally celebrating the deliverance of the Stuart King
James I from the Catholic plot to blow up parliament. Hogarth
includes a small bonfire in the foreground and a larger one being

prepared beside the bronze statue of Charles I in the mid distance. Of course 5 November was also the date that William III landed at Torbay, so if a 5 November circa 1736, then the bonfires could represent the liberation of England from the tyranny of James II. Yet in the early modern period, bonfires were a regular sight and used for a variety of reasons, whether in celebration or dissent. Hogarth's *Hudibras Burning Rumps at Temple Barr* (1726) depicts a bonfire as a form of popular protest, here against the 'Rump' parliament, reassembled between the death of Oliver Cromwell (1658) and Charles II's return two years later. Samuel Pepys refers to the bonfires and street celebrations across England in anticipation of the king's arrival, and ever after they formed part of the Oak Apple Day commemorations.

In the mid 1730s, when Hogarth's image was created, Britons could be forgiven for thinking that the Stuart cause was waning, like the moon in Hogarth's engraved version. Yet while France was prepared to sponsor an invasion, as in early 1744, the threat was clear and present. This image, in its deliberate ambiguities, sets out the opposing sides of the argument, both of which, if they only paused long enough to think, had their legitimacy – as the Mancunian poet John Byrom would encapsulate in his ironic ditty:

> GOD bless the King, I mean the Faith's Defender;
> God bless – no harm in blessing – the Pretender;
> But who Pretender is, or who is King,
> God bless us all – that's quite another Thing.[18]

To our pilgrims, as far as we know loyal to Hanover, the idea of the imminent arrival of a Stuart prince from faraway Rome would have seemed somewhat fantastical and, as their boat bobbed over the choppy water to the fort of Sheerness, the sound, smell and sight of the salutes would have appeared firmly in honour of the British monarchy and its current incumbent, not an exiled dynasty. But by the time Hogarth was putting *The Four Times of the Day* up for sale, at the turn of 1744 to 1745, he may have had reason to believe that Byrom's question and the nation's loyalties for Hanover or Stuart, whether entrenched or wavering, would very soon be put to the test.

CHAPTER SEVEN

TRUE PATRIOT

In late July 1745 the French ship, the *Dutillet*, had been skirting the coast of the western Highlands of Scotland. After several days of relentless buffeting, within sight of the islands of the Outer Hebrides, the weather shifted to mere driving rain and, grasping the opportunity, the captain dropped anchor and a young English clergyman and his companions made for land in a small boat. The bedraggled group found temporary shelter in one of the crofts near the beach.[1] Over the following days, rumours abounded that an unusually tall young man, called by the Gaelic-speaking locals *Prionnsa Tearlach*, had recently arrived in the area and since that time there were signs that the Western Highland clans were arming. So passed the first days on British soil of another Charles Stuart, determined to follow his great-uncle or die in the attempt.

The *Dutillet* had arrived off the island of Eriskay on 23 July, but it was not until 1 August that a proclamation offering a reward of £30,000 'to any Person who shall seize and secure the Eldest Son of the Pretender, in case He shall land, or attempt to land, in any of His Majesty's Dominions' was issued by the Lords Justices, including the Whig prime minster, Henry Pelham (Robert Walpole having been toppled in early 1742, dying on 18 March 1745) and his brother the Duke of Newcastle, acting as a Regency Council in the absence of the king, who was spending the summer in Hanover, as he often did.

At that time, in his painting room at the sign of the Golden Head, over four hundred miles away from the western Highlands, William Hogarth was busy working on a monumental portrait, more dramatic and ambitious still than that of Captain Coram five years earlier. Far from abandoning portraiture, he was, once again, aiming to prove himself Van Dyck's heir. The subject, whether by design or accident, would soon prove extremely apposite to current affairs. The situation in the Highlands was certainly disturbing, and with every fresh report the alarm increased. But great faith was placed in the British army troops stationed in the north, so in all likelihood this so-called rebellion would prove a mere cloud on the distant horizon, no bigger than a man's hand. With this comforting thought, to all appearances life in London continued more or less as usual.

At the turn of 1744 and 1745, George Vertue had penned an extended commentary on the 'remarkable circumstances' concerning the career of Mr William Hogarth to date, his character and behaviour, as well as charting where his ambition had led him and to what level of success: 'as all things have their spring from nature. time and cultivation – so Arts have their bloom & Fruite &, as well in other places in this Kingdom. on this observation at present a true English Genius in the Art of painting – has sprung and by natural strength of himself chiefly, begun with little & low-shrubb instructions, rose, to a surprizing hight in the publick esteem & opinion.'[2] Once again, Vertue surveys Hogarth's career from apprentice 'to a mean sort of Engraver of coats of arms' via expanding into engraving and painting, to wonderful success in 'humorous conversations', to portrait painting 'at large' and, finally, his attempts at history painting, working 'thro' all which with strong and powerful pursuits & studyes by boldness of his Genious'. This is a positive assessment and, after so many years charting Hogarth's steady rise, one senses that Vertue is weary of it. For then follows a fairly critical passage highlighting, as Vertue sees it, the way in which Hogarth set himself at odds or 'in opposition to all other professors of Painting' while, as the same time, developing a great reputation and esteem among 'the Lovers of Art', notably 'Nobles of the greatest consideration in the Nation'. Vertue believes Hogarth despised and undervalued all other artists, past and present, including, amazingly, Kneller, Lely and Van Dyck, along with his fellow English painters 'of the highest Reputation'. In addition to undermining his peers, Vertue accuses Hogarth of baiting them to their faces, actively encouraging confrontation, discord and strife. In Vertue's opinion, Hogarth was running roughshod over the battered egos of his fellows – no more a brotherhood, a fraternity of equals.

A case in point – how Hogarth's own recollections differ from the reality – can be seen once again in regard to portraiture. Over the years, despite his later protestations of abandoning the genre, a steady flow of clients continued to troop through Hogarth's front door at Leicester Fields, including Elizabeth Secker, later Mrs Samuel Salter, a jovial, twinkly-eyed young woman, swathed in saffron and green silk; the melancholic Captain Lord George Graham; James Ogilvy, Lord Deskford, later 3rd Earl of Seafield; and, following Bishop Hoadly, in 1744 Thomas Herring, the new Archbishop of York and second prelate of the Church of England.[3] This small selection of clients represent the usual professionals and their spouses who chose Hogarth over a plethora of other portrait painters such as Joseph Highmore and Thomas Hudson, through personal recommendation. Or, just as likely, they were attracted to this particular painter's style. Alongside a brace each of aristocrats and Anglican grandees, this was a haul of influential sitters with which any portrait painter would be delighted. And, as Archbishop Herring had subscribed to Hogarth's *Marriage A-la-Mode* series, it could provide a source of additional income through his other projects.

Yet not all was well. For although Hogarth was maintaining various strands and being successful with them, not everyone was convinced of his genius. For example, sounding a pessimistic note in an otherwise successful period for Hogarth, Archbishop Herring was compelled to admit that 'none of my friends can bear Hogarth's picture'.[4] We cannot now comment on what, precisely, those close to the archbishop found so odious, as the portrait would be reworked by Hogarth three years later in preparation for Herring's elevation to the Archbishopric of Canterbury. The Reverend John Duncombe (son-in-law of Joseph Highmore) described the archbishop's figure as 'gigantic' and the features 'all aggravated and outres' which, far from displaying Herring's 'engaging sweetness and benevolence' seemed more akin to the expressions of the notorious Edmund 'Bloody' Bonner, Bishop of London during the reign of the Catholic English monarch, Mary Tudor, 'who could burn a heretic'.[5]

Hogarth introduced great movement into the portrait, even after reworking it, and Herring's expression has a transitory quality. Hogarth's guiding principle was variety – which clearly suited most of his sitters very well – so it is unsurprising that in a clerical portrait, which could be a static, tediously limited range of black, white, pink and brown (indeed, in other hands, was often just this), he has introduced variety to raise it above the average or expected. Certainly the final version makes a virtue of the predominance of dense black and airy white in Anglican ecclesiastical dress, and it shimmers with movement, through the loose, freely applied brushstrokes of the archbishop's billowing sleeves and flowing body of the 'rochet' worn under a black chimere, which assist the impression that the prelate is in the very action of raising his extended hand while speaking. This effect would encourage the imaginative viewer to think that Herring was reaching forward, beyond the canvas, to gently grasp their hand in emphasis of the discursive point, or in empathy. Due to the circumstances and mounting crisis in 1745, the archbishop soon proved a most persuasive speaker in defence of the House of Hanover and the British government on the national stage – a Bonner indeed, when the situation called for it – a characteristic, by Duncombe's own admission, Hogarth had definitely captured.[6]

The only explanation for the chasm between what Hogarth was attempting to convey through such portraits and what his critics saw, is that the artist simply did not chime with that individual's taste or expectation. Herring does not say he himself disliked the portrait, but Hogarth's frustration at being misunderstood would grow, alongside a fear that the issue existed beyond specific individuals, that people, for whatever reason, refused to acknowledge his originality, his painterly skill, or simply could not see it. A prophet in his own land. But subsequent generations saw it – like David Wilkie – and, later in the nineteenth century, James Abbott McNeill Whistler, who described Hogarth as the greatest English painter. One of Whistler's students, who believed Hogarth was simply a graphic caricaturist, after viewing *Marriage A-la-Mode* at the National Gallery, scurried up to Whistler exclaiming 'Why!

– Hogarth! – He was a great Painter!' to which Whistler replied jokingly 'Sh--sh--yes! – I *know* it! ... *But don't you tell 'em!*'[7]

The outside world, Hogarth's contemporaries, saw the arrogance and dismissiveness, not the sensitivity, the self-doubt, the ghosts of poverty and family shame, in short the vulnerabilities which would have made him more universally liked, even loved, rather than grudgingly admired. George Vertue may have kept his thoughts to himself, but it is more likely that Hogarth's arrogance and dismissiveness was discussed, and in this critical, irritable tone, within art circles and beyond. Such accruing of embedded bad faith would work against Hogarth when he needed friends most, or, at the very least, found himself in situations where being given the benefit of the doubt would prove useful to his reputation and peace of mind.

However, if any self-doubt or sense of being out of step with the world – indeed despair at being misjudged – existed in 1745, it is not evident from his second major self-portrait, created some time in that pivotal year (Col. Fig. 19). It is bold and brazen. Here, as a development from that earlier image of a younger man, brimming with hope and warm enquiry, Hogarth presents his older, wiser and more affluent self as a gentleman at leisure, unwigged, a fur-trimmed cap and copper-silk house gown. The conspicuous and sturdy presence of the painter's pet pug, usually thought to be Trump, guards his master like a miniature Cerberus, even as both eye us with a mixture of resolve and defiance. An x-ray, revealing the ghostly lines of a previous composition, proves Hogarth's original idea was to be wigged, only to change his mind, shifting towards the manner of dress associated with gentlemanly intellectual and contemplative pursuits. The presence of volumes with the names of famed English and Anglo-Irish authors – upon which Hogarth, the intellect and artist, in the form of the oval portrait rests – is a significant hint as to the portrait's message and purpose. That his own image is a canvas within the canvas, supported by the works of Shakespeare, Milton and Swift, suggests allegory or metaphor – history, tragedy and comedy, epic poetry and the sublime, and, finally, satire. These three literary giants are his guiding spirits, his foundations, his intellectual kinsmen.

Hogarth

To add to the mystery – setting his own conundrum – in
the foreground is the painter's palette, with an enigmatic cypher
inscribed across it and the accompanying text, 'The Line of Beauty
and Grace' (the 'and Grace' now almost rubbed away), for observers to ponder. Returning to the choice of books, any visitor to
Hogarth's house would immediately understand the affinity with
Jonathan Swift, considered the greatest living literary satirist. In
fact, Dr Swift died in 1745, so this may be a memorial as well as recognition of influence and affinity. But John Milton and William
Shakespeare, in the opinion of his haughtier, more disdainful
contemporaries and critics, would have very little to do with
William Hogarth. Their inclusion, for Hogarth, combines ambition, emulation and empathy: to his critics it was simply a sign of
self-delusion and overweening pretension, way beyond his evident
gifts and talents from which he should not stray – as Vertue says,
damning with faint praise, the public like and expect the artist's
'humourous spritely diverting subjects'.

The boldness of the portrait suggests that Hogarth, quite
frankly, did not care or, in the face of such increasingly vocal
antipathy, was as determined as ever to prove his critics wrong.
The portrait remained as a painting for four years, until a print
was published, so only visitors to Hogarth's Leicester Fields house
could see it – but what did it mean, these books, that line, this
canine sentinel? (Perhaps here the spirit of Diogenes the Cynic,
the contrarian, lurks too.) Hogarth might simply stand by and
listen to the comments, testing the waters. Or perhaps, even at this
time, his close circle of friends and trusted colleagues were already
in on the plan and, around a flickering fire and a bowl of something
warming to stir the mental faculties, would debate, record, swap
notes and plot. The existence of this as yet undisclosed project,
evidently explaining what this curving, serpentine line might be
– even in this subtle way hinting at a move into art theory, so yet
another provocative gauntlet thrown down – would become clear
within the next decade.

Yet, the one thing a visitor to his home could immediately
surmise: Shakespeare and his English histories were uppermost
in Hogarth's mind. Aside from his own image and the 'Moses'

history painting for the Foundling Hospital, Hogarth's main focus at this moment was the monumental portrait of the new star of the English stage, the handsome young Davy Garrick in the role that had propelled him to stardom, King Richard III. The thwarted French invasion in early 1744 and the ongoing war with France in Flanders, coupled with the winning ways of Garrick and the 'infinite variety' of England's bard, had made the subject irresistible. But with the audacious, or reckless arrival of Charles Edward Stuart in the British Isles, the portrait had achieved on-the-button topical significance: civil war, regime change, rival dynasties and royal cousins at war.[8]

Raised in Lichfield, Garrick (b.1717) was schooled at the local grammar school, where he is credited with organising his fellow child actors into a performance of an old theatrical staple, George Farquhar's *The Recruiting Officer*, at the Bishop of Lichfield's palace, naturally playing the lead himself, the boozing soldier Sergeant Kite. Davy then moved to Samuel Johnson's school, Edial Hall, where the older man (although by only eight years) became his close friend and mentor. Davy often imitated Sam Johnson's ungainly appearance and heavy Staffordshire accent, most famously, on one occasion, while theatrically squeezing a lemon into a bowl and enquiring 'Who's for poonch?'[9] Dr Johnson would later describe Davy as having 'cultivated all the arts of gaity', and as a result he was 'brisk and lively'. 'Depend upon it, Sir,' he continued, speaking to James Boswell, 'vivacity is much an art, and depends greatly on habit.'[10] Garrick also required adulation and approbation. Despite the fact that, with Johnson as his guide, Garrick had received the education that had been denied Hogarth and while Hogarth was desperately clawing together a career, whereas the younger man was studying the arts of affability while dreaming of the stage, there is no indication of jealousy from Hogarth towards Garrick. He was perhaps too charming to be angry with, or hold a grudge against for any length of time. In fact Garrick and Hogarth were genuine, close and lifelong friends, and as a result it is easy to forget that there was a twenty-year difference in their ages. And while Garrick gave the impression that his success was effortless, in reality he worked damned hard for it.

Agreeing that Lichfield was too restricting to contain them any longer, Garrick and Johnson decided to venture to London, setting off together on 2 March 1737. Johnson later recalled that they had a single horse between them, so one rode while one walked, swapping occasionally the entire route, about 118 modern miles as the crow flies. If they followed the main road south they would have passed through Coventry, Daventry, Dunstable, St Albans and High Barnet. From Barnet, they would probably have walked over Finchley Common, a large area of heath where armies during the civil wars encamped, then passed the villages of Hampstead and Highgate – both commanding spectacular views to the south over the city of London from their hilltop location. Then downhill, arriving at Tottenham Court Turnpike, the informal gateway to the metropolis, the site of the future Foundling Hospital lying just to their left, and onwards, plunging from open fields, with the occasional farm building or inn, into the roaring streets of London itself.

Johnson never tired of London, living in the heart of the city, eventually, in the 1750s, at Gough Square with his cat, Hodge. Johnson suffered from a multitude of illness – some physical, some mental – and when young he had been brought into the presence of Queen Anne for the monarch to touch or cure him of the King's Evil, the condition commonly called scrofula. This was an extraordinary ceremony, revived by the seventeenth-century Stuarts, ignored by George I and his heirs, but continued by the Stuarts in exile. Whether Dr Johnson was an outright Jacobite is still debated. He certainly held an abiding, largely sentimental attachment to the Stuarts. And his dictionary definition of the opposing political 'parties', in reality, unlike modern strictly defined party politics, more affiliations ranging from loose to heartfelt, establishes in no uncertain terms where he stood: a Tory, Johnson declares, is 'One who adheres to the antient constitution of the state, and the apostolical hierarchy of the church of England, opposed to a whig', which is, 'The name of a faction.' That said, he does quote Jonathan Swift, 'Whoever has a true value for church and state, should avoid the extremes of *whig* for the sake of the former, and the extremes of tory on the account of the latter.'[11]

An impartial observer, Hogarth's friend André Rouquet, believed that 'Every thing is conducted in England by the spirit of party.' He acknowledges that the English can be reserved 'so great as to pass for timidity', but do not be deceived, for 'you should see the Englishman among his intimates ; you should see the principal persons of the nation in their *antigallican*', anti-French, 'and *anti-ministerial* clubs, or engaged in one of those political controversies of which they have an infinite number'. If you did 'you should hear him not indeed cooly reasoning in regard to the party which perhaps he has embraced merely by chance, but defending it with a noble warmth and vehemence', for to animate an Englishman 'there must be some party to defend or oppose. He is out of his element in an insipid medium ; he loves to place himself all at once in some remarkable extremity, from whence he seldom departs' – except, that is, 'to pass over to the opposite side.' This conduct, Rouquet concludes, 'is not perhaps the most rational, but it is the freest and the most shining ; as he is accustomed to an unlimited independence, all his actions shew his aversion to subjection'.[12] As Rouquet was an intimate of Hogarth's and a regular at, for example, Slaughter's, we can imagine this assessment is based on the particular, including the passionate declarations on one issue or another of his friend Hogarth, as well as the English in general.

Just four years after Davy and Samuel arrived in the capital, Garrick had made the transition from trainee lawyer at Lincoln's Inn to celebrity performer of Goodman's Fields Theatre. His professional London debut came on 19 October 1741 with *The Tragedy of King Richard III*, which broadly followed Shakespeare's text and narrative but was adapted (as was usual at the time) by Colley Cibber, with further tweaks by Garrick himself. Hogarth's portrait goes some way to explaining how and why Garrick commanded such love and adoration (Col. Fig. 20). This image exceeds all that could be hoped for in a portrait. It combines a good likeness of a living person with the gravitas and drama of a history painting – effectively creating a distinct genre, the theatrical portrait. Hogarth was very particular that the painting was a portrait – as he states in a letter dated 21 October 1746: 'The Picture ... was Painted from Mr. Garrick big as the life, & was sold for two Hundred pounds on account of its likeness, which was the reason it <u>was call'd Mr. Garrick in the Character of Richard the 3ᵈ</u> – & not any body else'[13] – as well as reflecting accurately the substance of the play and the history it sprang from. Ever the businessman, with a once poor man's sense of monetary value, Hogarth was particularly delighted at his portrait's £200 price tag, boasting it 'was more than any portrait painter was ever know[n] to receive for a portrait'.[14] In the summer of 1745 Garrick, now performing regularly at the Theatre Royal, Drury Lane, left London to tour the north of England en route to Dublin. He was at Buxton Hall, near Chapel-le-Frith in Derbyshire on 18 July, and by the end of October at Lichfield, his home town. So Hogarth must have begun the painting, or at least taken Garrick's likeness for the face section (analysis shows this is a separate canvas inserted into the larger one), by early July.[15]

The finished painting is spectacular and, as contemporaries remarked, even as it was recognisably a particular actor, through its scale and dramatic thrust it was also the tyrant king of history at a turning point.[16]

If *The Beggar's Opera* was a combination of current affairs, comedy and satire, then Richard III was history and tragedy – Hogarth as dramatic painter. The scene is a military encampment hours before a great battle, the creeping dawn revealing the gathering storm clouds. Foot soldiers warm themselves by a small fire, unaware of the personal drama a short distance away. For dominating the entire foreground is the solitary figure of their commander and king, awaking suddenly from a terrible dream in which his murdered wife and nephews appear: 'Have Mercy Heav'n! ha! Soft! 'twas but a Dream; But then so terrible, it shakes my Soul ... O Tyrant Conscience! how dost thou afflict me?'[17] Suspended mid action, the king's right hand is raised with fingers splayed – Hogarth's decision to isolate this hand at the very centre of the canvas is a *coup de théâtre* in itself, a device he used in *The Pool of Bethesda* – his wide eyes betraying confusion and fear. His left hand grasps the hilt of the sword lying at his side, which leads the eye towards the object located just above this hand: the contested crown of England. King Richard III of the Royal House of York will face his cousin, Henry Tudor of the Royal House of Lancaster on Bosworth Field: the nation is once more divided and the future of a kingdom hangs in the balance. But who pretender is, or who is king?

Elements of the composition, in particular the dominance of the tent structure, are certainly modelled on Charles Le Brun's *Alexander at the Tent of Darius*, painted in 1661 and displayed at Versailles (*salon de Mars*), so available to view when Hogarth was in Paris two years before.[18] If he had ventured to the French king's palace, then the scale of Le Brun's oil on canvas painting, nine feet eight inches in height and fourteen feet seven inches in length, would have left an impression on him. And once the idea for such a portrait of Garrick as Richard III had been made, one of the most famous tent scenes in art, in a military encampment after a crucial battle, would have sprung to mind.[19] The desire to paint at scale no doubt followed: Hogarth's canvas is seventy-five inches by ninety-eight. Hogarth mentions Le Brun's 'Alexander' series in *The Analysis of Beauty*, but in reference to the Gobelins tapestries that were woven from them.[20] More pertinent yet was the abbé le Blanc's use of Le Brun's paintings to bring down derision on Hogarth's *A Rake's Progress* – a 'compare and contrast' aiming to demonstrate the grandeur and dignity of the Frenchman and the seriousness of his audience, against Hogarth's poverty of ambition and the triviality of the English. So the connection to the Le Brun was also a riposte.

While Hogarth was wrestling with this immense painting, the news from the north was becoming more and more troubling. Charles Stuart had raised the Jacobite standard at Glenfinnan on 19 August, signalling the official beginning of the rebellion. He had then marched across Scotland to Edinburgh with little to bar his way, finally taking up residency at Holyroodhouse from 17 September. One of his officers, Alexander MacDonald, wrote, 'indeed the whole scene, as I have been told by many, was rather like a dream, so quick and amazing seemed the change'.[21]

And those troops who, everyone assumed, would extinguish this rising, led by the veteran commander Sir John Cope, were swiftly and spectacularly defeated near the village of Prestonpans, just south of Scotland's capital – the tales of fleeing British army troops, abandoning their officers and colours, was as sickening as it was frightening. The recall of regiments from Flanders was now accelerated, and eventually a new commander appointed; the king's own son, Prince William Augustus, Duke of Cumberland: the child that Hogarth had painted in 1732, with the martial trophy and grenadier, was now at twenty-four years old the focus of his father's hopes of holding on to the crown. (The king himself had returned early and in some haste from his sojourn in Germany.) Cumberland was also the brightest hope for the continuation of the settlement that had brought his family to the throne, alongside the Whig government which effectively kept them there. The single rain cloud no bigger than a man's hand had turned, almost overnight, into a deluge.

King George and the British government were not the only people undergoing a period of extreme anxiety. The upshot of Charles's decision, off his own bat and without warning, to attempt a Stuart restoration with no French invasion force, a handful of men, some arms and a modest war chest, was profound. Young men like Allan Ramsay and Alexander Cunyngham, who had travelled to Rome on their Grand Tours, shared a dram or two with their exiled compatriots, even raising a glass to King James III and VIII, and joined the Jacobite masonic lodge, had, no doubt, in the thrill of the moment, actually meant it. But they would now, unexpectedly, have their loyalty to the Stuarts severely challenged in a life-or-death struggle for the soul of the nation. Some would be true to the cause and sacrifice everything; some would prove that their enthusiastic toasts, at home or in private clubs to 'The King over the Water', or in the safe environment of a Roman tavern, had, when push came to shove, been nothing but empty gestures. The Jacobite cause had been kept very much alive – perhaps beyond its potency as a political force – through such displays of long-distance loyalty. Certainly Charles Stuart had grown tired of words. He demanded action.

And how his trust in the reality of those promises was tested. For it is a simple fact that the reception Charles received, even from those clan chiefs who were ardent Jacobites, was very far from enthusiastic. This was not the time, he was told. Where are your men and arms, where is your war chest? When, more to the point, will France invade England? In response, Charles charmed and dissembled; all Scotland will rise, he declared; her sister kingdom, England (ignoring, for now, the existence of Great Britain) will follow; and when our cousin in France invades, any moment now, the king shall enjoy his own again. Depending on his audience, a Stuart restoration would see the disbanding of the union between England and Scotland, or not, Catholicism would return as the state religion, or he, Charles, not being wedded to his father's faith, might just convert – like his cousin, Henry IV of France – to please his many Protestant adherents and sway the waverers. Or, at the very least, religious tolerance would be introduced under a benign king, who cared deeply for the conscience of his people. All and none of this was possible. The need for French support, during an international war which meant, in reality, a full-scale invasion with French troops, cash and arms, would make even the most ardent British Jacobite a little queasy. But, they might shrug and say apologetically, needs must when the devil drives. This need, smacking of a client or puppet monarchy, in hock to the wily, contrary and significantly more powerful cousin, King Louis, would come back again and again to haunt this young Stuart's progress, as it had done his father and would continue to do in the decades ahead.

But in the autumn of 1745 all seemed well for Charles Stuart as he held court at Holyroodhouse, the ancient seat of the Scottish Stuart kings, building his army and resources in preparation for an advance through the north-west of England, those counties that had the greatest residual support for the exiled dynasty – notably Lancashire, with its strong Roman Catholic population – and on to London in triumph.[22]

Meanwhile, in London, life went on. The west wing of the Foundling Hospital was nearing completion and was opened in October. At which point the babies who had been sent out to rural wet nurses in 1741 would now return as young children to a new life at the hospital (with the unavoidable consequence that these infants had, in the process, lost their surrogate mothers as well as their biological ones). Hogarth and his fellow governors had much to keep themselves occupied, the various subcommittee meetings, the ongoing need to raise money to complete the building work, plus other big plans and projects on which Hogarth was working. In some ways the current national crisis confirmed the rectitude and public benefit of such a refuge; these children will be raised as good, honest citizens, developing useful skills for the betterment of society, the nation and the glory of God. Supported by a large number of governors who now included the Dukes of Cumberland and Newcastle, the prime minister Henry Pelham and under the regal protection of George II, the hospital was avowedly patriotic, Protestant, Whig and pro-Hanoverian. Of course, that could all change, and the scale of what could be lost – or conversely regained, if you were a Tory or Jacobite – was for all to see on the ceiling and walls of the Great Hall at Greenwich.

One beneficiary, if such a thing were possible, of any mounting anxiety and desire to show loyalty to King George was the theatre. The evening of 28 September, at the end of a performance of Ben Jonson's *The Alchemist* at the Theatre Royal, Drury Lane, three famous soloists, Susannah Cibber – still flushed from her success at the premiere in Dublin of a new oratorio by George Handel called *Messiah* – John Beard and Thomas Reinhold (both also favourites of Handel) stepped forward to the front of the stage and, accompanied by a male choir, began to sing a traditional anthem arranged for the occasion by Thomas Arne, Susannah's brother, and with new words. The *General Advertiser* declared the 'universal Applause it met with, being encored with repeated Huzzas, sufficiently denoted in how just an Abhorrence they hold the arbitrary Schemes of our invidious Enemies, and detest the despotick Attempts of Papal Power'.[23] James Lacey, 'Master of his Majesty's Company of Comedians', was aiming, like other citizens, including members of the legal profession, to raise a volunteer company from among his players and associates to assist in the defence of London, the king and government. Perhaps both cursing and blessing his absence from the capital, although in his journey northwards he was hardly avoiding the action, David Garrick was in regular correspondence with friends and members of his company. In a letter to Francis Hayman (posted 10 October 1745) he declares, 'the Country is much allarm'd by the Rebels, for my own part I have little fear of 'em & intend offering my Service as a Volunteer as I have no other Engagements upon me & cannot be better employ'd ... till these Gentlemen have done playing the Knave in ye North, I can't think of playing the Fool'.[24] Garrick had thought that 'the Playhouses will find little Encouragement till these Clouds are blow over'. Yet Benjamin Victor, writing to Garrick two weeks after that first presentation of Arne's new-old anthem, describes, with a mixture of amusement and surprise, how Drury Lane and Covent Garden theatres had become the chief centres for piety and loyalty in the entire nation. 'Twenty men appear at the end of every play,' he writes, 'and one, stepping forward from the rest, with uplifted hands and eyes, begins singing, to an old anthem tune' with the words:

> God bless our noble King,
> God save great George our King,
> God save the King.
> Send him victorious,
> Happy and glorious,
> Long to reign over us,
> God save the King.[25]

Anthems, much like the names of Royal Navy ships, are adaptable to changing circumstances. According to the musicologist Dr Charles Burney, relaying information he had gleaned from the mother of Thomas Arne and Susannah Cibber, this tune had been composed, originally, to be sung on the streets and in the theatres in the late October of 1688 in support of James II, at the very moment when his crown and kingdom were under threat from the invading William of Orange, soon to be anointed King William III.[26] It had now been adapted and adopted – presumably in the hope that history would not repeat itself – for the purpose of rallying the supporters of King George. Pro-Hanoverian loyalism is too often underestimated by later generations, but as a demonstration of resistance to Charles Stuart and his advancing Jacobite army, theatrical productions, invariably ended with a rousing rendition of 'God Save the King', were bringing in the crowds and with them their cash. Susannah Cibber reported to Garrick that the 'Rebellion is so far from being a disadvantage to the playhouses, that, I assure you, it brings them very good houses'. Cibber had used her influence and crowd appeal to raise money to support the defence of London. At her instigation, the Theatre Royal, Covent Garden, put on three benefit performances of that guaranteed crowd-pleaser *The Beggar's Opera*, with Cibber in the lead role of Polly Peacham. As well as bringing some much-needed gaiety to the nation – those loyal to King George, at least, or those frankly indifferent to either party – proceeds amounted to a very welcome £602 7 shillings.[27] In early November Susannah writes to Garrick, in full Boudicca mode, or, perhaps more appropriately, Elizabeth at Tilbury, regarding the militia James Lacy had raised, that he was unable to 'enlist me in his ragged regiment. I should be very glad to command a body of regular troops, but I have no ambition to head the Drury-lane militia.'[28]

Garrick meanwhile, like Hogarth always thinking on his feet, was keen to know how his portrait was progressing and, perhaps more importantly, given the times, when a print might be available. An exchange of letters suggests that Hogarth was nearing completion of the painting at the end of October. Writing from Lichfield to Somerset Draper in London on 23 October, Garrick declares a mutual friend, William Wyndham, 'sends me a great account of *Hogarth*'s Picture; have you seen it lately?'[29] And then from Dublin on 1 December, again to Draper, 'Pray, does *Hogarth* go on with my picture, and does he intend a print from it?'[30]

Over the previous weeks and months London had been troubled by confusing intelligence of an imminent French invasion. Alone, Charles's army, 6,000 men and boys, was, frankly, less of an issue, now that a majority of British army troops had returned from Flanders. However, Prestonpans had proved that any complacency shown by the British army would be presumptuous, and the potential pincer movement on the capital of an advancing Jacobite army from the north and a French invasion force from the east, would be a game changer. Meanwhile Charles Stuart and his Jacobite army were proceeding at great speed, and with the element of surprise on their side. This was certainly the case in Manchester, where one of the most bizarre episodes occurred, in a situation that constantly oscillated between tragedy and farce. On 28 November, John Byrom recalled, 'I beheld this extraordinary event of two men and a half taking the famous town of Manchester without any resistance or opposition, which I suppose the apprehension of the rest being at their heels might inspire us, however courageous, with the prudence not to make.'[31] What Byrom, in his journal, is attempting to describe was the arrival of the advance party of the Jacobite army – namely a sergeant called John Dickson, apparently formerly of the British army, a deserter, his mistress and a second man. This absurd drama did not put Manchester in a good light and was widely reported, to the town's evident shame. And worse was to come, for in Manchester the Jacobite army achieved what it had singularly failed to do up to this point – to raise a regiment of Englishmen, commanded by a member of the Lancastrian gentry, Colonel Francis Towneley. With each step nearer to London, the hope increased that English Jacobites, finally, would find the courage to join in great numbers, or, at least instigate risings in their neighbourhoods. What would be named the Manchester Regiment, in reality up to three hundred men from all over Lancashire and beyond, seemed to indicate that the fabled English rising was at last nigh.[32]

A clergyman from near the market town of Derby wrote to his brother in London, recounting 'the Hurry, Confusion, and Frights we have been in in these Parts', as such reports of the swift approach of Charles and his army began to circulate. Local fears were intensifying, partly through the reports in London newspapers of 'such dismal Accounts of their Plundering, Pillaging, and barbarous Practices wherever they came'.[33] One such source was surely *The True Patriot*, a weekly journal published by Henry Fielding in response to the crisis. It was a mixture of fresh intelligence, reports from other newspapers, particularly local press in the Jacobite army's path, over the previous week, concerned readers' letters and editorial comment on the present situation. In his third issue, dated 19 November, Fielding shared with his readership a vision of what was coming: the streets of London overrun by marauding gangs in Highland kit, alien to most inhabitants of the capital, houses aflame, the bodies of men, women and children strewn everywhere, ladies of quality beaten and raped, examples of 'the Cruelty which now methought raged every where, with all the Fury which Rage, Zeal, Lust, and wanton Fierceness could inspire into the bloody Hearts of Popish Priests, Bigots and Barbarians'.[34] Such false propaganda, as Fielding himself later admitted, seemed necessary at the time to encourage British citizens, particularly those in the capital (who appeared sleepy to the threat), to finally rise up and defend themselves.

As the situation became more extreme, an indication of King George's resolve to stand and fight was announced: 'Yesterday thirty Field-Pieces were mounted on Carriages at the Tower, for the Army that is to rendezvous on Finchley Common; and we hear Orders are actually issued for getting ready his Majesty's Field Equipage and Baggage.'[35] Far from preparing for his escape aboard a yacht moored at the Tower of London, a rumour favoured among Jacobites, King George was actually preparing to travel north to Finchley Common to lead personally the army gathering there. George was no coward – he had led his troops at the Battle of Dettingen (Germany) in 1743. But in 1745 he was clearly and understandably under great pressure. Prior to his guards regiments leaving the capital for the encampment, the king held a military levee, an informal gathering of his officers. It was later reported that he declared, 'Gentlemen, you cannot be ignorant of the present precarious situation of our country, and though I have had so many recent instances of your exertions, the necessity of the times, and the knowledge I have of your hearts, induce me to demand your services again.' George then requested that 'all of you that are willing to meet the rebels, hold up your right hand; all those who may, from particular reasons, find it inconvenient, hold up your left hand'. To the king's evident relief, right hands were universally raised. King George found this signal of support so affecting 'that in attempting to thank the company, his feelings overpowered him, he burst into tears and retired'.[36]

Unsurprisingly, according to André Rouquet, Hogarth ventured the mile or so to Tottenham Court Turnpike, as he had done when an apprentice, to witness the scenes of civilian and military activity as the King's Guards marched north: 'M^r. Hogarth who never neglected being a Spectator on such like occasions, did not fail to mix with the Croud on the Spot.' As was his peculiar habit, so Rouquet continues, Hogarth noted everything that occurred, 'even to the most trifling ... which wou'd pass unobserv'd by the generality of the Spectators'.[37] No matter how prosaic, Hogarth sensed this was history in the making.

This crisis came to a head as Charles led his men into Derby on 4 December, just one hundred or so miles, or five days' march, from London. The arrival of express riders bearing intelligence to that effect meant the government were aware of this fact before London's citizenry. But by 6 December the word was out. Legends of universal panic in the capital, rather than anywhere else, are exaggerated. Those of a more nervous disposition had left every town and city, including Edinburgh, Carlisle, Preston, Manchester and Derby, well in advance of the Jacobite army's arrival. As Henry Fielding soon after sarcastically described it, when their entry into Derby was announced in London – meaning that Charles had appeared to slip past Cumberland's troops and was now 'in full March for this Town' – combined with the information (later found to be another false alarm) that the French had actually landed on the east coast of England, such terror was struck 'into several public-spirited Persons' who, for now, will remain nameless, 'that, to prevent their Money, Jewels, Plate, &c. falling into Rebellious or French Hands, they immediately began to pack up and secure the same'. They then prepared 'for Journies into the Country ... concluding, that the Plunder of what must remain behind in this City would satisfy the Victors, to prevent them at least for a long time from pursuing them'. However, while they were thus taking great care of themselves, 'another Spirit hath prevailed amongst the Men, particularly in the City of London, where many Persons of good Fortune having provided themselves with the Uniform, were on Saturday last inlisted as Volunteers in the Guards'.[38] These men, at least, knew what was at stake, and what they were willing to risk in the king's cause. The citizenry who remained to fight, with their 'Great George' at their head, awaited the issue.[39]

In the event, and very much against the desires of Charles

Stuart, the Jacobite army retreated from Derby, back through Lancashire and Westmorland, receiving a very different reception to that on their advance, and with the Duke of Cumberland and his men in hot pursuit. The Stuart prince's predominantly Scottish commanders, weary of an 'imminent' English rising that never quite happened and fearful of being surrounded and thus cut off from Scotland, won, by force of numbers, the argument. The majority of the Manchester Regiment were captured at Carlisle.

After eight long months, the 1745 Jacobite rebellion came to a bloody end at the Battle of Culloden on 16 April 1746, Charles escaping the field with a small mounted guard.[40] The defeat was a disaster, but the capture of the Stuart prince would have been a catastrophe. Through no fault of his own, fate would delay Charles's departure to France for five months, during which time he was a hunted fugitive, as his great-uncle had been before him. In the meantime, the Highlands, seen as fertile ground for any future rising, were now under martial law and the brutal pacification – burning villages, driving away livestock, rounding up rebels and worse – as directed by the vengeful victor of Culloden, 'Butcher' Cumberland, was rolled out.[41]

Even as tales of Charles Stuart's travails as a fugitive were circulating in London, Hogarth was finally publishing his engraving of *David Garrick as King Richard III*. A subscription ticket had been issued, decorated with a masque and palette – the unity of theatre and art.[42] George Vertue, ever fascinated by the activities of engravers and Hogarth in particular, noted that 'the end of June came out a Print of K. Richd 3 in the Character of Garrick the present famous player or Comedian. whose performances are much admired – by all persons – His picture is painted by Hogarth – and the engraved plate by him & Grignon [*sic*] a young man that first learnt of Gravelot to draw and Engrave.'[43] John Ireland recalled being told by Charles Grignion, the engraver mentioned by Vertue, that '*Hogarth* etched the head and hand, but finding the head too large, he erased it, and etched it a second time, when seeing it wrong placed upon the shoulders, he again rubbed it out, and replaced it as it now stands, remarking – "*I never was right, until I had been wrong*."'[44] Meanwhile in Dublin, George Faulkner, ever alert to any new production of Mr Hogarth's, announced, 'Just imported from London, and sold by the Printer hereof, The original Print of Mr. Garrick in Richard the Third.'[45]

The print proved extremely popular as the terror subsided to be replaced by relief and jubilation. Garrick was back in London by the end of May 1746, so witnessed the excitement around the publication of the Richard III print for himself. As a result, both artist and subject must have considered they deserved a celebration. In July, Garrick wrote to John Hoadly, then at his living in Old Arlesford, Hampshire, accepting an invitation to visit: '& the little-ingenious *Garrick* with the ingenious little *Hogarth*, will take the Opportunity of the *plump Doctor*'s being with You', that being the physician and renowned wit Messenger Monsey (b.1693), 'to get upon a Horse-block, mount a pair of Quadrupeds (or one if it carries double) & hie away to the Rev'd Rigdum Funnidos', a reference to the character from Henry Carey's farce *Chrononhotonthologos* 'at y[e] aforesaid Old Alresford [*sic*], there to be as Merry, facetious Mad & Nonsensical, as Liberty, Property & Old October can make Em! huzza! ... I am, in raptures at the Party! huzza again Boys!'[46] Garrick's infectious anticipation of a waggish sojourn with the 'boys', the Hoadly brothers, John and Benjamin, Monsey and Hogarth, reflects well on all concerned, and on the strong, easy-going friendship between them. It also hints that after a year weighed down by troubles, some light relief was desperately needed.

Inevitably the gathering involved some theatricals, for which the Hoadly family was famed, in this instance the premiere of Garrick's *Ragandjaw*, described by John Nichols as 'a laughable parody on the scene in *Julius Caesar*, where the *Ghost* appears to *Brutus*'.[47] Brutus was transformed into an English sergeant 'Brutarse', played by John, Cassius a corporal inevitably dubbed 'Cassiarse' played by Davy Garrick and Caesar's ghost, now the Devil's Cook 'Grilliardo' played by Hogarth. Grilliardo enters, accompanied by 'Thunder and Lightning', and declares 'I am Old Nick's Cook – & hither am I come/ To slice some Steaks from off thy Brawny Bum,/ Make Sausage of thy Guts, & Candles of thy Fat,/ And cut thy Cock off, to regale his Cat.'[48] This is only a sample of Hogarth's lines, which are ribald enough (also bearing in mind Hogarth's abilities in 'imitation'), and were made funnier still by the fact that Hogarth simply could not remember them in their entirety – unsurprisingly, his acute memory was for things figurative rather than literary – so, as recounted by Nichols, 'they hit on the following expedient in his favour. The verses he was to deliver were written in such large letters, on the outside of an illuminated paper-lanthorn, that he could read them when he entered with it in his hand on the stage.'[49] Given the props included a 'Pot of Beer', we can safely presume alcohol was consumed throughout, the opportunities for corpsing were manifold, with the likelihood of getting through the modest piece in one go diminishing by the second. Hogarth had also prepared a playbill for the occasion and painted the scenery, representing a sutling booth, a sutler being a civilian provisioner to the army, with a topical and irreverent allusion provided by 'the *Duck of Cumberland*'s head by way of sign'.[50] On another such occasion some years later, in the company of Hogarth and Garrick, John Hoadly declared in a letter to James Harris that he had 'laugh'd most shamefully', and there is every reason to think that he did here too, as did his companions.[51]

Four 'rebel' lords had been captured after Culloden: Kilmarnock, Balmerino, Cromarty and, most notorious of all, Simon Fraser, Lord Lovat.[52] Unlike the others, Lord Lovat had not raised a sword against King George, preferring to hedge his bets by sending his elder son – the Frasers would therefore appear to support whoever the winner might be. His ruse failing, Lord Lovat was found, as legend has it, hiding in a hollowed-out tree, his swollen, gouty legs made bulkier still by layers of rag protruding from the dead wood. More likely, however, he was found lying among the heather near Loch Morar, unable to walk or even move.[53] But the belittlingly comedic vision of the hollow tree prevailed in the popular imagination – a futile attempt to hide, when his bulk would not permit sanctuary, like Falstaff and the page boy. Despite his many historic crimes – ranging from kidnap and rape to spying, doubling dealing, dubious religious conversion, general dissembling for which he was notorious – he was, nonetheless, 11th Lord Lovat, the clan chief, and the local people honoured him accordingly. The Old Fox was carried in a cradle – some describe it as a cage-like basket, both comfortable and ridiculous – suspended between two horses, to Edinburgh and then south towards London for trial. By 12 August he was approaching St Albans in Hertfordshire, a mere twenty miles from Tottenham Court Turnpike. Here he rested for several days at a coaching inn, the White Hart on Holywell Street.[54]

Lovat was a hugely significant captive, and not only as a notorious clan chief; as an intimate of the Jacobite hierarchy and their plans, he might be the key to the entire Jacobite project and the means by which convictions for treason would be successfully prosecuted. The other captured lords, Cromarty, Balmerino and Kilmarnock, were second tier in comparison. Hogarth would have been aware of Lady Cromarty's desperate appeal for her husband's life to be spared. He may even have witnessed her ladyship's arrival at Leicester House, across the square from his own, the residence of Hogarth's one-time patron, Frederick, Prince of Wales and his family. According to Thomas Gray, when Lady Cromarty, with her four children, begged Augusta, Princess of Wales to intercede, the princess simply and poignantly brought her own children into the room: the women were now speaking mother to mother, but with the additional frisson that these were the very children, including the future George III, then only seven years old, whom Lord Cromarty had, only recently, wished to disinherit. But Lord Cromarty, on the intercession of Frederick with Augusta's support, was pardoned.

Lord Lovat was not so fortunate. In addition to his status, Lovat was a personality, a larger than life character and a genuine celebrity. As ever ready to supply a public demand, Hogarth would have hoped that, once nearing the capital, he could gain access to Lovat in order to take a likeness. Who else was up to the job? Given his reputation in the popular mind, it was almost incumbent on Hogarth to try. He had not created a portrait of this type of newsworthy individual since Sarah Malcolm, and Lovat was of a different order of significance. So keen, indeed, was Hogarth that the painting he had been lavishing all his attention on over the summer of 1746, the gift to the Foundling Hospital, *Moses Brought Before Pharaoh's Daughter*, destined for the Court Room, was temporarily abandoned so he could venture north. Perhaps cash flow, while working on *Moses*, had become an issue, and he required a quick injection to tide him and his family over, or, as likely, this was a business opportunity too good to miss.

Hogarth was alerted of Lovat's imminent arrival at St Albans by Dr Joshua Webster, a local physician who had the extraordinary or, as he might have seen it, dubious honour of tending to Lovat while he rested in the town, and to comment on Lovat's health.[55] It was the doctor's opinion that Lovat's condition, which, if sufficiently serious, might have delayed his trial appearance at Westminster Hall, was more feigned than real, brought on by apprehension of his arrival in London and the inevitability of his conviction and death. In reality Lovat suffered from a plethora of ongoing medical complaints, not least crippling gout which, even so, had not prevented his swift journey south.

According to Samuel Ireland, the artist and rebel lord had not met prior to the occasion at St Albans, although others believe that the two had been introduced some years before on one of Lovat's occasional trips to London.[56] This debate seems to have sprung from Lovat's reported reaction on being told that no less a personage than Mr William Hogarth begged leave to pay his respects and, if his lordship was amenable, to take his likeness. We are told that as the artist entered the chamber, he was received with an exuberant 'kiss fraternal' in the Gallic manner (in keeping with the French upbringing of many Highland chiefs).[57] This gesture could also be explained as Lovat's bonhomie, which, despite his many faults, kept fellow Highlanders like the pro-Hanoverian Duncan Forbes of Culloden fond of him, against their better judgement. It is also the reaction of someone attempting to belie his mounting anxiety for what lay before him, a bluff show of sangfroid mixed with delight at such a flattering distinction, a portrait, it can be argued, by the most famous artist in Great Britain – Sassenach or no. It could also hint at Lovat's self-evidently domineering and intimidating personality, establishing himself as the alpha male in the room and unsettling his guest. Samuel Ireland continues that

for Hogarth, being grabbed by this tall, bear of a man and forcefully kissed on each cheek 'was perhaps not very pleasant at that
moment'.[58] This was not because he was repulsed, necessarily, by
Lovat the rebel or man, but for the very prosaic reason that his
lordship was in the middle of being shaved. So without decorum,
Lovat immediately struggled to his feet, forgetting the barber, the
suds still clinging to his face and embraced Hogarth, leaving his
cheeks, in turn, lathered in soap.[59]

That Lovat was a singularly impressive if somewhat alarming
presence is captured superbly in Hogarth's portrait (overleaf): his
sheer bulk, from head to gouty toe, is exaggerated by the swollen
legs, full-skirted coat and large buckled wig, from which escapes
a single loose curl – all that might soften his intense expression.
Arched brows hover between earnestness and aggression, framing
heavy-lidded eyes that stare out hypnotically – as they would have
held Hogarth's own penetrating gaze – his mouth open as if speaking animatedly but, again, fluttering on the threshold of a sneer.
To be clear, this is not a caricature, but an example of Hogarth's
brilliance at defining his subject's complex physical and psycholog-
ical essence – a character – using an economy of well-chosen lines
and tonal hatching. The fruit of many years observing and sketching his fellow man, in the flesh, is here at its maturity. Hogarth
himself recalled that he caught Lord Lovat 'in the attitude of relating on his fingers the number of the rebel forces', muttering 'Such
a general had so many men, &c.' Hogarth, with the time to assess
every element, every pore of this famous man, observed that the
muscles in Lovat's neck appeared of unusual strength – greater, in
fact, than anyone else he had ever seen, indeed like a bull.[60] This
is the only detail Hogarth refers to, and happens to be pertinent
to Lovat's imminent execution by beheading – perhaps Hogarth's
second thought, as he analysed Lovat's physique.

The etching was published in August and, as with that of
Garrick as Richard III, was a huge success: the art-buying public
were keen still for mementoes of the rebellion. George Vertue
recorded that the original print run 'was greatly cryd up & sold
every where', priced one shilling and 'many many hundreds. <nay
thousands>' sold. He describes the image as 'from the life in his

46. *Simon Fraser, Lord Lovat*, etching, 1746

drole nature & manner' and 'thought to be surprisingly like'. Vertue seems affronted at this 'humourous Character' as depicted by Hogarth, who is, in reality, 'a Man that has the Vilest character. and the hatred of all partyes. & besides that a barefaced Rebel'. Given this, 'if some persons had Engravd and publisht his picture, it had been highly Criminal'. Yet, as 'the old saying' goes, 'as some are winkt at that steal a horse, whilst another is hang[e]d for looking over a hedge ... in this case Art overcomes Malice'.[61] Hogarth, in Vertue's opinion, gets away with murder, while Lovat, now immortalised as a 'character', a celebrity, gets away with High Treason.

William Harris, a friend of Hogarth's, had enclosed a copy of the Lovat print with his letter to Mrs Harris, declaring: 'Pray excuse my sending you such a very grotesque figure as the enclosed. It is really an exact resemblance of the person it was done for – Lord Lovat – as those who are well acquainted with him assure me ; and, as you see, it is neatly enough etched [...] The old Lord is represented in the very attitude he was in while telling Hogarth and the company some of his adventures.'[62] While Thomas Gray enquired of his friend Thomas Wharton, 'Have you seen Hogarth's print of Lord Lovat? it is admirable.'[63] John Nichols records that a printseller offered Hogarth the engraved plate's weight in gold to purchase it. In the event it was worth much more than this, given that Lovat's final moment on earth, a fresh opportunity for print sales, was still to come.

Beheadings were unusual. Hanging, drawing and quartering was technically the penalty for high treason, but it was usual for an aristocrat to have this waived in preference for the axe, considered a kindness. Indeed hanging, drawing and quartering itself had been modified, so that the condemned were hanged until dead and the corpse subjected to the degradations of disembowelling and butchering, rather than a living body. This is what had happened to the officers of the Manchester Regiment, the only designated English regiment in the Jacobite army. Its commander, Colonel Francis Towneley, was executed in July 1746 at the gallows on Kennington Common – one of the main southern approaches to London. Unfortunately for Towneley, he was still alive when he was placed on the block, and so had his chest beaten and finally his throat cut. The executioner then eviscerated the corpse, throwing the heart and intestines into a fire. And then the corpse was beheaded, the head dipped in tar, and, with that of Towneley's second in command, George Fletcher, impaled on the spikes atop Temple Bar, the place where the remains of traitors of the highest order were displayed.[64] Hogarth depicted the western gate into the City of London on Fleet Street in his engraving *Hudibras Burning Rumps at Temple Barr*, with two heads and a leg impaled. Meanwhile Lord Lovat sat in the Tower awaiting his fate, and Hogarth returned to his *Moses*, keen to complete the painting, as the other three artists had done, ready for a grand unveiling the following April.

In January 1747 a new publication was launched entitled, provocatively, *The Jacobite's Journal*, under the editorship of John Trott-Plaid, Esq. The headpiece was a rough wood-engraving, in the style of seventeenth-century broadsides, of a friar pulling the halter of a donkey, upon which sits a tartan-clad man and, perched on the animal's rear, a woman. The former holds a chalice-style cup with one hand, while raising his bonnet into the air with the other and shouting 'Huzzah'. The woman holds a back sword, part of the Highland warrior accoutrement now outlawed (as was tartan). In fact, as might be expected, the journal was a spoof written by Henry Fielding as a follow-up to *The True Patriot* – and the headpiece was designed by William Hogarth. The Jacobite couple may have reminded readers of Sergeant Dickson and his mistress entering Manchester, although here they are astride an ass and being led by a fat friar. A personification of the Roman Catholic Church, he turns his smirking face while pointing to his eye – a gesture for his audience to be watchful. The arrogant Scotsman of the Jacobite army's advance, boasting of the timidity and cowardice of the English as he took the town of Manchester singlehandedly, only days later had to return through the same streets on the army's retreat north: a greater example of hubris in action is difficult to imagine. Hogarth's preparatory drawing has the young male Jacobite, aka Dickson, almost punching the air, bonnet in hand, as he roars the second syllable of huz-zah! – the sketch is really that

47. *Design for the headpiece to 'The Jacobite's Journal'*, red chalk on paper, *c.*1747
Pretending to be written by a Jacobite for an empathetic audience, the
journal aimed to warn pro-Hanoverians of the ongoing danger.

specific. The group has the air of a 'skimmington', as seen in Hogarth's *Hudibras* engraving, although the couple appear ignorant of
their 'crime' and its punishment. Jacobite 'bluster' and 'delusion' is
here ridiculed, yet the friar acts as a warning that, if Britons do not
remain vigilant, it could happen all over again. After all, Britain

and France were still at war and, as the French were more than aware, even the whiff of a Stuart restoration attempt was extremely useful, leaving Great Britain always a little unstable.

The Foundling Hospital's Court Room history paintings were finally unveiled on 1 April 1747. George Vertue recalled 'an Entertainment. or publick dinner. of the Governors and other Gentlemen, that had inclination', about 170 persons, with 'great benefactions given then towards the hospital'. The four paintings 'by most people generally approvd and commended. as works of history painting in a higher degree of merit than has heretofore been done by English Painters'. Hogarth's project appeared to have succeeded. Better still, 'its Generally said and allowd that Hogarths peece gives the most strikeing satisfaction – & approbation' (Col. Fig. 21).[65] André Rouquet later wrote, now as an academician at the Académie royale in Paris, that 'History Painters have so seldom an opportunity of displaying their abilities in England, that it is surprizing there are any at all who apply themselves to this branch'. Yet, moving on to the display at the Foundling Hospital, 'This exhibition of skill, equally commendable and new, has afforded the public an opportunity of judging whether the English are such indifferent artists, as foreigners, and even the English themselves pretend.'[66]

　　John Nichols, spurred on by the opinion of Horace Walpole, followed his commentary on *The Happy Marriage* with an equally unpleasant observation, contrasting Hogarth's depiction of Pharaoh's daughter, the biblical child's rescuer and adoptive mother, with Moses's birth mother, the weeping figure, who, having reared her son, is now being paid off and dismissed. The frightened and distressed child clings to her skirts, even as Pharaoh's daughter offers her hand, like Christ at the Pool of Bethesda. Nichols states 'It must be allowed, that such an artist, however excellent in his walk, was better qualified to represent the low-born parent, than the royal preserver of a foundling.'[67] This may have been an opinion many held at the time, but Pharaoh's daughter is serene and elegant, as would be expected, the weeping mother displaying great dignity and selflessness in her misery, while Moses, with

12. *Mary Hogarth*, unfinished
oil on canvas, *c.*1735–40

13. *Ann Hogarth*, unfinished
oil on canvas, *c.*1735–40

14. *William Cavendish, Marquess of Hartington, Later
4th Duke of Devonshire*, oil on canvas, 1741

As well as a supporter of Hogarth, Hartington was a friend of David Garrick,
who was a regular visitor at Chatsworth, the family estate in Derbyshire. In 1757
Hartington, then Duke of Devonshire, used his influence as Lord Chamberlain
to help Hogarth achieve a position within the royal household.

15. *The Graham Children*, oil on canvas, 1742

16. *Marriage A-la-Mode I: The Marriage Settlement*, oil on canvas, 1743–4
Hogarth uses dogs as symbolic of human character (including his own) or
emotions and, as here, relationships. The chained dogs (bottom left) mimic the
betrothed, as previously seen at Tom Rakewell's wedding (Fig.22 p.138).

17. *Marriage A-la-Mode IV: The Countess's Levee or The Toilette*, oil on canvas, 1743–4
The countess prepares for the day in the company of (left to right) an Italian
castrato, two fops, a woman swooning at the former as a servant offers a cup of
chocolate, and her lover Silvertongue. Recognisable Old Master paintings heighten
the sexual atmosphere: (left to right) *The Rape of Ganymede* (Michelangelo),
Jupiter and Io (Correggio) and *Lot and his Daughters* (Bernardo Cavallino).

18. *The Happy Marriage: The Staymaker*, oil on canvas sketch, *c.*1745
As seen at the countess's levee, Hogarth may have filled the empty walls with
'paintings' that stress the reality of the situation depicted. Here the theme of domestic
happiness, with details such as the napping cat, will be echoed a few years later in
the sketch of a young couple (likely the Goodchilds) at home (Fig.39 p.265).

19. *Self-Portrait with Pug*, oil on canvas, 1745
Hogarth's friend, André Rouquet, painted a miniature *c.*1735 (National Portrait Gallery) that follows the original composition of the oval self-portrait, including wig, as revealed by an x-ray. This suggests that Hogarth took a much earlier image and adapted it to become a pictorial manifesto for *The Analysis of Beauty*.

20. *David Garrick as King Richard III*, oil on canvas, 1745
In 1749 Dr Samuel Drake described this painting in a poem about the owner's house, Duncombe Park: 'Within whose walls immortal Shakespeare shines,/ In Garrick's action, and in Hogarth's lines.'

21. *Moses Brought Before Pharaoh's Daughter*, oil on canvas, 1746
From Exodus 2:10: 'And the child grew, and she brought him unto Pharaoh's daughter, and he became her son. And she called his name Moses.' Moses, a vulnerable foundling, is rescued to become the leader of his people.

22. *The March of the Guards to Finchley*, oil on canvas, 1749–50
Hogarth's innovative use of this painting as a lottery prize generated huge interest in the engraving (1,833 subscription tickets were sold) and, according to George Vertue, a stunning £900 income. The painting was delivered to the winner, the Foundling Hospital, on 1 May 1750 and, despite offers to buy it, which Hogarth encouraged, remained in the collection, alongside *Captain Coram* and *Moses*.

23. *Heads of Six Servants of the Hogarth Household*, oil on canvas, 1750–55

24. *The Humours of an Election I: An Election Entertainment*, oil on canvas, 1754–5
This scene is based on seventeenth-century Netherlandish 'Merry Company' paintings by
artists such as Jan Steen and Jacob Jordaens. To the right are several instances of bloodletting,
most notably by a surgeon (centre right) considered a means of rebalancing the 'humours'.

25. *The Ascension Altarpiece (centrepiece): The Ascension*, oil on canvas, 1755–6
The three women in the triptych are mentioned in all four gospels and are usually named
as Jesus's mother, to whom St Mary Redcliffe church, Bristol (the destination of the
altarpiece) is dedicated, Mary Magdalene and Mary of Clopas. Hogarth spent six days in
Bristol to oversee the installation, which cost £800, including the charge for three frames
by local carver Thomas Patty and the transport of the enormous canvases from London.

26. *Sigismunda Mourning over the Heart of Guiscardo*, oil on canvas, 1759

27. *Self-Portrait Painting the Comic Muse*, oil on canvas, *c.*1757–8
This painting establishes the importance of comedy, elevated here by the
presence of the ancient Greek muse, Thalia, to Hogarth's art. The engraving,
published in 1758, includes *The Analysis of Beauty* leaning against the easel and,
in a later version, the mask Thalia holds has sprouted horns, like a satyr.

his face splotched with tears and mid sob, is recognisably a child who is losing the only mother he has known: the emotional experience of the modern foundling. Perhaps the complexities required of the painting's dual purpose – the biblical and modern stories combined in a single image – was not immediately evident to some contemporary observers. Once again, as seen at St Bartholomew's, in presenting the jarring realities of the foundling story, Hogarth was bringing a freshness and vitality to the subject, while attracting further opprobrium upon himself, decades after his death.

One person who would have appreciated Hogarth's unvarnished candour was, of course, no longer involved with the project. The story is told that Thomas Coram, from the time the hospital opened in its new building to his death in 1751, would 'comfort himself with a sight of the children', and 'he was often to be seen, clad in his well-worn red coat, seated on a bench under the Arcade, with tears in his eyes regaling small Foundlings with gingerbread'.[68] (Coram was buried under the altar of the hospital's chapel.)[69]

Eight days after the Court Room unveiling, Lord Lovat was beheaded on Tower Hill, next to the Tower of London, which is where he had been held since his arrival in the capital the year before. Such was his notoriety that additional seating stands had been constructed to accommodate the crowds eager to see how he carried himself in his final moments on earth and, of course, the manner of his grisly death – a much grander occasion than Hogarth depicts, that same year, at Tyburn in *Industry and Idleness*. The weaknesses inherent in these temporary 'grand stand' structures were severely tested, to the point that one of them collapsed. When Lovat was told this he apparently began to laugh uncontrollably and, it is said, was still laughing, all the way to the scaffold – from which, so the legend goes, we get the phrase 'to laugh your head off'. Rather than helpless merriment, according to one source his last action before laying his head on the block was to quote the ancient Roman poet Horace: '*Dulce & decorum est pro Patria mori.*'[70] After Lovat's execution on 9 April, and tapping into the popularity of Hogarth's etching, which had been given another sales boost at this time, an anonymous print was published entitled *Lovat's Ghost on Pilgrimage*.[71] Here Hogarth's portrait, reduced to

48. *The Stage Coach; Or The Country Inn Yard*, etching and engraving, 1747
Hogarth will return to depictions of farewell and departure
in *The March to Finchley*, and the political parade in *An
Election Entertainment* and *Chairing the Members*.

a wigless head, has assumed a spectral quality, as if Lovat were a restless spirit. Swapping his civilian's clothes for a monk's habit, Lovat aimlessly wanders between the tombstones, holding his severed head, where he will find no eternal rest.

In another example of a timely response, on 18 June a General Election was called, to be held at the end of the same month. Meanwhile, Hogarth had announced on the 26th that a print was imminent 'representing A Country Inn Yard at Election Time'.[72] The usual human mêlée can be seen – lovers kissing goodbye, drunks, squawking infants, a crone puffing on her pipe, all manner of folk large and small, as a woman shouts and rings the bell – just as the morning coach is preparing to set off. The inn, 'THE OLD ANGLE' or 'Angel', as pictured in the sign, serves the coaches to and from 'LUNDUN', as all true Londoners, including Hogarth and 'Tom Bates', the proprietor, pronounce it. The pair on top of the coach, a British tar from HMS *Centurion* teasing a despondent

Frenchman, relates, generally, to the ongoing war with France, but also specific encounters between this plucky Royal Navy man o' war and the enemy: how it passed safely through the French fleet during a fog in the English Channel and, more recently, in the May of 1747, managed to sail home with her main mast blown away. The only specific hint that an election is imminent is the parade in the background, where the effigy of a large child is being carried with the sign 'NO OLD BABY', a reference to recent election shenanigans, of little interest now. But, together, this effigy, with the Jack tar, Frenchman and the inn sign, tie this image directly into the recent rebellion and its reverberations. After all, Lovat had been executed only a few months before, and therefore he and the rebellion were still fresh in the mind; the French had (albeit grudgingly and late) supported the Jacobite effort, and were now harbouring Charles Edward Stuart in Paris (in reality, as grudgingly). The question of the Stuarts' legitimacy to rule Great Britain, specifically their religion, had come to the fore yet again, due to the ordination and then elevation to the College of Cardinals in Rome of Prince Henry Benedict, Jacobite Duke of York, in July. Even ardent Jacobites acknowledged the damage this had caused. 'No Old Baby', the sign being held aloft in the print, was also associated with his father, the Old Pretender and warming-pan child, so this election is as much about Jacobites and Loyalists as it was about Tories and Whigs. A dog, the symbol of loyalty, slumbers in his kennel despite the clamour around him.

By October 1747, Jacobites and rebellions aside, Hogarth was ready to launch yet another series. Rather than the focus on either vice or virtue separately, as seen with *Marriage A-la-Mode* and proposed in *The Happy Marriage*, this would focus on both. The twelve images that make up *Industry and Idleness* – no paintings, engraved prints only and so cutting the time from conception to delivery – presented, as already discussed, a clear choice between virtue and vice and their consequences in two dramatically diverging stories, following the two apprentices, Goodchild and Idle. Hogarth declared this clear message was 'calculated for the use & Instruction of youth w[h]erein every thing necessary to be known was to be made as inteligible as possible' both 'in words as well as figure',[73] that the price of the series should not be excessive, and therefore the cost would be 'within the reach of those for whom they [were] cheifly [*sic*] intended'. Hogarth aimed to deliver, simply and cheaply, what the unedifying parade from Newgate to Tyburn and its finale singularly failed to achieve. Fine engraving was not a requirement, reducing, again, the cost and plate preparation time. Hogarth stresses what is of far greater importance, and to the very nub of the prints' purpose, which is that 'the characters and Expressions' were well preserved, and to 'supose the whole were made into a kind of Tale', taking his characters from apprenticeship to Tyburn and the Lord Mayor's Show, via weaving lofts, civic banquets, tavern cellars and graveyards.[74] Fundamentally, in Hogarth's own words, the resulting juxtaposition of 'Industry' with 'Idleness' signalled 'the Advantages attending the former, and the miserable Effects of the latter'.[75]

Drawings survive which illustrate Hogarth's thought processes; his own journey, as he plots a course for these two young men. They also suggest a hardening towards both, as the manner of their progress is finalised. Using the drawings that will become scene six, 'The Industrious 'Prentice out of his Time, & Married to his Master's Daughter', in the first version just the perspective lines and figures in their surroundings set up the street scene; the house exterior of the newly-weds Mr and Mrs Francis Goodchild, the crowd with drums, The Monument in the mid distance – establishing it is a 'City' location – with charity being dispensed. To the right foreground a man pushes a wheelbarrow full of something like potatoes. By the next drawing, the basic structure remains but with much more detail. The key difference concerns the wheelbarrow man, who has now gone, and in his place a beautiful, gentle, very sympathetically observed pregnant woman and child, the infant holding a doll and a dog sitting expectantly before them both, hoping for a treat. By the final published version, the child and woman have been replaced by figures altogether different in tone and appearance: a crumpled beggar – identified by Reverend John Trusler as '*Philip-in-the-tub*', perhaps a 'Diogenes' figure, replete with dog – whom no one, including Goodchild, leaning out of his window, is paying much attention to. Although the

49. *Industry and Idleness Plate 6: The Industrious 'Prentice out of his Time and Married to his Master's Daughter*, etching and engraving, 1747
Traditionally, drummers awoke couples after their wedding night. The unused drawing (Fig. 39 p. 265) may have been an early idea for the modern newly-weds, but here the focus is custom and charity rather than homemaking.

message remains, that one path over the other is demonstrably advantageous, yet, Hogarth warns, any self-satisfaction should be avoided: honest 'Frank' Goodchild is duly warned.[76]

This new series offered a parallel progress to that of the *Harlot*, the *Rake* and the Squanderfields. At the very least, the enormous success of *Industry and Idleness* confirmed that Hogarth's commercial instinct was sound, in promoting the tale of a good and a bad apprentice rather than a happy marriage. Hogarth scrawled in his *Apology for Painters* the following cryptic note, 'the prentices bought at Christmas', which may be, as Ronald Paulson argues, a reference to masters buying sets to be dispersed as Christmas gifts to their apprentices.[77] This was certainly the intention.

The armistice in May 1748, after almost a decade of war, reopened the crossing from Dover to Calais, allowing passage to ordinary travellers across this narrowest route from Great Britain to the continent, for the first time in many years. The opportunity was too good to miss, and so a group of artists decided to grab this moment to journey to Paris in the August. Accompanying William Hogarth was his close friend Francis Hayman, fellow painters Thomas Hudson and the Van Aken brothers, Joseph and Alexander, and the sculptor Henry Cheere. Unlike his first trip to Paris in 1743, Hogarth was travelling in a sizeable group, surely, in part, for safety. Again, as with the first Paris trip, very little is known about the core part of the excursion to Paris, or where they went once in the city.

By this time, Charles Edward Stuart had been living in Paris for almost two years, initially under the protection of his cousin, King Louis, but increasingly, with a peace with Great Britain becoming desirable, as a very unwelcome guest. In fact, as negotiations for peace continued, the British government had already demanded the removal of the young Stuart from French territory as a condition. This would not have come as a surprise to the French – such clauses had been in every treaty between the two sides since 1688.

John Nichols offers a description of Hogarth's behaviour while in France, which he states was provided by an unnamed English engraver then also abroad:

> While *Hogarth* was in *France*, wherever he went, he was sure to be dissatisfied with all he saw. If an elegant circumstance either in furniture, or the ornaments of a room, was pointed out as deserving approbation, his narrow and constant reply was, 'What then? but it is *French*! Their houses are all gilt and b[eshi]t.' In the streets he was often clamourously rude. A tatter'd bag, or a pair of silk stockings with holes in them, drew a torrent of imprudent language from him. In vain did my informant (who knew that many *Scotch* and *Irish* were often within hearing of these reproaches, and would rejoice at least in an opportunity of getting our painter mobbed) advise him to be more cautious in his public remarks. He laughed at all such admonition, and treated the offerer of it as a pusillanimous wretch, unworthy of a residence in a free

country, making him the butt of his ridicule for several evenings afterwards.[78]

There is no reason to think that Hogarth did not behave in an obnoxious fashion while in France, although it does beg the question, why would he go to the bother of travelling all the way to Paris, only to denigrate everything, from the style of their buildings to the visible signs of poverty on their streets. It would come as no surprise that French architecture is in a French style, and deprivation and squalor were hardly unique to that nation, as Hogarth's own images of the human degradation seen in the streets of London make painfully clear.

The anecdote gives the impression that Hogarth went to Paris to strut about finding fault and taunting the locals – some of whom would be exiled Jacobites keen, in turn, to rise to the bait or, better still, for the infamous Paris mob to do so on their behalf. The source of this unedifying description, whom Hogarth apparently considered spineless, was clearly shocked enough to pass on their impression of what would have been both discourteous and foolish behaviour. Yes, Britain had just emerged from a terrible period of war with France and yes, King Louis had supported the rebellion. Every Briton had experienced this, but not all of them responded in this way. It is befuddling – although of a piece with some of his other behaviour, a man willing to cut off his nose to spite his face – and can only be explained by the possibility that Hogarth's unresolved anger, against everyone and no one, just life, which had always bubbled away under the surface, rising occasionally, was becoming more and more visible. However, we should remember that Nichols was recalling this anecdote decades later and in the full knowledge of what would come next: for Hogarth's reported bad behaviour would soon get its comeuppance.

According to George Vertue, Hogarth and Hayman returned home while the others ventured on to Flanders.[79] At Calais the two friends lodged at the English Inn, the Lion d'argent, and while awaiting the packet to Dover, Hogarth entertained himself by sketching, as was his habit, while observing various incidents playing out in the vicinity of the drawbridge and gate of the port.

What then occurred was reported by a variety of contemporaries, including Horace Walpole and Vertue, so it must have been a story that Hogarth – or Hayman – openly talked about on their return to London. As described by Walpole, who may have heard it from Hogarth himself or on the grapevine, one scene that gained the artist's attention was the arrival by boat from England of 'an immense piece of beef landing for the Lion d'Argent ... and several hungry friars following it'. Walpole describes the whole escapade as running 'a great risk' in the context of the peace, that Hogarth was 'imprudent as to be taking a sketch of the drawbridge at Calais'.[80] Imprudent, or impudent? Whichever it was, in his later recollections, Hogarth admits he spent some time sauntering about and looking at the gate itself 'which it seem[s] was build by the English when the place was in our possession still of the arms of England upon it'.[81] The presence of the English arms and its history, deemed important enough to comment on, might have lulled Hogarth into remaining in situ longer than was strictly necessary or wise. In any case, and unsurprisingly, he was presumed by local guards to be drawing the fortifications, rather than local monks and imported meat, and as a result he was arrested as a spy. He was escorted, at the point of a bayonet, to the governor for interrogation. In fact Vertue noted that both men, Hogarth and Hayman, were 'clapt into' the local 'Bastile'.[82] According to John Nichols, the commandant of Calais informed Hogarth that if the peace had not occurred 'he should have been obliged to have hung him up immediately on the ramparts'; in times of war, someone not in military uniform who is intelligence gathering could be summarily hanged for spying, so Hogarth's behaviour, just a few months after the secession of hostilities and while a treaty was being thrashed out, was at best naïve or misjudged. At worst, if brazen and consciously done, it was provocative and stupid, endangering himself and his English companion by association.[83]

Fortunately for Hogarth, Britain and France were at peace, but there was still the issue of why and what he was drawing. Eventually he was released on production of his sketches, the evidence in his defence, as clearly those of a 'painter for [my] own use', not useful to a military engineer or expert in ballistics.[84] They were still dangerous enough, however, as these drawings, described by Horace Walpole, were 'caricatures of the French', particularly the three hungry friars. But apparently the governor thought them amusing and released him. The Reverend Trusler offers a more positive version of events by stating that 'when it was known, who he was, he was speedily set at liberty'.[85] Hogarth was then confined to his lodgings, with his landlord, '*Grandsire*' in Nichols's account, as his gaoler, until the wind was favourable for a boat to Dover, on a clear day visible from Calais, from whence Vertue notes, Hogarth and Hayman 'were soon glad to return to England'.[86]

But the humiliation did not end there, for, as described by John Nichols, two guards were sent to escort Hogarth from the inn to the packet, which was presumably a French boat, because they 'did not quit him till he was three miles from the shore. They then spun him round like a top, on the deck' where everyone aboard could see 'and told him he was at liberty to proceed on his voyage without farther attendance or molestation'. Nichols then states that 'With the slightest allusion to the ludicrous particulars of this affair, poor *Hogarth* was by no means pleased.'[87] According to Nichols, Hogarth stayed at the Reverend Gostling's house in Canterbury the night he arrived back in England, and indeed it is from Gostling, via Hogarth himself, that Nichols's account of the incident in Calais comes.[88] Hogarth's sensitivities around his stature and dignity – both wounded by the manhandling he would have received as he was seized and marched to the governor's chambers, as well as, perhaps worse, on board ship – did not allow him to brazen it out, or laugh it off. Humiliating, even frightening, as it no doubt was at the time, it was certainly an adventure, a tale he lived to tell, which another might have packaged into an entertaining and hilarious story, full of jeopardy and derring-do, for an evening's amusement at Slaughter's or, more appropriate, the Beefsteak Club. Hogarth, put simply, was not that kind of man. The embarrassment, mixed with bitter disappointment at how his adventure to France had panned out, would quickly turn into a violent desire for revenge and result in one of his most vicious, chauvinistic and, frankly, grotesque images. For no sooner had he arrived in England than he 'set about the Picture'.

In his autobiographical notes, Hogarth prefaced his short recollection of the event with the following statement: 'The first time
any one goes from hence to france by way of Calais he cannot avoid
being struck with the Extreem different face things appear with at
so little a distance as from Dover' that is 'a farcical pomp of war,
parade of riligion and Bustle ... with very little bussiness in short
poverty slavery and Insolence <with an affectation of politeness>
give you even here the first specimen of the whole country.'[89] These
comments were written some years after the fact, so his humiliating experience demonstrably jarred still. But if this was Hogarth's
impressions of Calais and therefore the entire French nation on
arrival in the town in the August of 1748, then the reports of his
obnoxious behaviour during his time in the country make sense.
Hogarth would not have been unusual in holding such opinions
of the French. Rouquet includes the following observation within
his 'letters', unpacking Hogarth's prints for a French audience, as
to why, in his opinion, the English, generally speaking, view the
French as they do: 'The English never are as thoroughly pleas'd, as
when a Frenchman is deceiv'd' for 'their Theatre, their Conversation, the subject of their Pictures & above all, those of our Artist
carry this glorious mark of the Love of their Country, their Novells
even are deckt with entertaining strokes on this favourite subject ...
The pretended disgust & contempt with which the English treat
the French, explains itself to me in a very equivocal manner: Contempt rather indicates a wish of forgetfulness, but an Object that is
perpetually rail'd at, is an object that is continually in mind, Satire
constitutes an attention which makes me suspect that they do the
French the honor to hate them a little – '.[90] This would be the case,
particularly in the wake of or during yet another war – effectively
the situation for the entire eighteenth century. Indeed Hogarth's
two engravings for *The Invasion*, 'France' and 'England' of 1756
makes this explicit, with the English laughing at a stick-man caricature of King Louis. Even so, Hogarth's behaviour and attitude was
clearly considered extreme enough, by some of his contemporaries,
to be worthy of comment.

Hogarth's initial sketches of what passed in Calais had been
executed as an amusing comment on national difference, as his

statement suggests. And the incident, as recounted by Walpole to Horace Mann in Venice, of the arrival of the English beef destined for the English inn and the friars following after it, does appear at the centre of the painting *The Gate of Calais* (Tate). Hogarth is even seen sketching to the side, the pike, or halberd, hangs over his head, the arresting hand on Hogarth's shoulder, all leading the narrative on to what happened next at the governor's chambers. But, through the assortment of accompanying characters and characterisations, this whole depiction has escalated into a full-throttled visual assault on France and Roman Catholicism.

Hogarth's autobiographical notes observe that, in contrast to England, 'the fish wemen have faces of ... leather', while the soldiers he encountered are 'rag[g]ed and lean'. Hogarth goes on to state that after adding these characters, he 'introduced a poor highlander [the word 'exiled' scored through] fled thither on account of the Rebelion'. This Highlander is 'brozing on scanty french fair in sight [of] a Surloin of Beef a present from England which ... is opposed [to] the Kettle of soup meager'.[91] (Hogarth would reuse most of these elements in *The Invasion* prints seven years later.) So Hogarth's sense of indignation at his treatment by the governor and guards at Calais has metamorphosed into a somewhat triumphalist commentary on the recent Jacobite rebellion – a division within his native Britain which was nourished (he argues) by malignant foreign forces, Roman Catholicism and France to the detriment of 'gullible' Jacobites, here in the form of a tartan-clad Highlander whose only nourishment, now, is an onion. It is not difficult to see who the loser is in this scenario and who, Hogarth believes, has the last laugh.

In his fury Hogarth also set aside the sensitivities of his friend, John Pine, who modelled for the figure of the friar – a figure that Hogarth has already added to his repertoire of characters, as seen in *The Jacobite's Journal* headpiece – without (it is said) being told the purpose. Once placed at the centre of this scene, poor Pine was known thereafter as 'Friar Pine' – immediately connecting him to the *Calais Gate* painting and, after March 1749, the print – which he did not find amusing in the slightest. A few years later, in recompense, Hogarth painted his friend in the style of Rembrandt:

50. Charles Mosley and William Hogarth, *O the Roast Beef of Old England (The Gate of Calais)*, etching and engraving, 1749
Malice aside, the assembled characters are brilliantly depicted, some based on the sketches that caused Hogarth's arrest. The skate (bottom left) is a cheeky reference to Jean-Baptiste-Siméon Chardin's famous painting *The Ray* (1728, Louvre).

a deep brown background, with rich, heavy fabrics, also brown, highlighting John's strong face and the glint of an earring. It is a stunning portrait, published as a mezzotint, but also confirms the friar is a very close likeness.

Theodosius Forrest (Ebenezer's son) penned a cantata, *The Roast Beef of Old England*, which was published with a smaller version of the print as a headpiece. (The engraving of *Calais Gate* by Hogarth and Charles Mosley has the title 'O THE ROAST BEEF OF OLD ENGLAND'.) The cantata was likely to have been published with Hogarth's blessing – it commences ''Twas at the Gates of *Calais, Hogarth* tells' – and the contents of the libretto provides useful additional detail.[92] Here Forrest says that the man straining to carry the beef is 'Madam *Grandsire*'s cook' and the

two soldiers in white coats are Irish, both also wear white cock-
ades, the Jacobite emblem (the black cockade being Hanoverian),
one of whom 'From *Tyburn*'s fatal tree had hither fled, By honest
means to get his daily bread.' The white cockade is also worn by the
guard standing on the other side of the beef, striking a cocky 'inso-
lent' pose, seemingly unaware of the worn elbows of his shirt and
threadbare stockings. Perhaps he does not care. On the ground,
almost hidden in the shadows, sits 'poor *Sawney*', the Highlander,
with his 'dear lov'd mull ... thrown aside', all thoughts of drinking to King James VIII, 'The King Over the Water', forgotten. He
cries 'Ah, *Charley*! hadst thou not been seen, This ne'er had hapt
to me.'[93]

Forrest's words are closer in sentiment to Fielding's bluff 'Roast
Beef' ditty from his *Grub-Street Opera* of 1731. Less sympathetic
and perhaps more in tune with Hogarth's feelings, as expressed in
this image, was 'Beef and Liberty' published in the *Gentleman's
Magazine* in June 1748. Anti-Highland and anti-Jacobite feeling
is now applied to all Scots, despite the fact that Jacobitism was far
from a universal phenomenon in Scotland. Having described how,
'From steril rocks, and everlasting snow,/ When Scotia pour'd, in
swarms, the savage foe', the author declares, 'May this' – the beef
– 'still nerve the Briton's dreaded arm,/ When rude Rebellion
sounds the rash alarm!' Rebels 'cringe and starve on Gallia's envy'd
coast' and 'take the yoke, the slaves of tinsel state,/ And own your
shame in boasting Lewis great;/ There soups and sallads shall you
board supply,/ And the kind priest absolve ye when ye die.'[94]

Meanwhile in Edinburgh, the philosopher David Hume, a
self-professed sceptical Whig, was weighing up the situation for
post-rebellion Britain in an infinitely more measured and con-
structive way. Offering an alternative to Hogarth's attitude, in an
essay 'Of the Protestant Settlement', first penned in 1747, Hume
allows that, as a Scot, he speaks of the Stuarts as the dynasty who
had ruled over Scotland for several hundred years, whereas for
the English, the Stuarts were relatively recent, and James I, as a
Scot, was a foreigner when he acceded to the English throne,
after the death of his second cousin, Queen Elizabeth.[95] Nonetheless, James's succession was not disputed. Turning to the current

Stuart claim versus the House of Hanover's, he acknowledges that a settlement in favour of the former 'frees us from a disputed title', the latter 'from the claims of prerogative' or divine right. Hume was for liberty, which he considered 'so invaluable a blessing in society, that whatever favours its progress and security, can scarce be too fondly cherish'd by every one, who is a lover of human kind'. He is thus, on balance and happily, for Hanover, but, turning to recent upheavals, he includes a word of warning, for 'the claims of the banish'd family, I fear, are not yet antiquated; and who can foretel, that their future attempts will produce no greater disorder?'[96]

By 1749 Hogarth may have come around to a more conciliatory position, certainly less vicious than that expressed in the painting *Calais Gate*, forged in the summer's heat of 1748. Charles Stuart was at a safe distance, having been forcefully removed from France and, once more, being a wandering soul, having declared, after his brother and father's treachery, that he would never return to Rome during the latter's lifetime: a vow he kept, despite the pleading of a distraught parent.[97] If in *Calais Gate* Hogarth had visualised, in very stark terms, the young Stuart's defeat and exile, along with his followers, his next painting, with the 1745 rebellion as its starting point, would represent the events and the prince's adventure – already the stuff of legend, running parallel to the despairing, angry drunkard of reality – as a folk tale, wrapped up in a symbolic vision of national character and spirit at once patriotic and parody.

Henry Fielding, the pro-Hanoverian firebrand, was also pondering the rebellion and its meaning. While acknowledging that if Charles Stuart had won, he, Henry, would have been the first to swing, nonetheless, he too was softening: not in the politics of it (he would never be a Jacobite), but in an appreciation as to why the Stuart cause and the bonnie prince himself would have had appeal over the rival dynasty.[98] The *History of Tom Jones, a foundling* concerns legitimacy and inheritance, which cuts to the heart of the Stuart-Hanover conundrum. And alongside, with an abandoned infant as its hero, it challenges the prejudices that had prevented the creation of a refuge for such children – the 'Fondling Hospital' as wits described it – and which, ten years after its foundation, continued to be voiced in opposition to it.

Tom first appears, like a tiny miracle, as a newborn in the bed of Squire Allworthy, which, rather than kindness, immediately occasions a torrent of abuse from the squire's servant, Mrs Deborah Wilkins: firstly at the unknown mother or 'Hussy' who should be 'committed to *Bridewel*, and whipt at the Cart's Tail', and then the infant himself – 'Faugh, how it stinks! It doth not smell like a Christian.' Thankfully Allworthy, as his name declares, is more inclined to charity. As his servant spits and chides, 'There were some Strokes in this Speech which, perhaps, would have offended Mr. *Allworthy*, had he strictly attended to it ; but he had now got one of his Fingers into the Infant's Hand, which by its gentle pressure, seeming to implore his Assistance, had certainly out-pleaded the Eloquence of Mrs. *Deborah*, had it been ten times greater than it was.'[99] A foundling, with no identity or past, appearing in such a fashion, was a recognisable reference to the Stuart warming-pan baby. It is also the catalyst for the comic twists – Tom's parentage is incorrectly presumed to be Jenny Jones and Partridge, allowing for an Oedipal plot line when Tom and Jenny, unknowing, spend the night together. But the narrative, after the grown Tom, a charming and reckless youth, is disinherited and cast out of Paradise Hall, follows the adventures of another Stuart: Prince Charlie, the fugitive, the dispossessed.[100] Tom's ensuing wanderings are, on one level, a riff on Charles's own, whether the march to London to establish his claim, or the five months as a fugitive in Scotland. Tom's purpose is to regain his honour and reputation and to win back the fair maiden Sophia Western. Mixing recent history with fiction, Sophia, daughter of a Jacobite, is mistaken for Charles Stuart's mistress, Jenny Cameron – in itself a fabrication, intended to besmirch the 'Young Pretender' – and therefore becomes, herself, part of the fantasy of mistaken identities and alter egos.[101]

On the road Tom meets a company of soldiers who, it soon becomes apparent, are venturing elsewhere. The host of the inn responds to a thunderous knocking on his gate, as if the broader political issue of the day is about to crash into what has been, until this point, a modest domestic drama. The room is overwhelmed with military men in their red coats and, similarly, the rebellion has burst in upon everyday life. In conversation with one of the sergeants, Tom is informed that 'they were marching against the Rebels, and expected to be commanded by the glorious Duke of *Cumberland*', placing the narrative to late autumn 1745.[102] Tom declares 'The Cause of King *George* is the Cause of Liberty and true Religion. In other Words, it is the Cause of common Sense'.[103] Little wonder then, says Fielding, 'that in circumstances which would have warranted a much more romantic and wild Undertaking, it should occur to him to serve as a Volunteer in this Expedition'.[104]

With these connections to recent events, it is possible that *Tom Jones* was one stimulus for Hogarth's most famous image associated with the rebellion, *The March of the Guards to Finchley* (Col. Fig. 22). Rouquet breaks off his commentary on Hogarth's picture to make observations on Fielding's novel, the depth and variety of references, from 'Horace, Plato, M[r]. Hogarth, the Law, the Prophets, & Mademoiselle Sophia's Chambermaid' like a 'Shopkeepers Waste book, where they keep an account of all their Shop contains': establishing a connection, no matter how fluid, between the two.[105] Begun in 1749, the painting was completed in 1750, only a few years after the turmoil of 1745–6, but far enough away to bring some critical distance to bear.

The scene, as already noted, is the turnpike at Tottenham Court, where Hogarth had mingled with the crowd on those fateful days as the Jacobite army advanced. On the right is the King's Head, depicted as a bawdy house, with prostitutes at every window, whose sign is the womanising Stuart, King Charles II. To the left is the Adam and Eve tavern, perhaps a hint at the 'paradise' that may be 'lost', with one of the local boxing booths, as owned and run by Jack Broughton, winner of the watermen's prize and now a champion prize fighter, to which the sign 'Totenham Court Nursery' refers, the breeding ground for strong, battle-fit Britons. On the hill in the distance is the village of Highgate, and to the north of this, as every Londoner would know, lies Finchley. Some confusion has occurred over the date 1746 on the painting, which Hogarth changed to 1745 in the engraving. This is either a basic mistake on Hogarth's part, or a suggestion that, like *Tom Jones*, this is not a straightforward narrative following a clear chronology as it might first appear. What we are seeing is a conflation of events with several decipherable messages, and, no doubt, many more that are yet to be teased out – the painting and its meaning could be viewed as Hogarth's ultimate conundrum – and here, like the authors and poetasters of the Kentish tomb markers, he is shaking his head or smiling at us from beyond the grave.

That said, to those trying to make sense of it in 1750, the anchor date of early December 1745 will remind them, inevitably, of their feelings and reaction at that time – whether panic and fleeing, or calm resolve and standing firm – when faced with the very real possibility, considered implausible only six months before, of a Stuart prince marching into the British and English capital, at the head of a predominantly Scottish army. The monogram 'CR' on the King's Head pub sign, as the audience would be well aware, could as easily refer to another Charles Stuart who wanted to come home.

Cleverly, Hogarth places his audience with their backs to London itself, and therefore facing north towards an advancing army and an unknown future. Immediately before them are the troops charged with the defence of the capital, and all appears to be disorder, drunkenness and licentiousness, with distractions to the left and right, not unlike Bartholomew or Southwark fairs or, indeed, Bernard Mandeville's 'undisciplined Armies' at Tyburn. Bottom right, a soldier lolls in the mud, his uniform in disarray. To the left, a soldier grapples with a milkmaid, while another steals the milk from her pail: whichever side of the issue, rebellions are an abuse of civil society and a drain on commerce and resources.

On closer inspection, however, some hope for London's citizenry emerges. The drummer to the far left, his face battered and bruised from a recent encounter with a pugilist, a true British hero, strides off toward the centre of the canvas: the tat-tat of his drum drowns out the woman weeping behind him and, assisted by a fresh-faced boy piper, will soon summon the unruly ragtag before him.[106] The necessary transition from disorder to order is seen in the rows of grenadiers marching off in the mid distance. André Rouquet offers an intriguing explanation for the disorder within the composition, no doubt springing from Hogarth himself: 'dis-cipline is not much observ'd here & if you wou'd find fault with a want of it, you wou'd be told that subordination is for Slaves, for every thing that is call'd Licentious, in other Countries, bears here the sacred name of Liberty'.[107] Therefore the examples of indi-vidual misbehaviour and general mayhem are a reflection of the freedoms and liberty of the British people, who will transform when required – having dragged themselves away from boxing, whoring and drinking – into a disciplined fighting force. Rever-end Trusler observes that the narrow path the troops and baggage are attempting to move through hardly helps in their forming up in good order, but also that licence in behaviour is 'allowed to the sons of liberty, on quitting their home'.[108] And, after all, untrained (in military terminology 'undisciplined') civilians had volunteered to take the place of professional soldiers and guard London, freeing these troops to march north to meet the foe.

However, this painting is certainly not a piece of reportage specifically depicting events in early December 1745. Hogarth has set out a broader, multilayered interpretation of the '45 that can seem at times contradictory or even conflicted. However, as in *The Gate of Calais*, Hogarth is not willing to predict the future, simply to indicate what, in his opinion, is at stake – liberty and freedom – should another Jacobite rebellion occur. Loyal Britons must remain on their guard – as warned by David Hume and the friar in *The Jacobite's Journal* headpiece. Beneath the sign of Adam and Eve, an excitable Jacobite, wearing a tartan waistcoat, now a pro-hibited fabric, is tempted by another 'serpent', a Frenchman, who hisses of an imminent invasion by his countrymen. He holds the evidence in the form of a letter. To the right of these conspirators is the central group of a grenadier and two women: a love triangle, as first depicted in *The Beggar's Opera* twenty years ago. According to Rouquet, the 'handsome young Grenadier is the principal object' and 'is accompanied, or rather seiz'd & beset by two Women, one is a Ballad Singer the other a News Carrier, they are both with Child by our Hero'. Aside from this one connection, the women's 'figure & humour, are totally different, they are even of different parties', the one 'for, the other against Government'.[109] In other words, according to Rouquet, both women have a just claim over the grenadier, but, aside from this, they are poles apart. The younger woman standing to the left gazes up at him with tearful eyes, one hand gently holding his arm, while the other is placed on her swollen belly as a reference to their future hopes. Her basket contains the anthem 'God Save our Noble King' and a print of the Duke of Cumberland. The other, apparently older, woman, whose pregnancy is obscured, grasps his arm with her left hand, while raising with the other a rolled-up newspaper with which she will beat him. Her face is contorted with zeal, her wild eyes looking towards her rival. In her knapsack is the 'Jacobite Journal', and a cross is visible on her back.

The grenadier is both a young Briton and a representation of the young nation, Great Britain. In volunteering to defend his country, this grenadier may allude to the fictional volunteer, Tom Jones. Certainly this group, the most prominent in a composition bursting with action and noise, symbolises the central premise of the painting: the dynastic struggle for the body and soul of this new nation, composed of different peoples, different parties, Loyalist and Jacobite, now come to a crisis. The Jacobite's anger and violence – she uses 'The Remembrancer', an anti-Government paper, to beat the grenadier, a 'reminder' of past loyalty – reveals that the Stuarts will use aggression and force to assert their claim. The younger woman simply indicates towards their unborn child, suggesting that a more contented, stable, frankly more pleasant future awaits him. The inclusion of *The Jacobite's Journal*, penned by Henry Fielding, confirms that the Jacobite woman is delusional. Given the national trauma caused by the inability of recent Stuart monarchs, Mary II and Queen Anne, to produce heirs, and James II's 'miraculous' warming-pan son, the Jacobite's declared pregnancy cannot, or should not be relied upon. In any case, she is probably too late – the young Briton and her rival are already moving forward together and, in front of the Union Flag, a serjeant, with glowering eyes and a raised halberd pike, is about to silence the Jacobite for good, with one well-aimed swing. This man is a character who appears elsewhere in Hogarth's images – in *A Midnight Modern Conversation* and scene two of *A Rake's*

Progress – but here he takes on the role of the avenging Butcher Cumberland.

Tom Jones was translated into French in 1750, and among the readership was the now legendary hero, or anti-hero, of the '45, Bonnie Prince Charlie. What Charles Stuart made of this novel is not recorded, but his request, to an associate in Paris, to send him various publications on English subjects, including novels by his one-time detractor Henry Fielding, might simply be the Jacobite Prince of Wales displaying an interest in English literature and history. It might also suggest that Charles was preparing himself for another attempt – as unlikely as that might seem – despite the devastation of the most recent failed rebellion and its aftermath. The request by Charles was written at the turn of 1749/1750, exactly the time when Hogarth was painting *The March to Finchley*.[110] In addition to *Tom Jones*, Fielding's *Joseph Andrews* was also listed, both mentioning another detractor of the Stuarts, one William Hogarth. Meanwhile, in Hogarth's painting, standing under the King's Head sign is a tall, fair young man, blissfully unaware of what is going on around him, but gazing northwards: Charles Edward Stuart, or his Protestant alter ego Tom Jones?

In fact, in the summer of 1750, Charles Stuart finally arrived in London. His purpose was to encourage a fresh plot, later named after Lord Elibank, as David Hume had predicted. It is said he even converted to the Church of England in anticipation. Did the narrative of Tom Jones, and the softening of a once-fierce detractor, signal to this unhappy exile that another attempt might just succeed? A young handsome hero cast out from his home and from his true inheritance, left to journey to London to wrest both back, and, after much trial, tribulation and not a little ribaldry, to be acknowledged as the rightful heir all along? Sadly for Charles, it was another false dawn.

INTERLUDE EIGHT

MONDAY 29 MAY, OAK APPLE DAY. The travellers set out for Sheerness by boat, 'The Sea run High The Wind Blowing Hard at SW & by S' and landed just after twelve o'clock.[1] According to Edward Hasted, writing later in the century, the island's name came from the Saxon for 'Isle of Sheep', or Sceapige and, in describing the island, observed that 'by far the greatest part of it consists of upland pastures and marshes, the latter are much of them rich and fertile fatting land, the former are covered with ant hills, very wet in winter, and in summer subject to burn and split open eight or nine feet in depth'. That said, 'the whole face of the country exceeding pleasant in fine weather, being interspersed with much small hill and dale, and frequent houses and cottages [...] There is hardly any coppice wood throughout the whole of it ... The air is very thick and much subject to noxious vapours, arising from the large quantity of marshes in and near it, and the badness of the water, which make it very unwholesome, insomuch, that few people of substance live in it.' The Kent antiquarian makes an exception for the gentlemen in government service at the fort, garrison and dock of Sheerness, but 'in the low or marshy parts the inhabitants are very few indeed'.[2]

Writing in the 1720s, Daniel Defoe describes Sheerness as 'not only a Fortress, but a kind of Town, with several Streets in it, and inhabitants of several sorts ; but chiefly such whose business obliges them to reside here'.[3] The Navy Office was responsible for the building and repair of the ships at the dockyards at Sheerness, Chatham, Deptford, Woolwich, Portsmouth, Harwich and Plymouth, as well as the ports where the vessels arrived, for the victualling of the navy and therefore the appointing of pursers on ship and agents at ports. The Board of Ordnance, located at the Tower of London, was responsible for the castles, garrisons and the stores 'of Warlike Provision by Sea and Land'.[4]

There had been a square blockhouse at this most northerly tip of Sheppey since the last year of the reign of Henry VIII. This was destroyed during the raid on the Medway in 1667 and rebuilt by Bernard de Gomme in redbrick with later batteries, called 'the Half Moon' and 'Cavalier'. The company toured the fort, inspecting these impressive fortifications and batteries and, from this vantage, 'had a Delightful Prospect of the Sea' and over the whole of the Island of Sheppey. To the north of Sheerness, located in the estuary where the Thames meets the German Ocean, is the sandbank known as the Nore, a significant hazard to shipping entering and leaving the Thames, yet a rendezvous point for the northern fleet.[5]

During their tour, Sam Scott could not resist sniffing the large gun touchholes that had been recently fired, decidedly odd conduct, which made the others laugh heartily. Likewise, Hogarth raised some sniggers among his companions as he unceremoniously removed his shoes and stockings while in the garrison building to clip his toenails.[6] At one o'clock they began walking south to Queenborough, the main town of the island, strolling along the beach with the sea spray flying up and while admiring the vistas. Despite John Thornhill slipping over and hurting his leg, 'Wee all perambulated Merrily and arriv'd at Queenborough about Two.'[7]

Queenborough, according to Daniel Defoe, is 'a Town memorable for nothing, but that which is rather a dishonour to our Country than otherwise : Namely, *Queenborough* ; a miserable dirty, decay'd, poor, pitiful, fishing Town [...] sends two Burgesses to Parliament, as many as the Borough of *Southwark*, or the City of *Westminster* : Tho' it may be presumed all the Inhabitants are not possess'd of Estates answerable to the Rent of one good House in either of those Places I last mentioned.' He continues, the 'chief Business of this Town, as I could understand, consists in Ale-Houses, and Oyster-Catchers'.[8] Defoe's disdain for Queenborough's status as a town which, despite its scale and lack of useful activity, sends two members of parliament to Westminster, could as easily be directed to any number of constituencies up and down the country.

Queenborough, in fact, represented one of the most appalling perversions of the English electoral system at this time, known as 'rotten' or 'pocket' boroughs, by which ancient privilege continued to distort a process which was grossly unrepresentative of the populace as a whole. Such boroughs had tiny electorates yet sent one or even two members to parliament, as seen here, and where the selection of candidates was in the gift of a landowner or other 'interest'. Much of this was the result of anachronism, for example where a populous town in the medieval period had, by the eighteenth century, become greatly reduced or abandoned completely: the most infamous was Old Sarum in Wiltshire, an abandoned hill fort, where sheep safely grazed. Likewise, Queenborough had been able to return two members of parliament since it was granted to the town by Queen Elizabeth in 1571, making the queen something of a local hero in more ways than one. But by the early eighteenth century it had effectively joined the ignoble ranks of the 'rotten boroughs', the fifty-seven such constituencies who would finally lose separate representation with the Great Reform Act of 1832.

Unsurprisingly, the chief interest in this borough constituency was the Admiralty, on whom the vast majority of the electorate and inhabitants depended. Elections were organised through the corporation, who, by long-standing tradition, had the power to create new freemen who made up the electorate. In the period 1715–54, the electorate numbered between sixty and eighty men. At a by-election in January 1729, the Whig government supporter, Richard Evans, described at this time as 'Lieutenant-Governor of Chelsea Hospital'[9] as well as a 'Captain of Dragoons and lieutenant-governor of Sheerness',[10] was elected by one vote – thirty-seven, to the Tory, Sir Jeremy Sambrooke's thirty-six – and from that time until June 1747, the corporation managed to create enough new freemen to keep Evans and his fellow government candidates in position unopposed.[11] In addition to his other roles, which, you might think, would keep him fully occupied, on several occasions Evans was also mayor of Queenborough.[12]

Ebenezer Forrest and his friends were more kind to

Queenborough than was Daniel Defoe, declaring 'The Town is but One Street' which 'is Clean and Well Pav'd ... and answers the Descripcōn I have had of a Spanish Town, Viz'. There is no Sign of any Trade' – the last, probably information from the former prisoner of war Will Tothall, meaning no shop or trade signs, 'nor were many Human Creatures to be Seen at our first arrival.'[13] Forrest is not flattering about the church, Holy Trinity, considered 'Low and Ill Built', however, among the many tombstones, they spied one epitaph worth noting. The memorial was to Henry Knight, sometime mayor of Queenborough, who had died in 1657 aged fifty-three. The burial place also contained the remains of his first wife, Martha, with whom he had three sons and six daughters. Curiously, the memorial stone was commissioned by Henry's second wife, also Martha, who 'in token of the singalar [*sic*] love which she bare him hath erected this stone'.[14] All this information was carved into the memorial, but Forrest only quotes the following from the entire epitaph:

> Henry Knight Master of a Shipp to Greenland and Harpooneer
>   24 Voyages.
> In Greenland I whales Seahorse Bears did Slay
> Thoûgh Now my Body is Intombe in Clay.[15]

In addition to the West Indies, Will Tothall had travelled to New-foundland while in the sea service, which may have given him some experience of the whaling trade: a trade which had occurred since the seventeenth century, but much reduced of late, to the benefit of Dutch whalers. Even so, the British South Sea Company, in addition to their interests in the slave trade, financed 172 whaling trips to Greenland from London's Howland Dock between 1725 and 1732.[16]

Regarding the curiously named 'seahorse' and the bears mentioned on Henry Knight's gravestone, Henry Eking's *A View of the Greenland Trade* (London, 1725) states 'The Morse or Sea-Cow, some call it the Sea-Horse, is found here too, both in the Water and upon the Ice. It is as big as a large Bullock, and has two large Teeth in the upper Jaw sometimes Half a Yard long, hanging downwards, and bending inward like a Hook.' This description suggests a walrus. 'With these Teeth he will attack Men, and lay hold of a

Boat, and may sink it or tear it to pieces, unless the Men are nimble, and kill him before he can do Mischief.'[17] Eking's description of the many 'white Bears' which 'are found upon the Ice, swimming from one Island of Ice to another' and 'feed upon Fish, and the Flesh of the dead Whales, after our Fishermen have turn'd them adrift' must be what we now call polar bears. The whalers 'kill them with Lances, or shoot them with Musket-Balls. Some of them are as large as a Cow : Their Skin is valuable, and their Fat yields Train-Oyl too, but in small Quantity.'[18] Train oil is extracted from the boiling down of sea-animal blubber, mainly the whale.[19] In spite of such a gruelling existence and spending at least half the year, during twenty-four separate voyages, away from Sheppey, Henry still managed to have two wives and nine children.

Ebenezer Forrest offers a short description of Queenborough's Town House or, as it is known locally, the Clockhouse, which stands in the middle of the high street. They then visit the Red Lion Inn, locally called The Swans, no explanation given, which fronted the Swale and whose landlady was 'Civil' but 'prating', a gossip. Conversation aside, she had only one spare bed (which Will Tothall took), so they asked a 'Merry Woman' at a private house nearby, who was able to supply the want. That settled, they strolled once more along the main street, calling in at the church, where they had a cordial exchange with the chatty gravedigger, who, while leaning on his spade, perhaps still standing in the coffin-sized hole in the ground, offered some commentary on local life and folk. He considered the parson 'a Sad Dog'.[21] The pilgrims also discovered that despite two weekly markets, there was nothing to eat by way of fresh meat or fish, except lobsters, eggs and bacon, with which 'Wee Made our Supper'.[22] (With fresh lobster for supper, perhaps no one should feel sorry for them.) *The Cook's and Confectioner's Dictionary* lists recipes for baking, broiling, frying and roasting lobsters, one version for the last method while the unfortunate creatures are still, at the commencement, alive.[23] Bacon, according to Hannah Glasse, was created by rubbing salt into a side of pork, laying it down for a week and then rubbing it with bay-salt – great quantities were panned and available very locally – salt-petre, coarse sugar and common salt. The meat was basted regularly over two weeks with the 'pickle' that formed around it and then hung in wood smoke, 'where there is but little Fire, and a constant smoke for a month'. The bacon was then suspended in a dry place to be sliced as and when needed.[24] After this tasty repast, they walked to the top of a hill, where there was a well 'of Very Good Water', which was the only remnant of a royal palace, built by King Edward III for his Queen Philippa of Hainault, mother of the Black Prince and John of Gaunt, and after whom the palace, or castle, and town were named. Once a substantial building and part of England's coastal defences, it was declared beyond repair and pulled down. What remained, as Hogarth and his company discovered, was earthworks and this well.[25]

Wells were gathering places for locals who, at the end of the working day, refreshed themselves while admiring the pleasant country around them.[26] They are also, as we know from experience, where our travellers would be inspired to horse around. Only a decade before, the Royal Navy had inspected this well at Queenborough and noted it was two hundred feet deep and, digging deeper still, discovered excellent, drinkable water which was then used to supply the fort of Sheerness. Edward Hasted wrote later in the century, 'Fresh water is very scarce and the greatest part of it brackish, tho' between Eastchurch and Minster there are a few springs, which, notwithstanding they rise near the sea, the waters of them are perfectly good and fresh.'[27]

Ebenezer Forrest describes the group simply drinking at the well, rather than messing around, by drawing up a bucket. At that moment they meet two sailors who, along with four companions, were from the *Rose* man o' war. The day before, the sailors had escorted a midshipman (a junior officer-training position) who was the son of an army general, in a yawl, a ship's boat, usually four to six oars, up a nearby creek where the vessel ran ashore. The midshipman went to Sheerness, leaving the crew with a few cockles and one penny in cash between them. At the time Hogarth and friends encountered them, he still had not returned, and the men were 'Half Starv'd'.[28] Feeling sorry for them, the travellers gave them six pence, for which the sailors were very grateful, and immediately headed to the high street to buy food. Meanwhile Hogarth and company set off to take a look at the yawl still stuck in the mud. One sailor returned with some cockles for them, which 'Seem'd an Act of so much Gratitude that wee follow'd the Fellows into the Town and gave them another Sixpence and they fetch'd their Companions and all refresh'd themselves and were Very thankfull and Merry.' This is a heartening tale of fellow feeling, kindness and generosity, with the purchase and sharing of cockles as its heart. Cockles were a local crop, but within a peregrination the cockle was one symbol of the pilgrim. As observed, they make an appearance throughout the story.

Around seven o'clock, the pilgrims walked back through the town 'and Saw and Conversed with Severall pretty Women which wee did not Expect not having seen any at our Arrival'.[29] Descriptions of women are interesting, dividing, roughly, into two categories – they are either named, like Goody Hubbard, or simply 'half blind', 'merry', 'amiable', 'prating', etc. Returning to their main lodgings (the private house), a wooden chair was placed strategically in the street, and Hogarth, sitting in this prominent position, drew the scene (y^c 6th Drawing). In so doing 'he gather'd a great Many Men Women and Children ab^t. him to see his performance'. This must be something that Hogarth was used to, and it may be that some of those gathered about him knew who he was. But in any case – and note the use of 'performance', reminiscent of that other showman, Sir Godfrey Kneller – he entertained his audience with his speed and dexterity. The pretty women Ebenezer had noted on their arrival in the town are nowhere to be seen in the sketch, which draws attention to the church and clockhouse in the mid distance, the latter with its monumental flag, a castle, in celebration of the 'Oak Apple' holiday. Instead, the main group to the right are Hogarth, Forrest and the sailors, in their baggy trousers, coats and hats, and relates to a moment later in the evening, when he and Forrest met the sailors they had helped earlier, who were now standing 'at the Mayors Door'.[30] They were eager to give Forrest, a lawyer of course, an update on their predicament, regularly interspersed with the charmingly deferential 'your Worship':

the Midshipman was lately return'd from Sheerness & had been up the Creek to See how the Boat Lay and coming Back had mett a Sailor in Company with a Woman whom the Midshipman wanted to be free with and the Sailor opposed Insisting She was his Wife, & hindred him from being Rude, which ye Midshipman resenting was gone to ye. Mayor to redress his Greivances. Wee tho^r. this a Very odd affair, But Did not Stay to See the Result of it.[31]

To avoid getting embroiled in affairs of the heart, or, perhaps more accurately, loins, the five friends returned to the Red Lion Inn, where, in the communal room they 'Drank to our Friends as usuall and Emptied Severall Cans of Good Flip and all Sung Merrily'. The brew they were glugging from their cans (probably wooden drinking pots), called 'flip', was a potent mixture of beer, spirit and sugar, heated with a hot iron, which, as here, *The British Apollo* observed gets you 'most Damnably Typsie'.[32] Thus fortified, they sang, in an increasingly energetic fashion, their usual repertoire of ditties: a midnight modern conversation, albeit slightly earlier in the proceedings than that depicted in Hogarth's engraving just a year later. As they got tipsier and more boisterous, for the first time they found themselves with some competition in the singing stakes, in the guise of some men from the port of Harwich (further north along the east coast), who were drinking in the room next door. To the pilgrims' mounting dismay, 'They Sung Severall Sea Songs so agreably that our Sr John could not Come in Competicon Nor co^d. pishoken' – both songs that had served them so well throughout the journey thus far. So, to 'Save us from Disgrace' and 'after finishing the Evening as pleasant as possible', they called it a day and 'wee went out to ye House the Back Way to our Lodging at near Eleven',[33] a discreet, orderly and honourable retreat, out the back door, rather than passing through the tavern to the jeers of the maritime victors of this particular contest.

Their accommodation was split between the private house and the Red Lion Inn. Sam Scott's bed in the attic of the former 'made him grumble, and us Laugh'. This simply provoked Scott into a temper tantrum, with him then refusing to sleep there. So Will Tothall 'out of pure Good Nature offered him his Bed' at the Red Lion. Scott agreed and duly left for the inn, while Tothall ambled up the stairs to his eyrie, but discovered, to his horror, that he was expected to sleep 'in a Flock Bed without Curtains'.[34] The lack of curtains suggests a tester bed, usually with hangings that surround it, allowing for privacy, while cutting out light and sound – so the absence of curtains would be noticeable to anyone attempting to sleep there. Tothall followed Scott to the Red Lion. This made the others 'Very Merry and Slept upon it Till Six The Next Morning.'

TUESDAY 30 MAY, SIX O'CLOCK IN THE MORNING. At that time, Hogarth called up to Forrest, telling him that their landlady, or 'Good Woman', from the private house was insisting that the Flock Bed – whether used or not – was paid for, otherwise she would seek redress from the Mayor.[35] The idea that Scott should be dragged up before the local dignitary was encouraged by his friends, in recompense for making a fuss the night before, but in fact the woman simply wanted to be paid. Coming to the Red Lion, where Scott and Tothall were sleeping, they found the doors unlocked and no one awake. After rousing Scott, he offered the following in his defence: 'When he left us and was going to Bed he perceiv'd Something Stir under the Bedcloaths which he (collecting all his Courage) was resolv'd to Feel, at which Something Cry'd out (Seemingly affrighted) and Scar'd him out of his Witts, But resuming Courage enough to Enquire into the Nature of Affairs he found it to be a Litle Boy of the House who had Mistook ye Bed.'[36] This story, 'according to Custom made us Very Merry'. They ate the breakfast that Will Tothall had purchased, after which they quitted the Red Lion and walked to the place where their spare shirts were being laundered. Finding them still wet, they decided to carry them to the next town, where they would get them dried and ironed.

They left Queenborough at ten o'clock, and 'the Morning was Delighfull the Country Very Pleasant; through which wee pass'd Very agreeably,' aspying Minster in the distance, 'A Little Village on the Highest part of the Island. Wee Labour'd Hard to Climb the Hill to ye Church yard it being Very Steep'.[37] There are echoes here of Bunyan's pilgrim, Christian, and his companion, Faithful, climbing that hill, Difficulty, and reaching the summit, with spectacular views on all sides, where, as was their habit, they wandered around the graveyard, inspecting the markers, searching for one worthy of note. And, once again, they found it, 'On a Wooden Rail over a Grave the Following Epitaph in Verse',

Here Interr'd George Anderson Doth Lye
By fallen on an Anchor did Dye.
In Sheerness yard on Good Friday
y^e. 6th. of April, I Do Say –
All you that Read my Allegy [elegy]: Be alwaies
Ready for to Dye – aged 42 years.[38]

Nothing short of a warning, literally from the grave, to live life to the full, for you never know when or by what means you will die. Or simply, to expect the unexpected. In any case, that George Anderson died by falling on an anchor at the age of forty-two, would have particular and sobering resonance for a group of men in their thirties.

Several years later, Hogarth designed a grave marker, presumably intended to be carved into stone, for the famous pugilist and showman, George Taylor (d.1758). Taylor had been part of the company who fought at James Figg's boxing booth on Oxford Road from 1719, alongside Jack Broughton, and, in 1734, he took over the business, only for it to close when Broughton, with the Duke of Cumberland's encouragement, opened a rival amphitheatre nearby. These boxing clubs not only promoted bouts between professional pugilists, but taught gentlemen in the noble art. Hogarth's close friend John Ellys was a regular at the boxing academies, and by all accounts an accomplished pugilist. One such boxing booth – an arena – can be seen in *The March to Finchley*. Eventually Taylor retired, becoming the landlord of the Fountain Inn, Deptford, but, enticed back for one last and lucrative fight, on 5 August 1758 near St Albans, he was beaten soundly, and his pride, it is said, was left severely wounded. With his broken body and spirit beyond repair, he died in the December of that year. Perhaps knowing the end was approaching, Taylor asked Hogarth to design a suitable memorial – or perhaps Hogarth, as an admirer, volunteered.

The design contains two vignettes, to be situated below the

double-arched upper edge of the headstone, probably carved in relief, of 'George Taylor Triumphing over Death' on one side and 'Death Giving George Taylor a Cross-Buttock' on the other.[39] The first, symbolically, has the energetic boxer and athlete, in his physical prime, wrestling with death, a skeleton, and winning. George raises his eyes and hand heavenward, awaiting a favourable response from the bout's divine referee, which is given, in one version of the design (Tate), with a trumpet blast from the clouds. Yet, alas, he triumphs in one battle, only for death eventually and inevitably to turn the tables and win the next, whimsically and appropriately using a classic wrestling and, at this time, pugilist throw, the 'cross-buttock' manoeuvre. The skeleton prevails and has George pinned to the floor. Despite lying with his head flung back apparently in submission, George is struggling to the last. The intended epitaph reads:

To the Memory of
George Taylor
Whose
Skill and Courage
in the
Manual – Combat
would have done Honour
to the
Roman Circus
Incorruptable and Unconquerable
Learn
Heros of a higher class
From his Example
To render
British Bravery
Invincible

Vain all the Honours of my brow,
Victorious Wreaths forewell
One Trip from Death has laid me low
By whom such numbers fall

Still bravely I'll dispute the prize
Nor yield tho out of breath
'Tis but a fall I yet shall rise,
And vanquish even Death[40]

51. *George Taylor Breaking the Ribs of Death,* pen and brown
ink, graphite and red chalk on cream paper, *c.*1758
No stone has been identified, but a local historian, Thankfull Sturdee,
wrote in 1876 that Taylor's grave marker had been rejected by St Paul's,
Deptford, and was still displayed next to the mason yard in 1840.

52. *Death Giving George Taylor a Cross Buttock,* pen and brown
ink, graphite, and red chalk on cream paper, *c.*1758
Hogarth observed that a pugilist could advise a sculptor 'in what would give
the statue of an English-boxer a much better proportion, as to character, than
is to be seen, even in the famous group of antique boxers, (or as some call them,
Roman wrestlers), so much admired to this day.' (*The Analysis of Beauty*)

In the first tableau George is naked but for a loin cloth, like a demi-god of Classical Myth or a hero of 'the Roman Circus'. In the second, wearing breeches, stockings and shoes, he is, after all, human, like the gladiators of old, the men marching into battle who do not return, or those taking a pounding in the ring until their bodies can take no more. Even so, thus memorialised by Hogarth, a fellow self-made British hero, George Taylor is immortal: a trumpet blast from on high alludes both to the Day of Judgement, when all souls are equal before God, and Eternal Fame. Watch and learn you aristocrats, you so-called 'higher' class of beings. Remember the true image of British honour and bravery and aspire to rise to it, if you can.

To continue their search for divine or earthly inspiration, the group secured the key to the church, or more correctly abbey, from the landlord at the George Inn on the main Minster road nearby and within, they discovered a treasure trove of interesting tombs associated with local dignitaries and legends.[41] Minster Abbey, its full title 'The Abbey Church of the Blessed Virgin and St Sexburgha', was founded in the seventh century by the Saxon queen of that name. The abbey was spared from destruction during the dissolution of the monasteries, when ownership was transferred to Sir Thomas Cheyne.

The two tombs that captured the imagination of our pilgrims were those of 'a Spanish Embassador' and 'Lord Shorland', with Sam Scott sketching the first and Hogarth the second (Drawing yᵉ 7th and 8th). The identity of the occupant of the first tomb, called here 'The Spanish Ambassador', is in fact contested to this day, and Ebenezer Forrest does not venture to add any of the details. According to local legend, the Spanish Ambassador was one General Geronimo, mentioned in the church register, who was captured by Sir Edward Hoby in 1588 during the Armada crisis. The general was held hostage at Queenborough Castle, where he died. The issue regarding Scott's drawing of 1732 is that this, in fact, is a much earlier tomb dating to the late fifteenth rather than the sixteenth century, and furthermore, what is now thought to be the Spanish Ambassador's tomb was not unearthed until over one hundred years after *The Peregrination* took place (in 1833). It is therefore likely that a local legend, over the centuries and in the telling, has been applied erroneously to an anonymous tomb. Such is the nature of history versus legend, the latter often more powerful and enduring, even in the face of inconvenient facts.

The second tomb proved of particular interest, as it was associated with another yet more fantastical local legend. The story of Lord Shorland was so intriguing, so 'remarkable', that Ebenezer Forrest dedicated by far the longest description for any of the oddities noted on the entire journey to this single subject.[42]

The tale, according to Forrest, occurs, like that of the 'Spanish Ambassador', during the Armada crisis, with Queen Elizabeth in the vicinity of Sheerness 'on Board one of the Shipps at the Nore ... to take a Veiw of her Fleet'.[43] According to Ebenezer Forrest's retelling, which he must have noted down from a local, Lord Shorland was visiting a friend on the island and, passing Minster Abbey, came across a strange scene. The parson had refused to bury a body because there was no money to pay for it and was being remonstrated by a group of distressed mourners. Lord Shorland, 'being Extremely Mov'd', judged that the people should throw the parson into the open grave and then bury him, which they duly did and, unsurprisingly, 'he Died'. On reflection, his lordship felt the burden of his hasty decision, fearing he would be judged harshly himself – whether in this life or the next – and so, knowing the queen was nearby, he wrote a petition defending his actions and then, with great urgency, he mounted his horse, rode down the hill on which the church sits and, rather than waiting for a boat, continued, astride his steed, into the sea. Man and horse swam to the Nore ('above Three Miles off') and, arriving at the queen's ship, he begged an audience with Her Majesty, who 'reced, Read, and Granted it, and he without Quitting his Horse Swam back again to the Island.'[44] But this extraordinary feat (mainly, it should be said, carried out by the horse) was not the end of it. Arriving on the shore, Lord Shorland was met by an 'Old Woman', like a seer from some ancient Greek myth, or even (given the nature of her prophesy) like a dissembling witch from *Macbeth*, who told him that 'tho[h]. the Horse had then Saved his Life, he would be the cause of his Death'.[45] As a result, and in order to thwart 'the accomplishment of the Old Woman's Prophecy', Lord Shorland 'Alighted from his Horse Drew his Sword and kill'd him'. The horse's carcass was left exactly where it dropped, no honourable burial for this most faithful servant, until the tides forced the rotting body further inland. It is as if nature itself was correcting the unfairness of this brutal act – an act against a loyal companion, who had done all that was asked of him – in assisting the realisation of the prophecy, despite Lord Shorland's attempts to overturn his fate.

The story continued many years later. Lord Shorland found himself, once again, on the northern seashore near Minster. He spied the skull and bones of the horse, related the tale to his companions and, in a further act of casual contempt, kicked the skull. This action 'Hurt one of his Toes which Mortified and kill'd him.'[46] Much like George Anderson and his encounter with the anchor, an apparently minor incident has enormous ramifications. Be careful, both stories seem to say, actions, no matter how small, have effects, years or even decades on.

Lord Shorland was buried in the church at Minster, the very place where the incident, the burying alive of the priest, had occurred, therefore bringing the whole sorry episode full circle. Forrest concludes his extensive narrative by observing that 'a Monument is Erected Over his Grave, On which he is Figur'd, with a Horses Head (Supposed to be in the Waves) plac'd by him'.

The veracity of this legend is a given, among the locals, so much so 'That a Horses head Finely Gilt is plac'd as a Weathcock ... on the Church Steeple & the Figure of a Horse is Stuck upon the Spindle above that Weather cock, and the Church is Comōnly call'd the Horse Church.' There is a symmetry, whether coincidence or not, in the three references to horses connected to this church and the three cocks linked to the farm in Upper Stoke. Although the introduction of an oracle-type woman adds a supernatural quality to the legend – even the horse's six-mile round swim is extraordinary – the likelihood of dying from a self-inflicted wound or silly accident would, surely, have been far from unusual in the sixteenth century, even in the following seventeenth or eighteenth centuries, when basic modern medicines were unavailable. The story has a kernel of reality, and the presence of the horse's head within the tomb decoration, lying aside Lord Shorland with what look like waves around it, may further support the truth of the story.

However, it is not unusual in funerary monuments to have animals symbolically represented, or acting as foot cushions or used as ornament – which might suggest that the story came after Shorland's death, stimulated by the nature of his tomb effigy. In any case, 'Wee were so Well Satisfied of the Peoples Beleif that all they told us was true, That wee did not Dare to Declare our Disbeleif of one Tittle of the Story.' 'Tittle' is either a small stroke or minute part, a detail, but 'to tittle the tattle' is to spread gossip or falsehood.[47]

Hogarth's sketch depicts the knight lying on his side, legs crossed, his right foot touching a horse's head located behind and against the wall. Shorland holds a shield on his left arm and a sword is lying nearby. The knight's head rests on a pillow, but his expression, as rendered by Hogarth, is comical, as if he is turning his gaze towards the horse with an eternally petulant expression, in irritation that the Old Woman's prediction came true, in spite of all his best efforts. Above the knight's head, emerging from the decorative arch, is another face with a look contorted as if in empathy with Lord Shorland.[48]

In fact, Sir Robert de Shurland was the Lord Warden of the Cinque Ports during the reign of Edward I, that is, three hundred years before Queen Elizabeth. His horse was called Grey Dolphin, no doubt due to his colour rather than any prowess at swimming. The legend is still told, but now based firmly in the medieval rather than Tudor period. So, as we can see from Lord Shurland's story, the ways in which history is laid down are far from linear: from the moment of the event, stories branch and divide, are written by the victors or come to represent the version the teller prefers. In the process, inconvenient truths are ignored and embellishments accrue until myth has overtaken reality. Hogarth's own story, as we have seen – whether told by Hogarth himself, John Nichols or Horace Walpole – was not immune from this. And his last years would be marked by further contradictory accounts of the same event and, more fundamental still, by competing ideas as to how

Hogarth's life and work would be remembered, and for what he should be celebrated.

After pondering the fate of Lord Shurland and his horse, whether they believed any of it or not, the company dined at the George nearby until four o'clock, and then left Minster for Sheerness on foot, their pilgrimage coming to a close.

CHAPTER EIGHT

ORIGINAL GENIUS

It was usual in Hogarth's time, if affordable, to have a country house, in order to get away from the noise and bustle of the city. Many artists favoured areas to the west of London and invariably along-side – or at least near to – the river Thames. Sir Godfrey Kneller resided at Whitton in Middlesex, and one hundred years later, J. M. W. Turner would follow Sir Joshua Reynolds to the Richmond-Twickenham area, both inspired by Alexander Pope, whose villa and grotto nestled in a charming spot near the river. David Garrick purchased a villa at Hampton in 1754 and the Hogarths are said to have summered at Isleworth early in their marriage. But later they alighted on Chiswick, a world that we would not associate immediately with Hogarth – too countryfied, too placid – but it suited Billy, Jenny and their small family, Lady Judith Thornhill, sister Ann, cousin Mary Lewis and assorted staff, very well indeed. The lure of fields, large skies and the Thames at its gentlest and most rural was too enticing. At this time Chiswick village, with the buildings that dotted the countryside nearby, centred around St Nicholas's church, which sits close to the Thames. Church Street, passing St Nicholas's, turned into Burlington Lane, which were the two main thoroughfares. The Red Lion tavern, supplied by Thomas Mawson's brewery, was on the river, which was lined with fisherman's cottages. A 'Mr Webb' provided the Hogarths with regular fresh fish.[1]

Travelling to and from Chiswick would have required more regular use of a coach, and from a chalk drawing by Richard Livesay, said to be after an image by Hogarth, the latter's coachman was one David Jones, of whom little else is known.[2] Having spent most of his life walking around London, Hogarth seems, from an anecdote provided by 'one of his intimate friends' to John Nichols (intended to show his general absentmindedness) to have easily forgotten that he owned such a vehicle at all: 'he had occasion to pay a visit to the lord-mayor (I believe it was Mr. *Beckford*)', William Beckford, owner of *A Harlot's Progress* and *A Rake's Progress*: 'When he went, the weather was fine; but business detained him till a violent shower of rain came on. He was let out of the Mansion-house by a different door from that at which he entered; and, seeing the rain, began immediately to call for a hackney-coach. Not one was to be met with on any of the neighbouring stands ; and our artist sallied forth to brave the storm, and actually reached Leicester-fields without bestowing a thought on his own carriage, till Mrs. Hogarth (surprized to see him so wet and splashed) asked where he had left it.'[3]

From Leicester Fields, a coach would have travelled along Piccadilly, through Hyde Park Corner and Knight's Bridge, by which point the traveller had left London, then through the villages of Kensington, the location of the royal palace, through Hammersmith, eventually arriving at Chiswick, which was about seven miles due west of Leicester Fields. As fate would have it, Hogarth was now the close neighbour of Lord Burlington, whose Palladian-style villa, decorated by William Kent, adjoined his lordship's mansion.

William and Jane bought the house from the son of the first occupant, the Reverend George Andreas Ruperti, and this purchase, while maintaining the house in Leicester Fields, signifies Hogarth's status and wealth as he passed his fiftieth birthday. Originally built between 1713 and 1717, Hogarth extended the house around 1750 and established a painting room over the coach house at the end of the garden. The house sat aside Chiswick Common Field and, even with a small gathering of neighbours about them, was very much an idyll, yet still close to London. According to John Nichols, the Hogarths spent most of the summer season in Chiswick, and while there, Hogarth took on the largely honorary position of inspector of wet nurses for the area, on behalf of the Foundling Hospital.[4]

The house, according to Mrs Chapel who had worked there, was called 'the Cheese House' 'from its shape being said to be

very like that of a quarter of cheese'.[5] John Timbs recalled the
sign 'Hogarth's House' was inscribed on the piers of the gate, and
David Garrick provided two urn ornaments, which sat atop the
posts.[6] The interior, as would be expected of a house from the
early eighteenth century, was lined with wainscot, and a visitor in
1820 recalled seeing on the panelling in a ground floor room 'faint
traces of pen or pencil sketches'.[7] Much-loved pets were buried in
the grounds. A mulberry tree, according to Timbs, was struck by
lightning while Hogarth was in residence, and 'the iron braces or
girdles, by which it is held together, were made by his direction'.[8]
There were also other fruit trees and a nut tree walk, all within a
walled garden.

The Hogarths took possession of their house in September
1749, a year after the misadventure in Calais, and while William was
painting *The March to Finchley*. It is possible that they were encouraged to go there because of their friend, the surgeon John Ranby,
although Dr Thomas Morell, resident at Turnham Green, later
declared, 'I knew little of Hogarth before he came to Chiswick, not
long after his marriage',[9] which suggests that they were regular visitors for several decades before settling there. In 1748 John Ranby
had taken a large house on Burlington Lane, and around this time
Hogarth painted his friend's natural children, Hannah born in
1740 and George in 1743, both by his unnamed mistress.[10] And
in addition to Morell and Ranby, other close friends were neighbours. Around 1752/3, Henry Fielding, also a friend of Ranby's, in
the hope of improving his waning health was living at Fordhook, a
farm near Ealing less than three miles away.[11] James Ralph resided
at College House, Chiswick Mall, and Joshua Kirby, tutor in perspective to the royal children at Kew, also lived nearby.

Hogarth etched a view of his house, across the fields, which
John Nichols states was produced in 1750, and which was published by Jane after her husband's death.[12] The Cheese House is
the dark building centre left, with the garden wall, the pedestrian
and coach entrances visible.[13] Dominated by fields of ripened
corn, some of which has been harvested and placed into sheaves, a
pilgrim figure with staff rests in the left foreground with his dog.
The largest house, to the right of the Hogarths' home, was owned

53. *View across the cornfields to Hogarth's House,*
etching, published by Jane Hogarth in 1781

by the Earl of Northampton, with another residence alongside (to the left) probably the Ranby home, and little else but trees and open skies.[14]

Dated to this period is the beautiful group study of the Hogarth household servants (Col. Fig. 23). With the painting room located in the pleasant rural surroundings of Chiswick, it is an attractive thought, although it cannot be stated as fact, that this canvas was painted over a summer period, when the Hogarths were living predominantly at their retreat. It is likely that Hogarth began work on it at a time when his painting commissions had reduced – whether through happenstance or design will become clear – and this was an opportunity to capture a group of individuals who were part of his broader family, but under normal circumstances he simply would not have had the time to paint.

None of the sitters can be named with any accuracy, although the central figure is in a black coat with a white collar, dress associated with nonconformists such as Quakers, while the other man and the boy are pictured in what is likely to have been Hogarth's

livery, a brown frock or country coat with tan collar, green waistcoat, brass buttons and white neck stock. Samuel Ireland writes that
Jane and William had an old retainer called Ben Ives, and that Jane
had a servant called Samuel. It can be expected that the household
would have included a cook, had someone who would have helped
Jane and Lady Thornhill dress and style their hair, one of the men
to serve as a doorman and butler, a lad to run errands and perform
odd jobs, as well as a second maid who might serve at table, but
who would more probably assist the cook and do general cleaning
and laundry. The second man in the painting seems too old to be a
footman, and was perhaps a gardener and caretaker for Chiswick.
The portraits are sympathetic, even expressing great fondness, but
the boy is particularly compelling, with his slightly nervous, even
tearful expression, and again confirms what a wonderful painter of
children, or at least young people and their moods, Hogarth was.

Anecdotes concerning the Hogarths at Chiswick were provided by Mrs Chapel, at the time of her recollections aged in her
eighties.[15] The following story regarding one pet dog named as
Trump would make this animal at least sixteen years old at the
time, so the famous pug in his dotage. It is a charming description,
whichever of Hogarth's dogs it features, and indicates the companionship, reliance and mutual protection provided by man and pug:

> This faithful animal was remarkable for his intelligence.
> Hogarth was accustomed to smoke a pipe at different public
> houses in the neighbourhood, when he spent his evenings at
> Chiswick. A love of social conversation with his neighbours
> prompted this perhaps, but the necessity for studying nature
> was the pretext. He was in the habit of returning home about
> nine o'clock, and at that hour Trump, unbidden, would take
> upon himself to seek his master. From house to house the dog
> would take his way, till he found the object of his search. He
> was as well known in that vicinity as his master himself could
> be. Hogarth desired that no one should hurt him, wherever
> he intruded in quest of him ; and when Trump made his
> appearance, 'Your servant is come for you, sir,' was the cry.
> 'Yes, he knows my time,' was commonly Hogarth's reply, and

54. *Gulielmus Hogarth*, etching and engraving, 1749
There are references to 'Crab' in the 1750s, but Trump was
the celebrity pug. Using the Latin for William, this was
issued as a frontispiece to bound print volumes.

the animal with a sort of expostulating whine, would intimate
that it was time to go home, and they departed together.[16]

By this period Hogarth and his dog had become an established partnership. When the engraving of the 1745 self-portrait with pug was published in 1749, the same year as the move to Chiswick, the pamphlet *Scandalizade* declared, "'Tis *Hogarth* himself and his honest friend *Towser*,/ Inseparate companions ! [...] how boldly they strike,/ And I can't forbear thinking they're somewhat alike. – Oh fie ! to a dog would you *Hogarth* compare? – Not so – I say only they're alike as it were', concluding, 'they deserve a description below/ In capital letters, *Behold we are Two*.'[17]

One unusual portrait by Hogarth is of a black spaniel called Vulcan, sitting in a lush landscape, thought to be the companion of Thomas Wood of *The Daily Advertiser*, a man who, it is said, attended the same clubs as Hogarth.[18] This dog, like Trump, had a herding instinct when it came to his master, and would appear towards the end of an evening, at whichever tavern Thomas happened to be, holding a lantern in his mouth to guide Mr Wood through the late-night streets of London to his lodgings. This extraordinary intelligence appealed greatly to Hogarth, who has painted Vulcan, the most unlikely name for this fluffy animal, and possibly a nickname springing from his habit of carrying a flame (Vulcan the ancient Roman God of Fire) with a gently determined expression, eyes raised, vigilant. According to Mrs Chapel, Trump, Hogarth's 'great canine favourite', died of old age, but was not buried with the other pets in the garden at Chiswick. Rather, he was 'carefully stuffed, and long remained to the eye almost as perfect as when he lived. The ornament of the chimney piece in the hall of his master's residence.'[19] He remained, according to Mrs Chapel, at the centre of the household at Chiswick, a stoic and static sentinel, as seen in the portrait of man and dog hanging at Leicester Fields.

Another anecdote from Chiswick recalls Hogarth encountering a labourer who had one hand, the other replaced with a hook, probably a veteran of recent wars, who refused to beg while he could work: "'Such resolution does you credit," said Hogarth, and, slipping half-a-crown into his hand, he told him while he had a house that he might always claim a glass of beer when he wanted it. Like kindness was extended to many a poor deserving labourer, who was encouraged to call at "the Cheese House" for occasional aid or refreshment.'[20]

When Hogarth had completed *The March to Finchley* in 1750, he immediately arranged for it to be engraved by Luke Sullivan. The traced drawings (now at the British Museum) of the main faces in the painting, the grenadier, ballad seller and Jacobite, for example, were created to assist the young engraver in his endeavour, or so that Hogarth could 'fill in' these faces wherever he happened to be. Hogarth announced the imminent arrival of the print with a subscription ticket depicting a military trophy, and at the same time declared that the painting itself would be sold by auction, which rather resembled a raffle, via the subscriptions. Hogarth gave a number of the tickets to the Foundling Hospital, among which was the winning one.

In the meantime, King George, who, it is said, enjoyed looking at Hogarth's humorous prints, had asked to see, or was encouraged to see, the painting – with a view to dedicating the engraving to His Majesty – and the canvas was duly transported to Kensington Palace. The king's reported irritable response to Hogarth's painting is often quoted to prove him a complete philistine in matters to do with '*bainting* and *boetry*', as he, with his German accent, was held to pronounce it, which, as he continued, 'Neither the one nor the other ever did any good!'[21] In the event, as reported by William Pyne, '"There," said the king, "I have seen enough, take it away. This is not a march, this is all confusion and hurly-burly ; the painter has painted my guards all as drunk as roker-pokers," (his usual term for swine). His majesty, perhaps, was the only person who could not feel the wit and humour of that incomparable piece.'[22] In Pyne's opinion, 'His majesty's frigid indifference, and nonsensical observations on seeing the picture in question, naturally excited the resentment of the painter, who was sufficiently sensitive on the score of his reputation.'[23] Pyne continues that, soon after, Hogarth was at Slaughter's with some artist friends and associates and told them the king's reaction. 'Highmore,' he recalls, 'who had a slow, dry manner of expressing himself, observed, "I suppose his kingship would have preferred his rank and file marching along, two and two, pair and pair, as the Italian galanté showmen trundle the birds and beasts through the magic lanthern into Noah's ark." "No doubt, that exhibition would be more to his princely taste," said Hogarth ; "and so I shall dedicate my print of the drunken guards to the King of Prussia."'[24]

This anecdote, apocryphal or not, is interesting on several fronts; not least, that it recalls how admired *The March to Finchley* was among Hogarth's fellow artists, but also how the humour of the piece was expected to override any concerns as to the manner in which the King's Guards, his personal body guard, had been represented. Let us, just for a moment, consider the situation from George's point of view. He was certainly no royal connoisseur on the level of a Charles I – and much good it did that unfortunate monarch – but his interests lay elsewhere. He was extremely keen on all things military, and his favourite son was commander at the dramatic moment of crisis that *The March to Finchley* is, broadly, representing. He had also suffered extreme personal trauma during the 1745 rebellion, and it is easy to dismiss the impact on him as a human being, rather than as the occupant of the throne. His guards had displayed great loyalty to him and his dynasty at a time when the king must have wondered who he could or could not trust. His reaction to Hogarth's ribaldry, his misunderstanding of it, perhaps exacerbated by not sharing the humour, due to an upbringing in Hanover, is understandable. Rather than chastise the king for not having the wherewithal to laugh it off, we might wonder at Hogarth's naivety or arrogance in sending it to the king, without even considering what the response might be. This is not to say that Hogarth should have adapted his art in order to achieve royal favour, but, duty bound to send the painting once requested, he might have put himself in the king's shoes and braced himself for a less than favourable response.

As Hogarth warned, the engraving was 'most humbly Dedicated' '*To His MAIESTY the KING of PRUSIA, an Encourager of ARTS and SCIENCES!*' Far from being an irritable immediate response to the king's lack of enthusiasm, this inscription remained intact, the only correction (according to John Nichols) deemed necessary by the artist, still smarting from the rebuke and rebuff, concerned the missing second 's' in Prussia, whereby Hogarth added the accent '~' by hand on all the first edition prints.[25]

Also between 1748 and 1752, Hogarth was working on the history painting, *Paul before Felix* for Lincoln's Inn (where it still hangs), alongside the engravings *Gin Lane*, *Beer Street* and *The Four Stages of Cruelty*. The first two prints supported Henry Fielding, now a magistrate with his brother John, in his campaign against the so-called 'gin craze', and the four-image series was connected to the Murder Act of 1751, which sought, as suggested by Bernard Mandeville twenty-five years before, to add 'some further terror and peculiar mark of infamy' to the execution of murderers by hanging in chains and public dissection. For 'in no case whatsoever shall the body of any murderer be suffered to be buried'. In response to *Gin Lane* and *Beer Street*, someone describing themselves as 'an Englishman' was compelled to write to Hogarth, declaring 'When the advantage of Genius is made subservient to Publick Good it does Honour to the Professor, as it is expressive of Gratitude to his Creator by exerting itself to further the Happiness of his Creatures. The Poi[g]nancy and Delicacy of your Ridicule has perhaps been productious of more Reformation, than more elaborate Pieces would have effected.'[26]

On 28 May 1751 Hogarth announced that the paintings of *Marriage A-la-Mode* were to be sold by sealed bids, the result declared a week later. *The Daily Advertiser* offers the tantalising detail that the bids would be kept in a locked cabinet, but the current highest bid (without the bidder's name) would be viewable through the glass front, which fits the description of the 'linen' press in the front parlour at 'The Golden Head'. The advertisement also states that no dealer will be admitted. The paintings were purchased by John Lane of Hillingdon, Middlesex, for the bargain price of 120 guineas. The sale was not, for Hogarth, the success he had intended. John Lane told John Nichols how he had come to be the purchaser, offering the observation that the manner of the sale 'probably disobliged the public ; and there seemed to be at that time a combination against poor *Hogarth*, who perhaps, from the extraordinary and frequent approbation of his works, might have imbibed some degree of vanity, which the town in general, friends and foes, seemed resolved to mortify'. Another of Nichols's correspondents observed that Hogarth had asked his friends not to attend on the final day, as the room was small and likely to be crowded. The day itself arrived and he 'strutted away one hour, and fretted away two more, no bidder appearing'.[27] Mr Lane, continuing his account, arrived at the house on Leicester Fields expecting, like Hogarth, a lively crowd, but found instead only the artist and one other. Just before the clock struck midday, when the highest bid at that time was declared, to an empty room, to be £120, Mr Lane offered 120 guineas and then, seeing how downcast Hogarth was, declared that he would wait until three in the afternoon, to allow a higher bid to arrive, which the artist gratefully accepted.[28] But then, not wanting to continue the agony, Hogarth acknowledged Mr Lane as the successful bidder and wished him well with his purchase.[29]

In the autumn of 1752 André Rouquet, Hogarth's friend and neighbour, left London for Paris, but continued to be in contact with his old friend and was keen to hear news of the city he had lived in for thirty years. He would return, briefly, to look back over those years and produce an important book, *The Present State of the Arts in England* (published in 1755) where, like Voltaire before him (as already seen), he would try and make sense of the bewildering character of the English, as well as the environment for art in that country. In fact, Hogarth, too, had much to distract him in the years up to 1753. Not least the unveiling of his first foray into art theory, delivering on the promise of a sequence of tantalisingly obscure signals in his 1745 self-portrait. *The Analysis of Beauty* was yet another significant change of direction by Mr Hogarth.

As elegantly summarised by David Bindman, *The Analysis of Beauty* 'is a deliberate challenge to the idealism of academic theory, opposing nature against art as the true standard of beauty, present experience against antiquity, and variety against symmetry'.[30] Hogarth's method was to define and then analyse 'the principles of nature', under the headings fitness [appropriateness], variety, uniformity, simplicity, intricacy and quantity, 'by which we are directed to call forms of some bodies beautiful, others ugly; some graceful, and others the reverse'. At the heart was personal experience – observation, study, imitation – with one focus, nature and the natural world, whether the human form, the elements and landscape; and another focus the man-made, embracing everything from costume to architecture. 'Shakespear, who had the deepest penetration into nature,' Hogarth observed, 'has sum'd up all the charms of beauty in two words, INFINITE VARIETY ; where, speaking of Cleopatra's power over Anthony, he says, "– Nor custom stale/ Her infinite variety : – Act 2. Scene 3."'[31]

Beauty can stimulate feelings that range from the gentle to the intense, from the simply pleasing to the arresting. Hogarth also encouraged his readership to seek out the beautiful within the world before and around them, rather than rely on the mediation of self-appointed experts who, invariably, are not professional artists. It is a highly democratic proposition, stripped of jargon, of imposed judgement and overblown theorising, and therefore guaranteed to receive a very bumpy ride from certain quarters. Given this, particularly regarding Hogarth's overt sensitivities around his education, background and the mixed response to his forays into 'high' art, we might wonder what motivated him to expose himself, perhaps unnecessarily, to the brickbats of otherwise friendly critics, let alone the inevitable cannonades from his enemies.

He seems to have begun considering this move into art theory in a period when his power and influence were high, despite the disappointment of the auction of *Marriage A-la-Mode*. And we should recall the public backing of Henry Fielding, particularly in the preface to *Joseph Andrews*, as a further encouragement to put pen, as well as pencil, to paper. As ever, there is a mix of self-congratulation and self-promotion, with an even greater desire to do some genuine good, in particular, to release the young artist, the main intended reader (if not exclusively so), from the shackles of a rigid system of training. Hogarth had created a situation where he had a degree of independence, not complete, but certainly having a greater control over his art and therefore income than most other artists. He considered the truth of his opinions on art practice and appreciation as self-evident, so, from a position of strength and some authority, this was undoubtedly the moment to try to present his ideas and, by extension, sway others to his way of thinking. He was also inherently against the establishment of a formal 'royal' art academy, encouraging, he believed, the creation of more artists than the nation could sustain and where, as he perceived it, tired elite ideas around art would be inculcated into the young impressionable minds of the next generation of practitioners: and, arguably, when the Royal Academy was finally established in 1768, with Joshua Reynolds the presiding genius, that is exactly what happened – just ask Mr William Blake, who, on the title page of his copy of *The Works of Sir Joshua Reynolds*, scrawled 'This Man was Hired to Depress Art'.[32] (For balance, it should be noted that another of England's great artists also called William, that is Turner, thrived at the Royal Academy, as both student and academician.) Again, even as Hogarth was attempting to spread his ideas, those who wanted a continental-style academy would use his arguments against him, to undermine his attitude to that purpose. Of course, Hogarth could have been wrong. He was, by the 1750s, most certainly swimming against a very strong tide of opinion in the artistic community.

To establish that what he was saying was obvious, at least to those who had the wit and imagination to think differently (or for themselves), the subscription ticket for *The Analysis of Beauty* tells a story, in the form of a picture, associated with the explorer Christopher Columbus and his discovery of the 'New World'. His detractors declared this feat was not down to his personal ingenuity, because it could be done by anyone. Leaving aside the question of, if that is the case, why they had not done so, Columbus offers a conundrum by way of explanation: he asks them to stand an egg on its end. Despite repeated attempts, they fail to do so, but Columbus, able to focus on the issue and think practically, flattens the end of the egg by pressing it down quickly on to the table and, behold, it stood unaided. The answer may be obvious, once it has been pointed out, but, nonetheless, the person demonstrating the solution should be given due credit, if not, indeed, enthusiastic praise. The figure of Columbus is turning towards the two petulant men to his right, with an expression of hope that they might be convinced. The three to his left are all indicating degrees of delight and frustration at the solution: one is growling and pressing his

Rec'd of five Shillings being the first Payment for a short Tract in Quarto call'd the Analysis of Beauty; wherein Forms are consider'd in a new light, to which will be added two explanatory Prints serious and Comical Engrav'd on large Copper Plates fit to frame for Furniture.

55. *Columbus Breaking the Egg*, etching, 1752

clenched fist to his face – a version of a face palm – while another smiles with eyebrows raised in an 'Ah yes!' John Nichols declares, '*Hogarth* published this print as a sarcasm on those who had been inclined to laugh at his boasted line of beauty, as a discovery which every one might have made',[33] yet the figure of Columbus, surely Hogarth himself in this scenario, is imploring the doubters for a fair response, rather than demanding or sneering at them.

Hogarth recalls in the preface of *The Analysis of Beauty* that his inclusion of the waving or serpentine line of beauty – his personal hieroglyph named in his painted self-portrait – which achieved greater prominence through the engraving of 1749, was a ploy to

ease the various interested publics into the idea that Hogarth, of
all people, was, apparently, about to enter the lists of art theory.
'The bait soon took,' he declares, 'and no Egyptian hierogliphic
ever amused more than it did for a time, painters and sculptors
came to me to know the meaning of it, being as much puzzled with
it as other people, till it came to have some explanation.'[34] Hogarth
admits, in such matters, 'the torrent generally ran against me ; and
that several of my opponents had turn'd my arguments into ridicule, yet were daily availing themselves of their use, and venting
them even to my face as their own'.[35] He also anticipated that in
attempting to define something as slippery as 'Beauty' he may have
been on a hiding to nothing, but, he declared, so be it, and 'if the
reader shall think fit to rectify any mistakes, it will give me a sensible pleasure, and be doing great honour to the work'.[36] Certainly
on hearing that Mr Hogarth was about to publish his 'masterly
thoughts on the great Principles of your profession', the clergyman
and man of letters William Warburton eagerly subscribed for two
copies, and in his covering letter (dated 28 March 1752) to Hogarth
declares, 'You ow[e] this to your Country; for you are both an
Honour to your Profession, and a shame to that worthless crew
professing vertu & connoisseurship ; to whom, all that grovel is the
splendid poverty of wealth & taste are the miserable bubbles.' He
signs off 'with a true sense of your superior talents'.[37]

The substance of *The Analysis of Beauty* and its practical application was very much Hogarth's territory. The hieroglyph, for
example, was part of Hogarth's own system of memorising what
he had seen while out and about in the world: the three lines for
a pikeman and his dog entering the alehouse. His inclination to
pass on his straightforward method of observing and recording nature itself, whether in the countryside, in the street or in
a tavern, rather than copying 'nature' second-hand through the
art or theoretical writings of others, or, more broadly, adhering
to definitions of beauty derived from highly selective, restricted,
theoretical (rather than empirical) concepts, was evident from the
promise he gave Mary Pendarves as early as 1731. Hogarth's book
provides a method whereby artists could achieve beauty in their
art, but also guidance to anyone interested, like Mr Warburton,

in how we humans perceive and define beauty – in art, in each other and so on. Hogarth's basic tenet, to use the evidence of your own eyes and see beauty using your own judgement, with his treatise offering a sequence of pointers rather than a rigid template, did not just apply to the creators and buyers of art, even if (to a jobbing artist) they were paramount, but to everyone. To this end he was also keen to avoid imitating those inaccessible examples littered with untranslated Latin and Greek, oblique references to the type of literature that only those few with a gentleman's education would grasp.

But writing this down, in a manner that was intelligible and persuasive to as broad a readership as possible, while also responding to previous learned tracts touching on the subject – Aristotle, Giovanni Paolo Lomazzo, Charles-Alphonse du Fresnoy and Roger de Piles are mentioned within the text – was not his natural medium. In later life, he argued that he abandoned thoughts of following his father into a career as an author because of his parent's rough treatment at the hands of publishers, but it is also as clear that he was simply much better at drawing, which as he himself declared, was a natural talent, and then painting. He therefore approached a series of author friends, including Dr Thomas Morell and James Ralph, both neighbours in Chiswick and the latter at Leicester Fields too, to help him. Morell could easily have come to town, but we can imagine Hogarth's collaborators discussing various thoughts and drafts over a bowl in the rural ease of the Thameside village.

It is worth raising here, in the context of literature and literary men, that Hogarth was accused, notably by John Nichols, of deep ignorance and even a form of inverted snobbery: his 'anti-connoisseurship' extending to a disdain for all scholarship. The notion that Hogarth, 'a Scholar's son could be so ignorant', Jane Hogarth, addressing Nichols directly, declared 'false' and 'absurd'. Likewise that he 'despised <u>Books</u>, or Men, of Literati. <u>Most</u> of <u>his friends</u> <u>being</u> men of the first Genius as well as <u>Rank</u>, as is well known.'[38]

The Columbus subscription ticket announces that the first payment for 'a short tract ... wherein Forms are consider'd in a new light to which will be added two explanatory Prints serious and Comical' would be five shillings. As suggested, the two large accompanying prints were 'fit to frame for Furniture', that is framed up and put on the wall, although, in practice, as often they were bound into the volumes like maps. Either way, notations within the text connected to individual elements within the two prints, the latter visualising the descriptions and examples in the text and, in so doing, better explained Hogarth's meaning in practice. The title page included a quote from Milton's *Paradise Lost*: 'So vary'd be, and of his torturous train/ Curl'd many a wanton wreath, in sight of Eve, To Lure her eye. – Milton'. The key words are varied, curled, wanton, lure.

Plate 1 is a sculpture yard, perhaps suggested by James Ralph's comments in *The Weekly Register*, twenty years before, rather than depicting a specific place – the yard of John Cheere, Hogarth's companion to France in 1748, at Hyde Park Corner for example – although the yard is a space that allows the sculptures to be viewed on their own terms, rather than 'displayed' in an elevated fashion, such as within an art collector's gallery. The context also hints at the copyist's trade, the ubiquity of these particular sculptures, from houses and gardens, great and small, to drawing schools and academies. For here all exemplars of antiquity have been gathered – the Apollo (12), Antinous (6) and Torso Belvedere (54), the Medici Venus (13), the Farnese Hercules (3) and Laocoön (9) – alongside a modern tomb with weeping cherub, rubbing its tear-stained face with the robe of a judge in full-bottomed wig. Of them all, the Antinous (lover of the emperor Hadrian) and the central Venus offer the greatest visible reflections on Hogarth's serpentine line in action. A dancing master (7), whom John Nichols names as one '*Essex*',[39] thinks himself elegantly straight backed, feet at right angles in ballet first position, yet, in reality he appears clumsy aside Antinous, with his 'easy sway'. Around the edge are further diagrams, including our old friend Hudibras, with his beard 'composed of such plain lines as children make' or, as described by Samuel Butler himself, 'In cut and dye so like a tile, A sudden view it would beguile.'[40] This comical, rectangular 'roof tile' of a facial feature sits in contrast to a bust with entwined curls making up the beard, 'a varied play of serpentine lines, twisting together in a flame-like manner' appropriate for an Old Testament prophet or apostle.

56. *The Analysis of Beauty Plate 1*, etching and engraving, 1753
The copies after antique exemplars are, left to right, Farnese
Hercules, Antinous, Laocoön (centre back), Medici Venus
(centre), Torso Belvedere (centre front), Apollo Belvedere.

57. *The Analysis of Beauty Plate 2*, etching and engraving, 1753
The graceful couple (left) contrast with the ungainliness of the rest. The
dancers' hieroglyphs and floor movements (as diagrams) can be seen top left.

Further on, the squawking 'Old Baby' (17) makes an appearance, as an example of where improper or incompatible excesses meet, such as had always raised a belly laugh at Bartholomew Fair. Next to this is (18) 'a child with a man's wig and cap on' also seen at Bartholomew Fair, which has a similar ludicrous effect, as are, 'a Roman general, dress'd by a modern tailor and peruke-maker' intended 'for tragedy' but rather 'a comic figure' and 'Dancing-masters, representing deities, in their grand ballets on the stage, are no less ridiculous.'[41] The reference to the fey 'Jupiter', in first posi-tion, clutching his lightning bolts, who is the ballet dancer from *Taste in High Life*, and who, Nichols states, 'likewise meant for the celebrated *Desnoyer*, dancing in a grand ballet',[42] reiterates the comedic as well as stiffness of such figures, as opposed to appropri-ateness or grace.

Plate 2 is also familiar, with the main section, again surrounded by little vignettes, diagrams and examples, depicting 'The Country Dance' from *The Happy Marriage*. In engraved form, the commu-nity spirit of the original painting, the thump, squeak and gentle tap of shoed feet on wooden boards, the scrape and nasal hum of fiddle and bassoon, is still more than evident, but now corralled to a fresh purpose, with further details again illustrating Hoga-rth's text.[43] In the niches within the wall behind the dancers are figures of monarchs, most recognisably Henry VIII, Bluff King Hal, whose silhouette, as seen over the gate of St Bartholomew's Hospital and in the original by Hans Holbein, is a hieroglyph – 'a perfect X with his legs and arms',[44] as Hogarth has it – that many would recognise now. Next to him is the state portrait of Charles I by Van Dyck, as suggested in the figure of Christ at Bethesda's Pool and, further along, Queen Bess in full ruff and farthingale. On either side, an image after Charles-Antoine Coypel, of Sancho Panza astonished at Don Quixote destroying the puppet show – a figure Hogarth clearly liked because he used it several times in dif-ferent contexts, including *Masonry Delineated* – is contrasted with 'the effect of the serpentine lines in the fine turn of the Samaritan woman, fig.74. L. p.2, taken from one of the best pictures Annibal Carrache ever painted' – Scratchy Carracci himself.[45]

Within the border, the six or so dancing couples have been

reduced to a sequence of hieroglyphs too: 'The curve and two straight lines at right angles, gave the hint for the fat man's sprawling posture', 'The prim lady, his partner, in the riding-habit, by pecking back her elbows, as they call it, from the waste upwards, made a tolerable D, with a straight line under it, to signify the scanty stiffness of her pet[t]icoat ...'[46] and beneath, the pattern the most courtly of the couples is making on the floor, winds and curls.[47]

The Analysis of Beauty has been quoted extensively throughout this book, offering a hint as to its range, richness and variety. One further example is particularly telling, with regard to Hogarth's commitment to the utility of experience and constant observation, but also an indication of where our artist is personally, as a man in his mid fifties: a sequence of images of an individual, gradually adapting to the passing of time and the effects of ageing, as eternal a preoccupation of human kind as life itself.[48] Rembrandt, among others, made himself a particular study of the ageing process. Hogarth observes that from the age of twenty to thirty little changes, the bloom may 'go off a little', but the features have attained and retain a 'settled firmness'.[49] The gradual changes between thirty and fifty are described in Plate 2 figs 117 and 118, but 'what havock time continues to make after the age of fifty, is too remarkable to need describing : the strokes and cuts he then lays on are plain enough ; however, in spite of all his malice, those lineaments that have once been elegant, retain their flowing turns in venerable age, leaving to the last a comely piece of ruins.' Something to which most fifty-somethings across the ages must, with sadness, reconcile themselves.

In terms of positive responses to Hogarth's foray into art theory, John Nichols quotes Henrietta Knight, Baroness Luxborough, an example of an interested 'layman', declaring, 'It surprized me agreeably ; for I had conceived the performance to be a set of prints only, whereas I found a book which I did not imagine *Hogarth* capable of writing ; for in his pencil I always confided, but never imagined his pen would have afforded me so much pleasure. As to his not fixing *the precise degree of obliquity*, which constitutes beauty, I forgive him, because I think the task too hard to be performed literally : but yet he conveys an idea between his pencil and his pen, which makes one conceive his meaning pretty well.'[50] *The Analysis of Beauty* is wonderfully eclectic. Hogarth might be horrified at the comparison, but there is something of Don Saltero's museum about it – intellectuals may sniff, while those who enjoyed the breadth, inventiveness, imagination and humour as a means to enlightenment would be intrigued and delighted by it.

One such was Philip Yonge, vice chancellor of Cambridge University, who wrote to Hogarth confirming that he would find a place for the book in the library, that 'I have read it over with pleasure, & have no doubt but that many others will do the same, as there can be no one here to whom Mr Hogarth's name will not be an inducement to enquire into every thing that comes from his hand.'[51] Another was Benjamin Wilson, the scientist as well as former student at St Martin's Lane Academy, whom Hogarth had encouraged. Benjamin had been putting his friend and mentor's ideas into action: 'When you come to town I shall be very glad to shew you further advantages which I have gathered from your excellent Analysis. I assure you I think myself greatly indebted to you and know of no method to repay you than acknowledge it as I improve that the world may have one instance of your invariable principles being true.'[52]

John Nichols declares that the Hogarth family heaved a collective sigh of relief when the publication was finally ready.[53] Little did they know what was to come next. The attacks were not concerted as such, coming from a variety of sources, but the most overt and potentially damaging, for sales and reputation, came from a young artist, Paul Sandby. Sandby, with his brother Thomas, both draftsmen, had accompanied the Duke of Cumberland throughout the pacification of the Highlands after Culloden, during which Scotland would be mapped fully by the Board of Ordnance – no more would there be 'hiding places' for rebellion. At the same time Sandby was in the streets and towns of Scotland sketching the people and everyday scenes he encountered.[54] He would later produce some extremely striking etched portraits of London's street-criers: his 'Mackerel Seller' (1760), although closer in spirit to Ned Ward than Hogarth's *The Shrimp Girl*, is decidedly

Hogarthian in subject matter, and hints that Sandby's attack on the older artist – and it was a blisteringly vicious one, the weapon graphic satire, eight prints in total – sprang in part from his desire, at this time, to muscle in on what was seen as Hogarth's territory.[55]

Sandby, back in London by 1751, was between December 1753 and April 1754 hard at work on his anti-Hogarth prints. A natural development, while ranging around your victim's territory, would be to satirise the satirist, as John Aubrey had observed. Like Hogarth before him, there is an element of making your name by attacking a well-known figure, as well as challenging his deeply held beliefs. At the very least, Sandby aimed to illustrate that 'low' subjects, amusing and interesting as they might be, did not require the type of elevated learning and sophistication that a formal art academy could provide.

The sheer scale and severity of Paul Sandby's assault – the eight prints constitute a systematic programme of abuse – suggests that he felt there was a market for such things. The titles alone tell the sorry tale, ironically, as a progress: 'The Burlesquer burlesqued'; 'Puggs Graces Etched from his Original Daubing'; 'The Analyst Besh[itte]n in his own Taste'; 'The Author run Mad'; 'The Magic Lantern'; 'The Vile Ephesian' – here Hogarth is the Classical villain, Herostratus burning the Temple of Artemis at Ephesus, Hogarth's own symbol of Mother Nature; and, finally, the street hawker, 'A Mountebank Painter'. Hogarth was not completely friendless. Thomas Burgess responded with an engraving entitled 'A Collection of CONNOISEURS', where a gaggle of simpletons laugh over Sandby's caricatures with the text from Proverbs 1:22: 'How long ye Simple ones, will ye love Simplicity? And the Scorners delight in their Scorning, and Fools hate knowledge.'[56]

There is, admittedly, a difficulty in reducing beauty and grace, no matter how symbolic the intention, to a single waving line, elegant and pleasing as it might be, which can become strained in the application. This was an obvious place for the critics to start their demolition, before moving on to Hogarth's use of everyday accessible examples. Hogarth's very particular approach, which unusually if not uniquely includes humour, the stated 'serious and comical', allowed the earnest business of educating to be at the same time entertaining, even amusing: the dual role, as stated, of his modern moral subjects. Of course he does this, his critics like Sandby will declare, because he cannot raise his own eyes above street level, so little wonder he attempts to make a virtue of it.

Less overt, but still part of the opposition to Hogarth, was Joshua Reynolds. In 1748 Reynolds, former pupil of Thomas Hudson, returned from an extended period of study and travel around Italy and, like Ramsay a decade before, offered a new challenge to Hogarth's particular training – or lack of – and focus. Reynolds established himself as a portrait painter and, very soon after, as the leader of this new generation, which believed in Italy as central to an artist's training and the establishment of a formal art academy, on the continental lines, as the mechanism for teaching and exhibiting.[57] Unsurprisingly, Paul Sandby will be a founding member of the new Royal Academy, with Reynolds, as stated, the first president. Reynolds's early published arguments set out the correctness of 'the invariable, the great, and general ideas, which are fixed and inherent in universal nature' against, inferring this is Hogarth's fixation, 'a servile attention to minute exactness'.[58] Other than a desire to establish a continental-style academy, Sandby's two main accusations against Hogarth, as expressed in his eight satires – Hogarth's pretensions in publishing art theory and his inadequacies in grand history painting – could as easily be directed at Reynolds in the years ahead. There are many examples, particularly in history painting, where Reynolds singularly failed to rise to his own exacting standards as set out in his *Discourses on Art*. Which only goes to highlight the yawning gulf between writing about art and actually doing it – Hogarth's point against connoisseurs and art theorists in a nutshell.

Hogarth later observed, philosophically, 'it is a trite observation that as life is checquer'd ever[y] success or advantage in this world is attended with a reverse of one kind or other. So this work however well receiv'd both at home and abroad by the generality yet I sufferd more <uneasiness> from the abuse it occasions me than satisfaction from its success altho it was nothing less than I expected as may be seen by my preface to that work.'[59]

Perhaps Hogarth's detractors would have been less keen to

denigrate him so publicly if Henry Fielding had been available to defend his friend, as he had done before, vigorously and eloquently. Sadly, Fielding's health had been declining for several years, his workload as a magistrate, the various campaigns – gin was just one – having had severe consequences. Just after leaving England in the hope of recovering his health, he died in Lisbon on 8 October 1754. Hogarth's most likely literary champion was first indisposed and then gone forever: he would feel his loss now and for the remainder of his life.

It is fitting that just as he was contemplating life without his friend and defender, the highly political Henry Fielding, Hogarth should have been embarking on another modern moral series – as it turns out, his last. It may be that his focus on the political health of the nation was inspired, in part, by the tragic news of Fielding's death, aged just forty-seven. But in the first instance, Hogarth's new series, four canvases, and later prints (collaborating with three engravers), on *The Humours of an Election*, was undoubtedly in response to the Oxfordshire election of 1754, where the Whigs, with the help of the Duke of Marlborough, decided to challenge this Tory stronghold of some decades duration, with eye-watering amounts of money expended on both sides. Marlborough, no parliamentary reformer, had his own 'pocket' or 'rotten' borough, Woodstock, adjoining his palace of Blenheim. In brief, the Tories won both Oxfordshire seats by a narrow majority, so narrow in fact that when the legality of some of the votes was called into question, the decision was reverted to the House of Commons, where, unsurprisingly, the Whig majority voted in favour of their interest. But as ever, Hogarth's work is about electioneering, indeed British life in general, rather than charting a specific incident. In so doing, Hogarth brilliantly, once again, balances the particular with the generic, a point the painter Allan Ramsay makes in his *Essay on Ridicule* published in 1753. Describing Hogarth as 'incomparable', he declares that the strength of his fellow-artist's ridicule – its usefulness combined with comedic impact – lay in the targeting of general vices, rather than those of a particular individual, or for the purposes of a specific party or private grudge.[60] He notes that if Hogarth ever moved towards the latter (asking his subject's forgiveness for the suggestion), then those aware of the particular circumstance 'would withdraw from the author that esteem, which the rest of his conduct had so justly acquired'.

In this instance, Hogarth had moved from French contemporary art towards Dutch and Flemish genre scenes, a style of painting that connoisseurs, even if they collected them, considered very low down the artistic hierarchy and accused Hogarth of particularly emulating – having no greater ambition, intellect or talent, to soar any higher. So the conscious use of this specific style was, initially, a riposte. A certain 'Dutchness' suits the theme, with William III, who signed the Bill of Rights, recalled in the basic political symbolism, the orange cockade of the Whigs (the blue being Tory), and even making a cameo appearance in the first scene as a battered portrait, having received various undignified salutes from the Tory opposition. Like the scenes in his previous modern moral subjects, the four canvases are teeming with detail. But this series surpassed them all for scale, complexity and skill.[61] *Marriage A-la-Mode* may be better known, but here, ten years on, Hogarth really displayed his virtuosity as a painter as well as storyteller.

The range of detail is, to an extent, unravelled by a contemporary pamphlet, 'A Poetical description of Mr. *Hogarth*'s Election Prints', declaring itself 'Written under Mr. *Hogarth*'s sanction and inspection', although this is contested. Nonetheless it is a contemporary response and therefore of value in unpicking some of the dazzling wealth of detail the artist has presented. The pamphlet's introductory quote, 'Things unattempted yet in prose or rhime', again from John Milton, which establishes that Hogarth has, once again, achieved something totally original, could easily have been selected by the artist himself.[62]

The first is 'An Election Entertainment' (Col. Fig. 24), where the Whig candidates are socialising, in an unusually intimate manner with the urban electorate and their wives of Guzzledown, who are a veritable hotchpotch of smallholders, vicars and gentry. Bricks are being thrown through the window and one has found its target, in the guise of the secretary noting down the potential votes. He is collapsing backwards, arms outstretched, towards an assembly of vegetables, a large jug, pewter plates and a bright red lobster, as elegant a rendering in little of a Netherlandish 'still life' as you are ever likely to see. No one notices, above the scraping of fiddles, the rowdy drunkenness, the roar from the large crowds outside: Tories protesting against the Jewish Naturalisation Act of 1753, the effigy, according to John Nichols, is the Whig government minister responsible for the legislation, the Duke of Newcastle, as well as the 'loss' of eleven days, when England switched from the Julian to the Gregorian calendar and years commenced on 1 January, as had been the case in Scotland, rather than in March.[63] There is also an armed gang on the threshold of the room. Among the many characters brilliantly drawn, the three main groups located around the front of the large dining tables help to draw the otherwise bewildered eye through the melee: left to right, the young handsome candidate 'Sir Commodity Taxem Bart', his name declaring trade and taxation as two lynchpins of the Whig interest, is allowing himself to be kissed by the coachman's wife in the hope of her husband's vote. The electorate are keen to take advantage of this temporary secession of correct social behaviour, but there is no guarantee that support is forthcoming, suggested by the coachman carelessly setting fire to milord's wig. The two men at the centre we have met before; one is pouring alcohol, possibly gin, over the other's head wound, the latter grimacing while raising a firing glass to his bloodied lips (containing a shot, again likely to be gin). The eye then moves to the right, catching the flying secretary, where we might pause to imagine, in the moment after this, the next stage of that particular story line, the loud crash and squelch as the 'still life' unnaturally reanimates, every which way. Finally we arrive at the right-hand side, where Guzzledown's mayor is about to pass out, if not from overindulgence, then from the physician bleeding him.[64]

The second image shows canvassing in the countryside; money is changing hands, while two disfigured veterans of recent wars, sitting outside the 'Porto Bello' ale-house, as noted referring to Admiral Vernon's capture of the Spanish port in 1739, puff on pipes and animatedly share stories. The opposing parties are represented by the two public houses: The Crown, where the Whigs are assembled, in the distance, and the Royal Oak, the Tory tavern, in the

58. William Hogarth and François Antoine Aveline, *The Humours of an Election Plate 4: Chairing the Members*, etching and engraving, 1758
The parade, led by a blind fiddler and mimicked by the startled pigs, comes to a juddering halt courtesy of a butcher and a bear. All appear in Hogarth's earlier engraving (of another 'somebody') *Hudibras' First Adventure*.

foreground. Note the sign is of the Boscobel Oak, with the head of Charles II peering out. In the third, 'The Polling', every available elector is being herded to the vote, including a man in his winding sheet. Another veteran, severely maimed in action on behalf of king and country, is having his oath queried by an officious lawyer, who tries to argue that, as he has no hand, he cannot swear on the Bible. We can imagine this being a homage to the former serviceman that Hogarth had met in Chiswick, who had the pride and public spirit to refuse to beg while he could still work. No wonder, with all this corruption around her, Britannia's coach has collapsed. Finally, the winning Tory candidates are carried aloft in a street parade, a Roman Triumph of sorts, with the Whigs, gathering in the house next door, surprisingly (or unsurprisingly, given their majority in the House of Commons) unconcerned. However, a fight has broken out, and one victorious MP, plump and useless, is toppling from his elevated perch, mouth gaping, wig askew, to the rough music of a blind fiddler and the honk of a goose – the reality for this member is closer to a skimmington spouse than *vir triumphalis*.

If the subscription ledger (opened 28 March 1754) is anything to go by, with almost five hundred individual entries, the *Election* series was a success. Payments were either for the first print (the 'Entertainment') at five shillings down payment and a further five shillings and six pence when finished, or 'One Guinea paid down and one Guinea more'[65] for all four engravings. Top of the list is 'His Royal Highness the Prince of Wales', the future George III, his father Frederick having died unexpectedly in 1751, followed by George's mother, Augusta 'Her Royal Highness the Princess Dowager of Wales'. The Earl and Countess of Cardigan both subscribed to the complete set, as did the Duke and Duchess of Portland, Lord Cathcart, Somerset Draper, James Ralph, John Ranby, David Garrick and John Hoadly.[66] John Wilkes, the Archbishop of Canterbury Thomas Herring, 'Mr Pegge of Derby', the Earl and Countess of Shaftesbury and 'Miss Pattison' were among those opting for the single print in the first instance.[67] Various events will conspire to delay their publication, in fact, unusually, the four were issued individually between 1755 to 1758. But if anyone was under the illusion that Hogarth was a spent force, or that his sense of ambition was waning, his next project, crossing over with the *Election* series (one reason for delay) would swiftly disabuse them of it.

Twenty years on from his New Testament charity paintings at St Bartholomew's Hospital, Hogarth was commissioned to paint an altarpiece for St Mary Redcliffe in Bristol, for a £525 fee.[68] So in May 1755, only two years after *The Analysis of Beauty*, here was an opportunity to return to monumental history painting, which, undoubtedly, would be viewed as a demonstration of his own method and theories, now very much in the public domain. In his autobiographical notes Hogarth declares he did the commission 'as well as I could' and 'recollected some of these Ideas that I had pickt up when I vainly Imagind history painting might be brought into fasheon'.[69] The context of the Bristol commission, in contrast to St Bartholomew's, was a purely religious one.

The altarpiece would be the final element of the refurbishment of the church which had been ongoing since 1709. And in approaching Hogarth, the church authorities were signalling this artist's pre-eminence in such matters, as well as the principle, established by St Paul's Cathedral, that the commission ought to go to an Englishman and a Protestant. Although, given this, it is surprising that when an altarpiece was required for the chapel at the Foundling Hospital, the artist was one Andrea Casali (b.1705), a Roman trained under Fransesco Trevisani, a favoured painter of the Jacobite court, who arrived in England in 1741.[70] Of course Hogarth was extremely busy in the late 1740s and early 1750s, not least with his major publication, which effectively removed him from the painting fray for several years, aside from some very fine portraits, including his six servants, plus the *Election* series. Hogarth probably attended the concert, under the direction of George Handel, at the Foundling Hospital to raise money to complete the chapel, but there were no complaints from him regarding the altarpiece here being given to an Italian.

St Mary Redcliffe's vicar, the Reverend Thomas Boughton, was a learned and demonstrably ambitious man, well aware of Hogarth's reputation and abilities, including those paintings at St Bartholomew's and, indeed, his modern moral subjects. Here, at least, was a commissioner, and an Anglican clergyman at that, who believed in Hogarth's variety, but also that aspect of Hogarth's work that was essentially moral, educational, even spiritual, as well as entertaining in purpose – his own style of 'parabolic' teaching – no matter how lurid the image or subject.

The topic, the most dramatic and, in Christianity, crucial aspect of Jesus's story, his execution, burial, resurrection and ascension, gave Hogarth a totally new challenge, and one he approached in a very thoughtful and characteristically energetic manner. The scale alone is astounding: the left and right 'wings' of the triptych (three panels) measure over seventeen feet by fifteen feet; the middle panel a mighty twenty-eight feet seven inches by twenty-one feet eight inches. The finished work, with the side panels pulled in, so as to be slightly ajar, will aim to draw in and then enfold the church's faithful.

The first or left panel shows the sealing of the tomb with heavy stones as well as wax after Jesus's crucified body has been laid to rest within. The effort required to move these boulders, preventing anyone from stealing the body in fulfilment of the resurrection prophecy, is shown in the tensing figures to the right – one, even as he strains against the weight, an elegant, beautifully wrought academy figure.[71] The priest is also elegant as well as arrogant, his right hand on his hip, his left resting on the tomb in a downward pointing gesture. His robes are magnificent – as Hogarth observes in *The Analysis of Beauty* after discussing the grandeur of British robes of state and the 'awful dignity' of the figure of a judge in full sartorial pomp, 'The grandeur of the Eastern dress,' encompassing the Eastern Mediterranean, 'which so far surpasses the European, depends as much on quantity as on costliness. In a word, it is quantity which adds greatness to grace.' Although he adds the proviso, 'But then excess is to be avoided, or quantity will become clumsy, heavy, or ridiculous.'[72] The gesture confirms that the priest believes the subject of Jesus, tried and executed under the occupying Roman jurisdiction, is now buried here, along with the man. Moving to the right panel, the story continues with the tomb open, Jesus's body missing and his three mourners, by tradition all Marys including the Magdalene, asking where he is. The angel sits on the stone he has just cast aside – described in the gospel as 'His countenance like lightning'; Hogarth has indicated this with a dainty filigree of gold emanating from his head, 'his raiment was white as snow', again seen here in folding bright-white robes, loose dark-blond hair curling to the shoulders. He rests an elegant right arm on the tomb, while lifting the left and pointing heavenward saying, 'He is not here: for he is risen, as he said.'[73] In the distance, with the thunderous clouds lifting, the once forlorn crosses, the only suggestion of the crucifixion itself, are now bathed in a delicate ethereal pale pink and blue light.

The woman, probably Mary Magdalene, running across the centre canvas (Col. Fig. 25), while indicating back to the right panel, cleverly links this scene and the central panel, including the different time periods depicted. The centrepiece separates horizontally into three parts: the foreground has the gathered apostles witnessing Jesus's ascension. This occurs forty days after the events in the right panel, during which Jesus has appeared to several of his followers in a variety of contexts, including to Thomas, who doubted the resurrection until he touched Christ's fatal wounds. This apostle can be seen in shadow to the right. To the left is Peter, who denied Christ three times after his arrest prior to trial and execution, but is now Jesus's 'rock' on which he will build his church. The saint indicates with his left hand towards a rock in acknowledgement, while gazing in wonder, and some terror, at the ascended Christ.

Jesus correctly occupies his own space, a distinct sphere, literally and metaphorically, at the apex of the scene, with the power and glory of God emanating from his halo and setting the heavens ablaze. His robes are billowing dramatically around him and, overall, he is depicted in an other-worldly, softer manner to the remainder. Christ turns his head to gaze towards Peter, the chosen one. His arms imitate but in a more animated way the gesture of the angel by the tomb, as he appears in this moment to stride forward even as he is lifted up and will soon be enveloped in light. There are various possible models appropriate for this figure, including examples (available to Hogarth in engraving) of a resurrected or ascending Christ by, among others, Rubens and Raphael. In Sir James Thornhill's collection sale of 1734–5 were 'The Ascension' attributed to Sebastiano Ricci and the same subject by Thornhill himself.[74] There are two pen and ink drawings which were owned by Jonathan Richardson senior, then by Joshua Reynolds, of Christ posed in a similar manner to Hogarth's figure, by Polidoro da Caravaggio (*c.*1499–1563, no relation to Michelangelo Merisi, better known as 'Caravaggio').[75] The only hint of Christ's earthly presence and suffering – the crucifixion itself or descent from the cross would be too Catholic an image for a Protestant church – is a single wound, in his forward-placed foot, from one of the nails that attached him to the cross. The heavy black clouds that separate Christ from the earth hint at the Last Judgement, the terrible day when all men, kings and subjects would be weighed in the balance, so the image is a reminder of what is to come as well as what has passed. He is a figure of justice, redemption, hope and triumph.

*

Allan Ramsay had originally published some observations on *The Analysis of Beauty* in 1755, in the manner of a dialogue between various characters, including 'Lord Modish' and 'Colonel Freeman', where the latter observes that 'Hogarth owns that his line of beauty and grace is not to be seen in a toad', which should have encouraged him to wonder whether such a line, a universal cypher for beauty, exists, for 'a blooming she toad is the most beautiful sight in the creation, to all the crawling young gentlemen of her acquaintance; and that her crawl, or as they may possibly call it, her *pas grave*, is far before the minuet step, with all its wavings.' He concludes, 'An analysis or dissection can never be begun of any subject till the subject itself is ascertained, and consequently no analysis can be made of abstract beauty, nor of any abstraction whatsoever.'[76] Far from irritated, Hogarth appears to have appreciated the whimsical style of Ramsay's critique. It probably helped that the dialogue includes great praise for *The March to Finchley* as a representation 'of general manners and characters', coupled with his celebration of the 'incomparable' Hogarth in his *Essay on Ridicule* only a few years before. Hogarth offered a free copy of the dialogue on taste with every purchase of *The Analysis of Beauty* in an advertisement in the *London Evening Post*, dated 24–6 February 1757. He notes the author is 'a Friend to Mr. Hogarth, and eminent Portrait Painter', possibly a side swipe at Joshua Reynolds, whom, Hogarth might have considered, was neither. In 1757 Reynolds donated his full-length portrait of Lord Dartmouth to the Foundling Hospital, so a challenge of sorts to Hogarth's *Captain Coram*. In fact, in the same advertisement Hogarth announces, due to the ongoing frustrations of his *Election* engravings, that he has decided to concentrate on portrait painting. So perhaps, with Allan Ramsay now away in Italy, Hogarth had decided to do battle with Reynolds on his, Joshua's, own turf. John Hoadly wrote in April 1757, 'Hogarth has got again into Portraits; and has his hands full of business', although the evidence suggests otherwise. Nonetheless, 'He has almost finished a most noble one of our sprightly friend David Garrick and his Wife.' The portrait of Davy and Eva-Maria (Royal Collection) is affectionate and, indeed, 'sprightly'.[77]

In August 1758 Hogarth might have heard of the eviction of

his friend, André Rouquet, from his lodgings in the Louvre, where he had lived, as an academician, since July 1754.[78] Rouquet had lost his beloved wife, Jeanne, soon after he had arrived in France and had suffered from an apoplexy, recovered, but was then struck down again, this time with paralysing numbness. Unable to work, he convalesced in the countryside at Chaillot accompanied by an English governess, a friend of some twenty years' duration, who unexpectedly died. This appears to have caused a severe break-down. Addicted to drugs, even selling off his furniture to pay for them, Rouquet was found wandering the streets half-dressed, and had even set fire to his apartment at the Louvre on several occasions. For fear he might further harm himself and the com-munity of fellow academicians who resided at the Louvre, he was eventually taken to the asylum at Charenton, where he died in the December.

That same year, 1758, according to Hogarth's autobiographi-cal notes, 'An amiable nobleman', namely Lord Charlemont, 'prest before I entirely quitted the pencil to paint him a pickture le[a]ving the subject to me and any price I askd.' The paint-ing was of a virtuous married lady 'that had lost all at cards to a young officer', and who now wavers before allowing her pursuer to take his prize. The painting, dated 1758–60, called *Piquet* or *The Lady's Last Stake* (Albright Knox Art Gallery, Buffalo NY) is an attractive work; the main figure wears a stunning gold silk dress dramatically set against a deep-blue interior, the red of the hand-some young officer's military coat adding further vibrancy and all rendered elegantly enough, but perhaps, like the Garrick portrait, retracing past glories rather than attempting something fresh. That said, Lord Charlemont was delighted with his purchase, at a price Hogarth described as 'noble', and his effusive letter of thanks was a very welcome balm to Hogarth's increasingly wounded ego.[79] Even so, Hogarth, having sensed that he had performed well to an old tune and thus, with much-needed cash in the bag, now needed to astound the world once more. Another wealthy patron, Sir Richard Grosvenor, had asked for a painting on the same terms as Lord Charlemont, which Hogarth would work on in tandem. This would have added to the concern that he was now only fit for producing charming images of compromised young pretty women, the very essence of a victim of his own success. Indeed Hogarth's own comment that this new commission was 'much against my inclination' confirms his reticence to accept it, if the result was the same-old-same-old.

Yet, given the circumstances, Hogarth still decided to accept this offer. In a rush of enthusiasm, he embarked on a canvas depicting another young woman in distress, only this figure was from the annals of myth and fable, Giovanni Boccaccio's Sigismunda, as interpreted through the poet John Dryden.[80] Hogarth declared that his purpose was ever 'to fetch Tear[s] from the Spectator', and to that end 'my figure was the actor that was to do it'. So this was, once more, a 'cross-over' painting, not, this time, a portrait of an actor in the role, but the figure of legend, as a modern tragedian might interpret them. The particular scene, 'Sigismunda grieve over her lovers heart,' he declared 'I will aver as their [*sic*] are many living ladies especially that shed involuntary tears' so 'I was ... convinced that Peoples heart[s] were as easily touchd as I have seen them at a Tragedy.'[81]

The focus and laudable aim was to depict a woman's extreme grief at the loss of her love, on the orders of her father, Tancred. The latter chooses to not only kill Sigismunda's secret husband – Tancred's attendant Guiscardo, significantly beneath him in status and whom she had married against the wishes of her father – but to cut out his heart and present it to the grieving widow in a gold chalice, a mockingly kingly style: the father guilty of cruelty and tyranny stirred by pride.[82] Sigismunda weeps and laments over the heart, at one point kissing and holding it, although Dryden, in his poetical realisation, does not describe her inevitably bloodied lips or hand. This is an instance where the page, more able to veil such gory realities, succeeds over the canvas. Hogarth shows the princess bedecked in shimmering silks and pearls, with her father present as a miniature set in her bracelet; tears are visible in her slightly reddened eyes, which look out towards her audience. Guiscardo had presumed to take what was not his, and paid the ultimate price. Sigismunda, losing her beloved husband and then choosing to kill herself, also paid for her 'crime' of disobedience, but Tancred, in losing his daughter, gets his just deserts, and only redeems himself by repenting the actions that his pride has caused by burying the couple together in 'Royal State'.

It could be said that Hogarth's painting (Col. Fig. 26) would have had a better reception, for the disappointment and barely contained bitterness in his recollections are more than evident, if the idea and subject had simply come to him in isolation, rather than from some external influence or event. However, as expected with Hogarth, there was a competitive element, if not core, to most of what he set out to do. This time the competition was a painting by a long-dead Italian which had been auctioned at Sir Luke Schaub's collection sale in April 1758. Hogarth was dismissive of the attribution to Antonio Correggio, one of his favoured 'Old Master' artists (it has since been reassigned to Francesco Furini). So this lazy attribution – given by dealers or 'a set of cheats in ... the traffick of Pictures', 'the flatterers of Rich men ... who I am proud of ever haveing been at war with' and accepted by art buyers, or 'the great who love to be cheited [*sic*]' or indeed, worse still, who know no better – was enough to irritate Hogarth into action. Add to this that the so-called Correggio achieved the extraordinary price of £404 5 shillings at the sale, then Hogarth, still reeling from the unpleasantness surrounding Paul Sandby's prints and *The Analysis of Beauty*, felt the irresistible urge to respond publicly and blatantly. Hogarth would also have heard that Sir Richard Grosvenor had himself spent £1,000 at this auction. You do begin to feel that Hogarth would have had a far happier, albeit less interesting and even successful life, if he had restrained his desire to enter the boxing ring at every opportunity. And he was no longer the young bruiser, able to mentally pick himself up after each blow. Now in his early sixties, he was a little frayed around the edges and less able to move on from disappointments, as the tone of his autobiographical notes makes abundantly clear. Hogarth was, undeniably by this juncture, a successful 'grand old man' of British art, but his reference to retiring – before he 'entirely quitted the pencil' – suggests even he sensed that things were moving on, with or without him. Well, if so, he did nothing to assist an elegant exit: like George Taylor, he entered the ring for one further battle, in the hope of winning, finally, his very personal war.

Hogarth had written to William Huggins about the two pictures for Charlemont and Grosvenor on 4 November 1758, saying he had 'hardly been able to muster up spirits enough to go on' with them 'because they require so much exertion, if I would succeed in any tolerable degree in them'. This suggests he was weary of it all. But he had nothing but praise for the two commissioners: 'one should not conceal ... the name of such as behave so nobly'.[83] According to the former servant, Mrs Chapel, who must have received the information from either Mary Lewis or Jane Hogarth herself, Hogarth's depiction of the grieving Sigismunda was informed by a moment he secretly witnessed in his own home. Here are the circumstances:

> The mother of Mrs Hogarth, of whom she was exceedingly fond, was no more. The remains had been placed in a coffin preparatory to interment, when Mrs Hogarth withdrew unseen, as she supposed, to weep over the loved form of a parent whom, after a few hours, even in death she could never behold again. She was thus breathing her sorrows over the departed, when Hogarth found himself in the next apartment, and saw, through a small hole in the intervening wainscot, how his afflicted partner was engaged. Her distress, to him, appeared most interesting ; and, from what he then saw, he made his drawing of 'Sigismunda.' This was the real origin of the picture.[84]

This has all the signs of an apocryphal story, although Lady Thornhill had indeed died in November 1757, aged eighty-four, and Hogarth's memory for striking expressions or events, plus his ability to record them quickly on paper for future use, is well known. The immediate reasons for choosing this subject were confirmed by Hogarth himself: the inflated price at auction of a painting on this subject, coupled with a desire to do something different and extraordinary. Yet that still leaves the manner in which he depicted Sigismunda, and recalling his wife's anguish over the death of her beloved parent, as good an inspiration for an artist as any.

This period also, finally, saw a position at court as the king's sergeant painter (on 6 July 1757), just before the death after an illness of the previous incumbent and Hogarth's brother-in-law John Thornhill in the September. To compound a period of great personal loss for Jane and William, another close friend and collaborator, John Ellys, also died in the September of that year.[85] On his royal appointment Hogarth immediately painted his last self-portrait, seated at his easel (Col. Fig. 27), which was engraved with the new court title beneath. Those who thought this gross hypocrisy had clearly not followed closely Hogarth's career and attempts to gain royal commissions. They also did not realise that this position, of all positions, had personal meaning. It had been held by his mentor and father-in-law, then his friend and brother. Obviously the print of *The March to Finchley*, with its provocative dedication to the King of Prussia, who, unlike the British monarch, is a 'supporter of the arts and sciences' was conveniently glossed over, with the help of the new Duke of Devonshire (since 1755) formerly Lord Hartington, and briefly, between 1756 and 1757 prime minister, who agitated for the honour to be passed on to Hogarth. The role was worth around £200 per year.[86] The accounts for 1763 and 1764 show Hogarth receiving £561 and £581 respectively, and although not all clear profit, it was still a lucrative position.[87] George II may have grumbled in private about this abuser of his guards gaining a court position, but he did enjoy Hogarth's amusing prints so, why not? (George III was to confirm the appointment on his accession three years later, with Allan Ramsay as royal portrait painter.)

The status of a court position may have stirred Hogarth to attempt, once more, sublime history painting. Sigismunda weeping over Guiscardo's heart, as noted, is a curious story to visualise, full of the type of extreme pathos and gore of a Jacobean revenge play that, if not handled with care, could so easily slip into farce. It sits at the difficult tipping point, between a sense of horror and the desire to laugh. Furini, if only the connoisseurs and art buyers would use their eyes, does not fare well in this instance, with his princess, breast tantalisingly exposed, leaning on one hand while frowning, deeply. But this is not a level playing field, and no one was using their eyes, or applying an unbiased judgement. The desperate urge to own a 'Correggio', the kudos of such ownership, overrode every-thing. To say that Hogarth succeeds better than Furini is damning him with faint praise: his is an interesting and ambitious painting, but on balance it is a noble attempt. Unfortunately for Hogarth, the likelihood of people, particularly the connoisseurs and dealers he has spent his adult life attacking, admiring that ambition and then just shrugging their shoulders as to the execution, was negli-gible. Too many knew about it, too many knew how long he had laboured and worried over it. Disaster came with Sir Richard's response, who gently but firmly rejected it. Hogarth recalled he had 'ask four hundred' for it – the price of the Furini – which was cheap, 'as I had spent more time and anxiety upon [it] than would have got me double the money in any other way', besides, it was 'not half what a common face painter got in the time'. But, in the event, 'I kept my Picture' and 'he kept his mony'.[88]

As we have seen, vicious criticism had tipped the already fragile François Lemoyne into a spiral of despair, from which he could not and did not recover. Lemoyne is a reminder that artists, no matter how apparently robust and bullish on the outside, are sensi-tive to the critiquing of their creations, into which they have put their heart and soul – they are human after all. The older Hogarth, less resilient than his younger self, and with an eye, in his early sixties, to legacy and posterity, might now have fully understood that there was less time and fewer opportunities to assert his bril-liance and settle, on his own terms and with the next generation of arrogant pups yapping at his heels, his place in the pantheon of art.

This section of Hogarth's life can feel relentlessly negative. Perhaps if he had died, unexpectedly, in 1750, with *The March to Finchley* as his final triumphant work, he could have avoided com-pletely the idea that, like their political counterparts, artists lives, if too long, can end in failure. But then we would not have *Gin Lane*, *The Humours of an Election*, *The Ascension*, *The Analysis of Beauty* – the latter described by the second president (from 1792 to 1820) of the Royal Academy, the American Benjamin West, as a work 'of the highest value to every one studying the Art. Hogarth was a strut-ting, consequential little man, and made himself many enemies by that book ; but now that most of them are dead, it is examined by disinterested readers, unbiassed by personal animosities, and it will be yet more and more read, studied, and understood.'[89] When itemised in this way, the 1750s had been, objectively, a brilliant decade, demonstrating, once more, his extraordinary variety. Yet, as ever, it is all too human to remember the bad reviews, the hurtful and cruel, rather than the high praise and compliments.

Yet Hogarth was still finding joy in life and pleasure in the company of his many loyal friends. The occasion when John Hoadly recalled laughing 'most shamefully' was at Garrick's house at Hampton in the August of 1760, with Hogarth present 'to compleat the mess!'[90] An elegant retirement to Chiswick was still an option. It was also at this time that he received a welcome compliment, by way of an affectionate reference in a new work of fiction which was taking the literary world by storm. In March 1760, Laurence Sterne had ventured to London to discuss the second edition of volumes one and two of his inimitable *The Life and Opinions of Tristram Shandy, Gentleman* (first published in 1759, volumes three and four appearing in 1761, with five further volumes to come). *The Analysis of Beauty* is referred to twice; in both instances, like Ramsay with his comment on the toad, Sterne is being playful, even if a little critical, rather than irreverent or plain nasty. The first time is in regard to Dr Slop arriving at the Shandy abode (Volume 2, Chapter IX): 'Imagine to yourself a little squat, uncourtly figure of a Doctor *Slop*, of about four feet and a half perpendicular height, with a breadth of back, and a sesquipe-dality of belly, which might have done honour to a serjeant in the horse-guards. Such were the outlines of Dr. *Slop*'s figure, which, – if you have read *Hogarth*'s analysis of beauty, and if you have not, I wish you would, – you must know, may as certainly be caricatur'd and convey'd to the mind by three strokes as three hundred.'[91] Here Sterne seems to have grasped Hogarth's method of hieroglyphics exactly, alongside the humour – as seen in Plate 2 of *The Analysis of Beauty* in the country dancers, but also with Slop reduced to three strokes, like the pikeman and his dog entering the tavern. The second is less direct but, after the mention of Hogarth and his tract, unmistakable. Corporal Trim strikes a pose in preparation of reading out a 'Sermon on Conscience' to his audience, Walter

59. Simon François Ravenet I after William Hogarth, *Frontispiece to Laurence Sterne, 'The Life and Opinions of Tristram Shandy'*, engraving, 1760
The meandering style of Sterne's novel represents, to use Hogarth's phrase, a literary 'wanton kind of chace' and perhaps in further wry homage to *The Analysis of Beauty*, hieroglyphs and diagrams appear within the text.

Shandy, his brother Uncle Toby and Dr Slop (Volume 2, Chapter XVII): 'He stood, – for I repeat it, to take the picture of him in at one view, with his body sway'd', perhaps attempting Antinous's 'easy sway', 'and somewhat bent forwards, – his right-leg firm under him, sustaining seven-eighths of his whole weight, – the foot of his left-leg, the defect of which was no disadvantage to his attitude, advanced a little, – not laterally, nor forwards, but in a line betwixt them; – his knee bent, but that not violently, – but so as to fall within the limits of the line of beauty; – and I add, of the line of science too; – for consider, it had one eighth part of his body to bear up ...' and so it goes on, for several more lines, until 'This I recommend to painters? – need I add, – to orators? – I think not; for, unless they practise it, – they must fall upon their noses.'[92]

During a supper with David Garrick, Sterne met Richard Berenger, who was acquainted with Hogarth, and immediately asked Berenger to approach the artist on Sterne's behalf to supply an illustration for the new edition. He required 'no more than ten strokes of *Howgarth*'s witty Chissell',[93] knowing that such an ornament would boost the status and sales of this already famous work. Hogarth was sufficiently flattered to provide two illustrations free of charge, the first, the frontispiece to volume one, depicting Colonel Trim reading the sermon, and the second, from volume four, where Walter Shandy arrives late to Tristram's baptism, having passed on his choice of name – 'Tristmegistus' – to the maid Susannah, who cannot recall it and, thus, the baby is misnamed.[94] These delightful images were engraved by Simon François Ravenet.

George II died on 25 October 1760. As ever, a change of monarch signalled an assessment of what had gone, and an expectation of what will come. Hogarth started the new decade and reign thinking on his feet. Clearly in part due to his court position, which was soon confirmed, according to William Pyne he sat in the Golden Cross tavern at Charing Cross, awaiting the formal proclamation of the new king, George III, 'making sketches of the heralds, and the sergeant trumpeters' band, and the yeoman guard, in their splendid liveries, who rendezvous'd at Charing Cross' with the aim 'to paint a picture of the ceremony of proclaiming the new king'.[95]

This new work appears to have been conceived as a pendant, or companion piece, to *The March to Finchley*, which was certainly in Hogarth's mind in 1760. The death of the old king reopened the wound created by the king's rejection, coupled with a bout of serious illness, 'an inflammatory disorder, caught', again according to Pyne, while sketching 'at one of the windows of the Old Golden Cross, where he stood too long exposed to a current of air', which had laid him very low.[96] Dr Messenger Monsey, his companion in the theatricals at Old Arlesford with Garrick and Hoadly fourteen years before, now physician at the Royal Hospital Chelsea, attended to him: 'Hogarth got relief from his pain before daybreak, and dozed ; but suddenly awaking, began to talk of his projected picture : his fever high, and he wandered at times. We could not keep him still. "The old king knew no more painting," said he, "than that black man,"' pointing to Monsey, who, as a physician to the deceased monarch, was in court mourning. 'Monsey moved the candle, and said, "Hush, Hogarth, or Ephraim [Pyne's alter ego] and I will leave you, and then you must die." "What, for treason?" said he. "I say the old king scribbled all over my *March to Finchley*: see there', clearly hallucinating, 'it's black as a hearse." Poor Hogarth, notwithstanding his loyalty, never forgave the king for his indifference to that incomparable work.'[97] (The said painting, of course, had been at the Foundling Hospital since 1750.)

One rumour seems to have caused particular anxiety, that is Horace Walpole's stated ambition to write a critical history of painting in England up to and including Hogarth's generation. As it turned out, the first two volumes were published in 1762, the third in 1764 and volume four, covering the reigns of George I and II, including the careers of Thornhill and Hogarth, delayed until 1771. Walpole clearly held off publishing the last volume until all the main protagonists had died, presumably in order to get the full compass of the age thus described, but also to avoid any opprobrium from artists who felt he had treated them unfairly. And, in the event, most if not all the artists who had lived and worked in what will become the 'Age of Hogarth' had just reason to be concerned, for they would be dismissed in their entirety as 'the herd', with Hogarth as an isolated genius, but very much on Walpole's terms.

In 1761 Hogarth's particular worry was what Walpole might
say about Sir James Thornhill, which in effect is a sign that he
was anxious about his own entry in the series. In fact a discussion,
recalled by Walpole in a private letter written soon after on 5 May
1761, as a dialogue between 'H' and 'W', the artist and would-be
historian respectively, is sufficiently interesting and revealing that
it is worth quoting at length. The discussion came about while
Walpole was in Hogarth's painting room at Leicester Fields in front
of a portrait of 'Mr Fox', probably that of Henry Fox, to whom
the engraving of *An Election Entertainment* was dedicated, with
Hogarth saying that he would 'make as good a picture as Vandyke
or Rubens could'.[98] Walpole did not respond to this statement.
'"Why now," said [Hogarth], "you think this very vain, but why
should not one speak truth?" This *truth*,' Walpole says, turning, as
it were, to his correspondent, George Montagu, 'was uttered in the
face of his own Sigismunda, which is exactly a maudlin w[hore],
tearing off the trinkets that her keeper had given her, to fling at
his head ... her fingers are bloody with the heart, as if she had just
bought a sheep's pluck in St. James's Market.'[99] Now, given this is
how Walpole actually thought and no doubt did not restrict such
musings to the pages of a private letter, we can see why Hogarth,
indeed any artist, would fear the publishing of this man's survey of
their profession.

Walpole continues his letter: 'As I was going, Hogarth put on
a very grave face, and said, "Mr. Walpole, I want to speak to you",
concerning his proposed history, "I wish you would let me have
it, to correct ; I should be very sorry to have you expose yourself
to censure ; we painters must know more of those things than
other people. W. Do you think nobody understands painting but
painters? H. Oh! so far from it, there's Reynolds, who certainly
has genius; why, but t'other day he offered a hundred pounds for a
picture, that I would not hang in my cellar ; and indeed, to say truth,
I have generally found, that persons who had studied painting least
were the best judges of it.'[100] This was, obviously, Hogarth's well-
established opinion against connoisseurs, of which Walpole was a
prime example, so our painter was on difficult territory. Walpole
continued, quoting Hogarth, 'but what I particularly wished to say

to you was about Sir James Thornhill ... I would not have you say anything against him ... He was the first that attempted history in England, and, I assure you, some Germans have said that he was a very great painter.' At this time Walpole stated that he was unlikely to venture beyond the year 1700, and he had not decided whether Thornhill would be included. However, if he was, 'I fear you and I shall not agree upon his merits.' So Walpole here chose to add to Hogarth's anxiety, no doubt smarting at the artist's audacity in telling him, Walpole, what he could or could not do. But Hogarth, according to Walpole, persisted: 'H. I wish you would let me correct it ; besides, I am writing something of the same kind myself; I should be sorry we should clash.' Here Hogarth was referring to his notes for *Apology for Painters*, left incomplete at his death. Walpole stated it was not, as Hogarth believed, 'a critical history of painting' but 'an antiquarian history of it in England' based on George Vertue's notebooks, who had died in 1756, the manuscripts purchased by Walpole at Vertue's sale. Such a work, 'I believe ... will not give much offence'. Now here Walpole was either being disingenuous or blatantly lying, because Vertue's notebooks, as we know, were far more than simply antiquarian in interest. They covered a vast array of subjects, with extensive commentary, some factual, some personal. In the event, Walpole chose to wilfully ignore what Vertue had to say of the London art world of the late seventeenth to mid eighteenth century, replacing this thorough, albeit highly personal survey of the era with a severely fileted and therefore distorted version, to the detriment of art history for many centuries.

Moving on, Walpole added to Hogarth's concerns by saying, 'besides, if it does,' cause offence, 'I cannot help it : when I publish anything, I give it to the world to think of it as they please'.[101] This coming from a man of leisure, whose inherited wealth, privilege and power guaranteed him, not only an audience, but a far more pliant one than Hogarth could ever hope for. Walpole was exactly the type of aristocrat, highlighted by Hogarth over the years, who had the wherewithal to do so much for his fellow man, to have left the world a far better place than he found it, and yet chose to do very little indeed. And this was the person to whom Hogarth must leave his reputation, to do with as he will? No wonder he feared for Sir James and, by extension, himself. Hogarth appeared to accept Walpole's falsehood, although somewhat agitated still, to which Walpole declared 'My dear Mr. Hogarth, I must take my leave of you, you now grow too wild – and I left him. If I had stayed, there remained nothing but for him to bite me'. He concludes, 'I had consecrated a line to his genius (I mean, for wit) in my preface ; I shall not erase it ; but I hope nobody will ask me if he is not mad.'[102]

Hogarth was not mad, but he was clearly under strain, disillusioned and succumbing to regular bouts of illness. The malady in 1760, when Monsey was attending him, seems to have prevented Hogarth submitting to the first annual Society of Artists group exhibition in April that year, intended to imitate the salons of the Académie royale in Paris and springing from the annual artist gatherings at the Foundling Hospital. By the following year, around the time he was having his fraught 'debate' with Walpole, he was, however, sufficiently buoyant to submit several works, including *Calais Gate*, the single canvas *An Election Entertainment*, *The Lady's Last Stake*, *Sigismunda* and a smattering of portraits: effectively a modest survey of activity over the previous decade or so. His particular interest, unsurprisingly, was the public reaction to *Sigismunda*, until then only viewable at Hogarth's house. According to one anecdote, he posted a man next to the painting to hear what was said.[103] The reactions were sufficiently negative for Hogarth to withdraw the painting, replacing it with another canvas from the *Election* series, *Chairing the Members*, and for him to set about further agonised reworking. *Sigismunda* had clearly become a manifestation of all Hogarth's mounting unease, even paranoia. A satirical article in the *St. James's Chronicle* in late May 1761 would not have helped. Here a visitor to London meets a connoisseur who drags him to the Society of Artists exhibition 'to despise the wretched English dawbs'. The country visitor considers Hogarth 'the best Painter of Life and Manners in the Universe', having forked out £14 for his prints over the years. But according to the connoisseur, Hogarth is 'an absolute Bartholomew Droll, who paints Country Elections'. They arrive at the exhibiting space and the visitor cries 'Heavens', on seeing *Sigismunda*: 'Would my

Friend Dryden could but come to Life again to see his Thoughts so expressed, so coloured: – Who did it my Lord?' The connoisseur replies 'Hogarth ... and he is quite out of his Walk'. 'Hogarth! Said I, I could not indeed have expected this even of him.' And who, here, is compared to Van Dyck, Hogarth's totem since 1733? Not Hogarth, but the young pretender, Joshua Reynolds.[104]

Turning briefly to the section in *Anecdotes of Painting in England* where Horace Walpole recalls, within Hogarth's extensive entry, *Sigismunda*, the author effectively published his private opinion as expressed in his letter to George Montagu. Walpole rightly queried the *Sigismunda* as by 'Furino' (Furini) rather than Correggio, although he declares that it matters not by whom, for it is, after all, 'the celebrated Sigismonda of Sir Luke Schaub' and 'one of the finest pictures in England', which, demonstrably, it was and is not. Yet, according to Walpole, the aristocratic connoisseur, 'It is impossible to see the picture or read Dryden's inimitable tale, and not feel that the same soul animated both.' However, in Walpole's opinion, Hogarth's painting is 'no more like Sigismonda, than I to Hercules', a fleeting glimmer of self-awareness, 'Not to mention the wretchedness of the colouring, it was the representation of a maudlin strumpet ...' here repeating the description he had given George Montagu in 1761, concluding 'None of the sober grief, no dignity of suppressed anguish, no involuntary tear, no settled meditation on the fate she meant to meet, no amorous warmth turned holy by despair ...' and so on and so forth.[105] Silly, stupid, arrogant, hubristic Hogarth!

This attack on the painting, published when Hogarth was long dead but his widow very much alive, was extremely personal to Jane, who, according to Mrs Chapel, resented it 'as bitterly as ever after he was in his grave'.[106] Horace Walpole is described in this source as 'the heartless scoffer', an appellation it is difficult to argue against. Of course, this was all in the future, but it does show that, rather than being mad, Hogarth had read Walpole's character and intention precisely and accurately.

Recalling the *Sigismunda* affair, Hogarth writes in his autobiographical notes that 'Ill nature spread so fast' indeed 'now was the time for every little dog to bark in there [*sic*] profession and revive the old splene which appeard at the time my analysis came out.'[107] This really is the saddest section of the autobiographical notes. He continues, recounting 'the anxiety' in attempting, once more, history painting and the resulting ridicule 'coming at a time when perhaps nature rather wants a more quiet life and something to chere (?) it', something to enliven rather than depress the spirits. Having been 'sedentary' working on this painting, rather than taking care of himself and his health by regular exercise, unsurprisingly 'brought on an Illness which continue a year'. This is clearly the illness throughout 1760 and 1761. He emerged from this, and when sufficiently rested and well enough to ride (presumably at this juncture he was spending more and more time in Chiswick among the fields, the gentle river and fresh air), made a full recovery. However, this absence, through illness, he states, 'the loss of so much time and the inattention to Prints' from which a large part of his income derived, plus further difficulties springing from 'the wars ... abroad and contentions at home made it necessary to do some timed thing' that is a topical subject to 'stop a gap in my income'.[108]

It would be a relief to say, that thus ended Hogarth's difficulties, that he was able to put aside the less than enthusiastic response to this one painting, to focus on those who admired *The Analysis of Beauty*, and learn to enjoy the high esteem in which he and a vast majority of his works were clearly held. But, like a once unassailable, now wounded, pugilist, a little punch drunk, flailing around, Hogarth continued to stumble into further troubles and confrontation. Horace Walpole observed that 'The last memorable event in our artist's life was his quarrel with Mr. Wilkes, in which if Mr. Hogarth did not commence direct hostilities on the latter, he at least obliquely gave the first offence by an attack on the friends and party of that gentleman.'[109]

This was *The Times No.1*, 'the subject' Hogarth recalled 'of which tended to Peace and unanimity'. This was a rare, if unique, direct foray into contemporary politics, by overtly supporting one political interest over another – exactly what Allan Ramsay had warned him against. Hogarth's print was in support of the policy for peace over continuing the war, as advocated by the Scottish Tory John

60. *The Times No.1*, etching and engraving (third and final state), 1762
What became known as the Seven Years' War (1756–63) was a complex pan-
European conflict dovetailed with the escalating struggle between Great
Britain and France for colonial domination of North America and India.

Stuart, 3rd Earl of Bute, the new king's favourite and briefly prime
minister. The print included references to the 1745 Jacobite rebellion, but here, in a softening from the depiction of the Highlander
in *Calais Gate*, an English tar and clansman are shown working
together to put out the flames of conflict. He was thus, in his own
words, putting 'the opposers of this humane purpose in a light
which gave offence to the Fomenter of distruction in the minds of
the people'. The main 'fomenter', indeed the 'most notorious', was
John Wilkes, 'till now rather my friend'; since 1754 Wilkes had
been a member of the Beefsteak Club, had subscribed to the *Election* series and was 'a flatterer' to Hogarth. But now he attacked the
artist and former intimate 'in so infamous a manner that he himself
when pushd by even his best frinds ... was driven ... to so poor an
excuse as to say' when he wrote it 'he was drunck'. The situation,
Hogarth concluded sadly, 'could not but hurt ... a feeling mind'.[110]

As Walpole hints, Hogarth was not caught completely una-
wares. But despite a warning from Wilkes that an attack on his
friends Lord Temple and William Pitt, with a defence of Lord
Bute, would be taken as an attack on himself, Hogarth (perhaps in
desperate need of money) ploughed on regardless, and published
The Times No.1 in September 1762. Wilkes believed that in producing this print, Hogarth had sacrificed 'private friendship at the
altar of party madness',[111] while, in defence of Hogarth, the Reverend John Trusler (with Jane Hogarth's consent) declared that the
artist, then George III's sergeant painter, 'held with the court ; a
faithful servant to that master, in whose employment he was'.[112] At
that time David Garrick wrote to a mutual friend, the former Reverend now poet Charles Churchill, co-contributor with Wilkes to
the latter's anti-Bute journal *The North Briton*, begging him not to
get involved: 'I must intreat of You by ye Regard You profess to Me,
that You don't tilt at my Friend Hogarth before You See Me – You
cannot sure be angry at his Print? there is surely very harmless, tho
very Entertaining Stuff in it – He is a great & original Genius, I
love him as a Man & reverence him as an Artist – I would not for
all ye Politicks & Politicians in ye Universe that You two should
have the least Cause of Illwill to Each other. I am sure You will not
publish against him if You think twice – I am very unhappy at y^e
thoughts of it, pray Make Me quiet as soon as possibly by writing
to me at Hampton or Seeing Me here [i.e. Southampton Street,
Covent Garden].'[113] It is clear from the letter that Churchill, a
man with many faults, on a different issue was already attacking
someone else, the poet laureate William Whitehead. So, even
prior to his siding with Wilkes, Churchill had form – standing in
glass houses, lobbing stones.

The Times, hardly a vicious attack on anybody, was answered
by Wilkes, as Hogarth recalled, in 'a severe' edition of the *North
Briton* dated 25 September 1762. The contents of the print itself
was not, now, the sole subject, for Wilkes chose to attack Hogarth
on every front possible: as we all know, there is no enemy more
powerful, more able to hit their mark with greater accuracy, than a
former intimate. From sneering about *The Analysis of Beauty*, 'We
all titter the instant he takes up a *pen*, but we tremble when we see

the *pencil* in his hand', to describing his history paintings 'almost beneath all criticism'. *Sigismunda* gets a drubbing for she 'was not human ; and if the figure had any resemblance of any thing ever on earth, or had any pretence to meaning or expression, it was what he had seen, or perhaps made, in real life, his own wife in an agony of passion, but of what passion no connoisseur could guess'. Whether the expression of Sigismunda's grief was Jane's or not, this was an extremely unpleasant and unnecessary reference to Hogarth's wife. His summing up of Hogarth is as a painter obsessed with the most squalid aspects of human nature, 'to shew the *faulty* and *dark side* of every object. He never gives us in perfection the *fair face of nature*, but admirably well holds out her deformities to ridicule'. Even the abandoned *The Happy Marriage* series is brought in as evidence of a failed attempt at virtue, for the 'rancour and malevolence of his mind made him very soon turn with envy and disgust from objects of so pleasing contemplation'. Wilkes then moves on to berate Hogarth as a dying force, a '*setting sun*. He has long been very *dim*' and a man who 'will go all lengths to raise a laugh at your expence, and your whole life will be made miserable from his ambition of diverting the company for half an hour.' Perhaps there is something in this – what of poor Jonathan Richardson, Doctor Fidget? But what of Hogarth's instant regret, throwing the offending image into the fire? Wilkes fails to mention this, the regret. He was too busy mining every potential seam for slurs.

Perhaps predictably, Wilkes moves on to the painting, and particularly the engraving of *The March to Finchley*, stating 'when the *Guards* were ordered to march to *Finchley*, on the most important service they could be employed in, the extinguishing a *Scottish* rebellion, which threatened the intire ruin of the illustrious family on the throne, and, in consequence, of our liberties ... Mr. *Hogarth* came out with a print to make them ridiculous to their countrymen and to all *Europe*. Or was it to tell the *Scots* in his way how little these men were to be feared, and that they might safely advance?' A decidedly anti-Scottish stance, aimed at Lord Bute. Next he notes the dedication of the print to the King of Prussia – 'Is this patriotism ? In old *Rome*, or in any of the *Grecian* states, he would have been punished as a profligate citizen, totally devoid of

all principle. In *England* he is rewarded, and made *sergeant* painter
to that very king's grandson'. The charge against Hogarth here is
understandable – the dedication reveals his lack of empathy with
a king who had almost lost everything. Yet Wilkes is again indulging in fake offence – a nation at ease with itself can cope with a
little ribaldry. Having introduced Hogarth's court appointment,
which he ridicules as no better than a house or '*pannel-painter*',
the diatribe goes on and on.[114] The print that has stimulated this
outpouring is secondary to a complete personal and professional
assassination. Hogarth felt the blows, the sneering accusation that,
despite everything he had done to display variety, to unveil beauty,
in the end 'my women [are] harlot[s], and my men charicatures'.[115]

David Garrick, stuck in the unenviable position between these
two hostile camps, wrote a letter to Hogarth (unusual given they
lived so near), and it is clear why. Hogarth sensed that his friend
was hiding away from him and thus, by default, siding with the
Wilkes–Churchill party. In reality, Garrick probably felt he could
not afford to make enemies on either side. But Hogarth was a
solitary target in this crisis, and suffered his friend's absence more
keenly. The letter begins with reference to Benjamin Wilson:

[Saturday] 8 January 1763

Dear Hogarth.

Our friend *Wilson* hinted to me this Morning, that I had of
late been remiss in my visits to You – it may be so, tho upon
my Word, I am not conscious of it, for Such Ceremonies are
to Me, mere Counters, where there is no remission of Regard
& good Wishes – As *Wilson* is not an Accurate Observer of
things, not Ev'n of those which concerns him most, I must
imagine that yᵉ Hint came from You, & shall say a Word or
two to You upon it – *Montaigne*, who was a good Judge of
Human Nature, takes Notice, *that when Friends grow Exact,
& Ceremonious, it is a certain Sign of Coolness, for the true
Spirit of Friendship keeps no Account of Triffles* – We are, I
hope, a Strong exception to this Rule –

He offers another example where he has been accused of neglect, regarding Somerset Draper, who had asked Garrick how long it had been since he visited. Garrick offered a month or six weeks, but Draper confirmed it was 'a Year & some Days, reply'd he, but don't imagine that I have kept an Account; My Wife told Me so this Morning, & bid me Scold You for it – now', Garrick continues, 'if Mrs Hogarth has observ'd my Neglect, I am flatter'd by it, but if it is *Your* Observation, Woe betide You – Could I follow my inclinations I would see You Every day in ye week, without caring whether it was in Leicester Fields or Southampton Street', and he pleads poor health and the care of a large family, meaning his brother George's family, including many children. 'However Since You are grown a Polite Devil, & have a Mind to play at Lords & Ladies ... I will certainly call upon You soon & if you should not be at home, I will leave my *Card*.' Garrick then signs off, 'I am Yours Dear Hogy Most Sincerely D: Garrick.'[116] There are very few letters between the two friends, for the reasons that Garrick outlines in this missive, and because they lived so near each other in London. So, we could surmise, that to write such a long letter for a fault he was well known for, neglect of his friends, does suggest that Hogarth had been very affronted at this specific time. The use of the very personal nickname 'Hogy' is made more bittersweet in these circumstances.

In his own notes Hogarth states, 'when a man is cruelly and unjustly treated he naturally looks round and appeals to the standers by ... My Phylosophical friends bid me laugh at the Abusive nonsense of party writers.' Alas for his own peace of mind, he continues, 'But I cannot rest myself'.[117] In the event, 'my best was to return the complement & turn it to some adva[n]tage.'[118] Hogarth decided to address John Wilkes in kind, directly and personally. The result was one of the greatest political portraits of any age.

His opportunity came when Wilkes was arrested for sedition, after attacking the King's Speech in April 1763 in the *North Briton*, and then tried in Westminster Hall. Wilkes himself declared that when he made his second appearance in Westminster Hall, the place where Lord Lovat too had been tried, 'Mr. Hogarth skulked behind in a corner of the gallery of the court of Common Pleas', and while the great principles of Magna Carta and the English

61. *John Wilkes, Esq.*, etching, 1763

Wilkes's attack on the king's speech and, specifically, the treaty that ended
the Seven Years' War, led to his trial, although, due to a legal blunder,
he was released to the delight of a mob (whom he had incited) shouting
'Wilkes and Liberty'. Still MP for Aylesbury after bribing voters at the 1761
election, here Hogarth exposes him as a corrupt, self-serving 'patriot'.

constitution were being evoked, 'the painter was wholly employed in *caricaturing* the *person* of the man'. Wilkes concludes that the resulting image 'must be allowed to be an excellent ... *caricatura* of what nature had already *caricatured*.[119] The criticism of Hogarth for 'skulking' and ignoring the 'eloquence and courage' of the Lord Chief Justice seems a little rich from the man in the dock for sedition, but otherwise this is a good effort at deflecting the power of the print – note the jibe in the use of 'caricatura', which Hogarth had stated very publicly was not what he was about. Rather than skulking, Hogarth made a point of being at Wilkes's trial: mainly to get a fresh likeness, but it must have crossed his mind that it would heighten Wilkes's anxiety that some sort of reprisal was on its way, while stoking gleeful expectation in everyone else. In the event Hogarth aimed to delineate Wilkes's character, his external and internal traits, very far from 'the fair face of nature', to use Wilkes's words against him, which is why, unlike a caricature, it is true 'to nature', and therefore so devastating.[120]

The arrival of the image of the leering debauchee 'Squinting Jack' – a nod to Wilkes' membership of the Hellfire Club, with its ringleader, Sir Francis Dashwood – was announced in *The Public Advertiser* on 16 May 1763: 'This Day is published , Price 1s. A Whole-Length Print of JOHN WILKES, Esq; drawn from the Life, and etch'd by WILLIAM HOGARTH. To be had at the Golden Head in Leicester Fields. N.B. This Print is in direct Contrast to a Print of SIMON Lord LOVAT, first published in the Year 1746, and is of the same Size, and etch'd in the same Manner; which Print of Lord Lovat may be had, Price òne Shilling, at the same Place. Where also are sold, all the other engraved Works of the same Author, either bound together or otherwise.' The pairing up of Wilkes, rabidly anti-Scottish, with the Scots rebel, Lord Lovat, was a piece of genius – perhaps 'the two patriots' Hogarth refers to in his autobiographical notes.[121] *The Gazetteer and London Daily Advertiser*, 13 June 1763, 'On seeing the pictures of LOVAT and WILKES, drawn by HOGARTH' declared

FROM forty-five to sixty-three,
What changes *times* do bring?

'Tis now as bad to hate the Scot
As then to hate the King.
Old Lovat lov'd a Stuart well,
Hogarth his picture drew;
Wilkes hates a Stuart from his heart,
And Hogarth joins the two.[122]

As Hogarth recalled, his 'Portrait done as like as I could as to feature at the same time some indication of his mind fully answerd my purpose the ridiculous was apparent to every Eye', the self-proclaimed 'Brutus a saviour of his country with such an aspect' was so 'arrant … a Joke that tho it set every body else a laughing gauld him and his adherents to death', as was 'seen by the papers being every day stufft with evectives' – that is invectives – until, at length, everyone else had grown sick of the whole episode.[123]

In the meantime, though, Nichols declares that he was told by a printer that around four thousand copies were printed at its first publication, 'Being kept up for two or three following nights on the occasion, he has reason to remember it',[124] and this is a useful reminder that Hogarth's successes had a ripple effect through the industry, employing craftsmen, like printers, as well as keeping printsellers afloat.

The situation was far from over, for Squinting Jack and his chum at least, as Wilkes recalled; 'Mr. *Churchill* was exasperated at this personal attack on his friend'[125] – which was commensurate with Wilkes's attack on Hogarth, but no one is thinking clear-headedly at this juncture – who then published *An Epistle to William Hogarth*. Walpole described this latest Churchill poem as 'not the brightest of his works, and in which the severest strokes fell on a defect that the painter had neither caused nor could amend – his age'. David Garrick, writing (from Derbyshire) in alarm to George Colman, 'Pray write to me, & let me know how ye Town speaks of our Friend Churchill's Epistle – it is ye most bloody performance that has been publish'd in my time – I am very desirous to know the opinion of the People, for I am really much, very much hurt at it – his [Churchill's] description of his [Hogarth's] Age & infirmities is surely too shocking & barbarous – is Hogarth really ill, or does he meditate revenge? – Every article of news about these matters will be most agreeable to me – pray write me a heap of stuff for I cannot be Easy till I know all about Churchill, Hogarth, &c.'[126] John Nichols states, 'I have been assured by the friend who first carried the invective of *Churchill* to Hogarth', it was Thomas Morell, 'that he seemed quite insensible to the most sarcastical parts of it. He was so thoroughly wounded before by the *North Briton*, especially in regard to what related to domestic happiness, that he lay no where open to a fresh stroke.'[127] This indifference, relative to the shock of Wilkes's initial attack in the *North Briton*, is recalled by Hogarth himself: 'Churchill W[ilkes's] toadeater put the North Briton into verse in an Epistle to me, but as the abuse was ... the same except a little poetical heighting which always goes for nothing, it not only made no impression but in some measure effaced the Blacks stroke of the N[orth] B[riton].' However, sensing a quick rejoinder was required, and 'having an old plate by me with some parts ready such as the Back ground and a dog, I thought how I could turn so much work laid aside to account'. In this manner, using an old plate, he patched up 'a print of M^r. Churchill in the character of a Bear.'[128]

Much has been made of the fact that the plate Hogarth used was of himself and his pug (Fig. 54 p. 385), thus defacing his own image with that of Churchill as a loutish bear, entitled 'The Bruiser', with Trump now pissing on the author's anti-Hogarth missive. The many revisions of this print does suggest an intense period of activity and reworking. Although, with a new engraving of his most recent self-portrait in preparation, to replace the 1749 image as the frontispiece to a proposed complete works, and with the need for speed in responding to Churchill, Hogarth, as he says, having this old plate already there, simply patched it up, with no more emotion or bile or unintended self-immolation than that blasé comment might suggest. The sum, and here the old Hogarth comes to the fore, was to the artist's 'satisfaction <and pecuniary advantage> I receivd form [from] these two prints'; in other words he got his revenge on Wilkes and Churchill and made a lot of money out of it, which 'together with constant Riding on horse back restored me as much as health as can be expected at my time of life'. 'What

62. *The Bruiser*, etching and engraving, 1763
A volume of subscribers entitled *A New Way to Pay Old Debts* hints at the
poet's financial (as well as fraternal) motivation, echoing Tom Rakewell's
desperate literary attempt to pay his way out of the Fleet prison.

may follow,' he continues 'god knows ... Finis.'[129] This is not a man writing with the expectation that he will die imminently. The auto-biographical notes, no matter how angry, bitter or melancholic, can be viewed as a way of placing his career and life to date into the specific context of recent events. And given the unpleasantness, a level of resentment and even sorrow is understandable. That done, his spleen vented, here he seems to end on a less fraught note, for who knows what will happen next?

An admirer of Hogarth, writing anonymously from Bright-helmston (Brighton), enclosed a poem which opens: 'Dear Churchill! What ill-fated hour/ Has put thee into Hogarth's power?/ Your Railing shews how much you're hurt ; While Hogarth only was in sport.' Then, hitting on a fundamental truth, perhaps why Wilkes and then Churchill attacked the artist so vehemently: 'Epistles : Pho! They're tedious things/ Their very length disarms their stings ... The pencil, like contracted light/ Strikes with superior Force the sight,/ Takes every careless Eye, that passes,/ Which, without Reading, sees its lashes.'[130] Another letter, preserved among Hogarth's papers in the British Library, from the Quaker Ephraim Knox, declares admiration for 'thy compositions & handy works, & think them not only ingenious, but moral ; & even more than dramatic, perfectly Epic ; so that I think Thou deserves the Character of the Epic Painter ... & by which thou shalt be distinguished in future generations ; for I do not much mistake the matter, thy name will be had in honour, when thine adversaries are rotten.' Knox continues, 'Let not thy noble spirit that is in Thee, be diverted from its true & masterly Turn, of exposing licentiousness, Vice, Hypocrisy, Faction, & Apostacy'. He concludes with an epigram addressed to Charles Churchill, which includes the lines 'Judas himself was not so great a Fool;/ He sold for ready Cash – His paltry Soul.'[131]

Churchill's response to Hogarth's 'Bruiser' print was inevitable, and it is clear that, once again, the artist had hit his target straight between the eyes. Churchill, writing to Wilkes on 3 August 1763, exposes a bewildering absence of any sense of his own culpability for the situation's escalation: 'I take it for granted you have seen *Hogarth's Print* against me. Was ever any thing so contemptible?

I think he is fairly felo de se' (meaning suicidal or committing an act of self-destruction), 'I think not to let him off in that manner, although I might safely leave him to your notes', here referring to Wilkes's editorship of Churchill's works for publication. 'He has broke into my pale of private life,' Churchill continues, 'and set that example of illiberality which I wished – of that kind of attack which is ungenerous in the first instance, but justice in return. I intend an Elegy on him, supposing him dead.' Churchill then quotes an unnamed 'woman', probably Elizabeth Carr, the daughter of his landlord, whom, causing great public scandal, he seduced as a fifteen-year-old (they eloped in late 1763).[132] She 'tells me with a kiss, he will be really dead before it comes out : that I have already killed him, &c. How sweet is flattery from the woman we love, and how weak is our boasted strength when opposed to beauty and good sense with good nature !'[133] In this instance, Horace Walpole declared, 'Never did two angry men of their abilities throw mud with less dexterity.'[134]

John Nichols says that Hogarth spent the early part of 1764 retouching various printing plates 'with the assistance of several engravers whom he took with him to Chiswick', in preparation for the issue of a complete works.[135] Mrs Chapel describes engravers working in Hogarth's painting room at the end of the garden, 'and for recreation in their hours of leisure, he had a skittle ground prepared for them, that they might enjoy a healthy exercise without being tempted to drink by going to a public house'.[136] No doubt at the same time he was penning the autobiographical notes, intended in part as an introduction to the 'Complete Works', which appear on sheets of differing sizes, suggesting they were written at different times and in different places – whether Chiswick or Leicester Fields. One line, which he no doubt believed might serve as a final one, simply says 'Thus have I treated the most material circum[stanc]es of my life which passed on pre[t]ty much to my own liking < till lately > and I hope no ways injurious to any one.'[137] Alongside this introduction, containing details of his life to date, were to be short commentaries for each print (all quoted extensively here) and complementary to André Rouquet's earlier narratives as 'discriptive of the peculiar manners & characters of the

English nation' for the benefit of 'the Curious of other Countries'. Yet now Hogarth goes further, revealing a desire to be understood by generations to come, 'at home and abroad', for he hoped these explanations would 'be Instructive and amusing in future times when the customs manners fasheons Characters and Humours of the present age in this country may possibly be changed or lost to Posterity unless by this or some such means they are preserved'.[138]

Hogarth fell ill again while at Chiswick, but was moved to Leicester Fields on 25 October. John Nichols says he was 'in a very weak condition, yet remarkably cheerful; and, receiving an agreeable letter from the *American* Dr. *Franklin*', with enthusiasm 'drew up a rough draught of an answer to it'. Franklin was keen to order a set of Hogarth's prints for the Library Company of Philadelphia (Jane would supply this after her husband's death). Nichols also states that 'he boasted of having eaten a pound of beef-steaks for his dinner, and was to all appearance heartier than he had been for a long time before'.[139] This reference smacks, at best, of wishful thinking; that the creator of *Calais Gate or The Roast Beef of Old England* was to be finished off by such an ill-advised over indulgence – the ingesting of full-bloodied beef stirring an immediate restoration of his vigour, which proved to be temporary: even Hogarth would have seen the irony in that. But Nichols states, whether true or false, it was Mary Lewis, Jane Hogarth's cousin and companion, who was the source of the intelligence. In any case, within hours, as he was 'going to bed, he was seized with a vomiting, upon which he rung his bell with such a violence that he broke it, and expired about two hours afterwards in the arms of Mrs. *Mary Lewis*, who was called up on his being suddenly taken ill'.[140] His affliction was confirmed as an aneurysm, the swelling of the wall of an artery, which often has no symptoms, but if it ruptures, as seems to have happened here, the results can be fatal. Severe headaches might suggest a brain aneurysm, while vomiting blood a complaint of the stomach. John Nichols does not mention either. The main detail was that he was taken ill suddenly and died very soon after. Mrs Chapel recalled: 'It is not generally known that Hogarth's death was awfully sudden', albeit after periods over several years of ill health, and then, more remarkable still, 'that he was about to receive the honour of knighthood, and that had he lived one day longer he would have died Sir William Hogarth'.[141]

That George III esteemed Hogarth is plain from Benjamin Wilson's later testimony (a meeting at St James's in 1776), where the king 'made repeated inquiries respecting the personal history of Hogarth, and his paintings of which he was a great admirer', in particular *Marriage A-la-Mode*.[142] It was to the king that Wilson had relayed the anecdote of Hogarth telling the wrong story. Even so, Mrs Chapel's recollections of an imminent knighthood (it would have been as a 'knight bachelor' rather than of an order of chivalry) are extraordinary, and are likely to have been a misremembering. In this version of Hogarth's last twenty-four hours, she says Hogarth had acquired his court dress ready for the ceremony, on 25 October 1764, the anniversary of the king's accession, and that the day before he was at Chiswick trying on his finery 'that the ladies might see what sort of a figure he should make at court'. At this time he was 'in good health and spirits'.[143] That evening he returned to London with Mary, leaving Jane at Chiswick: '"I and Mary," said he, "will go to town, and I shall get a good night's rest to prepare the morrow."' Having delivered Jane to the home of some local ladies called Le Sage, Mary and he continued in the coach to Leicester Fields, where he said he would have 'a couple of eggs' before going to bed. He had not retired longer than an hour or two when Mary heard his bell ringing with such violence that she feared him ill. She burst into his room, at which he cried, '"Hot water! Hot water!" This was all he could say ; and in a short time, his head leaning on her shoulder, he expired.'[144] In this account the post-mortem found that 'the bursting of a polypus in his throat' was the immediate cause of death.

In any case, there is a fundamental issue with this version of Hogarth's final day on earth: most accounts confirm that he actually died some time during the night or early morning of 25 to 26 October, rather than late on the 24th or early on the 25th. Mrs Chapel may have confused an appearance at court, on the occasion of the king's accession to the throne, with Hogarth receiving a knighthood.[145] If he had been recommended, then surely his sponsor, as with his appointment as His Majesty's sergeant painter, would have been his long-term supporter, the Duke of Devon-shire.[146] The search for any evidence is ongoing, but there are two things we can say with certainty: firstly, such an honour would have been very acceptable indeed to Hogarth – both in emulation of his mentor and father Sir James, and as triumphant public recognition of his importance to art and the nation. And secondly, our artist died plain Billy Hogarth.

Hogarth was buried in the churchyard at St Nicolas's, Chiswick, with a tomb inscription by David Garrick:

> Farewell, great painter of mankind,
> Who reach'd the noblest point of art;
> Whose pictur'd morals charm the mind,
> And through the eye correct the heart.
> If *genius* fire thee, reader, stay,
> If *nature* touch thee, drop a tear;
> If neither move thee, turn away,
> For *Hogarth*'s honour'd dust lies here.[147]

As fate would have it, Hogarth's last adversary had come to a sad and little-mourned end only days after the artist. Horace Walpole, writing to Horace Mann on 15 November 1764, observed, 'Churchill the poet is dead, – to the great joy of the Ministry and the Scotch, and to the grief of very few indeed, I believe; for such a friend is not only a dangerous, but a ticklish possession.' He continues, 'This meteor blazed scarce four years ... and what is as remarkable, he died in nine days after his antagonist, Hogarth. Were I Charon, I should, without scruple, give the best place in my boat to the latter, who is an original genius.' Churchill apparently 'died of a drunken debauch at Calais, on a visit to his friend Wilkes', then in self-imposed exile to avoid arrest.[148] In fact, rather than in a blaze of sensual glory at Calais, Churchill had died painfully of typhus at Boulogne, to the sound of the uncontrollable sobbing of his dear friend. His corpse was delivered to St Martin's church in Dover, where the tombstone reads '1764. Here lies the Remains of the celebrated C CHURCHILL', with a line adapted from his poem, *The Candidate*, 'Life to the last enjoy'd, *Here* Churchill lies'.

Meanwhile, in the section of the garden in Chiswick which was given over to the graves of cherished pets, particularly birds and dogs, one grave marker dated 1760 exclaimed 'Alas, poor Dick!', possibly a bull finch.[149] Another, recalled by Mrs Chapel, dated 1764, was in memory of 'Pompey', 'a favourite dog', who was honoured with a somewhat longer and descriptive record – 'Life to the last enjoyed, here Pompey lies'[150] – a satirical play on Churchill's grave epitaph. Clearly, if true, Jane Hogarth had exacted a small but elegant revenge. And, as imagined by Walpole, wherever Charon, puffing on his pipe, had placed the two of them in that boat to the underworld, as they were carried across, Hogarth at least would be laughing, most shamefully.

EPILOGUE

'Go and do the same'

TUESDAY 30 MAY, AFTERNOON. At the fort of Sheerness the pilgrims hired a 'Bomb boat', vulgarly called, to Gravesend, leaving at five o'clock.[1] A 'bomboat' or 'bumboat' was a small trading craft which took provisions and cargo to and from ships. (The 'Bumboat Act' of 1762 was passed to prevent theft by bumboats from ships in harbours and at the docks on the Thames.[2]) The wind blew a fresh gale at east by south, both Billy Hogarth and Sam Scott suffered from seasickness, 'and Did what was Naturall in Such Cases'. Will Tothall went aboard one of the customs house sloops with Captain Robinson, 'who Furnish'd him with some Milk punch and us with some Fire to Light pipes which was greatly Wanted.'

The rain thundered down throughout the entire trip to Gravesend. As they bobbed along, looking out to sea, they spotted some porpoises (John Thornhill would include them in his map), who were 'Rolling in pursuit of their prey'. One appeared to be stranded on the shore, 'But he Deceiv'd our Expectations & gott off again'.[3]

At about seven o'clock, all the sick travellers having recovered, 'Wee Sail'd Merrily and Sang Sr John pishoken and Severall other Songs and Tunes our Selves, and our Cockswain Entertain'd us with Severall Sailors' Songs', no doubt the latter of a particularly salty nature. All was well until, that is, the boat ran aground on 'the Blye Sand', in the middle of the channel, at ebb tide and within an hour of the flood. The singing stopped.[4] This was a frankly dangerous position to be in, the boat and its passengers very vulnerable to being beaten by the winds and waves. However, the experience and skill of the crew, with the very able assistance of Will Tothall, saved the day. They got off the sandbank (albeit with the usual 'difficulty'), and the wind being favourable, they continued safely to Gravesend, arriving at about ten o'clock at night. That the journey included some danger and jeopardy is normal for any travel undertaken in this period, but adds to the idea of trial and tribulation being character-building – it also unveils the life-saving skills and calm behaviour of the group, Tothall being particularly useful in a crisis. A brush with the grim reaper is certainly life-affirming, and this tale, a wrestle with death, where all the British heroes, this time, are triumphant, would be told again and again.

In their relief, presumably back at Mrs Bramble's hostelry, 'Wee Sup'd and Drank Good Wine and tho^t. our Adventures and extraordinary Mirth ended'. But they discovered that their adventure was far from over, for 'a Great Coat Scott had borrow'd for this Journey and left at Gravesend (& travell'd without it)', which he thought would be still at the hostelry, 'Wee found (on our arrival here), could not be found. This tho^h. Greif to him was Sport to us and he Soon got the better of his uneasiness and Grew as Merry as wee, thus Wee continu'd till pretty Late and then Went to Bed.'[5]

WEDNESDAY 31 MAY, MORNING. They woke at eight o'clock, quite late, but a lie-in was allowed after their marine adventure. They had breakfast and then had a final walk about town. At ten o'clock they clambered on board a boat they had hired 'with a Truss of Clean Straw a Botle of Good Wine, Pipes Tobacco & Match'. They were ready for the final leg of their journey. The wind blew south-east, 'a Mackrell Gale', which was favourable for the passage back up the Thames to London. The journey was extremely pleasant indeed, drinking wine and puffing on their pipes, as the tilt-boat skimmed along, retracing their passage from a few days before. As they moved along the water the landscape around them changed, gradually becoming more and more developed with wharfs and associated buildings. Pleasant, that is, until they came to Erith. Scott was sitting at the edge of the craft happily sketching some shipping, when the boat tipped, causing the vessel to 'Ship a Sea', which drenched him and no one else from head to toe – the dunking made worse still because he had no protection (having lost his great coat): 'He Greatly Surpriz'd Got up, and Drawing the Fore tail of his Shirt from out his Breeches (wch. were also well Sous'd with Salt Water) he held it in both hands opposed to the Windward and the Sun Shining Warm he was soon Dry and recovering his Surprize Joyn'd with us in Laughing at ye Accid^t.'[6]

They travelled along the great river very merrily and, leaving the tilt-boat at Billingsgate, they clambered aboard a wherry. The broad-shouldered, spindle-shanked waterman rowed them from London's Old Bridge to Somerset House watergate, 'from whence Wee walk'd all together', Ebenezer Forrest concludes, 'and arrived at about Two at the Bedford Arms Covent Garden, in the same Good Humour wee left it to Set out on this Very Pleasant Expedition'.[7]

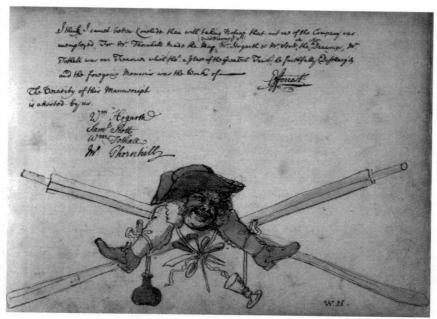

63. *No Body*, pen and brown ink, with grey wash and watercolour over graphite on paper, 1732

NOTES

BM British Museum
BL British Library
GM Gentleman's Magazine
ODNB Oxford Dictionary of National Biography
RCT Royal Collections Trust

Prologue

1   E. Forrest, *An account of what Seem'd most Remarkable in the Five Days Peregrination of the Five Following Persons Viz*. *Messieurs Tothall, Scott, Hogarth, Thornhill & Forrest ...*, 1732, BM 1847,0320.1-10.

2   W. Gostling, '*An Account of what seemed most remarkable in the five Days Peregrination ... Imitated In* HUDIBRASTICKS ...' in C. Mitchell ed., *Hogarth's Peregrination*, Oxford, 1952, pp. 21–47.

3   BL Add MS 27995 ff. 23–4, Rev. J. Hoadly to 'Billy' Hogarth, n.d.

4   J. Ireland, *Hogarth Illustrated*, 2nd edition, 3 Vols, London, 1793, Vol. I, p. cxx.

5   H. Fielding, *The History of Tom Jones, a foundling*, 6 Vols, London, 1749, Vol. I, p. 56.

6   J. T. Smith, *Nollekens and his Times*, 2 Vols, 2nd edition, London, 1829, Vol. I, p. 128.

7   RCT RCIN 913477, Letter from W. Hogarth to 'T. H.', 21 October 1746 .

8   Fielding, *Tom Jones*, Vol. II, p. 137.

9   Reproduced in facsimile in J. Ireland, *Supplement to Hogarth Illustrated*, 2nd edition, London, 1804, between p. xxiv and p. 2.

Interlude One

1   J. Nichols, *Biographical Anecdotes of William Hogarth*, 3rd edition, London, 1785, pp. 116–17: 'They set out at midnight, at a moment's warning, from the *Bedford Arms* Tavern, with each a shirt in his pocket.' It should be noted that Nichols was not the sole contributor to this biography. As stated George Steevens and Isaac Reed were involved over the three editions, but for simplicity and as the publisher, Nichols is named as the source throughout.

2   F. H. W. Sheppard ed., *Survey of London*, London, 1970, Vol. 36, p. 94. It was destroyed in 1769.

3   Inigo Jones was held in high regard throughout the eighteenth century. Hogarth was to paint a portrait of the architect in 1757–8 using the well-known engraving after Van Dyck, now at the National Maritime Museum BHC2810.

4   Horace Walpole quoting Speaker Onslow in Sheppard ed., *Survey of London*,
     Vol. 36, pp. 98–128.

5   E. Ward, *The Merry Travellers: or, A Trip upon Ten-Toes from Moorfields to
     Bromley An Humourous Poem. Intended as the Wandering Spy*, London, 1724.

6   G. Jacob, *The Poetical Register*, 2nd edition, London, 1723, pp. 225–6, p. 225.

7   E. Ward, *The London Spy Compleat, In Eighteen-Parts*, London, 1703,
     pp. 207–8.

8   S. Butler, *Hudibras. In Three Parts. Written in the Time of the Late Wars ...
     Adorn'd with a new Set of Cuts, Design'd and Engrav'd by Mr. HOGARTH.*,
     London, 1732, pp. 15–16.

9   Nichols, *Biographical Anecdotes*, p. 119.

10   Jacob, *The Poetical Register*, p. 225.

11   For Hogarth and graphic satire see M. Hallett, *The Spectacle of Difference:
     Graphic Satire in the Age of Hogarth*, New Haven & London, 1999.

12   Here it is called 'The Sailor's Ballad' see L. Theobald, *Perseus and Andromeda,
     As it is Performed at the Theatre Royal in Lincoln's-Inn-Fields*, 5th edition,
     London, 1731, pp. 23–4. Hogarth's illustrations are the Frontispiece, *Perseus
     Slaying Medusa* and opposite page 1, *Perseus Rescuing Andromeda* see R.
     Paulson, *Hogarth's Graphic Works*, 2 Vols, New Haven & London, 1965, Vol. I,
     pp. 139–40.

13   Theobald, *Perseus and Andromeda*, p. 23.

14   R. Paulson, *Hogarth*, 3 Vols, Cambridge, 1992–3, Vol. II, pp. 62–3.

15   For Doggett see T. A. Cook & G. Nickalls, *Thomas Doggett Deceased: A
     Famous Comedian*, London, 1908.

16   Doggett's Will 10 September 1721 in Cook & Nickalls, p. 52.

17   Winners include Edward Bishop (1716), John Dolbey of Rotherhithe (1719)
     and C. Gurney of Vauxhall (1721) see Cook & Nickalls, p. 82, p. 90; for Jack
     Broughton see *London Evening Post*, 1–4 August 1730.

18   [W. Hogarth] J. Burke ed., *The Analysis of Beauty with the rejected passages from
     the manuscript drafts and autobiographical notes*, Oxford, 1955, p. 99.

19   Ward, *The London Spy Compleat*, p. 146.

20   Hogarth continues 'whether I had the authority of an antique statue, or basso-
     relievo, for it or not.' Burke, *Analysis of Beauty*, pp. 99–100.

21   Jacob, *The Poetical Register*, Vol. II, pp. 26–30, p. 26.

22   The numerous starlings slowed the flow of the river through the bridge. This
     was particularly problematic in the severe winter months. In 1763 James Boswell
     described the 'rude and terrible appearance' of the river near London Bridge, on
     a mid January morning, as 'a pleasing horror ... partly frozen up, partly covered
     with enormous shoals of floating ice which crashed against each other'. See
     entry for 19 January 1763, F. A. Pottle ed., *Boswell's London Journal 1762–1763*,
     London, 1951, p. 153.

23   D. Defoe, *A Tour thro' the Whole Island of Great Britain*, 3 Vols, London,
     1724–7, Vol. I, Letter II, p. 33.

24   In a letter dated 23 February, 1711/12 Swift provides instructions for boiling
     oysters: 'Take oysters, wash them clean ; that is, wash their shells clean ; then
     put your oysters into an earthen pot, with their hollow sides down, then put

this pot covered into a great kettle with water, and so let them boil. Your oysters are boiled in their own liquor, and not mixed with water.' See J. Hawkesworth, *Letters, written by the late Jonathan Swift, D. D.*, 3 Vols, London, 1766–7, Vol. I, pp. 105–14, p. 113.

25 J. Boswell, *The Life of Samuel Johnson, LL.D.*, 2 Vols, London, 1791, Vol. II, p. 392.

26 *The Craftsman*, 5 December 1730, quoted in Paulson, *Hogarth*, 1992, Vol. I, pp. 202–3.

27 S. Ireland, *Graphic Illustrations of Hogarth*, 2 Vols, London, 1799, Vol. II, p. 3.

28 See H. Myers, 'William Henry Pyne' in *ODNB*, 3 January 2008.

29 W. H. Pyne [Ephraim Hardcastle], *Wine and Walnuts; or, After Dinner Chit-Chat*, 2 Vols, 2nd edition, London, 1824, Vol. I, p. 46.

30 Pyne, *Wine and Walnuts*, Vol. I, p. 57.

31 Pyne, *Wine and Walnuts*, Vol. I, p. 68.

32 Pyne, *Wine and Walnuts*, Vol. I, p. 68.

33 Ward, *The London Spy Compleat*, p. 48.

34 Ward, *The London Spy Compleat*, p. 48.

35 Forrest, f. 1.

36 Ward, *The London Spy Compleat*, pp. 38–9.

37 Forrest, f. 1.

38 Forrest, f. 1; Gostling, p. 21.

39 Forrest, f. 1.

40 Ward, *The London Spy Compleat*, p. 40.

1: Good Child

1 East Smithfield lies to the east of the Tower of London.

2 D. Bindman, 'William Hogarth' in *ODNB*, 21 May 2009.

3 *Grub Street Journal*, 24 November 1737.

4 Ward, *The London Spy Compleat*, p. 229.

5 Ward, *The London Spy Compleat*, pp. 229–30.

6 Ward, *The London Spy Compleat*, pp. 250–51.

7 Ward, *The London Spy Compleat*, p. 229.

8 Burke, *Analysis of Beauty* (Autobiographical Notes), p. 204.

9 Paulson, *Hogarth*, 1992, Vol. I, pp. 18–19.

10 Burke, *Analysis of Beauty* (Autobiographical Notes), p. 204.

11 Burke, *Analysis of Beauty*, p. 48.

12 Burke, *Analysis of Beauty*, p. 49.

13 Burke, *Analysis of Beauty* (Rejected Passages), p. 180.

14 E. Einberg, *William Hogarth: A Complete Catalogue of the Paintings*, New Haven & London, 2016, pp. 74–5.

15 Nichols, *Biographical Anecdotes*, p. 216.

16 Paulson, Hogarth, Vol. I, p. 6. That this marriage was not listed in the register of the Anglican Church of St Bartholomew the Great, suggests that the ceremony had taken place in a dissenting chapel, possibly because of Richard's religious inclinations rather than Anne's. The existence of the Gibbons family's

authorised version of the bible and Book of Common Prayer suggests she was raised an Anglican.

17 Paulson, *Hogarth*, 1992, Vol. I, pp. 5–7.

18 See E. A. Wrigley, R. S. Davies, J. E. Oeppen & R. S. Schofield, *English Population History from Family Reconstruction 1580–1836*, Cambridge, 1997, p. 218.

19 Paulson, *Hogarth*, 1992, Vol. I, p. 23.

20 *GM,* Vol. 95, Pt 1, Jan.–Jun. 1825, p. 516 regarding Westmorland: 'Of SHAP Abbey became tenants at the dissolution, the Hoggerd family, ancestors of the inimitable HOGARTH'.

21 T. Barber, 'Sir James Thornhill [Thornhull]' in *ODNB*, 3 January 2008.

22 Nichols, *Biographical Anecdotes*, pp. 5–6, note †.

23 Nichols, *Biographical Anecdotes*, p. 1, note †.

24 Lee, G., *Remnants of Rhyme by Thomas Hoggart of Troutbeck*, Kendal (printed for George Lee), 1853, p. 22. Thomas is said to have moved from Brampton to the village of Troutbeck, near Windermere, in early adulthood, where he worked as a joiner and farmer, married, through which he may have acquired a small property, had a large family (although only two children survived to adulthood) and died in 1709.

25 Lee, *Remnants of Rhyme*, p. 6.

26 Nichols, *Biographical Anecdotes*, p. 1, note †.

27 Nichols, *Biographical Anecdotes*, pp. 1–2 note †.

28 Lee, *Remnants of Rhyme*, p. 17.

29 Through the Latin for James, Jacobus.

30 The original in the Bodleian Library, Carte MSS 198, f. 9 quoted in E. Corp, *A Court in Exile: The Stuarts in France, 1689–1718*, Cambridge, 2004, p. 184.

31 R. Hogarth, *Thesaurarium Trilingue Publicum: Being an Introduction to English, Latin and Greek*, London, 1689, p. 57.

32 Hogarth, *Thesaurarium Trilingue Publicum,* pp. 63–4.

33 Hogarth, *Thesaurarium Trilingue Publicum,* p. 67.

34 Hogarth, *Thesaurarium Trilingue Publicum,* pp. 68–9.

35 Hogarth, *Thesaurarium Trilingue Publicum,* p. 71.

36 *Post Man and the Historical Account,* 8–11 January 1704.

37 J. E. Chaplin ed., *Benjamin Franklin's Autobiography* (A Norton Critical Edition), New York & London, 2012, p. 43; see also G. Goodwin, *Benjamin Franklin in London*, London, 2016, pp. 20–37.

38 *Evening Post,* 27–30 June 1713, 'Grammar Dispositions, or, An Examination of the Eights Parts of Speech, by Way of Questions and Answer, English and Latin; whereby Children, in a very little Time, will learn to speak and write Latin: To which is added a Chronological Table of Men and Things of great Note, from the Beginning of the World to the Year of Christ 1640 and downwards, by Richard Hogarth, Schoolmaster, All printed for W. Taylor at the Ship in Pater-Noster-Row'. See also Nichols, *Biographical Anecdotes*, p. 5.

39 Nichols, *Biographical Anecdotes*, p. 63, illustrated as a frontispiece.

40 Nichols, *Biographical Anecdotes*, p. 64. Among the manuscripts associated with Hogarth at the British Library, there is a curious item, professing to

be a 'Fragment from old Greek author' (BL Add MS 27995 f. 2) which may have been sent to Hogarth by his friend Rev. James Townley for use within *The Analysis of Beauty*. The document states: 'There was an antient Oracle delivered at Delphos, which says, "That the Source of Beauty should never be again rightly discovered, till a person should arise, whose Name was perfectly included in the Name of Pythagoras; which Person should again restore the antient Principle upon which all Beauty is founded." [Greek for 'Pythagoras'] Pythagoras [Greek for 'Hogarth'] Hogarth.' At the very least, the mature William Hogarth would have enjoyed this witty association between himself and Pythagoras, ancient philosopher and mathematician, immensely.

41 'Sold by Mrs. Anne Hogarth next Door to the Ship in Black and White Court, Old-Bailey' see *Daily Courant*, 13 January 1709 .

42 P. Rogers, 'Defoe in the Fleet Prison' in *The Review of English Studies*, Vol. 22, No.88 (Nov. 1971), pp. 451–5.

43 See the trial of John Restow, sentenced to death for 'deception' on 16 May 1711, *Old Bailey Proceedings Online* (t17110516-38).

44 Burke, *Analysis of Beauty* (Autobiographical Notes), pp. 204–5.

45 Nichols, *Biographical Anecdotes*, p. 6; *British Mercury*, 14 October 1713.

46 Burke, *Analysis of Beauty* (Autobiographical Notes), p. 204.

47 Paulson, *Hogarth*, 1992, Vol. I, p. 8.

48 Burke, *Analysis of Beauty* (Autobiographical Notes), p. 204.

49 Burke, *Analysis of Beauty* (Autobiographical Notes), p. 204.

50 A. Pope, *The Dunciad*, London, 1729, p. 81.

51 Burke, *Analysis of Beauty* (Autobiographical Notes), p. 205.

52 Burke, *Analysis of Beauty* (Autobiographical Notes), p. 201.

53 Nichols, *Biographical Anecdotes*, p. 6.

54 W. A. Littledale ed., *The Registers of Christ Church, Newgate, 1538 to 1754*, London, 1895, p. 212.

55 See 'Ellis Gamble' www.britishmuseum.org/collection/term/BIOG163066.

56 J. Strypes, *A Survey of the Cities of London and Westminster*, 2 Vols, London, 1720, Book 6, Chapter 5, p. 68.

57 For Highmore see J. Riding, *Joseph Highmore 1692–1780*, 2 Vols, Doctoral Thesis, University of York, 2012; and J. Riding, *Basic Instincts: Love, Passion and Violence in the Art of Joseph Highmore*, London, 2017.

58 Burke, *Analysis of Beauty* (Autobiographical Notes), p. 206.

59 Smith, *Nollekens*, Vol. II, p. 345. Smith must be referring to Old Nollekens, given Joseph Nollekens, the son, was not born until 1733.

60 See S. Ireland, *Graphic Illustrations of Hogarth*, London, 1794, pp. 22–3.

61 With reference to the events in Calais, summer 1748 Hogarth recalls 'as I was sauntering about'. Burke, *Analysis of Beauty* (Autobiographical Notes), p. 228.

62 Nichols, *Biographical Anecdotes*, p. 8.

63 Nichols, *Biographical Anecdotes*, p. 7.

64 Nichols, *Biographical Anecdotes*, p. 15.

65 Pyne, *Wine and Walnuts*, Vol. I, p. 268.

66 Nichols, *Biographical Anecdotes*, p. 63.

67 For Richardson see C. Gibson-Wood, *Jonathan Richardson: Art Theorist of the English Enlightenment*, New Haven & London, 2000.

68 *Public Advertiser*, 8 December 1764 quoted by Paulson, *Hogarth*, 1992, Vol. I, p. 63, where he discusses this event. Nichols, less dramatically, states Hogarth was 'distressed to raise so trifling a sum', although not so trifling in the 1720s. See also Paulson, *Hogarth*, 1992, Vol. I, pp. 63–4.

69 Nichols, *Biographical Anecdotes*, pp. 8–9.

70 Nichols, *Biographical Anecdotes*, pp. 8–9.

71 Burke, *Analysis of Beauty* (Autobiographical Notes), p. 201.

72 Burke, *Analysis of Beauty* (Rejected Passages), p. 177.

73 Burke, *Analysis of Beauty*, p. 52.

74 Burke, *Analysis of Beauty*, p. 53.

75 Burke, *Analysis of Beauty*, p. 82.

76 Burke, *Analysis of Beauty* (Rejected Passages), p. 187.

77 Burke, *Analysis of Beauty* (Autobiographical Notes), p. 202.

78 Chaplin ed., *Benjamin Franklin's Autobiography*, p. 42.

79 Chaplin ed., *Benjamin Franklin's Autobiography*, p. 40.

80 Chaplin ed., *Benjamin Franklin's Autobiography*, pp. 43–55.

81 Chaplin ed., *Benjamin Franklin's Autobiography*, p. 45.

82 Chaplin ed., *Benjamin Franklin's Autobiography*, p. 45.

83 Chaplin ed., *Benjamin Franklin's Autobiography*, pp. 45–6.

84 Chaplin ed., *Benjamin Franklin's Autobiography*, p. 46.

85 Examples include BM 1850,0525.7 and RCIN 811305.

86 Pyne, *Wine and Walnuts*, Vol. I, p. 230 note *.

87 Paulson, *Hogarth*, 1992, Vol. I, p. 52, 'he was back living with his mother "near the Black Bull" in Long Lane'.

88 Nichols, *Biographical Anecdotes*, p. 8.

89 Nichols, *Biographical Anecdotes*, p. 9.

90 Nichols, *Biographical Anecdotes*, p. 8.

91 Nichols, *Biographical Anecdotes*, p. 11.

92 See T. Clayton 'Overton family' in *ODNB*, 23 September 2004; Paulson, *Hogarth's Graphic Works*, Vol. I, pp. 5–6.

93 Chaplin ed., *Benjamin Franklin's Autobiography*, p. 47.

94 Burke, *Analysis of Beauty* (Autobiographical Notes), p. 215.

95 The Metropolitan Museum of Art, New York, has the copper plates for *Beer Street* and *Gin Lane*.

Interlude Two

1 N. Bailey, *Dictionarium Britannicum: Or a more Compleat Universal Etymological English Dictionary*, London, 1730, 'TILT-*Boat*' n.p.

2 S. Denne & W. Shrubsole, *History and Antiquities of Rochester and Its Environs*, Rochester, 1772, pp. 299–300.

3 [Anon.], *The Constitutions of the Company of Watermen and Lightermen*, London, 1730, p. 74.

4 Forrest, f. 17.

5   A. S. Marks, 'Hogarth's Mackinen Children' in *The British Art Journal*, Vol. IX, No.1 (Spring 2008), pp. 38–56, p. 39.

6   H. Sloane, *A Voyage to the Islands Madera, Barbados ... and Jamaica*, 2 Vols, London, 1707. See also A. MacGregor, 'Sir Hans Sloane' in *ODNB*, 23 September 2004.

7   For Tothall see Nichols, *Biographical Anecdotes*, pp. 116–18 note †; for the foundation of the British Museum see S. O'Connell, *London 1753*, London, 2003.

8   Nichols, *Biographical Anecdotes*, pp. 116–17 note †.

9   See Einberg, *Hogarth*, 2016, p. 134.

10   Bulstrode, via the Reverend Lyon of St Mary's Dover (in a letter to Nichols) states that Tothall bought a cottage in West Langdon near the port and 'Digging in a very small garden belonging to this cottage, he had the good fortune to find some valuable fossils; which to a man of taste was a singular treasure. He died *January 9, 1768*, at the age of 70 (possessed of about 1500l.), and was buried at *St. Mary's Church* at *Dover.*' The sale of Tothall's collection took place the following year, see Nichols, *Biographical Anecdotes*, p. 118.

11   A. S. Wensinger trans. & ed., *Hogarth on High Life: The Marriage à la Mode Series from Georg Christoph Lichtenberg's Commentaries*, Middleton, 1970, pp. 41–2.

12   Burke, *Analysis of Beauty* (Autobiographical Notes), p. 227.

13   When Steele visited it was based in Danvers Street.

14   Chaplin ed., *Benjamin Franklin's Autobiography*, p. 48 'went to Chelsea by Water to see ... Don Saltero's Curiosities'.

15   Pyne recalls such a donation, a carved and painted walking-cane handle, owned by 'Uncle Zachary', who 'was universally acknowledged to be as deeply skilled in *cane-ology* as any one'. The cane handle in question was known as a 'Funny Joe', modelled on 'a humourist, a half-witted fellow' who habitually sat on the carts taking the condemned to Tyburn. Salter was very keen to add Uncle Zachary's 'Funny Joe' to his collection, but his offer was refused. However, as a compromise, a cast was taken, which, according to Pyne, Hogarth painted, and this copy was sent to Chelsea. Pyne states that the cast was taken by Roubiliac, who is known to have arrived in England several years after Salter's death. Pyne, *Wine and Walnuts*, Vol. I, pp. 242–4.

16   R. Steele, *The Tatler*, No.34, 25–8 June 1709.

17   W. W. Wroth revised by P. E. Kell, 'James Salter [called Don Saltero]' in *ODNB*, 23 September 2004.

18   [Anon.], *A Catalogue of the Rarities to be seen at Don Saltero's Coffee-House in Chelsea*, London, 1738.

19   Burke, *Analysis of Beauty* (Rejected Passages), pp. 173–4.

20   Paulson, *Hogarth's Graphic Works*, Vol. I, pp. 99–102.

21   Franklin brought some 'curiosities' with him from America, including 'a Purse made of the Asbestos, which purifies by Fire', which he sold to Hans Sloane ('for which he paid me handsomely') see Chaplin ed., *Benjamin Franklin's Autobiography*, p. 44.

2: Mock King

1   Burke, *Analysis of Beauty* (Autobiographical Notes), p. 205.
2   M. Kitson, 'Hogarth's "Apology for Painters"' in *Walpole Society*, Oxford, Vol. 41, 1966–8, pp. 46–111, p. 93.
3   Kitson, *Hogarth's Apology for Painters*, p. 93.
4   George Vertue Notebooks I–VI, *Walpole Society*, Oxford, 1929–50, III, p. 11.
5   I. Bignamini, 'George Vertue, Art Historian and Art Institutions in London, 1689–1768: A Study of Clubs and Academies' in *Walpole Society*, Oxford, Vol. 54, 1988, pp. 1–148, p. 86. Bignamini suggests that Hogarth's nude at the British Museum was executed at the St Martin's Lane Academy of 1720, see p. 86.
6   B. Victor, *A Session of Painters*, London, 1725; see also J. Riding, '"A Session of Painters": Legacy, Succession, and the Prospects for British Portraiture after Kneller' in M. Hallett, N. Llewellyn & M. Myrone eds., *Court, Country, City: British Art and Architecture, 1660–1735*, New Haven & London, 2016, pp. 353–79.
7   Vertue, III, p. 98.
8   Kitson, *Hogarth's Apology for Painters*, p. 93.
9   Vertue, III, p. 20; Bignamini, *George Vertue*, p. 83.
10   Vertue, III, p. 20.
11   BM 1889,0706.63 to 74, set of tin-glazed earthenware Zodiac plates, painted by Sir James Thornhill 1711; K. Fremantle ed., *Sir James Thornhill's Sketch-Book Travel Journal of 1711: A visit to East Anglia and the Low Countries*, 2 Vols, Utrecht, 1975.
12   Vertue, I, p. 39.
13   *GM*, Vol. 86, Pt 1, April 1816, p. 302; see also R. Johns, '"An Air of Grandeur & Modesty": James Thornhill's Painting in the Dome of St. Paul's Cathedral' in *Eighteenth Century Studies*, Vol. 42, No. 4, 2009, pp. 501–527.
14   Sir James Thornhill, 'A Hue and Cry after Four of the King's Liege Subjects, who were lately suppos'd to be seen at Roystone in Hertfordshire 18 March 1720/1' in *Wren Society*, Vol. 17, 1940, pp. 12–13.
15   Thornhill, 'A Hue and Cry', p. 12.
16   Bignamini, *George Vertue*, p. 89.
17   J. Harris, 'William Kent' in *ODNB*, 24 May 2007.
18   J. Egerton, 'John Ellys' in *ODNB*, 23 September 2004.
19   Respectively *Nature and Her Followers* (*c.*1615) purchased by Thornhill in 1716/17 now at Kelvingrove Art Gallery and Museum and *Tancred and Erminia* (*c.*1634) purchased by Thornhill in 1717, now at the Barber Institute of Fine Arts, see Editorial, 'Sir James Thornhill's Collection' in *The Burlington Magazine*, June 1943, Vol. 82, No. 483, June 1943, pp. 133–7, p. 134.
20   Vertue, III, p. 73.
21   See T. Friedman, 'James Gibbs' in *ODNB*, 3 January 2008.
22   Ellis was now in partnership with the illustrious goldsmith Paul de Lamerie (1688–1751).
23   BM Cc,1.215 William Hogarth, *Ellis Gamble's Shop Card*, etching and engraving, 1723–33.

24   R. D. Hume, 'The Value of Money in eighteenth century England' in *Huntington Library Quarterly*, Vol. 77, No.4, December 2014, pp. 373–416, p. 373.

25   Burke, *Analysis of Beauty* (Autobiographical Notes), p. 205. See also Paulson, *Hogarth's Graphic Works*, 1965, Vol. I, p. 6 and p. 103.

26   Burke, *Analysis of Beauty* (Autobiographical Notes), p. 205.

27   In a fitting coda to the affair, John Nichols recalled that the altarpiece 'was for some years one of the ornaments of the music-room at *The Crown and Anchor* tavern in the *Strand*'. Nichols, *Biographical Anecdotes*, p. 138.

28   See Paulson, *Hogarth's Graphic Works*, 1965, Vol. I, p. 107; M. Hallett & C. Riding, *Hogarth*, London, 2007, p. 61.

29   J. Anderson, *The Constitutions of the Free-Masons*, London, 1723, published by order of the Duke of Wharton 'the present Right Worshipful GRAND-MASTER' and dedicated to the Duke of Montagu.

30   Burke, *Analysis of Beauty*, p. 136.

31   Paulson, *Hogarth's Graphic Works*, 1965, Vol. I, pp. 115–25.

32   *Daily Post*, 6 October 1725.

33   *Daily Post*, 25 February 1726.

34   M. G. H. Pittock, 'Allan Ramsay' in *ODNB*, 27 May 2010.

35   Ramsay certainly did this for his friend Sir John Clerk of Penicuik.

36   BM S,2.6 William Hogarth, *Frontispiece and its Explanation for Hudibras*, etching and engraving, 1726.

37   Nichols, *Biographical Anecdotes*, p. 10.

38   The outdoor version (Fizwilliam Museum, Cambridge) and indoor (The J. Paul Getty Musuem, Los Angeles) both painted *c.*1730–31. Chaplin ed., *Benjamin Franklin's Autobiography*, pp. 44–5.

39   B. Mandeville, *An Enquiry into the causes of the frequent executions at Tyburn*, London, 1725, p. 13 .

40   Mandeville, *Enquiry*, pp. 10–11.

41   Mandeville, *Enquiry*, pp. 20–21.

42   Mandeville, *Enquiry*, pp. 22–3.

43   J. Swift, *Works of J[onathan] S[wift ... Containing the Author's POETICAL WORKS*, 6 Vols, Dublin, 1735–8, Vol. II (1735), pp. 298–9.

44   Mandeville, *Enquiry*, p. 26.

45   J. Donne, *Devotions Upon Emergent Occasions*, London, 1624, (Meditation 17), pp. 415–16.

46   Mandeville, *Enquiry*, p. 16.

47   [D. Defoe], *A Narrative of all the Robberies, Escapes, &c. of John Sheppard : Giving an Exact Description of the manner of his wonderful Escape from the CASTLE in Newgate*, 2nd edition, London, 1724 .

48   Defoe, *John Sheppard*, p. 29.

49   Defoe, *John Sheppard*, p. 30.

50   *The British Journal*, 28 November 1724.

51   Vertue, IV, p. 29.

52   Vertue, I, p. 28.

53   Nichols, *Biographical Anecdotes*, p. 24.

54 Letter CCCCIX Dr Swift to Mr Gay, Dublin 23 November 1727 in J. Hawkesworth ed., *The Works of Jonathan Swift, D.D.*, 18 Vols, London, 1784, Vol. XVI, pp. 92–5, p. 95.

55 J. Swift, *The Intelligencer*, No 3, [May 1728], London, 1729, pp. 15–25, pp. 17–18.

56 Swift, *The Intelligencer*, pp. 21–2.

57 Swift, *The Intelligencer*, p. 25.

58 M. C. Battestin, 'Henry Fielding' in *ODNB*, 23 September 2004.

59 H. Fielding, *Tragedy of Tragedies*, London, 1731.

Interlude Three

1 No5450 Samuel Scott, *A Morning, with a View of Cuckold's Point*, oil on canvas, *c.*1750–1760, Tate.

2 F35 F37 F40 F45 F46 F48 Samuel Scott and George Lambert, oil on canvasses, *c.*1731, British Library.

3 No1224 Thomas Hudson, *Samuel Scott, the Marine Painter*, oil on canvas, *c.*1731–3, Tate.

4 See the popular medley, Thomas D'Urfey's *Wit and Mirth: Or, Pills to Purge Melancholy* published between 1698 and 1720, by 1720 it encompassed 6 volumes and over 1,000 songs and poems. Also Charles Mitchell, *Hogarth's Peregrination*, Oxford, 1952, p. 49 .

5 D'Urfey, *Wit and Mirth: Or, Pills to purge melancholy*, Vol. I, p. 26.

6 J. Brand, *Observations on Popular Antiquities*, Newcastle upon Tyne, 1777, p. 397.

7 Unknown, *Cuckolds Haven*, London, 1638, BL C.20.f. 7.46-47.

8 G. Ogle, *The Canterbury Tales of Chaucer. Modernis'd by several Hands*, 3 Vols, London, 1741, Vol. I, p. 30. This is a compilation of extant modernisations of the various elements of *The Canterbury Tales*, incomplete at George Ogle's death.

9 A. Pope & W. Warburton eds, *The Works of Shakespear: in Eight Volumes*, London, 1747, Vol. II, p. 286.

10 Ogle, *Canterbury Tales of Chaucer*, Vol. I, p. 186. See also B. Kalter, *Modern Antiques: The Material Past in England 1660–1780*, 2012, p. 86.

11 E. Ward, *A Frolick to Horn-Fair with a Walk from Cuckold's-Point Thro' Deptford and Greenwich*, London, 1700, p. 12.

12 M. Lincoln, *British Pirates and Society, 1680–1730*, Farnham, 2014, pp. 23–46.

13 *Weekly Journal or British Gazetteer*, 2 September 1721; [D. Defoe], *Captain Charles Johnson's General History of Pyrates*, London, 1724, pp. 157–73.

14 Lincoln, *British Pirates*, p. 34.

15 Trusler, *Hogarth Moralized*, p. 81 'the place, in the river, which they have just passed, that of Cuckold's Point'.

16 Forrest, f. 1; Gostling, p. 22.

17 M. Cole, *The Lady's Complete Guide*, London, 1789, p. 473.

18 J. Nott, *The Cook's and Confectioner's Dictionary*, London, 1723, BI no.86 'To make Biskets'.

19 Defoe, *A Tour*, Vol. I, Letter II, pp. 1–2.

20 Defoe, *A Tour*, Vol. I, Letter II, p. 2.

21   J. Thornhill, *An Explanation of the Painting in the Royal Hospital at Greenwich by Sir James Thornhill*, London, n.d., p. 5.

22   Thornhill, *An Explanation*, p. 14.

23   Thornhill, *An Explanation*, p. 16.

3 : Moral Subject

1   See D. Bindman 'William Hogarth' in *ODNB*, 21 May 2009 and C. S. Martinez 'Jane Hogarth' in *ODNB*, 9 July 2020. 'We find by Willis's Thesaurus of 1763, and by Lysons, that the Sheldon church was dedicated to St James.' W. Robins, *Paddington: Past and Present*, London, 1853, p. 134; D. Lysons, *The Environs of London: Volume 3, County of Middlesex*, London, 'Paddington' pp. 328–41, 'the former church, which was dedicated to St. James' built by Sir Joseph Sheldon, Lord Mayor of London around 1678.'

2   Fielding, *Tom Jones*, Vol. I, pp. 62–3.

3   Nichols, *Biographical Anecdotes*, p. 249.

4   *London Evening Post*, 1–3 April 1729.

5   Nichols, *Biographical Anecdotes*, p. 217. Also Trusler, *Hogarth Moralized*, p. 29.

6   See Einberg, *Hogarth*, 2016, p. 111.

7   Einberg, *Hogarth*, 2016, pp. 144–6.

8   Nichols, *Biographical Anecdotes*, p. 29: 'Soon after his marriage, *Hogarth* had summer-lodgings at *South-Lambeth*'.

9   RCT RCIN 913498 *Hogarth's lodging in South Lambeth*.

10   Tyers had acquired the lease on Spring Gardens in 1728, aged just twenty-one.

11   Now in the British Museum, 1913,0515.1.

12   Vertue, III, p. 38.

13   Vertue, III, p. 40.

14   Vertue, III, p. 41.

15   Vertue, III, p. 41.

16   H. Fielding, *The Historical Register, For the Year 1736*, London, 1737, pp. 10–11.

17   Vertue, III, p. 41.

18   Burke, *Analysis of Beauty* (Autobiographical Notes), pp. 215–16.

19   H. Walpole, *Anecdotes of Painting in England; With some account of the principal Artists*, 4 Vols, Strawberry Hill, 1762–71, Vol. IV, p. 75.

20   See Einberg, *Hogarth*, 2016: pp. 47–9; pp. 62–3; pp. 100–1; pp. 146–7; pp. 24–5.

21   Nichols, *Biographical Anecdotes*, p. 69.

22   Vertue, III, p. 50.

23   Identified in Nichols, *Biographical Anecdotes*, p. 69.

24   Vertue, III, p. 50.

25   BL Add MS 27995 f. 1, 'Account taken January the first 1731 of all ye Pictures that remain unfinishd'.

26   Private Collection see Einberg, *Hogarth*, 2016, pp. 91–3.

27   Mary Pendarves to Ann Granville, 13 July 1731 in A. Hall, Baroness Llanover ed., *The Autobiography and Correspondence of Mary Granville, Mrs. Delany*, 3 Vols, London, 1861, Vol. I, pp. 282–5, p. 283.

28 Hall ed., *Autobiography & Correspondence of Mary Granville*, 2nd series, London, 1862, Vol. I, p. 469.

29 Hall ed., *Autobiography & Correspondence of Mary Granville*, 2nd series, London, 1862, Vol. II, p. 215.

30 Quoted in R. Hayden, *Mrs. Delany: Her Life and Her Flowers*, 2nd ed, London, 2000, p. 155; M. Laird & A. Weisberg-Roberts, *Mrs. Delany & her Circle*, Newhaven & London, 2009, p. 234, n.2.

31 BL Add MS 2795 f. 1 'The Committy of the house of commons ... Sir Archibald Grant ... Nov 5th 1729' now in the National Portrait Gallery.

32 The Fitzwilliam Museum.

33 The prime version was at Clandon House, National Trust for England (NT 1441463), with another version in the Parliamentary Art Collection, WOA 354.

34 Vertue, III, p. 35. See also Barber, 'Sir James Thornhill', *ODNB*.

35 Group sketches at the Royal Collection (RCIN 401358) and National Gallery of Ireland (NGI.126) respectively; the Cumberland portrait at the Yale Center for British Art (B1977.14.59).

36 Vertue, III, p. 68.

37 *London Journal*, 17 November 1733.

38 The outdoor version (Fitzwilliam Musuem) and indoor (The J. Paul Getty Museum) both painted *c.* 1730–31. The Watteau is now in the National Gallery of Art, Washington.

39 *Jane Hogarth's sale catalogue*, 24 April 1790, Lugt 4574, 1790-04-24 p. 5, lot 30.

40 Vertue, VI, p. 193.

41 BM 1853,1210.540.

42 Burke, *Analysis of Beauty* (Autobiographical Notes), p. 216.

43 *The Sleeping Congregation* of 1728 was not engraved until 1736.

44 Vertue, III, p. 58.

45 Chaplin ed., *Benjamin Franklin's Autobiography,* p. 26.

46 BM Z,1.3, W. Hogarth, *A harlot in her garret*, 1731 (?), red and black chalk.

47 Vertue, III, p. 58.

48 Nichols, *Biographical Anecdotes*, p. 34.

49 *Old Bailey Proceedings Online*, 28 February 1730 'Receiv'd Sentence of Death 10' including Francis Hackabout (t17300228-71) and Francis Charteris (t17300228-69).

50 *Fog's Weekly Journal*, 14 March 1730.

51 Nichols, *Biographical Anecdotes*, p. 189.

52 Vertue, III, p. 53.

53 The source was Christopher Tillotson, a chief clerk of the Treasury and at the time Under-Secretary of State.

54 Nichols, *Biographical Anecdotes*, pp. 29–32. John Stagg, bookseller in London, Westminster Hall 1716?–1746 (died 1746?), *General Advertiser* 20–27 September 1746 'Yesterday Morning died at his House in Old Palace-yard, Westminster, after a long and tedious Indisposition, in the 52d Year of his Age, Mr. John Stagg, who has been near 30 Years an eminent Bookseller in Westminster Hall.' For their battles see Pyne, *Wine and Walnuts*, Vol. II, pp. 14–20.

55 Vertue, III, p. 58.

56 *Weekly Register*, 3 June 1732.

57 Nichols, *Biographical Anecdotes*, p. 32.

58 BM 1891,0713.519 and Art Institute Chicago 1947.144.

59 *Country Journal or The Craftsman*, 1 July 1732. For Martha Gamble see M. Volmert & D. Bucher, *European Fans in the seventeenth and eighteenth centuries: Images, Accessories, and Instruments of Gesture*, Berlin/Boston, 2020, pp. 214–16.

60 *London Evening Post*, 20–23 January 1733. Martha also sold wedding favours and watch papers see *Country Journal or The Craftsman*, 3 November 1733 and published a fan design based Hogarth's *Henry VIII and Anne Boleyn* in 1743, BM 1891,0713.409.

61 Nichols, *Biographical Anecdotes*, p. 33 note *.

62 'One morning early, Mrs. *Hogarth* undertook to convey several of them into his drawing-room. When he arose, he enquired from whence they came ; and being told ... cried out, "Very well ; the man who can furnish representations like these, can also maintain a wife without a portion."' Nichols, *Biographical Anecdotes*, p. 27.

63 Nichols, *Biographical Anecdotes*, p. 27.

64 Vertue, III, p. 58.

65 See Martinez, 'Jane Hogarth', *ODNB*.

66 *London Evening Post*, 16–18 May 1732.

67 Advertisement in the *Daily Post*, 26 April 1732. And then just a week later 'This Day is publish'd, The Second Edition, with Additions, particularly an Epistle to the Ingenious Mr. Hogarth, of The Harlot's Progress' *Daily Post*, 4 May 1732.

68 For the full story see K. Harvey, *The Impostress Rabbit Breeder: Mary Toft and Eighteenth-Century England*, Oxford, 2020 .

69 *Old Bailey Proceedings Online*, trial of Sarah Malcolm, 21 February 1733 (t17330221-52).

70 *Old Bailey Proceedings Online*, trial of Sarah Malcolm, 21 February 1733 (t17330221-52).

71 *Old Bailey Proceedings Online*, trial of Sarah Malcolm, 21 February 1733 (t17330221-52); *GM*, Vol. 3, February 1733, p. 97; Nichols, *Biographical Anecdotes*, pp. 172–3.

72 *The Craftsman or Country Journal* on 10 March 1732/3.

73 *GM*, Vol. 3, March 1733, p. 153. The report includes a rough woodcut after Hogarth's engraved portrait.

74 *Universal Spectator and Weekly Journal*, Saturday 10 March 1733.

75 J. Nichols & G. Steevens, *The Genuine Works of William Hogarth*, 3 Vols, London, 1808–17, Vol. II, p. 81.

76 Burke, *Analysis of Beauty*, p. 136.

77 Burke, *Analysis of Beauty*, p. 137.

78 Nichols, *Biographical Anecdotes*, p. 102.

79 Nichols, *Biographical Anecdotes*, pp. 17–18.

80 Nichols, *Biographical Anecdotes*, 1781, p. 68 quoted in Einberg, *Hogarth*, 2016, p. 144.

81 Elizabeth Einberg tentatively suggests that a portrait of an unknown man dated

1741 (Dulwich Picture Gallery) may be Ranby, see Einberg, *Hogarth*, 2016, p. 231.

82 J. Croker ed. John, Lord Hervey, *Memoirs of the reign of George the second*, 2 Vols, London, 1848, Vol. II, p. 526.

83 *London Journal*, 22 December 1733.

84 *Country Journal or The Craftsman*, 24 May 1735.

85 *London Daily Post and General Advertiser*, 30 June 1735.

86 Nichols, *Biographical Anecdotes*, p. 37 note *.

87 J. B. le Blanc, 'Letter XXIII To the Abbe du Bos; On the state of painting and sculpture in England' in *Letters on the English and French Nations*, London, 1747, pp. 155–63, p. 158.

88 Le Blanc, pp. 161–2.

89 Le Blanc, pp. 162–3.

90 'Description of the Legion Club' in J. Hawkesworth, *The Works of Dr. Jonathan Swift*, 17 Vols, London, 1765, Vol. VII, pp. 223–32, p. 231.

91 BL Add MS 27995 f. 4, G. Faulkner to W. Hogarth, Dublin 15 November 1740. The prints are certainly, according to an advertisement in the *London Daily Post and General Advertiser* of 24 November 1740, a revised state of *The Distressed Poet* (2nd state published March 1736/7, the third as 'The Distrest Poet' issued December 1740) its companion 'The Provok'd Musician', becoming *The Enraged Musician* (November 1741) and third to complete the set, but abandoned, 'on Painting'.

92 *General Evening Post*, 12–14 June 1735.

93 Elizabeth Galloway was found not guilty, see *Old Bailey Proceedings Online*, 2 July 1735 (t17350702-42).

94 *Weekly Miscellanies*, 18 May 1734.

95 Vertue, III, p. 70.

Interlude Four

1 'To encourage the others', that is other commanding officers.

2 Forrest, f. 1.

3 Forrest, f. 1; Gostling, p. 22.

4 Forrest, f. 1; Gostling, p. 22.

5 R. T. Wilson, *Life of General Sir Robert Wilson*, 2 vols, London, 1862, Vol. 1, p. 32.

6 Defoe, *A Tour*, Vol. I, Letter II, p. 10.

7 *OED* 'unlucky' 1.

8 'But as Virtue Surmounts all Obstacle's', Forrest, f. 1.

9 For one version see BL Harley 6798, f. 87.

10 Defoe, *A Tour*, Vol. I, Letter I, p. 8.

11 Gostling, p. 23; Forrest, f. 1.

12 Forrest, f. 1.

13 Defoe, *A Tour*, Vol. I, Letter II, pp. 13–14. The Horn Fair is mentioned on p. 6.

14 E. Hasted, *The History and Topographical Survey of Kent*, 6 Vols, Canterbury, 1797–8, Vol. I, p. 273. What we now call the North Sea was, in the eighteenth

century, known as the German sea or ocean. The name changed in the early
twentieth century due to hostilities between Britain and Germany.

15   The £5,000 drawn down via the act had been bolstered by donations of £2,000
from the new king, George II, and £500 from his consort, Queen Caroline.

16   See A. T. Vaughan, 'Pocahontas [Matoaka, Amonute]' in *ODNB*, 1 September
2017.

17   Forrest, f. 1; Gostling, p. 23.

18   Gostling, p. 23.

19   Forrest, f. 2.

20   Burke, *Analysis of Beauty* (Autobiographical Notes), p. 226.

21   See E. Cruickshanks, *Political Untouchables: The Tories and the '45*, London,
1979 and P. K. Monod, *Jacobitism and the English people, 1688–1788*,
Cambridge, 1993.

22   Forrest, f. 2.

23   Defoe, *A Tour*, Vol. I, Letter II, p. 20.

24   Indeed, Defoe introduces his *Tour* by declaring '*If* Antiquity *takes with you,
tho' the looking back into remote Things is studiously avoided, yet it is not wholly
omitted, nor any useful Observations neglected ; the learned Writers on the Subject
of Antiquity in* Great Britain *have so well discharg'd themselves, that we can never
over-value their Labours*'. Defoe, *A Tour*, Vol. I, Preface, p. iv.

25   Forrest, f. 2.

26   Forrest, f. 2; Denne & Shrubsole, *Rochester*, pp. 215–19.

27   S. Barter Bailey, 'Richard Watts' in *ODNB*, 3 January 2008.

28   The story was certainly believed at the time of *The Peregrination*, for when a
memorial was erected in 1736 to Richard Watts, in the cathedral where he is
buried, it declared that his mansion on Bolly Hill was 'call'd SATIS, so named
by Q. ELIZABETH of glorious memory'. The memorial includes a delightfully
grave-faced bust of Watts with full beard.

29   Forrest, f. 2.

30   *OED* 'proctor' 6.

31   Denne & Shrubsole, *Rochester*, p. 216.

32   *The Holy Bible*, London, 1743, Proverbs 14:21.

4: History Maker

1   Burke, *Analysis of Beauty* (Autobiographical Notes), p. 202.

2   A. Félibien, *Seven conferences held in the King of France's cabinet of paintings*,
London, 1740, pp. xxvii–xxviii.

3   Burke, *Analysis of Beauty* (Autobiographical Notes), p. 203.

4   For further on this see J. B. Shipley, 'Ralph. Ellys, Hogarth, and Fielding: The
Cabal Against Jacopo Amigoni' in *Eighteenth-Century Studies*, Vol. 1, No.4
(Summer, 1968), pp. 313–33.

5   Thornhill, 'A Hue and Cry', p. 12.

6   Quoted in Friedman, 'James Gibbs' in *ODNB*, 3 January 2008.

7   *General Evening Post*, 15–17 July 1735.

8   Burke, *Analysis of Beauty* (Autobiographical Notes), p. 202.

9   *The Holy Bible*, London, 1743, the Gospel of St Luke, Chap. 10, Verse 37.

10　Burke, *Analysis of Beauty* (Autobiographical Notes), pp. 202–3.

11　As well as Gibbs' backing, Hogarth may also have been supported by John Lloyd, bursar of the hospital, whose son Hogarth painted in 1738 and who would have been responsible for officially commissioning the artist.

12　Quoted in Paulson, *Hogarth*, 1992, II, p. 78.

13　Egerton, 'John Ellys' *ODNB*.

14　See Einberg, *Hogarth*, 2016, pp. 152–3. The sketch is in the Royal Collection, RCIN 913482.

15　Nichols, *Biographical Anecdotes*, p. 289.

16　Paulson, *Hogarth,* 1992, Vol. II, p. 87.

17　Courtesans as life models is not a new concept, but its inclusion by Nichols (a severe critic of what he presumes is Hogarth's moral code) seems designed to add weight to the idea that Hogarth, specifically, was incapable of elevated art. The statement that William and Ebenezer were intimately acquainted with Nell when they were young men, apparently before marriage, seems intended to suggest a sexual relationship, or, at the very least, to leave the potential hanging in the air.

18　One such sketch is now at Manchester Art Gallery, 1955.126.

19　Nichols, *Biographical Anecdotes*, p. 405.

20　Burke, *Analysis of Beauty*, pp. 109–10.

21　George Lambert was buried in St Paul's church. For Lambert's biography see E. Einberg, 'George Lambert' in *ODNB*, 19 May 2011.

22　Named as a member of the Fountain Lodge in the Strand in 1723; see Einberg, 'George Lambert' *ODNB*.

23　Quoted in Gibson-Wood, *Richardson*, p. 26.

24　In another parallel with Hogarth, Richardson's daughter, Mary, had married his apprentice, Thomas Hudson (Sam Scott's portraitist) in around 1724, a situation to which her father was never reconciled.

25　Pyne, *Wine and Walnuts*, Vol. I, p. 108.

26　Pyne, *Wine and Walnuts*, Vol. I, pp. 108–9.

27　A print professing to be by Hogarth is in the British Museum 1868,0808.3569.

28　S. Ireland, *Graphic Illustrations of Hogarth*, pp. 119–20.

29　Burke, *Analysis of Beauty*, p. 134.

30　Pyne, *Wine and Walnuts*, Vol. I, pp. 113–21.

31　*OED* 'catch' n.2, 3.

32　R. Stephens, 'Sublime Society of Beefsteaks' in *ODNB*, 19 May 2011.

33　Vertue, III, p. 78.

34　See *Analysis of Beauty Plate 2*, 'The Country Dance'.

35　The painting and sketch are now in the Tate: T00076 *The Good Samaritan*, 1744; and T04213.

36　Nichols & Steevens, *Genuine Works*, Vol. II, p. 263.

37　With many thanks to Will Palin, Chief Executive of Barts Heritage Trust, for providing access to the stairs and Great Hall, and for his thoughts on Hogarth's involvement with the hospital.

38　TA Highmore Gift 866/2/1, Joseph Highmore, *Paris Journal*, 26r–26v. For Highmore's 1734 trip see J. Riding, 'An Englishman in Paris: Joseph Highmore at the Académie Royale' in *Journal18*, Issue 2, Louvre Local (Fall 2016), http://www.journal18.org/841. Lemoyne was one of the most prominent artists in France and tutor to two leading painters of the next generation, François Boucher and Charles-Joseph Natoire.

39 *The Daily Post*, 2 June 1737.
40 'The following Piece, published in the St. James's Evening Post of June 7, is by the finest Painter in England; perhaps in the World in his Way', The London Magazine, or, Gentleman's Monthly Intelligencer, July 1737, pp. 385–6, p. 385.
41 Burke, *The Analysis of Beauty*, p. 106.
42 T. Nugent, *The Grand Tour, Containing an Exact Description of most of the Cities, Towns, and Remarkable Places of Europe*, 3 Vols, London, 1746, Vol. III, p. 43.
43 J. Upton ed., *The Schoolmaster or, A plain and perfect Way of teaching Children to Understand, Write, and Speak the Latin Tongue. By Roger Ascham ...*, London, 1711, p. 77.
44 Quoted in Paulson, *Hogarth*, 1993, Vol. III, pp. 101–2.
45 The Correggio painting is now in the Kunsthistorisches Museum, Vienna.
46 Burke, *Analysis of Beauty*, p. 132 note.
47 A. Forbes ed., *Curiosities of A Scots Charta Chest 1600–1800, With the Travels and Memoranda of Sir Alexander Dick [Cunyngham]*, Edinburgh, 1897, pp. 101–23.
48 Forbes ed., *Curiosities*, p. 114.
49 Quoted in J. Ingamells, 'Allan Ramsay, of Kinell' in *ODNB*, 17 September 2015.
50 Forbes, *Curiosities*, pp. 106–7.
51 Boswell, *Life of Samuel Johnson*, Vol. II, p. 61.
52 Vertue, III, pp. 97–8.

Interlude Five
1 Gostling, p. 25.
2 Denne & Shrubsole, *Rochester*, p. 16. The house which inspired Dickens is now called Restoration House.
3 Close to this same spot where the Crown stands, according to Denne and Shrubsole, 'has been an inn distinguished by the same sign upwards of four hundred and fifty years'. Denne & Shrubsole, *Rochester*, p. 303.
4 Forrest, f. 2.
5 From M. Davy, *Reformed Coquet*, London, 1752, p. 110 in *OED* 'flounder-mouthed' C2 adj.
6 H. Glasse, *The Art of Cookery Made Plain and Easy*, 2nd edition, London, 1747, p. 2.
7 Nott, *Cook's and Confectioner's Dictionary*, 'MU' no. 90.
8 Glasse, *Art of Cookery*, p. iii.
9 H. Fielding, *The Works of Henry Fielding*, 3rd edition, 12 Vols, London, 1766, Vol. II, pp. 179–242, p. 227.
10 Gostling, p. 25.
11 Forrest, f. 2.
12 Denne & Shrubsole, *Rochester*, p. 230.

13   For Shovell, see J. Macky, *Memoirs of the Secret Services*, London, 1733, p. 122; and for the events of 1707, J. H. Cooke, *The Shipwreck of Sir Cloudesley Shovell on the Scilly Islands*, London, 1883 and S. R. Pattison, 'Sir Cloudesley Shovell' in *Journal of the Royal Institute of Cornwall*, Vol. I, October 1864.

14   Forrest, f. 3.

15   Gostling, p. 26.

16   Forrest, f. 3; Gostling, p. 26.

17   Defoe, *A Tour*, Vol. I, Letter II, p. 20.

18   N. A. M. Rodger, *The Command of the Ocean: A Naval History of Britain, 1649–1815*, London, 2006, p. 227.

19   Samuel Scott, *The Capture of Puerto Bello, 21 November 1739*, 1740, National Maritime Museum BHC0354; see E. Hughes ed., *Spreading Canvas: Eighteenth-Century British Marine Painting*, New Haven & London, 2016, pp. 1–4.

20   Defoe, *A Tour*, Vol. I, Letter II, pp. 20–21.

21   Forrest, f. 3.

22   The painting is in the National Maritime Museum, BHC3614.

23   Defoe, *A Tour*, Vol. I, Letter II, p. 24.

24   Defoe, *A Tour*, Vol. I, Letter II p. 24.

25   An early commission, the painting is now in the Commissioner's House at Chatham Dockyard.

26   J. Swift, *Travels into Several Remote Nations of the World. In Four Parts. By Lemuel Gulliver ...*, London, 1726, Vol. I, p. 206; p. 268.

27   Forrest, f. 3.

28   Forrest, f. 3.

5: Feeling Fellow

1   For the tokens, see J. Bright & G. Clark, *An Introduction to the Tokens at the Foundling Museum*, 2nd edition, London, 2014 and J. Styles, *Threads of Feeling: The London Foundling Hospital's Textile Tokens 1740–79*, London, 2010.

2   'Minutes of the Daily Committee 25 March 1741' transcribed in R. H. Nichols & F. A. Wray, *The History of the Foundling Hospital*, London, 1935, pp. 37–8.

3   Burke, *Analysis of Beauty* (Autobiographical Notes), p. 213.

4   Rodger, *Command of the Ocean*, p. 310.

5   Defoe, *A Tour*, Vol. I, Letter III, p. 59.

6   For a reassessment of Monmouth's life see A. Keay, *The Last Royal Rebel: The Life and Death of James, Duke of Monmouth*, London, 2016.

7   S. E. Morison, 'Letters of Thomas Coram' in *Proceedings of the Massachusetts Historical Society October Meeting, 1922*, Third Series, Boston, Vol. 56 (Oct. 1922–Jun. 1923), pp. 1–68, T. Coram to B. Colman, London 30 April 1734, pp. 19–24, p. 20. The book was *Ecclesiastes, sive de Ratione concionandi*, 1730.

8   [R. Brocklesby], *Private VIRTUE and publick SPIRIT display'd. In a Succinct ESSAY ON THE CHARACTER OF Capt. Thomas Coram*, London, 1751, p. 4. For parentage see J. S. Taylor, 'Thomas Coram' in *ODNB*, 28 September 2006, also G. Wagner, *Thomas Coram, Gent., 1668–1751*, Woodbridge, 2015, p. 8.

9 D. Defoe, *Review of the State of the British Nation*, Vol. IV, No. 126 (2 December 1707), p. 504.

10 Morison, *Letters of Thomas Coram*, Liverpool, 23 September 1735, pp. 27–31, p. 27.

11 Both Harvard College and Yale were founded to train congregationalist clergy.

12 There is also a reference to him living in the Parish of St Botolph Without, Aldgate, and knowing the vicar there, Dr Bray (1656–1730).

13 W. Coxe, *Memoirs of the Administration of Sir Robert Walpole*, 3 Vols, London, 1798, Vol. III, p. 243.

14 Morison, *Letters of Thomas Coram*, T. Coram to Dr Colman, London, 21 September 1738, pp. 38–42, p. 41.

15 Morison, *Letters of Coram*, T. Coram to Dr Colman, London, 21 September 1738, pp. 38–42, p. 42.

16 Brocklesby, *Private VIRTUE*, pp. 4–6.

17 *Daily Courant*, 13 December 1732.

18 *Daily Journal*, 23 December 1729.

19 *London Evening Post*, 28–30 September 1738.

20 *London Evening Post*, 18–20 May 1738.

21 *Old Bailey Proceedings Online*, 12 July 1720 (t17200712-27).

22 Morison, *Letters from Coram*, T. Coram to Dr Colman, London, 2 March 1736/7, pp. 33–5, p. 33. He was still regularly sending books of a religious nature, specifically of a Protestant nature, to the colonies, one bundle from the Society for Propagating Christian Knowledge. Far less attractive to our thinking now, but standard in this period, he was a supporter of encouraging conversion to Christianity among Native Americans and enslaved Africans.

23 Morison, *Letters of Thomas Coram*, T. Coram to Dr Colman, London 22 September 1738, pp. 42–51, p. 43.

24 Morison, *Letters of Thomas Coram*, T. Coram to Dr Colman, London 22 September 1738, pp. 42–51, p. 43.

25 Morison, *Letters of Thomas Coram*, T. Coram to Dr Colman, London 22 September 1738, pp. 42–51, p. 43.

26 See Riding, *Basic Instincts*, pp. 101–2.

27 Riding, *Basic Instincts*, particularly pp. 93–118.

28 *London Evening Post*, 25–7 October 1739.

29 London, 24 August 1739, *Letters by Coram*, p. 53.

30 *General Evening Post*, 20–22 November 1739.

31 Vertue, III, p. 102; Einberg, *Hogarth*, 2016, pp. 209–11.

32 Burke, *Analysis of Beauty* (Autobiographical Notes), p. 214.

33 Burke, *Analysis of Beauty* (Autobiographical Notes), p. 215.

34 Burke, *Analysis of Beauty* (Autobiographical Notes), p. 217.

35 Burke, *Analysis of Beauty* (Autobiographical Notes), p. 217.

36 Burke, *Analysis of Beauty* (Autobiographical Notes), p. 217.

37 H. Diack Johnstone, 'Maurice Greene' in *Oxford Music Online: Grove Music Online*, 20 January 2016.

38 Nichols, *Biographical Anecdotes*, p. 57.

39 Both sets, Sir Peter Lely's 'Windsor Beauties' and Sir Godfrey Kneller's 'Hampton Court Beauties' are still in the Royal Collection.

40 Burke, *Analysis of Beauty* (Autobiographical Notes), p. 218.

41 Regarding the site of the permanent building, Coram had written in August 1739, 'I think I may say I am sure of having 34 acres of Land in the fields before Queens Square in Ormond Street for a Scite for our Hospital and every thing proper belonging thereto it is about an equal Distance from Aldgate and from Whitehall or St. James Palace.' Morison, *Letters of Thomas Coram*, T. Coram to Dr Colman, London, 24 August 1739, pp. 51–4, p. 54.

42 Nichols & Wray, *History of the Foundling Hospital*, pp. 37–8.

43 Nichols & Wray, *History of the Foundling Hospital*, p. 40. See also A. Levene, *Childcare, Health and Mortality at the London Foundling Hospital, 1741–1800*, Manchester, 2012.

44 Coram quoted in Nichols & Wray, *History of the Foundling Hospital*, p. 24.

45 For the art collection see B. Nicholson, *The Treasures of the Foundling Hospital*, Oxford, 1972.

46 As first argued in Riding, *Joseph Highmore*, Vol. 1, pp. 240–45, and Riding, *Basic Instincts*, pp. 104–10.

Interlude Six

1 Forrest, f. 3.

2 Forrest, f. 3.

3 Gostling, p. 27.

4 Gostling, p. 27.

5 Forrest, f. 4.

6 Gostling, p. 28.

7 Burke, *Analysis of Beauty* (Autobiographical Notes), p.228. The last English foothold on the continent, lost in the final months of the reign of Mary I, who famously declared, 'when I am dead & opened, you shall find Calice [Calais] lying in my hart', see John Foxe, *TAMO* (1585 edition), The Digital Humanities Institute, Sheffield, 2011.

8 BM 1967,0211.3 and 1969,0111.1.

9 Forrest, f. 4.

10 Defoe, *A Tour*, Vol. I, Letter II, p. 27.

11 Forrest, f. 4.

12 And even the shells had their uses. For example, Charles II's thoroughfare called the 'Mall', running across the northside of St James's Palace, where the king played the new game, Pell Mell (a kind of croquet), was covered in crushed cockle shells.

13 In the Reverend Gostling's doggerel verse 'Now growing frolicksome and gay, Like boys, we, after dinner play,/ But, as the scene lay in a fort,/ Something like war must be our sport.' Gostling, p. 28.

14 Forrest, f. 4.

15 Forrest, f. 4.

16 Daughter of King Wulfhere of Mercia and niece of his brother and successor, King Aethelred.

17 For the interest in commemoration via benefactions, tombs and grave markers see K. Thomas, *The Ends of Life: Roads to Fulfilment in Early Modern England*, Oxford, 2009, pp. 245–62.

18 Burke, *Analysis of Beauty*, p. 42.

19 Chaplin ed., *Benjamin Franklin's Autobiography*, p. 40.

20 E. Rowe, *Friendship in Death: In Twenty Letters from the Dead to the Living*, 2nd edition, London, 1729. See Thomas, *Ends of Life*, pp. 226–31.

21 Gostling, p. 29.

22 *OED* 'poetaster', n. .

23 Forrest, f. 4.

24 T. Gray, *Designs by Mr. Bentley, For Six Poems by Mr. T. Gray*, London, 1753, pp. 28–36, p. 33.

25 Forrest, f. 5.

26 Gostling, p. 29.

27 See C. Probyn, 'Jonathan Swift' in *ODNB*, 23 September 2004.

28 Ned Ward, before his adventures in London, describes being in 'a tedious Confinement to a Country *Hutt*, where I dwelt like Diogenes in his *Tub*', *The London Spy Compleat*, p. 1.

29 Both Jonathan Richardson and Hans Sloane had drawings on the subject of Diogenes in their collections, see BM ff,2.180 and SL,5214.133.

30 Forrest, f. 5. The current tavern near the church is called The Chequers.

31 Gostling, p. 29.

32 Ogle, *Canterbury Tales*, Vol. I, p. 30. We might also get a sense of the landlady's agreeableness, 'Of Jests she had an unexhausted Store;/ Her Talk did notably Love's Art advance;/ For she had practis'd long that old, new Dance'. Ogle, *Canterbury Tales*, Vol. I, p. 31.

33 'Behold the Woes of Matrimonial Life,/ And hear with Rev'rence an experience'd Wife!/ To dear-bought Wisdom give the Credit due,/ And think, for once, a Woman tells you true.' Ogle, *Canterbury Tales*, Vol. III, p. 51.

34 Forrest, f. 5.

35 Forrest, f. 5.

36 Forrest, f. 5.

37 Forrest, f. 5.

38 Forrest, f. 5; 'This triple alliance gave occasion/ To much improving speculation'. Gostling, p. 30.

39 Named '*Northfleet*' by the Reverend Gostling. Gostling, p. 30.

40 Forrest, f. 5.

41 Hasted, *History of Kent*, Vol. IV, map.

42 A pub of that name stands on the site, built during the nineteenth century. There is a detached stable block.

43 Forrest, f. 6.

44 Forrest, f. 6.

45 [Anon.], *Hymen: An accurate Description of the Ceremonies used in Marriage, By every Nation in the Known World*, London, 1760, p. 174.

46 Forrest, f. 6.

6: Nature's Dramatist

1   ['Truth'], '"Billy and Jenny," or Souvenirs of the Celebrated Hogarth and his Lady' in *The Mirror of Literature, Amusement and Instruction*, London, 1843, (New Series) Vol. III, pp. 306–7, pp. 322–4.

2   Bienecke Rare Book and Manuscript Library, Yale University, GEN MSS 1429 Box 9 Folder 258, J. Hogarth to A. Walker, 29 May 1781. With gratitude to Cristina S. Martinez who discovered this letter, part quoting it in her article 'Jane Hogarth' in *ODNB*, 9 July 2020. Also TNA PROB 1/66.

3   Rev. J. Trusler, *Hogarth Moralized, being A Complete Edition of Hogarth's Works*, London, 1768: 'Now First Published, With the Approbation of JANE HOGARTH, Widow of the late Mr. HOGARTH'.

4   TNA PROB 1/66 Nichols, *Biographical Anecdotes*, p. 98.

5   J. Ireland, *Supplement to Hogarth Illustrated*, London, 1804, p. 368. According to Ireland they were presented to him by Mary Lewis, Jane Hogarth's cousin, who inherited the estate after her death.

6   TNA PROB 1/66; Nichols, *Biographical Anecdotes*, pp. 99–100.

7   The Zodiac Plates are listed as Lot 66 in Jane Hogarth's sale catalogue; see Lugt 4575, 1790-04-24 p. 6.

8   Vertue, III, p. 105.

9   John Hoadly mentions the 'painting-room' at Leicester Fields in his undated letter to Hogarth see BL Add MS 27995 f. 23.

10 *Country Journal*, 16 April 1737.

11 Jane Hogarth's Sale Catalogue, Lugt 4575, 1790-04-24 p. 6 lot 65.

12 Lugt 4575, 1790-04-24 p. 6 lots 60 and 59.

13 E. Einberg, *Manner & Morals: Hogarth and British Painting 1700–1760*, London, 1987, pp. 23–4.

14 Kitson, *Hogarth's Apology for Painters*, p. 98.

15 The Royal Academy of Arts, presented to the institution in 1831 by J. M. W. Turner as having been owned by Hogarth. It is 415 mm × 230 mm × 24 mm. A similar item in the collection was owned by Sir Joshua Reynolds.

16 Royal Academy of Arts, 970 mm long, 30 mm diameter.

17 During a discussion about Hogarth, Wilkie declared that 'I have had them so often present to my mind in my waking dreams ... that all the incidents are commonly passing before me in my sleep.' Quoted from an unsigned memoir 'Sir David Wilkie and Friends' in *Fraser's Magazine for Town and Country*, Vol. 24 (No.139–44), London, Oct. 1841, pp. 443–54, p. 453.

18 Einberg, *Hogarth*, 2016, p. 11.

19 As seen when X-rayed; see Einberg, *Hogarth*, 2016, pp. 283–4.

20 ['Truth'], 'Billy and Jenny', *Mirror of Literature*, p. 307.

21 A. Rouquet, *The Present State of the Arts in England*, London, 1755, pp. 42–3.

22 Nichols, *Biographical Anecdotes*, p. 14. A few years later (1735–8) Western would commission a family conversation, now at the National Gallery of Ireland; see Einberg, *Hogarth*, 2016, pp. 156–8.

23 Quoted in Nichols, *Biographical Anecdotes*, p. 14.

24 All private collections; see Einberg, *Hogarth*, 2016: pp. 124–6; pp. 186–8; and pp. 192–3.

25   Einberg, *Hogarth*, 2016, pp. 335–6.

26   The painting remains in the Boyne family by descent; see Einberg, *Hogarth*, 2016, p. 186.

27   Q. Valerius Maximus, *His Collections of the Memorable Acts and Sayings of ... the Antient Romans*, London, 1684, p. 232.

28   It is possible that art was the means of introduction between Hogarth and the Hoadlys. Bishop Hoadly's first wife, the mother of Ben and John, was the Yorkshire-born professional portrait painter Sarah Curtis (1676?–1743) see Vertue, III, p. 113; Vertue, V, p. 1 and p. 14; J. Egerton, 'Sarah Curtis' in *ODNB*, 23 September 2004; for Bishop Hoadly's portrait; see Einberg, *Hogarth*, 2016, pp. 234–6.

29   See S. Taylor, 'Benjamin Hoadly' in *ODNB*, 3 January 2008.

30   See Einberg, *Hogarth*, 2016: p. 282; pp. 184–5; 203–4; pp. 223–4; pp. 233–4.

31   Nichols, *Biographical Anecdotes*, p. 57.

32   Einberg, *Hogarth*, 2016, pp. 115–16.

33   Quoted in Einberg, *Hogarth*, 2016, p. 246, note 4.

34   *GM*, Vol. 1, London, 1732, p. 501. Curiously, in the version viewed, the original announcement does not appear on page 311.

35   Einberg, *Hogarth*, 2016, p. 246, making reference to R. Simon, *Hogarth, France and British Art*, London, 2007, pp. 42–6.

36   Burke, *Analysis of Beauty* (Autobiographical Notes), p. 216.

37   Burke, *Analysis of Beauty* (Autobiographical Notes), p. 216.

38   Burke, *Analysis of Beauty* (Autobiographical Notes), p. 216.

39   Burke, *Analysis of Beauty* (Autobiographical Notes), p. 203.

40   Mary Edward's Sale, C. Cock's 28–9 May 1746, 1st day (49) 'Mr Hogarth Taste a-la-Mode'.

41   P. Mansell, *Dressed to Rule: Royal and Court Costume from Louis XIV to Elizabeth II*, Yale 2005, p. 15. John Nichols identifies this figure as being an actual person, 'Lord *Portmore*' (as a long-serving member of parliament the 2nd earl does not fit the youthful character here ridiculed), while the woman to the left is, according to the same source, an unnamed but celebrated courtesan. Nichols, *Biographical Anecdotes*, pp. 259–60.

42   Nichols, *Biographical Anecdotes*, p. 259.

43   *Daily Advertiser*, 2 April 1743.

44   This puts paid to Georg Lichtenberg's assertion that Hogarth had a particular 'Lord W' in mind when creating the character of Lord Squander, although it cannot be discounted that, conversely and as seen in the print lampooning William Kent's altarpiece of 1725, this is actually a ploy, or sleight of hand, to draw attention to any correspondences to living people; see Wensinger trans. & ed., *Hogarth on High Life*, p. 19.

45   *Daily Advertiser*, 8 November 1744.

46   BL Add MS 27,994 12v; also Einberg, *Hogarth*, 2016, pp. 259–60.

47   Le Bas had engraved book illustrations after Hubert Gravelot, *La game d'Amour* after Watteau (engraving 1726 for *Recueil Julienne*), *The Four Elements* (1734–6) and *The Five Senses* (1736).

48   Vertue, III, p. 41.

49   Ravenet had moved to London by 1750, setting up a school of line engraving and among the pupils was William Wynne Ryland. Died in London, buried at the Old St Pancras Churchyard on 6 April 1764.

50   George Vertue was unimpressed – noting at the turn of 1743 to 1744 'to begin this year M^r. Hogarth I am told has got a young Engraver from Paris to assist him in his plates or to work for him – this according to custom was told to me – not to comfort me – so much as to shew (their malicious) envy'. Vertue, III, p. 120. Vertue's evident hurt, against those who told him of Hogarth's plans, as well as the arrival of French competitors, is understandable.

51   *Daily Advertiser*, 4 April 1743.

52   Vertue, III, p. 137.

53   Riding, *Basic Instincts*, pp. 57–91; for Chardin see J. Carey, *Taking Time: Chardin's Boy Building a House of Cards and other paintings*, London, 2012.

54   H. Fielding, *The history of the adventures of Joseph Andrews ... Written in imitation of the manner of Cervantes, etc*, 2nd edition, 2 Vols, London, 1742, Vol. I, p. viii.

55   Fielding, *Joseph Andrews*, Vol. I, pp. viii–ix.

56   W. Somervile, *Hobbinol, or the Rural Games. A Burlesque Poem*, London, 1740, 'Dedication' before p. i.

57   Burke, *Analysis of Beauty* (Autobiographical Notes), p. 206.

58   Burke, *Analysis of Beauty* (Autobiographical Notes), p. 209.

59   Burke, *Analysis of Beauty* (Autobiographical Notes), p. 210.

60   Burke, *Analysis of Beauty* (Autobiographical Notes), p. 212.

61   Fielding, *Joseph Andrews*, Vol. I, pp. 42–3 .

62   Fielding, *Joseph Andrews*, Vol. II, p. 90.

63   Burke, *Analysis of Beauty*, p. 5.

64   Jane Hogarth's Sale Catalogue Lugt 4575, 1790-04-24 p. 5 lot 31 'Ghezzi's caricatures'.

65   Nichols, *Biographical Anecdotes*, p. 259: 'As he designed after her ideas, he had little kindness for his performance, and never would permit a print to be taken from it.'

66   Vertue, III, p. 124, date of the sale 1 March 1744–5.

67   Einberg, *Hogarth*, 2016, p. 56.

68   Vertue, III, p. 124.

69   ['Truth'], 'Billy and Jenny', *Mirror of Literature*, p. 307.

70   Nichols, *Biographical Anecdotes*, p. 46.

71   Nichols, *Biographical Anecdotes*, p. 46.

72   Nichols, *Biographical Anecdotes*, p. 48.

73   Nichols & Steevens, *Genuine Works*, Vol. I, p. 127 note *.

74   Beinecke Library, Yale GEN MSS 1429, Box 9, Folder 258, J. Hogarth to A. Walker, 29 May 1781.

75   BL Add MS 30803 B, f. 58 quoted in Einberg, *Hogarth*, 2016, p. 88.

Interlude Seven

1   Forrest, f. 6.

2   Forrest, f. 6.

3 Gostling, p. 32.
4 Forrest, f. 7.
5 Forrest, f. 7.
6 [Anon.], *A Discourse on Witchcraft*, London, 1736, p. 26.
7 Forrest, f. 7; Gostling, p. 32.
8 T. Dyche & W. Pardon, *A New General English Dictionary*, London, 1765.
9 A fathom is six feet.
10 Hasted, *History of Kent*, Vol. VI, pp. 229–33.
11 Forrest, f. 7.
12 By the seventeenth century there was a significant salt-panning works at this location on the shore. The 'Salt houses' Forrest refers to would include 'pans', a basin (whether natural or man-made) where sea water stands and, through evaporation creates residue salt which is harvested, a storehouse and wharf, windmill sluices and a 'good dwelling house' called Saltpans House. P. Macdougall, *The story of the Hoo Peninsula*, Rochester, 1980, p. 151; *Post Man and historical Account*, 30 May 1710. Also re Hogarth *Daily Advertiser* 22 March 1773, *Gazetteer and New Daily Advertiser*, 29 November 1791. Also, C. B. Burnett, *A History of the isle of Grain*, 1906.
13 Forrest, f. 7.
14 Fremantle, *Thornhill's Sketch-Book Travel Journal*, p. 22.
15 Ward, *The London Spy Compleat*, p. 202.
16 G. H. Gater & E. P. Wheeler, *Survey of London*, London, 1935, Vol. XVI, pp. 258–68.
17 W. Matthews ed., *Charles II's Escape from Worcester: A Collection of Narratives Assembled by Samuel Pepys*, London, 1967, pp. 5–6. This collection includes Charles's own account of his escape as transcribed by Pepys, pp. 34–84.
18 J. Byrom, *Miscellaneous Poems*, 2 Vols, Manchester, 1773, Vol. II, p. 342.

7: True Patriot
1 See J. Riding, *Jacobites: A New History of the '45 Rebellion*, London, 2016, Chapter 8 'Eriskay'; 'Duncan Cameron's Journal' in H. Paton ed., *The Lyon in Mourning*, 3 Vols, Edinburgh, 1896, Vol. I, pp. 201–11 and 'Aeneas MacDonald's Journal' in Paton ed., *The Lyon in Mourning*, Vol. I, pp. 288–9.
2 Vertue, III, pp. 123–4.
3 Einberg, *Hogarth*, 2016: 1741, Tate, pp. 239–40; a group depicted unusually in a ship's cabin, c.1742–4, National Maritime Museum, pp. 253–5; Private Collection, c.1742–5, pp. 255–6.
4 See Einberg, *Hogarth*, 2016, pp. 270–71.
5 Quoted Einberg, *Hogarth*, 2016, p. 271.
6 Apparently a portrait of the same date, by Thomas Hudson, was more attuned to the taste of Herring's social circle.
7 Quoted in E. R. Pennell & J. Pennell, *The life of James McNeill Whistler*, 2 Vols, London (3rd Impression), 1909, Vol. II, p. 22.
8 See J. Riding, 'From Bosworth Field to Finchley Common: Britain, Hogarth and the 1745 Jacobite Rebellion' in S. Parissien ed., *Celebrating Britain: Canaletto, Hogarth and Patriotism*, London, 2015, pp. 70–95.

9   P. H. Fitzgerald, *The Life of David Garrick*, 2 Vols, London, 1868, Vol. I, p. 34.

10   J. Boswell, *Life of Samuel Johnson*, Vol. II, p. 34.

11   S. Johnson, *A Dictionary of the English Language*, 2 Vols, London, 1755, Vol. II, 'TOS-TOT' and 'WHI'.

12   A. Rouquet, *The Present State of the Arts in England*, London, 1755, pp. 41–2.

13   RCIN 913477, W. Hogarth to 'T. H.' 21 October 1746 .

14   Burke, *Analysis of Beauty* (Autobiographical Notes), p. 213. Paid by a Mr Duncombe, identified as Thomas of Duncombe Park in Yorkshire; see Einberg, *Hogarth*, 2016, p. 274.

15   D. M. Little & G. M. Kahrl ed., *The Letters of David Garrick*, 3 Vols, London, 1963–5, Vol. 1, p. 65 and p. 70.

16   The painting's equally magnificent frame, which adds greater emphasis to its scale, would have fitted the grandeur of Duncombe's house, as one visitor expressed it: 'Within those walls immortal Shakespeare shines,/ In Garrick's action, and in Hogarth's lines; Th'expressive features speak the tortur'd breast,/ And all the savage tyrant stands confest.' Dr Samuel Drake to Thomas Duncombe the younger in 1749, quoted in Einberg, *Hogarth*, 2016, p. 274 and the frame illustrated on p. 275.

17   See W. Shakespeare, *The Tragical History of King Richard the Third ... As it is now Acted at the Theatre-Royal in Drury-Lane. Reviv'd, with Alterations, by Mr. Cibber*, London, 1718, p. 64; also Einberg, *Hogarth*, 2016, pp. 274–5.

18   See collections.chateauversailles.fr MV 6165.

19   An engraving by Sébastien Leclerc I after Le Brun, dated 1696, with the composition as per the painting, not reversed, was also available for guidance.

20   Burke, *Analysis of Beauty*, p. 11.

21   Riding, *Jacobites*, pp. 91–169; G. Lockhart, 'Alexander MacDonald's Journall and Memoirs' in *The Lockhart Papers*, 2 Vols, London, 1817, Vol. II, pp. 479–510, p. 489.

22   Riding, *Jacobites*, pp. 169–221.

23   *Daily Advertiser*, 30 September 1745.

24   Little & Kahrl, *Letters of David Garrick*, Vol. I, p. 54.

25   P. Scholes, *God Save the Queen!*, Oxford, 1954, p. 7.

26   S. Klima, G. Bowers & K. S. Grant eds., *Memoirs of Dr. Charles Burney, 1726–1769*, Lincoln & London, 1988, p. 55.

27   J. Boaden, *The private correspondence of David Garrick*, 2nd edition, 2 Vols, London, 1835, Vol. I, p. xv .

28   Boaden, *Private correspondence of David Garrick*, Vol. I, p. 39.

29   Little & Kahrl, *Letters of David Garrick*, Vol. I, p. 65.

30   Little & Kahrl, *Letters of David Garrick*, Vol. I, p. 70.

31   'John Byrom to Mr. Vigor, Manchester 1 March 1745/6 OS' in R. Parkinson ed., *The private journal and literary remains of John Byrom*, 4 Vols (32, 34, 40, 44), Chetham Society, Manchester, 1854–7, Vol. 44, pp. 411–14, p. 411.

32   Riding, *Jacobites*, pp. 227–51.

33   'Copy of a letter from a Clergyman near Derby, to his Brother in London, 9 December 1745' in *The Chester Miscellany. Being a collection of several pieces,*

both in priose and verse, which were in the Chester Courant from January 1745, to May 1750, Chester, 1750, pp. 65–9, p. 65.

34 H. Fielding, *The True Patriot: and History of Our Own Times*, 19 November 1745.

35 *Daily Post*, 6 December 1745.

36 E. Cock, *The Soldier's Companion or Martial Recorder*, London, 1824, Vol. I, pp. 292–3.

37 BL Add MS 27,994, Anonymous translation, *Letter from Mr [Rouquet] to one of his Friends in Paris in order to explain Mr. Hogarth's Prints*, 16v.

38 H. Fielding, *The True Patriot: and History of Our Own Times*, 10 December 1745, p. 2.

39 Fielding, *The True Patriot*, 10 December 1745, p. 2.

40 Riding, *Jacobites*, pp. 413–27.

41 For Charles as fugitive see Riding, *Jacobites*, pp. 429–39; 453–7; pp. 465–9; p. 479; pp. 491–3; for the pacification of the Highlands, pp. 441–9; pp. 459–62.

42 One version is written out to John Ranby.

43 Vertue, III, p. 130.

44 J. Ireland, *Hogarth Illustrated*, Vol. III, p. 337.

45 *George Faulkner, The Dublin Journal*, 15–18 November 1746.

46 Little & Kahrl eds., *Letters of David Garrick*, Vol. I, pp. 78–9.

47 Nichols, *Biographical Anecdotes*, pp. 57–8.

48 Transcription of the manuscript then in the possession of R. W. Ketton-Cremer (n.30, p. 429) in Paulson, *Hogarth*, 1992, Vol. II, pp. 259–60, p. 259.

49 Nichols, *Biographical Anecdotes*, pp. 57–8.

50 Nichols, *Biographical Anecdotes*, p. 58.

51 HRO Malmesbury Papers 9M73/G485/27, letter from J. Hoadly to J. Harris, 27 August 1760; also quoted in Einberg, *Hogarth*, 2016, p. 237.

52 For details on Lovat's life see S. Fraser, *The Last Highlander*, London, 2012.

53 Fraser, *The Last Highlander*, p. 333.

54 Now Holy Hill. The inn was a timber-framed building dating back to 1470.

55 *GM*, Vol. 86, December 1799, p. 1,014, thought to be the author of *The Beggar's Petition* (Rev. Thomas Moss also put forward as author): 'Dr. Joshua Webster (M.D.) ... written at St. Alban's [*sic*] in the year 1764'. By 1799 Webster was resident in Chelsea.

56 Nichols, *Biographical Anecdotes*, p. 283.

57 Lovat, who spoke reasonable French and, at a moment when he was keen to promote himself as a Jacobite, had spent time at James VII of Scotland's court at Saint-Germain-en-Laye, converting to Catholicism in the bargain.

58 S. Ireland, *Graphic Illustrations*, Vol. I, p. 146.

59 Nichols says Lovat 'received his old friend with a salute, which left much of the lather on his face'. Nichols, *Biographical Anecdotes*, p. 283.

60 Nichols, *Biographical Anecdotes*, p. 283.

61 Vertue, III, p. 131.

62 J. Harris [Earl of Malmesbury] ed., *A Series of Letters of the First Earl of Malmesbury*, 2 Vols, London, 1870, Vol. I, p. 46.

63   N. Nichols ed., *The Works of Thomas Gray*, London, 1835, Vol. III, p. 11.

64   Riding, *Jacobites*, pp. 472–7.

65   Vertue, III, p. 135.

66   Rouquet, *The Present State of the Arts in England*, p. 21 and p. 27.

67   Nichols, *Biographical Anecdotes*, p. 47.

68   Nichols & Wray, *History of the Foundling Hospital*, pp. 23–4.

69   When the hospital was demolished in the 1920s, Coram's remains were moved to St Andrew's church, High Holborn, along with the font and the organ case donated by Handel.

70   [Anon.], *A Candid and Impartial Account of the Behaviour of Simon Lord Lovat from the Time his Death-Warrant was deliver'd, to the Day of his Execution*, London, 1747, p. 28.

71   The subscript states it was published on 15 June 1747, with the lines: 'Disguis'd thro' Life, a Layman at ye Block,/ My headless Trunk resumes ye Monkish Frock,/ Doom'd, for my Crimes in Pilgrimage to roam,/ With weary steps I seek my Native Home',/ 'Where Vanity inscribes my Father's Tomb/ But Justice now denies my Carcase Room'.

72   *Daily and General Advertiser*, 26 June 1747.

73   Burke, *Analysis of Beauty* (Autobiographical Notes), p. 225.

74   Burke, *Analysis of Beauty* (Autobiographical Notes), p. 225.

75   *London Evening Post*, 15–17 October 1747.

76   Trusler, *Hogarth Moralized*, pp. 83–4.

77   Kitson, *Hogarth's Apology for Painters*, p. 81; Paulson, *Hogarth*, 1992, Vol. II, p. 290; See also M. Hallett & C. Riding, *Hogarth*, London, 2007, p. 181.

78   Nichols, *Biographical Anecdotes*, pp. 49–50.

79   Vertue, III, pp. 141–2.

80   J. Wright ed., *The Letters of Horace Walpole, Earl of Orford*, 6 Vols, London, 1840, Vol. II, pp. 250–53, 252–3, H. Walpole to H. Mann, Arlington Street London, 15 December 1748.

81   Burke, *Analysis of Beauty*, p. 227.

82   Vertue, III, p. 142.

83   Nichols, *Biographical Anecdotes*, p. 50.

84   Burke, *Analysis of Beauty* (Autobiographical Notes), p. 228.

85   Trusler, *Hogarth Moralized*, p. 106.

86   Vertue, III, p. 142.

87   Nichols, *Biographical Anecdotes*, p. 50.

88   Nichols, *Biographical Anecdotes*, p. 49.

89   Burke, *Analysis of Beauty* (Autobiographical Notes), p. 227 .

90   BL Add MS 27,994 *Letter from Mr [Rouquet]*, 17v.

91   Burke, *Analysis of Beauty* (Autobiographical Notes), p. 228.

92   Nichols, *Biographical Anecdotes*, pp. 291–5.

93   Nichols, *Biographical Anecdotes*, p. 294.

94   *GM*, Vol. 18, London, 1748, p. 277. This poem was first noted in E. Einberg & J. Egerton, *Tate Gallery Collections: The Age of Hogarth*, London, 1988, p. 129.

95   D. Hume, 'Discourse XI, Of the Protestant Succession' in *Political Discourses*, 2nd edition, Edinburgh, 1752, pp. 263–79.

96   Hume, *Political Discourses*, p. 277 and p. 272.

97   James Francis Edward died in 1766, on which Charles took up residence at the Palazzo del Re as King Charles III.

98   For an exploration see J. A. Stevenson, *The Real History of Tom Jones*, New York & Basingstoke, 2005, Chapter 1: 'Stuart Ghosts', pp. 17–46.

99   Fielding, *Tom Jones*, Vol. I, pp. 13–15.

100   Fielding, *Tom Jones*, Vol. II, p. 305.

101   Fielding, *Tom Jones*, Vol. IV, pp. 107–10.

102   Fielding, *Tom Jones*, Vol. III, pp. 82–5.

103   Fielding, *Tom Jones*, Vol. III, p. 215.

104   Fielding, *Tom Jones*, Vol. III, p. 85.

105   BL Add MS 27,994 *Letter from Mr. [Rouquet]*, f. 18r.

106   Hanging beneath the Adam and Eve image and directly above the drummer is the name 'Giles Gardiner': 'Gardiner' apt, or ironic, placed near the 'Garden' of Eden.

107   BL Add MS 27,994 *Letter from Mr. [Rouquet]*, ff. 16r–19r, f. 17r. Another translation for this section was published in *The Midwife: or, The Old Woman's Magazine*, Vol. I, London, 1751, p. 183.

108   Trusler, *Hogarth Moralized*, p. 171.

109   BL Add MS 27,994 *Letter from Mr. [Rouquet]*, f. 17r.

110   RA, Stuart Papers/MAIN/307/128 Mlle Luci or Ferrand not dated [23 February 1750 NS or the British date (OS) 12 February 1749/50].

Interlude Eight

1   Forrest, f. 7.

2   Hasted, *History of Kent*, Vol. VI, pp. 207–8.

3   Defoe, *A Tour*, Vol. I, Letter II, p. 27.

4   J. Macky, *A Journey Through England*, 4th edition, 2 Vols, London, 1724, Vol. I, pp. 223–4.

5   From the battlements, the pilgrims may have seen a very recent innovation to allay the dangers to shipping. In around 1731–2, and so possibly just before the visit to Sheerness, the entrepreneurial Robert Hamblin and David Avery had stationed a lightboat, the first of its kind in the world, at the Nore sandbank as a private venture. The idea proved a great success, and continued to be used until the early nineteenth century, with the Nore lightboat appearing in marine paintings by J. M. W. Turner.

6   Forrest, f. 8.

7   Forrest, f. 8.

8   Defoe, *A Tour*, Vol. I, Letter II, p. 29.

9   *Flying Post or The Weekly Medley*, 1 February 1729.

10   Quoted in *Cobbett's Parliamentary History of England*, Vol IX. 1733–7, London, 1811, p. 622; or 'deputy governor of Sheerness' in C. H. Green, *Historical Register*, Vol. XVIII, London, 1733, p. 301.

11   A. N. Newman, 'Queenborough' in R. Sedgwick ed., *History of Parliament: the House of Commons 1715–1754*, 1970.

12   A. N. Newman, 'Richard Evans' in Sedgwick ed., *The History of Parliament: the*

House of Commons 1715–1754. The source is an unsigned letter to Geo. Wellard, town clerk of Queenborough, Wellard mss, Kent AO.

13   Forrest, f. 8.

14   Charles Mitchell's note in *Hogarth's Peregrination*, p. 50.

15   Forrest, f. 8. This grave marker, called locally 'the Whale tablet', is now displayed inside the church.

16   H. Eking, *A View of the Greenland Trade*, London, 1725, p. 23.

17   Eking, p. 30.

18   Eking, p. 31.

19   *OED* 'train oil', n.

20   Forrest, f. 8.

21   Forrest, ff. 8–9.

22   Forrest, f. 9.

23   Nott, *Cook's and Confectioner's Dictionary*, 'LO 52–7'.

24   Glasse, *Art of Cookery*, p. 257 and p. 259.

25   Forrest, f. 9.

26   See Brand, *Popular Antiquities*, p. 82.

27   Hasted, *History of Kent*, Vol. VI, pp. 207–16.

28   Forrest, f. 9.

29   Forrest, f. 9.

30   There is also a figure sitting on a chair next to the door of a building on the left, which seems to relate to Forrest's description of Hogarth sketching in the street.

31   Forrest, f. 10.

32   *OED* 'can' 1.a 1731 'N. Bailey Universal Etymol. Eng Dict '*Cann*, a wooden Pot to drink out of' and *OED* 'flip' 2. *The British Apollo*, 8–10 June 1709.

33   Forrest, f. 10.

34   *OED* 'flock-bed' C1 a. n. Mattress made of or stuffed with flock, tufts of wool or cotton, seen as low-quality and not made for comfort.

35   Forrest, f. 11.

36   Forrest, f. 11.

37   Forrest, f. 11.

38   Forrest, f. 11.

39   Tate T08211 and T08212; YCBA versions B1975.4.1257 and B1975.4.1256. For Taylor see D. Brailsford, 'George Taylor' in *ODNB*, 23 September 2004.

40   BM Cc,1.189, Richard Livesay, *George Taylor epitaph*, etching, 1782. Copy of Hogarth's manuscript, published by Jane Hogarth.

41   Forrest, f. 12. The George, until recently the Prince of Waterloo, is now a private house. It has been dated back to 1633.

42   Forrest, ff. 12–13.

43   So resonant was the repelling of the Armada that the ten great tapestries woven in Flanders to celebrate the event, commissioned by Charles, Lord Howard of Effingham, Lord High Admiral in 1591, then purchased in 1616 by James I to hang at his Palace of Whitehall and then the Tower of London, were considered national treasures. Placed in the House of Lords debating chamber on special occasions, they were displayed there permanently by Oliver Cromwell in 1651 as a symbol of English resistance to foreign invasion, of a military, religious or

philosophical nature. They remained there throughout the Georgian period, as reminders of the might of the English, later the British, navy and its role in the defence, strength, spirit and glory, as they then would view it, of the nation. Just seven years after *The Peregrination*, Hogarth's friend John Pine published engravings of the ten tapestries. Pine had supported Hogarth's copyright act of 1735, in which there was a clause (inserted at the third reading in parliament) giving him exclusive permission to reproduce the design of these tapestries. The engravings were produced by Pine and Bernard Baron, Hogarth's collaborator, after drawings by Hubert Gravelot after Clement Lemprière, very much an English and French affair. In the introduction Pine declared 'because Time, or Accident, or Moths may deface these valuable shadows, we have endeavoured to preserve their Likeness', a prophetic statement indeed, for these national treasures would be destroyed one hundred years later, in the Great Fire at the Palace of Westminster – and, apart from a few oblique views of them within images of the House of Lords chamber, Pine's engravings are all that remain. They were used to reproduce the tapestries, in oil on canvas, for the Prince's Chamber, House of Lords.

44   Forrest, f. 12.
45   Forrest, f. 12.
46   Forrest, f. 13.
47   Forrest, f. 13; *OED* 'tittle' 1. n. and 2. v.1. 1.a .
48   The effigy is much marked by old graffiti; there are a few 'WH's but none verifiable to 1732.

8: Original Genius

1   ['Truth'], 'Billy and Jenny', *Mirror of Literature*, p. 307.
2   Einberg, *Hogarth*, 2016, p. 329.
3   Nichols, *Biographical Anecdotes*, pp. 58–9.
4   Nichols, *Biographical Anecdotes*, p. 51.
5   ['Truth'], 'Billy and Jenny', *Mirror of Literature*, p. 307.
6   J. Timbs, *Anecdote Biography or, Scenes and Events in the Lives of Distinguished Persons*, London, 1860, p. 74.
7   Timbs, *Anecdote Biography*, p. 75.
8   Timbs, *Anecdote Biography*, p. 75.
9   Nichols & Steevens, *Genuine Works*, Vol. I, p. 127, note *.
10   G. Clegg, 'Mr Ranby and his House' in *Brentford & Chiswick Local History Journal* 8 (1999). Ranby had accommodation in London and from 1752 he used an apartment associated with his role as surgeon to Chelsea Hospital, which is where he died and is buried. In a travel journal dated June–August 1741, George writes 'This is an account of a tour made by my Mother'. He goes on, 'She died in 1746 when I was only three years old. But I have always had a strong and filial remembrance of being taken to the side of her bed to take leave of me & bless me which (God be thanked) she seemed to do with great composure.' Her descendants in the nineteenth century removed her name from the journal, quoted in Einberg, *Hogarth*, 2016, p. 298.
11   Fielding provided a short pen portrait of John Ranby in *Tom Jones*: 'This

Surgeon, whose Name I have forgot, tho' I remember it began with an *R*, had the first Character in his Profession, and was Serjeant-Surgeon to the King. He had moreover many good Qualities, and was a very generous, good-natured Man, and ready to do any Service to his Fellow Creatures.' Fielding, *Tom Jones*, Vol. II, p. 261.

12   It had been thought to be a view of John Ranby's home, from a handwritten note on one impression which states, 'A View of Mr. Ranby the Surgeon's house Taken from Hogarth's window at Chiswick'. As the engraving was published during Jane's lifetime (1781), this was assumed to be correct.

13   See V. Bott, 'Hogarth's House as Hogarth saw it' in *The British Art Journal*, Autumn 2007, Vol. 8, No.2, pp. 34–8.

14   Intriguingly a domed building to the furthest right may be Burlington's villa, or a temple in his extensive gardens.

15   'Sir, – Your readers will be surprised to learn that there is now living at Brompton an aged female who was the favourite servant of Mrs Hogarth during the long period of fifteen years'; see ['Truth'], 'Billy and Jenny', *Mirror of Literature*, p. 306.

16   ['Truth'], 'Billy and Jenny', *Mirror of Literature*, p. 307.

17   Transcribed in Nichols, *Biographical Anecdotes*, pp. 296–7.

18   Private Collection, *c.*1735–45, see Einberg, *Hogarth*, 2016, p. 163.

19   ['Truth'], 'Billy and Jenny', *Mirror of Literature*, p. 307.

20   ['Truth'], 'Billy and Jenny', *Mirror of Literature*, p. 307.

21   T. Cook, *Anecdotes of Mr. Hogarth, and Explanatory Descriptions of the Plates of Hogarth Restored*, London, 1803, p. 262.

22   Pyne, *Wine and Walnuts*, Vol. I, pp. 173–4.

23   Pyne, *Wine and Walnuts*, Vol. I, p. 173.

24   Pyne, *Wine and Walnuts*, Vol. I, p. 174.

25   Nichols, *Biographical Anecdotes*, p. 299 note †. The engraving stages show the change of date on the 'Totenham Court Nursery' sign, from '1746' in Luke Sullivan's proofs, to 1745, and with the clarifying title 'A Representation of the March of the Guards towards Scotland in the Year 1745' in the final published print, which anchors the main action to the autumn/winter of that year, even, as discussed, as it plays around with time and sequence.

26   BL Add MS 27995 f. 16r, Letter from 'An Englishman' to W Hogarth, 12 December 1759.

27   Nichols, *Biographical Anecdotes*, p. 281 note *.

28   The bid of £120 had come from Charles Perry, who wrote to Hogarth on 15 May 1751 declaring his astonishment that the highest bid at that point was only £75, see BL Add MS 27995 f. 6.

29   John Lane's account in Nichols, *Biographical Anecdotes*, pp. 279–81 note *.

30   Bindman, 'William Hogarth' *ODNB*; also D. Bindman, *Hogarth and his Times*, London, 1997, pp. 168–81.

31   Burke, *Analysis of Beauty*, p. 15.

32   'Of the impossibility to there ever being a market in this kingdom or in any part of the world that can maintain more than twelve artists in a way that may be thought an adiquate recompense for so tedious a study'; see BL Add MS

27993 W. Hogarth, *Observations on the institution of the Royal Academy and on the practice of art in England*, n.d. f. 2; Blake's annotated copy BL C.45.e.18–20, E. Malone ed., *The Works of Sir Joshua Reynolds, Knight*, 2nd edition, London, 1798, Vol. I, titlepage. Also R. Hamlyn, *William Blake*, London, 2000, pp. 186–7.

33 Nichols, *Biographical Anecdotes*, p. 324.

34 Burke, *Analysis of Beauty*, p. 10.

35 Burke, *Analysis of Beauty*, p. 19.

36 Burke, *Analysis of Beauty*, p. 20.

37 BL Add MS 27995 f. 6r, W. Warburton to W. Hogarth 28 March 1752. See also B. W. Young 'William Warburton' in *ODNB*, 24 May 2007.

38 Beinecke Library, Yale, GEN MSS 1429 box 9 f. 258 J. Hogarth to A. Walker, 29 May 1781. Jane is responding to the first edition of Nichols's biography.

39 Nichols, *Biographical Anecdotes*, p. 325.

40 Burke, *Analysis of Beauty*, p. 136.

41 Burke, *Analysis of Beauty*, pp. 48–9.

42 Nichols, *Biographical Anecdotes*, p. 325.

43 Burke, *Analysis of Beauty*, p. 147.

44 Burke, *Analysis of Beauty*, p. 148.

45 Burke, *Analysis of Beauty*, p. 148.

46 Burke, *Analysis of Beauty*, p. 147.

47 James Beattie, writing the year Hogarth died, declared, 'A country-dance of men and women, like those exhibited by Hogarth in his *Analysis of Beauty*, could hardly fail to make a beholder merry, whether he believed their union to be the effect of design, or of accident.' He observes how Hogarth has artfully entwined the opposites of 'incongruity' with 'relation', or connection, which exist together happily here for 'all of them are incongruous in respect of one another ; thus far the assemblage displays contrariety or want of relation : and they are all united in the same place, and in the same dance ; and thus far they are mutually related.' J. Beattie, 'On LAUGHTER, and LUDICROUS COMPOSITION' in *Essays*, Edinburgh, 1776, p. 353.

48 Burke, *Analysis of Beauty*, p. 144.

49 Burke, *Analysis of Beauty*, p. 145.

50 'Lady *Luxborough*'s Letters p. 380', quoted in Nichols, *Biographical Anecdotes*, p. 327. H. Knight, Baroness Luxborough, *Letters written by the Late Right Honourable Lady Luxborough, to William Shenstone, Esq.*, London, 1775, Letter CVIII 16 March 1754, pp. 324–6, section quoted by Nichols, *Biographical Anecdotes*, p. 324.

51 BL Add MS 27995, f. 10r, P. Yonge to W. Hogarth, Cambridge, 28 November 1753.

52 BL Add MS 27995, f. 14r, B. Wilson to W. Hogarth (at Chiswick), *c*.1754; see also E. I. Carlyle & J. Hargreaves 'Benjamin Wilson' in *ODNB*, 26 May 2005.

53 Nichols, *Biographical Anecdotes*, p. 53.

54 For a survey of Sandby's life and career see J. Bonehill & S. Daniels, *Paul Sandby: Picturing Britain*, London, 2009 with street scenes, pp. 120–40. For

Sandby's satires against Hogarth see Bonehill & Daniels, *Sandby*, pp. 38–47 and D. Bindman, *Hogarth and his Times*, London, 1997, pp. 168–81.

55 Bonehill & Daniels, *Sandby*, pp. 106–18.

56 See Bindman, *Hogarth and his Times*, pp. 168–81.

57 For Sandby's role in the formation of the Royal Academy see Bonehill & Daniels, *Sandby*, pp. 29–31.

58 *The Idler*, No.82, 10 November 1759; *The Idler*, No.76, 26 September 1759, see Bindman, 'William Hogarth', *ODNB*.

59 Burke, *Analysis of Beauty* (Autobiographical Notes), p. 203.

60 A. Ramsay, *An Essay on Ridicule*, London, 1753, pp. 74–5.

61 The canvases are forty inches by fifty inches, rather than the twenty-eight by thirty-six for *Marriage A-la-Mode*.

62 Nichols, *Biographical Anecdotes*, p. 338, complete poem transcription pp. 338–60.

63 Nichols, *Biographical Anecdotes*, p. 335.

64 Hogarth had declared this series contained no portraits, nor were the characters based on any specific person, excepting, as he confirmed to John Nichols, the figure sitting near the open window: 'that is the Irish gentleman [the present Sir *John Parnell*, nephew to the poet, and remarkable for his very flat nose], who is diverting the company by a face drawn with a burnt cork upon the back of his hand', perhaps a trick Hogarth himself had seen, or did himself, 'while he is supposed to be singing – *An old woman cloathed in grey*. This gentleman (then an eminent attorney) begged it as a favour ; declaring, at the same time, he was so generally known, that the introduction of his face would be of service to our artist in the sale of his prints at *Dublin*.' Nichols, *Biographical Anecdotes*, p. 335.

65 BL Add MS 22394 *Names of subscribers to the four prints of An Election*, f. 1.

66 BL Add MS 22394, f. 2 except Cathcart (f. 5) and Portland (f. 8) Garrick (f. 20) Hoadly (f. 21).

67 BL Add MS 22394, f. 7 Wilkes; f. 5 Canterbury; f. 6 Pegge; f. 7 Shaftesbury; f. 10 Pattison.

68 John Nichols observes, 'A sum of money was left to defray the expence of these ornaments, and it found its way into *Hogarth's* pocket. The original sketches in oil for these performances, are now at Mrs. *Hogarth's* house at *Leicester-fields*.' Nichols, *Biographical Anecdotes*, p. 111. Nichols seems to dislike the idea that an artist should need to earn money, a curiously unrealistic attitude given the nature of the world. For the fee, see Paulson, *Hogarth*, 1993, Vol. III, p. 205.

69 'To shew how little it may be expected that history painting well [will] ever be requird in the way it has been on accounts of religion abroad there have been but two Public demands in within the forty years'; that is *Paul Before Felix*, the large canvas for Lincoln's Inn and this altarpiece for St Mary Redcliffe, 'for both which I was applied to'. Burke, *Analysis of Beauty* (Autobiographical Notes), p. 219.

70 The subject was *The Adoration of the Magi*, which George Vertue observed was 'tho't to be not strong enough, by some & of a pale weakly colouring' see Vertue, III, p. 157. Also J. Ingamells, 'Andrea Casali' in *ODNB*, 23 September 2004.

71   The red chalk preparatory drawing (III, 32a) is now at the Morgan Library, New York.

72   Burke, *Analysis of Beauty*, pp. 47–8.

73   For the complete passage see *The Holy Bible*, London, 1743, the Gospel of St Matthew 28:1–6.

74   Editorial, 'Sir James Thornhill's Collection' in *The Burlington Magazine*, pp. 134–5.

75   BM 1918, 0615.2 and 1936, 1010.3.

76   Ramsay's tract was republished as *A Dialogue on Taste*, 2nd edition, London, 1762, p. 29.

77   Einberg, *Hogarth*, 2016, pp. 337–9.

78   D. Maskill, 'The Neighbor from Hell: André Rouquet's Eviction from the Louvre,' *Journal18*, Issue 2 *Louvre Local* (Fall 2016), http://www.journal18. org/822. DOI: 10.30610/2.2016.1.

79   The artist himself declared the nobleman's gratitude 'was far more pleasing' than the money 'to one of my turn'. Burke, *Analysis of Beauty* (Autobiographical Notes), p. 219.

80   J. Dryden, *Fables Ancient and Modern; Translated into Verse, from Homer, Ovid, Boccace, & Chaucer: with Original Poems*, London, 1700, pp. 123–51.

81   Burke, *Analysis of Beauty* (Autobiographical Notes), p. 220.

82   'Now, though the sullen Sire had eas'd his Mind,/ The Pomp of his Revenge was yet behind,/ A Pomp prepar'd to grace the Present he design'd./ A Goblet rich with Gems, and rough with Gold,/ Of Depth, and Breadth, the precious Pledge to hold,/ With cruel Care he chose : The hollow Part Inclos'd; the Lid conceal'd the Lover's Heart.' Dryden, *Fables*, p. 146.

83   Einberg, *Hogarth*, 2016, p. 353, quoting from a manuscript in the collection of Mrs Donald F. Hyde .

84   ['Truth'], 'Billy and Jenny', *Mirror of Literature*, p. 323.

85   Bindman, 'William Hogarth' in *ODNB*, Barber, 'Sir James Thornhill' in *ODNB* and Egerton, 'John Ellys' in *ODNB*.

86   Burke, *Analysis of Beauty* (Autobiographical Notes), p. 219: 'I have had at least one way or other L200 with this competency'.

87   RCT RCIN 401358 files.

88   Burke, *Analysis of Beauty* (Autobiographical Notes), p. 220.

89   Smith, *Nollekens*, Vol. II, p. 350.

90   HRO Malmesbury Papers 9M73/G485/27, letter from J. Hoadly to J. Harris, 27 August 1760.

91   L. Sterne, *The Life and Opinions of Tristram Shandy, Gentleman*, 2nd edition, London, 1760, Vol. II, pp. 58–9.

92   Sterne, *Tristram Shandy*, Vol. II, pp. 99–100.

93   See W. Holtz, 'Pictures for Parson Yorick: Laurence Sterne's London visit of 1760' in *Eighteenth century studies*, Vol. I, No.2 (Winter 1967), pp. 169–84.

94   Sterne, *Tristram Shandy*, 2nd edition, London, 1761, Vol. IV, pp. 111–12.

95   Pyne, *Wine and Walnuts*, Vol. I, p. 163.

96   The Golden Cross – first mentioned in 1643 – was a large coaching inn from where coaches departed for Dover, Brighton and York.

97   Pyne, *Wine and Walnuts*, Vol. I, pp. 172–3. This agitation for the offence Hogarth still felt, a decade on, is borne out by the republishing of a *March to Finchley* engraving, 'retouched and improved' by himself, on 12 June 1761, but still dedicated to the King of Prussia.

98   For the portrait see Einberg, *Hogarth*, 2016, pp. 359–60.

99   Wright ed., *Letters of Horace Walpole*, Vol. IV, pp. 140–42, H. Walpole to G. Montagu, London, 5 May 1761, pp. 140–41.

100 Wright ed., *Letters of Horace Walpole*, Vol. IV, pp. 140–42, H. Walpole to G. Montagu, London, 5 May 1761, p. 141.

101 Wright ed., *Letters of Horace Walpole*, Vol. IV, pp. 140–42, H. Walpole to G. Montagu, London, 5 May 1761, p. 141.

102 Wright ed., *Letters of Horace Walpole*, Vol. IV, pp. 140–42, H. Walpole to G. Montagu, London, 5 May 1761, pp. 141–2.

103 Paulson, *Hogarth*, 1993, Vol. III, p. 324.

104 *St James's Chronicle*, 23–6 May 1761 .

105 Walpole, *Anecdotes of Painting in England*, Vol. IV, pp. 77–9, p. 78.

106 ['Truth'], 'Billy and Jenny', *Mirror of Literature*, p. 323.

107 Burke, *Analysis of Beauty* (Autobiographical Notes), p. 220.

108 Burke, *Analysis of Beauty* (Autobiographical Notes), p. 221.

109 Walpole, *Anecdotes of Painting in England*, Vol. IV, p. 79.

110 Burke, *Analysis of Beauty* (Autobiographical Notes), p. 221.

111 J. Wilkes, *English Liberty: Being a Collection of Interesting Tracts, From the Year 1762 to 1769*, London, 1769, p. 366 n.*.

112 Trusler, *Hogarth Moralized*, p. iii.

113 Little & Kahrl, *Letters of David Garrick*, Vol. I, pp. 366–7, posted 7 September 1762.

114 J. Wilkes, *The North Briton*, No. XVII, 25 September 1762, pp. 97–102.

115 Burke, *Analysis of Beauty* (Autobiographical Notes), p. 218.

116 Little & Kahrl, *Letters of David Garrick*, Vol. I, pp. 369–70.

117 Burke, *Analysis of Beauty* (Autobiographical Notes), p. 222.

118 Burke, *Analysis of Beauty* (Autobiographical Notes), p. 221.

119 Wilkes, *English* Liberty, p. 367.

120 Nichols states that the original drawing for the latter 'which was thrown by *Hogarth* into the fire, was snatched out of it by Mrs *Lewis*, and is now in the possession of Mr S. *Ireland*.' Nichols, *Biographical Anecdotes*, p. 386 note †.

121 Burke, *Analysis of Beauty* (Autobiographical Notes), p. 231.

122 *Gazetteer and London Daily Advertiser*, 13 June 1763.

123 Burke, *Analysis of Beauty* (Autobiographical Notes), p. 221.

124 Nichols, *Biographical Anecdotes*, p. 387.

125 Wilkes, *English Liberty*, p. 368.

126 Little & Kahrl, *Letters of David Garrick*, Vol. I, pp. 378–9, p. 378.

127 Nichols, *Biographical Notes*, p. 90.

128 Burke, *Analysis of Beauty* (Autobiographical Notes), pp. 221–2.

129 Burke, *Analysis of Beauty* (Autobiographical Notes), pp. 221–2.

130 BL Add MS 27995, f. 17 Anon letter and poem to W. Hogarth, Brighthelmston, 9 July 1763.

131 BL Add MS 27995 f. 21r, E. Knox to W. Hogarth, 20 August 1763 and epigram f. 22r.

132 See J. Sambrook, 'Charles Churchill' in *ODNB*, 28 September 2006.

133 Churchill is quoted in Wilkes, *English Liberty*, pp. 366–8; also quoted in Nichols, *Biographical Anecdotes*, p. 387 note *.

134 R. Bentley, *Letters of Horace Walpole, Earl of Orford, to Sir Horace Mann 1760–1785*, 3 Vols, London, 1843, Vol. I, p. 108 n.*.

135 Nichols, *Biographical Anecdotes*, p. 93.

136 ['Truth'], 'Billy and Jenny', *Mirror of Literature*, p. 307.

137 BL Add MS 27991, 'Fragments of an autobiography, etc., by William Hogarth'; Burke, *Analysis of Beauty* (Autobiographical Notes), p. 219.

138 Burke, *Analysis of Beauty* (Autobiographical Notes), p. 201 and p. 208.

139 Nichols, *Biographical Anecdotes*, pp. 93–4.

140 Nichols, *Biographical Anecdotes*, p. 94.

141 ['Truth'], 'Billy and Jenny', *Mirror of Literature*, p. 323.

142 R. T. Wilson, *The Life of General Sir Robert Wilson*, 2 Vols, London, 1862, Vol. 1, pp. 30–31.

143 ['Truth'], 'Billy and Jenny', *Mirror of Literature*, p. 324.

144 ['Truth'], 'Billy and Jenny', *Mirror of Literature*, p. 324.

145 I am grateful to Timothy Duke, Norroy and Ulster King at Arms for his thoughts, and to Rosie Razzall at the Royal Collection Trust .

146 Burke, *Analysis of Beauty* (Autobiographical Notes), p. 219.

147 Nichols, *Biographical Anecdotes*, p. 95.

148 P. Cunningham ed., *The Letters of Horace Walpole: Earl of Orford*, 9 Vols, London, 1861, Vol. IV, H. Walpole to H. Mann, 15 November 1764, pp. 291–2, p. 291.

149 Timbs, *Anecdote Biography*, p. 75.

150 ['Truth'], 'Billy and Jenny', *Mirror of Literature,* pp. 306–7.

Epilogue

1   Forrest, f. 13.

2   *OED* 'bumboat' 1.a.

3   Forrest, f. 13.

4   Forrest, f. 14.

5   Forrest, f. 14.

6   Forrest, f. 14.

7   Forrest, f. 14.

BIBLIOGRAPHY

Manuscripts

Bienecke Rare Book & Manuscript Library, Yale University.
GEN MSS 1429   Box 9 Folder 258, J. Hogarth to A. Walker, 29 May 1781.

British Library
BL Add MS 22394   *Names of subscribers to the four prints of An Election, by*
                      William Hogarth 1754–1757; together with the names of
                      subscribers to the intended print of Sigismonda ...; notes,
                      copies of letters, etc., relating to Sigismonda, in Hogarth's own
                      handwriting ...; and original letters, 1754–1764, folio.
BL Add MS 27991   *Fragments of an autobiography, etc., by William Hogarth,*
                      eighteenth century, small folio.
BL Add MS 27993   *Observations on the institution of the Royal Academy and on*
                      the practice of art in England, by William Hogarth, eighteenth
                      century, folio.
BL Add MS 27994   Anonymous translation, *Letters from Mr. [Rouquet] to one of*
                      his Friends in Paris in order to explain Mr. Hogarth's Prints,
                      eighteenth century.
BL Add MS 27995   *Original letters and papers relating to William Hogarth,*
                      1731–91.

British Museum
1847,0320.1–10   Ebenezer Forrest, *An account of what Seem'd most Remarkable*
                      in the Five Days Peregrination of the Five Following Persons
                      Viz^t. Messieurs Tothall, Scott, Hogarth, Thornhill & Forrest ...,
                      bound manuscript with drawings by William Hogarth,
                      Samuel Scott and John Thornhill, 1732.

Hampshire Record Office
Malmesbury Papers   9M73/G485/1–32 letters from John Hoadly to James Harris
                      1737–72.

National Archives
TNA PROB 1/66   Will of William Hogarth 16 August, proved 9 November
                      1764.

Royal Archives
RA Stuart Papers/MAIN

Royal Collection Trust
RCT RCIN 913477   Letter from W. Hogarth to 'T. H.', 21 October 1746.
RCT RCIN 913498   [J. T. Smith?] *Hogarth's lodging in South Lambeth.*
RCT RCIN 401358   Object Record File.

Tate Archive
TA Highmore Gift   866/2/1 Joseph Highmore, *Paris Journal*, 1734.

Primary Sources (Printed)
Anderson, J., *The Constitutions of the Free-Masons*, London, 1723.
[Anon.], *A Candid and Impartial Account of the Behaviour of Simon Lord Lovat from the Time his Death-Warrant was deliver'd, to the Day of his Execution*, London, 1747.
[Anon.], *A Catalogue of the Rarities to be seen at Don Saltero's Coffee-House in Chelsea*, 12th edition, London, 1738.
[Anon.], *A Discourse on Witchcraft*, London, 1736.
[Anon.], *Hymen: An accurate Description of the Ceremonies used in Marriage, By every Nation in the Known World*, London, 1760.
[Anon.], *The Constitutions of the Company of Watermen and Lightermen*, London, 1730.
Aubrey, J., R. Barber ed., *Brief Lives*, Woodbridge, 2009.
Bailey, N., *Dictionarium Britannicum: Or a more Compleat Universal Etymological English Dictionary*, London, 1730.
Beattie, J., *Essays*, Edinburgh, 1776.
Bentley, R., *Letters of Horace Walpole, Earl of Orford, to Sir Horace Mann 1760–1785*, 3 Vols, London, 1843.
Boaden, J., *The private correspondence of David Garrick*, 2nd edition, 2 Vols, London, 1835.
Boswell, J., *The Life of Samuel Johnson, LL.D.*, 2 Vols, London, 1791.
Brand, J., *Observations on Popular Antiquities*, Newcastle upon Tyne, 1777.
British Mercury, 14 October 1713.
Brocklesby, R., *Private VIRTUE and publick SPIRIT display'd. In a Succinct ESSAY ON THE CHARACTER OF Capt. Thomas Coram*, London, 1751.
Burke, J. ed. [W. Hogarth], *The Analysis of Beauty with the rejected passages from the manuscript drafts and autobiographical notes*, Oxford, 1955.
Butler, S., *Hudibras. In Three Parts. Written in the Time of the Late Wars ... Adorn'd with a new Set of Cuts, Design'd and Engrav'd by Mr. HOGARTH*, London, 1732.
Byrom, J., *Miscellaneous Poems*, 2 Vols, Manchester, 1773.
Chaplin, J. E. ed., *Benjamin Franklin's Autobiography* (A Norton Critical Edition), New York & London, 2012.
Cobbett, W., *Cobbett's Parliamentary History of England*, Vol. IX, 1733–7, London, 1811.

Cole, M., *The Lady's Complete Guide*, London, 1789.

Cook, T., *Anecdotes of Mr. Hogarth, and Explanatory Descriptions of the Plates of Hogarth Restored*, London, 1803.

Country Journal or The Craftsman, 1 July 1732.

Country Journal or The Craftsman, 10 March 1732/3.

Country Journal or The Craftsman, 3 November 1733.

Country Journal or The Craftsman, 24 May 1735.

Country Journal or The Craftsman, 16 April 1737.

Coxe, W., *Memoirs of the Administration of Sir Robert Walpole*, 3 Vols, London, 1798.

Croker, J. ed. [John, Lord Hervey], *Memoirs of the reign of George the second*, 2 Vols, London, 1848.

Cunningham, P. ed., *The Letters of Horace Walpole: Earl of Orford*, 9 Vols, London, 1861.

Daily Advertiser, 2 April 1743.

Daily Advertiser, 4 April 1743.

Daily Advertiser, 8 November 1744.

Daily Advertiser, 30 September 1745.

Daily Advertiser, 22 March 1773.

Daily and General Advertiser, 26 June 1747.

Daily Courant, 13 January 1709.

Daily Courant, 13 December 1732.

Daily Journal, 23 December 1729.

Daily Post, 6 October 1725.

Daily Post, 25 February 1726.

Daily Post, 26 April 1732.

Daily Post, 4 May 1732.

Daily Post, 2 June 1737.

Daily Post, 6 December 1745.

Defoe, D., *Review of the State of the British Nation*, Vol. IV, No. 126, London, 2 December 1707.

[Defoe, D.], *A Narrative of all the Robberies, Escapes, &c. of John Sheppard : Giving an Exact Description of the manner of his wonderful Escape from the CASTLE in Newgate*, 2nd edition, London, 1724.

[Defoe, D.], *Captain Charles Johnson's General History of Pyrates*, London, 1724.

Defoe, D., *A Tour thro' the Whole Island of Great Britain*, 3 Vols, London, 1724–7.

Denne, S. & W. Shrubsole, *History and Antiquities of Rochester and Its Environs*, Rochester, 1772.

Donne, J., *Devotions Upon Emergent Occasions*, London, 1624.

Dryden, J., *Fables Ancient and Modern; Translated into Verse, from Homer, Ovid, Boccace, & Chaucer: with Original Poems*, London, 1700.

D'Urfey, T., *Wit and Mirth: Or, Pills to Purge Melancholy*, 6 Vols, London, 1698–1720.

Dyche, T. & W. Pardon, *A New General English Dictionary*, London, 1765.

Eking, H., *A View of the Greenland Trade*, London, 1725.

Evening Post, 27–30 June 1713.

Félibien, A. & A. Testelin trans., *Seven conferences held in the King of France's cabinet of paintings*, London, 1740.

Fielding, H., *Tragedy of Tragedies*, London, 1731.

Fielding, H., *The Historical Register, For the Year 1736*, London, 1737.

Fielding, H., *An Apology for the Life of Mrs. Shamela Andrews*, London, 1741.

Fielding, H., *The History of the Adventures of Joseph Andrews...Written in imitation of the manner of Cervantes, etc.*, 2nd edition, 2 Vols, London, 1742.

Fielding, H., *Les avantures de Joseph Andrews*, 2 Vols, London, 1743.

Fielding, H., *The True Patriot: and History of Our Own Times*, 19 November 1745.

Fielding, H., *The True Patriot: and History of Our Own Times*, 10 December 1745.

[Fielding, H.], 'John Trott-Plaid', *The Jacobite's Journal*, Issue 1, 5 December 1747.

Fielding, H., *The History of Tom Jones, a foundling*, 6 Vols, London, 1749.

Fielding, H., *Histoire de Tom Jones ou L'enfant trouvé*, 4 Vols, London, 1750.

Fielding, H., *An Enquiry into the Causes of the late Increase of Robbers, &c., with some Proposals for Remedying this Growing Evil.*, London, 1751.

Fielding, H., *The Works of Henry Fielding*, 3rd edition, 12 Vols, London, 1766.

Flying Post or The Weekly Medley, 1 February 1729.

Fog's Weekly Journal, 14 March 1730.

Forbes, A. ed., *Curiosities of A Scots Charta Chest 1600–1800, With the Travels and Memoranda of Sir Alexander Dick [Cunyngham]*, Edinburgh, 1897.

Fraser's Magazine for town and country, Vol. 24 (No. 139–144), London, October 1841, pp. 443–54.

Fremantle, K. ed., *Sir James Thornhill's Sketch-Book Travel Journal of 1711: A visit to East Anglia and the Low Countries*, 2 Vols, Utrecht, 1975.

Gazetteer and London Daily Advertiser, 13 June 1763.

Gazetteer and New Daily Advertiser, 29 November 1791.

General Advertiser, 20–27 September 1746.

General Evening Post, 12–14 June 1735.

General Evening Post, 15–17 July 1735.

General Evening Post, 20–22 November 1739.

Gentleman's Magazine, Vol. 1, London, 1732.

Gentleman's Magazine, Vol. 3, March 1733.

Gentleman's Magazine, Vol. 18, London, 1748.

Gentleman's Magazine, Vol. 86, December 1799.

Gentleman's Magazine, Vol. 86, Pt 1, April 1816.

Gentleman's Magazine, Vol. 95, Pt 1, Jan–Jun 1825.

George Faulkner, The Dublin Journal, 15–18 November 1746.

Glasse, H., *The Art of Cookery Made Plain and Easy*, 2nd edition, London, 1747.

Gostling, W., 'An Account of what seemed most remarkable in the five Days Peregrination ... Imitated In HUDIBRASTICKS ...' in C. Mitchell ed., *Hogarth's Peregrination*, Oxford, 1952, pp. 21–47.

Gray, T., *Designs by Mr. Bentley, For Six Poems by Mr. T. Gray*, London, 1753.

Green, C. H., *Historical Register*, Vol. XVIII, London, 1733.

Grub Street Journal, 24 November 1737.

Hall, A., Baroness Llanover ed., *The Autobiography and Correspondence of Mary Granville, Mrs. Delany*, 3 Vols, London, 1861.

Harris, J. [Earl of Malmesbury] ed., *A Series of Letters of the First Earl of Malmesbury*, 2 Vols, London, 1870.

Hasted, E., *The History and Topographical Survey of Kent*, 6 Vols, Canterbury, 1797–8.

Hawkesworth, J. ed., *The Works of Dr. Jonathan Swift*, 17 Vols, London, 1765.

Hawkesworth, J. ed., *Letters, written by the late Jonathan Swift, D.D.*, 3 Vols, London, 1766–7.

Hawkesworth, J. ed., *The Works of Jonathan Swift, D.D.*, 18 Vols, London, 1784.

Hogarth, R., *Thesaurarium Trilingue Publicum: Being an Introduction to English, Latin and Greek*, London, 1689.

Hughes, J., *The Ecstasy*, London, 1720.

Hume, D., *Political Discourses*, 2nd edition, Edinburgh, 1752.

Ireland, J., *Hogarth Illustrated*, 2nd edition, 3 Vols, London, 1793.

Ireland, J., *Supplement to Hogarth Illustrated*, 2nd edition, London, 1804.

Ireland, S., *Graphic Illustrations of Hogarth*, London, 1794.

Ireland, S., *Graphic Illustrations of Hogarth*, 2 Vols, London, 1799.

Jacob, G., *The Poetical Register*, 2 Vols, London, 1723.

Jane Hogarth's sale catalogue, 24 April 1790 (Lugt 4574, 1790-04-24).

Johnson, S., *A Dictionary of the English Language*, 2 Vols, London, 1755.

Kitson, M. ed., 'Hogarth's "Apology for Painters"', *Walpole Society*, Oxford, Vol. 41, 1966–8, pp. 46–111.

Klima, S., G. Bowers & K. S. Grant eds., *Memoirs of Dr. Charles Burney, 1726–1769*, Lincoln & London, 1988.

Knight, H., Baroness Luxborough, *Letters written by the Late Right Honourable Lady Luxborough, to William Shenstone, Esq.*, London, 1775.

La Motraye, A. de, *Travels through Europe, Asia, and into Parts of Africa*, London, 1723/4.

Le Blanc, Abbé J. B., 'Letter XXIII To the Abbe du Bos; On the state of painting and sculpture in England' in *Letters on the English and French Nations*, London, 1747, pp. 155–63.

Lee, G. ed., *Remnants of Rhyme by Thomas Hoggart of Troutbeck*, Kendal (printed for George Lee), 1853.

Little, D. M. & G. M. Kahrl ed., *The Letters of David Garrick*, 3 Vols, London, 1963–5.

Livesay, R., *George Taylor epitaph*, etching, 1782, a copy of Hogarth's manuscript, published by Jane Hogarth (BM Cc,1.189).

Lockhart, G., 'Alexander MacDonald's Journall and Memoirs' in *The Lockhart Papers*, 2 Vols, London, 1817, Vol. II, pp. 479–510.

London Daily Post and General Advertiser, 30 June 1735.

London Daily Post and General Advertiser, 24 November 1740.

London Evening Post, 1–3 April 1729.

London Evening Post, 1–4 August 1730.

London Evening Post, 16–18 May 1732.

London Evening Post, 20–23 January 1733.

London Evening Post, 18–20 May 1738.

London Evening Post, 28–30 September 1738.

London Evening Post, 25–7 October 1739.

London Evening Post, 15–17 October 1747.

London Journal, 17 November 1733.

London Journal, 22 December 1733.

Lysons, D., *The Environs of London: Volume 3, County of Middlesex,* London, 1795.

Macky, J., *A Journey Through England*, 4th edition, 2 Vols, London, 1724.

Macky, J., *Memoirs of the Secret Services*, London, 1733.

Malone, E. ed., *The Works of Sir Joshua Reynolds, Knight*, 2nd edition, London, 1798.

Mandeville, B., *An Enquiry into the causes of the frequent executions at Tyburn*, London, 1725.

Mary Edward's Sale, C. Cock's, 28–9 May 1746.

Matthews, W. ed., *Charles II's Escape from Worcester: A Collection of Narratives Assembled by Samuel Pepys*, London, 1967.

Maximus, Q. Valerius, *His Collections of the Memorable Acts and Sayings of ... the Antient Romans*, London, 1684.

Mitchell, C., *Hogarth's Peregrination*, Oxford, 1952.

Nichols, J., *Biographical Anecdotes of William Hogarth*, 3rd edition, London, 1785.

Nichols, J. & G. Steevens, *The Genuine Works of William Hogarth*, 3 Vols, London, 1808–17.

Nichols, N. ed., *The Works of Thomas Gray*, London, 1835.

Nott, J., *The Cook's and Confectioner's Dictionary*, London, 1723.

Nugent, T., *The Grand Tour, Containing an Exact Description of most of the Cities, Towns, and Remarkable Places of Europe*, 3 Vols, London, 1746.

Ogle, G., *The Canterbury Tales of Chaucer. Modernis'd by several Hands*, 3 Vols, London, 1741.

Old Bailey Proceedings Online, trial of John Restow for deception (bankruptcy), 16 May 1711 (t17110516–38).

Old Bailey Proceedings Online, trial of Ann Jones for infanticide, 12 July 1720 (t17200712–27).

Old Bailey Proceedings Online, trial of Francis Charteris for rape, 28 February 1730 (t17300228–69).

Old Bailey Proceedings Online, trial of Francis Hackabout for highway robbery, 28 February 1730 (t17300228–71).

Old Bailey Proceedings Online, trial of Sarah Malcolm for murder, 21 February 1733 (t17330221–52).

Old Bailey Proceedings Online, trial of Elizabeth Calloway for arson, 2 July 1735 (t17350702–42).

Parkinson, R. ed., *The private journal and literary remains of John Byrom*, 4 Vols (32, 34, 40, 44), Chetham Society, Manchester, 1854–7.

Paton, H. ed., *The Lyon in Mourning*, 3 Vols, Edinburgh, 1896.

Pennell, E. R. & J. Pennell, *The life of James McNeill Whistler*, 2 Vols, London (3rd Impression), 1909.

Pope, A., *The Dunciad*, London, 1729.

Pope, A. & W. Warburton eds, *The Works of Shakespear: in Eight Volumes*, London, 1747.

Post Man and the Historical Account, 8–11 January 1704.

Post Man and the Historical Account, 30 May 1710.

Pottle, F. A. ed., *Boswell's London Journal 1762–1763*, London, 1951.

Public Advertiser, 8 December 1764.

Pyne, W. H. [Ephraim Hardcastle], *Wine and Walnuts; or, After Dinner Chit-Chat*, 2nd edition, 2 Vols, London, 1824.

Ramsay, A. (senior), *Tea-Table Miscellany: a Collection of Scots Sangs*, 10th edition, London, 1740.

Ramsay, A., *An Essay on Ridicule*, London, 1753.

Ramsay, A., *A Dialogue on Taste*, 2nd edition, London, 1762.

Richardson, J., *An essay on the theory of painting ... Enlarg'd and Corrected*, 2nd edition, London, 1725.

Richardson, J. & J. Richardson, *An account of some of the statues, bas-reliefs, drawings and pictures in Italy. &c.*, London, 1722.

Richardson, J. & J. Richardson, *Explanatory Notes and Remarks on Milton's Paradise Lost*, London, 1734.

Richardson, S., *Pamela: or, Virtue rewarded ... and afterwards, in her exalted condition ... and embellish'd with copper plates, design'd and engrav'd by Mr. Hayman, and Mr. Gravelot*, 6th edition, London, 1742.

Rouquet, A., *The Present State of the Arts in England*, London, 1755.

Rowe, E., *Friendship in Death: In Twenty Letters from the Dead to the Living*, 2nd edition, London, 1729.

St. James's Chronicle, 23–6 May 1761.

Shakespeare, W., *The Tragical History of King Richard the Third ... As it is now Acted at the Theatre-Royal in Drury-Lane. Reviv'd, with Alterations, by Mr. Cibber*, London, 1718.

Sloane, H., *A Voyage to the Islands Madera, Barbados ... and Jamaica*, 2 Vols, London, 1707.

Smith, J. T., *Nollekens and his Times*, 2 Vols, 2nd edition, London, 1829.

Somervile, W., *Hobbinol, or the Rural Games. A Burlesque Poem*, London, 1740.

Steele, R., *The Tatler*, No. 34, 25–8 June 1709.

Sterne, L., *The Life and Opinions of Tristram Shandy, Gentleman*, 2nd edition, 4 Vols, London, 1760–61.

Strypes, J., *A Survey of the Cities of London and Westminster*, 2 Vols, London, 1720.

Swift, J., *Travels into Several Remote Nations of the World. In Four Parts. By Lemuel Gulliver ...*, London, 1726.

Swift, J., *The Intelligencer*, No. 3, [May 1728], London, 1729.

Swift, J., *Works of J[onathan] S[wift] ... Containing the Author's POETICAL WORKS*, 6 Vols, Dublin, 1735–8.

The British Journal, 28 November 1724.

The Chester Miscellany. Being a collection of several pieces, both in prose and verse, which were in the Chester Courant from January 1745, to May 1750, Chester, 1750.

The Craftsman, 5 December 1730.

The Holy Bible, London, 1743.

The Idler, No. 76, 26 September 1759.

The Idler, No. 82, 10 November 1759.

The London Magazine, or, Gentleman's Monthly Intelligencer, July 1737.

The Midwife: or, The Old Woman's Magazine, Vol. I, London, 1751.

Theobald, L., *Perseus and Andromeda, As it is Performed at the Theatre Royal in Lincoln's-Inn-Fields*, 5th edition, London, 1731.

Thornhill, Sir J., 'A Hue and Cry after Four of the King's Liege Subjects, who were lately suppos'd to be seen at Roystone in Hertfordshire 18 March 1720/1', *Wren Society*, Vol. 17, 1940, pp. 12–13.

Thornhill, J., *An Explanation of the Painting in the Royal Hospital at Greenwich by Sir James Thornhill*, London, n.d.

Trusler, Rev. J., *Hogarth Moralized, being A Complete Edition of Hogarth's Works*, London, 1768.

['Truth'], '"Billy and Jenny," or Souvenirs of the Celebrated Hogarth and his Lady' in *The Mirror of Literature, Amusement and Instruction*, London, 1843, (New Series) Vol. III, pp. 306–7, pp. 322–4.

Universal Spectator and Weekly Journal, Saturday 10 March 1733.

Unknown, *Cuckolds haven*, London, 1638 (British Library C.20.f. 7.46–7).

Upton, J. ed., *The Schoolmaster or, A plain and perfect Way of teaching Children to Understand, Write, and Speak the Latin Tongue. By Roger Ascham ...*, London, 1711.

Vertue, G, Notebooks I–VI, *Walpole Society*, Oxford, 1929–50.

Victor, B., *A Session of Painters*, London, 1725.

Walpole, H., *Anecdotes of Painting in England; With some account of the principal Artists*, 4 Vols, Strawberry Hill, 1762–71.

Ward, E., *A Frolick to Horn-Fair with a Walk from Cuckold's-Point Thro' Deptford and Greenwich*, London, 1700.

Ward, E., *The London Spy Compleat, In Eighteen-Parts. By the Author of the Trip to JAMAICA*, London, 1703.

Ward, E., *The Merry Travellers: or, A Trip upon Ten-Toes from Moorfields to Bromley An Humourous Poem. Intended as the Wandering Spy*, 2nd edition, London, 1724.

Weekly Journal or British Gazetteer, 2 September 1721.

Weekly Miscellanies, 18 May 1734.

Weekly Register, 3 June 1732.

Wensinger, A. S. trans. & ed., *Hogarth on High Life: The Marriage à la Mode Series from Georg Christoph Lichtenberg's Commentaries*, Middleton, 1970.

Wilkes, J., *The North Briton*, No. XVII, 25 September 1762, pp. 97–102.

Wilkes, J., *English Liberty: Being a Collection of Interesting Tracts, From the Year 1762 to 1769*, London, 1769.

Wright, J. ed., *The Letters of Horace Walpole, Earl of Orford*, 6 Vols, London, 1840.

Secondary Sources

Allen, B., *Francis Hayman*, New Haven & London, 1987.

Allin., D. S., *The Early Years of the Foundling Hospital 1739/41–1773*, London, 2010.

Antal, F. , *Hogarth and his place in European Art*, London, 1962.

Bailey, J., *Unquiet Lives: Marriage and Marriage Breakdown in England, 1660–1800*, Cambridge, 2003.

Barber, T., 'Sir James Thornhill [Thornhull]' in *ODNB*, 3 January 2008.

Barber, T. ed., [contributors T. Batchelor, A. Geraghty, L. Hamlett, J. Legard, A. Lim & D. A. H. B. Taylor], *British Baroque: Power and Illusion*, London, 2020.

Barter Bailey, S., 'Richard Watts' in *ODNB*, 3 January 2008.

Battestin, M. C., 'Henry Fielding' in *ODNB*, 23 September 2004.

Berry, H., *Orphans of Empire: The fate of London's foundlings*, Oxford, 2019.

Bignamini, I., 'George Vertue, Art Historian and Art Institutions in London, 1689–1768: A Study of Clubs and Academies', *Walpole Society*, Oxford, Vol. 54, 1988, pp. 1–148.

Bignamini, I. & M. Postle, *The artist's model: its role in British art from Lely to Etty*, Nottingham & London, 1991.

Bindman, D., *Hogarth and his Times: serious comedy*, London, 1997.

Bindman, D., 'William Hogarth' in *ODNB*, 21 May 2009.

Bindman, D. ed., *Hogarth: Place and Progress*, London, 2019.

Bonehill, J. & S. Daniels, *Paul Sandby: Picturing Britain*, London, 2009.

Black, J., *Eighteenth-century Britain 1688–1783*, Basingstoke, 2001.

Bott, V., 'Hogarth's House as Hogarth saw it' in *The British Art Journal*, Autumn 2007, Vol. 8, No. 2, pp. 34–8 .

Brailsford, D., 'George Taylor' in *ODNB*, 23 September 2004.

Bright, J. & G. Clark, *An Introduction to the Tokens at the Foundling Museum*, 2nd edition, London, 2014.

Bucholz, R. O. & J. P. Ward, *London: A Social and Cultural History, 1550–1750*, Cambridge, 2012.

Burnett, C. B., *A History of the isle of Grain*, 1906.

Carey, J., *Taking Time: Chardin's Boy Building a House of Cards and other paintings*, London, 2012.

Carlyle, E. I. & J. Hargreaves 'Benjamin Wilson' in *ODNB*, 26 May 2005.

Clayton, T., 'Overton family' in *ODNB*, 23 September 2004.

Clegg, G., 'Mr Ranby and his House' in *Brentford & Chiswick Local History Journal* 8, 1999.

Cock, E., *The Soldier's Companion or Martial Recorder*, London, 1824.

Colley, L., *Britons: Forging the Nation 1707–1837*, New Haven & London, 1992.

Cook, T., *Anecdotes of Mr. Hogarth, and Explanatory Descriptions of the Plates of Hogarth Restored*, London, 1803.

Cook, T. A. & G. Nickalls, *Thomas Doggett Deceased: A Famous Comedian*, London, 1908.

Cooke, J. H., *The Shipwreck of Sir Cloudesley Shovell on the Scilly Islands*, London, 1883.

Corp, E., *A Court in Exile: The Stuarts in France, 1689–1718*, Cambridge, 2004.

Corp, E., *The Stuarts in Italy, 1719–1766: A Royal Court in Permanent Exile*, Cambridge, 2011.

Craske, M., *William Hogarth*, London, 2000.

Cruickshanks, E., *Political Untouchables: The Tories and the '45*, London, 1979.

Diack Johnstone, H., 'Maurice Greene' in *Oxford Music Online: Grove Music Online*, 20 January 2016.

[Editorial], 'Sir James Thornhill's Collection' in *The Burlington Magazine*, June 1943, Vol. 82, No. 483, June 1943, pp. 133–7.

[Editorial], 'Mrs. Hogarth's Collection' in *The Burlington Magazine*, June 1943, Vol. 85, No. 499, October 1944, pp. 237–9.

Egerton, J., *National Gallery Catalogues: The British School*, London, 1998.

Egerton, J., 'John Ellys' in *ODNB*, 23 September 2004.

Egerton, J., 'Sarah Curtis' in *ODNB*, 23 September 2004.

Einberg, E., *Manner & Morals: Hogarth and British Painting 1700–1760*, London, 1987.

Einberg, E., 'George Lambert' in *ODNB*, 19 May 2011.

Einberg, E., *William Hogarth: A Complete Catalogue of the Paintings*, New Haven & London, 2016.

Einberg, E. & J. Egerton, *Tate Gallery Collections: The Age of Hogarth*, London, 1988.

'Ellis Gamble' in www.britishmuseum.org/collection/term/BIOG163066.

Fitzgerald, P. H., *The Life of David Garrick*, 2 Vols, London, 1868.

Fordham, D., *British art and the Seven Years' War: allegiance and autonomy*, Philadelphia, 2010.

Fraser, S., *The Last Highlander*, London, 2012.

Friedman, T., *James Gibbs*, New Haven & London, 1984.

Friedman, T., 'James Gibbs' in *ODNB*, 3 January 2008.

Gater, G. H. & E. P. Wheeler, *Survey of London*, Vol. XVI, London, 1935.

Gatrell, V., *The First Bohemians: Life and Art in London's Golden Age*, London, 2013.

Gibson-Wood, C., *Jonathan Richardson: Art Theorist of the English Enlightenment*, New Haven & London, 2000.

Goodwin, G., *Benjamin Franklin in London*, London, 2016.

Hallett, M., *The Spectacle of Difference: Graphic Satire in the Age of Hogarth*, New Haven & London, 1999.

Hallett, M., *Hogarth*, London, 2000.

Hallett, M. & C. Riding, *Hogarth*, London, 2007.

Hallett, M., N. Llewellyn & M. Myrone eds., *Court, Country, City: British Art and Architecture, 1660–1735*, New Haven & London, 2016.

Hamlett, L., *Mural Painting in Britain 1630–1730: Experiencing Histories*, New York & Abingdon, 2020.

Hamlyn, R., *William Blake*, London, 2000.

Harris, J., 'William Kent' in *ODNB*, 24 May 2007.

Harris, R. & R. Simon eds., *Enlightened Self-Interest: The Foundling Hospital and Hogarth*, London, 1997.

Harvey, K., *The Impostress Rabbit Breeder: Mary Toft and Eighteenth-Century England*, Oxford, 2020.

Hayden, R., *Mrs. Delany: Her Life and Her Flowers*, 2nd edition, London, 2000.

Holtz, W., 'Pictures for Parson Yorick: Laurence Sterne's London visit of 1760' in *Eighteenth century studies*, Vol. I, No. 2 (Winter 1967), pp. 169–84.

Hotten, J. C. [E. Forrest], *Hogarth's Frolic. The five day's peregrination around the isle of Sheppey of William Hogarth and his fellow pilgrims, Scott, Tothall, Thornhill, and Forrest*, London, 1872.

Hughes, E. ed., *Spreading Canvas: Eighteenth-Century British Marine Painting*, New Haven & London, 2016.

Hume, R. D., 'The Value of Money in eighteenth century England' in *Huntington Library Quarterly*, Vol. 77, No. 4, December 2014, pp. 373–416.

Hyde, R., *The A to Z of Georgian London*, London, 1982.

Ingamells, J., 'Andrea Casali' in *ODNB*, 23 September 2004.

Ingamells, J., 'Allan Ramsay, of Kinell' in *ODNB*, 17 September 2015.

Johns, R., *James Thornhill and Decorative History Painting in England after 1688*, 2 Vols, Doctoral Thesis, University of York, 2004.

Johns, R., '"An Air of Grandeur & Modesty": James Thornhill's Painting in the Dome of St. Paul's Cathedral' in *Eighteenth Century Studies*, Vol. 42, No. 4, 2009.

Kalter, B., *Modern Antiques: The Material Past in England 1660–1780*, Lewisburg, 2011.

Keay, A., *The Last Royal Rebel: The Life and Death of James, Duke of Monmouth*, London, 2016.

Krysmanski, B. W., *Hogarth's Hidden Parts: Satiric Allusion, Erotic Wit, Blasphemous Bawdiness and Dark Humour in Eighteenth-Century English Art*, Hildesheim, Zurich & New York, 2010.

Laird, M. & A. Weisberg-Roberts, *Mrs. Delany & her Circle*, Newhaven & London, 2009.

Langford, P. , *Englishness Identified: Manners and Characters 1650–1850*, Oxford, 2000.

Lawson, J. ed., *Historic England: The Hoo Peninsula Landscape*, Swindon, 2015.

Levene, A., *Childcare, Health and Mortality at the London Foundling Hospital, 1741–1800*, Manchester, 2012.

Lincoln, M., *British Pirates and Society, 1680–1730*, Farnham, 2014.

Littledale, W. A. ed., *The Registers of Christ Church, Newgate, 1538 to 1754*, London, 1895.

Lucas, A., R. Johns, S. Stewart & S. Paine, *The Painted Hall: Sir James Thornhill's Masterpiece at Greenwich*, London & New York, 2019.

Macdougall, P. , *The story of the Hoo Peninsula*, Rochester, 1980.

MacGregor, A., 'Sir Hans Sloane' in *ODNB*, 23 September 2004.

McClure, R. K., *Coram's Children: The London Foundling Hospital in the Eighteenth Century*, New Haven & London, 1981.

Mansell, P. , *Dressed to Rule: Royal and Court Costume from Louis XIV to Elizabeth II*, New Haven, 2005.

Marks, A. S., 'Hogarth's Mackinen Children' in *The British Art Journal*, Vol. IX, No. 1 (Spring 2008), pp. 38–56.

Martinez, C. S., 'Jane Hogarth' in *ODNB*, 9 July 2020.

Maskill, D., 'The Neighbor from Hell: André Rouquet's Eviction from the Louvre,' *Journal18*, Issue 2, *Louvre Local* (Fall 2016), http://www.journal18. org/822.

Morison, S. E., 'Letters of Thomas Coram' in *Proceedings of the Massachusetts Historical Society October Meeting, 1922*, Third Series, Boston, Vol. 56 (October 1922–June 1923), pp. 1–68.

Monod, P. K., *Jacobitism and the English people, 1688–1788*, Cambridge, 1993.

Myers, H., 'William Henry Pyne' in *ODNB*, 3 January 2008.

Newman, A. N., 'Queenborough' in R. Sedgwick ed., *The History of Parliament: the House of Commons 1715–1754*, 1970.

Newman, A. N., 'Richard Evans' in R. Sedgwick ed., *The History of Parliament: the House of Commons 1715–1754*, 1970.

Nichols, R. H. & F. A. Wray, *The History of the Foundling Hospital*, London, 1935.

Nicholson, B., *The Treasures of the Foundling Hospital*, Oxford, 1972.

O'Brien, J., *Harlequin Britain, Pantomime and Entertainment, 1690–1760*, Baltimore & London, 2004.

O'Connell, S., *London 1753*, London, 2003.

Parissien, S. ed., *Celebrating Britain: Canaletto, Hogarth and Patriotism*, London, 2015.

Pattison, S. R., 'Sir Cloudesley Shovell' in *Journal of the Royal Institute of Cornwall*, Vol. I, October 1864.

Paulson, R., *Hogarth's Graphic Works*, 2 Vols, New Haven & London, 1965.

Paulson, R., *Hogarth: His Life, Art, and Times*, 2 Vols, Newhaven & London, 1971 .

Paulson, R., *Popular and polite art in the age of Hogarth and Fielding*, Notre Dame & London, 1979.

Paulson, R., *Hogarth*, 3 Vols, Cambridge, 1992–3.

Pittock, M. G. H., 'Allan Ramsay' in *ODNB*, 27 May 2010.

Pointon, M., *Hanging the Head: Portraiture and Social Formation in Eighteenth-Century England*, New Haven & London, 1993.

Pointon, M., *William Hogarth's 'Sigismunda' in Focus, with a technical essay by Rica Jones*, London, 2000.

Probyn, C., 'Jonathan Swift' in *ODNB*, 23 September 2004.

Retford, K., *The Conversation Piece: Making Modern Art in Eighteenth-century Britain*, New Haven & London, 2017.

Riding, J., 'Captain Thomas Coram: "Private Virtue and publick Spirit"' in R. Harris & R. Simon eds., *Enlightened Self-Interest: The Foundling Hospital and Hogarth*, London, 1997, pp. 16–19.

Riding, J., *Joseph Highmore 1692–1780*, 2 Vols, Doctoral Thesis, University of York, 2012.

Riding, J., 'From Bosworth Field to Finchley Common: Britain, Hogarth and the 1745 Jacobite Rebellion' in S. Parissien ed., *Celebrating Britain: Canaletto, Hogarth and Patriotism*, London, 2015.

Riding, J., *Jacobites: A New History of the '45 Rebellion*, London, 2016.

Riding, J., '"A Session of Painters": Legacy, Succession, and the Prospects for British Portraiture after Kneller' in M. Hallett, N. Llewellyn & M. Myrone eds., *Court, Country, City: British Art and Architecture, 1660–1735*, New Haven & London, 2016, pp. 353–79.

Riding, J., 'An Englishman in Paris: Joseph Highmore at the Académie Royale' in *Journal18*, Issue 2, *Louvre Local* (Fall 2016), http://www.journal18.org/841.

Riding, J., *Basic Instincts: Love, Passion and Violence in the Art of Joseph Highmore*, London, 2017.

Riding, J., 'Rewards of Virtue: Hogarth's *The Happy Marriage*' in D. Bindman ed., *Hogarth: Place and Progress*, London, 2019, pp. 42–51.

Robins, W., *Paddington: Past and Present*, London, 1853.

Rodger, N. A. M., *The Command of the Ocean: A Naval History of Britain, 1649–1815*, London, 2006.

Rogers, P. , 'Defoe in the Fleet Prison', *The Review of English Studies*, Vol. 22, No. 88 (November 1971), pp. 451–5.

Rubenhold, H., *Harris's List of Covent-Garden Ladies: Sex in the City in Georgian Britain*, London, 2005.

Sambrook, J., 'Charles Churchill' in *ODNB*, 28 September 2006.

Scholes, P. , *God Save the Queen!*, Oxford, 1954.

Sedgwick, R. ed., *History of Parliament: the House of Commons 1715–1754*, 1970.

Sheppard, F. H. W. ed., *Survey of London*, Vol. 36, London, 1970.

Shipley, J. B., 'Ralph. Ellys, Hogarth, and Fielding: The Cabal Against Jacopo Amigoni' in *Eighteenth-Century Studies*, Vol. 1, No. 4 (Summer, 1968), pp. 313–33.

Simon, R., *Hogarth, France and British Art*, London, 2007.

Smart, A., *The life and art of Allan Ramsay*, London, 1952.

Smart, A., *Allan Ramsay: painter, essayist and man of the Enlightenment*, New Haven & London, 1992.

Solkin, D. H., *Painting for Money: The Visual Arts and the Public Sphere in Eighteenth-century England*, New Haven & London, 1992.

Stephens, R., 'Sublime Society of Beefsteaks' in *ODNB*, 19 May 2011.

Stevenson, J. A., *The Real History of Tom Jones*, New York & Basingstoke, 2005.

Stewart, J. D., *Sir Godfrey Kneller and the English Baroque Portrait*, Oxford, 1983.

Styles, J., *Threads of Feeling: The London Foundling Hospital's Textile Tokens 1740–1779*, London, 2010.

Sweet, R., *Antiquaries: The Discovery of the Past in Eighteenth-Century Britain*, London & New York, 2004.

Taylor, J. S., 'Thomas Coram' in *ODNB*, 28 September 2006.

Taylor, S., 'Benjamin Hoadly' in *ODNB*, 3 January 2008.

Thomas, K., *The Ends of Life: Roads to Fulfilment in Early Modern England*, Oxford, 2009.

Thompson, A. C., *George II: King and Elector*, New Haven & London, 2011 .

Timbs, J., *Anecdote Biography or, Scenes and Events in the Lives of Distinguished Persons*, London, 1860.

Uglow, J., *Hogarth: A Life and a World*, London, 1997.

Vaughan, A. T., 'Pocahontas [Matoaka, Amonute]' in *ODNB*, 1 September 2017.

Vaughan, W., *British Painting: The Golden Age from Hogarth to Turner*, London, 1999.

Vickery, A., *Behind Closed Doors: At Home in Georgian England*, New Haven & London, 2009.

Volmert, M. & D. Bucher, *European Fans in the seventeenth and eighteenth centuries: Images, Accessories, and Instruments of Gesture*, Berlin/Boston, 2020.

Wagner, G., *Thomas Coram, Gent., 1668–1751*, Woodbridge, 2015.

Waterhouse, E., *Painting in Britain 1530–1790* (1953), New Haven & London, 1994.

White, J., *London in the Eighteenth Century: A Great and Monstrous Thing*, 2012.

Whitley, W. T., *Artists and their Friends in England 1700–1799*, 2 Vols, London & Boston, 1928.

Wilson, R. T., *Life of General Sir Robert Wilson*, 2 Vols, London, 1862.

Worsley, L., *Courtiers: The Secret History of the Georgian Court at Kensington Palace*, London, 2011.

Wrigley, E. A., R. S. Davies, J. E. Oeppen & R. S. Schofield, *English Population History from Family Reconstruction 1580–1836*, Cambridge, 1997.

Wroth, W. W. revised by P. E. Kell, 'James Salter [called Don Saltero]', *ODNB*, 23 September 2004.

Young, B. W., 'William Warburton' in *ODNB*, 24 May 2007.

Websites

Art Sales Catalogue Online, including Frits Lugt's *Répertoire des Catalogues de Ventes Publiques*

britishmuseum.org/collection/term/BIOG163066

collections.chateauversailles.fr

Early English Books Online

History of Parliament Online

Old Bailey Proceedings Online (www.oldbaileyonline.org, version 6.0, 17 April 2011)

Oxford Dictionary of National Biography Online

Oxford English Dictionary Online

Oxford Music Online: Grove Music Online

Seventeenth and Eighteenth century Burney Newspapers Collection

LIST OF ILLUSTRATIONS

Unless otherwise specified, all works are by William Hogarth

Colour Plates

Black-and-white illustrations

ACKNOWLEDGEMENTS

It may seem strange that this is the first biography of William Hogarth – one of the most famous and recognisable of all British artists – for a quarter century. This, in part, is testament to the high regard in which Jenny Uglow's *Hogarth: A Life and a World* (1997) is held – one spur (when contemplating a new biography) for a different approach in structure, style and content. Further, according to received wisdom, publishing on eighteenth-century subjects (i.e. neither 'Henry' nor 'Hitler') is, like Bunyan's hill, fraught with difficulty. So my heartfelt gratitude to previous editors Michael Fishwick (*Jacobites*) and Richard Milbank (*Peterloo*) for helping me to gain a toehold. My first meeting with Andrew Franklin and Cecily Gayford was characterised by laughter and gravity in equal measure – a good omen given the subject of our discussion. My profound thanks to them and the team at Profile, particularly Graeme Hall, who managed brilliantly the book's journey to publication. And guiding me through the entire process, my agent Bill Hamilton: still patient, wise and bewilderingly buoyant.

The time to research and write was in part supported by a Paul Mellon Centre Mid-Career Fellowship, for which I am extremely grateful to the Advisory Council members. The following institutions and the assistance of their staff were crucial – increasingly so as 2020 advanced: Barts Heritage (St Bartholomew's Hospital); Beinecke Rare Book & Manuscript Library; the British Library Rare Books & Music and Manuscripts Reading Rooms; the British Museum Department for Prints and Drawings; Hampshire Record Office; the London Library; Rev. Jeanette McLaren, and the volunteers of Minster Abbey and the parish of West Sheppey; the National Archives; the Priory Church of St Bartholomew the Great; the Royal Collection Trust; St Mary Redcliffe Church, Bristol; St Paul's Church, Covent Garden. It is impossible to publish a book on Hogarth – a beautiful book at least, particularly when the author shares or carries the cost of illustrations – without the generosity of owners and custodians who are willing to reduce significantly or waive completely often eye-watering reproduction fees. My eternal gratitude to Barts Heritage and Opus Conservation, the Foundling Museum, the Metropolitan Museum of Art, New York, the National Gallery, London, Sir John Soane's Museum and the Yale Center for British Art. In particular, I encourage you to support Barts and the Foundling, as did Hogarth himself.

I am indebted to Mark Hallett and Christine Riding: first, because they co-curated the great Hogarth retrospective at Tate Britain in 2007 and second, for their kindness in reading and commenting on an early and even longer draft. The wealth of curatorship and scholarship consulted is humbly acknowledged within the endnotes and bibliography. Special thanks to Brian Allen, Susanna Avery-Quash, Tabitha Barber, Emma Barker, David Bindman, Martin Caiger-Smith, Caroline Campbell, Juliet Carey, Hugo Chapman, Tim Clayton, Amy Concannon, Janet Dickinson, Helen Dorey, Alison Duke, Timothy Duke, David Forsyth, Sarah Fraser, Ruth Gill, John Goodall, George Goodwin, Janet Graffius, Lydia Hamlett, Robin Hamlyn, Jeannie Hobhouse, Caro Howell, David Fraser Jenkins, Richard Johns, Anna Keay, Tim Knox, Darren S. Layne, Andrew Loukes, Anne Lyles, Cristina S. Martinez, Frances Morris, Franny Moyle, Lynda Nead, Sheila O'Connell, Will Palin, Kathleen Palmer, Clare Pardy, Steven Parissien, Lucy Peltz, Martin Postle, Ricky Pound, Rosie Razzall, Kate Retford, Rebecca Rideal, James Robinson, Hallie Rubenhold, Jennifer Scott, Desmond Shawe-Taylor, Robin Simon, Kate Smith, Kathleen Soriano, David Souden, Chris Stephens, Martin Stiles, David H. B. Taylor, Simon Thurley, Jo Tinworth, Peter Trippi, Nicholas Tromans, Sarah Turner, William Vaughan, Lucy Whittaker, Rhys Williams, Lucy Worsley, all of whom have given advice, support and encouragement over the years; and to Ronald Paulson, whose extensive publishing record remains the starting point for any foray into Hogarth's life, and his graphic work in particular. I have benefitted immensely from the scholarship, generosity and camaraderie of Elizabeth Einberg, who started me off on my journey in eighteenth-century art over thirty years ago. And through her magnificent catalogue raisonné of Hogarth's paintings, Elizabeth, like Billy, has been my constant companion over recent years. Additional thanks to my fellow 'Jacobite' Sarah Fraser, for joining me on a joyously madcap day in the summer of 2020 as we travelled around Hoo, the Isle of Grain and Sheppey in the steps of Hogarth and his fellow pilgrims, ending with barbeque shrimps and ice cream on a windswept Whitstable jetty. As I have noted before, I endeavour to put into action the tools of storytelling that I have learned by knowing and working with Mike Leigh – I hope I am getting better at it ...

To my family and friends who have sustained me through a tough period for everyone with their affection, enduring faith and humour. In addition to those already named, my parents Jack and Pat, to whom this volume is dedicated with much love, the Ridings and Johnsons, Danielle Brandon, Nick Devison, Susanna Eastburn, Matthew Fox, Nancy Granese, Helen Grearson, Charlotte Higgins, Sarah Hodgson, Tim Knapman, Georgina Lowe, Sarah McBryde, David McCulloch, Caroline Meer, Keith Miller, Ned Palmer, Stephen Pardy, Matthew Peacock, Mona Penner, Matthew Plampin, Eileen Read, Imogen Robertson, Sara Robinson, David Teather, Will Tuckett and Tim Wright.

Finally, Hogarth was a man of his age and firmly middle class. He was certainly no 'man of the people' as so often described. Undeniably, some of the attitudes he expressed in word and image are deeply problematic for twenty-first-century audiences. Yet, it seems, some of these attitudes – prevalent across Britain three hundred years ago – along with a certain style of self-serving tinpot patriot, as Hogarth saw them, are with us still: to paraphrase one Tory sage, patriotism is a fine thing, until it becomes the last refuge of scoundrels. Unlike them and on balance, Hogarth, despite his many faults, remains an Englishman and a Briton who can be described as heroic: for his immense creativity, of course, but also for the strength and energy he harnessed to causes which demonstrably improved the lives of his fellow citizens; his dogged determination to shine a penetrating light on the shameless misbehaviour of the entitled elite; a man of great deeds as well as words. Given this, my last thanks must go to Hogarth's spiritual descendants – the likes of *Private Eye*, indeed all those who, like Hogarth, speak truth to power with precision and wit, while (for now) the rest of us can only laugh until we cry.

JR
London, April 2021

INDEX

Note: Page references in *italics* indicate images. WH indicates William Hogarth.

Peregrination, The (cont.)

Chequer Alehouse, Isle of Grain 306–7

churches, visits to 252–5. *See also individual church name*

Crown Inn, Rochester 214–17, 222, 247–8

Cuckold's Point 121–8, 129, 130, 132, 227, 256, 263

Dark House, Billingsgate 28–9, 30, 60, 71, 251

Drawing ye 2d 247

Drawing ye 3d 249–51, 262

Drawing ye 4th: The Nag's Head 304–5, *305*

Drawing ye 5th: The Manner of our Embarking 307, *308*, *308*

Drawing ye 6th 369

Drawing ye 7th and 8th 375–9

'Duke of Puddle Dock' sketch 28–9

Execution Dock, Wapping 129–31

food eaten on 214–16, 306, 367–8

Frindsbury, Church of All Saints 248–9

Gostling poem 3, 19, 29, 181, 182, 214, 217, 248, 251, 253, 254, 255, 259–60

Gravesend 13, 25, 26, 28, 71–2, 135, 177, 178, 179–82, 443–4

Greenwich 132–5, 177

Hoo 252–9

Hop Scotch (or scoring) (game) 216, 217

Isle of Grain 248, 261, 306, 309

Isle of Sheppey 2–3, 4, 12, 25, 121, 133, 181, 307, 363–6, 367

Kings Ferry 307

Lower Stoke 261, 304

manuscript 3, 4, 187, 250. *See also* Forrest, Ebenezer

map, John Thornhill's 3, 180, 182

Marlborough, boarding of 219–20

Milton 182, 184

Minster Abbey 375–9

Nag's Head, Lower Stoke 261–3, 304

No Body drawing 9–10, *445*

'Pishoken' (song) 131, 370, 443

playfights 252, 255, 261, 262, 263

Purfleet 177–9

Queenborough 364–71, 375

Rochester 181, 184–7, 214–17, 222, 247–8

Royal Sovereign, boarding of 220

Some Body drawing 9, 186, 249

Scott's philosophical conundrum 260

Sheerness 306–11, *308*, 312, 363–4, 365, 368, 379, 443

Sign of the Dover Castle 182–4

'Sir John got him an ambling nag' (song) 122, 370, 443

Some Body drawing 9, 186, 249

Somerset Watergate, catch boat at 21–6

St Catherine's Hospital, Rochester 186–7, 214, 216

St Werburgh's, Hoo 252–5, 258, 263

St Peter's church, Stoke (or Upper Stoke) 260–1

'Stroud' or Strood 187, 248

Three Cocks 261, 263, 377

Tilt-boat 71–2, 133, 444, 445

'Unlucky Boy' 179

Upnor Castle 249–51

WH 'Motion', St Werburgh's, Hoo 254–8

'Why shou'd wee Quarrell for Riches', or 'The Sailor's Rant' (song) 20–1

See also individual participant name

Perseus and Andromeda (pantomime entertainment) 20

Pett, Christopher 222

Pett, Peter 220

Pett, Phineas 177

Philippa of Hainault, Queen Consort of England 368

Pine, John 98, 353–4

pirates 128–30, 131, 180, 256

'Pishoken' (song) 131, 370, 443

Pitt, William (the Elder) 428

Pocahontas (Rebecca Rolfe) 182

Pope, Alexander 8, 53–4, 119, 380; *The Dunciad* 117

Prestonpans, battle of (1745) 323–4, 328